DATE DUE			
APR 17 1979			
FEB 1 1982 ILL 3-1-82			
MAR 24 1983			
JAN 16 1984			
DEC 18 1989			
JUL 2 1990			
MAY 28 1991 APR 28 2000			

Collected Poems

W. H. AUDEN

Collected Poems

Edited by
EDWARD MENDELSON

Random House
New York

Library of Congress Cataloging in Publication Data

Auden, Wystan Hugh, 1907-1973.
Collected poems.

Includes index.
I. Mendelson, Edward.
√ PR6001.U4A17 1976   821'.9'12   76-14155
ISBN 0-394-40895-0

Manufactured in the United States of America
2 4 6 8 9 7 5 3

A limited edition of this book has been privately printed.
First Trade Edition

66184

Contents

Editor's Preface   *page* 11
Author's Forewords   15
Dedicatory Poem   17

PART I   PART III
Paid on Both Sides (*1928*)   19   Letter to Lord Byron (*1936*)   75

PART II   PART IV
1927–1932   *1933–1938*
The Letter   39   A Summer Night   103
Taller To-day   39   Paysage Moralisé   104
Missing   40   O What is That Sound   105
The Secret Agent   41   Our Hunting Fathers   106
The Watershed   41   Through the Looking-Glass   107
No Change of Place   42   Two Climbs   108
Let History Be My Judge   42   Meiosis   108
Never Stronger   43   A Misunderstanding   109
This Loved One   44   Who's Who   109
Easy Knowledge   44   Schoolchildren   109
Too Dear, Too Vague   45   May   110
Between Adventure   46   A Bride in the 30's   111
A Free One   46   On This Island   112
Family Ghosts   47   Night Mail   113
The Questioner Who Sits So   As I Walked Out One Evening 114
   Sly   47   Twelve Songs   116
Venus Will Now Say a   His Excellency   122
   Few Words   49   Casino   123
1929   50   Oxford   124
The Bonfires   53   Dover   124
On Sunday Walks   54   Journey to Iceland   126
Shorts   55   Detective Story   127
Happy Ending   57   Death's Echo   128
This Lunar Beauty   57   The Price   129
The Question   58   Danse Macabre   129
Five Songs   59   Lullaby   131
Uncle Henry   60   Orpheus   132
Consider   61   Miss Gee   132
The Wanderer   62   James Honeyman   134
The Watchers   63   Victor   138
Adolescence   64   As He Is   142
The Exiles   64   A Voyage   143
The Decoys   66   The Capital   145
Have a Good Time   66   Brussels in Winter   146
Half Way   67   Musée des Beaux Arts   146
Ode   68   Gare du Midi   147
Legend   70   The Novelist   147
The Witnesses   71   The Composer   148

Rimbaud	148	Few and Simple	253
A. E. Housman	148	The Lesson	253
Edward Lear	149	A Healthy Spot	254
Epitaph on a Tyrant	149	The Model	255
Sonnets from China	149	Canzone	256
		Anthem	257
		The Fall of Rome	257
PART V		Nursery Rhyme	258
New Year Letter (*1940*)	159	In Schrafft's	259
		Under Which Lyre	259
		Music is International	263
PART VI		The Duet	264
1939–1947		Pleasure Island	265
In Memory of W. B. Yeats	197	A Walk After Dark	267
In Memory of Ernst Toller	198		
Voltaire at Ferney	199		
Herman Melville	200	PART VII	
The Unknown Citizen	201	For the Time Being	
They	201	(*1941–1942*)	269
The Prophets	203		
Like a Vocation	203		
The Riddle	204	PART VIII	
Heavy Date	205	The Sea and the Mirror	
Law Like Love	208	(*1942–1944*)	309
The Hidden Law	209		
Ten Songs	210		
In Memory of Sigmund		PART IX	
Freud	215	The Age of Anxiety	343
Another Time	218	(*1944–1946*)	
Our Bias	218		
Hell	219		
Lady Weeping at the		PART X	
Crossroads	219	*1948–1957*	
Anthem for St. Cecilia's Day	220	In Transit	413
The Dark Years	222	In Praise of Limestone	414
The Quest	224	Ischia	416
Shorts	231	Under Sirius	417
No Time	234	Cattivo Tempo	419
Diaspora	234	Hunting Season	420
Luther	235	Fleet Visit	420
Montaigne	235	An Island Cemetery	421
The Council	236	Not in Baedeker	422
The Maze	236	Ode to Gaea	423
Blessed Event	238	Bucolics	426
Kairos and Logos	238	Shorts	435
At the Grave of Henry		Five Songs	437
James	242	Three Occasional Poems	440
Alone	243	Their Lonely Betters	444
Leap Before You Look	244	First Things First	444
If I Could Tell You	244	The More Loving One	445
Atlantis	245	A Permanent Way	445
In Sickness and in Health	247	Nocturne	446
Many Happy Returns	249	Precious Five	447
Mundus Et Infans	252	Memorial for The City	450

The Shield of Achilles 454
Secondary Epic 455
Makers of History 456
T the Great 457
The Managers 459
The Epigoni 460
Bathtub Thoughts 461
The Old Man's Road 461
The History of Science 462
The History of Truth 463
Homage to Clio 463
The Love Feast 466
The Chimeras 466
Merax & Mullin 467
Limbo Culture 468
There Will Be No Peace 468
A Household 469
'The Truest Poetry is the
   Most Feigning' 470
We Too Had Known Golden
   Hours 471
Secrets 472
Numbers and Faces 473
Objects 473
Words 473
The Song 474
One Circumlocution 474
Horae Canonicae 475
Good-Bye To The Mezzogiorno 486

PART XI
Dichtung und Wahrheit (1959) 489

PART XII
1958–1971
Dame Kind 503
Reflections in a Forest 504
Hands 505
The Sabbath 507
Walks 507
Friday's Child 509
Academic Graffiti 510
Thanksgiving for a Habitat 518
Shorts I 539
Two Don Quixote Lyrics 541
A Change of Air 542
You 543
Et in Arcadia Ego 544
Hammerfest 545
Iceland Revisited 546
On the Circuit 548
Symmetries & Asymmetries 549

The Maker 554
At the Party 555
Bestiaries are Out 556
After Reading a Child's Guide
   to Modern Physics 557
Ascension Day, 1964 558
Whitsunday in Kirchstetten 559
Three Posthumous Poems 561
City Without Walls 562
Eleven Occasional Poems 565
The Horatians 579
Profile 581
Since 584
Amor Loci 585
Bird-Language 586
Two Songs 586
Forty Years On 588
Marginalia 589
In Due Season 603
Rois Fainéants 603
Partition 604
August 1968 604
Fairground 605
River Profile 605
Insignificant Elephants 607
Ode to Terminus 608
Six Commissioned Texts 609
Prologue at Sixty 622
Epistle to a Godson 624
The Art of Healing 626
A New Year Greeting 628
Smelt and Tasted 629
Heard and Seen 630
I Am Not a Camera 630
A Bad Night 631
Moon Landing 632
The Garrison 633
Pseudo-Questions 634
Stark bewölkt 634
Natural Linguistics 636
The Aliens 637
Doggerel by a Senior Citizen 638
Shorts II 639
Old People's Home 645
Circe 646
Short Ode to the Cuckoo 647
Ode to the Medieval Poets 647
An Encounter 648
A Shock 649
Loneliness 649
Talking to Dogs 650
Talking to Mice 651
Talking to Myself 652

9

Part XIII
1972–1973

Thank You, Fog	657	Ode to the Diencephalon	664
Aubade	658	Shorts	665
Unpredictable But		Posthumous Letter to	
Providential	659	Gilbert White	667
Address to the Beasts	660	A Contrast	668
Archaeology	662	The Question	668
Progress?	663	No, Plato, No	669
A Curse	664	Nocturne	669
		A Thanksgiving	671
		A Lullaby	672

Appendix I: Titles of Poems Excluded from this
  Edition   677
Appendix II: Variant Titles   680
Index of Titles   685
Index of First Lines   689

Editor's Preface

This edition includes all the poems that W. H. Auden wished to preserve, in a text that represents his final revisions. It thus omits the poems Auden published in his early years but finally discarded. Normally the decision to print an author's latest text needs no defence; and when an editor works under the final instructions of his author, he is morally obliged to respect the dead man's intentions. Some of Auden's readers have objected that his late revisions weaken the force of his early poems, and that the original versions are always to be preferred. Yet the history of Auden's reputation has consistently followed a pattern in which initial outrage at new developments in manner and subject is supplanted by gradual acceptance and understanding of the merits of Auden's changes. The same pattern has informed the reception of Auden's revisions: as they lose their unsettling novelty, it becomes increasingly possible to recognize them as the improvements that, on the whole, they are. Fortunately, obligation and judgement are agreed in requiring that this first posthumous collected edition conform to its author's wishes to the extent that they can be determined.

The excluded poems, and the early versions of revised poems, retain nonetheless great literary and historical interest, and, for those readers who want them, may be found in *The English Auden*, a selection of Auden's early work in prose and verse, some unpublished, which will appear shortly after publication of the present volume.

Auden's late revisions are, for the most part, extensions of his methods of composition and revision from his earlier years. The poems Auden wrote from the start of his career until around 1942 were subject throughout their history to elaborate reworking, cutting, and rearrangement; frequently they lost or gained stanzas between first appearance in a periodical and first book publication, then endured further transformations before being collected, or banished, or set in the larger context of a play or longer poem. The late poems, whose final shape Auden had more clearly in mind while composing them, seldom were subjected to more than minor verbal adjustments. The many early poems that Auden printed in his books, but rejected from this edition, are listed in Appendix I. After 1942 Auden never wrote a poem that he disowned after publication.

This book is the third of Auden's major collected editions. Auden proposed a collection to his initially reluctant American publisher early in 1942, and delivered the manuscript at the end of the following year. Wartime delays permitted further additions and changes during 1944, and *The Collected Poetry of W. H. Auden* appeared at last in April 1945. Auden had wanted the title *Poems 1928–1945*—'The word Collected suggests finality which, I *hope* anyway, is incorrect'—but his objections to the publisher's title went unheeded. A British version of the book, titled *Collected Shorter Poems 1930–1944*, appeared in 1950. The poems in these editions were arranged in alphabetical order of first lines; many poems were revised or truncated; and some lyrics that had once found their way into longer works re-emerged as separate poems.

For a Penguin/Modern Library selection published in 1958 Auden made some further revisions, and began to plan more extensive changes for a new collected volume. Encouraged by his British publisher, during the summer of 1965 he prepared the text of *Collected Shorter Poems 1927–1957*—whose title finally gave the correct *terminus a quo*. The book was published in England in November 1966 and in America the year after. Many of the early poems were further revised, and an alarming number were omitted, among them 'Petition', 'Spain' and 'September 1, 1939'. Auden's justification for this surgery appears in the preface reprinted in the present edition.

In 1968, at the suggestion of his British publisher, Auden collected his longer poems, making major revisions only to the extent of cutting some autobiographical passages (and some dead wood) from 'Letter to Lord Byron'—which he had chosen to omit altogether in 1945.

The present collection includes all the poems Auden reprinted in 1966 and 1968, and all the original verse he printed after the *terminus ad quem* of the 1966 collection—the later poems in *Homage to Clio* (1960), all of *About the House* (1965), *City Without Walls* (1969), *Academic Graffiti* (1971), *Epistle to a Godson* (1972), and the posthumous *Thank You, Fog* (1974). Three poems that Auden referred to as 'posthumous poems' are printed here for the first time, and four poems that Auden had omitted in 1966 are here restored in revised versions—'James Honeyman', 'They' (originally 'Crisis'), 'Kairos and Logos', and 'Canzone'. The 'addenda' to the poem titled 'Profile' are also printed for the first time.

Auden excluded translations from his earlier collections, and I have therefore omitted the four 'Transliterations' of Polish and Russian poems from *About the House* and the versions of Brecht songs from *City Without Walls*. I have omitted also the late masque written in collaboration with Chester Kallman, 'The Entertainment of the Senses', which I had added to the unfinished typescript of *Thank You, Fog*, as its proper place is in a future edition of Auden's collected plays.

I have included Auden's brief and elegant preface to his 1945 (and 1950) collection, and the longer foreword printed in 1966. The dates appended to these texts, like those appended to many of the poems, are dates of composition, not of publication.

*   *   *

For convenience in the remaining notes I shall refer to the earlier collected editions by their (italicized) dates of publication: *1945*, *1950*, and *1966*.

ORDER OF POEMS In *1966* Auden arranged his poems in roughly chronological sequence and divided them among four sections, which are preserved in this edition as Parts II, IV, VI and X. His foreword implied that each section represented 'a new chapter in my life', and all but one of his chapter-divisions mark events in the public realm—Auden's departure from England to America in January 1939, the beginning of his first summer in Ischia in 1948, and his departure from Ischia to his new summer home in Austria in the summer of 1958. The division between the first two sections almost certainly marks an intensely private event, the 'Vision of Agape' Auden describes in *Forewords and Afterwords*. (He does not explicitly claim the experience as his own, but writes that he will 'quote from an unpublished account for the authenticity of which I can vouch'—of course, he could hardly vouch for the authenticity of *someone else's* account of a mystical vision.) 'One fine summer night in June 1933,' he writes, '. . . I felt myself invaded by a power which, though I consented

12

to it, was irresistible and certainly not mine. For the first time in my life I knew exactly—because, thanks to the power, I was doing it—what it means to love one's neighbour as oneself. . . .' (p. 69). The experience was the occasion—although interestingly not the subject—of 'A Summer Night', the poem that opens the section with the poems of 1933–1938.

The order of the poems of 1958–1973 is my own, but I have tried to follow Auden's procedures from the earlier sections. The division between the two final sections of the book commemorates Auden's departure for Oxford from his winter home in New York early in 1972. In the 1958–1971 section the arrangement is derived, as far as possible, from the separate volumes in which Auden first gathered these poems. The order of poems in the final section, corresponding to the posthumous *Thank You, Fog*, is entirely editorial, as Auden did not leave the unfinished typescript in a coherent or chronological sequence.

One or two minor changes and omissions in the earlier sections have proved necessary. In *1966* Auden printed some excerpts from his longer poems, and these excerpts I have now omitted, to avoid duplication with the complete texts elsewhere in the book. I have added the four restored poems, mentioned above, at the points that seemed most appropriate. The poem printed as 'Anthem' in *Epistle to a Godson* now appears among the poems of 1939–1947, as it derives from an early draft of 'The Age of Anxiety', and was written probably around 1945.

The dedicatory poem is reprinted from *1966*.

TEXT Auden made some slight revisions and corrections in copies of *1966* and the later volumes. In one or two places he made different changes at different times; I have used the version I believe to be the last. Many other minor changes in this edition derive from Auden's letters and conversations during the last two years of his life. I have corrected various misprints, restored two lines dropped by earlier printers, emended misspellings, and in two or three instances—added a mark of punctuation where the addition transformed nonsense into sense. I hope the words and phrases in foreign languages are at last correct—although nothing could be done with the garble of '*codex gentium*' in 'New Year Letter'. Auden's spelling in his early work tends to be British, in his later work American, and I have let the inconsistencies stand. (There is sufficient evidence to demonstrate that these changes in spelling are mostly the results of changes in Auden's own practice, and not the consequence of different printing-house rules.)

In 'Letter to Lord Byron' I have restored the original version of a line (Part I, stanza 15, line 4) that was altered in the proofs of the poem's first publication in order to avoid libel.

Because Auden sometimes prepared slightly different texts for his British and American publishers, and tended to make revisions on one side of the Atlantic that he later forgot on the other, various textual problems arise whose complexity is quite disproportionate to their importance: the reader should feel free, therefore, to ignore the rest of this paragraph. In *1945* Auden printed, and slightly revised, excerpts from 'Paid on Both Sides' as separate short poems; and in *1966* he similarly excerpted and revised portions of other longer works. The revisions that he made in the excerpts never found their way into his reprintings of the full texts, but I have incorporated them (save one that seems to be a misprint) in the present edition. A knottier problem involves the British and American textual traditions of the sonnet sequence 'The Quest'. The first appearance of the sequence in book form was in *The Double Man* (1941), published in London as *New Year Letter*. The British edition appeared two months after the American, but it is by no means certain that the British text represents Auden's later intentions. In the American text the sonnets of 'The Quest' bear individual titles; in the British text they bear only numbers. Later, when preparing the text of *1945* for his American publisher, Auden used the American edition of *The Double Man*, and reprinted the separate titles—attentively not mechanically, as he altered one of them. However, when, still later, he compiled *1966* for his British publisher, the publisher provided him with a copy of the British collection *1950* (which, unlike *1945*, did not include 'The Quest') and a copy of the 1941 British edition of *New Year Letter*—which, as I said, printed 'The Quest' without the separate titles. That is: the circumstances of publishing caused Auden to return, for *1966*, to a 1941 text that lacked the titles, and to ignore his *1945* revision which had included them. As I cannot, of course, be certain that Auden would have retained the titles had he worked from *1945*—the later text—I have not presumed to restore them to the body of the present edition, but they are far too valuable to lose, and I have listed them in a note to Appendix II.

DATES OF COMPOSITION Where provided, these represent the dates on which the poems first achieved approximately their present form, although many of the poems, especially those of the 1930s, were later subject to drastic reworking. Evidence for the dates derives from notebooks and manuscripts (in the early poems) and from Auden's letters (in the more recent work). No doubt further evidence will emerge in time, but I thought it preferable to list partial information now rather than wait until a complete chronology becomes feasible.

Dates given to the month and year are, I believe, accurate to within one month. Where only a year is given, the date is based on Auden's later recollection (not always reliable) or on my own surmise, based on the evidence available. Although the printed dates demonstrate that the order of poems is far from strictly chronological—as Auden acknowledges in his foreword to *1966*—I have not attempted to correct Auden's sequence.

TITLES In his early years Auden was reluctant to assist his readers with titles any more precise than 'Song' or 'Chorus', but his attitude softened by the end of the 1930s. When preparing *1945* Auden gave many of his earlier poems ironic and distancing titles whose tone was (depending upon the reader's point of view) either tellingly or irritatingly at variance with the poems they headed. Auden replaced a few of the more flippant titles with neutral ones in *1950*, and the *1966* titles were more sober still. This edition uses the latest available titles, some of them taken from a 1968 *Selected Poems*, but for the convenience of those readers who are familiar with Auden's earlier collections, Appendix II provides an index of variants.

In Part XII the title 'Two *Don Quixote* Lyrics' is a sole example of editorial explanation. And while Auden's typescript for *Thank You, Fog* titled one of its poems 'Lullaby', I have here reverted to the apparently earlier reading '*A* Lullaby' better to avoid confusion with a celebrated earlier poem.

*   *   *

It is a pleasure to record my gratitude to Ellen Wertheimer for invaluable help in preparing the text. Readers will recognize that my preface and appendices are modelled after those in *The Collected Poems of Louis MacNeice*, edited by Professor E. R. Dodds, to whom I am indebted for example and encouragement. I am grateful also to many friends of W. H. Auden who provided information on dates of composition, and offered assistance with textual problems: especially generous help came from Professor A. H. Campbell, Professor Wendell Johnson, Mrs Isabella Levitin, and Mrs Ursula Niebuhr.

EDWARD MENDELSON

Author's Forewords

In the eyes of every author, I fancy, his own past work falls into four classes. First, the pure rubbish which he regrets ever having conceived; second—for him the most painful—the good ideas which his incompetence or impatience prevented from coming to much (*The Orators* seems to me such a case of the fair notion fatally injured); third, the pieces he has nothing against except their lack of importance; these must inevitably form the bulk of any collection since, were he to limit it to the fourth class alone, to those poems for which he is honestly grateful, his volume would be too depressingly slim.

1944

*   *   *

In 1944, when I first assembled my shorter pieces, I arranged them in the alphabetical order of their first lines. This may have been a silly thing to do, but I had a reason. At the age of thirty-seven I was still too young to have any sure sense of the direction in which I was moving, and I did not wish critics to waste their time, and mislead readers, making guesses about it which would almost certainly turn out to be wrong. To-day, nearing sixty, I believe that I know myself and my poetic intentions better and, if anybody wants to look at my writings from an historical perspective, I have no objection. Consequently, though I have sometimes shuffled poems so as to bring together those related by theme or genre, in the main their order is chronological.

Some poems which I wrote and, unfortunately, published, I have thrown out because they were dishonest, or bad-mannered, or boring.

A dishonest poem is one which expresses, no matter how well, feelings or beliefs which its author never felt or entertained. For example, I once expressed a desire for 'New styles of architecture'; but I have never liked modern architecture. I prefer *old* styles, and one must be honest even about one's prejudices. Again, and much more shamefully, I once wrote:

History to the defeated
May say alas but cannot help nor pardon.

To say this is to equate goodness with success. It would have been bad enough if I had ever held this wicked doctrine, but that I should have

15

stated it simply because it sounded to me rhetorically effective is quite inexcusable.

In art as in life, bad manners, not to be confused with a deliberate intention to cause offence, are the consequence of an over-concern with one's own ego and a lack of consideration for (and knowledge of) others. Readers, like friends, must not be shouted at or treated with brash familiarity. Youth may be forgiven when it is brash or noisy, but this does not mean that brashness and noise are virtues.

Boredom is a subjective reaction but, if a poem makes its author yawn, he can hardly expect a less partial reader to wade through it.

A good many of the poems have been revised. Critics, I have observed, are apt to find revisions ideologically significant. One, even, made a great to-do about what was in fact a typographical error. I can only say that I have never, consciously at any rate, attempted to revise my former thoughts or feelings, only the language in which they were first expressed when, on further consideration, it seemed to me inaccurate, lifeless, prolix or painful to the ear. Re-reading my poems, I find that in the nineteen-thirties I fell into some very slovenly verbal habits. The definite article is always a headache to any poet writing in English, but my addiction to German usages became a disease. Again, it makes me wince when I see how ready I was to treat *-or* and *-aw* as homophones. It is true that in the Oxonian dialect I speak they are, but that isn't really an adequate excuse. I also find that my ear will no longer tolerate rhyming a voiced *S* with an unvoiced. I have had to leave a few such rhymes because I cannot at the moment see a way to get rid of them, but I promise not to do it again. On revisions as a matter of principle, I agree with Valéry: 'A poem is never finished; it is only abandoned.'

This collection stops at the year nineteen-fifty-seven. In the following year I transferred my summer residence from Italy to Austria, so starting a new chapter in my life which is not yet finished. The poems included cover a span of thirty years, there are, if I've counted rightly, three hundred of them, I was twenty when I wrote the earliest, fifty when I wrote the latest: four nice round numbers. Besides, the volume looks alarmingly big already.

1965

For
CHRISTOPHER ISHERWOOD
and
CHESTER KALLMAN

Although you be, as I am, one of those
Who feel a Christian ought to write in prose,
For poetry is magic: born in sin, you
May read it to exorcise the Gentile in you.

Part I

Paid on Both Sides

A Charade

To Cecil Day-Lewis

Characters

Lintzgarth
JOHN NOWER
DICK
GEORGE****
WALTER
KURT
CULLEY
STEPHEN**
ZEPPEL—JOHN NOWER'S SERVANT
NUMBER SIX
JOAN—MOTHER OF JOHN NOWER
TRUDY***

Nattrass
AARON SHAW*****
SETH SHAW
THE SPY—SETH'S BROTHER
BERNARD
SETH'S MOTHER***
ANNE SHAW

FATHER CHRISTMAS*
THE DOCTOR
BO****
PO*****
THE MAN-WOMAN
THE DOCTOR'S BOY**
THE ANNOUNCER*
THE CHIEF GUEST*
THE BUTLER*

THE CHORUS

The starred parts should be doubled

[*No scenery is required. The stage should have a curtained-off recess. The distinction between the two hostile parties should be marked by different coloured arm-bands.* THE CHORUS, *which should not consist of more than three persons, wear similar and distinctive clothing.*]

[*Enter* TRUDY *and* WALTER.]
TRUDY: You've only just heard?
WALTER: Yes. A breakdown at the Mill needed attention, kept me all morning. I guessed no harm. But lately, riding at leisure, Dick met me, panted disaster. I came here at once. How did they get him?
TRUDY: In Kettledale above Colefangs road passes where high banks overhang dangerous from ambush. To Colefangs had to go, would speak with Layard, Jerry and Hunter with him only. They must have stolen news, for Red Shaw waited with ten, so Jerry said, till for last time unconscious. Hunter was killed at first shot. They fought, exhausted ammunition, a brave defence but fight no more.
WALTER: Has Joan been told yet?
TRUDY: Yes. It couldn't be helped. Shock, starting birth pangs, caused a premature delivery.
WALTER: How is she?
TRUDY: Bad, I believe. But here's the doctor.
[*Enter* DOCTOR.]
Well, Doctor, how are things going?

21

DOCTOR: Better thanks. We've had a hard fight, but it's going to be all
right. She'll pull through and have a fine infant as well. My God, I'm
thirsty after all that. Where can I get a drink?
WALTER: Here in the next room, Doctor.
[*Exeunt. Back curtains draw.* JOAN *with child and corpse.*]
JOAN:

Not from this life, not from this life is any
To keep; sleep, day and play would not help there,
Dangerous to new ghost; new ghost learns from many,
Learns from old termers what death is, where.

Who's jealous of his latest company,
From one day to the next final to us,
A changed one, would use sorrow to deny
Sorrow, to replace death? Sorrow is sleeping thus.

Unforgetting is not today's forgetting
For yesterday, not bedrid scorning,
But a new begetting,
An unforgiving morning.

[*Baby squeals.*]

O see, he is impatient
To pass beyond this pretty lisping time:
There'll be some crying out when he's come there.

[*Back curtains close.*]
CHORUS:

Can speak of trouble, pressure on men
Born all the time, brought forward into light
For warm dark moan.
Though heart fears all heart cries for, rebuffs with mortal beat
Skyfall, the legs sucked under, adder's bite.
That prize held out of reach
Guides the unwilling tread,
The asking breath,
Till on attended bed
Or in untracked dishonour comes to each
His natural death.

We pass our days
Speak, man to men, easy, learning to point,
To jump before ladies, to show our scars:
But no,
We were mistaken, these faces are not ours.
They smile no more when we smile back:
Eyes, ears, tongue, nostrils bring
News of revolt, inadequate counsel to
An infirm king.

O watcher in the dark, you wake
Our dream of waking, we feel
Your finger on the flesh that has been skinned,
By your bright day

22

See clear what we were doing, that we were vile.
Your sudden hand
Shall humble great
Pride, break it, wear down to stumps old systems which await
The last transgression of the sea.

[*Enter* JOHN NOWER *and* DICK.]

JOHN NOWER : If you have really made up your mind, Dick, I won't try and persuade you to stop. But I shall be sorry to lose you.

DICK : I have thought it all over and I think it is the best thing to do. My cousin writes that the ranch is a thoroughly good proposition. I don't know how I shall like the Colonies but I feel I must get away from here. There is not room enough . . . but the actual moving is unpleasant.

JOHN NOWER : I understand. When are you thinking of sailing?

DICK : My cousin is sailing tomorrow. If I am going I am to join him at the Docks.

JOHN NOWER : Right. Tell one of the men to go down to the post-office and send a wire for you. If you want anything else, let me know.

DICK : Thank you.

[*Exit* DICK. *Enter* ZEPPEL.]

ZEPPEL : Number Six wishes to see you, sir.

JOHN NOWER : All right, show him in.

[*Enter* NUMBER SIX.]

Well, what is it?

NUMBER SIX : My area is Rookhope. Last night at Horse and Farrier, drank alone, one of Shaw's men. I sat down friendly next till muzzed with drink and lateness he was blabbing. Red Shaw goes to Brandon Walls today, visits a woman.

JOHN NOWER : Alone?

NUMBER SIX : No, sir. He takes a few. I got no numbers.

JOHN NOWER : This is good news. Here is a pound for you.

NUMBER SIX : Thank you very much, sir.

[*Exit* NUMBER SIX.]

JOHN NOWER : Zeppel.

ZEPPEL : Sir.

JOHN NOWER : Ask George to come here at once.

ZEPPEL : Very good, sir.

[JOHN *gets a map out. Enter* GEORGE.]

JOHN NOWER : Red Shaw is spending the day at Brandon Walls. We must get him. You know the ground well, don't you, George?

GEORGE : Pretty well. Let me see the map. There's a barn about a hundred yards from the house. Yes, here it is. If we can occupy that without attracting attention it will form a good base for operations, commands both house and road. If I remember rightly, on the other side of the stream is a steep bank. Yes, you can see from the contours. They couldn't get out that way, but lower down is marshy ground and possible. You want to post some men there to catch those who try.

JOHN NOWER : Good. Who do you suggest to lead that party?

GEORGE : Send Sturton. He knows the whole district blindfold. He and I as boys fished all those streams together.

JOHN NOWER : I shall come with you. Let's see: it's dark now about five. Fortunately there's no moon and it's cloudy. We'll start then about half-past. Pick your men and get some sandwiches made up in the kitchen. I'll see about the ammunition if you will remember to bring a

23

compass. We meet outside at a quarter past.

[*Exeunt. Enter* KURT *and* CULLEY.]

KURT: There's time for a quick one before changing. What's yours?

CULLEY: I'll have a sidecar, thanks.

KURT: Zeppel, one sidecar and one C.P.S. I hear Chapman did the lake in eight.

CULLEY: Yes, he is developing a very pretty style. I am not sure though that Pepys won't beat him next year if he can get out of that double kick. Thanks. Prosit.

KURT: Cheerio.

[*Enter* WALTER *and* TRUDY.]

WALTER: Two half pints, Zeppel, please. [*To* KURT.] Can you let me have a match? How is the Rugger going?

KURT: All right, thank you. We have not got a bad team this season.

WALTER: Where do you play yourself?

KURT: Wing 3Q.

WALTER: Did you ever see Warner? No, he'd be before your time. You remember him don't you, Trudy?

TRUDY: He was killed in the fight at Colefangs, wasn't he?

WALTER: You are muddling him up with Hunter. He was the best three-quarter I have ever seen. His sprinting was marvellous to watch.

ZEPPEL (*producing Christmas turkey*): Not bad eh?

TRUDY (*feeling it*): Oh a fine one. For tomorrow's dinner?

ZEPPEL: Yes. Here, puss . . . gobble, gobble . . .

TRUDY (*to* WALTER): What have you got Ingo for Christmas?

WALTER: A model crane. Do you think he will like it?

TRUDY: He loves anything mechanical. He's so excited he can't sleep.

KURT: Come on, Culley, finish your drink. We must be getting along. [*To* WALTER.] You must come down to the field on Monday and see us.

WALTER: I will if I can.

[*Exit* KURT *and* CULLEY.]

TRUDY: Is there any news yet?

WALTER: Nothing has come through. If things are going right they may be back any time now.

TRUDY: I suppose they will get him?

WALTER: It's almost certain. Nower has waited long enough.

TRUDY:

I am sick of this feud. What do we want to go on killing each other for?
We are all the same. He's trash, yet if I cut my finger it bleeds like his.
But he's swell, keeps double shifts working all night by flares:
His mother squealed like a pig when he came crouching out.
Sometimes we read a sign, cloud in the sky,
The wet tracks of a hare, quicken the step
Promise the best day. But here no remedy
Is to be thought of, no news but the new death;
A Nower dragged out in the night, a Shaw
Ambushed behind the wall. Blood on the ground
Would welcome fighters. Last night at Hammergill
A boy was born fanged like a weasel. I am old,
Shall die before next winter, but more than once shall hear
The cry for help, the shooting round the house.

WALTER:
The best are gone.

24

Often the man, alone shut, shall consider
The killings in old winters, death of friends.
Sitting with stranger shall expect no good.

Spring came, urging to ships, a casting off,
But one would stay, vengeance not done; it seemed
Doubtful to them that they would meet again.

Fording in the cool of the day they rode
To meet at crossroads when the year was over:
Dead is Brody, such a man was Maul.

I will say this not falsely; I have seen
The just and the unjust die in the day,
All, willing or not, and some were willing.

Here they are.
[*Enter* JOHN NOWER, GEORGE, STURTON *and others. The three speak
alternately*.]

Day was gone, Night covered sky,
Black over earth, When we came there,
To Brandon Walls, Where Red Shaw lay
Hateful and sleeping, Unfriendly visit.
I wished to revenge, Quit fully
Who my father at Colefangs valley,
Lying in ambush, Cruelly shot,
With life for life.

Then watchers saw They were attacked,
Shouted in fear, A night alarm
To men asleep, Doomed men awoke,
Felt for their guns, Ran to the doors,
Would wake their master Who lay with woman,
Upstairs together, Tired after love.
He saw then There would be shooting
Hard fight.

Shot answered shot, Bullets screamed,
Guns shook, Hot in the hand,
Fighters lay, Groaning on ground
Gave up life. Edward fell,
Shot through the chest, First of our lot,
By no means refused fight, Stephen was good,
His first encounter, Showed no fear,
Wounded many.

Then Shaw knew We were too strong,
Would get away Over the moor,
Return alive, But found at the ford
Sturton waiting, Greatest gun-anger,
There he died, Nor any came,
Fighters home, Nor wives shall go
Smiling to bed. They boast no more.

[STEPHEN *suddenly gets up*.]

STEPHEN: A forward forward can never be a backward backward.

GEORGE: Help me put Stephen to bed, somebody. He got tight on the way back. Hullo, they've caught a spy.

VOICES OUTSIDE: Look out. There he is. Catch him. Got you.

[*Enter* KURT *and others with prisoner*.]

KURT: We found this chap hiding in an outhouse.

JOHN NOWER: Bring him here. Who are you?

STEPHEN: I know him. I saw him once at Eickhamp. He's Seth Shaw's brother.

JOHN NOWER: He is, is he. What do you come here for? You know what we do to spies. I'll destroy the whole lot of you. Take him out.

SPY: You may look big, but we'll get you one day, Nower.

[*Exeunt all but* JOHN NOWER, STEPHEN *following*.]

STEPHEN: Don't go, darling.

[JOHN NOWER *sits. A shot outside followed by cheers*.]

[*Enter* ZEPPEL.]

ZEPPEL: Will you be wanting anything more tonight, sir?

JOHN NOWER: No, that will be all thank you.

ZEPPEL: Good night, sir.

JOHN NOWER:

Always the following wind of history
Of others' wisdom makes a buoyant air
Till we come suddenly on pockets where
Is nothing loud but us; where voices seem
Abrupt, untrained, competing with no lie
Our fathers shouted once. They taught us war,
To scamper after darlings, to climb hills,
To emigrate from weakness, find ourselves
The easy conquerors of empty bays:
But never told us this, left each to learn,
Hear something of that soon-arriving day
When to gaze longer and delighted on
A face or idea be impossible.
Could I have been some simpleton that lived
Before disaster sent his runners here:
Younger than worms, worms have too much to bear.
Yes, mineral were best: could I but see
These woods, these fields of green, this lively world
Sterile as moon.

CHORUS:

The Spring unsettles sleeping partnerships,
Foundries improve their casting process, shops
Open a further wing on credit till
The winter. In summer boys grow tall
With running races on the froth-wet sand,
War is declared there, here a treaty signed;
Here a scrum breaks up like a bomb, there troops
Deploy like birds. But proudest into traps
Have fallen. These gears which ran in oil for week
By week, needing no look, now will not work;
Those manors mortgaged twice to pay for love
Go to another.
                    O how shall man live

Whose thought is born, child of one farcical night,
To find him old? The body warm but not
By choice, he dreams of folk in dancing bunches,
Of tart wine spilt on home-made benches,
Where learns, one drawn apart, a secret will
Restore the dead; but comes thence to a wall.
Outside on frozen soil lie armies killed
Who seem familiar but they are cold.
Now the most solid wish he tries to keep
His hands show through; he never will look up,
Say 'I am good'. On him misfortune falls
More than enough. Better where no one feels,
The out-of-sight, buried too deep for shafts.

[*Enter* FATHER CHRISTMAS. *He speaks to the audience.*]
FATHER CHRISTMAS: Ladies and Gentlemen: I should like to thank you
all very much for coming here tonight. Now we have a little surprise for
you. When you go home, I hope you will tell your friends to come and
bring the kiddies, but you will remember to keep this a secret, won't
you? Thank you. Now I will not keep you waiting any longer.
[*Lights. A trial.* JOHN NOWER *as the accuser. The* SPY *as accused.* JOAN *as his
warder with a gigantic feeding bottle.* FATHER CHRISTMAS *as president, the
rest as jury, wearing school caps.*]
FATHER CHRISTMAS: Is there any more evidence?
JOHN NOWER: Yes. I know we have and are making terrific sacrifices, but
we cannot give in. We cannot betray the dead. As we pass their graves
can we be deaf to the simple eloquence of their inscriptions, those who
in the glory of their early manhood gave up their lives for us? No, we
must fight to the finish.
FATHER CHRISTMAS: Very well. Call the witness.
[*Enter* BO.]
BO:
In these days during the migrations, days
Freshening with rain reported from the mountains,
By loss of memory we are reborn,
For memory is death; by taking leave,
Parting in anger and glad to go
Where we are still unwelcome, and if we count
What dead the tides wash in, only to make
Notches for enemies. On northern ridges
Where flags fly, seen and lost, denying rumour
We baffle proof, speakers of a strange tongue.
[*The* SPY *groans. His cries are produced by jazz instruments at the back of the
stage.* JOAN *brandishes her bottle.*]
JOAN: Be quiet, or I'll give you a taste of this.
FATHER CHRISTMAS: Next, please.
[*Enter* PO.]
PO:
Past victory is honour, to accept
An island governorship, back to estates
Explored as child; coming at last to love
Lost publicly, found secretly again
In private flats, admitted to a sign.
An understanding sorrow knows no more,

Sits waiting for the lamp, far from those hills
Where rifts open unfenced, mark of a fall,
And flakes fall softly softly burying
Deeper and deeper down her loving son.

[*The* SPY *groans.* JOHN NOWER *produces a revolver.*]

JOHN NOWER: Better to get it over.

JOAN: This way for the Angel of Peace.

FATHER CHRISTMAS: Leave him alone. This fellow is very very ill. But he
  will get well.

[*The* MAN-WOMAN *appears as a prisoner of war behind barbed wire, in the
snow.*]

MAN-WOMAN:
  Because I'm come it does not mean to hold
  An anniversary, think illness healed,
  As to renew the lease, consider costs
  Of derelict iron works on deserted coasts.
  Love was not love for you but episodes,
  Traffic in memoirs, views from different sides;
  You thought oaths of comparison a bond,
  And though you had your orders to disband,
  Refused to listen, but remained in woods,
  Poorly concealed your profits under wads.
  Nothing was any use; therefore I went
  Hearing you call for what you did not want.
  I lay with you; you made that an excuse
  For playing with yourself, but homesick because
  Your mother told you that's what flowers did,
  And thought you lived since you were bored, not dead,
  And could not stop. So I was cold to make
  No difference, but you were quickly meek,
  Altered for safety. I tried then to demand
  Proud habits, protestations called your mind
  To show you it was extra, but instead
  You overworked yourself, misunderstood,
  Adored me for the chance. Lastly I tried
  To teach you acting, but always you had nerves
  To fear performances as some fear knives.
  Now I shall go. No, you if you come,
  Will not enjoy yourself, for where I am
  All talking is forbidden. . . .

[*The* SPY *groans.*]

JOHN NOWER: I can't bear it.

[*Shoots him. Lights out.*]

VOICES:
  Quick, fetch a doctor.
  Ten pounds for a doctor.
  Ten pounds to keep him away.
  Coming, coming.

[*Lights.* FATHER CHRISTMAS, JOHN NOWER *and the* SPY *remain. The* JURY
has gone, but there is a PHOTOGRAPHER.]

FATHER CHRISTMAS: Stand back there. Here comes the doctor.

[*Enter* DOCTOR *and his* BOY.]

BOY: Tickle your arse with a feather, sir.

DOCTOR: What's that?

BOY: Particularly nasty weather, sir.

DOCTOR: Yes, it is. Tell me, is my hair tidy? One must always be careful with a new client.

BOY: It's full of lice, sir.

DOCTOR: What's that?

BOY: It's looking nice, sir. [*For the rest of the scene the* BOY *fools about.*]

FATHER CHRISTMAS: Are you the doctor?

DOCTOR: I am.

FATHER CHRISTMAS: What can you cure?

DOCTOR: Tennis elbow, Graves' Disease, Derbyshire neck and Housemaid's knees.

FATHER CHRISTMAS: Is that all you can cure?

DOCTOR: No, I have discovered the origin of life. Fourteen months I hesitated before I concluded this diagnosis. I received the morning star for this. My head will be left at death for clever medical analysis. The laugh will be gone and the microbe in command.

FATHER CHRISTMAS: Well, let's see what you can do.

[DOCTOR *takes circular saws, bicycle pumps, etc., from his bag.*]

BOY: You need a pill, sir.

DOCTOR: What's that.

BOY: You'll need your skill, sir. O sir you're hurting.

[BOY *is kicked out.*]

[JOHN NOWER *tries to get a look.*]

DOCTOR: Go away. Your presence will be necessary at Scotland Yard when the criminals of the war are tried, but your evidence will not be needed. It is valueless. Cages will be provided for some of the more interesting specimens. [*Examines the body.*] Um, yes. Very interesting. The conscious brain appears normal except under emotion. Fancy it. The Devil couldn't do that. This advances and retreats under control and poisons everything round it. My diagnosis is: Adamant will, cool brain and laughing spirit. Hullo, what's this? [*Produces a large pair of pliers and extracts an enormous tooth from the body.*] Come along, that's better. Ladies and Gentlemen, you see I have nothing up my sleeve. This tooth was growing ninety-nine years before his great grandmother was born. If it hadn't been taken out today he would have died yesterday. You may get up now.

[*The* SPY *gets up. The* PHOTOGRAPHER *gets ready.*]

PHOTOGRAPHER: Just one minute, please. A little brighter, a little brighter. No, moisten the lips and start afresh. Hold it.

[PHOTOGRAPHER *lets off his flash. Lights out.* FATHER CHRISTMAS *blows a whistle.*]

FATHER CHRISTMAS: All change.

[*Lights.* SPY *behind a gate guarded by* FATHER CHRISTMAS. *Enter* JOHN NOWER *running.*]

JOHN NOWER: I'm late, I'm late. Which way is it? I must hurry.

FATHER CHRISTMAS: You can't come in here, without a pass.

[JOHN NOWER *turns back his coat lapel.*]

FATHER CHRISTMAS: O I beg your pardon, sir. This way, sir.

[*Exit* FATHER CHRISTMAS. *The* ACCUSER *and* ACCUSED *plant a tree.*]

JOHN NOWER:

Sometime sharers of the same house,
We know not the builder nor the name of his son.
Now cannot mean to them; boy's voice among dishonoured portraits
To dockside barmaid speaking,

Sorry through wires, pretended speech.
SPY:
    Escaped
    Armies' pursuit, rebellion and eclipse
    Together in a cart,
    After all journeys
    We stay and are not known.
[*Lights out.*]
    Sharers of the same house,
    Attendants on the same machine,
    Rarely a word, in silence understood.

[*Lights.* JOHN NOWER *alone in his chair. Enter* DICK.]
DICK:
    Hullo. I've come to say goodbye.
    Yesterday we sat at table together,
    Fought side by side at enemies face-to-face meeting.
    Today we take our leave, time for departure.
    I'm sorry.
JOHN NOWER:
    Here, give me your knife and take mine. By these
    We may remember each other.
    There are two chances, but more of one
    Parting for ever, not hearing the other
    Though he need help.
    Have you got everything you want?
DICK: Yes, thanks. Goodbye, John.
JOHN NOWER: Goodbye.
[*Exit* DICK.]
    There is the city,
    Lighted and clean once, pleasure for builders,
    And I,
    Letting to cheaper tenants, have made a slum,
    Houses at which the passer shakes his fist,
    Remembering evil.
    Pride and indifference have shared with me, and I
    Have kissed them in the dark, for mind has dark,
    Shaded commemorations, midnight accidents
    In streets where heirs may dine.

    But love, sent east for peace
    From tunnels under those
    Bursts now to pass
    On trestles over meaner quarters
    A noise and flashing glass.

    Feels morning streaming down,
    Wind from the snows,
    Nowise withdrawn by doubting flinch
    Nor joined to any by belief's firm flange,
    Refreshed sees all,
    The tugged-at teat,
    The hopper's steady feed, the frothing leat.
    Zeppel.

[*Enter* ZEPPEL.]

ZEPPEL : Sir.

JOHN NOWER : Get my horse ready at once, please.

[*Exeunt.*]

CHORUS :

To throw away the key and walk away,
Not abrupt exile, the neighbours asking why,
But following a line with left and right,
An altered gradient at another rate,
Learns more than maps upon the whitewashed wall,
The hand put up to ask; and makes us well
Without confession of the ill. All pasts
Are single old past now, although some posts
Are forwarded, held looking on a new view;
The future shall fulfil a surer vow,
Not smiling at queen over the glass rim,
Nor making gunpowder in the top room,
Not swooping at the surface still like gulls
But with prolonged drowning shall develop gills.

But there are still to tempt; areas not seen
Because of blizzards or an erring sign,
Whose guessed at wonders would be worth alleging,
And lies about the cost of a night's lodging.
Travellers may sleep at inns but not attach,
They sleep one night together, not asked to touch;
Receive no normal welcome, not the pressed lip,
Children to lift, not the assuaging lap.
Crossing the pass descend the growing stream,
Too tired to hear except the pulses' strum,
Reach villages to ask for a bed in,
Rock shutting out the sky, the old life done.

[CULLEY *enters right and squats in the centre of the stage, looking left through field glasses. Several shots are heard off. Enter* GEORGE *and* KURT.]

GEORGE : Are you much hurt?

KURT : Nothing much, sir. Only a slight flesh wound. Did you get him, sir?

GEORGE : On ledge above the gulley, aimed at, seen moving, fell; looked down on, sprawls in the stream.

KURT : Good. He sniped poor Billy last Easter, riding to Flash.

GEORGE : I have some lint and bandages in my haversack, and there is a spring here. I'll dress your arm.

[*Enter* SETH *finds* BERNARD, *left.*]

SETH : Did you find Tom's body?

BERNARD : Yes, sir. It's lying in the Hangs.

SETH : Which way did they go?

BERNARD : Down there, sir.

[CULLEY *observes them and runs right.*]

CULLEY : There are twenty men from Nattrass, sir, over the gap, coming at once.

GEORGE : Have they seen us?

CULLEY : Not yet.

GEORGE : We must get out. You go down to the copse and make for the

31

Barbon road. We'll follow the old tramway. Keep low and run like hell.
[*Exeunt right.* SETH *watches through field glasses.*]
SETH: Yes. No. No. Yes, I can see them. They are making for the Barbon road. Go down and cut them off. There is good cover by the bridge. We've got them now.

[*A whistle. The back curtains draw, showing* JOHN NOWER, ANNE *and* AARON *and the* ANNOUNCER *grouped. Both sides enter left and right.*]
AARON:
    There is a time for peace; too often we
    Have gone on cold marches, have taken life,
    Till wrongs are bred like flies; the dreamer wakes
    Who beats a smooth door, behind footsteps, on the left
    The pointed finger, the unendurable drum,
    To hear of horses stolen or a house burned.
    Now this shall end with marriage as it ought:
    Love turns the wind, brings up the salt smell,
    Shadow of gulls on the road to the sea.
ANNOUNCER: The engagement is announced of John Nower, eldest son of the late Mr. and Mrs. George Nower of Lintzgarth, Rookhope, and Anne Shaw, only daughter of the late Mr. and Mrs. Joseph Shaw of Nattrass, Garrigill.
ALL: Hurrah.
[GEORGE *and* SETH *advance to the centre, shake hands and cross over the stage to their opposite sides. Back curtains close. Exeunt in different directions, talking as they go.*]
GEORGE: It was a close shave that time. We had a lucky escape. How are you feeling?
KURT: The arm is rather painful. I owe Bernard one for that.
BERNARD: It's a shame. Just when we had them fixed.
SETH: Don't you worry. You'll get your chance.
BERNARD: But what about this peace?
SETH: That remains to be seen. Only wait.

[*Exeunt. Back curtains draw.* JOHN NOWER *and* ANNE *alone.* JOHN *blows on a grass held between the thumbs and listens.*]
JOHN NOWER: On Cautley where a peregrine has nested, iced heather hurt the knuckles. Fell on the ball near time, the forward stopped. Goodbye now, he said, would open the swing doors. . . . These I remember, but not love till now. We cannot tell where we shall find it, though we all look for it till we do, and what others tell us is no use to us.
    Some say that handsome raider still at large,
    A terror to the Marches, in truth is love;
    And we must listen for such messengers
    To tell us daily: 'Today a saint came blessing
    The huts': 'Seen lately in the provinces,
    Reading behind a tree and people passing.'
    But love returns;
    At once all heads are turned this way, and love
    Calls order—silenced the angry sons—
    Steps forward, greets, repeats what he has heard
    And seen, feature for feature, word for word.
ANNE:
    Yes, I am glad this evening that we are together.

The silence is unused, death seems
    An axe's echo.

The summer quickens all,
Scatters its promises
To you and me no less
Though neither can compel.
JOHN NOWER:
  The wish to last the year,
  The longest look to live,
  The urgent word survive
  The movement of the air.
ANNE:
  But, loving now, let none
  Think of divided days
  When we shall choose from ways,
  All of them evil, one.
JOHN NOWER:
  Look on with stricter brows
  The sacked and burning town,
  The ice-sheet moving down,
  The fall of an old house.
ANNE: John, I have a car waiting. There is time to join Dick before the boat sails. We sleep in beds where men have died howling.
JOHN NOWER: You may be right, but we shall stay.
ANNE:
  Tonight the many come to mind,
  Sent forward in the thaw with anxious marrow,
  For such might now return with a bleak face,
  An image, pause half-lighted in the door,
  A greater but not fortunate in all;
  Come home deprived of an astonishing end—
  Morgan's who took a clean death in the north
  Shouting against the wind, or Cousin Dodds',
  Passed out in her chair, the snow falling—
  The too-loved clays, borne over by diverse drifts,
  Fallen upon the far side of all enjoyment,
  Unable to move closer, shall not speak
  Out of that grave, stern on no capital fault;
  Enough to have lightly touched the unworthy thing.
JOHN NOWER: We live still.
ANNE: But what has become of the dead? They forget.
JOHN NOWER: These. Smilers, all who stand on promontories, slinkers, whisperers, deliberate approaches, echoes, time, promises of mercy, what dreams or goes masked, embraces that fail, insufficient evidence, touches of the old wound.
  But let us not think of things which we hope will be long in coming.
CHORUS:
  The Spring will come,
  Not hesitate for one employer who
  Though a fine day and every pulley running
  Would quick lie down; nor save the wanted one
  That, wounded in escaping, swam the lake
  Safe to the reeds, collapsed in shallow water.

You have tasted good and what is it? For you,
Sick in the green plain, healed in the tundra, shall
Turn westward back from your alone success,
Under a dwindling Alp to see your friends
Cut down the wheat.

JOHN NOWER: It's getting cold, dear, let's go in.

[*Exeunt. Back curtains close.*]

CHORUS:
For where are Basley who won the Ten,
Dickon so tarted by the House,
Thomas who kept a sparrow-hawk?
The clock strikes, it is time to go,
The tongue ashamed, deceived by a shake of the hand.

[*Enter* BRIDAL PARTY *left,* GUESTS *right.*]

GUESTS: Ssh.

[*The* CHIEF GUEST *comes forward and presents a bouquet to the bride.*]

CHIEF GUEST:
With gift in hand we come
From every neighbour farm
To celebrate in wine
The certain union of
A woman and a man;
And may their double love
Be shown to the stranger's eye
In a son's symmetry.
Now hate is swallowed down,
All anger put away;
The spirit comes to its own,
The beast to its play.

[ALL *clap. The* CHIEF GUEST *addresses the* AUDIENCE.]

CHIEF GUEST: Will any lady be so kind as to oblige us with a dance?... Thank you very much... This way miss... What tune would you like?

[*Gramophone. A dance. As the dance ends, the back curtains draw and the* BUTLER *enters centre.*]

BUTLER: Dinner is served.

[AARON *goes to the* DANCER.]

AARON: You'll dine with us, of course?

[*Exeunt all except* SETH *and his* MOTHER.]

GUESTS (*as they go out*): It will be a good year for them, I think.
You don't mean that he ... well, you know what.
Rather off his form lately.
The vein is showing good in the Quarry Hazel.
One of Edward's friends.
You must come and have a look at the Kennels some day.
Well it does seem to show.
    [*Etc., etc.*]

[*Back curtains close.*]

MOTHER: Seth.

SETH: Yes, Mother.

MOTHER: John Nower is here.

SETH: I know that. What do you want me to do?

MOTHER: Kill him.

SETH: I can't do that. There is peace now; besides he is a guest in our house.

MOTHER: Have you forgotten your brother's death . . . taken out and shot like a dog? It is a nice thing for me to hear people saying that I have a coward for a son. I am thankful your father is not here to see it.

SETH: I'm not afraid of anything or anybody, but I don't want to.

MOTHER: I shall have to take steps.

SETH: It shall be as you like. Though I think that much will come of this, chiefly harm.

MOTHER: I have thought of that.

[*Exit* MOTHER.]

SETH: The little funk. Sunlight on sparkling water, its shades dissolved, reforming, unreal activity where others laughed but he blubbed clinging, homesick, an undeveloped form. I'll do it. Men point in after days. He always was. But wrongly. He fought and overcame, a stern self-ruler. You didn't hear. Hearing they look ashamed too late for shaking hands. Of course I'll do it.

[*Exit* SETH.]

[*A shot. More shots. Shouting.*]

VOICES OUTSIDE: A trap. I might have known.
Take that, damn you.
Open the window.
You swine.
Jimmy, O my God.

[*Enter* SETH *and* BERNARD.]

BERNARD: The Master's killed. So is John Nower, but some of them got away, fetching help, will attack in an hour.

SETH: See that all the doors are bolted.

[*Exeunt right and left. The back curtains draw.* ANNE *with the dead.*]

ANNE:
Now we have seen the story to its end.
The hands that were to help will not be lifted,
And bad followed by worse leaves to us tears,
An empty bed, hope from less noble men.
I had seen joy
Received and given, upon both sides, for years.
Now not.

CHORUS:
Though he believe it, no man is strong.
He thinks to be called the fortunate,
To bring home a wife, to live long.

But he is defeated; let the son
Sell the farm lest the mountain fall;
His mother and her mother won.

His fields are used up where the moles visit,
The contours worn flat; if there show
Passage for water he will miss it:

Give up his breath, his woman, his team;
No life to touch, though later there be
Big fruit, eagles above the stream.

CURTAIN

January–December 1928

35

Part II

1927–1932

The Letter

From the very first coming down
Into a new valley with a frown
Because of the sun and a lost way,
You certainly remain: to-day
I, crouching behind a sheep-pen, heard
Travel across a sudden bird,
Cry out against the storm, and found
The year's arc a completed round
And love's worn circuit re-begun,
Endless with no dissenting turn.
Shall see, shall pass, as we have seen
The swallow on the tile, spring's green
Preliminary shiver, passed
A solitary truck, the last
Of shunting in the Autumn. But now,
To interrupt the homely brow,
Thought warmed to evening through and through,
Your letter comes, speaking as you,
Speaking of much but not to come.

Nor speech is close nor fingers numb,
If love not seldom has received
An unjust answer, was deceived.
I, decent with the seasons, move
Different or with a different love,
Nor question overmuch the nod,
The stone smile of this country god
That never was more reticent,
Always afraid to say more than it meant.

December 1927

Taller To-day

Taller to-day, we remember similar evenings,
Walking together in a windless orchard
Where the brook runs over the gravel, far from the glacier.

Nights come bringing the snow, and the dead howl
Under headlands in their windy dwelling
Because the Adversary put too easy questions
On lonely roads.

But happy now, though no nearer each other,
We see farms lighted all along the valley;
Down at the mill-shed hammering stops
And men go home.

Noises at dawn will bring
Freedom for some, but not this peace
No bird can contradict: passing but here, sufficient now
For something fulfilled this hour, loved or endured.

March 1928

Missing

From scars where kestrels hover,
The leader looking over
Into the happy valley,
Orchard and curving river,
May turn away to see
The slow fastidious line
That disciplines the fell,
Hear curlew's creaking call
From angles unforeseen,
The drumming of a snipe
Surprise where driven sleet
Had scalded to the bone
And streams are acrid yet
To an unaccustomed lip;
The tall unwounded leader
Of doomed companions, all
Whose voices in the rock
Are now perpetual,
Fighters for no one's sake,
Who died beyond the border.

Heroes are buried who
Did not believe in death,
And bravery is now,
Not in the dying breath
But resisting the temptations
To skyline operations.
Yet glory is not new;
The summer visitors
Still come from far and wide,
Choosing their spots to view
The prize competitors,
Each thinking that he will
Find heroes in the wood,
Far from the capital,
Where lights and wine are set
For supper by the lake,
But leaders must migrate:
'Leave for Cape Wrath to-night,'
And the host after waiting
Must quench the lamps and pass
Alive into the house.

January 1929

The Secret Agent

Control of the passes was, he saw, the key
To this new district, but who would get it?
He, the trained spy, had walked into the trap
For a bogus guide, seduced by the old tricks.

At Greenhearth was a fine site for a dam
And easy power, had they pushed the rail
Some stations nearer. They ignored his wires:
The bridges were unbuilt and trouble coming.

The street music seemed gracious now to one
For weeks up in the desert. Woken by water
Running away in the dark, he often had
Reproached the night for a companion
Dreamed of already. They would shoot, of course,
Parting easily two that were never joined.

January 1928

The Watershed

Who stands, the crux left of the watershed,
On the wet road between the chafing grass
Below him sees dismantled washing-floors,
Snatches of tramline running to a wood,
An industry already comatose,
Yet sparsely living. A ramshackle engine
At Cashwell raises water; for ten years
It lay in flooded workings until this,
Its latter office, grudgingly performed.
And, further, here and there, though many dead
Lie under the poor soil, some acts are chosen,
Taken from recent winters; two there were
Cleaned out a damaged shaft by hand, clutching
The winch a gale would tear them from; one died
During a storm, the fells impassable,
Not at his village, but in wooden shape
Through long abandoned levels nosed his way
And in his final valley went to ground.

Go home, now, stranger, proud of your young stock,
Stranger, turn back again, frustrate and vexed:
This land, cut off, will not communicate,
Be no accessory content to one
Aimless for faces rather there than here.
Beams from your car may cross a bedroom wall,
They wake no sleeper; you may hear the wind
Arriving driven from the ignorant sea
To hurt itself on pane, on bark of elm
Where sap unbaffled rises, being spring;
But seldom this. Near you, taller than grass,
Ears poise before decision, scenting danger.

August 1927

41

No Change of Place

Who will endure
Heat of day and winter danger,
Journey from one place to another,
Nor be content to lie
Till evening upon headland over bay,
Between the land and sea
Or smoking wait till hour of food,
Leaning on chained-up gate
At edge of wood?

Metals run,
Burnished or rusty in the sun,
From town to town,
And signals all along are down;
Yet nothing passes
But envelopes between these places,
Snatched at the gate and panting read indoors,
And first spring flowers arriving smashed,
Disaster stammered over wires,
And pity flashed.

For should professional traveller come,
Asked at the fireside, he is dumb,
Declining with a secret smile,
And all the while
Conjectures on our maps grow stranger
And threaten danger.

There is no change of place:
No one will ever know
For what conversion brilliant capital is waiting,
What ugly feast may village band be celebrating;
For no one goes
Further than railhead or the ends of piers,
Will neither go nor send his son
Further through foothills than the rotting stack
Where gaitered gamekeeper with dog and gun
Will shout 'Turn back'.

? April 1929

Let History Be My Judge

We made all possible preparations,
Drew up a list of firms,
Constantly revised our calculations
And allotted the farms,

Issued all the orders expedient
In this kind of case:
Most, as was expected, were obedient,
Though there were murmurs, of course;

Chiefly against our exercising
Our old right to abuse:
Even some sort of attempt at rising,
But these were mere boys.

For never serious misgiving
Occurred to anyone,
Since there could be no question of living
If we did not win.

The generally accepted view teaches
That there was no excuse,
Though in the light of recent researches
Many would find the cause

In a not uncommon form of terror;
Others, still more astute,
Point to possibilities of error
At the very start.

As for ourselves there is left remaining
Our honour at least,
And a reasonable chance of retaining
Our faculties to the last.

December 1928

Never Stronger

Again in conversations
Speaking of fear
And throwing off reserve
The voice is nearer
But no clearer
Than first love
Than boys' imaginations.

For every news
Means pairing off in twos and twos,
Another I, another You,
Each knowing what to do
But of no use.

Never stronger
But younger and younger,
Saying good-bye but coming back, for fear
Is over there,
And the centre of anger
Is out of danger.

January 1929

This Loved One

Before this loved one
Was that one and that one,
A family
And history
And ghost's adversity,
Whose pleasing name
Was neighbourly shame.
Before this last one
Was much to be done,
Frontiers to cross
As clothes grew worse,
And coins to pass
In a cheaper house,
Before this last one,
Before this loved one.

Face that the sun
Is lively on
May stir but here
Is no new year;
This gratitude for gifts is less
Than the old loss,
Touching a shaking hands
On mortgaged lands,
And smiling of
This gracious greeting,
'Good day. Good luck',
Is no real meeting,
But instinctive look,
A backward love.

March 1929

Easy Knowledge

Between attention and attention,
The first and last decision,
Is mortal distraction
Of earth and air,
Further and nearer,
The vague wants
Of days and nights,
And personal error;
And the fatigued face,
Taking the strain
Of the horizontal force
And the vertical thrust,
Makes random answer
To the crucial test;
The uncertain flesh,
Scraping back chair
For the wrong train,

44

Falling in slush
Before a friend's friends
Or shaking hands
With a snub-nosed winner.

The opening window, closing door,
Open, close, but not
To finish or restore;
These wishes get
No further than
The edges of the town,
And leaning asking from the car
Cannot tell us where we are;
While the divided face
Has no grace
No discretion,
No occupation
But registering
Acreage, mileage,
The easy knowledge
Of the virtuous thing.   *May 1930*

Too Dear, Too Vague

Love by ambition
Of definition
Suffers partition
And cannot go
From yes to no,
For no is not love; no is no,
The shutting of a door,
The tightening jaw,
A wilful sorrow;
And saying yes
Turns love into success,
Views from the rail
Of land and happiness;
Assured of all,
The sofas creak,
And were this all, love were
But cheek to cheek
And dear to dear.

Voices explain
Love's pleasure and love's pain,
Still tap the knee
And cannot disagree,
Hushed for aggression
Of full confession,
Likeness to likeness
Of each old weakness;
Love is not there,

45

Love has moved to another chair,
Aware already
Of what stands next,
And is not vexed,
And is not giddy,
Leaves the North in place
With a good grace,
And would not gather
Another to another,
Designs his own unhappiness
Foretells his own death and is faithless.

March 1929

Between Adventure

Upon this line between adventure
Prolong the meeting out of good nature
Obvious in each agreeable feature.

Calling of each other by name,
Smiling, taking a willing arm,
Has the companionship of a game.

But should the walk do more than this
Out of bravado or drunkenness,
Forward or back are menaces.

On neither side let foot slip over,
Invading Always, exploring Never,
For this is hate and this is fear.

On narrowness stand, for sunlight is
Brightest only on surfaces;
No anger, no traitor, but peace.

June 1929

A Free One

Watch any day his nonchalant pauses, see
His dextrous handling of a wrap as he
Steps after into cars, the beggar's envy.

'There is a free one,' many say, but err.
He is not that returning conqueror,
Nor ever the poles' circumnavigator.

But poised between shocking falls on razor-edge
Has taught himself this balancing subterfuge
Of an accosting profile, an erect carriage.

The song, the varied action of the blood,
Would drown the warning from the iron wood,
Would cancel the inertia of the buried:

Travelling by daylight on from house to house
The longest way to an intrinsic peace,
With love's fidelity and with love's weakness.

March 1929

Family Ghosts

The strings' excitement, the applauding drum,
Are but the initiating ceremony
That out of cloud the ancestral face may come,

And never hear their subaltern mockery,
Graffiti-writers, moss-grown with whimsies,
Loquacious when the watercourse is dry.

It is your face I see, and morning's praise
Of you is ghost's approval of the choice,
Filtered through roots of the effacing grass.

Fear, taking me aside, would give advice
'To conquer her, the visible enemy,
It is enough to turn away the eyes.'

Yet there's no peace in the assaulted city,
But speeches at the corners, hope for news,
Outside the watchfires of a stronger army.

And all emotions to expression come,
Recovering the archaic imagery:
This longing for assurance takes the form

Of a hawk's vertical stooping from the sky;
These tears, salt for a disobedient dream,
The lunatic agitation of the sea;

While this despair with hardened eyeballs cries
'A Golden Age, a Silver . . . rather this,
Massive and taciturn years, the Age of Ice'.

April 1929

The Questioner Who Sits So Sly

Will you turn a deaf ear
To what they said on the shore,
Interrogate their poises
In their rich houses;

Of stork-legged heaven-reachers,
Of the compulsory touchers,
The sensitive amusers,
And masked amazers?

Yet wear no ruffian badge,
Nor lie behind the hedge,
Waiting with bombs of conspiracy
In arm-pit secrecy;

Carry no talisman
For germ or the abrupt pain,
Needing no concrete shelter
Nor porcelain filter?

Will you wheel death anywhere
In his invalid chair,
With no affectionate instant
But his attendant?

For to be held as friend
By an undeveloped mind,
To be joke for children is
Death's happiness:

Whose anecdotes betray
His favourite colour as blue,
Colour of distant bells
And boy's overalls.

His tales of the bad lands
Disturb the sewing hands;
Hard to be superior
On parting nausea;

To accept the cushions from
Women against martyrdom,
Yet applauding the circuits
Of racing cyclists.

Never to make signs,
Fear neither maelstrom nor zones,
Salute with soldiers' wives
When the flag waves;

Remembering there is
No recognized gift for this;
No income, no bounty,
No promised country.

But to see brave sent home
Hermetically sealed with shame,
And cold's victorious wrestle
With molten metal.

A neutralizing peace
And an average disgrace
Are honour to discover
For later other.

September 1929

Venus Will Now Say a Few Words

Since you are going to begin to-day
Let us consider what it is you do.
You are the one whose part it is to lean,
For whom it is not good to be alone.
Laugh warmly turning shyly in the hall
Or climb with bare knees the volcanic hill,
Acquire that flick of wrist and after strain
Relax in your darling's arms like a stone,
Remembering everything you can confess,
Making the most of firelight, of hours of fuss;
But joy is mine not yours—to have come so far,
Whose cleverest invention was lately fur;
Lizards my best once who took years to breed,
Could not control the temperature of blood.
To reach that shape for your face to assume,
Pleasure to many and despair to some,
I shifted ranges, lived epochs handicapped
By climate, wars, or what the young men kept,
Modified theories on the types of dross,
Altered desire and history of dress.

You in the town now call the exile fool
That writes home once a year as last leaves fall,
Think—Romans had a language in their day
And ordered roads with it, but it had to die:
Your culture can but leave—forgot as sure
As place-name origins in favourite shire—
Jottings for stories, some often mentioned Jack,
And references in letters to a private joke,
Equipment rusting in unweeded lanes,
Virtues still advertised on local lines;
And your conviction shall help none to fly,
Cause rather a perversion on next floor.

Nor even is despair your own, when swiftly
Comes general assault on your ideas of safety:
That sense of famine, central anguish felt
For goodness wasted at peripheral fault,
Your shutting up the house and taking prow
To go into the wilderness to pray,
Means that I wish to leave and to pass on,
Select another form, perhaps your son;
Though he reject you, join opposing team
Be late or early at another time,
My treatment will not differ—he will be tipped,
Found weeping, signed for, made to answer, topped.
Do not imagine you can abdicate;
Before you reach the frontier you are caught;
Others have tried it and will try again
To finish that which they did not begin:
Their fate must always be the same as yours,

To suffer the loss they were afraid of, yes,
Holders of one position, wrong for years.

November 1929

1929

I

It was Easter as I walked in the public gardens,
Hearing the frogs exhaling from the pond,
Watching traffic of magnificent cloud
Moving without anxiety on open sky—
Season when lovers and writers find
An altering speech for altering things,
An emphasis on new names, on the arm
A fresh hand with fresh power.
But thinking so I came at once
Where solitary man sat weeping on a bench,
Hanging his head down, with his mouth distorted
Helpless and ugly as an embryo chicken.

So I remember all of those whose death
Is necessary condition of the season's putting forth,
Who, sorry in this time, look only back
To Christmas intimacy, a winter dialogue
Fading in silence, leaving them in tears.
And recent particulars come to mind;
The death by cancer of a once hated master,
A friend's analysis of his own failure,
Listened to at intervals throughout the winter
At different hours and in different rooms.
But always with success of others for comparison,
The happiness, for instance, of my friend Kurt Groote,
Absence of fear in Gerhart Meyer
From the sea, the truly strong man.

A 'bus ran home then, on the public ground
Lay fallen bicycles like huddled corpses:
No chattering valves of laughter emphasised
Nor the swept gown ends of a gesture stirred
The sessile hush; until a sudden shower
Fell willing into grass and closed the day,
Making choice seem a necessary error.

April 1929

II

Coming out of me living is always thinking,
Thinking changing and changing living,
Am feeling as it was seeing—
In city leaning on harbour parapet
To watch a colony of duck below
Sit, preen, and doze on buttresses
Or upright paddle on flickering stream,
Casually fishing at a passing straw.

Those find sun's luxury enough,
Shadow know not of homesick foreigner
Nor restlessless of intercepted growth.

All this time was anxiety at night,
Shooting and barricade in street.
Walking home late I listened to a friend
Talking excitedly of final war
Of proletariat against police—
That one shot girl of nineteen through the knees
They threw that one down concrete stair—
Till I was angry, said I was pleased.

Time passes in Hessen, in Gutensberg,
With hill-top and evening holds me up,
Tiny observer of enormous world.
Smoke rises from factory in field,
Memory of fire: On all sides heard
Vanishing music of isolated larks:
From village square voices in hymn,
Men's voices, an old use.
And I above standing, saying in thinking:

'Is first baby, warm in mother,
Before born and is still mother,
Time passes and now is other,
Is knowledge in him now of other,
Cries in cold air, himself no friend.
In grown man also, may see in face,
In his day-thinking and in his night-thinking,
Is wareness and is fear of other,
Alone in flesh, himself no friend.'

He says, 'We must forgive and forget,'
Forgetting saying but is unforgiving
And unforgiving is in his living;
Body reminds in him to loving,
Reminds but takes no further part,
Perfunctorily affectionate in hired room
But takes no part and is unloving
But loving death. May see in dead,
In face of dead that loving wish,
As one returns from Africa to wife
And his ancestral property in Wales.

Yet sometimes men look and say good
At strict beauty of locomotive,
Completeness of gesture or unclouded eye;
In me so absolute unity of evening
And field and distance was in me for peace
Was over me in feeling without forgetting
Those ducks' indifference, that friend's hysteria,
Without wishing and with forgiving,

To love my life, not as other,
Not as bird's life, not as child's,
'Cannot', I said, 'being no child now nor a bird.'

May 1929

III

Order to stewards and the study of time,
Correct in books, was earlier than this
But joined this by the wires I watched from train,
Slackening of wire and posts' sharp reprimand,
In month of August to a cottage coming.

Being alone, the frightened soul
Returns to this life of sheep and hay
No longer his: he every hour
Moves further from this and must so move,
As child is weaned from his mother and leaves home
But taking the first steps falters, is vexed,
Happy only to find home, a place
Where no tax is levied for being there.

So, insecure, he loves and love
Is insecure, gives less than he expects.
He knows not if it be seed in time to display
Luxuriantly in a wonderful fructification
Or whether it be but a degenerate remnant
Of something immense in the past but now
Surviving only as the infectiousness of disease
Or in the malicious caricature of drunkenness;
Its end glossed over by the careless but known long
To finer perception of the mad and ill.

Moving along the track which is himself,
He loves what he hopes will last, which gone,
Begins the difficult work of mourning,
And as foreign settlers to strange country come,
By mispronunciation of native words
And intermarriage create a new race,
A new language, so may the soul
Be weaned at last to independent delight.

Startled by the violent laugh of a jay
I went from wood, from crunch underfoot,
Air between stems as under water;
As I shall leave the summer, see autumn come
Focusing stars more sharply in the sky,
See frozen buzzard flipped down the weir
And carried out to sea, leave autumn,
See winter, winter for earth and us,
A forethought of death that we may find ourselves at
    death
Not helplessly strange to the new conditions.

August 1929

IV

It is time for the destruction of error.
The chairs are being brought in from the garden,
The summer talk stopped on that savage coast
Before the storms, after the guests and birds:
In sanatoriums they laugh less and less,
Less certain of cure; and the loud madman
Sinks now into a more terrible calm.

The falling leaves know it, the children,
At play on the fuming alkali-tip
Or by the flooded football ground know it—
This is the dragon's day, the devourer's:
Orders are given to the enemy for a time
With underground proliferation of mould,
With constant whisper and with casual question,
To haunt the poisoned in his shunned house,
To destroy the efflorescence of the flesh,
The intricate play of the mind, enforce
Conformity with the orthodox bone.

You whom I gladly walk with, touch,
Or wait for as one certain of good,
We know it, know that love
Needs more than the admiring excitement of union,
More than the abrupt self-confident farewell,
The heel on the finishing blade of grass,
The self-confidence of the falling root,
Needs death, death of the grain, our death,
Death of the old gang; would leave them
In sullen valley where is made no friend,
The old gang to be forgotten in the spring,
The hard bitch and the riding-master,
Stiff underground; deep in clear lake
The lolling bridegroom, beautiful, there.

October 1929

The Bonfires

Look there! The sunk road winding
To the fortified farm.
Listen! The cock's alarm
In the strange valley.

Are we the stubborn athletes;
Are we then to begin
The run between the gin
And bloody falcon?

The horns of the dark squadron
Converging to attack;
The sound behind our back
Of glaciers calving.

53

In legend all were simple,
And held the straitened spot;
But we in legend not,
Are not simple.

In weakness how much further;
Along what crooked route
By hedgehog's gradual foot,
Or fish's fathom.

Bitter the blue smoke rises
From garden bonfires lit,
To where we burning sit:
Good, if it's thorough,

Leaving no double traitor
In days of luck and heat,
To time the double beat,
At last together.

January 1931

On Sunday Walks

On Sunday walks
Past the shut gates of works
The conquerors come
And are handsome.

Sitting all day
By the open window,
Say what they say,
Know what to know,
Who brought and taught
Unusual images
And new tunes to old cottages,
With so much done,
Without a thought
Of the anonymous lampoon,
The cellar counterplot,
Though in the night,
Pursued by eaters,
They clutch at gaiters
That straddle and deny
Escape that way,
Though in the night
Is waking fright.

Father by son
Lives on and on,
Though over date
And motto on the gate
The lichen grows
From year to year,

Still here and there
That Roman nose
Is noticed in the villages,
And father's son
Knows what they said
And what they did.

Not meaning to deceive,
Wish to give suck
Enforces make-believe,
And what was fear
Of fever and bad-luck
Is now a scare
At certain names,
A need for charms,
For certain words
At certain fords,
And what was livelihood
Is tallness, strongness,
Words and longness,
All glory and all story,
Solemn and not so good.

August 1929

Shorts

Pick a quarrel, go to war,
Leave the hero in the bar;
Hunt the lion, climb the peak:
No one guesses you are weak.

*   *   *

The friends of the born nurse
Are always getting worse.

*   *   *

When he is well
She gives him hell,
But she's a brick
When he is sick.

*   *   *

You're a long way off becoming a saint
So long as you suffer from any complaint;
But, if you don't, there's no denying
The chances are that you're not trying.

*   *   *

I'm afraid there's many a spectacled sod
Prefers the British Museum to God.

* * *

I'm beginning to lose patience
With my personal relations:
They are not deep,
And they are not cheap.

* * *

Those who will not reason
Perish in the act:
Those who will not act
Perish for that reason.

* * *

Let us honour if we can
The vertical man,
Though we value none
But the horizontal one.

* * *

These had stopped seeking
But went on speaking,
Have not contributed
But have diluted.

These ordered light
But had no right,
These handed on
War and a son.

Wishing no harm
But to be warm,
These fell asleep
On the burning heap.

* * *

Private faces in public places
Are wiser and nicer
Than public faces in private places.

1929–1931

Happy Ending

The silly fool, the silly fool
Was sillier in school
But beat the bully as a rule.

The youngest son, the youngest son
Was certainly no wise one
Yet could surprise one.

Or rather, or rather,
To be posh, we gather,
One should have no father.

Simple to prove
That deeds indeed
In life succeed,
But love in love,
And tales in tales
Where no one fails.

August 1929

This Lunar Beauty

This lunar beauty
Has no history,
Is complete and early;
If beauty later
Bear any feature,
It had a lover
And is another.

This like a dream
Keeps other time,
And daytime is
The loss of this;
For time is inches
And the heart's changes,
Where ghost has haunted
Lost and wanted.

But this was never
A ghost's endeavour
Nor, finished this,
Was ghost at ease;
And till it pass
Love shall not near
The sweetness here,
Nor sorrow take
His endless look.

April 1930

The Question

To ask the hard question is simple;
Asking at meeting
With the simple glance of acquaintance
To what these go
And how these do:
To ask the hard question is simple,
The simple act of the confused will.

But the answer
Is hard and hard to remember:
On steps or on shore
The ears listening
To words at meeting,
The eyes looking
At the hands helping,
Are never sure
Of what they learn
From how these things are done.
And forgetting to listen or see
Makes forgetting easy;
Only remembering the method of remembering,
Remembering only in another way,
Only the strangely exciting lie,
Afraid
To remember what the fish ignored,
How the bird escaped, or if the sheep obeyed.

Till, losing memory,
Bird, fish, and sheep are ghostly,
And ghosts must do again
What gives them pain.
Cowardice cries
For windy skies,
Coldness for water,
Obedience for a master.

Shall memory restore
The steps and the shore,
The face and the meeting place;
Shall the bird live,
Shall the fish dive,
And sheep obey
In a sheep's way;
Can love remember
The question and the answer,
For love recover
What has been dark and rich and warm all over?

                                    ? August 1930

58

Five Songs

I

What's in your mind, my dove, my coney;
Do thoughts grow like feathers, the dead end of life;
Is it making of love or counting of money,
Or raid on the jewels, the plans of a thief?

Open your eyes, my dearest dallier;
Let hunt with your hands for escaping me;
Go through the motions of exploring the familiar;
Stand on the brink of the warm white day.

Rise with the wind, my great big serpent;
Silence the birds and darken the air;
Change me with terror, alive in a moment;
Strike for the heart and have me there.

November 1930

II

That night when joy began
Our narrowest veins to flush,
We waited for the flash
Of morning's levelled gun.

But morning let us pass,
And day by day relief
Outgrows his nervous laugh,
Grown credulous of peace,

As mile by mile is seen
No trespasser's reproach,
And love's best glasses reach
No fields but are his own.

November 1931

III

For what as easy
For what though small,
For what is well
Because between,
To you simply
From me I mean.

Who goes with who
The bedclothes say,
As I and you
Go kissed away,
The data given,
The senses even.

Fate is not late,
Nor the speech rewritten,
Nor one word forgotten,
Said at the start
About heart,
By heart, for heart.

October 1931

IV

Seen when nights are silent,
The bean-shaped island,
And our ugly comic servant,
Who was observant.

O the veranda and the fruit,
The tiny steamer in the bay
Startling summer with its hoot:—
You have gone away.

V

'O where are you going?' said reader to rider,
'That valley is fatal when furnaces burn,
Yonder's the midden whose odours will madden,
That gap is the grave where the tall return.'

'O do you imagine,' said fearer to farer,
'That dusk will delay on your path to the pass,
Your diligent looking discover the lacking,
Your footsteps feel from granite to grass?'

'O what was that bird,' said horror to hearer,
'Did you see that shape in the twisted trees?
Behind you swiftly the figure comes softly,
The spot on your skin is a shocking disease.'

'Out of this house'—said rider to reader,
'Yours never will'—said farer to fearer,
'They're looking for you'—said hearer to horror,
As he left them there, as he left them there.

October 1931

Uncle Henry

When the Flyin' Scot
fills for shootin', I go southward,
wisin' after coffee, leavin'
Lady Starkie.

Weady for some fun,
visit yearly Wome, Damascus,
in Mowocco look for fwesh a-
-musin' places.

Where I'll find a fwend,
don't you know, a charmin' cweature,
like a Gweek God and devoted:
   how delicious!

All they have they bwing,
Abdul, Nino, Manfwed, Kosta:
here's to women for they bear such
   lovely kiddies!

? 1931

Consider

Consider this and in our time
As the hawk sees it or the helmeted airman:
The clouds rift suddenly—look there
At cigarette-end smouldering on a border
At the first garden party of the year.
Pass on, admire the view of the massif
Through plate-glass windows of the Sport Hotel;
Join there the insufficient units
Dangerous, easy, in furs, in uniform,
And constellated at reserved tables,
Supplied with feelings by an efficient band,
Relayed elsewhere to farmers and their dogs
Sitting in kitchens in the stormy fens.

Long ago, supreme Antagonist,
More powerful than the great northern whale,
Ancient and sorry at life's limiting defect,
In Cornwall, Mendip, or the Pennine moor
Your comments on the highborn mining-captains,
Found they no answer, made them wish to die
—Lie since in barrows out of harm.
You talk to your admirers every day
By silted harbours, derelict works,
In strangled orchards, and a silent comb
Where dogs have worried or a bird was shot.
Order the ill that they attack at once:
Visit the ports and, interrupting
The leisurely conversation in the bar
Within a stone's throw of the sunlit water,
Beckon your chosen out. Summon
Those handsome and diseased youngsters, those women
Your solitary agents in the country parishes;
And mobilize the powerful forces latent
In soils that make the farmer brutal,
In the infected sinus, and the eyes of stoats.
Then, ready, start your rumour, soft
But horrifying in its capacity to disgust
Which, spreading magnified, shall come to be
A polar peril, a prodigious alarm,
Scattering the people, as torn-up paper

Rags and utensils in a sudden gust,
Seized with immeasurable neurotic dread.

Seekers after happiness, all who follow
The convolutions of your simple wish,
It is later than you think; nearer that day
Far other than that distant afternoon
Amid rustle of frocks and stamping feet
They gave the prizes to the ruined boys.
You cannot be away, then, no
Not though you pack to leave within an hour,
Escaping humming down arterial roads:
The date was yours; the prey to fugues,
Irregular breathing and alternate ascendancies
After some haunted migratory years
To disintegrate on an instant in the explosion of mania
Or lapse for ever into a classic fatigue.

March 1930

The Wanderer

Doom is dark and deeper than any sea-dingle.
Upon what man it fall
In spring, day-wishing flowers appearing,
Avalanche sliding, white snow from rock-face,
That he should leave his house,
No cloud-soft hand can hold him, restraint by women;
But ever that man goes
Through place-keepers, through forest trees,
A stranger to strangers over undried sea,
Houses for fishes, suffocating water,
Or lonely on fell as chat,
By pot-holed becks
A bird stone-haunting, an unquiet bird.

There head falls forward, fatigued at evening,
And dreams of home,
Waving from window, spread of welcome,
Kissing of wife under single sheet;
But waking sees
Bird-flocks nameless to him, through doorway voices
Of new men making another love.

Save him from hostile capture,
From sudden tiger's leap at corner;
Protect his house,
His anxious house where days are counted
From thunderbolt protect,
From gradual ruin spreading like a stain;
Converting number from vague to certain,
Bring joy, bring day of his returning,
Lucky with day approaching, with leaning dawn.

August 1930

The Watchers

Now from my window-sill I watch the night,
The church clock's yellow face, the green pier light
Burn for a new imprudent year;
The silence buzzes in my ear;
The lights of near-by families are out.

Under the darkness nothing seems to stir;
The lilac bush like a conspirator
Shams dead upon the lawn, and there
Above the flagstaff the Great Bear
Hangs as a portent over Helensburgh.

O Lords of Limit, training dark and light
And setting a tabu 'twixt left and right,
The influential quiet twins
From whom all property begins,
Look leniently upon us all to-night.

No one has seen you: none can say, 'Of late
Here. You can see the marks—They lay in wait,'
But in my thoughts to-night you seem
Forms which I saw once in a dream,
The stocky keepers of a wild estate.

With guns beneath your arms, in sun and wet,
At doorways posted or on ridges set,
By copse or bridge we know you there
Whose sleepless presences endear
Our peace to us with a perpetual threat.

Look not too closely, be not over-quick;
We have no invitation, but we are sick,
Using the mole's device, the carriage
Of peacock or rat's desperate courage,
And we shall only pass you by a trick.

Deeper towards the summer the year moves on.
What if the starving visionary have seen
The carnival within our gates,
Your bodies kicked about the streets,
We need your power still: use it, that none,

O, from their tables break uncontrollably away,
Lunging, insensible to injury,
Dangerous in a room or out wild-
-ly spinning like a top in the field,
Mopping and mowing through the sleepless day.

February 1932

Adolescence

By landscape reminded once of his mother's figure
The mountain heights he remembers get bigger and bigger:
With the finest of mapping pens he fondly traces
All the family names on the familiar places.

In a green pasture straying, he walks by still waters;
Surely a swan he seems to earth's unwise daughters,
Bending a beautiful head, worshipping not lying,
'Dear' the dear beak in the dear concha crying.

Under the trees the summer bands were playing;
'Dear boy, be brave as these roots,' he heard them saying:
Carries the good news gladly to a world in danger,
Is ready to argue, he smiles, with any stranger.

And yet this prophet, homing the day is ended,
Receives odd welcome from the country he so defended:
The band roars 'Coward, Coward,' in his human fever,
The giantess shuffles nearer, cries 'Deceiver'.

March 1931

The Exiles

What siren zooming is sounding our coming
Up frozen fjord forging from freedom,
    What shepherd's call
    When stranded on hill,
    With broken axle
    On track to exile?

With labelled luggage we alight at last,
Joining joking at the junction on the moor,
    With practised smile
    And harmless tale
    Advance to meet
    Each new recruit.

Expert from uplands, always in oilskins,
Recliner from library, laying down law,
    Owner from shire,
    All meet on this shore,
    Facing each prick
    With ginger pluck.

Our rooms are ready, the register signed,
There is time to take a turn before dark,
    See the blistering paint
    On the scorching front,
    Or icicle sombre
    On pierhead timber.

To climb the cliff path to the coastguard's point
Past the derelict dock deserted by rats,
      Look from concrete sill
      Of fort for sale
      To the bathers' rocks,
      The lovers' ricks.

Our boots will be brushed, our bolsters pummelled,
Cupboards are cleared for keeping our clothes:
      Here we shall live
      And somehow love
      Though we only master
      The sad posture.

Picnics are promised and planned for July
To the wood with the waterfall, walks to find
      Traces of birds,
      A mole, a rivet,
      In factory yards
      Marked strictly private.

There will be skating and curling at Christmas—indoors
Charades and ragging; then riders pass
      Some afternoons
      In snowy lanes,
      Shut in by wires,
      Surplus from wars.

In Spring we shall spade the soil on the border
For blooming of bulbs; we shall bow in Autumn,
      When trees make passes,
      As high gale pushes,
      And bewildered leaves
      Fall on our lives.

Watching through windows the wastes of evening,
The flare of foundries at fall of the year,
      The slight despair
      At what we are,
      The marginal grief
      Is source of life.

In groups forgetting the gun in the drawer
Need pray for no pardon, are proud till recalled
      By music on water
      To lack of stature,
      Saying Alas
      To less and less.

Till holding our hats in our hands for talking,
Or striding down streets for something to see,
      Gas-light in shops,
      The fate of ships,
      And the tide-wind
      Touch the old wound.

Till our nerves are numb and their now is a time
Too late for love or for lying either,
    Grown used at last
    To having lost,
    Accepting dearth,
    The shadow of death.

October 1930

The Decoys

There are some birds in these valleys
Who flutter round the careless
With intimate appeal,
By seeming kindness trained to snaring,
They feel no falseness.

Under the spell completely
They circle can serenely,
And in the tricky light
The masked hill has a purer greenness.
Their flight looks fleeter.

But fowlers, O, like foxes,
Lie ambushed in the rushes.
Along the harmless tracks
The madman keeper crawls through brushwood,
Axe under oxter.

Alas, the signal given,
Fingers on trigger tighten.
The real unlucky dove
Must smarting fall away from brightness
Its love from living.

May 1931

Have a Good Time

'We have brought you,' they said, 'a map of the country;
Here is the line that runs to the vats,
This patch of green on the left is the wood,
We've pencilled an arrow to point out the bay.
No thank you, no tea; why look at the clock.
Keep it? Of course. It goes with our love.

We shall watch your future and send our love.
We lived for years, you know, in the country.
Remember at week-ends to wind up the clock.
We've wired to our manager at the vats.
The tides are perfectly safe in the bay,
But whatever you do don't go to the wood.

There's a flying trickster in that wood,
And we shan't be there to help with our love.
Keep fit by bathing in the bay,
You'll never catch fever then in the country.
You're sure of a settled job at the vats
If you keep their hours and live by the clock.'

He arrived at last; it was time by the clock.
He crossed himself as he passed the wood;
Black against evening sky the vats
Brought tears to his eyes as he thought of their love;
Looking out over the darkening country,
He saw the pier in the little bay.

At the week-ends the divers in the bay
Distracted his eyes from the bandstand clock;
When down with fever and in the country
A skein of swans above the wood
Caused him no terror; he came to love
The moss that grew on the derelict vats.

And he has met sketching at the vats
Guests from the new hotel in the bay;
Now, curious, following his love,
His pulses differing from the clock,
Finds consummation in the wood
And sees for the first time the country.

Sees water in the wood and trees by the bay,
Hears a clock striking near the vats;
'This is your country and the hour of love'.

                                        September 1931

Half Way

Having abdicated with comparative ease
And dismissed the greater part of your friends,
Escaping by submarine
In a false beard, half-hoping the ports were watched,
You have got here, and it isn't snowing:
How shall we celebrate your arrival?

Of course we shall mention
Your annual camp for the Tutbury glass-workers,
Your bird-photography phase, your dream at the Hook,
Even your winter in Prague, though not very fully:
Your public refusal of a compass
Is fixed for to-morrow.

Now look at this map.
Red means a first-class, yellow a second-class road,
Crossed swords are for battlefields, gothic characters
For places of archaeological interest.

Our man will drive you as far as the Shot Tower;
Further than that, we fear, is impossible.
At Bigsweir look out for the Kelpie.
If you meet Mr Wren it is wiser to hide.
Consult before leaving a water-doctor.
Do you wish to ask any questions?

Good. You may go.

January 1930

Ode

Though aware of our rank and alert to obey orders,
Watching with binoculars the movement of the grass for an ambush,
The pistol cocked, the code-word committed to memory;
      The youngest drummer
Knows all the peace-time stories like the oldest soldier,
      Though frontier-conscious,

About the tall white gods who landed from their open boat,
Skilled in the working of copper, appointing our feast-days,
Before the islands were submerged, when the weather was calm,
      The maned lion common,
An open wishing-well in every garden;
      When love came easy.

Perfectly certain, all of us, but not from the records,
Not from the unshaven agent who returned to the camp:
The pillar dug from the desert recorded only
      The sack of a city,
The agent clutching his side collapsed at our feet,
      'Sorry! They got me!'

Yes, they were living here once but do not now,
Yes, they are living still but do not here;
Lying awake after Lights Out a recruit may speak up:
      'Who told you all this?'
The tent-talk pauses a little till a veteran answers
      'Go to sleep, Sonny!'

Turning over he closes his eyes, and then in a moment
Sees the sun at midnight bright over cornfield and pasture,
Our hope. . . . Someone jostles him, fumbling for boots,
      Time to change guard:
Boy, the quarrel was before your time, the aggressor
      No one you know.

Your childish moments of awareness were all of our world,
At five you sprang, already a tiger in the garden,
At night your mother taught you to pray for our Daddy
      Far away fighting,
One morning you fell off a horse and your brother mocked you:
      'Just like a girl!'

Now we're due to parade on the square in front of the Cathedral,
When the bishop has blessed us, to file in after the choirboys,
To stand with the wine-dark conquerors in the roped-off pews,
          Shout ourselves hoarse:
'They ran like hares; we have broken them up like firewood;
          They fought against God'.

While in a great rift in the limestone miles away
At the same hour they gather, tethering their horses beside them;
A scarecrow prophet from a boulder foresees our judgment,
          Their oppressors howling;
And the bitter psalm is caught by the gale from the rocks:
          'How long shall they flourish?'

What have we all been doing to have made from Fear
That laconic war-bitten captain addressing them now?
Heart and head shall be keener, mood the more
          As our might lessens:
To have caused their shout 'We will fight till we lie down beside
          The Lord we have loved'.

There's Wrath who has learnt every trick of guerrilla warfare,
The shamming dead, the night-raid, the feinted retreat;
Envy their brilliant pamphleteer, to lying
          As husband true,
Expert impersonator and linguist, proud of his power
          To hoodwink sentries.

Gluttony living alone, austerer than us,
Big simple Greed, Acedia famed with them all
For her stamina, keeping the outposts, and somewhere Lust,
          That skilful sapper,
Muttering to his fuses in a tunnel 'Could I meet here with Love,
          I would hug her to death'.

There are faces there for which for a very long time
We've been on the look-out, though often at home we imagined
Catching sight of a back or hearing a voice through a doorway
          We had found them at last;
Put our arms round their necks and looked in their eyes and discovered
          We were unlucky.

And some of them, surely, we seem to have seen before:
Why, that girl who rode off on her bicycle one fine summer evening
And never returned, she's there; and the banker we'd noticed
          Worried for weeks;
Till he failed to arrive one morning and his room was empty,
          Gone with a suitcase.

They speak of things done on the frontier we were never told,
The hidden path to their squat Pictish tower
They will never reveal though kept without sleep, for their code is
          'Death to the squealer':
They are brave, yes, though our newspapers mention their bravery
          In inverted commas.

But careful; back to our lines; it is unsafe there,
Passports are issued no longer; that area is closed;
There's no fire in the waiting-room now at the climbers' Junction,
    And all this year
Work has been stopped on the power-house; the wind whistles under
    The half-built culverts.

All leave is cancelled to-night; we must say good-bye.
We entrain at once for the North; we shall see in the morning
The headlands we're doomed to attack; snow down to the tide-line:
    Though the bunting signals
'Indoors before it's too late; cut peat for your fires,'
    We shall lie out there.

November 1931

Legend

Enter with him
These legends, Love;
For him assume
Each diverse form,
To legend native,
As legend queer;
That he may do
What these require,
Be, Love, like him
To legend true.

When he to ease
His heart's disease
Must cross in sorrow
Corrosive seas,
As dolphin go;
As cunning fox
Guide through the rocks,
Tell in his ear
The common phrase
Required to please
The guardians there;
And when across
The livid marsh
Big birds pursue,
Again be true,
Between his thighs
As pony rise,
And swift as wind
Bear him away
Till cries and they
Are left behind.

But when at last,
These dangers passed,
His grown desire
Of legend tire,
Then, Love, standing
At legend's ending,
Claim your reward;
Submit your neck
To the ungrateful stroke
Of his reluctant sword,
That, starting back,
His eyes may look
Amazed on you,
Find what he wanted
Is faithful too
But disenchanted,
Love as love.

December 1931

The Witnesses

Young men late in the night
    Toss on their beds,
Their pillows do not comfort
    Their uneasy heads,
The lot that decides their fate
    Is cast to-morrow,
One must depart and face
    Danger and sorrow.

Is it me? Is it me?

Look in your heart and see:
    There lies the answer.
Though the heart like a clever
    Conjuror or dancer
Deceive you often with many
    A curious sleight,
And motives like stowaways
    Are found too late.

What shall he do, whose heart
    Chooses to depart?

He shall against his peace
    Feel his heart harden,
Envy the heavy birds
    At home in a garden,
For walk he must the empty
    Selfish journey
Between the needless risk
    And the endless safety.

Will he safe and sound
Return to his own ground?

Clouds and lions stand
  Before him dangerous,
And the hostility of dreams.
  Then let him honour Us,
Lest he should be ashamed
  In the hour of crisis,
In the valley of corrosion
  Tarnish his brightness.

Who are You, whose speech
Sounds far out of reach?

? 1934

You are the town and We are the clock.
We are the guardians of the gate in the rock,
  The Two.
On your left and on your right,
In the day and in the night,
  We are watching you.

Wiser not to ask just what has occurred
To them who disobeyed our word;
  To those
We were the whirlpool, we were the reef,
We were the formal nightmare, grief
  And the unlucky rose.

Climb up the crane, learn the sailor's words
When the ships from the islands laden with birds
  Come in;
Tell your stories of fishing and other men's wives,
The expansive dreams of constricted lives,
  In the lighted inn.

But do not imagine We do not know,
Or that what you hide with such care won't show
  At a glance:
Nothing is done, nothing is said,
But don't make the mistake of believing us dead;
  I shouldn't dance.

We're afraid in that case you'll have a fall;
We've been watching you over the garden wall
  For hours:
The sky is darkening like a stain;
Something is going to fall like rain,
  And it won't be flowers.

When the green field comes off like a lid,
Revealing what was much better hid—
    Unpleasant:
And look, behind you without a sound
The woods have come up and are standing round
    In deadly crescent.

The bolt is sliding in its groove;
Outside the window is the black remov-
    -er's van:
And now with sudden swift emergence
Come the hooded women, the hump-backed surgeons
    And the Scissor Man.

This might happen any day;
So be careful what you say
    And do:
Be clean, be tidy, oil the lock,
Weed the garden, wind the clock;
    Remember the Two.

1932

Part III

Letter to Lord Byron

Excuse, my lord, the liberty I take
  In thus addressing you. I know that you
Will pay the price of authorship and make
  The allowances an author has to do.
  A poet's fan-mail will be nothing new.
And then a lord—Good Lord, you must be peppered,
Like Gary Cooper, Coughlin, or Dick Sheppard,

With notes from perfect strangers starting, 'Sir,
  I liked your lyrics, but *Childe Harold's* trash,'
'My daughter writes, should I encourage her?'
  Sometimes containing frank demands for cash,
  Sometimes sly hints at a platonic pash,
And sometimes, though I think this rather crude,
The correspondent's photo in the rude.

And as for manuscripts—by every post . . .
  I can't improve on Pope's shrill indignation,
But hope that it will please his spiteful ghost
  To learn the use in culture's propagation
  Of modern methods of communication;
New roads, new rails, new contacts, as we know
From documentaries by the G.P.O.

For since the British Isles went Protestant
  A church confession is too high for most.
But still confession is a human want,
  So Englishmen must make theirs now by post
  And authors hear them over breakfast toast.
For, failing them, there's nothing but the wall
Of public lavatories on which to scrawl.

So if ostensibly I write to you
  To chat about your poetry or mine,
There's many other reasons: though it's true
  That I have, at the age of twenty-nine
  Just read *Don Juan* and I found it fine.
I read it on the boat to Reykjavik
Except when eating or asleep or sick.

Now home is miles away, and miles away
  No matter who, and I am quite alone
And cannot understand what people say,
  But like a dog must guess it by the tone;
  At any language other than my own
I'm no great shakes, and here I've found no tutor
Nor sleeping lexicon to make me cuter.

The thought of writing came to me today
   (I like to give these facts of time and space);
The bus was in the desert on its way
   From Möthrudalur to some other place:
   The tears were streaming down my burning face;
I'd caught a heavy cold in Akureyri,
And lunch was late and life looked very dreary.

Professor Housman was I think the first
   To say in print how very stimulating
The little ills by which mankind is cursed,
   The colds, the aches, the pains are to creating;
   Indeed one hardly goes too far in stating
That many a flawless lyric may be due
Not to a lover's broken heart, but 'flu.

But still a proper explanation's lacking;
   Why write to you? I see I must begin
Right at the start when I was at my packing.
   The extra pair of socks, the airtight tin
   Of China tea, the anti-fly were in;
I asked myself what sort of books I'd read
In Iceland, if I ever felt the need.

I can't read Jefferies on the Wiltshire Downs,
   Nor browse on limericks in a smoking-room;
Who would try Trollope in cathedral towns,
   Or Marie Stopes inside his mother's womb?
   Perhaps you feel the same beyond the tomb.
Do the celestial highbrows only care
For works on Clydeside, Fascists, or Mayfair?

In certain quarters I had heard a rumour
   (For all I know the rumour's only silly)
That Icelanders have little sense of humour.
   I knew the country was extremely hilly,
   The climate unreliable and chilly;
So looking round for something light and easy
I pounced on you as warm and *civilisé.*

There is one other author in my pack:
   For some time I debated which to write to.
Which would least likely send my letter back?
   But I decided that I'd give a fright to
   Jane Austen if I wrote when I'd no right to,
And share in her contempt the dreadful fates
Of Crawford, Musgrove, and of Mr Yates.

Then she's a novelist. I don't know whether
   You will agree, but novel writing is
A higher art than poetry altogether
   In my opinion, and success implies
   Both finer character and faculties.
Perhaps that's why real novels are as rare
As winter thunder or a polar bear.

The average poet by comparison
　Is unobservant, immature, and lazy.
You must admit, when all is said and done,
　His sense of other people's very hazy,
　His moral judgements are too often crazy,
A slick and easy generalization
Appeal too well to his imagination.

I must remember, though, that you were dead
　Before the four great Russians lived, who brought
The art of novel writing to a head;
　The Book Society had not been bought.
　But now the art for which Jane Austen fought,
Under the right persuasion bravely warms
And is the most prodigious of the forms.

She was not an unshockable blue-stocking;
　If shades remain the characters they were,
No doubt she still considers you as shocking.
　But tell Jane Austen, that is, if you dare,
　How much her novels are beloved down here.
She wrote them for posterity, she said;
'Twas rash, but by posterity she's read.

You could not shock her more than she shocks me;
　Beside her Joyce seems innocent as grass.
It makes me most uncomfortable to see
　An English spinster of the middle class
　Describe the amorous effect of 'brass',
Reveal so frankly and with such sobriety
The economic basis of society.

So it is you who is to get this letter.
　The experiment may not be a success.
There're many others who could do it better,
　But I shall not enjoy myself the less.
　Shaw of the Air Force said that happiness
Comes in absorption: he was right, I know it;
Even in scribbling to a long-dead poet.

Every exciting letter has enclosures,
　And so shall this—a bunch of photographs,
Some out of focus, some with wrong exposures,
　Press cuttings, gossip, maps, statistics, graphs;
　I don't intend to do the thing by halves.
I'm going to be very up to date indeed.
It is a collage that you're going to read.

I want a form that's large enough to swim in,
　And talk on any subject that I choose,
From natural scenery to men and women,
　Myself, the arts, the European news:
　And since she's on a holiday, my Muse
Is out to please, find everything delightful
And only now and then be mildly spiteful.

Ottava Rima would, I know, be proper,
    The proper instrument on which to pay
My compliments, but I should come a cropper;
    Rhyme-royal's difficult enough to play.
    But if no classics as in Chaucer's day,
At least my modern pieces shall be cheery
Like English bishops on the Quantum Theory.

Light verse, poor girl, is under a sad weather;
    Except by Milne and persons of that kind
She's treated as *démodé* altogether.
    It's strange and very unjust to my mind
    Her brief appearances should be confined,
Apart from Belloc's *Cautionary Tales*,
To the more bourgeois periodicals.

'The fascination of what's difficult',
    The wish to do what one's not done before,
Is, I hope, proper to *Quicunque Vult*,
    The proper card to show at Heaven's door.
    Gerettet not *Gerichtet* be the Law,
Et cetera, et cetera. O curse,
That is the flattest line in English verse.

Parnassus after all is not a mountain,
    Reserved for A.1. climbers such as you;
It's got a park, it's got a public fountain.
    The most I ask is leave to share a pew
    With Bradford or with Cottam, that will do:
To pasture my few silly sheep with Dyer
And picnic on the lower slopes with Prior.

A publisher's an author's greatest friend,
    A generous uncle, or he ought to be.
(I'm sure we hope it pays him in the end.)
    I love my publishers and they love me,
    At least they paid a very handsome fee
To send me here. I've never heard a grouse
Either from Russell Square or Random House.

But now I've got uncomfortable suspicions,
    I'm going to put their patience out of joint.
Though it's in keeping with the best traditions
    For Travel Books to wander from the point
    (There is no other rhyme except anoint),
They well may charge me with—I've no defences—
Obtaining money under false pretences.

I know I've not the least chance of survival
    Beside the major travellers of the day.
I am no Lawrence who, on his arrival,
    Sat down and typed out all he had to say;
    I am not even Ernest Hemingway.
I shall not run to a two-bob edition,
So just won't enter for the competition.

And even here the steps I flounder in
   Were worn by most distinguished boots of old.
Dasent and Morris and Lord Dufferin,
   Hooker and men of that heroic mould
   Welcome me icily into the fold;
I'm not like Peter Fleming an Etonian,
But, if I'm Judas, I'm an old Oxonian.

The Haig Thomases are at Myvatn now,
   At Hvitarvatn and at Vatnajökull
Cambridge research goes on, I don't know how:
   The shades of Asquith and of Auden Skökull
   Turn in their coffins a three-quarter circle
To see their son, upon whose help they reckoned,
Being as frivolous as Charles the Second.

So this, my opening chapter, has to stop
   With humbly begging everybody's pardon.
From Faber first in case the book's a flop,
   Then from the critics lest they should be hard on
   The author when he leads them up the garden,
Last from the general public he must beg
Permission now and then to pull their leg.

II

I'm writing this in pencil on my knee,
   Using my other hand to stop me yawning,
Upon a primitive, unsheltered quay
   In the small hours of a Wednesday morning.
   I cannot add the summer day is dawning;
In Seythisfjördur every schoolboy knows
That daylight in the summer never goes.

To get to sleep in latitudes called upper
   Is difficult at first for Englishmen.
It's like being sent to bed before your supper
   For playing darts with father's fountain-pen,
   Or like returning after orgies, when
Your breath's like luggage and you realize
You've been more confidential than was wise.

I've done my duty, taken many notes
   Upon the almost total lack of greenery,
The roads, the illegitimates, the goats:
   To use a rhyme of yours, there's handsome scenery
   But little agricultural machinery;
And with the help of Sunlight Soap the Geysir
Affords to visitors le plus grand plaisir.

The North, though, never was your cup of tea;
   'Moral' you thought it so you kept away.
And what I'm sure you're wanting now from me
   Is news about the England of the day,

81

What sort of things *La Jeunesse* do and say.
Is Brighton still as proud of her pavilion,
And is it safe for girls to travel pillion?

I'll clear my throat and take a Rover's breath
    And skip a century of hope and sin—
For far too much has happened since your death.
    Crying went out and the cold bath came in,
    With drains, bananas, bicycles, and tin,
And Europe saw from Ireland to Albania
The Gothic revival and the Railway Mania.

We're entering now the Eotechnic Phase
    Thanks to the Grid and all those new alloys;
That is, at least, what Lewis Mumford says.
    A world of Aertex underwear for boys,
    Huge plate-glass windows, walls absorbing noise,
Where the smoke nuisance is utterly abated
And all the furniture is chromium-plated.

Well, you might think so if you went to Surrey
    And stayed for week-ends with the well-to-do,
Your car too fast, too personal your worry
    To look too closely at the wheeling view.
    But in the north it simply isn't true.
To those who live in Warrington or Wigan,
It's not a white lie, it's a whacking big 'un.

There on the old historic battlefield,
    The cold ferocity of human wills,
The scars of struggle are as yet unhealed;
    Slattern the tenements on sombre hills,
    And gaunt in valleys the square-windowed mills
That, since the Georgian house, in my conjecture
Remain our finest native architecture.

On economic, health, or moral grounds
    It hasn't got the least excuse to show;
No more than chamber pots or otter hounds;
    But let me say before it has to go,
    It's the most lovely country that I know;
Clearer than Scafell Pike, my heart has stamped on
The view from Birmingham to Wolverhampton.

Long, long ago, when I was only four,
    Going towards my grandmother, the line
Passed through a coal-field. From the corridor
    I watched it pass with envy, thought 'How fine!
    Oh how I wish that situation mine.'
Tramlines and slagheaps, pieces of machinery,
That was, and still is, my ideal scenery.

Hail to the New World! Hail to those who'll love
    Its antiseptic objects, feel at home.

Lovers will gaze at an electric stove,
   Another *poésie de départ* come
Centred round bus-stops or the aerodrome.
But give me still, to stir imagination
The chiaroscuro of the railway station.

Preserve me from the Shape of Things to Be;
   The high-grade posters at the public meeting,
The influence of Art on Industry,
   The cinemas with perfect taste in seating;
   Preserve me, above all, from central heating.
It may be D. H. Lawrence hocus-pocus,
But I prefer a room that's got a focus.

But you want facts, not sighs. I'll do my best
   To give a few; you can't expect them all.
To start with, on the whole we're better dressed;
   For chic the difference to-day is small
   Of barmaid from my lady at the Hall.
It's sad to spoil this democratic vision
With millions suffering from malnutrition.

Again, our age is highly educated;
   There is no lie our children cannot read,
And as MacDonald might so well have stated
   We're growing up and up and up indeed.
   Advertisements can teach us all we need;
And death is better, as the millions know,
Than dandruff, night-starvation, or B.O.

We've always had a penchant for field sports,
   But what do you think has grown up in our towns?
A passion for the open air and shorts;
   The sun is one of our emotive nouns.
   Go down by chara' to the Sussex Downs,
Watch the manoeuvres of the week-end hikers
Massed on parade with Kodaks or with Leicas.

These movements signify our age-long rule
   Of insularity has lost its powers;
The cult of salads and the swimming pool
   Comes from a climate sunnier than ours,
   And lands which never heard of licensed hours.
The south of England before very long
Will look no different from the Continong.

You lived and moved among the best society
   And so could introduce your hero to it
Without the slightest tremor of anxiety;
   Because he was your hero and you knew it,
   He'd know instinctively what's done, and do it.
He'd find our day more difficult than yours
For industry has mixed the social drawers.

We've grown, you see, a lot more democratic,
    And Fortune's ladder is for all to climb;
Carnegie on this point was most emphatic.
    A humble grandfather is not a crime,
    At least, if father made enough in time!
Today, thank God, we've got no snobbish feeling
Against the more efficient modes of stealing.

The porter at the Carlton is my brother,
    He'll wish me a good evening if I pay,
For tips and men are equal to each other.
    I'm sure that *Vogue* would be the first to say
    Que le Beau Monde is socialist today;
And many a bandit, not so gently born
Kills vermin every winter with the Quorn.

Adventurers, though, must take things as they find them
    And look for pickings where the pickings are.
The drives of love and hunger are behind them,
    They can't afford to be particular:
    And those who like good cooking and a car,
A certain kind of costume or of face,
Must seek them in a certain kind of place.

Don Juan was a mixer and no doubt
    Would find this century as good as any
For getting hostesses to ask him out,
    And mistresses that need not cost a penny.
    Indeed our ways to waste time are so many,
Thanks to technology, a list of these
Would make a longer book than *Ulysses*.

Yes, in the smart set he would know his way
    By second nature with no tips from me.
Tennis and Golf have come in since your day;
    But those who are as good at games as he
    Acquire the back-hand quite instinctively,
Take to the steel-shaft and hole out in one,
Master the books of Ely Culbertson.

I see his face in every magazine.
    'Don Juan at lunch with one of Cochran's ladies.'
'Don Juan with his red setter May MacQueen.'
    'Don Juan, who's just been wintering in Cadiz,
    Caught at the wheel of his maroon Mercedes.'
'Don Juan at Croydon Aerodrome.' 'Don Juan
Snapped in the paddock with the Aga Khan.'

But if in highbrow circles he would sally
    It's just as well to warn him there's no stain on
Picasso, all-in wrestling, or the Ballet.
    Sibelius is the man. To get a pain on
    Listening to Elgar is a sine qua non.
A second-hand acquaintance of Pareto's
Ranks higher than an intimate of Plato's.

The vogue for Black Mass and the cult of devils
  Has sunk. The Good, the Beautiful, the True
Still fluctuate about the lower levels.
  Joyces are firm and there there's nothing new.
Eliots have hardened just a point or two.
Hopkins are brisk, thanks to some recent boosts.
There's been some further weakening in Prousts.

I'm saying this to tell you who's the rage,
  And not to loose a sneer from my interior.
Because there's snobbery in every age,
  Because some names are loved by the superior,
  It does not follow they're the least inferior:
For all I know the Beatific Vision's
On view at all Surrealist Exhibitions.

Now for the spirit of the people. Here
  I know I'm treading on more dangerous ground:
I know there're many changes in the air,
  But know my data too slight to be sound,
  I know, too, I'm inviting the renowned
Retort of all who love the Status Quo:
'You can't change human nature, don't you know!'

We've still, it's true, the same shape and appearance,
  We haven't changed the way that kissing's done;
The average man still hates all interference,
  Is just as proud still of his new-born son:
  Still, like a hen, he likes his private run,
Scratches for self-esteem, and slyly pecks
A good deal in the neighbourhood of sex.

But he's another man in many ways:
  Ask the cartoonist first, for he knows best.
Where is the John Bull of the good old days,
  The swaggering bully with the clumsy jest?
  His meaty neck has long been laid to rest,
His acres of self-confidence for sale;
He passed away at Ypres and Passchendaele.

Turn to the work of Disney or of Strube;
  There stands our hero in his threadbare seams;
The bowler hat who strap-hangs in the tube,
  And kicks the tyrant only in his dreams,
  Trading on pathos, dreading all extremes;
The little Mickey with the hidden grudge;
Which is the better, I leave you to judge.

Begot on Hire Purchase by Insurance,
  Forms at his christening worshipped and adored;
A season ticket schooled him in endurance,
  A tax collector and a waterboard
  Admonished him. In boyhood he was awed
By a matric, and complex apparatuses
Keep his heart conscious of Divine Afflatuses.

'I am like you,' he says, 'and you, and you,
    I love my life, I love the home-fires, have
To keep them burning. Heroes never do.
    Heroes are sent by ogres to the grave.
    I may not be courageous, but I save.
I am the one who somehow turns the corner,
I may perhaps be fortunate Jack Horner.

'I am the ogre's private secretary;
    I've felt his stature and his powers, learned
To give his ogreship the raspberry
    Only when his gigantic back is turned.
    One day, who knows, I'll do as I have yearned.
The short man, all his fingers on the door,
With repartee shall send him to the floor.'

One day, which day? O any other day,
    But not today. The ogre knows his man.
To kill the ogre—that would take away
    The fear in which his happy dreams began,
    And with his life he'll guard dreams while he can.
Those who would really kill his dream's contentment
He hates with real implacable resentment.

He dreads the ogre, but he dreads yet more
    Those who conceivably might set him free,
Those the cartoonist has no time to draw.
    Without his bondage he'd be all at sea;
    The ogre need but shout 'Security',
To make this man, so lovable, so mild,
As madly cruel as a frightened child.

Byron, thou should'st be living at this hour!
    What would you do, I wonder, if you were?
Britannia's lost prestige and cash and power,
    Her middle classes show some wear and tear,
    We've learned to bomb each other from the air;
I can't imagine what the Duke of Wellington
Would say about the music of Duke Ellington.

Suggestions have been made that the Teutonic
    Führer-Prinzip would have appealed to you
As being the true heir to the Byronic—
    In keeping with your social status too
    (It has its English converts, fit and few),
That you would, hearing honest Oswald's call,
Be gleichgeschaltet in the Albert Hall.

'Lord Byron at the head of his storm-troopers!'
    Nothing, says science, is impossible:
The Pope may quit to join the Oxford Groupers,
    Nuffield may leave one farthing in his Will,
    There may be someone who trusts Baldwin still,
Someone may think that Empire wines are nice,
There may be people who hear Tauber twice.

You liked to be the centre of attention,
    The gay Prince Charming of the fairy story,
Who tamed the Dragon by his intervention.
    In modern warfare, though it's just as gory,
    There isn't any individual glory;
The Prince must be anonymous, observant,
A kind of lab-boy, or a civil servant.

You never were an Isolationist;
    Injustice you had always hatred for,
And we can hardly blame you, if you missed
    Injustice just outside your lordship's door:
    Nearer than Greece were cotton and the poor.
Today you might have seen them, might indeed
Have walked in the United Front with Gide,

Against the ogre, dragon, what you will;
    His many shapes and names all turn us pale,
For he's immortal, and today he still
    Swinges the horror of his scaly tail.
    Sometimes he seems to sleep, but will not fail
In every age to rear up to defend
Each dying force of history to the end.

Milton beheld him on the English throne,
    And Bunyan sitting in the Papal chair;
The hermits fought him in their caves alone,
    At the first Empire he was also there,
    Dangling his Pax Romana in the air:
He comes in dreams at puberty to man,
To scare him back to childhood if he can.

Banker or landlord, booking-clerk or Pope,
    Whenever he's lost faith in choice and thought,
When a man sees the future without hope,
    Whenever he endorses Hobbes' report
    'The life of man is nasty, brutish, short,'
The dragon rises from his garden border
And promises to set up law and order.

He that in Athens murdered Socrates,
    And Plato then seduced, prepares to make
A desolation and to call it peace
    Today for dying magnates, for the sake
    Of generals who can scarcely keep awake,
And for that doughy mass in great and small
That doesn't want to stir itself at all.

Forgive me for inflicting all this on you,
    For asking you to hold the baby for us;
It's easy to forget that where you've gone, you
    May only want to chat with Set and Horus,
    Bored to extinction with our earthly chorus:
Perhaps it sounds to you like a trunk-call,
Urgent, it seems, but quite inaudible.

Yet though the choice of what is to be done
　　Remains with the alive, the rigid nation
Is supple still within the breathing one;
　　Its sentinels yet keep their sleepless station,
　　And every man in every generation,
Tossing in his dilemma on his bed,
Cries to the shadows of the noble dead.

We're out at sea now, and I wish we weren't;
　　The sea is rough, I don't care if it's blue;
I'd like to have a quick one, but I daren't.
　　And I must interrupt this screed to you,
　　For I've some other little jobs to do;
I must write home or mother will be vexed,
So this must be continued in our next.

III
My last remarks were sent you from a boat.
　　I'm back on shore now in a warm bed-sitter,
And several friends have joined me since I wrote;
　　So though the weather out of doors is bitter,
　　I feel a great deal cheerier and fitter.
A party from a public school, a poet,
Have set a rapid pace, and make me go it.

We're starting soon on a big expedition
　　Into the desert, which I'm sure is corking:
Many would like to be in my position.
　　I only hope there won't be too much walking.
　　Now let me see, where was I? We were talking
Of Social Questions when I had to stop;
I think it's time now for a little shop.

In setting up my brass plate as a critic,
　　I make no claim to certain diagnosis,
I'm more intuitive than analytic,
　　I offer thought in homoeopathic doses
　　(But someone may get better in the process).
I don't pretend to reasoning like Pritchard's
Or the logomachy of I. A. Richards.

I like your muse because she's gay and witty,
　　Because she's neither prostitute nor frump,
The daughter of a European city,
　　And country houses long before the slump;
　　I like her voice that does not make me jump:
And you I find sympatisch, a good townee,
Neither a preacher, ninny, bore, nor Brownie.

A poet, swimmer, peer, and man of action,
　　—It beats Roy Campbell's record by a mile—
You offer every possible attraction.
　　By looking into your poetic style

88

And love-life on the chance that both were vile,
Several have earned a decent livelihood,
Whose lives were uncreative but were good.

You've had your packet from the critics, though:
    They grant you warmth of heart, but at your head
Their moral and aesthetic brickbats throw.
    A 'vulgar genius' so George Eliot said,
    Which doesn't matter as George Eliot's dead,
But T. S. Eliot, I am sad to find,
Damns you with: 'an uninteresting mind'.

A statement which I must say I'm ashamed at;
    A poet must be judged by his intention,
And serious thought you never said you aimed at.
    I think a serious critic ought to mention
    That one verse style was really your invention,
A style whose meaning does not need a spanner,
You are the master of the airy manner.

By all means let us touch our humble caps to
    La poésie pure, the epic narrative;
But comedy shall get its round of claps, too.
    According to his powers, each may give;
    Only on varied diet can we live.
The pious fable and the dirty story
Share in the total literary glory.

There's every mode of singing robe in stock,
    From Shakespeare's gorgeous fur coat, Spenser's muff,
Or Dryden's lounge suit to my cotton frock,
    And Wordsworth's Harris tweed with leathern cuff.
    Firbank, I think, wore just a just-enough;
I fancy Whitman in a reach-me-down,
But you, like Sherlock, in a dressing-gown.

I'm also glad to find I've your authority
    For finding Wordsworth a most bleak old bore,
Though I'm afraid we're in a sad minority
    For every year his followers get more,
    Their number must have doubled since the war.
They come in train-loads to the Lakes, and swarms
Of pupil-teachers study him in Storm's.

'I hate a pupil-teacher,' Milton said,
    Who also hated bureaucratic fools;
Milton may thank his stars that he is dead,
    Although he's learnt by heart in public schools,
    Along with Wordsworth and the list of rules;
For many a don while looking down his nose
Calls Pope and Dryden classics of our prose.

And new plants flower from that old potato.
    They thrive best in a poor industrial soil,

Are hardier crossed with Rousseaus or a Plato;
  Their cultivation is an easy toil.
William, to change the metaphor, struck oil;
His well seems inexhaustible, a gusher
That saves old England from the fate of Russia.

The mountain-snob is a Wordsworthian fruit;
  He tears his clothes and doesn't shave his chin,
He wears a very pretty little boot,
  He chooses the least comfortable inn;
  A mountain railway is a deadly sin;
His strength, of course, is as the strength of ten men,
He calls all those who live in cities wen-men.

I'm not a spoil-sport, I would never wish
  To interfere with anybody's pleasures;
By all means climb, or hunt, or even fish,
  All human hearts have ugly little treasures;
  But think it time to take repressive measures
When someone says, adopting the 'I know' line,
The Good Life is confined above the snow-line.

Besides, I'm very fond of mountains, too;
  I like to travel through them in a car;
I like a house that's got a sweeping view;
  I like to walk, but not to walk too far.
  I also like green plains where cattle are,
And trees and rivers, and shall always quarrel
With those who think that rivers are immoral.

Not that my private quarrel gives quietus to
  The interesting question that it raises;
Impartial thought will give a proper status to
  This interest in waterfalls and daisies,
  Excessive love for the non-human faces,
That live in hearts from Golders Green to Teddington;
It's all bound up with Einstein, Jeans, and Eddington.

It is a commonplace that's hardly worth
  A poet's while to make profound or terse,
That now the sun does not go round the earth,
  That man's no centre of the universe;
  And working in an office makes it worse.
The humblest is acquiring with facility
A Universal-Complex sensibility.

For now we've learnt we mustn't be so bumptious
  We find the stars are one big family,
And send out invitations for a scrumptious
  Simple, old-fashioned, jolly romp with tea
  To any natural objects we can see.
We can't, of course, invite a Jew or Red
But birds and nebulae will do instead.

The Higher Mind's outgrowing the Barbarian,
    It's hardly thought hygienic now to kiss;
The world is surely turning vegetarian;
    And as it grows too sensitive for this,
    It won't be long before we find there is
A Society of Everybody's Aunts
For the Prevention of Cruelty to Plants.

I dread this like the dentist, rather more so:
    To me Art's subject is the human clay,
And landscape but a background to a torso;
    All Cézanne's apples I would give away
    For one small Goya or a Daumier.
I'll never grant a more than minor beauty
To pudge or pilewort, petty-chap or pooty.

Art, if it doesn't start there, at least ends,
    Whether aesthetics like the thought or not,
In an attempt to entertain our friends;
    And our first problem is to realize what
    Peculiar friends the modern artist's got;
It's possible a little dose of history
May help us in unravelling this mystery.

At the Beginning I shall *not* begin,
    Not with the scratches in the ancient caves;
Heard only knows the latest bulletin
    About the finds in the Egyptian graves;
    I'll skip the war-dance of the Indian braves;
Since, for the purposes I have in view,
The English eighteenth century will do.

We find two arts in the Augustan age:
    One quick and graceful, and by no means holy,
Relying on his lordship's patronage;
    The other pious, sober, moving slowly,
    Appealing mainly to the poor and lowly.
So Isaac Watts and Pope, each forced his entry
To lower middle class and landed gentry.

Two arts as different as Jews and Turks,
    Each serving aspects of the Reformation,
Luther's division into faith and works:
    The God of the unique imagination,
    A friend of those who have to know their station;
And the Great Architect, the Engineer
Who keeps the mighty in their higher sphere.

The important point to notice, though, is this:
    Each poet knew for whom he had to write,
Because their life was still the same as his.
    As long as art remains a parasite
    On any class of persons it's alright;
The only thing it must be is attendant,
The only thing it mustn't, independent.

But artists, though, are human; and for man
  To be a scivvy is not nice at all:
So everyone will do the best he can
  To get a patch of ground which he can call
  His own. He doesn't really care how small,
So long as he can style himself the master:
Unluckily for art, it's a disaster.

To be a highbrow is the natural state:
  To have a special interest of one's own,
Rock gardens, marrows, pigeons, silver plate,
  Collecting butterflies or bits of stone;
  And then to have a circle where one's known
Of hobbyists and rivals to discuss
With expert knowledge what appeals to us.

But to the artist this is quite forbidden:
  On this point he must differ from the crowd,
And, like a secret agent, must keep hidden
  His passion for his shop. However proud,
  And rightly, of his trade, he's not allowed
To etch his face with his professional creases,
Or die from occupational diseases.

Until the great Industrial Revolution
  The artist had to earn his livelihood:
However much he hated the intrusion
  Of patron's taste or public's fickle mood,
  He had to please or go without his food;
He had to keep his technique to himself
Or find no joint upon his larder shelf.

But Savoury and Newcomen and Watt
  And all those names that I was told to get up
In history preparation and forgot,
  A new class of creative artist set up,
  On whom the pressure of demand was let up:
He sang and painted and drew dividends,
But lost responsibilities and friends.

Those most affected were the very best:
  Those with originality of vision,
Those whose technique was better than the rest,
  Jumped at the chance of a secure position
  With freedom from the bad old hack tradition,
Leave to be sole judges of the artist's brandy,
Be Shelley, or Childe Harold, or the Dandy.

So started what I'll call the Poet's Party:
  (Most of the guests were painters, never mind)—
The first few hours the atmosphere was hearty,
  With fireworks, fun, and games of every kind;
  All were enjoying it, no one was blind;
Brilliant the speeches improvised, the dances,
And brilliant, too, the technical advances.

How nice at first to watch the passers-by
   Out of the upper window, and to say
'How glad I am that though I have to die
   Like all those cattle, I'm less base than they!'
   How we all roared when Baudelaire went fey.
'See this cigar,' he said, 'it's Baudelaire's.
What happens to perception? Ah, who cares?'

Today, alas, that happy crowded floor
   Looks very different: many are in tears:
Some have retired to bed and locked the door;
   And some swing madly from the chandeliers;
   Some have passed out entirely in the rears;
Some have been sick in corners; the sobering few
Are trying hard to think of something new.

I've made it seem the artist's silly fault,
   In which case why these sentimental sobs?
In fact, of course, the whole tureen was salt.
   The soup was full of little bits of snobs.
   The common clay and the uncommon nobs
Were far too busy making piles or starving
To look at pictures, poetry, or carving.

I've simplified the facts to be emphatic,
   Playing Macaulay's favourite little trick
Of lighting that's contrasted and dramatic;
   Because it's true Art feels a trifle sick,
   You mustn't think the old girl's lost her kick.
And those, besides, who feel most like a sewer
Belong to Painting not to Literature.

You know the terror that for poets lurks
   Beyond the ferry when to Minos brought.
Poets must utter their Collected Works,
   Including Juvenilia. So I thought
   That you might warn him. Yes, I think you ought,
In case, when my turn comes, he shall cry 'Atta boys,
Off with his bags, he's crazy as a hatter, boys!'

The clock is striking and it's time for lunch;
   We start at four. The weather's none too bright.
Some of the party look as pleased as Punch.
   We shall be travelling, as they call it, light:
   We shall be sleeping in a tent tonight.
You know what Baden-Powell's taught us, don't you,
Ora pro nobis, please, this evening, won't you?

IV
A ship again; this time the *Dettifoss*.
   Grierson can buy it; all the sea I mean,
All this Atlantic that we've now to cross
   Heading for England's pleasant pastures green.

Pro tem I've done with the Icelandic scene;
I watch the hills receding in the distance,
I hear the thudding of an engine's pistons.

I hope I'm better, wiser for the trip:
    I've had the benefit of northern breezes,
The open road and good companionship,
    I've seen some very pretty little pieces;
    And though the luck was almost all MacNeice's,
I've spent some jolly evenings playing rummy—
No one can talk at Bridge, unless it's Dummy.

I've learnt to ride, at least to ride a pony,
    Taken a lot of healthy exercise,
On barren mountains and in valleys stony,
    I've tasted a hot spring (a taste was wise),
    And foods a man remembers till he dies.
All things considered, I consider Iceland,
Apart from Reykjavik, a very nice land.

The part can stand as symbol for the whole:
    So ruminating in these last few weeks,
I see the map of all my youth unroll,
    The mental mountains and the psychic creeks,
    The towns of which the master never speaks,
The various parishes and what they voted for,
The colonies, their size, and what they're noted for.

A child may ask when our strange epoch passes,
    During a history lesson, 'Please, sir, what's
An intellectual of the middle classes?
    Is he a maker of ceramic pots
    Or does he choose his king by drawing lots?'
What follows now may set him on the rail,
A plain, perhaps a cautionary, tale.

My passport says I'm five feet and eleven,
    With hazel eyes and fair (it's tow-like) hair,
That I was born in York in 1907,
    With no distinctive markings anywhere.
    Which isn't quite correct. Conspicuous there
On my right cheek appears a large brown mole,
I think I don't dislike it on the whole.

My father's forbears were all Midland yeomen
    Till royalties from coal mines did them good;
I think they must have been phlegmatic slowmen.
    My mother's ancestors had Norman blood,
    From Somerset I've always understood;
My grandfathers on either side agree
In being clergymen and C. of E.

Father and Mother each was one of seven,
    Though one died young and one was not all there;

Their fathers both went suddenly to Heaven
　　While they were still quite small and left them here
　　To work on earth with little cash to spare;
A nurse, a rising medico, at Bart's
Both felt the pangs of Cupid's naughty darts.

My home then was professional and 'high'.
　　No gentler father ever lived, I'll lay
All Lombard Street against a shepherd's pie.
　　We imitate our loves: well, neighbours say
　　I grow more like my mother every day.
I don't like business men. I know a Prot
Will never really kneel, but only squat.

In pleasures of the mind they both delighted;
　　The library in the study was enough
To make a better boy than me short-sighted;
　　Our old cook Ada surely knew her stuff;
　　My elder brothers did not treat me rough;
We lived at Solihull, a village then;
Those at the gasworks were my favourite men.

My earliest recollection to stay put
　　Is of a white stone doorstep and a spot
Of pus where father lanced the terrier's foot;
　　Next, stuffing shag into the coffee pot
　　Which nearly killed my mother, but did not;
Both psychoanalyst and Christian minister
Will think these incidents extremely sinister.

With northern myths my little brain was laden,
　　With deeds of Thor and Loki and such scenes;
My favourite tale was Andersen's *Ice Maiden*;
　　But better far than any kings or queens
　　I liked to see and know about machines:
And from my sixth until my sixteenth year
I thought myself a mining engineer.

The mine I always pictured was for lead,
　　Though copper mines might, *faute de mieux*, be sound.
Today I like a weight upon my bed;
　　I always travel by the Underground;
　　For concentration I have always found
A small room best, the curtains drawn, the light on;
Then I can work from nine till tea-time, right on.

I must admit that I was most precocious
　　(Precocious children rarely grow up good).
My aunts and uncles thought me quite atrocious
　　For using words more adult than I should;
　　My first remark at school did all it could
To shake a matron's monumental poise;
'I like to see the various types of boys.'

The Great War had begun: but masters' scrutiny
    And fists of big boys were the war to us;
It was as harmless as the Indian Mutiny,
    A beating from the Head was dangerous.
    But once when half the form put down *Bellus*
We were accused of that most deadly sin,
Wanting the Kaiser and the Huns to win.

The way in which we really were affected
    Was having such a varied lot to teach us.
The best were fighting, as the King expected,
    The remnant either elderly grey creatures,
    Or characters with most peculiar features.
Many were raggable, a few were waxy,
One had to leave abruptly in a taxi.

Surnames I must not write—O Reginald,
    You at least taught us that which fadeth not,
Our earliest visions of the great wide world;
    The beer and biscuits that your favourites got,
    Your tales revealing you a first-class shot,
Your riding breeks, your drama called *The Waves*,
A few of us will carry to our graves.

'Half a lunatic, half a knave.' No doubt
    A holy terror to the staff at tea;
A good headmaster must have soon found out
    Your moral character was all at sea;
    I question if you'd got a pass degree:
But little children bless your kind that knocks
Away the edifying stumbling blocks.

How can I thank you? For it only shows
    (Let me ride just this once my hobby-horse),
There're things a good headmaster never knows.
    There must be sober schoolmasters, of course,
    But what a prep school really puts across
Is knowledge of the world we'll soon be lost in:
Today it's more like Dickens than Jane Austen.

I hate the modern trick, to tell the truth,
    Of straightening out the kinks in the young mind,
Our passion for the tender plant of youth,
    Our hatred for all weeds of any kind.
    Slogans are bad: the best that I can find
Is this: 'Let each child have that's in our care
As much neurosis as the child can bear.'

In this respect, at least, my bad old Adam is
    Pigheadedly against the general trend;
And has no use for all these new academies
    Where readers of the better weeklies send
    The child they probably did not intend,
To paint a lampshade, marry, or keep pigeons,
Or make a study of the world religions.

Goddess of bossy underlings, Normality!
  What murders are committed in thy name!
Totalitarian is thy state Reality,
  Reeking of antiseptics and the shame
  Of faces that all look and feel the same.
Thy Muse is one unknown to classic histories,
The topping figure of the hockey mistress.

From thy dread Empire not a soul's exempted:
  More than the nursemaids pushing prams in parks,
By thee the intellectuals are tempted,
  O, to commit the treason of the clerks,
  Bewitched by thee to literary sharks.
But I must leave thee to thy office stool,
I must get on now to my public school.

Men had stopped throwing stones at one another,
  Butter and Father had come back again;
Gone were the holidays we spent with Mother
  In furnished rooms on mountain, moor, and fen;
  And gone those summer Sunday evenings, when
Along the seafronts fled a curious noise,
'Eternal Father', sung by three young boys.

Nation spoke Peace, or said she did, with nation;
  The sexes tried their best to look the same;
Morals lost value during the inflation,
  The great Victorians kindly took the blame;
  Visions of Dada to the Post-War came,
Sitting in cafés, nostrils stuffed with bread,
Above the recent and the straight laced dead.

I've said my say on public schools elsewhere:
  Romantic friendship, prefects, bullying,
I shall not deal with, *c'est une autre affaire*.
  Those who expect them, will get no such thing,
  It is the strictly relevant I sing.
Why should they grumble? They've the Greek Anthology,
And all the spicier bits of Anthropology.

We all grow up the same way, more or less;
  Life is not known to give away her presents;
She only swops. The unselfconsciousness
  That children share with animals and peasants
  Sinks in the *Sturm und Drang* of adolescence.
Like other boys I lost my taste for sweets,
Discovered sunsets, passion, God, and Keats.

I shall recall a single incident,
  No more. I spoke of mining engineering
As the career on which my mind was bent,
  But for some time my fancies had been veering;
  Mirages of the future kept appearing;
Crazes had come and gone in short, sharp gales,
For motor-bikes, photography, and whales.

But indecision broke off with a clean cut end
　　One afternoon in March at half past three
When walking in a ploughed field with a friend;
　　Kicking a little stone, he turned to me
　　And said, 'Tell me, do you write poetry?'
I never had, and said so, but I knew
That very moment what I wished to do.

Without a bridge passage this leads me straight
　　Into the theme marked 'Oxford' on my score
From pages twenty-five to twenty-eight.
　　Aesthetic trills I'd never heard before
　　Rose from the strings, shrill poses from the cor;
The woodwind chattered like a pre-war Russian,
'Art' boomed the brass, and 'Life' thumped the percussion.

A raw provincial, my good taste was tardy,
　　And Edward Thomas I as yet preferred;
I was still listening to Thomas Hardy
　　Putting divinity about a bird;
　　But Eliot spoke the still unspoken word;
For gasworks and dried tubers I forsook
The clock at Grantchester, the English rook.

All youth's intolerant certainty was mine as
　　I faced life in a double-breasted suit;
I bought and praised but did not read Aquinas,
　　At the *Criterion's* verdict I was mute,
　　Though Arnold's I was ready to refute;
And through the quads dogmatic words rang clear,
'Good poetry is classic and austere.'

So much for Art. Of course Life had its passions too;
　　The student's flesh like his imagination
Makes facts fit theories and has fashions too.
　　We were the tail, a sort of poor relation
　　To that debauched, eccentric generation
That grew up with their fathers at the War,
And made new glosses on the noun Amor.

Three years passed quickly while the Isis went
　　Down to the sea for better or for worse;
Then to Berlin, not Carthage, I was sent
　　With money from my parents in my purse,
　　And ceased to see the world in terms of verse.
I met a chap called Layard and he fed
New doctrines into my receptive head.

Part came from Lane, and part from D. H. Lawrence;
　　Gide, though I didn't know it then, gave part.
They taught me to express my deep abhorrence
　　If I caught anyone preferring Art
　　To Life and Love and being Pure-in-Heart.
I lived with crooks but seldom was molested;
The Pure-in-Heart can never be arrested.

He's gay; no bludgeonings of chance can spoil it,
  The Pure-in-Heart loves all men on a par,
And has no trouble with his private toilet;
  The Pure-in-Heart is never ill; catarrh
  Would be the yellow streak, the brush of tar;
Determined to be loving and forgiving,
I came back home to try and earn my living.

The only thing you never turned your hand to
  Was teaching English in a boarding school.
Today it's a profession that seems grand to
  Those whose alternative's an office stool;
  For budding authors it's become the rule.
To many an unknown genius postmen bring
Typed notices from Rabbitarse and String.

The Head's M.A., a bishop is a patron,
  The assistant staff is highly qualified;
Health is the care of an experienced matron,
  The arts are taught by ladies from outside;
  The food is wholesome and the grounds are wide;
The aim is training character and poise,
With special coaching for the backward boys.

I found the pay good and had time to spend it,
  Though others may not have the good luck I did:
For you I'd hesitate to recommend it;
  Several have told me that they can't abide it.
  Still, if one tends to get a bit one-sided,
It's pleasant as it's easy to secure
The hero worship of the immature.

More, it's a job, and jobs today are rare:
  All the ideals in the world won't feed us
Although they give our crimes a certain air.
  So barons of the press who know their readers
  Employ to write their more appalling leaders,
Instead of Satan's horned and hideous minions,
Clever young men of liberal opinions.

Which brings me up to nineteen thirty-five;
  Six months of film work is another story
I can't tell now. But, here I am, alive,
  Knowing the true source of that sense of glory
  That still surrounds the England of the Tory,
Come only to the rather tame conclusion
That no man by himself has life's solution.

I know—the fact is really not unnerving—
  That what is done is done, that no past dies,
That what we see depends on who's observing,
  And what we think on our activities,
  That envy warps the virgin as she dries
But *Post coitum, homo tristis* means
The lover must go carefully with the greens.

The boat has brought me to the landing-stage,
　Up the long estuary of mud and sedges;
The line I travel has the English gauge;
　The engine's shadow vaults the little hedges;
　And summer's done. I sign the usual pledges
To be a better poet, better man;
I'll really do it this time if I can.

I hope this reaches you in your abode,
　This letter that's already far too long,
Just like the Prelude or the Great North Road;
　But here I end my conversational song.
　I hope you don't think mail from strangers wrong.
As to its length, I tell myself you'll need it,
You've all eternity in which to read it.

? August–October 1936

Part IV

1933–1938

A Summer Night

(to Geoffrey Hoyland)

Out on the lawn I lie in bed,
Vega conspicuous overhead
   In the windless nights of June,
As congregated leaves complete
Their day's activity; my feet
   Point to the rising moon.

Lucky, this point in time and space
Is chosen as my working-place,
   Where the sexy airs of summer,
The bathing hours and the bare arms,
The leisured drives through a land of farms
   Are good to a newcomer.

Equal with colleagues in a ring
I sit on each calm evening
   Enchanted as the flowers
The opening light draws out of hiding
With all its gradual dove-like pleading,
   Its logic and its powers:

That later we, though parted then,
May still recall these evenings when
   Fear gave his watch no look;
The lion griefs loped from the shade
And on our knees their muzzles laid,
   And Death put down his book.

Now north and south and east and west
Those I love lie down to rest;
   The moon looks on them all,
The healers and the brilliant talkers
The eccentrics and the silent walkers,
   The dumpy and the tall.

She climbs the European sky,
Churches and power-stations lie
   Alike among earth's fixtures:
Into the galleries she peers
And blankly as a butcher stares
   Upon the marvellous pictures.

To gravity attentive, she
Can notice nothing here, though we
   Whom hunger does not move,
From gardens where we feel secure
Look up and with a sigh endure
   The tyrannies of love:

And, gentle, do not care to know,
Where Poland draws her eastern bow,
   What violence is done,
Nor ask what doubtful act allows
Our freedom in this English house,
   Our picnics in the sun.

Soon, soon, through dykes of our content
The crumpling flood will force a rent
   And, taller than a tree,
Hold sudden death before our eyes
Whose river dreams long hid the size
   And vigours of the sea.

But when the waters make retreat
And through the black mud first the wheat
   In shy green stalks appears,
When stranded monsters gasping lie,
And sounds of riveting terrify
   Their whorled unsubtle ears,

May these delights we dread to lose,
This privacy, need no excuse
   But to that strength belong,
As through a child's rash happy cries
The drowned parental voices rise
   In unlamenting song.

After discharges of alarm
All unpredicted let them calm
   The pulse of nervous nations,
Forgive the murderer in his glass,
Tough in their patience to surpass
   The tigress her swift motions.

June 1933

Paysage Moralisé

Hearing of harvests rotting in the valleys,
Seeing at end of street the barren mountains,
Round corners coming suddenly on water,
Knowing them shipwrecked who were launched for islands,
We honour founders of these starving cities
Whose honour is the image of our sorrow,

Which cannot see its likeness in their sorrow
That brought them desperate to the brink of valleys;
Dreaming of evening walks through learned cities
They reined their violent horses on the mountains,
Those fields like ships to castaways on islands,
Visions of green to them who craved for water.

They built by rivers and at night the water
Running past windows comforted their sorrow;
Each in his little bed conceived of islands
Where every day was dancing in the valleys
And all the green trees blossomed on the mountains,
Where love was innocent, being far from cities.

But dawn came back and they were still in cities;
No marvellous creature rose up from the water;
There was still gold and silver in the mountains
But hunger was a more immediate sorrow,
Although to moping villages in valleys
Some waving pilgrims were describing islands . . .

'The gods,' they promised, 'visit us from islands,
Are stalking, head-up, lovely, through our cities;
Now is the time to leave your wretched valleys
And sail with them across the lime-green water,
Sitting at their white sides, forget your sorrow,
The shadow cast across your lives by mountains.'

So many, doubtful, perished in the mountains,
Climbing up crags to get a view of islands,
So many, fearful, took with them their sorrow
Which stayed them when they reached unhappy cities,
So many, careless, dived and drowned in water,
So many, wretched, would not leave their valleys.

It is our sorrow. Shall it melt? Then water
Would gush, flush, green these mountains and these valleys,
And we rebuild our cities, not dream of islands.

May 1933

O What is That Sound

O what is that sound which so thrills the ear
    Down in the valley drumming, drumming?
Only the scarlet soldiers, dear,
    The soldiers coming.

O what is that light I see flashing so clear
    Over the distance brightly, brightly?
Only the sun on their weapons, dear,
    As they step lightly.

O what are they doing with all that gear,
    What are they doing this morning, this morning?
Only their usual manoeuvres, dear,
    Or perhaps a warning.

O why have they left the road down there,
    Why are they suddenly wheeling, wheeling?
Perhaps a change in their orders, dear.
    Why are you kneeling?

105

O haven't they stopped for the doctor's care,
    Haven't they reined their horses, their horses?
Why, they are none of them wounded, dear,
    None of these forces.

O is it the parson they want, with white hair,
    Is it the parson, is it, is it?
No, they are passing his gateway, dear,
    Without a visit.

O it must be the farmer who lives so near.
    It must be the farmer so cunning, so cunning?
They have passed the farmyard already, dear,
    And now they are running.

O where are you going? Stay with me here!
    Were the vows you swore deceiving, deceiving?
No, I promised to love you, dear,
    But I must be leaving.

O it's broken the lock and splintered the door,
    O it's the gate where they're turning, turning;
Their boots are heavy on the floor
    And their eyes are burning.

                                    October 1932

Our Hunting Fathers

Our hunting fathers told the story
    Of the sadness of the creatures,
Pitied the limits and the lack
    Set in their finished features;
Saw in the lion's intolerant look,
Behind the quarry's dying glare,
Love raging for the personal glory
    That reason's gift would add,
The liberal appetite and power,
    The rightness of a god.

Who, nurtured in that fine tradition,
    Predicted the result,
Guessed Love by nature suited to
    The intricate ways of guilt,
That human ligaments could so
His southern gestures modify
And make it his mature ambition
    To think no thought but ours,
To hunger, work illegally,
    And be anonymous?

                                    ? May 1934

Through the Looking-Glass

Earth has turned over; our side feels the cold,
And life sinks choking in the wells of trees,
A faint heart here and there stops ticking, killed,
Icing on ponds entrances village boys:
Among wreathed holly and wrapped gifts I move,
Old carols on the piano, a glowing hearth,
All our traditional sympathy with birth,
Put by your challenge to the shifts of love.

Your portrait hangs before me on the wall,
And there what view I wish for I shall find,
The wooded or the stony, though not all
The painter's gifts can make its flatness round;
Through each blue iris greet the heaven of failures,
That mirror world where Logic is reversed,
Where age becomes the handsome child at last,
The glass wave parted for the country sailors.

There move the enormous comics, drawn from life—
My father as an Airedale and a gardener,
My mother chasing letters with a knife.
You are not present as a character;
(Only the family have speaking parts).
You are a valley or a river-bend,
The one an aunt refers to as a friend,
The tree from which the weasel racing starts.

Behind me roars that other world it matches,
Love's daytime kingdom which I say you rule,
His total state where all must wear your badges,
Keep order perfect as a naval school.
Noble emotions, organized and massed,
Line the straight flood-lit tracks of memory
To cheer your image as it flashes by,
All lust at once informed on and suppressed.

Yours is the only name expressive there,
And family affection speaks in cypher.
Lay-out of hospital and street and square
That comfort to its homesick children offer,
As I, their author, stand between these dreams,
Unable to choose either for a home,
Your would-be lover who has never come
In a great bed at midnight to your arms.

Such dreams are amorous; they are indeed:
But no one but myself is loved in these,
While time flies on above the dreamer's head,
Flies on, flies on, and with your beauty flies,
And pride succeeds to each succeeding state,
Still able to buy up the life within,
License no liberty except his own,
Order the fireworks after the defeat.

Language of moderation cannot hide:—
My sea is empty and its waves are rough;
Gone from the map the shore where childhood played,
Tight-fisted as a peasant, eating love;
Lost in my wake the archipelago,
Islands of self through which I sailed all day
Planting a pirate's flag, a generous boy;
And lost my way to action and to you.

Lost if I steer. Tempest and tide may blow
Sailor and ship past the illusive reef,
And I yet land to celebrate with you
The birth of natural order and true love:
With you enjoy the untransfigured scene,
My father down the garden in his gaiters,
My mother at her bureau writing letters,
·Free to our favours, all our titles gone.

December 1933

Two Climbs

Fleeing from short-haired mad executives,
The sad and useless faces round my home,
Upon the mountains of my fear I climb:
Above, a breakneck scorching rock; no caves,
No col, no water. With excuse concocted,
Soon on a lower alp I fall and pant,
Cooling my weariness in faults that flaunt
A life which they have stolen and perfected.

Climbing with you was easy as a vow.
We reached the top not hungry in the least,
But it was eyes we looked at, not the view,
Saw nothing but ourselves, left-handed, lost,
Returned to shore, the rich interior still
Unknown: love gave the power, but took the will.

1933

Meiosis

Love had him fast but though he fought for breath
He struggled only to possess Another,
The snare forgotten in their little death,
Till you, the seed to which he was a mother,
That never heard of love, through love was free,
While he within his arms a world was holding,
To take the all-night journey under sea,
Work west and northward, set up building.

Cities and years constricted to your scope,
All sorrow simplified though almost all
Shall be as subtle when you are as tall:
Yet clearly in that 'almost' all his hope
That hopeful falsehood cannot stem with love
The flood on which all move and wish to move.

1933

A Misunderstanding

Just as his dream foretold, he met them all:
The smiling grimy boy at the garage
Ran out before he blew his horn; the tall
Professor in the mountains with his large
Tweed pockets full of plants addressed him hours
Before he would have dared; the deaf girl too
Seemed to expect him at her green chateau;
A meal was laid, the guest-room full of flowers.

More, their talk always took the wished-for turn,
Dwelt on the need for someone to advise,
Yet, at each meeting, he was forced to learn
The same misunderstanding would arise.
Which was in need of help? Were they or he
The physician, bridegroom and incendiary?

May 1934

Who's Who

A shilling life will give you all the facts:
How Father beat him, how he ran away,
What were the struggles of his youth, what acts
Made him the greatest figure of his day:
Of how he fought, fished, hunted, worked all night,
Though giddy, climbed new mountains; named a sea:
Some of the last researchers even write
Love made him weep his pints like you and me.

With all his honours on, he sighed for one
Who, say astonished critics, lived at home;
Did little jobs about the house with skill
And nothing else; could whistle; would sit still
Or potter round the garden; answered some
Of his long marvellous letters but kept none.

? 1934

Schoolchildren

Here are all the captivities, the cells are as real,
but these are unlike the prisoners we know,
who are outraged or pining or wittily resigned
   or just wish all away.

For these dissent so little, so nearly content
with the dumb play of dogs, with licking and rushing;
the bars of love are so strong, their conspiracies
   weak like the vows of drunkards.

Indeed, their strangeness is difficult to watch:
the condemned see only the fallacious angels of a vision,
so little effort lies behind their smiling,
   the beast of vocation is afraid.

But watch them, set against our size and timing
their almost neuter, their slightly awkward perfection;
for the sex is there, the broken bootlace is broken:
   the professor's dream is not true.

Yet the tyranny is so easy. An improper word
scribbled upon a fountain, is that all the rebellion?
A storm of tears wept in a corner, are these
   the seeds of a new life?

May 1937

May

May with its light behaving
Stirs vessel, eye and limb,
The singular and sad
Are willing to recover,
And to each swan-delighting river
The careless picnics come
In living white and red.

Our dead, remote and hooded,
In hollows rest, but we
From their vague woods have broken,
Forests where children meet
And the white angel-vampires flit,
Stand now with shaded eye,
The dangerous apple taken.

The real world lies before us,
Brave motions of the young,
Abundant wish for death,
The pleasing, pleasured, haunted:
A dying Master sinks tormented
In his admirers' ring,
The unjust walk the earth.

And love that makes impatient
Tortoise and roe, that lays
The blonde beside the dark,
Urges upon our blood,
Before the evil and the good
How insufficient is
Touch, endearment, look.

1934

A Bride in the 30's

Easily you move, easily your head,
And easily, as through leaves of an album, I'm led
Through the night's delights and the day's impressions,
Past tenement, river, upland, wood,
Though sombre the sixteen skies of Europe
   And the Danube flood.

Looking and loving, our behaviours pass
Things of stone, of steel and of polished glass;
Lucky to Love the strategic railway,
The run-down farms where his looks are fed,
And in each policed unlucky city
   Lucky his bed.

He from these lands of terrifying mottoes
Makes worlds as innocent as Beatrix Potter's;
Through bankrupt countries where they mend the roads,
Along unending plains his will is,
Intent as a collector, to pursue
   His greens and lilies.

Easy for him to find in your face
A pool of silence or a tower of grace,
To conjure a camera into a wishing-rose,
Simple to excite in the air from a glance
Horses, fountains, a side-drum, a trombone,
   The cosmic dance.

Summoned by such a music from our time,
Such images to sight and audience come
As Vanity cannot dispel or bless,
Hunger and fear in their variations,
Grouped invalids watching movements of birds,
   And single assassins,

Ten desperate million marching by,
Five feet, six feet, seven feet high,
Hitler and Mussolini in their wooing poses,
Churchill acknowledging the voters' greeting,
Roosevelt at the microphone, van der Lubbe laughing,
   And our first meeting.

But Love except at our proposal
Will do no trick at his disposal,
Without opinions of his own performs
The programme that we think of merit,
And through our private stuff must work
   His public spirit.

Certain it became, while still incomplete,
There were prizes for which we would never compete:
A choice was killed by each childish illness,
The boiling tears amid the hot-house plants,
The rigid promise fractured in the garden,
    And the long aunts.

While every day there bolted from the field
Desires to which we could not yield,
Fewer and clearer grew our plans,
Schemes for a life-time, sketches for a hatred,
And early among my interesting scrawls
    Appeared your portrait.

You stand now before me, flesh and bone
That ghosts would like to make their own:
Beware them, look away, be deaf,
When rage would proffer her immediate pleasure
Or glory swap her fascinating rubbish
    For your one treasure.

Be deaf, too, standing uncertain now,
A pine-tree shadow across your brow,
To what I hear and wish I did not,
The voice of Love saying lightly, brightly,
'Be Lubbe, be Hitler, but be my good,
    Daily, nightly.'

Trees are shaken, mountains darken,
But the heart repeats, though we would not hearken:
'Yours the choice to whom the gods awarded
The language of learning, the language of love,
Crooked to move as a money-bug, as a cancer,
    Or straight as a dove'.

November 1934

On This Island

Look, stranger, on this island now
The leaping light for your delight discovers,
Stand stable here
And silent be,
That through the channels of the ear
May wander like a river
The swaying sound of the sea.

Here at the small field's ending pause
When the chalk wall falls to the foam and its tall ledges
Oppose the pluck
And knock of the tide,
And the shingle scrambles after the suck-
-ing surf,
And the gull lodges
A moment on its sheer side.

112

Far off like floating seeds the ships
Diverge on urgent voluntary errands,
And the full view
Indeed may enter
And move in memory as now these clouds do,
That pass the harbour mirror
And all the summer through the water saunter.

1935

Night Mail
(Commentary for a G.P.O. Film)

I
This is the Night Mail crossing the Border,
Bringing the cheque and the postal order,

Letters for the rich, letters for the poor,
The shop at the corner, the girl next door.

Pulling up Beattock, a steady climb:
The gradient's against her, but she's on time.

Past cotton-grass and moorland border,
Shovelling white steam over her shoulder,

Snorting noisily, she passes
Silent miles of wind-bent grasses.

Birds turn their heads as she approaches,
Stare from bushes at her blank-faced coaches.

Sheep-dogs cannot turn her course;
They slumber on with paws across.

In the farm she passes no one wakes,
But a jug in a bedroom gently shakes.

II
Dawn freshens. Her climb is done.
Down towards Glasgow she descends,
Towards the steam tugs yelping down a glade of cranes,
Towards the fields of apparatus, the furnaces
Set on the dark plain like gigantic chessmen.
All Scotland waits for her:
In dark glens, beside pale-green lochs,
Men long for news.

III
Letters of thanks, letters from banks,
Letters of joy from girl and boy,
Receipted bills and invitations
To inspect new stock or to visit relations,

And applications for situations,
And timid lovers' declarations,
And gossip, gossip from all the nations,
News circumstantial, news financial,
Letters with holiday snaps to enlarge in,
Letters with faces scrawled on the margin,
Letters from uncles, cousins and aunts,
Letters to Scotland from the South of France,
Letters of condolence to Highlands and Lowlands,
Written on paper of every hue,
The pink, the violet, the white and the blue,
The chatty, the catty, the boring, the adoring,
The cold and official and the heart's outpouring,
Clever, stupid, short and long,
The typed and the printed and the spelt all wrong.

IV

Thousands are still asleep,
Dreaming of terrifying monsters
Or a friendly tea beside the band in Cranston's or Crawford's:
Asleep in working Glasgow, asleep in well-set Edinburgh,
Asleep in granite Aberdeen,
They continue their dreams,
But shall wake soon and hope for letters,
And none will hear the postman's knock
Without a quickening of the heart.
For who can bear to feel himself forgotten?

? July 1935

As I Walked Out One Evening

As I walked out one evening,
  Walking down Bristol Street,
The crowds upon the pavement
  Were fields of harvest wheat.

And down by the brimming river
  I heard a lover sing
Under an arch of the railway:
  'Love has no ending.

'I'll love you, dear, I'll love you
  Till China and Africa meet,
And the river jumps over the mountain
  And the salmon sing in the street,

'I'll love you till the ocean
  Is folded and hung up to dry
And the seven stars go squawking
  Like geese about the sky.

The years shall run like rabbits,
    For in my arms I hold
The Flower of the Ages,
    And the first love of the world.'

But all the clocks in the city
    Began to whirr and chime:
'O let not Time deceive you,
    You cannot conquer Time.

'In the burrows of the Nightmare
    Where Justice naked is,
Time watches from the shadow
    And coughs when you would kiss.

'In headaches and in worry
    Vaguely life leaks away,
And Time will have his fancy
    To-morrow or to-day.

'Into many a green valley
    Drifts the appalling snow;
Time breaks the threaded dances
    And the diver's brilliant bow.

'O plunge your hands in water,
    Plunge them in up to the wrist;
Stare, stare in the basin
    And wonder what you've missed.

'The glacier knocks in the cupboard,
    The desert sighs in the bed,
And the crack in the tea-cup opens
    A lane to the land of the dead.

'Where the beggars raffle the banknotes
    And the Giant is enchanting to Jack,
And the Lily-white Boy is a Roarer,
    And Jill goes down on her back.

'O look, look in the mirror,
    O look in your distress;
Life remains a blessing
    Although you cannot bless.

'O stand, stand at the window
    As the tears scald and start;
You shall love your crooked neighbour
    With your crooked heart.'

It was late, late in the evening,
    The lovers they were gone;
The clocks had ceased their chiming,
    And the deep river ran on.

November 1937

115

Twelve Songs

I. SONG OF THE BEGGARS

—'O for doors to be open and an invite with gilded edges
  To dine with Lord Lobcock and Count Asthma on the
    platinum benches,
  With somersaults and fireworks, the roast and the smacking
    kisses'—
      Cried the cripples to the silent statue,
      The six beggared cripples.

—'And Garbo's and Cleopatra's wits to go astraying,
  In a feather ocean with me to go fishing and playing,
  Still jolly when the cock has burst himself with crowing'—
      Cried the cripples to the silent statue,
      The six beggared cripples.

—'And to stand on green turf among the craning yellow faces
  Dependent on the chestnut, the sable, and Arabian horses,
  And me with a magic crystal to foresee their places'—
      Cried the cripples to the silent statue,
      The six beggared cripples.

—'And this square to be a deck and these pigeons canvas to rig,
  And to follow the delicious breeze like a tantony pig
  To the shaded feverless islands where the melons are big'—
      Cried the cripples to the silent statue,
      The six beggared cripples.

—'And these shops to be turned to tulips in a garden bed,
  And me with my crutch to thrash each merchant dead
  As he pokes from a flower his bald and wicked head'—
      Cried the cripples to the silent statue,
      The six beggared cripples.

—'And a hole in the bottom of heaven, and Peter and Paul
  And each smug surprised saint like parachutes to fall,
  And every one-legged beggar to have no legs at all'—
      Cried the cripples to the silent statue,
      The six beggared cripples.

? 1935

II

O lurcher-loving collier, black as night,
Follow your love across the smokeless hill;
Your lamp is out, the cages all are still;
Course for her heart and do not miss,
For Sunday soon is past and, Kate, fly not so fast,
For Monday comes when none may kiss:
Be marble to his soot, and to his black be white.

June 1935

III

Let a florid music praise,
   The flute and the trumpet,
Beauty's conquest of your face:
In that land of flesh and bone,
Where from citadels on high
Her imperial standards fly,
     Let the hot sun
     Shine on, shine on.

O but the unloved have had power,
   The weeping and striking,
Always: time will bring their hour;
Their secretive children walk
Through your vigilance of breath
To unpardonable Death,
     And my vows break
     Before his look.

February 1936

IV

Dear, though the night is gone,
Its dream still haunts to-day,
That brought us to a room
Cavernous, lofty as
A railway terminus,
And crowded in that gloom
Were beds, and we in one
In a far corner lay.

Our whisper woke no clocks,
We kissed and I was glad
At everything you did,
Indifferent to those
Who sat with hostile eyes
In pairs on every bed,
Arms round each other's necks,
Inert and vaguely sad.

What hidden worm of guilt
Or what malignant doubt
Am I the victim of,
That you then, unabashed,
Did what I never wished,
Confessed another love;
And I, submissive, felt
Unwanted and went out.

1936

V

Fish in the unruffled lakes
Their swarming colours wear,
Swans in the winter air
A white perfection have,
And the great lion walks
Through his innocent grove;
Lion, fish and swan
Act, and are gone
Upon Time's toppling wave.

We, till shadowed days are done,
We must weep and sing
Duty's conscious wrong,
The Devil in the clock,
The goodness carefully worn
For atonement or for luck;
We must lose our loves,
On each beast and bird that moves
Turn an envious look.

Sighs for folly done and said
Twist our narrow days,
But I must bless, I must praise
That you, my swan, who have
All gifts that to the swan
Impulsive Nature gave,
The majesty and pride,
Last night should add
Your voluntary love.

1936

VI. AUTUMN SONG

Now the leaves are falling fast,
Nurse's flowers will not last,
Nurses to their graves are gone,
But the prams go rolling on.

Whispering neighbours left and right
Daunt us from our true delight,
Able hands are forced to freeze
Derelict on lonely knees.

Close behind us on our track,
Dead in hundreds cry Alack,
Arms raised stiffly to reprove
In false attitudes of love.

Scrawny through a plundered wood,
Trolls run scolding for their food,
Owl and nightingale are dumb,
And the angel will not come.

118

Clear, unscaleable, ahead
Rise the Mountains of Instead,
From whose cold cascading streams
None may drink except in dreams.

1936

VII

Underneath an abject willow,
　Lover, sulk no more:
Act from thought should quickly follow.
　What is thinking for?
Your unique and moping station
　Proves you cold;
　Stand up and fold
Your map of desolation.

Bells that toll across the meadows
　From the sombre spire
Toll for these unloving shadows
　Love does not require.
All that lives may love; why longer
　Bow to loss
　With arms across?
Strike and you shall conquer.

Geese in flocks above you flying,
　Their direction know,
Icy brooks beneath you flowing,
　To their ocean go.
Dark and dull is your distraction:
　Walk then, come,
　No longer numb
Into your satisfaction.

1936

VIII

At last the secret is out, as it always must come in the end,
The delicious story is ripe to tell to the intimate friend;
Over the tea-cups and in the square the tongue has its desire;
Still waters run deep, my dear, there's never smoke without fire.

Behind the corpse in the reservoir, behind the ghost on the links,
Behind the lady who dances and the man who madly drinks,
Under the look of fatigue, the attack of migraine and the sigh
There is always another story, there is more than meets the eye.

For the clear voice suddenly singing, high up in the convent wall,
The scent of elder bushes, the sporting prints in the hall,
The croquet matches in summer, the handshake, the cough, the kiss,
There is always a wicked secret, a private reason for this.

? 1936

IX

Stop all the clocks, cut off the telephone,
Prevent the dog from barking with a juicy bone,
Silence the pianos and with muffled drum
Bring out the coffin, let the mourners come.

Let aeroplanes circle moaning overhead
Scribbling on the sky the message He Is Dead,
Put crêpe bows round the white necks of the public doves,
Let the traffic policemen wear black cotton gloves.

He was my North, my South, my East and West,
My working week and my Sunday rest,
My noon, my midnight, my talk, my song;
I thought that love would last for ever: I was wrong.

The stars are not wanted now: put out every one;
Pack up the moon and dismantle the sun;
Pour away the ocean and sweep up the wood;
For nothing now can ever come to any good.

? 1936

X

O the valley in the summer where I and my John
Beside the deep river would walk on and on
While the flowers at our feet and the birds up above
Argued so sweetly on reciprocal love,
And I leaned on his shoulder; 'O Johnny, let's play':
But he frowned like thunder and he went away.

O that Friday near Christmas as I well recall
When we went to the Charity Matinee Ball,
The floor was so smooth and the band was so loud
And Johnny so handsome I felt so proud;
'Squeeze me tighter, dear Johnny, let's dance till it's day':
But he frowned like thunder and he went away.

Shall I ever forget at the Grand Opera
When music poured out of each wonderful star?
Diamonds and pearls they hung dazzling down
Over each silver or golden silk gown;
'O John I'm in heaven,' I whispered to say:
But he frowned like thunder and he went away.

O but he was as fair as a garden in flower,
As slender and tall as the great Eiffel Tower,
When the waltz throbbed out on the long promenade
O his eyes and his smile they went straight to my heart;
'O marry me, Johnny, I'll love and obey':
But he frowned like thunder and he went away.

O last night I dreamed of you, Johnny, my lover,
You'd the sun on one arm and the moon on the other,
The sea it was blue and the grass it was green,
Every star rattled a round tambourine;
Ten thousand miles deep in a pit there I lay:
But you frowned like thunder and you went away.

April 1937

XI. ROMAN WALL BLUES

Over the heather the wet wind blows,
I've lice in my tunic and a cold in my nose.

The rain comes pattering out of the sky,
I'm a Wall soldier, I don't know why.

The mist creeps over the hard grey stone,
My girl's in Tungria; I sleep alone.

Aulus goes hanging around her place,
I don't like his manners, I don't like his face.

Piso's a Christian, he worships a fish;
There'd be no kissing if he had his wish.

She gave me a ring but I diced it away;
I want my girl and I want my pay.

When I'm a veteran with only one eye
I shall do nothing but look at the sky.

October 1937

XII

Some say that love's a little boy,
    And some say it's a bird,
Some say it makes the world go round,
    And some say that's absurd,
And when I asked the man next-door,
    Who looked as if he knew,
His wife got very cross indeed,
    And said it wouldn't do.

Does it look like a pair of pyjamas,
    Or the ham in a temperance hotel?
Does its odour remind one of llamas,
    Or has it a comforting smell?
Is it prickly to touch as a hedge is,
    Or soft as eiderdown fluff?
Is it sharp or quite smooth at the edges?
    O tell me the truth about love.

Our history books refer to it
    In cryptic little notes,
It's quite a common topic on
    The Transatlantic boats;
I've found the subject mentioned in
    Accounts of suicides,
And even seen it scribbled on
    The backs of railway-guides.

    Does it howl like a hungry Alsatian,
      Or boom like a military band?
    Could one give a first-rate imitation
      On a saw or a Steinway Grand?
    Is its singing at parties a riot?
      Does it only like Classical stuff?
    Will it stop when one wants to be quiet?
      O tell me the truth about love.

I looked inside the summer-house;
    It wasn't ever there:
I tried the Thames at Maidenhead,
    And Brighton's bracing air.
I don't know what the blackbird sang,
    Or what the tulip said;
But it wasn't in the chicken-run,
    Or underneath the bed.

    Can it pull extraordinary faces?
      Is it usually sick on a swing?
    Does it spend all its time at the races,
      Or fiddling with pieces of string?
    Has it views of its own about money?
      Does it think Patriotism enough?
    Are its stories vulgar but funny?
      O tell me the truth about love.

    When it comes, will it come without warning
      Just as I'm picking my nose?
    Will it knock on my door in the morning,
      Or tread in the bus on my toes?
    Will it come like a change in the weather?
      Will its greeting be courteous or rough?
    Will it alter my life altogether?
      O tell me the truth about love.

January 1938

His Excellency

    As it is, plenty;
    As it's admitted
    The children happy,
    And the car, the car
    That goes so far,

And the wife devoted:
To this as it is,
To the work and the banks
Let his thinning hair
And his hauteur
Give thanks, give thanks.

All that was thought
As like as not, is not;
When nothing was enough
But love, but love,
And the rough future
Of an intransigeant nature,
And the betraying smile,
Betraying, but a smile:
That that is not, is not;
Forget, forget.

Let him not cease to praise,
Then, his lordly days;
Yes, and the success
Let him bless, let him bless:
Let him see in this
The profit larger
And the sin venial,
Lest he see as it is
The loss as major
And final, final.

1936

Casino

Only their hands are living, to the wheel attracted,
are moved, as deer trek desperately towards a creek
   through the dust and scrub of a desert, or gently,
      as sunflowers turn to the light,

and, as night takes up the cries of feverish children,
the cravings of lions in dens, the loves of dons,
   gathers them all and remains the night, the
      great room is full of their prayers.

To a last feast of isolation self-invited,
they flock, and in a rite of disbelief are joined;
   from numbers all their stars are recreated,
      the enchanted, the worldly, the sad.

Without, calm rivers flow among the wholly living
quite near their trysts, and mountains part them, and birds,
   deep in the greens and moistures of summer,
      sing towards their work.

But here no nymph comes naked to the youngest shepherd,
the fountain is deserted, the laurel will not grow;
   the labyrinth is safe but endless, and broken
     is Ariadne's thread,

as deeper in these hands is grooved their fortune: lucky
were few, and it is possible that none was loved,
   and what was god-like in this generation
     was never to be born.

1936

Oxford

Nature invades: old rooks in each college garden
Still talk, like agile babies, the language of feeling,
By towers a river still runs coastward and will run,
   Stones in those towers are utterly
   Satisfied still with their weight.

Mineral and creature, so deeply in love with themselves
Their sin of accidie excludes all others,
Challenge our high-strung students with a careless beauty,
   Setting a single error
   Against their countless faults.

Outside, some factories, then a whole green county
Where a cigarette comforts the evil, a hymn the weak,
Where thousands fidget and poke and spend their money:
   Eros Paidagogos
   Weeps on his virginal bed.

And over this talkative city like any other
Weep the non-attached angels. Here too the knowledge of death
Is a consuming love, and the natural heart refuses
   A low unflattering voice
   That sleeps not till it find a hearing.

December 1937

Dover

Steep roads, a tunnel through chalk downs, are the approaches;
A ruined pharos overlooks a constructed bay;
The sea-front is almost elegant; all the show
Has, inland somewhere, a vague and dirty root:
   Nothing is made in this town.

A Norman castle, dominant, flood-lit at night,
Trains which fume in a station built on the sea,
Testify to the interests of its regular life:
Here dwell the experts on what the soldiers want,
   And who the travellers are

Whom ships carry in or out between the lighthouses,
Which guard for ever the made privacy of this bay
Like twin stone dogs opposed on a gentleman's gate.
Within these breakwaters English is properly spoken,
      Outside an atlas of tongues.

The eyes of departing migrants are fixed on the sea,
Conjuring destinies out of impersonal water:
'I see an important decision made on a lake,
An illness, a beard, Arabia found in a bed,
      Nanny defeated, Money.'

Red after years of failure or bright with fame,
The eyes of homecomers thank these historical cliffs:
'The mirror can no longer lie nor the clock reproach;
In the shadow under the yew, at the children's party,
      Everything must be explained.'

The Old Town with its Keep and Georgian houses
Has built its routine upon such unusual moments;
Vows, tears, emotional farewell gestures,
Are common here, unremarkable actions
      Like ploughing or a tipsy song.

Soldiers crowd into the pubs in their pretty clothes,
As pink and silly as girls from a high-class academy;
The Lion, The Rose, The Crown, will not ask them to die,
Not here, not now: all they are killing is time,
      A pauper civilian future.

Above them, expensive, shiny as a rich boy's bike,
Aeroplanes drone through the new European air
On the edge of a sky that makes England of minor importance;
And tides warn bronzing bathers of a cooling star
      With half its history done.

High over France, a full moon, cold and exciting
Like one of those dangerous flatterers we meet and love
When we are utterly wretched, returns our stare:
The night has found many recruits; to thousands of pilgrims
      The Mecca is coldness of heart.

The cries of the gulls at dawn are sad like work:
The soldier guards the traveller who pays for the soldier,
Each prays in a similar way for himself, but neither
Controls the years or the weather. Some may be heroes:
      Not all of us are unhappy.

                                        August 1937

Journey to Iceland

Each traveller prays *Let me be far from any*
physician, every port has its name for the sea,
   the citiless, the corroding, the sorrow,
     and North means to all *Reject*.

These plains are for ever where cold creatures are hunted
and on all sides: white wings flicker and flaunt;
   under a scolding flag the lover
     of islands may see at last,

in outline, his limited hope, as he nears a glitter
of glacier, sterile immature mountains intense
   in the abnormal northern day, and a river's
     fan-like polyp of sand.

Here let the citizen, then, find natural marvels,
a horse-shoe ravine, an issue of steam from a cleft
   in the rock, and rocks, and waterfalls brushing
     the rocks, and among the rocks birds;

the student of prose and conduct places to visit,
the site of a church where a bishop was put in a bag,
   the bath of a great historian, the fort where
     an outlaw dreaded the dark,

remember the doomed man thrown by his horse and crying
Beautiful is the hillside. I will not go,
   the old woman confessing *He that I loved the*
     best, to him I was worst.

Europe is absent: this is an island and should be
a refuge, where the affections of its dead can be bought
   by those whose dreams accuse them of being
     spitefully alive, and the pale

from too much passion of kissing feel pure in its deserts.
But is it, can they, as the world is and can lie?
   A narrow bridge over a torrent,
     a small farm under a crag

are natural settings for the jealousies of a province:
a weak vow of fidelity is made at a cairn,
   within the indigenous figure on horseback
     on the bridle-path down by the lake

his blood moves also by furtive and crooked inches,
asks all our questions: *Where is the homage? When*
   shall justice be done? Who is against me?
     Why am I always alone?

Our time has no favourite suburb, no local features
are those of the young for whom all wish to care;
    its promise is only a promise, the fabulous
        country impartially far.

Tears fall in all the rivers: again some driver
pulls on his gloves and in a blinding snowstorm starts
    upon a fatal journey, again some writer
        runs howling to his art.

July 1936

Detective Story

Who is ever quite without his landscape,
The straggling village street, the house in trees,
All near the church? Or else, the gloomy town-house,
The one with the Corinthian pillars, or
The tiny workmanlike flat, in any case
A home, a centre where the three or four things
That happen to a man do happen?
Who cannot draw the map of his life, shade in
The country station where he meets his loves
And says good-bye continually, mark the spot
Where the body of his happiness was first discovered?

An unknown tramp? A magnate? An enigma always,
With a well-buried past: and when the truth,
The truth about our happiness comes out,
How much it owed to blackmail and philandering.

What follows is habitual. All goes to plan:
The feud between the local common sense
And intuition, that exasperating amateur
Who's always on the spot by chance before us;
All goes to plan, both lying and confession,
Down to the thrilling final chase, the kill.

Yet, on the last page, a lingering doubt:
The verdict, was it just? The judge's nerves,
That clue, that protestation from the gallows,
And our own smile . . . why, yes . . .

But time is always guilty. Someone must pay for
Our loss of happiness, our happiness itself.

July 1936

Death's Echo

'O who can ever gaze his fill,'
  Farmer and fisherman say,
'On native shore and local hill,
Grudge aching limb or callus on the hand?
Father, grandfather stood upon this land,
And here the pilgrims from our loins will stand.'
  So farmer and fisherman say
  In their fortunate hey-day:
But Death's low answer drifts across
Empty catch or harvest loss
  Or an unlucky May.
The earth is an oyster with nothing inside it,
  Not to be born is the best for man;
The end of toil is a bailiff's order,
  Throw down the mattock and dance while you can.

'O life's too short for friends who share,'
  Travellers think in their hearts,
'The city's common bed, the air,
The mountain bivouac and the bathing beach,
Where incidents draw every day from each
Memorable gesture and witty speech.'
  So travellers think in their hearts,
  Till malice or circumstance parts
Them from their constant humour:
And slyly Death's coercive rumour
  In that moment starts.
A friend is the old old tale of Narcissus,
  Not to be born is the best for man;
An active partner in something disgraceful,
  Change your partner, dance while you can.

'O stretch your hands across the sea,'
  The impassioned lover cries,
'Stretch them towards your harm and me.
Our grass is green, and sensual our brief bed,
The stream sings at its foot, and at its head
The mild and vegetarian beasts are fed.'
  So the impassioned lover cries
  Till the storm of pleasure dies:
From the bedpost and the rocks
Death's enticing echo mocks,
    And his voice replies.
The greater the love, the more false to its object,
  Not to be born is the best for man;
After the kiss comes the impulse to throttle,
  Break the embraces, dance while you can.

'I see the guilty world forgiven,'
  Dreamer and drunkard sing,
'The ladders let down out of heaven,
The laurel springing from the martyr's blood,
The children skipping where the weeper stood,
The lovers natural and the beasts all good.'
  So dreamer and drunkard sing
  Till day their sobriety bring:
Parrotwise with Death's reply
From whelping fear and nesting lie,
  Woods and their echoes ring.
The desires of the heart are as crooked as corkscrews,
  Not to be born is the best for man;
The second-best is a formal order,
  The dance's pattern; dance while you can.
Dance, dance, for the figure is easy,
  The tune is catching and will not stop;
Dance till the stars come down from the rafters;
  Dance, dance, dance till you drop.

1936

The Price

Who can ever praise enough
The world of his belief?
Harum-scarum childhood plays
In the meadows near his home,
In his woods love knows no wrong,
Travellers ride their placid ways,
In the cool shade of the tomb
Age's trusting footfalls ring.
Who can paint the vivid tree
And grass of phantasy?

But to create it and to guard
Shall be his whole reward:
He shall watch and he shall weep,
All his father's love deny,
To his mother's womb be lost,
Eight nights with a wanton sleep,
Then upon the ninth shall be
Bride and victim to a ghost,
And in the pit of terror thrown
Shall bear the wrath alone.

July 1936

Danse Macabre

It's farewell to the drawing-room's mannerly cry,
The professor's logical whereto and why,
The frock-coated diplomat's polished aplomb,
Now matters are settled with gas and with bomb.

The works for two pianos, the brilliant stories
Of reasonable giants and remarkable fairies,
The pictures, the ointments, the frangible wares
And the branches of olive are stored upstairs.

For the Devil has broken parole and arisen,
He has dynamited his way out of prison,
Out of the well where his Papa throws
The rebel angel, the outcast rose.

Like influenza he walks abroad,
He stands by the bridge, he waits by the ford,
As a goose or a gull he flies overhead,
He hides in the cupboard and under the bed.

O were he to triumph, dear heart, you know
To what depths of shame he would drag you low;
He would steal you away from me, yes, my dear,
He would steal you and cut off your beautiful hair.

Millions already have come to their harm,
Succumbing like doves to his adder's charm;
Hundreds of trees in the wood are unsound:
I'm the axe that must cut them down to the ground.

For I, after all, am the Fortunate One,
The Happy-Go-Lucky, the spoilt Third Son;
For me it is written the Devil to chase
And to rid the earth of the human race.

The behaving of man is a world of horror,
A sedentary Sodom and slick Gomorrah;
I must take charge of the liquid fire
And storm the cities of human desire.

The buying and selling, the eating and drinking,
The disloyal machines and irreverent thinking,
The lovely dullards again and again
Inspiring their bitter ambitious men.

I shall come, I shall punish, the Devil be dead,
I shall have caviar thick on my bread,
I shall build myself a cathedral for home
With a vacuum cleaner in every room.

I shall ride the parade in a platinum car,
My features will shine, my name will be Star,
Day-long and night-long the bells I shall peal,
And down the long street I shall turn the cartwheel.

So Little John, Long John, Peter and Paul,
And poor little Horace with only one ball,
You shall leave your breakfast, your desk and your play
On a fine summer morning the Devil to slay.

For it's order and trumpet and anger and drum
And power and glory command you to come;
The graves will fly open to let you all in,
And the earth be emptied of mortal sin.

The fishes are silent deep in the sea,
The skies are lit up like a Christmas tree,
The star in the West shoots its warning cry:
'Mankind is alive, but Mankind must die.'

So good-bye to the house with its wallpaper red,
Good-bye to the sheets on the warm double bed,
Good-bye to the beautiful birds on the wall,
It's good-bye, dear heart, good-bye to you all.

January 1937

Lullaby

Lay your sleeping head, my love,
Human on my faithless arm;
Time and fevers burn away
Individual beauty from
Thoughtful children, and the grave
Proves the child ephemeral:
But in my arms till break of day
Let the living creature lie,
Mortal, guilty, but to me
The entirely beautiful.

Soul and body have no bounds:
To lovers as they lie upon
Her tolerant enchanted slope
In their ordinary swoon,
Grave the vision Venus sends
Of supernatural sympathy,
Universal love and hope;
While an abstract insight wakes
Among the glaciers and the rocks
The hermit's carnal ecstasy.

Certainty, fidelity
On the stroke of midnight pass
Like vibrations of a bell
And fashionable madmen raise
Their pedantic boring cry:
Every farthing of the cost,
All the dreaded cards foretell,
Shall be paid, but from this night
Not a whisper, not a thought,
Not a kiss nor look be lost.

Beauty, midnight, vision dies:
Let the winds of dawn that blow
Softly round your dreaming head
Such a day of welcome show
Eye and knocking heart may bless,
Find our mortal world enough;
Noons of dryness find you fed
By the involuntary powers,
Nights of insult let you pass
Watched by every human love.

January 1937

Orpheus

What does the song hope for? And his moved hands
A little way from the birds, the shy, the delightful?
    To be bewildered and happy,
    Or most of all the knowledge of life?

But the beautiful are content with the sharp notes of the air;
The warmth is enough. O if winter really
    Oppose, if the weak snowflake,
    What will the wish, what will the dance do?

April 1937

Miss Gee

Let me tell you a little story
    About Miss Edith Gee;
She lived in Clevedon Terrace
    At Number 83.

She'd a slight squint in her left eye,
    Her lips they were thin and small,
She had narrow sloping shoulders
    And she had no bust at all.

She'd a velvet hat with trimmings,
    And a dark grey serge costume;
She lived in Clevedon Terrace
    In a small bed-sitting room.

She'd a purple mac for wet days,
    A green umbrella too to take,
She'd a bicycle with shopping basket
    And a harsh back-pedal brake.

The Church of Saint Aloysius
    Was not so very far;
She did a lot of knitting,
    Knitting for that Church Bazaar.

132

Miss Gee looked up at the starlight
  And said, 'Does anyone care
That I live in Clevedon Terrace
  On one hundred pounds a year?'

She dreamed a dream one evening
  That she was the Queen of France
And the Vicar of Saint Aloysius
  Asked Her Majesty to dance.

But a storm blew down the palace,
  She was biking through a field of corn,
And a bull with the face of the Vicar
  Was charging with lowered horn.

She could feel his hot breath behind her,
  He was going to overtake;
And the bicycle went slower and slower
  Because of that back-pedal brake.

Summer made the trees a picture,
  Winter made them a wreck;
She bicycled to the evening service
  With her clothes buttoned up to her neck.

She passed by the loving couples,
  She turned her head away;
She passed by the loving couples
  And they didn't ask her to stay.

Miss Gee sat down in the side-aisle,
  She heard the organ play;
And the choir it sang so sweetly
  At the ending of the day,

Miss Gee knelt down in the side-aisle,
  She knelt down on her knees;
'Lead me not into temptation
  But make me a good girl, please.'

The days and nights went by her
  Like waves round a Cornish wreck;
She bicycled down to the doctor
  With her clothes buttoned up to her neck.

She bicycled down to the doctor,
  And rang the surgery bell;
'O, doctor, I've a pain inside me,
  And I don't feel very well.'

Doctor Thomas looked her over,
  And then he looked some more;
Walked over to his wash-basin,
  Said, 'Why didn't you come before?'

133

Doctor Thomas sat over his dinner,
    Though his wife was waiting to ring,
Rolling his bread into pellets;
    Said, 'Cancer's a funny thing.

'Nobody knows what the cause is,
    Though some pretend they do;
It's like some hidden assassin
    Waiting to strike at you.

'Childless women get it,
    And men when they retire;
It's as if there had to be some outlet
    For their foiled creative fire.'

His wife she rang for the servant,
    Said, 'Don't be so morbid, dear';
He said: 'I saw Miss Gee this evening
    And she's a goner, I fear.'

They took Miss Gee to the hospital,
    She lay there a total wreck,
Lay in the ward for women
    With the bedclothes right up to her neck.

They laid her on the table,
    The students began to laugh;
And Mr. Rose the surgeon
    He cut Miss Gee in half.

Mr. Rose he turned to his students,
    Said, 'Gentlemen, if you please,
We seldom see a sarcoma
    As far advanced as this.'

They took her off the table,
    They wheeled away Miss Gee
Down to another department
    Where they study Anatomy.

They hung her from the ceiling,
    Yes, they hung up Miss Gee;
And a couple of Oxford Groupers
    Carefully dissected her knee.

                                        April 1937

James Honeyman

James Honeyman was a silent child;
He didn't laugh or cry:
He looked at his mother
With curiosity.

134

Mother came up to the nursery,
Peeped through the open door,
Saw him striking matches,
Sitting on the nursery floor.

He went to the children's party,
The buns were full of cream,
Sat there dissolving sugar
In his tea-cup in a dream.

On his eighth birthday
Didn't care that the day was wet,
For by his bedside
Lay a ten-shilling chemistry set.

Teacher said: 'James Honeyman
Is the cleverest boy we've had,
But he doesn't play with the others,
And that, I think, is sad.'

While the other boys played football,
He worked in the laboratory,
Got a scholarship to college
And a first-class degree,

Kept awake with black coffee,
Took to wearing glasses,
Writing a thesis
On the toxic gases,

Went out into the country,
Went by a Green Line bus,
Walked upon the Chilterns,
Thought about phosphorus,

Said: 'Lewisite in its day
Was pretty decent stuff,
But, under modern conditions,
It's not nearly strong enough.'

His Tutor sipped his port,
Said: 'I think it's clear
That young James Honeyman's
The most brilliant man of the year.'

He got a job in research
With Imperial Alkali,
Said to himself while shaving:
'I'll be famous before I die.'

His landlady said: 'Mr. Honeyman,
You've only got one life,
You ought to have some fun, Sir,
You ought to find a wife.'

At Imperial Alkali
There was a girl called Doreen,
One day she cut her finger,
Asked him for iodine.

'I'm feeling faint,' she said.
He led her to a chair,
Fetched her a glass of water,
Wanted to stroke her hair.

They took a villa on the Great West Road,
Painted green and white;
On their left a United Dairy,
A cinema on their right.

At the bottom of the garden
He built a little shed.
'He's going to blow us up,'
All the neighbours said.

Doreen called down at midnight:
'Jim, dear, it's time for bed.'
'I'll finish my experiment,
And then I'll come,' he said.

Caught influenza at Christmas.
The doctor said: 'Go to bed.'
'I'll finish my experiment,
And then I'll go,' he said.

Walked out on Sundays,
Helped to push the pram,
Said, 'I'm looking for a gas, dear,
A whiff will kill a man.

'I'm going to find it,
That's what I'm going to do.'
Doreen squeezed his hand and said:
'Jim, I believe in you.'

In the hot nights of summer,
When the roses all were red,
James Honeyman was working
In his little garden shed.

Came upstairs at midnight,
Kissed his sleeping son,
Held up a sealed glass test-tube,
Said: 'Look, Doreen, I've won!'

They stood together by the window,
The moon was bright and clear.
He said: 'At last I've done something
That's worthy of you, dear.'

He took a train next morning,
Went up to Whitehall
With the phial in his pocket
To show it to them all.

He sent in his card,
The officials only swore:
'Tell him we're very busy
And show him the door.'

Doreen said to the neighbours:
'Isn't it a shame!
My husband's so clever,
And they didn't know his name.'

One neighbour was sympathetic,
Her name was Mrs. Flower:
She was the agent
Of a Foreign Power.

One evening they sat at supper,
There came a gentle knock:
'A gentleman to see Mr. Honeyman.'
He stayed till eleven o'clock.

They walked down the garden together,
Down to the little shed:
'We'll see you, then, in Paris.
Good night,' the gentleman said.

The boat was nearing Dover,
He looked back at Calais,
Said: 'Honeyman's N.P.C.
Will be heard of some day.'

He was sitting in the garden,
Writing notes on a pad:
Their little son was playing
Round his Mum and Dad.

Suddenly out of the east
Some aeroplanes appeared.
Somebody screamed: 'They're bombers!
War must have been declared!'

The first bomb hit the Dairy,
The second the cinema,
The third fell in the garden
Just like a falling star.

'O kiss me, Mother, kiss me,
And tuck me up in bed,
For Daddy's invention
Is going to choke me dead!'

'Where are you, Jim, where are you?
O put your arms round me,
For my lungs are full
Of Honeyman's N.P.C.!'

'I wish I were a salmon,
Swimming in the sea,
I wish I were the dove
That coos upon the tree.'

'O you are not a salmon,
O you are not the dove:
But you invented the vapour
That is killing those you love.'

'O hide me in the mountains,
O drown me in the sea:
Lock me in a dungeon
And throw away the key.'

'O you can't hide in the mountains,
O you can't drown in the sea,
But you must die, and you know why,
By Honeyman's N.P.C.!'

August 1937

Victor

Victor was a little baby,
    Into this world he came;
His father took him on his knee and said:
    'Don't dishonour the family name.'

Victor looked up at his father
    Looked up with big round eyes:
His father said: 'Victor, my only son,
    Don't you ever ever tell lies.'

Victor and his father went riding
    Out in a little dog-cart;
His father took a Bible from his pocket and read,
    'Blessed are the pure in heart.'

It was a frosty December,
    It wasn't the season for fruits;
His father fell dead of heart disease
    While lacing up his boots.

It was a frosty December
    When into his grave he sank;
His uncle found Victor a post as cashier
    In the Midland Counties Bank.

It was a frosty December
  Victor was only eighteen,
But his figures were neat and his margins straight
  And his cuffs were always clean.

He took a room at the Peveril,
  A respectable boarding-house;
And Time watched Victor day after day
  As a cat will watch a mouse.

The clerks slapped Victor on the shoulder;
  'Have you ever had a woman?' they said,
'Come down town with us on Saturday night'.
  Victor smiled and shook his head.

The manager sat in his office,
  Smoked a Corona cigar;
Said: 'Victor's a decent fellow but
  He's too mousey to go far'.

Victor went up to his bedroom,
  Set the alarum bell;
Climbed into bed, took his Bible and read
  Of what happened to Jezebel.

It was the First of April,
  Anna to the Peveril came;
Her eyes, her lips, her breasts, her hips
  And her smile set men aflame.

She looked as pure as a schoolgirl
  On her First Communion day,
But her kisses were like the best champagne
  When she gave herself away.

It was the Second of April,
  She was wearing a coat of fur;
Victor met her upon the stairs
  And he fell in love with her.

The first time he made his proposal,
  She laughed, said: 'I'll never wed';
The second time there was a pause;
  Then she smiled and shook her head.

Anna looked into her mirror,
  Pouted and gave a frown;
Said: 'Victor's as dull as a wet afternoon
  But I've got to settle down.'

The third time he made his proposal,
  As they walked by the Reservoir;
She gave him a kiss like a blow on the head,
  Said: 'You are my heart's desire.'

They were married early in August,
      She said: 'Kiss me, you funny boy';
Victor took her in his arms and said:
      'O my Helen of Troy.'

It was the middle of September,
      Victor came to the office one day;
He was wearing a flower in his buttonhole,
      He was late but he was gay.

The clerks were talking of Anna,
      The door was just ajar;
One said: 'Poor old Victor, but where ignorance
      Is bliss, et cetera.'

Victor stood still as a statue,
      The door was just ajar;
One said: 'God, what fun I had with her
      In that Baby Austin car.'

Victor walked out into the High Street,
      He walked to the edge of the town;
He came to the allotments and the rubbish heap,
      And his tears came tumbling down.

Victor looked up at the sunset
      As he stood there all alone;
Cried: 'Are you in Heaven, Father?'
      But the sky said 'Address not known'.

Victor looked up at the mountains,
      The mountains all covered with snow;
Cried: 'Are you pleased with me, Father?'
      And the answer came back, 'No'.

Victor came to the forest,
      Cried: 'Father, will she ever be true?'
And the oaks and the beeches shook their heads
      And they answered: 'Not to you.'

Victor came to the meadow
      Where the wind went sweeping by;
Cried: 'O Father, I love her so',
      But the wind said: 'She must die'.

Victor came to the river
      Running so deep and so still;
Cried: 'O Father, what shall I do?'
      And the river answered: 'Kill'.

Anna was sitting at a table,
      Drawing cards from a pack;
Anna was sitting at table
      Waiting for her husband to come back.

It wasn't the Jack of Diamonds
    Nor the Joker she drew at first;
It wasn't the King or the Queen of Hearts
    But the Ace of Spades reversed.

Victor stood in the doorway,
    He didn't utter a word;
She said: 'What's the matter, darling?'
    He behaved as if he hadn't heard.

There was a voice in his left ear,
    There was a voice in his right,
There was a voice at the base of his skull
    Saying: 'She must die to-night'.

Victor picked up a carving-knife,
    His features were set and drawn,
Said: 'Anna, it would have been better for you
    If you had not been born.'

Anna jumped up from the table,
    Anna started to scream,
But Victor came slowly after her
    Like a horror in a dream.

She dodged behind the sofa,
    She tore down a curtain rod,
But Victor came slowly after her;
    Said: 'Prepare to meet thy God.'

She managed to wrench the door open,
    She ran and she didn't stop.
But Victor followed her up the stairs
    And he caught her at the top.

He stood there above the body,
    He stood there holding the knife;
And the blood ran down the stairs and sang:
    'I'm the Resurrection and the Life'.

They tapped Victor on the shoulder,
    They took him away in a van;
He sat as quiet as a lump of moss
    Saying, 'I am the Son of Man'.

Victor sat in a corner
    Making a woman of clay;
Saying: 'I am Alpha and Omega, I shall come
    To judge the earth one day.'

June 1937

As He Is

Wrapped in a yielding air, beside
  The flower's noiseless hunger,
Close to the tree's clandestine tide,
  Close to the bird's high fever,
  Loud in his hope and anger,
Erect about a skeleton,
  Stands the expressive lover,
  Stands the deliberate man.

Beneath the hot unasking sun,
  Past stronger beasts and fairer
He picks his way, a living gun,
  With gun and lens and Bible,
  A militant enquirer,
The friend, the rash, the enemy,
  The essayist, the able,
  Able at times to cry.

The friendless and unhated stone
  Lies everywhere about him,
The Brothered-One, the Not-Alone,
  The brothered and the hated
  Whose family have taught him
To set against the large and dumb,
  The timeless and the rooted,
  His money and his time.

For mother's fading hopes become
  Dull wives to his dull spirits,
Soon dulled by nurse's moral thumb,
  That dullard fond betrayer,
  And, childish, he inherits,
So soon by legal father tricked,
  The tall imposing tower,
  Imposing, yes, but locked.

And ruled by dead men never met,
  By pious guess deluded,
Upon the stool of mania set
  Or stool of desolation,
  Sits murderous and clear-headed;
Enormous beauties round him move,
  For grandiose is his vision
  And grandiose his love.

Determined on Time's truthful shield
  The lamb must face the tigress,
Their faithful quarrel never healed
  Though, faithless, he consider
  His dream of vaguer ages,
Hunter and victim reconciled,
  The lion and the adder,
  The adder and the child.

Fresh loves betray him, every day
   Over his green horizon
A fresh deserter rides away,
   And miles away birds mutter
   Of ambush and of treason;
To fresh defeats he still must move,
   To further griefs and greater,
   And the defeat of grief.

May 1937

A Voyage

I. WHITHER?

Where does this journey look which the watcher upon the quay,
Standing under his evil star, so bitterly envies,
As the mountains swim away with slow calm strokes
And the gulls abandon their vow? Does it promise a juster life?

Alone with his heart at last, does the fortunate traveller find
In the vague touch of a breeze, the fickle flash of a wave,
Proofs that somewhere exists, really, the Good Place,
Convincing as those that children find in stones and holes?

No, he discovers nothing: he does not want to arrive.
His journey is false, his unreal excitement really an illness
On a false island where the heart cannot act and will not suffer:
He condones his fever; he is weaker than he thought; his weakness
    is real.

But at moments, as when real dolphins with leap and panache
Cajole for recognition or, far away, a real island
Gets up to catch his eye, his trance is broken: he remembers
Times and places where he was well; he believes in joy,

That, maybe, his fever shall find a cure, the true journey an end
Where hearts meet and are really true, and crossed this ocean, that
    parts
Hearts which alter but is the same always, that goes
Everywhere, as truth and falsehood go, but cannot suffer.

1938

II. THE SHIP

All streets are brightly lit; our city is kept clean;
Her Third-Class deal from greasy packs, her First bid high;
Her beggars banished to the bows have never seen
What can be done in state-rooms: no one asks why.

Lovers are writing letters, athletes playing ball,
One doubts the virtue, one the beauty of his wife,
A boy's ambitious: perhaps the Captain hates us all;
Someone perhaps is leading a civilised life.

Slowly our Western culture in full pomp progresses
Over the barren plains of a sea; somewhere ahead
A septic East, odd fowl and flowers, odder dresses:

Somewhere a strange and shrewd To-morrow goes to bed,
Planning a test for men from Europe; no one guesses
Who will be most ashamed, who richer, and who dead.

1938

III. THE SPHINX

Did it once issue from the carver's hand
Healthy? Even the earliest conqueror saw
The face of a sick ape, a bandaged paw,
An ailing lion crouched on dirty sand.

We gape, then go uneasily away:
It does not like the young nor love nor learning.
Time hurt it like a person: it lies turning
A vast behind on shrill America,

And witnesses. The huge hurt face accuses
And pardons nothing, least of all success:
What counsel it might offer it refuses
To those who face akimbo its distress.

'Do people like me?' *No*. The slave amuses
The lion. 'Am I to suffer always?' *Yes*.

1938

IV. HONG KONG

Its leading characters are wise and witty,
Their suits well-tailored, and they wear them well,
Have many a polished parable to tell
About the *mores* of a trading city.

Only the servants enter unexpected,
Their silent movements make dramatic news;
Here in the East our bankers have erected
A worthy temple to the Comic Muse.

Ten thousand miles from home and What's-Her-Name
A bugle on this Late Victorian hill
Puts out the soldier's light; off-stage, a war

Thuds like the slamming of a distant door:
Each has his comic role in life to fill,
Though Life be neither comic nor a game.

December 1938

V. MACAO

A weed from Catholic Europe, it took root
Between some yellow mountains and a sea,
Its gay stone houses an exotic fruit,
A Portugal-cum-China oddity.

Rococo images of Saint and Saviour
Promise its gamblers fortunes when they die,
Churches alongside brothels testify
That faith can pardon natural behavior.

A town of such indulgence need not fear
Those mortal sins by which the strong are killed
And limbs and governments are torn to pieces:

Religious clocks will strike, the childish vices
Will safeguard the low virtues of the child,
And nothing serious can happen here.

December 1938

VI. A MAJOR PORT

No guidance can be found in ancient lore:
Banks jostle in the sun for domination,
Behind them stretch like sorry vegetation
The low recessive houses of the poor.

We have no destiny assigned us,
No data but our bodies: we plan
To better ourselves; bleak hospitals alone remind us
Of the equality of man.

Children are really loved here, even by police:
They speak of years before the big were lonely.
Here will be no recurrence.

Only
The brass-bands throbbing in the parks foretell
Some future reign of happiness and peace.

We learn to pity and rebel.

1938

The Capital

Quarter of pleasures where the rich are always waiting,
Waiting expensively for miracles to happen,
Dim-lighted restaurant where lovers eat each other,
Café where exiles have established a malicious village:

145

You with your charm and your apparatus have abolished
The strictness of winter and the spring's compulsion;
Far from your lights the outraged punitive father,
The dullness of mere obedience here is apparent.

So with orchestras and glances, soon you betray us
To belief in our infinite powers; and the innocent
Unobservant offender falls in a moment
Victim to his heart's invisible furies.

In unlighted streets you hide away the appalling;
Factories where lives are made for a temporary use
Like collars or chairs, rooms where the lonely are battered
Slowly like pebbles into fortuitous shapes.

But the sky you illumine, your glow is visible far
Into the dark countryside, enormous and frozen,
Where, hinting at the forbidden like a wicked uncle,
Night after night to the farmer's children you beckon.

December 1938

Brussels in Winter

Wandering through cold streets tangled like old string,
Coming on fountains rigid in the frost,
Its formula escapes you; it has lost
The certainty that constitutes a thing.

Only the old, the hungry and the humbled
Keep at this temperature a sense of place,
And in their misery are all assembled;
The winter holds them like an Opera-House.

Ridges of rich apartments loom to-night
Where isolated windows glow like farms,
A phrase goes packed with meaning like a van,

A look contains the history of man,
And fifty francs will earn a stranger right
To take the shuddering city in his arms.

December 1938

Musée des Beaux Arts

About suffering they were never wrong,
The Old Masters: how well they understood
Its human position; how it takes place
While someone else is eating or opening a window or just walking
        dully along;
How, when the aged are reverently, passionately waiting
For the miraculous birth, there always must be

146

Children who did not specially want it to happen, skating
On a pond at the edge of the wood:
They never forgot
That even the dreadful martyrdom must run its course
Anyhow in a corner, some untidy spot
Where the dogs go on with their doggy life and the torturer's horse
Scratches its innocent behind on a tree.

In Breughel's *Icarus*, for instance: how everything turns away
Quite leisurely from the disaster; the ploughman may
Have heard the splash, the forsaken cry,
But for him it was not an important failure; the sun shone
As it had to on the white legs disappearing into the green
Water; and the expensive delicate ship that must have seen
Something amazing, a boy falling out of the sky,
Had somewhere to get to and sailed calmly on.

December 1938

Gare du Midi

A nondescript express in from the South,
Crowds round the ticket barrier, a face
To welcome which the mayor has not contrived
Bugles or braid: something about the mouth
Distracts the stray look with alarm and pity.
Snow is falling. Clutching a little case,
He walks out briskly to infect a city
Whose terrible future may have just arrived.

December 1938

The Novelist

Encased in talent like a uniform,
The rank of every poet is well known;
They can amaze us like a thunderstorm,
Or die so young, or live for years alone.

They can dash forward like hussars: but he
Must struggle out of his boyish gift and learn
How to be plain and awkward, how to be
One after whom none think it worth to turn.

For, to achieve his lightest wish, he must
Become the whole of boredom, subject to
Vulgar complaints like love, among the Just

Be just, among the Filthy filthy too,
And in his own weak person, if he can,
Dully put up with all the wrongs of Man.

December 1938

147

The Composer

All the others translate: the painter sketches
A visible world to love or reject;
Rummaging into his living, the poet fetches
The images out that hurt and connect,

From Life to Art by painstaking adaption,
Relying on us to cover the rift;
Only your notes are pure contraption,
Only your song is an absolute gift.

Pour out your presence, a delight cascading
The falls of the knee and the weirs of the spine,
Our climate of silence and doubt invading;

You alone, alone, imaginary song,
Are unable to say an existence is wrong,
And pour out your forgiveness like a wine.

December 1938

Rimbaud

The nights, the railway-arches, the bad sky,
His horrible companions did not know it;
But in that child the rhetorician's lie
Burst like a pipe: the cold had made a poet.

Drinks bought him by his weak and lyric friend
His five wits systematically deranged,
To all accustomed nonsense put an end;
Till he from lyre and weakness was estranged.

Verse was a special illness of the ear;
Integrity was not enough; that seemed
The hell of childhood: he must try again.

Now, galloping through Africa, he dreamed
Of a new self, a son, an engineer,
His truth acceptable to lying men.

December 1938

A. E. Housman

No one, not even Cambridge, was to blame
(Blame if you like the human situation):
Heart-injured in North London, he became
The Latin Scholar of his generation.

Deliberately he chose the dry-as-dust,
Kept tears like dirty postcards in a drawer;
Food was his public love, his private lust
Something to do with violence and the poor.

In savage foot-notes on unjust editions
He timidly attacked the life he led,
And put the money of his feelings on

The uncritical relations of the dead,
Where only geographical divisions
Parted the coarse hanged soldier from the don.

December 1938

Edward Lear

Left by his friend to breakfast alone on the white
Italian shore, his Terrible Demon arose
Over his shoulder; he wept to himself in the night,
A dirty landscape-painter who hated his nose.

The legions of cruel inquisitive They
Were so many and big like dogs: he was upset
By Germans and boats; affection was miles away:
But guided by tears he successfully reached his Regret.

How prodigious the welcome was. Flowers took his hat,
And bore him off to introduce him to the tongs;
The demon's false nose made the table laugh; a cat
Soon had him waltzing madly, let him squeeze her hand;
Words pushed him to the piano to sing comic songs;

And children swarmed to him like settlers. He became a land.

January 1939

Epitaph on a Tyrant

Perfection, of a kind, was what he was after,
And the poetry he invented was easy to understand;
He knew human folly like the back of his hand,
And was greatly interested in armies and fleets;
When he laughed, respectable senators burst with laughter,
And when he cried the little children died in the streets.

January 1939

Sonnets from China

I

So from the years their gifts were showered: each
Grabbed at the one it needed to survive;
Bee took the politics that suit a hive,
Trout finned as trout, peach moulded into peach,

And were successful at their first endeavour.
The hour of birth their only time in college,
They were content with their precocious knowledge,
To know their station and be right for ever.

149

Till, finally, there came a childish creature
On whom the years could model any feature,
Fake, as chance fell, a leopard or a dove,

Who by the gentlest wind was rudely shaken,
Who looked for truth but always was mistaken,
And envied his few friends, and chose his love.

II

They wondered why the fruit had been forbidden:
It taught them nothing new. They hid their pride,
But did not listen much when they were chidden:
They knew exactly what to do outside.

They left. Immediately the memory faded
Of all they'd known: they could not understand
The dogs now who before had always aided;
The stream was dumb with whom they'd always planned.

They wept and quarrelled: freedom was so wild.
In front maturity as he ascended
Retired like a horizon from the child,

The dangers and the punishments grew greater,
And the way back by angels was defended
Against the poet and the legislator.

III

Only a smell had feelings to make known,
Only an eye could point in a direction,
The fountain's utterance was itself alone:
He, though, by naming thought to make connection

Between himself as hunter and his food;
He felt the interest in his throat and found
That he could send a servant to chop wood
Or kiss a girl to rapture with a sound.

They bred like locusts till they hid the green
And edges of the world: confused and abject,
A creature to his own creation subject,

He shook with hate for things he'd never seen,
Pined for a love abstracted from its object,
And was oppressed as he had never been.

IV

He stayed, and was imprisoned in possession:
By turns the seasons guarded his one way,
The mountains chose the mother of his children,
In lieu of conscience the sun ruled his day.

Beyond him, his young cousins in the city
Pursued their rapid and unnatural courses,
Believed in nothing but were easy-going,
Far less afraid of strangers than of horses.

He, though, changed little,
But took his colour from the earth,
And grew in likeness to his fowls and cattle.

The townsman thought him miserly and simple,
Unhappy poets took him for the truth,
And tyrants held him up as an example.

V

His care-free swagger was a fine invention:
Life was too slow, too regular, too grave.
With horse and sword he drew the girls' attention,
A conquering hero, bountiful and brave,

To whom teen-agers looked for liberation:
At his command they left behind their mothers,
Their wits were sharpened by the long migration,
His camp-fires taught them all the horde were brothers.

Till what he came to do was done: unwanted,
Grown seedy, paunchy, pouchy, disappointed,
He took to drink to screw his nerves to murder,

Or sat in offices and stole,
Boomed at his children about Law and Order,
And hated life with heart and soul.

VI

He watched the stars and noted birds in flight;
A river flooded or a fortress fell:
He made predictions that were sometimes right;
His lucky guesses were rewarded well.

Falling in love with Truth before he knew Her,
He rode into imaginary lands,
By solitude and fasting hoped to woo Her,
And mocked at those who served Her with their hands.

Drawn as he was to magic and obliqueness,
In Her he honestly believed, and when
At last She beckoned to him he obeyed,

Looked in Her eyes: awe-struck but unafraid,
Saw there reflected every human weakness,
And knew himself as one of many men.

VII

He was their servant (some say he was blind),
Who moved among their faces and their things;
Their feeling gathered in him like a wind
And sang. They cried 'It is a God that sings',

And honoured him, a person set apart,
Till he grew vain, mistook for personal song
The petty tremors of his mind or heart
At each domestic wrong.

Lines came to him no more; he had to make them
(With what precision was each strophe planned):
Hugging his gloom as peasants hug their land,

He stalked like an assassin through the town,
And glared at men because he did not like them,
But trembled if one passed him with a frown.

VIII

He turned his field into a meeting-place,
Evolved a tolerant ironic eye,
Put on a mobile money-changer's face,
Took up the doctrine of Equality.

Strangers were hailed as brothers by his clocks,
With roof and spire he built a human sky,
Stored random facts in a museum box,
To watch his treasure set a paper spy.

All grew so fast his life was overgrown,
Till he forgot what all had once been made for:
He gathered into crowds but was alone,

And lived expensively but did without,
No more could touch the earth which he had paid for,
Nor feel the love which he knew all about.

IX

He looked in all His wisdom from His throne
Down on the humble boy who herded sheep,
And sent a dove. The dove returned alone:
Song put a charmed rusticity to sleep.

But He had planned such future for this youth:
Surely, His duty now was to compel,
To count on time to bring true love of truth
And, with it, gratitude. His eagle fell.

It did not work: His conversation bored
The boy, who yawned and whistled and made faces,
And wriggled free from fatherly embraces,

But with His messenger was always willing
To go where it suggested, and adored,
And learned from it so many ways of killing.

X

So an age ended, and its last deliverer died
In bed, grown idle and unhappy; they were safe:
The sudden shadow of a giant's enormous calf
Would fall no more at dusk across their lawns outside.

They slept in peace: in marshes here and there no doubt
A sterile dragon lingered to a natural death,
But in a year the slot had vanished from the heath;
A kobold's knocking in the mountain petered out.

Only the sculptors and the poets were half-sad,
And the pert retinue from the magician's house
Grumbled and went elsewhere. The vanquished powers were
        glad

To be invisible and free; without remorse
Struck down the silly sons who strayed into their course,
And ravished the daughters, and drove the fathers mad.

                                                    1936

XI

Certainly praise: let song mount again and again
For life as it blossoms out in a jar or a face,
For vegetal patience, for animal courage and grace:
Some have been happy; some, even, were great men.

But hear the morning's injured weeping and know why:
Ramparts and souls have fallen; the will of the unjust
Has never lacked an engine; still all princes must
Employ the fairly-noble unifying lie.

History opposes its grief to our buoyant song,
To our hope its warning. One star has warmed to birth
One puzzled species that has yet to prove its worth:

The quick new West is false, and prodigious but wrong
The flower-like Hundred Families who for so long
In the Eighteen Provinces have modified the earth.

XII

Here war is harmless like a monument:
A telephone is talking to a man;
Flags on a map declare that troops were sent;
A boy brings milk in bowls. There is a plan

For living men in terror of their lives,
Who thirst at nine who were to thirst at noon,
Who can be lost and are, who miss their wives
And, unlike an idea, can die too soon.

Yet ideas can be true, although men die:
For we have seen a myriad faces
Ecstatic from one lie,

And maps can really point to places
Where life is evil now.
Nanking. Dachau.

XIII

Far from a cultural centre he was used:
Abandoned by his general and his lice,
Under a padded quilt he turned to ice
And vanished. He will never be perused

When this campaign is tidied into books:
No vital knowledge perished in that skull;
His jokes were stale; like wartime, he was dull;
His name is lost for ever like his looks.

Though runeless, to instructions from headquarters
He added meaning like a comma when
He joined the dust of China, that our daughters

Might keep their upright carriage, not again
Be shamed before the dogs, that, where are waters,
Mountains and houses, may be also men.

XIV

They are and suffer; that is all they do:
A bandage hides the place where each is living,
His knowledge of the world restricted to
A treatment metal instruments are giving.

They lie apart like epochs from each other
(Truth in their sense is how much they can bear;
It is not talk like ours but groans they smother),
From us remote as plants: we stand elsewhere.

For who when healthy can become a foot?
Even a scratch we can't recall when cured,
But are boisterous in a moment and believe

Reality is never injured, cannot
Imagine isolation: joy can be shared,
And anger, and the idea of love.

XV

As evening fell the day's oppression lifted;
Tall peaks came into focus; it had rained:
Across wide lawns and cultured flowers drifted
The conversation of the highly trained.

Thin gardeners watched them pass and priced their shoes;
A chauffeur waited, reading in the drive,
For them to finish their exchange of views:
It looked a picture of the way to live.

Far off, no matter what good they intended,
Two armies waited for a verbal error
With well-made implements for causing pain,

And on the issue of their charm depended
A land laid waste with all its young men slain,
Its women weeping, and its towns in terror.

XVI

Our global story is not yet completed,
Crime, daring, commerce, chatter will go on,
But, as narrators find their memory gone,
Homeless, disterred, these know themselves defeated.

Some could not like nor change the young and mourn for
Some wounded myth that once made children good,
Some lost a world they never understood,
Some saw too clearly all that man was born for.

Loss is their shadow-wife, Anxiety
Receives them like a grand hotel, but where
They may regret they must: their doom to bear

Love for some far forbidden country, see
A native disapprove them with a stare
And Freedom's back in every door and tree.

XVII

Simple like all dream-wishes, they employ
The elementary rhythms of the heart,
Speak to our muscles of a need for joy:
The dying and the lovers bound to part

Hear them and have to whistle. Ever new,
They mirror every change in our position,
They are our evidence of how we do,
The very echoes of our lost condition.

Think in this year what pleased the dancers best,
When Austria died, when China was forsaken,
Shanghai in flames and Teruel re-taken.

France put her case before the world: *Partout*
Il y a de la joie. America addressed
Mankind: *Do you love me as I love you?*

XVIII

Chilled by the Present, its gloom and its noise,
On waking we sigh for an ancient South,
A warm nude age of instinctive poise,
A taste of joy in an innocent mouth.

At night in our huts we dream of a part
In the balls of the Future: each ritual maze
Has a musical plan, and a musical heart
Can faultlessly follow its faultless ways.

We envy streams and houses that are sure,
But, doubtful, articled to error, we
Were never nude and calm as a great door,

And never will be faultless like our fountains:
We live in freedom by necessity,
A mountain people dwelling among mountains.

XIX

When all our apparatus of report
Confirms the triumph of our enemies,
Our frontier crossed, our forces in retreat,
Violence pandemic like a new disease,

And Wrong a charmer everywhere invited,
When Generosity gets nothing done,
Let us remember those who looked deserted:
To-night in China let me think of one

Who for ten years of drought and silence waited,
Until in Muzot all his being spoke,
And everything was given once for all.

Awed, grateful, tired, content to die, completed,
He went out in the winter night to stroke
That tower as one pets an animal.

XX

Who needs their names? Another genus built
Those dictatorial avenues and squares,
Gigantic terraces, imposing stairs,
Men of a sorry kennel, racked by guilt,

Who wanted to persist in stone for ever:
Unloved, they had to leave material traces,
But these desired no statues but our faces,
To dwell there incognito, glad we never

Can dwell on what they suffered, loved or were.
Earth grew them as a bay grows fishermen
Or hills a shepherd. While they breathed, the air

All breathe took on a virtue; in our blood,
If we allow them, they can breathe again:
Happy their wish and mild to flower and flood.

XXI
(To E. M. Forster)

Though Italy and King's are far away,
And Truth a subject only bombs discuss,
Our ears unfriendly, still you speak to us,
Insisting that the inner life can pay.

As we dash down the slope of hate with gladness,
You trip us up like an unnoticed stone,
And, just when we are closeted with madness,
You interrupt us like the telephone.

Yes, we are Lucy, Turton, Philip: we
Wish international evil, are delighted
To join the jolly ranks of the benighted

Where reason is denied and love ignored,
But, as we swear our lie, Miss Avery
Comes out into the garden with a sword.

1938

Part V

New Year Letter

(January 1, 1940)

TO ELIZABETH MAYER

PART ONE

Under the familiar weight
Of winter, conscience and the State,
In loose formations of good cheer,
Love, language, loneliness and fear,
Towards the habits of next year,
Along the streets the people flow,
Singing or sighing as they go:
Exalté, piano, or in doubt,
All our reflections turn about
A common meditative norm,
Retrenchment, Sacrifice, Reform.

Twelve months ago in Brussels, I
Heard the same wishful-thinking sigh
As round me, trembling on their beds,
Or taut with apprehensive dreads,
The sleepless guests of Europe lay
Wishing the centuries away,
And the low mutter of their vows
Went echoing through her haunted house,
As on the verge of happening
There crouched the presence of The Thing.
All formulas were tried to still
The scratching on the window-sill,
All bolts of custom made secure
Against the pressure on the door.
But up the staircase of events
Carrying his special instruments,
To every bedside all the same
The dreadful figure swiftly came.

Yet Time can moderate his tone
When talking to a man alone,
And the same sun whose neutral eye
All florid August from the sky
Had watched the earth behave and seen
Strange traffic on her brown and green,
Obedient to some hidden force
A ship abruptly change her course,
A train make an unwonted stop,
A little crowd smash up a shop,
Suspended hatreds crystallize
In visible hostilities,
Vague concentrations shrink to take
The sharp crude patterns generals make,
The very morning that the war
Took action on the Polish floor,
Lit up America and on
A cottage in Long Island shone
Where Buxtehude as we played

161

One of his *passacaglias* made
Our minds a *civitas* of sound
Where nothing but assent was found,
For art had set in order sense
And feeling and intelligence,
And from its ideal order grew
Our local understanding too.

To set in order—that's the task
Both Eros and Apollo ask;
For Art and Life agree in this
That each intends a synthesis,
That order which must be the end
That all self-loving things intend
Who struggle for their liberty,
Who use, that is, their will to be.
Though order never can be willed
But is the state of the fulfilled,
For will but wills its opposite
And not the whole in which they fit,
The symmetry disorders reach
When both are equal each to each,
Yet in intention all are one,
Intending that their wills be done
Within a peace where all desires
Find each in each what each requires,
A true *Gestalt* where indiscrete
Perceptions and extensions meet.
Art in intention is mimesis
But, realized, the resemblance ceases;
Art is not life and cannot be
A midwife to society,
For art is a *fait accompli*.
What they should do, or how or when
Life-order comes to living men
It cannot say, for it presents
Already lived experience
Through a convention that creates
Autonomous completed states.
Though their particulars are those
That each particular artist knows,
Unique events that once took place
Within a unique time and space,
In the new field they occupy,
The unique serves to typify,
Becomes, though still particular,
An algebraic formula,
An abstract model of events
Derived from past experiments,
And each life must itself decide
To what and how it be applied.

Great masters who have shown mankind
An order it has yet to find,
What if all pedants say of you
As personalities be true?
All the more honour to you then
If, weaker than some other men,
You had the courage that survives
Soiled, shabby, egotistic lives,
If poverty or ugliness,
Ill-health or social unsuccess
Hunted you out of life to play
At living in another way;
Yet the live quarry all the same
Were changed to huntsmen in the game,
And the wild furies of the past,
Tracked to their origins at last,
Trapped in a medium's artifice,
To charity, delight, increase.
Now large, magnificent, and calm,
Your changeless presences disarm
The sullen generations, still
The fright and fidget of the will,
And to the growing and the weak
Your final transformations speak,
Saying to dreaming 'I am deed.'
To striving 'Courage. I succeed.'
To mourning 'I remain. Forgive,'
And to becoming 'I am. Live.'

They challenge, warn and witness. Who
That ever has the rashness to
Believe that he is one of those
The greatest of vocations chose,
Is not perpetually afraid
That he's unworthy of his trade,
As round his tiny homestead spread
The grand constructions of the dead,
Nor conscious, as he works, of their
Complete uncompromising stare,
And the surveillance of a board
Whose warrant cannot be ignored?
O often, often must he face,
Whether the critics blame or praise,
Young, high-brow, popular or rich,
That summary tribunal which
In a perpetual session sits,
And answer, if he can, to its
Intense interrogation. Though
Considerate and mild and low
The voices of the questioners,
Although they delegate to us
Both prosecution and defence,
Accept our rules of evidence
And pass no sentence but our own,

Yet, as he faces them alone,
O who can show convincing proof
That he is worthy of their love?
Who ever rose to read aloud
Before that quiet attentive crowd
And did not falter as he read,
Stammer, sit down, and hang his head?
Each one, so liberal is the law,
May choose whom he appears before,
Pick any influential ghost
From those whom he admires the most.
So, when my name is called, I face,
Presiding coldly on my case,
That lean hard-bitten pioneer
Who spoiled a temporal career
And to the supernatural brought
His passion, senses, will and thought,
By *Amor Rationalis* led
Through the three kingdoms of the dead,
In concrete detail saw the whole
Environment that keeps the soul,
And grasped in its complexity
The Catholic ecology,
Described the savage fauna he
In Malebolge's fissure found,
And fringe of blessed flora round
A juster nucleus than Rome,
Where love had its creative home.
Upon his right appears, as I
Reluctantly must testify
And weigh the sentence to be passed,
A choleric enthusiast,
Self-educated WILLIAM BLAKE
Who threw his spectre in the lake,
Broke off relations in a curse
With the Newtonian Universe,
But even as a child would pet
The tigers VOLTAIRE never met,
Took walks with them through Lambeth, and
Spoke to Isaiah in the Strand,
And heard inside each mortal thing
Its holy emanation sing,
While to his left upon the bench,
Muttering that terror is not French,
Frowns the young RIMBAUD guilt demands,
The adolescent with red hands,
Skilful, intolerant and quick,
Who strangled an old rhetoric.
The court is full; I catch the eyes
Of several I recognize,
For as I look up from the dock
Embarrassed glances interlock.
There DRYDEN sits with modest smile,
The master of the middle style,

Conscious CATULLUS who made all
His gutter-language musical,
Black TENNYSON whose talents were
For an articulate despair,
Trim, dualistic BAUDELAIRE,
Poet of cities, harbours, whores,
Acedia, gaslight and remorse,
HARDY whose Dorset gave much joy
To one unsocial English boy,
And RILKE whom *die Dinge* bless,
The Santa Claus of loneliness.
And many others, many times,
For I relapse into my crimes,
Time and again have slubbered through
With slip and slapdash what I do,
Adopted what I would disown,
The preacher's loose immodest tone;
Though warned by a great sonneteer
Not to sell cheap what is most dear,
Though horrible old KIPLING cried
'One instant's toil to Thee denied
Stands all eternity's offence,'
I would not give them audience.
Yet still the weak offender must
Beg still for leniency and trust
His power to avoid the sin
Peculiar to his discipline.

The situation of our time
Surrounds us like a baffling crime.
There lies the body half-undressed,
We all had reason to detest,
And all are suspects and involved
Until the mystery is solved
And under lock and key the cause
That makes a nonsense of our laws.
O Who is trying to shield Whom?
Who left a hairpin in the room?
Who was the distant figure seen
Behaving oddly on the green?
Why did the watchdog never bark?
Why did the footsteps leave no mark?
Where were the servants at that hour?
How did a snake get in the tower?
Delayed in the democracies
By departmental vanities,
The rival sergeants run about
But more to squabble than find out,
Yet where the Force has been cut down
To one inspector dressed in brown,
He makes the murderer whom he pleases
And all investigation ceases.
Yet our equipment all the time
Extends the area of the crime

Until the guilt is everywhere,
And more and more we are aware,
However miserable may be
Our parish of immediacy,
How small it is, how, far beyond,
Ubiquitous within the bond
Of an impoverishing sky,
Vast spiritual disorders lie.
Who, thinking of the last ten years,
Does not hear howling in his ears
The Asiatic cry of pain,
The shots of executing Spain,
See stumbling through his outraged mind
The Abyssinian, blistered, blind,
The dazed uncomprehending stare
Of the Danubian despair,
The Jew wrecked in the German cell,
Flat Poland frozen into hell,
The silent dumps of unemployed
Whose *areté* has been destroyed,
And will not feel blind anger draw
His thoughts towards the Minotaur,
To take an early boat for Crete
And rolling, silly, at its feet
Add his small tidbit to the rest?
It lures us all; even the best,
Les hommes de bonne volonté, feel
Their politics perhaps unreal
And all they have believed untrue,
Are tempted to surrender to
The grand apocalyptic dream
In which the persecutors scream
As on the evil Aryan lives
Descends the night of the long knives,
The bleeding tyrant dragged through all
The ashes of his capitol.

Though language may be useless, for
No words men write can stop the war
Or measure up to the relief
Of its immeasurable grief,
Yet truth, like love and sleep, resents
Approaches that are too intense,
And often when the searcher stood
Before the Oracle, it would
Ignore his grown-up earnestness
But not the child of his distress,
For through the Janus of a joke
The candid psychopompos spoke.
May such heart and intelligence
As huddle now in conference
Whenever an impasse occurs
Use the Good Offices of verse;
May an Accord be reached, and may

This *aide-mémoire* on what they say,
This private minute for a friend,
Be the dispatch that I intend;
Although addressed to a Whitehall,
Be under Flying Seal to all
Who wish to read it anywhere,
And, if they open it, *En Clair*.

PART TWO

Tonight a scrambling decade ends,
And strangers, enemies and friends
Stand once more puzzled underneath
The signpost on the barren heath
Where the rough mountain track divides
To silent valleys on all sides,
Endeavouring to decipher what
Is written on it but cannot,
Nor guess in what direction lies
The overhanging precipice.
Through the pitch-darkness can be heard
Occasionally a muttered word,
And intense in the mountain frost
The heavy breathing of the lost;
Far down below them whence they came
Still flickers feebly a red flame,
A tiny glow in the great void
Where an existence was destroyed;
And now and then a nature turns
To look where her whole system burns
And with a last defiant groan
Shudders her future into stone.

How hard it is to set aside
Terror, concupiscence and pride,
Learn who and where and how we are,
The children of a modest star,
Frail, backward, clinging to the granite
Skirts of a sensible old planet,
Our placid and suburban nurse
In SITTER's swelling universe,
How hard to stretch imagination
To live according to our station.
For we are all insulted by
The mere suggestion that we die
Each moment and that each great I
Is but a process in a process
Within a field that never closes;
As proper people find it strange
That we are changed by what we change,

That no event can happen twice
And that no two existences
Can ever be alike; we'd rather
Be perfect copies of our father,
Prefer our *idées fixes* to be
True of a fixed Reality.
No wonder, then, we lose our nerve
And blubber when we should observe:
The patriots of an old idea,
No longer sovereign this year,
Get angry like LABELLIÈRE,
Who, finding no invectives hurled
Against a topsy-turvy world
Would right it, earned a quaint renown
By being buried upside-down;
Unwilling to adjust belief,
Go mad in a fantastic grief
Where no adjustment need be done,
Like SARAH WHITEHEAD, the Bank Nun,
For, loving a live brother, she
Wed an impossibility,
Pacing Threadneedle Street in tears,
She watched one door for twenty years,
Expecting, what she dared not doubt,
Her hanged embezzler to walk out.

But who, though, is the Prince of Lies
If not the Spirit-that-denies,
The shadow just behind the shoulder
Claiming it's wicked to grow older,
Though we are damned if we turn round
Thinking salvation has been found?
Yet in his very effort to
Prevent the actions we could do,
He has to make the here and now
As marvellous as he knows how
And so engrossing we forget
To drop attention for regret;
Defending relaxation, he
Must show impassioned energy,
And all through tempting us to doubt
Point us the way to find truth out.
Poor cheated MEPHISTOPHELES,
Who think you're doing as you please
In telling us by doing ill
To prove that we possess free will,
Yet do not will the will you do,
For the Determined uses you,
Creation's errand-boy creator,
Diabolus egredietur
Ante pedes ejus—foe,
But so much more effective, though,
Than our well-meaning stupid friends
In driving us towards good ends.

Lame fallen shadow, *retro me*,
Retro but do not go away:
Although, for all your fond insistence,
You have no positive existence,
Are only a recurrent state
Of fear and faithlessness and hate,
That takes on from becoming me
A legal personality,
Assuming your existence is
A rule-of-thumb hypostasis,
For, though no person, you can damn,
So, *credo ut intelligam.*
For how could we get on without you
Who give the *savoir-faire* to doubt you
And keep you in your proper place,
Which is, to push us into grace?

Against his paralysing smile
And honest realistic style
Our best protection is that we
In fact live in eternity.
The sleepless counter of our breaths
That chronicles the births and deaths
Of pious hopes, the short careers
Of dashing promising ideas,
Each congress of the Greater Fears,
The emigration of beliefs,
The voyages of hopes and griefs,
Has no direct experience
Of discontinuous events,
And all our intuitions mock
The formal logic of the clock.
All real perception, it would seem,
Has shifting contours like a dream,
Nor have our feelings ever known
Any discretion but their own.
Suppose we love, not friends or wives,
But certain patterns in our lives,
Effects that take the cause's name,
Love cannot part them all the same;
If in this letter that I send
I write 'Elizabeth's my friend,'
I cannot but express my faith
That I is Not-Elizabeth.
For though the intellect in each
Can only think in terms of speech
We cannot practise what we preach.
The cogitations of DESCARTES
Are where all sound semantics start;
In Ireland the great BERKELEY rose
To add new glories to our prose,
But when in the pursuit of knowledge,
Risking the future of his college,
The bishop hid his anxious face,

'Twas more by grammar than by grace
His modest Church-of-England God
Sustained the fellows and the quad.

But the Accuser would not be
In his position, did not he,
Unlike the big-shots of the day,
Listen to what his victims say.
Observing every man's desire
To warm his bottom by the fire
And state his views on Education,
Art, Women, and The Situation,
Has learnt what every woman knows,
The wallflower can become the rose,
Penelope the homely seem
The Helen of Odysseus' dream
If she will look as if she were
A fascinated listener,
Since men will pay large sums to whores
For telling them they are not bores.
So when with overemphasis
We contradict a lie of his,
The great Denier won't deny
But purrs: 'You're cleverer than I;
Of course you're absolutely right,
I never saw it in that light.
I see it now: The intellect
That parts the Cause from the Effect
And thinks in terms of Space and Time
Commits a legalistic crime,
For such an unreal severance
Must falsify experience.
Could one not almost say that the
Cold serpent on the poisonous tree
Was *l'esprit de géométrie*,
That Eve and Adam till the Fall
Were totally illogical,
But as they tasted of the fruit
The syllogistic sin took root?
Abstracted, bitter refugees,
They fought over their premises,
Shut out from Eden by the bar
And Chinese Wall of *Barbara*.
O foolishness of man to seek
Salvation in an *ordre logique*!
O cruel intellect that chills
His natural warmth until it kills
The roots of all togetherness!
Love's vigour shrinks to less and less,
On sterile acres governed by
Wage's abstract prudent tie
The hard self-conscious particles
Collide, divide like numerals
In knock-down drag-out *laissez-faire*,

And build no order anywhere.
O when will men show common sense
And throw away intelligence,
That killjoy which discriminates,
Recover what appreciates,
The deep unsnobbish instinct which
Alone can make relation rich,
Upon the *Beischlaf* of the blood
Establish a real neighbourhood
Where art and industry and *mœurs*
Are governed by an *ordre du cœur*?'

The Devil, as is not surprising—
His business is self-advertising—
Is a first-rate psychologist
Who keeps a conscientious list,
To help him in his ticklish deals,
Of what each client thinks and feels,
His school, religion, birth and breeding,
Where he has dined and who he's reading,
By every name he makes a note
Of what quotations to misquote,
And flings at every author's head
Something a favourite author said.
'The Arts? Well, FLAUBERT didn't say
Of artists: "*Ils sont dans le vrai*."
Democracy? Ask BAUDELAIRE:
"*Un esprit belge*," a soiled affair
Of gas and steam and table-turning.
Truth? ARISTOTLE was discerning:
"In crowds I am a friend of myth." '
Then, as I start protesting, with
The air of one who understands
He puts a RILKE in my hands.
'You know the *Elegies*, I'm sure—
O Seligkeit der Kreatur
Die immer bleibt im Schosse—womb,
In English, is a rhyme to tomb.'
He moves on tiptoe round the room,
Turns on the radio to mark
Isolde's *Sehnsucht* for the dark.

But all his tactics are dictated
By problems he himself created,
For as the great schismatic who
First split creation into two
He did what it could never do,
Inspired it with the wish to be
Diversity in unity,
An action which has put him in,
Pledged as he is to Rule-by-Sin,
As ambiguous a position
As any Irish politician,
For, torn between conflicting needs,

He's doomed to fail if he succeeds,
And his neurotic longing mocks
Him with its self-made paradox,
To be both god and dualist.
For, if dualities exist,
What happens to the god? If there
Are any cultures anywhere
With other values than his own,
How can it possibly be shown
That his are not subjective or
That all life is a state of war?
While, if the monist view be right,
How is it possible to fight?
If love has been annihilated
There's only hate left to be hated.
To say two different things at once,
To wage offensives on two fronts,
And yet to show complete conviction,
Requires the purpler kinds of diction
And none appreciate as he
Polysyllabic oratory.
All vague idealistic art
That coddles the uneasy heart
Is up his alley, and his pigeon
The woozier species of religion,
Even a novel, play or song,
If loud, lugubrious and long;
He knows the bored will not unmask him
But that he's lost if someone ask him
To come the hell in off the links
And say exactly what he thinks.
To win support of any kind
He has to hold before the mind
Amorphous shadows it can hate,
Yet constantly postpone the date
Of what he's made The Grand Attraction,
Putting an end to them by action,
Because he knows, were he to win,
Man could do evil but not sin.
To sin is to act consciously
Against what seems necessity,
A possibility cut out
In any world that excludes doubt.
So victory could do no more
Than make us what we were before,
Beasts with a Rousseauistic charm
Unconscious we were doing harm.
Politically, then, he's right
To keep us shivering all night,
Watching for dawn from Pisgah's height,
And to sound earnest as he paints
The new Geneva of the saints,
To strike the poses as he speaks
Of DAVID's too too Empire Greeks,

Look forward with the cheesecake air
Of one who crossed the Delaware.
A realist, he has always said:
'It is Utopian to be dead,
For only on the Other Side
Are Absolutes all satisfied
Where, at the bottom of the graves,
Low Probability behaves.'

The False Association is
A favourite strategy of his:
Induce men to associate
Truth with a lie, then demonstrate
The lie and they will, in truth's name,
Treat babe and bath-water the same,
A trick that serves him in good stead
At all times. It was thus he led
The early Christians to believe
All Flesh unconscious on the eve
Of the Word's temporal interference
With the old Adam of Appearance;
That almost any moment they
Would see the trembling consuls pray,
Knowing that as their hope grew less
So would their heavenly worldliness,
Their early agape decline
To a late lunch with Constantine.
Thus WORDSWORTH fell into temptation
In France during a long vacation,
Saw in the fall of the Bastille
The Parousia of liberty,
And weaving a platonic dream
Round a provisional régime
That sloganized the Rights of Man,
A liberal fellow-traveller ran
With Sans-culotte and Jacobin,
Nor guessed what circles he was in,
But ended as the Devil knew
An earnest Englishman would do,
Left by Napoleon in the lurch,
Supporting the Established Church,
The Congress of Vienna and
The Squire's paternalistic hand.

Like his, our lives have been coeval
With a political upheaval,
Like him, we had the luck to see
A rare discontinuity,
Old Russia suddenly mutate
Into a proletarian state,
The odd phenomenon, the strange
Event of qualitative change.
Some dreamed, as students always can,
It realized the potential Man,

A higher species brought to birth
Upon a sixth part of the earth,
While others settled down to read
The theory that forecast the deed
And found their humanistic view
In question from the German who,
Obscure in gaslit London, brought
To human consciousness a thought
It thought unthinkable, and made
Another consciousness afraid.
What if his hate distorted? Much
Was hateful that he had to touch.
What if he erred? He flashed a light
On facts where no one had been right.
The father-shadow that he hated
Weighed like an Alp; his love, frustrated,
Negating as it was negated,
Burst out in boils; his animus
Outlawed him from himself; but thus,
And only thus, perhaps, could he
Have come to his discovery.
Heroic charity is rare;
Without it, what except despair
Can shape the hero who will dare
The desperate catabasis
Into the snarl of the abyss
That always lies just underneath
Our jolly picnic on the heath
Of the agreeable, where we bask,
Agreed on what we will not ask,
Bland, sunny and adjusted by
The light of the accepted lie?
As he explored the muttering tomb
Of a museum reading room,
The Dagon of the General Will
Fell in convulsions and lay still;
The tempting Contract of the rich,
Revealed as an abnormal witch,
Fled with a shriek, for as he spoke
The justifying magic broke;
The garden of the Three Estates
Turned desert, and the Ivory Gates
Of Pure Idea to gates of horn
Through which the Governments are born.
But his analysis reveals
The other side to Him-who-steals
Is He-who-makes-what-is-of-use,
Since, to consume, man must produce;
By Man the Tough Devourer sets
The nature his despair forgets
Of Man Prolific since his birth,
A race creative on the earth,
Whose love of money only shows
That in his heart of hearts he knows

His love is not determined by
A personal or tribal tie
Or colour, neighbourhood, or creed,
But universal, mutual need;
Loosed from its shroud of temper, his
Determinism comes to this:
None shall receive unless they give;
All must co-operate to live.
Now he is one with all of those
Who brought an epoch to a close,
With him who ended, as he went
Past an archbishop's monument,
The slaveowners' mechanics; one
With the ascetic farmer's son
Who, while the Great Plague ran its course,
Drew up a Roman code for Force;
One with the naturalist, who fought
Pituitary headaches, brought
Man's pride to heel at last and showed
His kinship with the worm and toad,
And Order as one consequence
Of the unfettered play of Chance.

Great sedentary Caesars who
Have pacified some dread tabu,
Whose wits were able to withdraw
The *numen* from some local law
And with a single concept brought
Some ancient rubbish heap of thought
To rational diversity,
You are betrayed unless we see
No *codex gentium* we make
Is difficult for Truth to break;
The *Lex Abscondita* evades
The vigilantes in the glades,
Now here, now there, one leaps and cries
'I've got her and I claim the prize,'
But when the rest catch up, he stands
With just a torn blouse in his hands.

We hoped; we waited for the day
The State would wither clean away,
Expecting the Millennium
That theory promised us would come:
It didn't. Specialists must try
To detail all the reasons why;
Meanwhile at least the layman knows
That none are lost so soon as those
Who overlook their crooked nose,
That they grow small who imitate
The mannerisms of the great,
Afraid to be themselves, or ask
What acts are proper to their task,
And that a tiny trace of fear

Is lethal in man's atmosphere.
The rays of Logos take effect,
But not as theory would expect,
For, sterile and diseased by doubt,
The dwarf mutations are thrown out
From Eros' weaving centrosome.

O Freedom still is far from home,
For MOSCOW is as far as ROME
Or PARIS. Once again we wake
With swimming heads and hands that shake
And stomachs that keep nothing down.
Here's where the devil goes to town,
Who knows that nothing suits his book
So well as the hang-over look,
That few drunks feel more awful than
The Simon-pure Utopian.
He calls at breakfast in the role
Of blunt but sympathetic soul:
'Well, how's our Socialist this morning?
I could say "Let this be a warning,"
But no, why should I? Students must
Sow their wild oats at times or bust.
Such things have happened in the lives
Of all the best Conservatives.
I'll fix you something for your liver.'
And thus he sells us down the river.
Repenting of our last infraction
We seek atonement in reaction
And cry, nostalgic like a whore,
'I was a virgin still at four.'
Perceiving that by sailing near
The Hegelian whirlpool of Idea
Some foolish aliens have gone down,
Lest our democracy should drown
We'd wreck her on the solid rock
Of genteel anarchists like LOCKE,
Wave at the mechanized barbarian
The vorpal sword of an Agrarian.

O how the devil who controls
The moral asymmetric souls
The either-ors, the mongrel halves
Who find truth in a mirror, laughs.
Yet time and memory are still
Limiting factors on his will;
He cannot always fool us thrice,
For he may never tell us lies,
Just half-truths we can synthesize.
So, hidden in his hocus-pocus,
There lies the gift of double focus,
That magic lamp which looks so dull
And utterly impractical
Yet, if Aladdin use it right,
Can be a sesame to light.

PART THREE

Across East River in the night
Manhattan is ablaze with light.
No shadow dares to criticize
The popular festivities,
Hard liquor causes everywhere
A general *détente*, and Care
For this state function of Good Will
Is diplomatically ill:
The Old Year dies a noisy death.

Warm in your house, Elizabeth,
A week ago at the same hour
I felt the unexpected power
That drove our ragged egos in
From the dead-ends of greed and sin
To sit down at the wedding feast,
Put shining garments on the least,
Arranged us so that each and all,
The erotic and the logical,
Each felt the *placement* to be such
That he was honoured overmuch,
And SCHUBERT sang and MOZART played
And GLUCK and food and friendship made
Our privileged community
That real republic which must be
The State all politicians claim,
Even the worst, to be their aim.

O but it happens every day
To someone. Suddenly the way
Leads straight into their native lands,
The *temenos'* small wicket stands
Wide open, shining at the centre
The well of life, and they may enter.
Though compasses and stars cannot
Direct to that magnetic spot,
Nor Will nor willing-not-to-will,
For there is neither good nor ill,
But free rejoicing energy.
Yet anytime, how casually,
Out of his organized distress
An accidental happiness,
Catching man off his guard, will blow him
Out of his life in time to show him
The field of Being where he may,
Unconscious of Becoming, play
With the Eternal Innocence
In unimpeded utterance.
But perfect Being has ordained
It must be lost to be regained,

And in its orchards grow the tree
And fruit of human destiny,
And man must eat it and depart
At once with gay and grateful heart,
Obedient, reborn, re-aware;
For, if he stop an instant there,
The sky grows crimson with a curse,
The flowers change colour for the worse,
He hears behind his back the wicket
Padlock itself, from the dark thicket
The chuckle with no healthy cause,
And, helpless, sees the crooked claws
Emerging into view and groping
For handholds on the low round coping,
As Horror clambers from the well:
For he has sprung the trap of Hell.

Hell is the being of the lie
That we become if we deny
The laws of consciousness and claim
Becoming and Being are the same,
Being in time, and man discrete
In will, yet free and self-complete;
Its fire the pain to which we go
If we refuse to suffer, though
The one unnecessary grief
Is the vain craving for relief,
When to the suffering we could bear
We add intolerable fear,
Absconding from remembrance, mocked
By our own partial senses, locked
Each in a stale uniqueness, lie
Time-conscious for eternity.

We cannot, then, will Heaven where
Is perfect freedom; our wills there
Must lose the will to operate.
But will is free not to negate
Itself in Hell; we're free to will
Ourselves up Purgatory still,
Consenting parties to our lives,
To love them like attractive wives
Whom we adore but do not trust;
We cannot love without their lust,
And need their stratagems to win
Truth out of Time. In Time we sin.
But Time is sin and can forgive;
Time is the life with which we live
At least three quarters of our time,
The purgatorial hill we climb,
Where any skyline we attain
Reveals a higher ridge again.
Yet since, however much we grumble,
However painfully we stumble,

Such mountaineering all the same
Is, it would seem, the only game
At which we show a natural skill,
The hardest exercises still
Just those our muscles are the best
Adapted to, its grimmest test
Precisely what our fear suspected,
We have no cause to look dejected
When, wakened from a dream of glory,
We find ourselves in Purgatory,
Back on the same old mountain side
With only guessing for a guide.
To tell the truth, although we stifle
The feeling, are we not a trifle
Relieved to wake on its damp earth?
It's been our residence since birth,
Its inconveniences are known,
And we have made its flaws our own.
Is it not here that we belong,
Where everyone is doing wrong,
And normal our freemartin state,
Half angel and half *petite bête*?
So, perched upon the sharp *arête*,
Where if we do not move we fall,
Yet movement is heretical,
Since over its ironic rocks
No route is truly orthodox,
O once again let us set out,
Our faith well balanced by our doubt,
Admitting every step we make
Will certainly be a mistake,
But still believing we can climb
A little higher every time,
And keep in order, that we may
Ascend the penitential way
That forces our wills to be free,
A reverent frivolity
That suffers each unpleasant test
With scientific interest,
And finds romantic, *faute de mieux*,
The sad *nostalgie des adieux*.

Around me, pausing as I write,
A tiny object in the night,
Whichever way I look, I mark
Importunate along the dark
Horizon of immediacies
The flares of desperation rise
From signallers who justly plead
Their cause is piteous indeed:
Bewildered, how can I divine
Which is my true Socratic Sign,
Which of these calls to conscience is
For me the *casus fœderis*,

179

From all the tasks submitted, choose
The *athlon* I must not refuse?
A particle, I must not yield
To particles who claim the field,
Nor trust the demagogue who raves,
A quantum speaking for the waves,
Nor worship blindly the ornate
Grandezza of the Sovereign State.
Whatever wickedness we do
Need not be, orators, for you;
We can at least serve other ends,
Can love the *polis* of our friends
And pray that loyalty may come
To serve mankind's *imperium*.

But where to serve and when and how?
O none escape these questions now:
The future which confronts us has
No likeness to that age when, as
Rome's huggermugger unity
Was slowly knocked to pieces by
The unco-ordinated blows
Of artless and barbaric foes,
The stressed and rhyming measures rose;
The cities we abandon fall
To nothing primitive at all;
This lust in action to destroy
Is not the pure instinctive joy
Of animals, but the refined
Creation of machines and mind,
As out of Europe comes a Voice,
Compelling all to make their choice,
A theologian who denies
What more than twenty centuries
Of Europe have assumed to be
The basis of civility,
Our evil *Daimon* to express
In all its ugly nakedness
What none before dared say aloud,
The metaphysics of the Crowd,
The Immanent Imperative
By which the lost and injured live
In mechanized societies
Where natural intuition dies,
The international result
Of Industry's *Quicunque vult*,
The hitherto-unconscious creed
Of little men who half succeed.

Yet maps and languages and names
Have meaning and their proper claims.
There are two atlases: the one
The public space where acts are done,
In theory common to us all,

180

Where we are needed and feel small,
The *agora* of work and news
Where each one has the right to choose
His trade, his corner and his way,
And can, again in theory, say
For whose protection he will pay,
And loyalty is help we give
The place where we prefer to live;
The other is the inner space
Of private ownership, the place
That each of us is forced to own,
Like his own life from which it's grown,
The landscape of his will and need
Where he is sovereign indeed,
The state created by his acts
Where he patrols the forest tracts
Planted in childhood, farms the belt
Of doings memorized and felt,
And even if he find it hell
May neither leave it nor rebel.
Two worlds describing their rewards,
That one in tangents, this in chords;
Each lives in one, all in the other,
Here all are kings, there each a brother:
In politics the Fall of Man
From natural liberty began
When, loving power or sloth, he came
Like Burke to think them both the same.

England to me is my own tongue,
And what I did when I was young.
If now, two aliens in New York,
We meet, Elizabeth, and talk
Of friends who suffer in the torn
Old Europe where we both were born,
What this refutes or that confirms,
I can but think our talk in terms
Of images that I have seen,
And England tells me what we mean.
Thus, squalid beery Burton stands
For shoddy thinking of-all brands;
The wreck of Rhondda for the mess
We make when for a short success
We split our symmetry apart,
Deny the Reason or the Heart;
Ye Oldë Tudor Tea-Shoppe for
The folly of dogmatic law,
While graceless Bournemouth is the sloth
Of men or bureaucrats or both.

No matter where, or whom I meet,
Shop-gazing in a Paris street,
Bumping through Iceland in a bus,
At teas when clubwomen discuss

The latest Federation Plan,
In Pullman washrooms, man to man,
Hearing how circumstance has vexed
A broker who is oversexed,
In houses where they do not drink,
Whenever I begin to think
About the human creature we
Must nurse to sense and decency,
An English area comes to mind,
I see the nature of my kind
As a locality I love,
Those limestone moors that stretch from BROUGH
To HEXHAM and the ROMAN WALL,
There is my symbol of us all.
There, where the EDEN leisures through
Its sandstone valley, is my view
Of green and civil life that dwells
Below a cliff of savage fells
From which original address
Man faulted into consciousness.
Along the line of lapse the fire
Of life's impersonal desire
Burst through his sedentary rock
And, as at DUFTON and at KNOCK,
Thrust up between his mind and heart
Enormous cones of myth and art.
Always my boy of wish returns
To those peat-stained deserted burns
That feed the WEAR and TYNE and TEES,
And, turning states to strata, sees
How basalt long oppressed broke out
In wild revolt at CAULDRON SNOUT,
And from the relics of old mines
Derives his algebraic signs
For all in man that mourns and seeks,
For all of his renounced techniques,
Their tramways overgrown with grass,
For lost belief, for all Alas,
The derelict lead-smelting mill,
Flued to its chimney up the hill,
That smokes no answer any more
But points, a landmark on BOLTS LAW,
The finger of all questions. There
In ROOKHOPE I was first aware
Of Self and Not-self, Death and Dread:
Adits were entrances which led
Down to the Outlawed, to the Others,
The Terrible, the Merciful, the Mothers;
Alone in the hot day I knelt
Upon the edge of shafts and felt
The deep *Urmutterfurcht* that drives
Us into knowledge all our lives,
The far interior of our fate
To civilize and to create,

Das Weibliche that bids us come
To find what we're escaping from.
There I dropped pebbles, listened, heard
The reservoir of darkness stirred;
'*O deine Mutter kehrt dir nicht*
Wieder. Du selbst bin ich, dein' Pflicht
Und Liebe. Brach sie nun mein Bild.'
And I was conscious of my guilt.

But such a bond is not an Ought,
Only a given mode of thought,
Whence my imperatives were taught.
Now in that other world I stand
Of fully alienated land,
An earth made common by the means
Of hunger, money, and machines,
Where each determined nature must
Regard that nature as a trust
That, being chosen, he must choose,
Determined to become of use;
For we are conscripts to our age
Simply by being born; we wage
The war we are, and may not die
With POLYCARP's despairing cry,
Desert or become ill: but how
To be the patriots of the Now?
Here all, by rights, are volunteers,
And anyone who interferes
With how another wills to fight
Must base his action, not on right,
But on the power to compel;
Only the 'Idiot' can tell
For which state office he should run,
Only the Many make the One.

Eccentric, wrinkled, and ice-capped,
Swarming with parasites and wrapped
In a peculiar atmosphere,
Earth wobbles on down her career
With no ambition in her heart;
Her loose land-masses drift apart,
Her zone of shade and silence crawls
Steadily westward. Daylight falls
On Europe's frozen soldiery
And millions brave enough to die
For a new day; for each one knows
A day is drawing to a close.
Yes, all of us at least know that,
All from the seasoned diplomat
Used to the warm Victorian summers
Down to the juveniles and drummers.
Whatever nonsense we believe,
Whomever we can still deceive,
Whatever language angers us,

Whoever seems the poisonous
Old dragon to be killed if men
Are ever to be rich again,
We know no fuss or pain or lying
Can stop the moribund from dying,
That all the special tasks begun
By the Renaissance have been done.

When unity had come to grief
Upon professional belief
Another unity was made
By equal amateurs in trade.
Out of the noise and horror, the
Opinions of artillery,
The barracks chatter and the yell
Of charging cavalry, the smell
Of poor opponents roasting, out
Of LUTHER's faith and MONTAIGNE's doubt,
The epidemic of translations,
The Councils and the navigations,
The confiscations and the suits,
The scholars' scurrilous disputes
Over the freedom of the Will
And right of Princes to do ill,
Emerged a new *Anthropos*, an
Empiric Economic Man,
The urban, prudent, and inventive,
Profit his rational incentive
And Work his whole *exercitus*,
The individual let loose
To guard himself, at liberty
To starve or be forgotten, free
To feel in splendid isolation
Or drive himself about creation
In the closed cab of Occupation.

He did what he was born to do,
Proved some assumptions were untrue.
He had his half-success; he broke
The silly and unnatural yoke
Of famine and disease that made
A false necessity obeyed;
A Protestant, he found the key
To Catholic economy,
Subjected earth to the control
And moral choices of the soul;
And in the training of each sense
To serve with joy its evidence
He founded a new discipline
To fight an intellectual sin,
Reason's depravity that takes
The useful concepts that she makes
As universals, as the *kitsch*,
But worshipped statues upon which

She leaves her effort and her crown,
And if his half-success broke down,
All failures have one good result:
They prove the Good is difficult.

He never won complete support;
However many votes he bought.
He could not silence all the cliques,
And no miraculous techniques
Could sterilize all discontent
Or dazzle it into assent,
But at the very noon and arch
Of his immense triumphal march
Stood prophets pelting him with curses
And sermons and satiric verses,
And ostentatious beggars slept.
BLAKE shouted insults, ROUSSEAU wept,
Ironic KIERKEGAARD stared long
And muttered 'All are in the wrong,'
While BAUDELAIRE went mad protesting
That progress is not interesting
And thought he was an albatross,
The great Erotic on the cross
Of Science, crucified by fools
Who sit all day on office stools,
Are fairly faithful to their wives
And play for safety all their lives,
For whose *Verbürgerlichung* of
All joy and suffering and love
Let the grand pariah atone
By dying hated and alone.

The World ignored them; they were few.
The careless victor never knew
Their grapevine rumour would grow true,
Their alphabet of warning sounds
The common grammar all have grounds
To study; for their guess is proved:
It is the Mover that is moved.
Whichever way we turn, we see
Man captured by his liberty,
The measurable taking charge
Of him who measures, set at large
By his own actions, useful facts
Become the user of his acts,
And Chance the choices of his soul;
The beggar put out by his bowl,
Boys trained by factories for leading
Unusual lives as nurses, feeding
Helpless machines, girls married off
To typewriters, old men in love
With prices they can never get,
Homes blackmailed by a radio set,
Children inherited by slums

And idiots by enormous sums.
We see, we suffer, we despair:
The well-armed children everywhere
Who envy the self-governed beast
Now know that they are bound at least,
Die Aufgeregten without pity
Destroying the historic city,
The ruined showering with honours
The blind Christs and the mad Madonnas,
The Gnostics in the brothels treating
The flesh as secular and fleeting,
The *dialegesthai* of the rich
At cocktail parties as to which
Technique is most effective in
Enforcing labour discipline,
What Persian Apparatus will
Protect their privileges still
And safely keep the living dead
Entombed, hilarious, and fed,
The Disregarded in their shacks
Upon the wrong side of the tracks,
Poisoned by reasonable hate,
Are symptoms of one common fate.
All in their morning mirrors face
A member of a governed race.
Each recognizes what LEAR saw,
And he and THURBER like to draw,
The neuter outline that's the plan
And icon of Industrial Man,
The Unpolitical afraid
Of all that has to be obeyed.

But still each private citizen
Thanks God he's not as other men:
O all too easily we blame
The politicians for our shame
And the hired officers of state
For all those customs that frustrate
Our own intention to fulfil
Eros's legislative will.
Yet who must not, if he reflect,
See how unserious the effect
That he to love's volition gives,
On what base compromise he lives?
Even true lovers on some bed
The graceful god has visited
Find faults at which to hang the head,
And know the morphon full of guilt
Whence all community is built,
The cryptozoön with two backs
Whose sensibility that lacks
True reverence contributes much
Towards the soldier's violent touch.
For, craving language and a myth

And hands to shape their purpose with,
In shadow round the fond and warm
The possible societies swarm,
Because their freedom as their form
Upon our sense of style depends,
Whose eyes alone can seek their ends,
And they are impotent if we
Decline responsibility.
O what can love's intention do
If all his agents are untrue?
The politicians we condemn
Are nothing but our L. C. M.
The average of the average man
Becomes the dread Leviathan,
Our million individual deeds,
Omissions, vanities, and creeds,
Put through the statistician's hoop
The gross behaviour of a group:
Upon each English conscience lie
Two decades of hypocrisy,
And not a German can be proud
Of what his apathy allowed.

The flood of tyranny and force
Arises at a double source:
In PLATO's lie of intellect
That all are weak but the Elect
Philosophers who must be strong,
For, knowing Good, they will no Wrong,
United in the abstract Word
Above the low anarchic herd;
Or ROUSSEAU's falsehood of the flesh
That stimulates our pride afresh
To think all men identical
And strong in the Irrational.
And yet, although the social lie
Looks double to the dreamer's eye,
The rain to fill the mountain streams
That water the opposing dreams
By turns in favour with the crowd
Is scattered from one common cloud.
Up in the Ego's atmosphere
And higher altitudes of fear
The particles of error form
The shepherd-killing thunderstorm,
And our political distress
Descends from her self-consciousness,
Her cold *concupiscence d'esprit*
That looks upon her liberty
Not as a gift from life with which
To serve, enlighten, and enrich
The total creature that could use
Her function of free-will to choose
The actions that this world requires

To educate its blind desires,
But as the right to lead alone
An attic life all on her own,
Unhindered, unrebuked, unwatched,
Self-known, self-praising, self-attached.
All happens as she wishes till
She asks herself why she should will
This more than that, or who would care
If she were dead or gone elsewhere,
And on her own hypothesis
Is powerless to answer this.
Then panic seizes her; the glance
Of mirrors shows a countenance
Of wretched empty-brilliance. How
Can she escape self-loathing now?
What is there left for pride to do
Except plunge headlong *vers la boue*,
For freedom except suicide,
The self-asserted self-denied?
A witch self-tortured as she spins
Her whole devotion widdershins,
She worships in obscene delight
The Not, the Never, and the Night,
The formless Mass without a Me,
The Midnight Women and the Sea.
The genius of the loud Steam Age,
Loud WAGNER, put it on the stage:
The mental hero who has swooned
With sensual pleasure at his wound,
His intellectual life fulfilled
In knowing that his doom is willed,
Exists to suffer; borne along
Upon a timeless tide of song,
The huge doll roars for death or mother,
Synonymous with one another;
And Woman, passive as in dreams,
Redeems, redeems, redeems, redeems.

Delighted with their takings, bars
Are closing under fading stars;
The revellers go home to change
Back into something far more strange,
The tightened self in which they may
Walk safely through their bothered day,
With formal purpose up and down
The crowded fatalistic town,
And dawn sheds its calm candour now
On monasteries where they vow
An economic abstinence.
Modern in their impenitence,
Blonde, naked, paralysed, alone,
Like rebel angels turned to stone
The secular cathedrals stand
Upon their valuable land,

Frozen forever in a lie,
Determined always to deny
That man is weak and has to die,
And hide the huge phenomena
Which must decide America,
That culture that had worshipped no
Virgin before the Dynamo,
Held no Nicea nor Canossa,
Hat keine verfallenen Schlösser,
Keine Basalte, the great Rome
To all who lost or hated home.

A long time since it seems to-day
The Saints in Massachusetts Bay
Heard theocratic COTTON preach
And legal WINTHROP's Little Speech;
Since MISTRESS HUTCHINSON was tried
By those her Inner Light defied,
And WILLIAMS questioned Moses' law
But in Rhode Island waited for
The Voice of the Beloved to free
Himself and the Democracy;
Long since inventive JEFFERSON
Fought realistic HAMILTON,
Pelagian versus Jansenist;
But the same heresies exist.
Time makes old formulas look strange,
Our properties and symbols change,
But round the freedom of the Will
Our disagreements centre still,
And now as then the voter hears
The battle cries of two ideas.
Here, as in Europe, is dissent,
This raw untidy continent
Where the Commuter can't forget
The Pioneer; and even yet
A *Völkerwanderung* occurs:
Resourceful manufacturers
Trek southward by progressive stages
For sites with no floor under wages,
No ceiling over hours; and by
Artistic souls in towns that lie
Out in the weed and pollen belt
The need for sympathy is felt,
And east to hard New York they come;
And self-respect drives Negroes from
The one-crop and race-hating delta
To northern cities helter-skelter;
And in jalopies there migrates
A rootless tribe from windblown states
To suffer further westward where
The tolerant Pacific air
Makes logic seem so silly, pain
Subjective, what he seeks so vain

The wanderer may die; and kids,
When their imagination bids,
Hitch-hike a thousand miles to find
The Hesperides that's on their mind,
Some Texas where real cowboys seem
Lost in a movie-cowboy's dream.
More even than in Europe, here
The choice of patterns is made clear
Which the machine imposes, what
Is possible and what is not,
To what conditions we must bow
In building the Just City now.

However we decide to act,
Decision must accept the fact
That the machine has now destroyed
The local customs we enjoyed,
Replaced the bonds of blood and nation
By personal confederation.
No longer can we learn our good
From chances of a neighbourhood
Or class or party, or refuse
As individuals to choose
Our loves, authorities, and friends,
To judge our means and plan our ends;
For the machine has cried aloud
And publicized among the crowd
The secret that was always true
But known once only to the few,
Compelling all to the admission,
Aloneness is man's real condition,
That each must travel forth alone
In search of the Essential Stone,
'The Nowhere-without-No' that is
The justice of societies.
Each salesman now is the polite
Adventurer, the landless knight
GAWAINE-QUIXOTE, and his goal
The *Frauendienst* of his weak soul;
Each biggie in the Canning Ring
An unrobust lone FISHER-KING;
Each subway face the PEQUOD of
Some ISHMAEL hunting his lost love,
To harpoon his unhappiness
And turn the whale to a princess;
In labs the puzzled KAFKAS meet
The inexplicable defeat:
The odd behaviour of the law,
The facts that suddenly withdraw,
The path that twists away from the
Near-distant CASTLE they can see,
The Truth where they will be denied
Permission ever to reside;
And all the operatives know
190

Their factory is the *champ-clos*
And drawing-room of HENRY JAMES,
Where the *débat* decides the claims
Of liberty and justice; where,
Like any Jamesian character,
They learn to draw the careful line,
Develop, understand, refine.

A weary Asia out of sight
Is tugging gently at the night,
Uncovering a restless race;
Clocks shoo the childhood from its face,
And accurate machines begin
To concentrate its adults in
A narrow day to exercise
Their gifts in some cramped enterprise.
How few pretend to like it: O
Three quarters of these people know
Instinctively what ought to be
The nature of society
And how they'd live there if they could.
If it were easy to be good,
And cheap, and plain as evil how,
We all would be its members now:
How readily would we become
The seamless live continuum
Of supple and coherent stuff,
Whose form is truth, whose content love,
Its pluralist interstices
The homes of happiness and peace,
Where in a unity of praise
The largest *publicum's* a *res*,
And the least *res* a *publicum*;
How grandly would our virtues bloom
In a more conscionable dust
Where Freedom dwells because it must,
Necessity because it can,
And men confederate in Man.

But wishes are not horses, this
Annus is not *mirabilis*;
Day breaks upon the world we know
Of war and wastefulness and woe;
Ashamed civilians come to grief
In brotherhoods without belief,
Whose good intentions cannot cure
The actual evils they endure,
Nor smooth their practical career,
Nor bring the far horizon near.
The New Year brings an earth afraid,
Democracy a ready-made
And noisy tradesman's slogan, and
The poor betrayed into the hand
Of lackeys with ideas, and truth

Whipped by their elders out of youth,
The peaceful fainting in their tracks
With martyrs' tombstones on their backs,
And culture on all fours to greet
A butch and criminal *élite*,
While in the vale of silly sheep
Rheumatic old patricians weep.

Our news is seldom good: the heart,
As ZOLA said, must always start
The day by swallowing its toad
Of failure and disgust. Our road
Gets worse and we seem altogether
Lost as our theories, like the weather,
Veer round completely every day,
And all that we can always say
Is: true democracy begins
With free confession of our sins.
In this alone are all the same,
All are so weak that none dare claim
'I have the right to govern,' or
'Behold in me the Moral Law,'
And all real unity commences
In consciousness of differences,
That all have wants to satisfy
And each a power to supply.
We need to love all since we are
Each a unique particular
That is no giant, god, or dwarf,
But one odd human isomorph;
We can love each because we know
All, all of us, that this is so:
Can live since we are lived, the powers
That we create with are not ours.

O Unicorn among the cedars,
To whom no magic charm can lead us,
White childhood moving like a sigh
Through the green woods unharmed in thy
Sophisticated innocence,
To call thy true love to the dance,
O Dove of science and of light,
Upon the branches of the night,
O Ichthus playful in the deep
Sea-lodges that forever keep
Their secret of excitement hidden,
O sudden Wind that blows unbidden,
Parting the quiet reeds, O Voice
Within the labyrinth of choice
Only the passive listener hears,
O Clock and Keeper of the years,
O Source of equity and rest,
Quando non fuerit, non est,
It without image, paradigm

Of matter, motion, number, time,
The grinning gap of Hell, the hill
Of Venus and the stairs of Will,
Disturb our negligence and chill,
Convict our pride of its offence
In all things, even penitence,
Instruct us in the civil art
Of making from the muddled heart
A desert and a city where
The thoughts that have to labour there
May find locality and peace,
And pent-up feelings their release,
Send strength sufficient for our day,
And point our knowledge on its way,
O da quod jubes, Domine.

Dear friend Elizabeth, dear friend
These days have brought me, may the end
I bring to the grave's dead-line be
More worthy of your sympathy
Than the beginning; may the truth
That no one marries lead my youth
Where you already are and bless
Me with your learned peacefulness,
Who on the lives about you throw
A calm *solificatio*,
A warmth throughout the universe
That each for better or for worse
Must carry round with him through life,
A judge, a landscape, and a wife.
We fall down in the dance, we make
The old ridiculous mistake,
But always there are such as you
Forgiving, helping what we do.
O every day in sleep and labour
Our life and death are with our neighbour,
And love illuminates again
The city and the lion's den,
The world's great rage, the travel of young men.

January–October 1940

Part VI

1939–1947

In Memory of W. B. Yeats
(d. Jan. 1939)

I

He disappeared in the dead of winter:
The brooks were frozen, the airports almost deserted,
And snow disfigured the public statues;
The mercury sank in the mouth of the dying day.
What instruments we have agree
The day of his death was a dark cold day.

Far from his illness
The wolves ran on through the evergreen forests,
The peasant river was untempted by the fashionable quays;
By mourning tongues
The death of the poet was kept from his poems.

But for him it was his last afternoon as himself,
An afternoon of nurses and rumours;
The provinces of his body revolted,
The squares of his mind were empty,
Silence invaded the suburbs,
The current of his feeling failed; he became his admirers.

Now he is scattered among a hundred cities
And wholly given over to unfamiliar affections,
To find his happiness in another kind of wood
And be punished under a foreign code of conscience.
The words of a dead man
Are modified in the guts of the living.

But in the importance of noise of to-morrow
When the brokers are roaring like beasts on the floor of the Bourse,
And the poor have the sufferings to which they are fairly accustomed,
And each in the cell of himself is almost convinced of his freedom,
A few thousand will think of this day
As one thinks of a day when one did something slightly unusual.
What instruments we have agree
The day of his death was a dark cold day.

II

You were silly like us; your gift survived it all:
The parish of rich women, physical decay,
Yourself. Mad Ireland hurt you into poetry.
Now Ireland has her madness and her weather still,
For poetry makes nothing happen: it survives
In the valley of its making where executives
Would never want to tamper, flows on south
From ranches of isolation and the busy griefs,
Raw towns that we believe and die in; it survives,
A way of happening, a mouth.

III

Earth, receive an honoured guest:
William Yeats is laid to rest.
Let the Irish vessel lie
Emptied of its poetry.

In the nightmare of the dark
All the dogs of Europe bark,
And the living nations wait,
Each sequestered in its hate;

Intellectual disgrace
Stares from every human face,
And the seas of pity lie
Locked and frozen in each eye.

Follow, poet, follow right
To the bottom of the night,
With your unconstraining voice
Still persuade us to rejoice;

With the farming of a verse
Make a vineyard of the curse,
Sing of human unsuccess
In a rapture of distress;

In the deserts of the heart
Let the healing fountain start,
In the prison of his days
Teach the free man how to praise.

February 1939

In Memory of Ernst Toller
(*d. May 1939*)

The shining neutral summer has no voice
To judge America, or ask how a man dies;
And the friends who are sad and the enemies who rejoice

Are chased by their shadows lightly away from the grave
Of one who was egotistical and brave,
Lest they should learn without suffering how to forgive.

What was it, Ernst, that your shadow unwittingly said?
Did the small child see something horrid in the woodshed
Long ago? Or had the Europe which took refuge in your head

Already been too injured to get well?
For just how long, like the swallows in that other cell,
Had the bright little longings been flying in to tell

198

About the big and friendly death outside,
Where people do not occupy or hide;
No towns like Munich; no need to write?

Dear Ernst, lie shadowless at last among
The other war-horses who existed till they'd done
Something that was an example to the young.

We are lived by powers we pretend to understand:
They arrange our loves; it is they who direct at the end
The enemy bullet, the sickness, or even our hand.

It is their to-morrow hangs over the earth of the living
And all that we wish for our friends: but existence is believing
We know for whom we mourn and who is grieving.

May 1939

Voltaire at Ferney

Almost happy now, he looked at his estate.
An exile making watches glanced up as he passed,
And went on working; where a hospital was rising fast
A joiner touched his cap; an agent came to tell
Some of the trees he'd planted were progressing well.
The white alps glittered. It was summer. He was very great.

Far off in Paris, where his enemies
Whispered that he was wicked, in an upright chair
A blind old woman longed for death and letters. He would write
'Nothing is better than life'. But was it? Yes, the fight
Against the false and the unfair
Was always worth it. So was gardening. Civilize.

Cajoling, scolding, scheming, cleverest of them all,
He'd led the other children in a holy war
Against the infamous grown-ups, and, like a child, been sly
And humble when there was occasion for
The two-faced answer or the plain protective lie,
But, patient like a peasant, waited for their fall.

And never doubted, like D'Alembert, he would win:
Only Pascal was a great enemy, the rest
Were rats already poisoned; there was much, though, to be done,
And only himself to count upon.
Dear Diderot was dull but did his best;
Rousseau, he'd always known, would blubber and give in.

So, like a sentinel, he could not sleep. The night was full of wrong,
Earthquakes and executions. Soon he would be dead,
And still all over Europe stood the horrible nurses
Itching to boil their children. Only his verses
Perhaps could stop them: He must go on working. Overhead
The uncomplaining stars composed their lucid song.

February 1939

Herman Melville
(for Lincoln Kirstein)

Towards the end he sailed into an extraordinary mildness,
And anchored in his home and reached his wife
And rode within the harbour of her hand,
And went across each morning to an office
As though his occupation were another island.

Goodness existed: that was the new knowledge.
His terror had to blow itself quite out
To let him see it; but it was the gale had blown him
Past the Cape Horn of sensible success
Which cries: 'This rock is Eden. Shipwreck here.'

But deafened him with thunder and confused with lightning:
—The maniac hero hunting like a jewel
The rare ambiguous monster that had maimed his sex,
Hatred for hatred ending in a scream,
The unexplained survivor breaking off the nightmare—
All that was intricate and false; the truth was simple.

Evil is unspectacular and always human,
And shares our bed and eats at our own table,
And we are introduced to Goodness every day,
Even in drawing-rooms among a crowd of faults;
He has a name like Billy and is almost perfect,
But wears a stammer like a decoration:
And every time they meet the same thing has to happen;
It is the Evil that is helpless like a lover
And has to pick a quarrel and succeeds,
And both are openly destroyed before our eyes.

For now he was awake and knew
No one is ever spared except in dreams;
But there was something else the nightmare had distorted—
Even the punishment was human and a form of love:
The howling storm had been his father's presence
And all the time he had been carried on his father's breast.

Who now had set him gently down and left him.
He stood upon the narrow balcony and listened:
And all the stars above him sang as in his childhood
'All, all is vanity,' but it was not the same;
For now the words descended like the calm of mountains—
—Nathaniel had been shy because his love was selfish—
Reborn, he cried in exultation and surrender
'The Godhead is broken like bread. We are the pieces.'

And sat down at his desk and wrote a story.

March 1939

The Unknown Citizen

(To JS/07/M/378
This Marble Monument
Is Erected by the State)

He was found by the Bureau of Statistics to be
One against whom there was no official complaint,
And all the reports on his conduct agree
That, in the modern sense of an old-fashioned word, he was a saint,
For in everything he did he served the Greater Community.
Except for the War till the day he retired
He worked in a factory and never got fired,
But satisfied his employers, Fudge Motors Inc.
Yet he wasn't a scab or odd in his views,
For his Union reports that he paid his dues,
(Our report on his Union shows it was sound)
And our Social Psychology workers found
That he was popular with his mates and liked a drink.
The Press are convinced that he bought a paper every day
And that his reactions to advertisements were normal in every way.
Policies taken out in his name prove that he was fully insured,
And his Health-card shows he was once in hospital but left it cured.
Both Producers Research and High-Grade Living declare
He was fully sensible to the advantages of the Instalment Plan
And had everything necessary to the Modern Man,
A phonograph, a radio, a car and a frigidaire.
Our researchers into Public Opinion are content
That he held the proper opinions for the time of year;
When there was peace, he was for peace; when there was war, he went.
He was married and added five children to the population,
Which our Eugenist says was the right number for a parent of his
    generation,
And our teachers report that he never interfered with their education.
Was he free? Was he happy? The question is absurd:
Had anything been wrong, we should certainly have heard.

March 1939

They

Where do they come from? Those whom we so much dread,
as on our dearest location falls the chill
    of their crooked wing and endangers
    the melting friend, the aqueduct, the flower.

Terrible Presences that the ponds reflect
back at the famous and, when the blond boy
    bites eagerly into the shining
    apple, emerge in their shocking fury,

and we realize the woods are deaf and the sky
nurses no one, and we are awake and these,
    like farmers, have purpose and knowledge,
    but towards us their hate is directed.

We are the barren pastures to which they bring
the resentment of outcasts; on us they work
   out their despair; they wear our weeping
   as the disgraceful badge of their exile.

We have conjured them here like a lying map;
desiring the extravagant joy of life,
   we lured with a mirage of orchards,
   fat in the lazy climate of refuge.

Our money sang like streams on the aloof peaks
of our thinking that beckoned them on like girls;
   our culture like a West of wonder
   shone a solemn promise in their faces.

We expected the beautiful or the wise,
ready to see a charm in our childish fibs,
   pleased to find nothing but stones, and
   able at once to create a garden.

But those who come are not even children with
the big indiscriminate eyes we had lost,
   occupying our narrow spaces
   with their anarchist vivid abandon.

They arrive, already adroit, having learned
restraint at the table of a father's rage;
   in a mother's distorting mirror
   they discovered the Meaning of Knowing.

For a future of marriage nevertheless
the bed is prepared; though all our whiteness shrinks
   from the hairy and clumsy bridegroom,
   we conceive in the shuddering instant.

For the barren must wish to bear though the Spring
punish; and the crooked that dreads to be straight
   cannot alter its prayer but summons
   out of the dark a horrible rector.

The tawny and vigorous tiger can move
with style through the borough of murder; the ape
   is really at home in the parish
   of grimacing and licking: but we have

failed as their pupils. Our tears well from a love
we have never outgrown; our armies predict
   more than we hope; even our armies
   have to express our need for forgiveness.

April 1939

The Prophets

Perhaps I always knew what they were saying:
Even those earliest messengers who walked
Into my life from books where they were staying,
Those beautiful machines that never talked
But let the small boy worship them and learn
All their long names whose hardness made him proud;
Love was the word they never said aloud
As nothing that a picture can return.

And later when I hunted the Good Place,
Abandoned lead-mines let themselves be caught;
There was no pity in the adit's face,
The rusty winding-engine never taught
One obviously too apt, to say Too Late:
Their lack of shyness was a way of praising
Just what I didn't know, why I was gazing,
While all their lack of answer whispered 'Wait,'
And taught me gradually without coercion,
And all the landscape round them pointed to
The calm with which they took complete desertion
As proof that you existed.

     It was true.
For now I have the answer from the face
That never will go back into a book
But asks for all my life, and is the Place
Where all I touch is moved to an embrace,
And there is no such thing as a vain look.

            May 1939

Like a Vocation

Not as that dream Napoleon, rumour's dread and centre,
Before whose riding all the crowds divide,
Who dedicates a column and withdraws,
Nor as that general favourite and breezy visitor
To whom the weather and the ruins mean so much,
Nor as any of those who always will be welcome,
As luck or history or fun,
Do not enter like that: all these depart.

Claim, certainly, the stranger's right to pleasure:
Ambassadors will surely entertain you
With knowledge of operas and men,
Bankers will ask for your opinion
And the heiress' cheek lean ever so slightly towards you,
The mountains and the shopkeepers accept you
And all your walks be free.

But politeness and freedom are never enough,
Not for a life. They lead
Up to a bed that only looks like marriage;
Even the disciplined and distant admiration
For thousands who obviously want nothing
Becomes just a dowdy illness. These have their moderate success;
They exist in the vanishing hour.

But somewhere always, nowhere particularly unusual,
Almost anywhere in the landscape of water and houses,
His crying competing unsuccessfully with the cry
Of the traffic or the birds, is always standing
The one who needs you, that terrified
Imaginative child who only knows you
As what the uncles call a lie,
But knows he has to be the future and that only
The meek inherit the earth, and is neither
Charming, successful, nor a crowd;
Alone among the noise and policies of summer,
His weeping climbs towards your life like a vocation.

May 1939

The Riddle

Underneath the leaves of life,
Green on the prodigious tree,
   In a trance of grief
Stand the fallen man and wife:
Far away a single stag
Banished to a lonely crag
Gazes placid out to sea,
While from thickets round about
Breeding animals look in
   On Duality,
And small birds fly in and out
   Of the world of man.

Down in order from a ridge,
Bayonets glittering in the sun,
   Soldiers who will judge
Wind towards a little bridge:
Even orators may speak
Truths of value to the weak,
Necessary acts are done
By the ill and the unjust;
But the Judgment and the Smile,
   Though these two-in-one
See creation as they must,
   None shall reconcile.

Bordering our middle earth
Kingdoms of the Short and Tall,
  Rivals for our faith,
Stir up envy from our birth:
So the giant who storms the sky
In an angry wish to die
Wakes the hero in us all,
While the tiny with their power
To divide and hide and flee,
  When our fortunes fall,
Tempt to a belief in our
  Immortality.

Lovers running each to each
Feel such timid dreams catch fire
  Blazing as they touch,
Learn what love alone can teach:
Happy on a tousled bed
Praise Blake's acumen who said:
'One thing only we require
Of each other; we must see
In another's lineaments
  Gratified desire';
That is our humanity;
  Nothing else contents.

Nowhere else could I have known
Than, beloved, in your eyes
  What we have to learn,
That we love ourselves alone:
All our terrors burned away
We can learn at last to say:
'All our knowledge comes to this,
That existence is enough,
That in savage solitude
  Or the play of love
Every living creature is
  Woman, Man, and Child'.

June 1939

✓ Heavy Date

Sharp and silent in the
Clear October lighting
Of a Sunday morning
  The great city lies;
And I at a window
Looking over water
At the world of Business
  With a lover's eyes.

All mankind, I fancy,
When anticipating
Anything exciting
    Like a rendezvous,
Occupy the time in
Purely random thinking,
For when love is waiting
    Logic will not do.

Much as he would like to
Concentrate completely
On the precious Object,
    Love has not the power:
Goethe put it neatly;
No one cares to watch the
Loveliest sunset after
    Quarter of an hour.

Malinowski, Rivers,
Benedict and others
Show how common culture
    Shapes the separate lives:
Matrilineal races
Kill their mothers' brothers
In their dreams and turn their
    Sisters into wives.

Who when looking over
Faces in the subway,
Each with its uniqueness,
    Would not, did he dare,
Ask what forms exactly
Suited to their weakness
Love and desperation
    Take to govern there:

Would not like to know what
Influence occupation
Has on human vision
    Of the human fate:
Do all clerks for instance
Pigeon-hole creation,
Brokers see the Ding-an-
    -sich as Real Estate?

When a politician
Dreams about his sweetheart,
Does he multiply her
    Face into a crowd,
Are her fond responses
All-or-none reactions,
Does he try to buy her,
    Is the kissing loud?

Strange are love's mutations:
Thus, the early poem
Of the flesh sub rosa
   Has been known to grow
Now and then into the
Amor intellectu-
-alis of Spinoza;
   How we do not know.

Slowly we are learning,
We at least know this much,
That we have to unlearn
   Much that we were taught,
And are growing chary
Of emphatic dogmas;
Love like Matter is much
   Odder than we thought.

Love requires an Object,
But this varies so much,
Almost, I imagine,
   Anything will do:
When I was a child, I
Loved a pumping-engine,
Thought it every bit as
   Beautiful as you.

Love has no position,
Love's a way of living,
One kind of relation
   Possible between
Any things or persons
Given one condition,
The one sine qua non
   Being mutual need.

Through it we discover
An essential secret
Called by some Salvation
   And by some Success;
Crying for the moon is
Naughtiness and envy,
We can only love what-
   -ever we possess.

I believed for years that
Love was the conjunction
Of two oppositions;
   That was all untrue;
Every young man fears that
He is not worth loving:
Bless you, darling, I have
   Found myself in you.

When two lovers meet, then
There's an end of writing
Thought and Analytics:
    Lovers, like the dead,
In their loves are equal;
Sophomores and peasants,
Poets and their critics
    Are the same in bed.

October 1939

Law Like Love

Law, say the gardeners, is the sun,
Law is the one
All gardeners obey
To-morrow, yesterday, to-day.

Law is the wisdom of the old,
The impotent grandfathers feebly scold;
The grandchildren put out a treble tongue,
Law is the senses of the young.

Law, says the priest with a priestly look,
Expounding to an unpriestly people,
Law is the words in my priestly book,
Law is my pulpit and my steeple.
Law, says the judge as he looks down his nose,
Speaking clearly and most severely,
Law is as I've told you before,
Law is as you know I suppose,
Law is but let me explain it once more,
Law is The Law.

Yet law-abiding scholars write:
Law is neither wrong nor right,
Law is only crimes
Punished by places and by times,
Law is the clothes men wear
Anytime, anywhere,
Law is Good morning and Good night.

Others say, Law is our Fate;
Others say, Law is our State;
Others say, others say
Law is no more,
Law has gone away.

And always the loud angry crowd,
Very angry and very loud,
Law is We,
And always the soft idiot softly Me.

If we, dear, know we know no more
Than they about the Law,
If I no more than you
Know what we should and should not do
Except that all agree
Gladly or miserably
That the Law is
And that all know this,
If therefore thinking it absurd
To identify Law with some other word,
Unlike so many men
I cannot say Law is again,
No more than they can we suppress
The universal wish to guess
Or slip out of our own position
Into an unconcerned condition.
Although I can at least confine
Your vanity and mine
To stating timidly
A timid similarity,
We shall boast anyway:
Like love I say.

Like love we don't know where or why,
Like love we can't compel or fly,
Like love we often weep,
Like love we seldom keep.

September 1939

The Hidden Law

The Hidden Law does not deny
Our laws of probability,
But takes the atom and the star
And human beings as they are,
And answers nothing when we lie.

It is the only reason why
No government can codify,
And legal definitions mar
    The Hidden Law.

Its utter patience will not try
To stop us if we want to die:
When we escape It in a car,
When we forget It in a bar,
These are the ways we're punished by
    The Hidden Law.

1940

Ten Songs

Say this city has ten million souls,
Some are living in mansions, some are living in holes:
Yet there's no place for us, my dear, yet there's no place for us.

Once we had a country and we thought it fair,
Look in the atlas and you'll find it there:
We cannot go there now, my dear, we cannot go there now.

In the village churchyard there grows an old yew,
Every spring it blossoms anew:
Old passports can't do that, my dear, old passports can't do that.

The consul banged the table and said:
'If you've got no passport you're officially dead':
But we are still alive, my dear, but we are still alive.

Went to a committee; they offered me a chair;
Asked me politely to return next year:
But where shall we go to-day, my dear, but where shall we go to-day?

Came to a public meeting; the speaker got up and said:
'If we let them in, they will steal our daily bread';
He was talking of you and me, my dear, he was talking of you and me.

Thought I heard the thunder rumbling in the sky;
It was Hitler over Europe, saying: 'They must die';
We were in his mind, my dear, we were in his mind.

Saw a poodle in a jacket fastened with a pin,
Saw a door opened and a cat let in:
But they weren't German Jews, my dear, but they weren't
    German Jews.

Went down to the harbour and stood upon the quay,
Saw the fish swimming as if they were free:
Only ten feet away, my dear, only ten feet away.

Walked through a wood, saw the birds in the trees;
They had no politicians and sang at their ease:
They weren't the human race, my dear, they weren't the
    human race.

Dreamed I saw a building with a thousand floors,
A thousand windows and a thousand doors;
Not one of them was ours, my dear, not one of them was ours.

Stood on a great plain in the falling snow;
Ten thousand soldiers marched to and fro:
Looking for you and me, my dear, looking for you and me.

March 1939

II. (CALYPSO)

Dríver drive fáster and máke a good rún
Down the Spríngfield Line únder the shíning sún.

Flý like an aéroplane, dón't pull up shórt
Till you bráke for Grand Céntral Státion, New Yórk.

For thére in the míddle of thát waiting-háll
Should be stánding the óne that Í love best of áll.

If he's nót there to méet me when Í get to tówn,
I'll stánd on the síde-walk with téars rolling dówn.

For hé is the óne that I lóve to look ón,
The ácme of kíndness and pérfectión.

He présses my hánd and he sáys he loves mé,
Which I fínd an admiráble pecúliaritý.

The wóods are bright gréen on both sídes of the líne;
The trées have their lóves though they're dífferent from míne.

But the póor fat old bánker in the sún-parlor cár
Has nó one to lóve him excépt his cigár.

If Í were the Héad of the Chúrch or the Státe,
I'd pówder my nóse and just téll them to wáit.

For lóve's more impórtant and pówerful thán
Éven a príest or a póliticián.

May 1939

III

Warm are the still and lucky miles,
White shores of longing stretch away,
A light of recognition fills
  The whole great day, and bright
The tiny world of lovers' arms.

Silence invades the breathing wood
Where drowsy limbs a treasure keep,
Now greenly falls the learned shade
  Across the sleeping brows
And stirs their secret to a smile.

Restored! Returned! The lost are borne
On seas of shipwreck home at last:
See! In a fire of praising burns
  The dry dumb past, and we
Our life-day long shall part no more.

October 1939

IV

Carry her over the water,
  And set her down under the tree,
Where the culvers white all day and all night,
  And the winds from every quarter,
Sing agreeably, agreeably, agreeably of love.

Put a gold ring on her finger,
  And press her close to your heart,
While the fish in the lake their snapshots take,
  And the frog, that sanguine singer,
Sings agreeably, agreeably, agreeably of love.

The streets shall all flock to your marriage,
  The houses turn round to look,
The tables and chairs say suitable prayers,
  And the horses drawing your carriage
Sing agreeably, agreeably, agreeably of love.

? 1939

V

DOG The single creature leads a partial life,
    Man by his mind, and by his nose the hound;
    He needs the deep emotions I can give,
    I scent in him a vaster hunting ground.

CATS Like calls to like, to share is to relieve
    And sympathy the root bears love the flower;
    He feels in us, and we in him perceive
    A common passion for the lonely hour.

CATS We move in our apartness and our pride
    About the decent dwellings he has made:
DOG In all his walks I follow at his side,
    His faithful servant and his loving shade.

December 1939

VI

Eyes look into the well,
Tears run down from the eye;
The tower cracked and fell
From the quiet winter sky.

Under a midnight stone
Love was buried by thieves;
The robbed heart begs for a bone,
The damned rustle like leaves.

Face down in the flooded brook
With nothing more to say,
Lies One the soldiers took,
And spoiled and threw away.

1940

212

VII. DOMESDAY SONG

Jumbled in one common box
Of their dark stupidity,
Orchid, swan, and Caesar lie;
Time that tires of everyone
Has corroded all the locks
Thrown away the key for fun.

In its cleft the torrent mocks
Prophets who in days gone by
Made a profit on each cry,
Persona grata now with none;
And a jackass language shocks
Poets who can only pun.

Silence settles on the clocks;
Nursing mothers point a sly
Index finger at a sky,
Crimson in the setting sun;
In the valley of the fox
Gleams the barrel of a gun.

Once we could have made the docks,
Now it is too late to fly;
Once too often you and I
Did what we should not have done;
Round the rampant rugged rocks
Rude and ragged rascals run.

January 1941

VIII

Though determined Nature can
Only offer human eyes
One alternative to sleep,
Opportunity to weep,
    Who can refuse her?
Error does not end with youth
But increases in the man;
    All truth, only truth,
Carries the ambiguous lies
    Of the Accuser.

Though some sudden fire of grace
Visit our mortality
Till a whole life tremble for
Swans upon a river or
    Some passing stranger,
Hearts by envy are possessed
From the moment that they praise;
    To rejoice, to be blessed,
Places us immediately
    In mortal danger.

213

Though we cannot follow how
Evil miracles are done
Through the medium of a kiss,
Aphrodite's garden is
    A haunted region;
For the very signs whereby
Lovers register their vow,
    With a look, with a sigh,
Summon to their meetings One
    Whose name is Legion.

We, my darling, for our sins
Suffer in each other's woe,
Read in injured eyes and hands
How we broke divine commands
    And served the Devil.
Who is passionate enough
When the punishment begins?
    O my love, O my love,
In the night of fire and snow
    Save me from evil.

July 1941

IX

My second thoughts condemn
And wonder how I dare
To look you in the eye.
What right have I to swear
Even at one a.m.
To love you till I die?

Earth meets too many crimes
For fibs to interest her;
If I can give my word,
Forgiveness can recur
Any number of times
In Time. Which is absurd.

Tempus fugit. Quite.
So finish up your drink.
All flesh is grass. It is.
But who on earth can think
With heavy heart or light
Of what will come of this?

September 1942

X

On and on and on
The forthright catadoup
Shouts at the stone-deaf stone;
Over and over again,
Singly or as a group,
Weak diplomatic men
With a small defiant light
Salute the incumbent night.

With or without a mind,
Chafant or outwardly calm,
Each thing has an axe to grind
And exclaims its matter-of-fact;
The child with careful charm
Or a sudden opprobrious act,
The tiger, the griping fern,
Extort the world's concern.

All, all, have rights to declare,
Not one is man enough
To be, simply, publicly, there
With no private emphasis;
So my embodied love
Which, like most feeling, is
Half humbug and half true,
Asks neighbourhood of you.

June 1947

In Memory of Sigmund Freud
(d. Sept. 1939)

When there are so many we shall have to mourn,
when grief has been made so public, and exposed
    to the critique of a whole epoch
    the frailty of our conscience and anguish,

of whom shall we speak? For every day they die
among us, those who were doing us some good,
    who knew it was never enough but
    hoped to improve a little by living.

Such was this doctor: still at eighty he wished
to think of our life from whose unruliness
    so many plausible young futures
    with threats or flattery ask obedience,

but his wish was denied him: he closed his eyes
upon that last picture, common to us all,
    of problems like relatives gathered
    puzzled and jealous about our dying.

For about him till the very end were still
those he had studied, the fauna of the night,
    and shades that still waited to enter
    the bright circle of his recognition

turned elsewhere with their disappointment as he
was taken away from his life interest
    to go back to the earth in London,
    an important Jew who died in exile.

Only Hate was happy, hoping to augment
his practice now, and his dingy clientele
    who think they can be cured by killing
    and covering the gardens with ashes.

They are still alive, but in a world he changed
simply by looking back with no false regrets;
    all he did was to remember
    like the old and be honest like children.

He wasn't clever at all: he merely told
the unhappy Present to recite the Past
    like a poetry lesson till sooner
    or later it faltered at the line where

long ago the accusations had begun,
and suddenly knew by whom it had been judged,
    how rich life had been and how silly,
    and was life-forgiven and more humble,

able to approach the Future as a friend
without a wardrobe of excuses, without
    a set mask of rectitude or an
    embarrassing over-familiar gesture.

No wonder the ancient cultures of conceit
in his technique of unsettlement foresaw
    the fall of princes, the collapse of
    their lucrative patterns of frustration:

if he succeeded, why, the Generalised Life
would become impossible, the monolith
    of State be broken and prevented
    the co-operation of avengers.

Of course they called on God, but he went his way
down among the lost people like Dante, down
    to the stinking fosse where the injured
    lead the ugly life of the rejected,

and showed us what evil is, not, as we thought,
deeds that must be punished, but our lack of faith,
    our dishonest mood of denial,
    the concupiscence of the oppressor.

If some traces of the autocratic pose,
the paternal strictness he distrusted, still
    clung to his utterance and features,
    it was a protective coloration

for one who'd lived among enemies so long:
if often he was wrong and, at times, absurd,
    to us he is no more a person
    now but a whole climate of opinion

under whom we conduct our different lives:
Like weather he can only hinder or help,
    the proud can still be proud but find it
    a little harder, the tyrant tries to

make do with him but doesn't care for him much:
he quietly surrounds all our habits of growth
    and extends, till the tired in even
    the remotest miserable duchy

have felt the change in their bones and are cheered,
till the child, unlucky in his little State,
    some hearth where freedom is excluded,
    a hive whose honey is fear and worry,

feels calmer now and somehow assured of escape,
while, as they lie in the grass of our neglect,
    so many long-forgotten objects
    revealed by his undiscouraged shining

are returned to us and made precious again;
games we had thought we must drop as we grew up,
    little noises we dared not laugh at,
    faces we made when no one was looking.

But he wishes us more than this. To be free
is often to be lonely. He would unite
    the unequal moieties fractured
    by our own well-meaning sense of justice,

would restore to the larger the wit and will
the smaller possesses but can only use
    for arid disputes, would give back to
    the son the mother's richness of feeling:

but he would have us remember most of all
to be enthusiastic over the night,
    not only for the sense of wonder
    it alone has to offer, but also

because it needs our love. With large sad eyes
its delectable creatures look up and beg
    us dumbly to ask them to follow:
    they are exiles who long for the future

217

that lies in our power, they too would rejoice
if allowed to serve enlightenment like him,
        even to bear our cry of 'Judas',
    as he did and all must bear who serve it.

One rational voice is dumb. Over his grave
the household of Impulse mourns one dearly loved:
        sad is Eros, builder of cities,
    and weeping anarchic Aphrodite.

November 1939

Another Time

For us like any other fugitive,
Like the numberless flowers that cannot number
And all the beasts that need not remember,
It is to-day in which we live.

So many try to say Not Now,
So many have forgotten how
To say I Am, and would be
Lost, if they could, in history.

Bowing, for instance, with such old-world grace
To a proper flag in a proper place,
Muttering like ancients as they stump upstairs
Of Mine and His or Ours and Theirs.

Just as if time were what they used to will
When it was gifted with possession still,
Just as if they were wrong
In no more wishing to belong.

No wonder then so many die of grief,
So many are so lonely as they die;
No one has yet believed or liked a lie:
Another time has other lives to live.

October 1939

Our Bias

The hour-glass whispers to the lion's roar,
The clock-towers tell the gardens day and night
How many errors Time has patience for,
How wrong they are in being always right.

Yet Time, however loud its chimes or deep,
However fast its falling torrent flows,
Has never put one lion off his leap
Nor shaken the assurance of a rose.

For they, it seems, care only for success:
While we choose words according to their sound
And judge a problem by its awkwardness;

And Time with us was always popular.
When have we not preferred some going round
To going straight to where we are?

September 1939

✓ Hell

Hell is neither here nor there,
Hell is not anywhere,
Hell is hard to bear.

It is so hard to dream posterity
Or haunt a ruined century
And so much easier to be.

Only the challenge to our will,
Our pride in learning any skill,
Sustains our effort to be ill.

To talk the dictionary through
Without a chance word coming true
Is more than Darwin's apes could do.

Yet pride alone could not insist
Did we not hope, if we persist,
That one day Hell might actually exist.

In time, pretending to be blind
And universally unkind
Might really send us out of our mind.

If we were really wretched and asleep
It would be then *de trop* to weep,
It would be natural to lie,
There'd be no living left to die.

September 1939

Lady Weeping at the Crossroads

Lady, weeping at the crossroads,
Would you meet your love
In the twilight with his greyhounds,
And the hawk on his glove?

Bribe the birds then on the branches,
Bribe them to be dumb,
Stare the hot sun out of heaven
That the night may come.

219

Starless are the nights of travel,
Bleak the winter wind;
Run with terror all before you
And regret behind.

Run until you hear the ocean's
Everlasting cry;
Deep though it may be and bitter
You must drink it dry,

Wear out patience in the lowest
Dungeons of the sea,
Searching through the stranded shipwrecks
For the golden key,

Push on to the world's end, pay the
Dread guard with a kiss,
Cross the rotten bridge that totters
Over the abyss.

There stands the deserted castle
Ready to explore;
Enter, climb the marble staircase
Open the locked door.

Cross the silent empty ballroom,
Doubt and danger past;
Blow the cobwebs from the mirror,
See yourself at last.

Put your hand behind the wainscot,
You have done your part;
Find the penknife there and plunge it
Into your false heart.

1940

Anthem for St. Cecilia's Day
(for Benjamin Britten)

I

In a garden shady this holy lady
With reverent cadence and subtle psalm,
Like a black swan as death came on
Poured forth her song in perfect calm:
And by ocean's margin this innocent virgin
Constructed an organ to enlarge her prayer,
And notes tremendous from her great engine
Thundered out on the Roman air.

Blonde Aphrodite rose up excited,
Moved to delight by the melody,
White as an orchid she rode quite naked
In an oyster shell on top of the sea;

At sounds so entrancing the angels dancing
Came out of their trance into time again,
And around the wicked in Hell's abysses
The huge flame flickered and eased their pain.

Blessed Cecilia, appear in visions
To all musicians, appear and inspire:
Translated Daughter, come down and startle
Composing mortals with immortal fire.

II

I cannot grow;
I have no shadow
To run away from,
I only play.

I cannot err;
There is no creature
Whom I belong to,
Whom I could wrong.

I am defeat
When it knows it
Can now do nothing
By suffering.

All you lived through,
Dancing because you
No longer need it
For any deed.

I shall never be
Different. Love me.

III

O ear whose creatures cannot wish to fall,
Calm spaces unafraid of wear or weight,
Where Sorrow is herself, forgetting all
The gaucheness of her adolescent state,
Where Hope within the altogether strange
From every outworn image is released,
And Dread born whole and normal like a beast
Into a world of truths that never change:
Restore our fallen day; O re-arrange.

O dear white children casual as birds,
Playing among the ruined languages,
So small beside their large confusing words,
So gay against the greater silences
Of dreadful things you did: O hang the head,
Impetuous child with the tremendous brain,
O weep, child, weep, O weep away the stain,
Lost innocence who wished your lover dead,
Weep for the lives your wishes never led.

221

O cry created as the bow of sin
Is drawn across our trembling violin.
O weep, child, weep, O weep away the stain.
O law drummed out by hearts against the still
Long winter of our intellectual will.
That what has been may never be again.
O flute that throbs with the thanksgiving breath
Of convalescents on the shores of death.
O bless the freedom that you never chose.
O trumpets that unguarded children blow
About the fortress of their inner foe.
O wear your tribulation like a rose.

July 1940

The Dark Years

Returning each morning from a timeless world,
the senses open upon a world of time:
    after so many years the light is
    novel still and immensely ambitious,

but, translated from her own informal world,
the ego is bewildered and does not want
    a shining novelty this morning,
    and does not like the noise or the people.

For behind the doors of this ambitious day
stand shadows with enormous grudges, outside
    its chartered ocean of perception
    misshapen coastguards drunk with foreboding,

and whispering websters, creeping through this world,
discredit so much literature and praise.
    Summer was worse than we expected:
    now an Autumn cold comes on the water,

as lesser lives retire on their savings, their
small deposits of starches and nuts, and soon
    will be asleep or travelling
    or dead. But this year the towns of our childhood

are changing complexion along with the woods,
and many who have shared our conduct will add
    their pinches of detritus to the
    nutritive chain of determined being,

and even our uneliminated decline
to a vita minima, huddling for warmth,
    the hard- and the soft-mouthed together
    in a coma of waiting, just breathing

in a darkness of tribulation and death,
while blizzards havoc the garden and the old
      Folly becomes unsafe, the mill-wheels
   rust, and the weirs fall slowly to pieces.

Will the inflamed ego attempt as before
to migrate again to her family place,
      to the hanging gardens of Eros
   and the moons of a magical summer?

The local train does not run any more,
the heretical roses have lost their scent,
      and her Cornish Hollow of tryst is
   swarming now with discourteous villains

whom Father's battered hat cannot wave away,
and the fancy-governed sequence leads us all
      back to the labyrinth where either
   we are found or lose ourselves for ever.

What signs ought we to make to be found, how can
we will the knowledge that we must know to will?
      The waste is a suburb of prophets,
   but who has seen Jesus and who only

Judas the Abyss? The rocks are big and bad,
death all too substantial in the thinning air,
      learning screams in the narrow gate where
   events are traded with time but cannot

tell what logic must and must not leave to fate,
or what laws we are permitted to obey:
      there are no birds now, predatory
   glaciers glitter in a chilly evening,

and death is probable. Nevertheless,
whatever the situation and the blame,
      let the lips make formal contrition
   for whatever is going to happen,

time remembered bear witness to time required,
the positive and negative ways through time
      embrace and encourage each other
   in a brief moment of intersection,

that the spirit orgulous may while it can
conform to its temporal focus with praise,
      acknowledging the attributes of
   one immortal, one infinite Substance,

and the shabby structure of indolent flesh
give a resonant echo to the Word which was
      from the beginning, and the shining
   Light be comprehended by the darkness.

                                    ? October 1940

223

The Quest

I

Out of its steps our future, through this door
Enigmas, executioners and rules,
Her Majesty in a bad temper or
A red-nosed Fool who makes a fool of fools.

Great persons eye it in the twilight for
A past it might so carelessly let in,
A widow with a missionary grin,
The foaming inundation at a roar.

We pile our all against it when afraid,
And beat upon its panels when we die:
By happening to be open once, it made

Enormous Alice see a wonderland
That waited for her in the sunshine and,
Simply by being tiny, made her cry.

II

All had been ordered weeks before the start
From the best firms at such work, instruments
To take the measure of all queer events,
And drugs to move the bowels or the heart.

A watch, of course, to watch impatience fly,
Lamps for the dark and shades against the sun;
Foreboding, too, insisted on a gun,
And coloured beads to soothe a savage eye.

In theory they were sound on Expectation,
Had there been situations to be in;
Unluckily they were their situation:

One should not give a poisoner medicine,
A conjurer fine apparatus, nor
A rifle to a melancholic bore.

III

Two friends who met here and embraced are gone,
Each to his own mistake; one flashes on
To fame and ruin in a rowdy lie,
A village torpor holds the other one,
Some local wrong where it takes time to die:
This empty junction glitters in the sun.

So at all quays and crossroads: who can tell
These places of decision and farewell
To what dishonour all adventure leads,
What parting gift could give that friend protection,
So orientated his vocation needs
The Bad Lands and the sinister direction?

All landscapes and all weathers freeze with fear,
But none have ever thought, the legends say,
The time allowed made it impossible;
For even the most pessimistic set
The limit of their errors at a year.
What friends could there be left then to betray,
What joys take longer to atone for; yet
Who would complete without the extra day
The journey that should take no time at all?

IV

No window in his suburb lights that bedroom where
A little fever heard large afternoons at play:
His meadows multiply; that mill, though, is not there
Which went on grinding at the back of love all day.

Nor all his weeping ways through weary wastes have found
The castle where his Greater Hallows are interned;
For broken bridges halt him, and dark thickets round
Some ruin where an evil heritage was burned.

Could he forget a child's ambition to be old
And institutions where it learned to wash and lie,
He'd tell the truth for which he thinks himself too young,

That everywhere on his horizon, all the sky,
Is now, as always, only waiting to be told
To be his father's house and speak his mother tongue.

V

In villages from which their childhoods came
Seeking Necessity, they had been taught
Necessity by nature is the same
No matter how or by whom it be sought.

The city, though, assumed no such belief,
But welcomed each as if he came alone,
The nature of Necessity like grief
Exactly corresponding to his own.

And offered them so many, every one
Found some temptation fit to govern him,
And settled down to master the whole craft

Of being nobody; sat in the sun
During the lunch-hour round the fountain rim,
And watched the country kids arrive and laughed.

VI

Ashamed to be the darling of his grief,
He joined a gang of rowdy stories where
His gift for magic quickly made him chief
Of all these boyish powers of the air;

225

Who turned his hungers into Roman food,
The town's asymmetry into a park;
All hours took taxis; any solitude
Became his flattered duchess in the dark.

But, if he wished for anything less grand,
The nights came padding after him like wild
Beasts that meant harm, and all the doors cried Thief;

And when Truth met him and put out her hand,
He clung in panic to his tall belief
And shrank away like an ill-treated child.

VII

His library annoyed him with its look
Of calm belief in being really there;
He threw away a rival's boring book,
And clattered panting up the spiral stair.

Swaying upon the parapet he cried:
'O Uncreated Nothing, set me free,
Now let Thy perfect be identified,
Unending passion of the Night, with Thee.'

And his long-suffering flesh, that all the time
Had felt the simple cravings of the stone
And hoped to be rewarded for her climb,

Took it to be a promise when he spoke
That now at last she would be left alone,
And plunged into the college quad, and broke.

VIII

He watched with all his organs of concern
How princes walk, what wives and children say,
Re-opened old graves in his heart to learn
What laws the dead had died to disobey,

And came reluctantly to his conclusion:
'All the arm-chair philosophies are false;
To love another adds to the confusion;
The song of mercy is the Devil's Waltz.'

All that he put his hand to prospered so
That soon he was the very King of creatures,
Yet, in an autumn nightmare trembled, for,

Approaching down a ruined corridor,
Strode someone with his own distorted features
Who wept, and grew enormous, and cried Woe.

IX

This is an architecture for the odd;
Thus heaven was attacked by the afraid,
So once, unconsciously, a virgin made
Her maidenhead conspicuous to a god.

Here on dark nights while worlds of triumph sleep
Lost Love in abstract speculation burns,
And exiled Will to politics returns
In epic verse that makes its traitors weep.

Yet many come to wish their tower a well;
For those who dread to drown, of thirst may die,
Those who see all become invisible:

Here great magicians, caught in their own spell,
Long for a natural climate as they sigh
'Beware of Magic' to the passer-by.

X

They noticed that virginity was needed
To trap the unicorn in every case,
But not that, of those virgins who succeeded,
A high percentage had an ugly face.

The hero was as daring as they thought him,
But his peculiar boyhood missed them all;
The angel of a broken leg had taught him
The right precautions to avoid a fall.

So in presumption they set forth alone
On what, for them, was not compulsory,
And stuck half-way to settle in some cave
With desert lions to domesticity,

Or turned aside to be absurdly brave,
And met the ogre and were turned to stone.

XI

His peasant parents killed themselves with toil
To let their darling leave a stingy soil
For any of those fine professions which
Encourage shallow breathing, and grow rich.

The pressure of their fond ambition made
Their shy and country-loving child afraid
No sensible career was good enough,
Only a hero could deserve such love.

So here he was without maps or supplies,
A hundred miles from any decent town;
The desert glared into his blood-shot eyes,
The silence roared displeasure:

                              looking down,
He saw the shadow of an Average Man
Attempting the exceptional, and ran.

XII

Incredulous, he stared at the amused
Official writing down his name among
Those whose request to suffer was refused.

The pen ceased scratching: though he came too late
To join the martyrs, there was still a place
Among the tempters for a caustic tongue

To test the resolution of the young
With tales of the small failings of the great,
And shame the eager with ironic praise.

Though mirrors might be hateful for a while,
Women and books would teach his middle age
The fencing wit of an informal style,
To keep the silences at bay and cage
His pacing manias in a worldly smile.

XIII

The over-logical fell for the witch
Whose argument converted him to stone,
Thieves rapidly absorbed the over-rich,
The over-popular went mad alone,
And kisses brutalized the over-male.

As agents their importance quickly ceased;
Yet, in proportion as they seemed to fail,
Their instrumental value was increased
For one predestined to attain their wish.

By standing stones the blind can feel their way,
Wild dogs compel the cowardly to fight,
Beggars assist the slow to travel light,
And even madmen manage to convey
Unwelcome truths in lonely gibberish.

XIV

Fresh addenda are published every day
To the encyclopedia of the Way,

Linguistic notes and scientific explanations,
And texts for schools with modernized spelling and illustrations.

Now everyone knows the hero must choose the old horse,
Abstain from liquor and sexual intercourse,

And look out for a stranded fish to be kind to:
Now everyone thinks he could find, had he a mind to,

The way through the waste to the chapel in the rock
For a vision of the Triple Rainbow or the Astral Clock,

Forgetting his information comes mostly from married men
Who like fishing and a flutter on the horses now and then.

And how reliable can any truth be that is got
By observing oneself and then just inserting a Not?

XV

Suppose he'd listened to the erudite committee,
He would have only found where not to look;
Suppose his terrier when he whistled had obeyed,
It would not have unearthed the buried city;
Suppose he had dismissed the careless maid,
The cryptogram would not have fluttered from the book.

'It was not I,' he cried as, healthy and astounded,
He stepped across a predecessor's skull;
'A nonsense jingle simply came into my head
And left the intellectual Sphinx dumbfounded;
I won the Queen because my hair was red;
The terrible adventure is a little dull.'

Hence Failure's torment: 'Was I doomed in any case,
Or would I not have failed had I believed in Grace?'

XVI

He parried every question that they hurled:
'What did the Emperor tell you?' 'Not to push.'
'What is the greatest wonder of the world?'
'The bare man Nothing in the Beggar's Bush.'

Some muttered: 'He is eager for effect.
A hero owes a duty to his fame.
He looks too like a grocer for respect.'
Soon they slipped back into his Christian name.

The only difference that could be seen
From those who'd never risked their lives at all
Was his delight in details and routine:

For he was always glad to mow the grass,
Pour liquids from large bottles into small,
Or look at clouds through bits of coloured glass.

XVII

Others had found it prudent to withdraw
Before official pressure was applied,
Embittered robbers outlawed by the Law,
Lepers in terror of the terrified.

But no one else accused these of a crime;
They did not look ill: old friends, overcome,
Stared as they rolled away from talk and time
Like marbles out into the blank and dumb.

The crowd clung all the closer to convention,
Sunshine and horses, for the sane know why
The even numbers should ignore the odd:

The Nameless is what no free people mention;
Successful men know better than to try
To see the face of their Absconded God.

XVIII
Spinning upon their central thirst like tops,
They went the Negative Way towards the Dry;
By empty caves beneath an empty sky
They emptied out their memories like slops,

Which made a foul marsh as they dried to death,
Where monsters bred who forced them to forget
The lovelies their consent avoided; yet,
Still praising the Absurd with their last breath,

They seeded out into their miracles:
The images of each grotesque temptation
Became some painter's happiest inspiration,

And barren wives and burning virgins came
To drink the pure cold water of their wells,
And wish for beaux and children in their name.

XIX
Poet, oracle, and wit
Like unsuccessful anglers by
The ponds of apperception sit,
Baiting with the wrong request
The vectors of their interest,
At nightfall tell the angler's lie.

With time in tempest everywhere,
To rafts of frail assumption cling
The saintly and the insincere;
Enraged phenomena bear down
In overwhelming waves to drown
Both sufferer and suffering.

The waters long to hear our question put
Which would release their longed-for answer, but.

XX
Within these gates all opening begins:
White shouts and flickers through its green and red,
Where children play at seven earnest sins
And dogs believe their tall conditions dead.

Here adolescence into number breaks
The perfect circle time can draw on stone,
And flesh forgives division as it makes
Another's moment of consent its own.

All journeys die here: wish and weight are lifted:
Where often round some old maid's desolation
Roses have flung their glory like a cloak,

The gaunt and great, the famed for conversation
Blushed in the stare of evening as they spoke
And felt their centre of volition shifted.

Summer 1940

Shorts

Motionless, deep in his mind, lies the past the poet's forgotten,
Till some small experience wake it to life and a poem's begotten,
Words its presumptive primordia, Feeling its field of induction,
Meaning its pattern of growth determined during construction.

*　*　*

Whether determined by God or their neural structure, still
All men have one common creed, account for it as you will:
The Truth is one and incapable of self-contradiction;
All knowledge that conflicts with itself is Poetic Fiction.

*　*　*

His ageing nature is the same
As when childhood wore its name
In an atmosphere of love,
And to itself appeared enough:
Only now, when he has come
In walking distance of his tomb,
He at last discovers who
He had always been to whom
He so often was untrue.

*　*　*

Babies in their mothers' arms
Exercise their budding charms
On their fingers and their toes,
Striving ever to enclose
In the circle of their will
Objects disobedient still,
But the boy comes fast enough
To the limits of self-love,
And the adult learns what small
Forces rally at his call.
Large and paramount the State

231

That will not co-operate
With the Duchy of his mind:
All his lifetime he will find
Swollen knee or aching tooth
Hostile to his quest for truth;
Never will his prick belong
To his world of right and wrong,
Nor its values comprehend
Who is foe and who is friend.

*   *   *

Do we want to return to the womb? Not at all.
No one really desires the impossible:
That is only the image out of our past
We practical people use when we cast
Our eyes on the future, to whom freedom is
The absence of all dualities.
Since there never can be much of that for us
In the universe of Copernicus,
Any heaven we think it decent to enter
Must be Ptolomaic with ourselves at the centre.

*   *   *

Once for candy Cook had stolen
    X was punished by Papa;
When he asked where babies come from,
    He was lied to by Mama.

Now the city streets are waiting
    To mislead him, and he must
Keep an eye on ageing beggars
    Lest they strike him in disgust.

*   *   *

With what conviction the young man spoke
When he thought his nonsense rather a joke;
Now, when he doesn't doubt any more,
No one believes the booming old bore.

*   *   *

To the man-in-the-street who, I'm sorry to say,
    Is a keen observer of life,
The word *intellectual* suggests right away
    A man who's untrue to his wife.

*   *   *

Base words are uttered only by the base
And can for such at once be understood,
But noble platitudes:—ah, there's a case
Where the most careful scrutiny is needed
To tell a voice that's genuinely good
From one that's base but merely has succeeded.

*   *   *

These public men who seem so to enjoy their dominion,
With their ruined faces and voices treble with hate,
Are no less martyrs because unaware of their fetters:
What would *you* be like, were you never allowed to create
Or reflect, but compelled to give an immediate opinion,
Condemned to destroy or distribute the works of your betters?

*   *   *

The Champion smiles—What Personality!
The Challenger scowls—How horrid he must be!
But let the Belt change hands and they change places,
Still from the same old corners come the same grimaces.

*   *   *

When Statesmen gravely say 'We must be realistic',
The chances are they're weak and, therefore, pacifistic,
But when they speak of Principles, look out: perhaps
Their generals are already poring over maps.

*   *   *

Who will cure the nation's ill?
A leader with a selfless will.
But how will you find this leader of yours?
By process of Natural Selection, of course.

*   *   *

Standing among the ruins, the horror-struck conqueror exclaimed:
'Why do they have to attempt to refuse me my destiny? Why?'

*   *   *

Why are the public buildings so high? How come you don't know?
Why, that's because the spirits of the public are so low.

*   *   *

'Hard cases make bad law', as the politician learns to his cost:
Yet just is the artist's reproach—'Who generalises is lost.'

*   *   *

Don't you dream of a world, a society, with no coercion?
Yes: where a foetus is able to refuse to be born.

*   *   *

Hans-in-Kelder, Hans-in-Kelder,
    What are you waiting for?
We need your strong arm to look after the farm,
    And keep the wolf from the door.

Hans-in-Kelder, Hans-in-Kelder,
    Came out of the parsley-bed;
Came out at a run and levelled a gun
    And shot his old parents dead.

1940

No Time

Clocks cannot tell our time of day
For what event to pray,
Because we have no time, because
We have no time until
We know what time we fill,
Why time is other than time was.

Nor can our question satisfy
The answer in the statue's eye.
Only the living ask whose brow
May wear the Roman laurel now:
The dead say only how.

What happens to the living when they die?
Death is not understood by death: nor you, nor I.

1940

Diaspora

How he survived them they could never understand:
Had they not beggared him themselves to prove
They could not live without their dogmas or their land?

No worlds they drove him from were ever big enough:
How *could* it be the earth the Unconfined
Meant when It bade them set no limits to their love?

And he fulfilled the role for which he was designed:
On heat with fear, he drew their terrors to him,
And was a godsend to the lowest of mankind,

Till there was no place left where they could still pursue him
Except that exile which he called his race.
But, envying him even that, they plunged right through him

234

Into a land of mirrors without time or space,
And all they had to strike now was the human face.

1940

Luther

With conscience cocked to listen for the thunder,
He saw the Devil busy in the wind,
Over the chiming steeples and then under
The doors of nuns and doctors who had sinned.

What apparatus could stave off disaster
Or cut the brambles of man's error down?
Flesh was a silent dog that bites its master,
World a still pond in which its children drown.

The fuse of Judgement spluttered in his head:
'Lord, smoke these honeyed insects from their hives.
All works, Great Men, Societies are bad.
The Just shall live by Faith. . .' he cried in dread.

And men and women of the world were glad,
Who'd never cared or trembled in their lives.

1940

Montaigne

Outside his library window he could see
A gentle landscape terrified of grammar,
Cities where lisping was compulsory,
And provinces where it was death to stammer.

The hefty sprawled, too tired to care: it took
This donnish undersexed conservative
To start a revolution and to give
The Flesh its weapons to defeat the Book.

When devils drive the reasonable wild,
They strip their adult century so bare,
Love must be re-grown from the sensual child,

To doubt becomes a way of definition,
Even belles lettres legitimate as prayer,
And laziness a movement of contrition.

1940

235

The Council

In gorgeous robes befitting the occasion,
For weeks their spiritual and temporal lordships met
To reconcile eternity with time and set
Our earth of marriage on a sure foundation.
The little town was full of spies: corrupt mankind
Waited on tenterhooks.

                    With ostentation
Doors were at last flung back; success had been complete:
The formulae essential to salvation
Were phrased for ever and the true relation
Of Agape to Eros finally defined.
The burghers hung out flags in celebration;
The peasants danced and roasted oxen in the street.

Into their joy four heralds galloped up with news.
'Fierce tribes are moving on the Western Marches.
Out East a virgin has conceived a son again.
The Southern shipping-lanes are in the hands of Jews.
The Northern Provinces are much deluded
By one who claims there are not seven stars but ten.'

Who wrote upon the council-chamber arches
That sad exasperated cry of tired old men:
Postremum Sanctus Spiritus effudit?

                                        1940

The Maze

Anthropos apteros for days
Walked whistling round and round the maze,
Relying happily upon
His temperament for getting on.

The hundredth time he sighted, though,
A bush he left an hour ago,
He halted where four alleys crossed
And recognised that he was lost.

'Where am I? Metaphysics says
No question can be asked unless
It has an answer, so I can
Assume this maze has got a plan.

'If theologians are correct,
A Plan implies an Architect:
A God-built maze would be, I'm sure,
The Universe in Miniature.

'Are data from the world of sense,
In that case, valid evidence?
What, in the universe I know,
Can give directions how to go?

'All Mathematics would suggest
A steady straight line as the best,
But left and right alternately
Is consonant with History.

'Aesthetics, though, believes all Art
Intends to gratify the heart:
Rejecting disciplines like these,
Must I, then, go which way I please?

'Such reasoning is only true
If we accept the classic view,
Which we have no right to assert
According to the introvert.

'His absolute presupposition
Is: Man creates his own condition.
This maze was not divinely built
But is secreted by my guilt.

'The centre that I cannot find
Is known to my unconscious mind;
I have no reason to despair
Because I am already there.

'My problem is how not to will;
They move most quickly who stand still:
I'm only lost until I see
I'm lost because I want to be.

'If this should fail, perhaps I should,
As certain educators would,
Content myself with this conclusion:
In theory there is no solution.

'All statements about what I feel,
Like I-am-lost, are quite unreal:
My knowledge ends where it began;
A hedge is taller than a man.'

Anthropos apteros, perplexed
To know which turning to take next,
Looked up and wished he were a bird
To whom such doubts must seem absurd.

1940

Blessed Event

Round the three actors in any blessed event
Is always standing an invisible audience of four,
The double twins, the fallen natures of man.

On the Left they remember difficult childhoods,
On the Right they have forgotten why they were so happy,
Above sit the best decisive people,
Below they must kneel all day so as not to be governed.

Four voices just audible in the hush of any Christmas:
Accept my friendship or die.
I shall keep order and not very much will happen.
Bring me luck and of course I'll support you.
I smell blood and an era of prominent madmen.

But the Three hear nothing and are blind even to the landscape
With its towns and rivers and pretty pieces of nonsense.
He, all father, repenting their animal nights,
Cries: *Why did She have to be tortured? It is all my fault.*
Once more a virgin, She whispers: *The Future shall never suffer.*
And the New Life awkwardly touches its home, beginning to fumble
About in the Truth for the straight successful Way
Which will always appear to end in some dreadful defeat.

February 1939

Kairos and Logos

I

Around them boomed the rhetoric of time,
The smells and furniture of the known world
Where conscience worshipped an aesthetic order
And what was unsuccessful was condemned;
While, at the centre of its vast self-love,
Sat Caesar with his pleasures, dreading death.

In clanging verse that military order,
Transferring its obsession onto time,
Besieged the body and cuckolded love;
Puzzling the boys of an athletic world,
These only feared another kind of Death
To which the time-obsessed are all condemned.

Night and the rivers sang a chthonic love,
Destroyer of cities and of daylight order,
But seemed to them weak argument for death.
The apple tree that cannot measure time
Might taste the apple yet not be condemned:
They, to enjoy it, must renounce the world.

Friendly to what the multitudes call death,
Placing their lives below the dogs who love
Their fallen masters and are not condemned,
They came to life within a dying order;
Outside the sunshine of its civil world
Barbarians waited their appointed time.

Its flagrant self-assertions were condemned
To interest the forest and draw death
On aqueducts and learning; yet the world,
Through them, had witnessed, when predestined love
Fell like a daring meteor into time,
The condescension of eternal order.

So, sown in little clumps about the world,
The just, the faithful and the uncondemned
Broke out spontaneously all over time,
Setting against the random facts of death
A ground and possibility of order,
Against defeat the certainty of love.

And never, like its own, condemned the world
Or hated time, but sang until their death:
'O Thou who lovest, set its love in order.'

II

Quite suddenly her dream became a word:
There stood the unicorn, declaring—'Child';
She kissed her dolls good-bye and one by one
Embraced the faithful roses in the garden,
Waved for the last time to her mother's home,
And tiptoed out into the silent forest.

And seemed the lucky, the predestined one
For whom the stones made way without a word;
And sparrows fought to make her feel at home,
And winds restrained their storms before the child;
And all the children of that mother-forest
Were told to let her treat it as her garden.

Till she forgot that she was not at home
Where she was loved, of course, by everyone,
Could always tell the rose-bush—'Be a forest,'
Or make dolls guess when she had thought a word,
Or play at being Mother in the garden
And have importance as her only child.

So, scampering like a sparrow through the forest,
She piled up stones, pretending they were Home,
Called the wild roses that she picked 'My Garden,'
Made any wind she chose the Naughty One,
Talked to herself as to a doll, a child
Whose mother-magic knew the Magic Word.

And took the earth for granted as her garden:
Till the day came the children of the forest
Ceased to regard or treat her as a child;
The roses frowned at her untidy home,
The sparrows laughed when she misspelt a word,
Winds cried: 'A mother should behave like one.'

Frightened and cruel like a guilty child,
She shouted all the roses from her garden,
And threw stones at the winds: without a word
The unicorn slipped off into the forest
Like an offended doll, and one by one
The sparrows flew back to her mother's home.

Of course the forest overran her garden,
Yet, though, like everyone, she lost her home,
The Word still nursed Its motherhood, Its child.

III

If one could name the father of these things,
They would not happen to decide one's fate:
He woke one morning and the verbal truth
He went to bed with was no longer there;
The years of reading fell away; his eyes
Beheld the weights and contours of the earth.

One must be passive to conceive the truth:
The bright and brutal surfaces of things
Awaited the decision of his eyes,
These pretty girls, to be embraced by fate
And mother all the objects of the earth;
The fatherhood of knowledge stood out there.

One notices, if one will trust one's eyes,
The shadow cast by language upon truth:
He saw his rôle as father to an earth
Whose speechless, separate, and ambiguous things
Married at his decision; he was there
To show a lucid passion for their fate.

One has good reason to award the earth
The dog-like dumb devotion of the eyes;
Death, love, dishonour are predicted there,
Her arbitrary moments are the truth:
No, he was not the father of his fate;
The power of decision lay with things.

To know, one must decide what is not there,
Where sickness is, and nothing: all that earth
Presented was a challenge to his fate
To father dreams of talking oaks, of eyes
In walls, catastrophes, sins, poems, things
Whose possibilities excluded truth.

What one expects is not, of course, one's fate:
When he had finished looking at them, there
Were helpless images instead of things
That had looked so decided; instead of earth
His fatherless creation; instead of truth
The luckiest convention of his eyes:

That saw himself there with an exile's eyes,
Missing his Father, a thing of earth
On whose decision hung the fate of truth.

IV

Castle and crown are faded clean away,
The fountain sinks into a level silence;
What kingdom can be reached by the occasions
That climb the broken ladders of our lives?
We are imprisoned in unbounded spaces,
Defined by an indefinite confusion.

We should have wept before for these occasions,
We should have given what is snatched away;
Tall columns, acrobats of cheering spaces,
Loud hymns that were the royal wives of silence,
Now you are art and part of our confusion;
We are at loggerheads with our own lives.

The order of the macrocosmic spaces,
The outward calm of their remote occasions,
Have lost all interest in our confusion;
Our inner regimen has given way;
The subatomic gulfs confront our lives
With the cold stare of their eternal silence.

Where are the kings who routed all confusion,
The bearded gods who shepherded the spaces,
The merchants who poured gold into our lives?
Where the historic routes, the great occasions?
Laurel and language wither into silence;
The nymphs and oracles have fled away.

And cold and absence echo on our lives:
'We are your conscience of your own confusion
That made a stricken widow of the silence
And weeping orphans of the unarmed spaces,
That laid time waste behind you, stole away
The birthright of innumerable occasions.'

Reproach, though, is a blessing, proof that silence
And condemnation presuppose our lives:
We are not lost but only run away,
The authors and the powers of confusion;
We are the promise of unborn occasions;
Our presence is required by all the spaces.

The flora of our lives could guide occasions
Without confusion on their frisking way
Through all the silences and all the spaces.

? 1940

At the Grave of Henry James

The snow, less intransigeant than their marble,
Has left the defence of whiteness to these tombs,
    And all the pools at my feet
Accommodate blue now, echo such clouds as occur
To the sky, and whatever bird or mourner the passing
    Moment remarks they repeat.

While rocks, named after singular spaces
Within which images wandered once that caused
    All to tremble and offend,
Stand here in an innocent stillness, each marking the spot
Where one more series of errors lost its uniqueness
    And novelty came to an end.

To whose real advantage were such transactions,
When worlds of reflection were exchanged for trees?
    What living occasion can
Be just to the absent? Noon but reflects on itself,
And the small taciturn stone, that is the only witness
    To a great and talkative man,

Has no more judgement than my ignorant shadow
Of odious comparisons or distant clocks
    Which challenge and interfere
With the heart's instantaneous reading of time, time that is
A warm enigma no longer to you for whom I
    Surrender my private cheer,

As I stand awake on our solar fabric,
That primary machine, the earth, which gendarmes, banks
    And aspirin pre-suppose,
On which the clumsy and sad may all sit down, and any who will
Say their a-ha to the beautiful, the common locus
    Of the Master and the rose.

Shall I not especially bless you as, vexed with
My little inferior questions, I stand
    Above the bed where you rest,
Who opened such passionate arms to your *Bon* when It ran
Towards you with its overwhelming reasons pleading
    All beautifully in Its breast?

With what an innocence your hand submitted
To those formal rules that help a child to play,
    While your heart, fastidious as
A delicate nun, remained true to the rare noblesse
Of your lucid gift and, for its love, ignored the
    Resentful muttering Mass,

Whose ruminant hatred of all that cannot
Be simplified or stolen is yet at large:
    No death can assuage its lust
To vilify the landscape of Distinction and see
The heart of the Personal brought to a systolic standstill,
    The Tall to diminished dust.

Preserve me, Master, from its vague incitement;
Yours be the disciplinary image that holds
    Me back from agreeable wrong
And the clutch of eddying Muddle, lest Proportion shed
The alpine chill of her shrugging editorial shoulder
    On my loose impromptu song.

All will be judged. Master of nuance and scruple,
Pray for me and for all writers, living or dead:
    Because there are many whose works
Are in better taste than their lives, because there is no end
To the vanity of our calling, make intercession
    For the treason of all clerks.

                                                    1941

Alone

            Each lover has a theory of his own
            About the difference between the ache
            Of being with his love, and being alone:

            Why what, when dreaming, is dear flesh and bone
            That really stirs the senses, when awake,
            Appears a simulacrum of his own.

            Narcissus disbelieves in the unknown;
            He cannot join his image in the lake
            So long as he assumes he is alone.

            The child, the waterfall, the fire, the stone,
            Are always up to mischief, though, and take
            The universe for granted as their own.

            The elderly, like Proust, are always prone
            To think of love as a subjective fake;
            The more they love, the more they feel alone.

Whatever view we hold, it must be shown
Why every lover has a wish to make
Some other kind of otherness his own:
Perhaps, in fact, we never are alone.

1940

Leap Before You Look

The sense of danger must not disappear:
The way is certainly both short and steep,
However gradual it looks from here;
Look if you like, but you will have to leap.

Tough-minded men get mushy in their sleep
And break the by-laws any fool can keep;
It is not the convention but the fear
That has a tendency to disappear.

The worried efforts of the busy heap,
The dirt, the imprecision, and the beer
Produce a few smart wisecracks every year;
Laugh if you can, but you will have to leap.

The clothes that are considered right to wear
Will not be either sensible or cheap,
So long as we consent to live like sheep
And never mention those who disappear.

Much can be said for social savoir-faire,
But to rejoice when no one else is there
Is even harder than it is to weep;
No one is watching, but you have to leap.

A solitude ten thousand fathoms deep
Sustains the bed on which we lie, my dear:
Although I love you, you will have to leap;
Our dream of safety has to disappear.

December 1940

If I Could Tell You

Time will say nothing but I told you so,
Time only knows the price we have to pay;
If I could tell you I would let you know.

If we should weep when clowns put on their show,
If we should stumble when musicians play,
Time will say nothing but I told you so.

There are no fortunes to be told, although,
Because I love you more than I can say,
If I could tell you I would let you know.

The winds must come from somewhere when they blow,
There must be reasons why the leaves decay;
Time will say nothing but I told you so.

Perhaps the roses really want to grow,
The vision seriously intends to stay;
If I could tell you I would let you know.

Suppose the lions all get up and go,
And all the brooks and soldiers run away;
Will Time say nothing but I told you so?
If I could tell you I would let you know.

October 1940

Atlantis

Being set on the idea
　Of getting to Atlantis,
You have discovered of course
　Only the Ship of Fools is
Making the voyage this year,
As gales of abnormal force
　Are predicted, and that you
　Must therefore be ready to
Behave absurdly enough
　To pass for one of The Boys,
At least appearing to love
　Hard liquor, horseplay and noise.

Should storms, as may well happen,
　Drive you to anchor a week
In some old harbour-city
　Of Ionia, then speak
With her witty scholars, men
Who have proved there cannot be
　Such a place as Atlantis:
　Learn their logic, but notice
How their subtlety betrays
　A simple enormous grief;
Thus they shall teach you the ways
　To doubt that you may believe.

If, later, you run aground
　Among the headlands of Thrace
Where with torches all night long
　A naked barbaric race
Leaps frenziedly to the sound
Of conch and dissonant gong;
　On that stony savage shore
　Strip off your clothes and dance, for
Unless you are capable
　Of forgetting completely
About Atlantis, you will
　Never finish your journey.

245

Again, should you come to gay
   Carthage or Corinth, take part
In their endless gaiety;
   And if in some bar a tart,
As she strokes your hair, should say
'This is Atlantis, dearie,'
   Listen with attentiveness
   To her life-story: unless
You become acquainted now
   With each refuge that tries to
Counterfeit Atlantis, how
   Will you recognize the true?

Assuming you beach at last
   Near Atlantis, and begin
The terrible trek inland
   Through squalid woods and frozen
Tundras where all are soon lost;
If, forsaken then, you stand,
   Dismissal everywhere,
   Stone and snow, silence and air,
Remember the noble dead
   And honour the fate you are,
Travelling and tormented,
   Dialectic and bizarre.

Stagger onward rejoicing;
   And even then if, perhaps
Having actually got
   To the last col, you collapse
With all Atlantis gleaming
Below you yet you cannot
   Descend, you should still be proud
   Even to have been allowed
Just to peep at Atlantis
   In a poetic vision:
Give thanks and lie down in peace,
   Having seen your salvation.

All the little household gods
   Have started crying, but say
Good-bye now, and put to sea.
   Farewell, dear friend, farewell: may
Hermes, master of the roads
And the four dwarf Kabiri,
   Protect and serve you always;
   And may the Ancient of Days
Provide for all you must do
   His invisible guidance,
Lifting up, friend, upon you
   The light of His countenance.

January 1941

In Sickness and in Health

(for Maurice and Gwen Mandelbaum)

Dear, all benevolence of fingering lips
That does not ask forgiveness is a noise
  At drunken feasts where Sorrow strips
To serve some glittering generalities:
Now, more than ever, we distinctly hear
The dreadful shuffle of a murderous year
And all our senses roaring as the Black
Dog leaps upon the individual back.

Whose sable genius understands too well
What code of famine can administrate
  Those inarticulate wastes where dwell
Our howling appetites: dear heart, do not
Think lightly to contrive his overthrow;
No, promise nothing, nothing, till you know
The kingdom offered by the love-lorn eyes
A land of condors, sick cattle, and dead flies.

And how contagious is its desolation,
What figures of destruction unawares
  Jump out on Love's imagination
And chase away the castles and the bears;
How warped the mirrors where our worlds are made;
What armies burn up honour, and degrade
Our will-to-order into thermal waste;
What goods are smashed that cannot be replaced.

Let no one say I Love until aware
What huge resources it will take to nurse
  One ruining spoek, one tiny hair
That casts a shadow through the universe:
We are the deaf immured within a loud
And foreign language of revolt, a crowd
Of poaching hands and mouths who out of fear
Have learned a safer life than we can bear.

Nature by nature in unnature ends:
Echoing each other like two waterfalls,
  Tristan, Isolde, the great friends,
Make passion out of passion's obstacles,
Deliciously postponing their delight,
Prolong frustration till it lasts all night,
Then perish lest Brangaene's worldly cry
Should sober their cerebral ecstasy.

But, dying, conjure up their opposite,
Don Juan, so terrified of death he hears
  Each moment recommending it
And knows no argument to counter theirs:
Trapped in their vile affections, he must find
Angels to keep him chaste; a helpless, blind,
Unhappy spook, he haunts the urinals,
Existing solely by their miracles.

247

That syllogistic nightmare must reject
The disobedient phallus for the sword;
    The lovers of themselves collect,
And Eros is politically adored:
New Machiavellis, flying through the air,
Express a metaphysical despair,
Murder their last voluptuous sensation,
All passion in one passionate negation.

Beloved, we are always in the wrong,
Handling so clumsily our stupid lives,
    Suffering too little or too long,
Too careful even in our selfish loves:
The decorative manias we obey
Die in grimaces round us every day,
Yet through their tohu-bohu comes a voice
Which utters an absurd command—Rejoice.

Rejoice. What talent for the makeshift thought
A living corpus out of odds and ends?
    What pedagogic patience taught
Pre-occupied and savage elements
To dance into a segregated charm?
Who showed the whirlwind how to be an arm,
And gardened from the wilderness of space
The sensual properties of one dear face?

Rejoice, dear love, in Love's peremptory word;
All chance, all love, all logic, you and I,
    Exist by grace of the Absurd,
And without conscious artifice we die:
So, lest we manufacture in our flesh
The lie of our divinity afresh,
Describe round our chaotic malice now,
The arbitrary circle of a vow.

That reason may not force us to commit
That sin of the high-minded, sublimation,
    Which damns the soul by praising it,
Force our desire, O Essence of creation,
To seek Thee always in Thy substances,
Till the performance of those offices
Our bodies, Thine opaque enigmas, do,
Configure Thy transparent justice too.

Lest animal bias should decline our wish
For Thy perfection to identify
    Thee with Thy things, to worship fish,
Or solid apples, or the wavering sky,
Our intellectual motions with Thy light
To such intense vibration, Love, excite,
That we give forth a quiet none can tell
From that in which the lichens live so well.

That this round O of faithfulness we swear
May never wither to an empty nought
   Nor petrify into a square,
Mere habits of affection freeze our thought
In their inert society, lest we
Mock virtue with its pious parody
And take our love for granted, Love permit
Temptations always to endanger it.

Lest, blurring with old moonlight of romance
The landscape of our blemishes, we try
   To set up shop on Goodwin Sands,
That we, though lovers, may love soberly,
O Fate, O *Felix Osculum*, to us
Remain nocturnal and mysterious:
Preserve us from presumption and delay,
And hold us to the ordinary way.

                        1940

Many Happy Returns
(for John Rettger)

Johnny, since to-day is
February the twelfth when
Neighbours and relations
   Think of you and wish,
Though a staunch Aquarian,
Graciously accept the
Verbal celebrations
   Of a doubtful Fish.

Seven years ago you
Warmed your mother's heart by
Making a successful
   Début on our stage;
Naïveté's an act that
You already know you
Cannot get away with
   Even at your age.

So I wish you first a
Sense of theatre; only
Those who love illusion
   And know it will go far:
Otherwise we spend our
Lives in a confusion
Of what we say and do with
   Who we really are.

You will any day now
Have this revelation:
'Why, we're all like people
   Acting in a play.'

249

And will suffer, Johnny,
Man's unique temptation
Precisely at the moment
    You utter this cliché.

Remember if you can then,
Only the All-Father
Can change the cast or give them
    Easier lines to say;
Deliberate interference
With others for their own good
Is not allowed the author
    Of the play within The Play.

Just because our pride's an
Evil there's no end to,
Birthdays and the arts are
    Justified, for when
We consciously pretend to
Own the earth or play at
Being gods, thereby we
    Own that we are men.

As a human creature
You will all too often
Forget your proper station,
    Johnny, like us all;
Therefore let your birthday
Be a wild occasion
Like a Saturnalia
    Or a Servants' Ball.

What else shall I wish you?
Following convention
Shall I wish you Beauty,
    Money, Happiness?
Or anything you mention?
No, for I recall an
Ancient proverb:—Nothing
    Fails like a success.

What limping devil sets our
Head and heart at variance,
That each time the Younger
    Generation sails,
The old and weather-beaten
Deny their own experience
And pray the gods to send them
    Calm seas, auspicious gales?

I'm not such an idiot
As to claim the power
To peer into the vistas
    Of your future, still

I'm prepared to guess you
Have not found your life as
Easy as your sister's
    And you never will.

If I'm right about this,
May you in your troubles,
Neither (like so many
    In the U.S.A.)
Be ashamed of any
Suffering as vulgar,
Nor bear them like a hero
    In the biggest way.

All the possibilities
It had to reject are
What give life and warmth to
    An actual character;
The roots of wit and charm tap
Secret springs of sorrow,
Every brilliant doctor
    Hides a murderer.

Then, since all self-knowledge
Tempts man into envy,
May you, by acquiring
    Proficiency in what
Whitehead calls the art of
Negative Prehension,
Love without desiring
    All that you are not.

Tao is a tightrope,
So to keep your balance,
May you always, Johnny,
    Manage to combine
Intellectual talents
With a sensual gusto,
The Socratic Doubt with
    The Socratic Sign.

That is all that I can
Think of at this moment
And it's time I brought these
    Verses to a close:
Happy Birthday, Johnny,
Live beyond your income,
Travel for enjoyment,
    Follow your own nose.

February 1942

Mundus et Infans

(for Albert and Angelyn Stevens)

Kicking his mother until she let go of his soul
Has given him a healthy appetite: clearly, her rôle
   In the New Order must be
To supply and deliver his raw materials free;
   Should there be any shortage,
She will be held responsible; she also promises
To show him all such attentions as befit his age.
   Having dictated peace,

With one fist clenched behind his head, heel drawn up to thigh
The cocky little ogre dozes off, ready,
   Though, to take on the rest
Of the world at the drop of a hat or the mildest
   Nudge of the impossible,
Resolved, cost what it may, to seize supreme power and
Sworn to resist tyranny to the death with all
   Forces at his command.

A pantheist not a solipsist, he co-operates
With a universe of large and noisy feeling-states
   Without troubling to place
Them anywhere special, for, to his eyes, Funnyface
   Or Elephant as yet
Mean nothing. His distinction between Me and Us
Is a matter of taste; his seasons are Dry and Wet;
   He thinks as his mouth does.

Still, his loud iniquity is still what only the
Greatest of saints become—someone who does not lie:
   He because he cannot
Stop the vivid present to think, they by having got
   Past reflection into
A passionate obedience in time. We have our Boy-
Meets-Girl era of mirrors and muddle to work through,
   Without rest, without joy.

Therefore we love him because his judgments are so
Frankly subjective that his abuse carries no
   Personal sting. We should
Never dare offer our helplessness as a good
   Bargain, without at least
Promising to overcome a misfortune we blame
History or Banks or the Weather for: but this beast
   Dares to exist without shame.

Let him praise our Creator with the top of his voice,
Then, and the motions of his bowels; let us rejoice
   That he lets us hope, for
He may never become a fashionable or
   Important personage:
However bad he may be, he has not yet gone mad;
Whoever we are now, we were no worse at his age;
   So of course we ought to be glad

When he bawls the house down. Has he not a perfect right
To remind us at every moment how we quite
    Rightly expect each other
To go upstairs or for a walk, if we must cry over
    Spilt milk, such as our wish
That, since apparently we shall never be above
Either or both, we had never learned to distinguish
    Between hunger and love?

? August 1942

Few and Simple

Whenever you are thought, the mind
Amazes me with all the kind
Old such-and-such it says about you
As if I were the one that you
Attach unique importance to,
Not one who would but didn't get you.

Startling us both at certain hours,
The flesh that mind insists is ours,
Though I, for one, by now know better,
Gets ready for no-matter-what
As if it had forgotten that
What happens is another matter.

Few as they are, these facts are all
The richest moment can recall,
However it may choose to group them,
And, simple as they look, enough
To make the most ingenious love
Think twice of trying to escape them.

February 1944

The Lesson

The first time that I dreamed, we were in flight,
And fagged with running; there was civil war,
A valley full of thieves and wounded bears.

Farms blazed behind us; turning to the right,
We came at once to a tall house, its door
Wide open, waiting for its long-lost heirs.

An elderly clerk sat on the bedroom stairs
Writing; but we had tiptoed past him when
He raised his head and stuttered—'Go away'.
We wept and begged to stay:
He wiped his pince-nez, hesitated, then
Said no, he had no power to give us leave;
Our lives were not in order; we must leave.

*   *   *

The second dream began in a May wood;
We had been laughing; your blue eyes were kind,
Your excellent nakedness without disdain.

Our lips met, wishing universal good;
But, on their impact, sudden flame and wind
Fetched you away and turned me loose again

To make a focus for a wide wild plain,
Dead level and dead silent and bone dry,
Where nothing could have suffered, sinned, or grown.
On a high chair alone
I sat, a little master, asking why
The cold and solid object in my hands
Should be a human hand, one of your hands.

*   *   *

And the last dream was this: we were to go
To a great banquet and a Victory Ball
After some tournament or dangerous test.

Our cushions were of crimson velvet, so
We must have won; though there were crowns for all,
Ours were of gold, of paper all the rest.

Fair, wise or funny was each famous guest,
Love smiled at Courage over priceless glass,
And rockets died in hundreds to express
Our learned carelessness.
A band struck up; all over the green grass
A sea of paper crowns rose up to dance:
Ours were too heavy; we did not dance.

*   *   *

I woke. You were not there. But as I dressed
Anxiety turned to shame, feeling all three
Intended one rebuke. For had not each
In its own way tried to teach
My will to love you that it cannot be,
As I think, of such consequence to want
What anyone is given, if they want?

October 1942

A Healthy Spot

They're nice—one would never dream of going over
Any contract of theirs with a magnifying
Glass, or of locking up one's letters—also
Kind and efficient—one gets what one asks for.
Just what is wrong, then, that, living among them,

254

One is constantly struck by the number of
Happy marriages and unhappy people?
They attend all the lectures on Post-War Problems,
For they do mind, they honestly want to help; yet,
As they notice the earth in their morning papers,
What sense do they make of its folly and horror
Who have never, one is convinced, felt a sudden
Desire to torture the cat or do a strip-tease
In a public place? Have they ever, one wonders,
Wanted so much to see a unicorn, even
A dead one? Probably. But they won't say so,
Ignoring by tacit consent our hunger
For eternal life, that caged rebuked question
Occasionally let out at clambakes or
College reunions, and which the smoking-room story
Alone, ironically enough, stands up for.

? February 1944

The Model

Generally, reading palms or handwriting or faces
   Is a job of translation, since the kind
      Gentleman often is
   A seducer, the frowning schoolgirl may
      Be dying to be asked to stay;
But the body of this old lady exactly indicates her mind;

Rorschach or Binet could not add to what a fool can see
   From the plain fact that she is alive and well;
      For when one is eighty
   Even a teeny-weeny bit of greed
      Makes one very ill indeed,
And a touch of despair is instantaneously fatal:

Whether the town once drank bubbly out of her shoes or whether
   She was a governess with a good name
      In Church circles, if her
   Husband spoiled her or if she lost her son,
      Is by this time all one.
She survived whatever happened; she forgave; she became.

So the painter may please himself; give her an English park,
   Rice-fields in China, or a slum tenement;
      Make the sky light or dark;
   Put green plush behind her or a red brick wall.
      She will compose them all,
Centring the eye on their essential human element.

1942

Canzone

When shall we learn, what should be clear as day,
We cannot choose what we are free to love?
Although the mouse we banished yesterday
Is an enraged rhinoceros today,
Our value is more threatened than we know:
Shabby objections to our present day
Go snooping round its outskirts; night and day
Faces, orations, battles, bait our will
As questionable forms and noises will;
Whole phyla of resentments every day
Give status to the wild men of the world
Who rule the absent-minded and this world.

We are created from and with the world
To suffer with and from it day by day:
Whether we meet in a majestic world
Of solid measurements or a dream world
Of swans and gold, we are required to love
All homeless objects that require a world.
Our claim to own our bodies and our world
Is our catastrophe. What can we know
But panic and caprice until we know
Our dreadful appetite demands a world
Whose order, origin, and purpose will
Be fluent satisfaction of our will?

Drift, Autumn, drift; fall, colours, where you will:
Bald melancholia minces through the world.
Regret, cold oceans, the lymphatic will
Caught in reflection on the right to will:
While violent dogs excite their dying day
To bacchic fury; snarl, though, as they will,
Their teeth are not a triumph for the will
But utter hesitation. What we love
Ourselves for is our power not to love,
To shrink to nothing or explode at will,
To ruin and remember that we know
What ruins and hyaenas cannot know.

If in this dark now I less often know
That spiral staircase where the haunted will
Hunts for its stolen luggage, who should know
Better than you, beloved, how I know
What gives security to any world,
Or in whose mirror I begin to know
The chaos of the heart as merchants know
Their coins and cities, genius its own day?
For through our lively traffic all the day,
In my own person I am forced to know
How much must be forgotten out of love,
How much must be forgiven, even love.

Dear flesh, dear mind, dear spirit, dearest love,
In the depths of myself blind monsters know
Your presence and are angry, dreading Love
That asks its images for more than love;
The hot rampageous horses of my will,
Catching the scent of Heaven, whinny: Love
Gives no excuse to evil done for love,
Neither in you, nor me, nor armies, nor the world
Of words and wheels, nor any other world.
Dear fellow-creature, praise our God of Love
That we are so admonished, that no day
Of conscious trial be a wasted day.

Or else we make a scarecrow of the day,
Loose ends and jumble of our common world,
And stuff and nonsense of our own free will;
Or else our changing flesh may never know
There must be sorrow if there can be love.

September 1942

Anthem

Let us praise our Maker, with true passion extol Him.
Let the whole creation give out another sweetness,
Nicer in our nostrils, a novel fragrance
From cleansed occasions in accord together
As one feeling fabric, all flushed and intact,
Phenomena and numbers announcing in one
Multitudinous oecumenical song
Their grand giveness of gratitude and joy,
Peaceable and plural, their positive truth
An authoritative This, an unthreatened Now
When, in love and in laughter, each lives itself,
For, united by His Word, cognition and power,
System and Order, are a single glory,
And the pattern is complex, their places safe.

? 1945

The Fall of Rome
(for Cyril Connolly)

The piers are pummelled by the waves;
In a lonely field the rain
Lashes an abandoned train;
Outlaws fill the mountain caves.

Fantastic grow the evening gowns;
Agents of the Fisc pursue
Absconding tax-defaulters through
The sewers of provincial towns.

257

Private rites of magic send
The temple prostitutes to sleep;
All the literati keep
An imaginary friend.

Cerebrotonic Cato may
Extol the Ancient Disciplines,
But the muscle-bound Marines
Mutiny for food and pay.

Caesar's double-bed is warm
As an unimportant clerk
Writes *I DO NOT LIKE MY WORK*
On a pink official form.

Unendowed with wealth or pity,
Little birds with scarlet legs,
Sitting on their speckled eggs,
Eye each flu-infected city.

Altogether elsewhere, vast
Herds of reindeer move across
Miles and miles of golden moss,
Silently and very fast.

? February 1947

Nursery Rhyme

Their learned kings bent down to chat with frogs;
This was until the Battle of the Bogs.
The key that opens is the key that rusts.

Their cheerful kings made toffee on their stoves;
This was until the Rotting of the Loaves.
The robins vanish when the ravens come.

That was before the coaches reached the bogs;
Now woolly bears pursue the spotted dogs.
A witch can make an ogre out of mud.

That was before the weevils ate the loaves;
Now blinded bears invade the orange groves.
A witch can make an ogre out of mud.

The woolly bears have polished off the dogs;
Our bowls of milk are full of drowning frogs.
The robins vanish when the ravens come.

The blinded bears have rooted up the groves;
Our poisoned milk boils over on our stoves.
The key that opens is the key that rusts.

January 1947

In Schrafft's

Having finished the Blue-plate Special
And reached the coffee stage,
Stirring her cup she sat,
A somewhat shapeless figure
Of indeterminate age
In an undistinguished hat.

When she lifted her eyes it was plain
That our globular furore,
Our international rout
Of sin and apparatus
And dying men galore,
Was not being bothered about.

Which of the seven heavens
Was responsible her smile
Wouldn't be sure but attested
That, whoever it was, a god
Worth kneeling-to for a while
Had tabernacled and rested.

July 1947

Under Which Lyre

A REACTIONARY TRACT FOR THE TIMES
(*Phi Beta Kappa Poem, Harvard, 1946*)

Ares at last has quit the field,
The bloodstains on the bushes yield
    To seeping showers,
And in their convalescent state
The fractured towns associate
    With summer flowers.

Encamped upon the college plain
Raw veterans already train
    As freshman forces;
Instructors with sarcastic tongue
Shepherd the battle-weary young
    Through basic courses.

Among bewildering appliances
For mastering the arts and sciences
    They stroll or run,
And nerves that steeled themselves to slaughter
Are shot to pieces by the shorter
    Poems of Donne.

Professors back from secret missions
Resume their proper eruditions,
        Though some regret it;
They liked their dictaphones a lot,
They met some big wheels, and do not
        Let you forget it.

But Zeus' inscrutable decree
Permits the will-to-disagree
        To be pandemic,
Ordains that vaudeville shall preach
And every commencement speech
        Be a polemic.

Let Ares doze, that other war
Is instantly declared once more
        'Twixt those who follow
Precocious Hermes all the way
And those who without qualms obey
        Pompous Apollo.

Brutal like all Olympic games,
Though fought with smiles and Christian names
        And less dramatic,
This dialectic strife between
The civil gods is just as mean,
        And more fanatic.

What high immortals do in mirth
Is life and death on Middle Earth;
        Their a-historic
Antipathy forever gripes
All ages and somatic types,
        The sophomoric

Who face the future's darkest hints
With giggles or with prairie squints
        As stout as Cortez,
And those who like myself turn pale
As we approach with ragged sail
        The fattening forties.

The sons of Hermes love to play,
And only do their best when they
        Are told they oughtn't;
Apollo's children never shrink
From boring jobs but have to think
        Their work important.

Related by antithesis,
A compromise between us is
        Impossible;
Respect perhaps but friendship never:
Falstaff the fool confronts forever
        The prig Prince Hal.

If he would leave the self alone,
Apollo's welcome to the throne,
    Fasces and falcons;
He loves to rule, has always done it;
The earth would soon, did Hermes run it,
    Be like the Balkans.

But jealous of our god of dreams,
His common-sense in secret schemes
    To rule the heart;
Unable to invent the lyre,
Creates with simulated fire
    Official art.

And when he occupies a college,
Truth is replaced by Useful Knowledge;
    He pays particular
Attention to Commercial Thought,
Public Relations, Hygiene, Sport,
    In his curricula.

Athletic, extrovert and crude,
For him, to work in solitude
    Is the offence,
The goal a populous Nirvana:
His shield bears this device: *Mens sana
    Qui mal y pense*.

Today his arms, we must confess,
From Right to Left have met success,
    His banners wave
From Yale to Princeton, and the news
From Broadway to the Book Reviews
    Is very grave.

His radio Homers all day long
In over-Whitmanated song
    That does not scan,
With adjectives laid end to end,
Extol the doughnut and commend
    The Common Man.

His, too, each homely lyric thing
On sport or spousal love or spring
    Or dogs or dusters,
Invented by some court-house bard
For recitation by the yard
    In filibusters.

To him ascend the prize orations
And sets of fugal variations
    On some folk-ballad,
While dietitians sacrifice
A glass of prune-juice or a nice
    Marsh-mallow salad.

Charged with his compound of sensational
Sex plus some undenominational
    Religious matter,
Enormous novels by co-eds
Rain down on our defenceless heads
    Till our teeth chatter.

In fake Hermetic uniforms
Behind our battle-line, in swarms
    That keep alighting,
His existentialists declare
That they are in complete despair,
    Yet go on writing.

No matter; He shall be defied;
White Aphrodite is on our side:
    What though his threat
To organize us grow more critical?
Zeus willing, we, the unpolitical,
    Shall beat him yet.

Lone scholars, sniping from the walls
Of learned periodicals,
    Our facts defend,
Our intellectual marines,
Landing in little magazines,
    Capture a trend.

By night our student Underground
At cocktail parties whisper round
    From ear to ear;
Fat figures in the public eye
Collapse next morning, ambushed by
    Some witty sneer.

In our morale must lie our strength:
So, that we may behold at length
    Routed Apollo's
Battalions melt away like fog,
Keep well the Hermetic Decalogue,
    Which runs as follows:—

Thou shalt not do as the dean pleases,
Thou shalt not write thy doctor's thesis
    On education,
Thou shalt not worship projects nor
Shalt thou or thine bow down before
    Administration.

Thou shalt not answer questionnaires
Or quizzes upon World-Affairs,
    Nor with compliance
Take any test. Thou shalt not sit
With statisticians nor commit
    A social science.

Thou shalt not be on friendly terms
With guys in advertising firms,
    Nor speak with such
As read the Bible for its prose,
Nor, above all, make love to those
    Who wash too much.

Thou shalt not live within thy means
Nor on plain water and raw greens.
    If thou must choose
Between the chances, choose the odd:
Read *The New Yorker*, trust in God;
    And take short views.

1946

Music is International
(*Phi Beta Kappa Poem, Columbia, 1947*)

Orchestras have so long been speaking
This universal language that the Greek
    And the Barbarian have both mastered
Its enigmatic grammar which at last
    Says all things well. But who is worthy?
What is sweet? What is sound? Much of the earth
    Is austere, her temperate regions
Swarming with cops and robbers; germs besiege
    The walled towns and among the living
The captured outnumber the fugitive.
    Where silence is coldest and darkest,
Among those staring blemishes that mark
    War's havocking slot, it is easy
To guess what dreams such vaulting cries release:
    The unamerican survivor
Hears angels drinking fruit-juice with their wives
    Or making money in an open
Unpolicied air. But what is our hope,
    As with an ostentatious rightness
These gratuitous sounds like water and light
    Bless the Republic? Do they sponsor
In us the mornes and motted mammelons,
    The sharp streams and sottering springs of
A commuter's wish, where each frescade rings
    With melodious booing and hooing
As some elegant lovejoy deigns to woo
    And nothing dreadful ever happened?
Probably yes. We are easy to trap,
    Being Adam's children, as thirsty
For mere illusion still as when the first
    Comfortable heresy crooned to
The proud flesh founded on the self-made wound,
    And what we find rousing or touching
Tells us little and confuses us much.
    As Shaw said—Music is the brandy

Of the damned. It was from the good old grand
    Composers the progressive kind of
Tyrant learned how to melt the legal mind
    With a visceral A-ha; fill a
Dwarf's ears with sforzandos and the dwarf will
    Believe he's a giant; the orchestral
Metaphor bamboozles the most oppressed
    —As a trombone the clerk will bravely
Go oompah-oompah to his minor grave—,
    So that today one recognises
The Machiavel by the hair in his eyes,
    His conductor's hands. Yet the jussive
Elohim are here too, asking for us
    Through the noise. To forgive is not so
Simple as it is made to sound; a lot
    Of time will be quite wasted, many
Promising days end badly, and again
    We shall offend: but let us listen
To the song which seems to absorb all this,
    For these halcyon structures are useful
As structures go—though not to be confused
    With anything really important
Like feeding strays or looking pleased when caught
    By a bore or a hideola;
Deserving nothing, the sensible soul
    Will rejoice at the sudden mansion
Of any joy; besides, there is a chance
    We may some day need very much to
Remember when we were happy—one such
    Future would be the exile's ending
With no graves to visit, no socks to mend,
    Another to be short of breath yet
Staying on to oblige, postponing death—
    Listen! Even the dinner waltz in
Its formal way is a voice that assaults
    International wrong, so quickly,
Completely delivering to the sick,
    Sad, soiled prosopon of our ageing
Present the perdition of all her rage.

? June 1947

The Duet

All winter long the huge sad lady
Sang to her warm house of the heart betrayed:
    Love lies delirious and a-dying,
The purlieus are shaken by his wild cry.
    But back across the fret dividing
His wildernesses from her floral side,
    All winter long a scrunty beggar
With one glass eye and one hickory leg,
    Stumping about half-drunk through stony
Ravines and over dead volcanic cones,
    Refused her tragic hurt, declaring

264

A happy passion to the freezing air,
  Turning his barrel-organ, playing
Lanterloo, my lovely, my First-of-May.

  Louder on nights when in cold glory
The full moon made its meditative tour,
  To rich chords from her grand black piano
She sang the disappointment that is Man
  For all her lawns and orchards: *Slowly*
The spreading ache bechills the rampant glow
  Of fortune-hunting blood, time conjures
The moskered ancestral tower to plunge
  From its fastidious cornice down to
The pigsties far below, the oaks turn brown,
  The cute little botts of the sailors
Are snapped up by the sea. But to her gale
  Of sorrow from the moonstruck darkness
That ragged runagate opposed his spark,
  For still his scrannel music-making
In tipsy joy across the gliddered lake,
  Praising for all those rocks and craters
The green refreshments of the watered state,
  Cried Nonsense to her large repining:
The windows have opened, a royal wine
  Is poured out for the subtle pudding;
Light Industry is humming in the wood
  And blue birds bless us from the fences:
We know the time and where to find our friends.

                        1947

Pleasure Island

What there is as a surround to our figures
  Is very old, very big,
Very formidable indeed; the ocean
  Stares right past us as though
No one here was worth drowning, and the eye, true
  Blue all summer, of the sky
Would not miss a huddle of huts related
  By planks, a dock, a state
Of undress and improvised abandon
  Upon unshadowed sand.
To send a cry of protest or a call for
  Protection up into all
Those dazzling miles, to add, however sincerely,
  One's occasional tear
To that volume, would be rather silly,
  Nor is there one small hill
For the hopeful to climb, one tree for the hopeless
  To sit under and mope;
The coast is a blur and without meaning
  The churches and routines

Which stopped there and never cared or dared to
   Cross over to interfere
With this outpost where nothing is wicked
   But to be sorry or sick,
But one thing unneighbourly, work. Sometimes
   A visitor may come
With notebooks intending to make its quiet
   Emptiness his ally
In accomplishing immortal chapters,
   But the hasty tap-tap-tap
Of his first day becomes by the second
   A sharp spasmodic peck
And by the third is extinct; we find him
   Next improving his mind
On the beach with a book, but the dozing
   Afternoon is opposed
To rhyme and reason and chamber music,
   The plain sun has no use
For the printing press, the wheel, the electric
   Light, and the waves reject
Sympathy: soon he gives in, stops stopping
   To think, lets his book drop
And lies, like us, on his stomach watching
   As bosom, backside, crotch
Or other sacred trophy is borne in triumph
   Past his adoring by
Souls he does not try to like; then, getting
   Up, gives all to the wet
Clasps of the sea or surrenders his scruples
   To some great gross braying group
That will be drunk till Fall. The tide rises
   And falls, our household ice
Drips to death in the dark and our friendships
   Prepare for a weekend
They will probably not survive: for our
   Lenient amusing shore
Knows in fact about all the dyings, is in
   Fact our place, namely this
Place of a skull, a place where the rose of
   Self-punishment will grow.
The sunset happens, the bar is copious
   With fervent life that hopes
To make sense, but down the beach some decaying
   Spirit shambles away,
Kicking idly at driftwood and dead shellfish
   And excusing itself
To itself with evangelical gestures
   For having failed the test:
The moon is up there, but without warning,
   A little before dawn,
Miss Lovely, life and soul of the party,
   Wakes with a dreadful start,
Sure that whatever—O God!—she is in for
   Is about to begin,

Or hearing, beyond the hushabye noises
  Of sea and Me, just a voice
Ask, as one might the time or a trifle
  Extra, her money and her life.

1948

A Walk After Dark

A cloudless night like this
Can set the spirit soaring:
After a tiring day
The clockwork spectacle is
Impressive in a slightly boring
Eighteenth-century way.

It soothed adolescence a lot
To meet so shameless a stare;
The things I did could not
Be so shocking as they said
If that would still be there
After the shocked were dead.

Now, unready to die
But already at the stage
When one starts to resent the young,
I am glad those points in the sky
May also be counted among
The creatures of middle-age.

It's cosier thinking of night
As more an Old People's Home
Than a shed for a faultless machine,
That the red pre-Cambrian light
Is gone like Imperial Rome
Or myself at seventeen.

Yet however much we may like
The stoic manner in which
The classical authors wrote,
Only the young and the rich
Have the nerve or the figure to strike
The lacrimae rerum note.

For the present stalks abroad
Like the past and its wronged again
Whimper and are ignored,
And the truth cannot be hid;
Somebody chose their pain,
What needn't have happened did.

Occurring this very night
By no established rule,
Some event may already have hurled
Its first little No at the right
Of the laws we accept to school
Our post-diluvian world:

But the stars burn on overhead,
Unconscious of final ends,
As I walk home to bed,
Asking what judgment waits
My person, all my friends,
And these United States.

August 1948

Part VII

For the Time Being

A Christmas Oratorio

IN MEMORIAM
CONSTANCE ROSALIE AUDEN
1869–1941

*What shall we say then? Shall we continue
in sin, that grace may abound? God forbid.*
                                        ROMANS VI

Advent

CHORUS

Darkness and snow descend;
The clock on the mantelpiece
Has nothing to recommend,
Nor does the face in the glass
Appear nobler than our own
As darkness and snow descend
On all personality.
Huge crowds mumble—'Alas,
Our angers do not increase,
Love is not what she used to be;'
Portly Caesar yawns—'I know;'
He falls asleep on his throne,
They shuffle off through the snow:
Darkness and snow descend.

SEMI-CHORUS

Can great Hercules keep his
Extraordinary promise
To reinvigorate the Empire?
Utterly lost, he cannot
Even locate his task but
Stands in some decaying orchard
Or the irregular shadow
Of a ruined temple, aware of
Being watched from the horrid mountains
By fanatical eyes yet
Seeing no one at all, only hearing
The silence softly broken
By the poisonous rustle
Of famishing Arachne.

CHORUS

Winter completes an age
With its thorough levelling;
Heaven's tourbillions of rage
Abolish the watchman's tower
And delete the cedar grove.
As winter completes an age,
The eyes huddle like cattle, doubt
Seeps into the pores and power
Ebbs from the heavy signet ring;
The prophet's lantern is out
And gone the boundary stone,
Cold the heart and cold the stove,
Ice condenses on the bone:
Winter completes an age.

SEMI-CHORUS

Outside the civil garden
Of every day of love there

Crouches a wild passion
   To destroy and be destroyed.
O who to boast their power
Have challenged it to charge? Like
Wheat our souls are sifted
   And cast into the void.

The evil and armed draw near;
The weather smells of their hate
And the houses smell of our fear;
Death has opened his white eye
And the black hole calls the thief
As the evil and armed draw near.
Ravens alight on the wall,
Our plans have all gone awry,
The rains will arrive too late,
Our resourceful general
Fell down dead as he drank
And his horses died of grief,
Our navy sailed away and sank;
The evil and armed draw near.

II
NARRATOR
If, on account of the political situation,
There are quite a number of homes without roofs, and men
Lying about in the countryside neither drunk nor asleep,
If all sailings have been cancelled till further notice,
If it's unwise now to say much in letters, and if,
Under the subnormal temperatures prevailing,
The two sexes are at present the weak and the strong,
That is not at all unusual for this time of year.
If that were all we should know how to manage. Flood, fire,
The desiccation of grasslands, restraint of princes,
Piracy on the high seas, physical pain and fiscal grief,
These after all are our familiar tribulations,
And we have been through them all before, many, many times.
As events which belong to the natural world where
The occupation of space is the real and final fact
And time turns round itself in an obedient circle,
They occur again and again but only to pass
Again and again into their formal opposites,
From sword to ploughshare, coffin to cradle, war to work,
So that, taking the bad with the good, the pattern composed
By the ten thousand odd things that can possibly happen
Is permanent in a general average way.

   Till lately we knew of no other, and between us we seemed
To have what it took—the adrenal courage of the tiger,
The chameleon's discretion, the modesty of the doe,
Or the fern's devotion to spatial necessity:
To practise one's peculiar civic virtue was not

So impossible after all; to cut our losses
And bury our dead was really quite easy: That was why
We were always able to say: 'We are children of God,
And our Father has never forsaken His people.'

    But then we were children: That was a moment ago,
Before an outrageous novelty had been introduced
Into our lives. Why were we never warned? Perhaps we were.
Perhaps that mysterious noise at the back of the brain
We noticed on certain occasions—sitting alone
In the waiting room of the country junction, looking
Up at the toilet window—was not indigestion
But this Horror starting already to scratch Its way in?
Just how, just when It succeeded we shall never know:
We can only say that now It is there and that nothing
We learnt before It was there is now of the slightest use,
For nothing like It has happened before. It's as if
We had left our house for five minutes to mail a letter,
And during that time the living room had changed places
With the room behind the mirror over the fireplace;
It's as if, waking up with a start, we discovered
Ourselves stretched out flat on the floor, watching our shadow
Sleepily stretching itself at the window. I mean
That the world of space where events re-occur is still there,
Only now it's no longer real; the real one is nowhere
Where time never moves and nothing can ever happen:
I mean that although there's a person we know all about
Still bearing our name and loving himself as before,
That person has become a fiction; our true existence
Is decided by no one and has no importance to love.

    That is why we despair; that is why we would welcome
The nursery bogey or the winecellar ghost, why even
The violent howling of winter and war has become
Like a juke-box tune that we dare not stop. We are afraid
Of pain but more afraid of silence; for no nightmare
Of hostile objects could be as terrible as this Void.
This is the Abomination. This is the wrath of God.

                         III
                        CHORUS
        Alone, alone, about a dreadful wood
        Of conscious evil runs a lost mankind,
        Dreading to find its Father lest it find
        The Goodness it has dreaded is not good:
        Alone, alone, about our dreadful wood.

        Where is that Law for which we broke our own,
        Where now that Justice for which Flesh resigned
        Her hereditary right to passion, Mind
        His will to absolute power? Gone. Gone.
        Where is that Law for which we broke our own?

                         273

The Pilgrim Way has led to the Abyss.
Was it to meet such grinning evidence
We left our richly odoured ignorance?
Was the triumphant answer to be this?
The Pilgrim Way has led to the Abyss.

We who must die demand a miracle.
How could the Eternal do a temporal act,
The Infinite become a finite fact?
Nothing can save us that is possible:
We who must die demand a miracle.

IV
RECITATIVE

If the muscle can feel repugnance, there is still a false move to be made;
If the mind can imagine tomorrow, there is still a defeat to remember;
As long as the self can say 'I', it is impossible not to rebel;
As long as there is an accidental virtue, there is a necessary vice:
And the garden cannot exist, the miracle cannot occur.

For the garden is the only place there is, but you will not find it
Until you have looked for it everywhere and found nowhere that is not a
    desert;
The miracle is the only thing that happens, but to you it will not be
    apparent,
Until all events have been studied and nothing happens that you cannot
    explain;
And life is the destiny you are bound to refuse until you have consented to
    die.

Therefore, see without looking, hear without listening, breathe without
    asking:
The Inevitable is what will seem to happen to you purely by chance;
The Real is what will strike you as really absurd;
Unless you are certain you are dreaming, it is certainly a dream of your
    own;
Unless you exclaim—'There must be some mistake'—you must be
    mistaken.

V
CHORUS

O where is that immortal and nameless Centre from which our points of
    Definition and death are all equi-distant? Where
The well of our wish to wander, the everlasting fountain
    Of the waters of joy that our sorrow uses for tears?
O where is the garden of Being that is only known in Existence
    As the command to be never there, the sentence by which
Alephs of throbbing fact have been banished into position,
    The clock that dismisses the moment into the turbine of time?

O would I could mourn over Fate like the others, the resolute creatures,
  By seizing my chance to regret. The stone is content
With a formal anger and falls and falls; the plants are indignant
  With one dimension only and can only doubt
Whether light or darkness lies in the worse direction; and the subtler
  Exiles who try every path are satisfied
With proving that none have a goal: why must Man also acknowledge
  It is not enough to bear witness, for even protest is wrong?

Earth is cooled and fire is quenched by his unique excitement,
  All answers expire in the clench of his questioning hand,
His singular emphasis frustrates all possible order:
  Alas, his genius is wholly for envy; alas,
The vegetative sadness of lakes, the locomotive beauty
  Of choleric beasts of prey, are nearer than he
To the dreams that deprive him of sleep, the powers that compel him to
    idle,
  To his amorous nymphs and his sanguine athletic gods.

How can his knowledge protect his desire for truth from illusion?
  How can he wait without idols to worship, without
Their overwhelming persuasion that somewhere, over the high hill,
  Under the roots of the oak, in the depths of the sea,
Is a womb or a tomb wherein he may halt to express some attainment?
  How can he hope and not dream that his solitude
Shall disclose a vibrating flame at last and entrust him forever
  With its magic secret of how to extemporize life?

The Annunciation

I

THE FOUR FACULTIES
Over the life of Man
We watch and wait,
The Four who manage
His fallen estate:
We who are four were
Once but one,
Before his act of
Rebellion;
We were himself when
His will was free,
His error became our
Chance to be.
Powers of air and fire,
Water and earth,
Into our hands is given
Man from his birth:

INTUITION
As a dwarf in the dark of
His belly I rest;

FEELING
A nymph, I inhabit
The heart in his breast;

SENSATION
A giant, at the gates of
His body I stand;

THOUGHT
His dreaming brain is
My fairyland.

TUTTI
Invisible phantoms,
The forms we assume are
Adapted to each
Individual humour,
Beautiful facts or true
Generalizations,
Test cases in Law or
Market quotations:
As figures and formulae
Chemists have seen us,
Who to true lovers were
Putti of Venus.

Ambiguous causes
Of all temptation,
We lure men either
To death or salvation:
We alone may look over
The wall of that hidden
Garden whose entrance
To him is forbidden;
Must truthfully tell him
What happens inside,
But what it may mean he
Alone must decide.

II
THOUGHT
The garden is unchanged, the silence is unbroken.
Truth has not yet intruded to possess
Its empty morning nor the promised hour
Shaken its lasting May.

INTUITION
            The human night,
Whose messengers we are, cannot dispel
Its wanton dreams, and they are all we know.

SENSATION

My senses are still coarse
From late engrossment in a fair. Old tunes
Reiterated, lights with repeated winks,
Were fascinated like a tic and brought
Whole populations running to a plain,
Making its lush alluvial meadows
One boisterous preposter. By the river
A whistling crowd had waited many hours
To see a naked woman swim upstream;
Honours and reckless medicines were served
In booths where interest was lost
As easily as money; at the back,
In a wet vacancy among the ash cans,
A waiter coupled sadly with a crow.

FEELING

I have but now escaped a raging landscape:
There woods were in a tremor from the shouts
Of hunchbacks hunting a hermaphrodite;
A burning village scampered down a lane;
Insects with ladders stormed a virgin's house;
On a green knoll littered with picnics
A mob of horses kicked a gull to death.

INTUITION

Remembrance of the moment before last
Is like a yawning drug. I have observed
The sombre valley of an industry
In dereliction. Conduits, ponds, canals,
Distressed with weeds; engines and furnaces
At rust in rotting sheds; and their strong users
Transformed to spongy heaps of drunken flesh.
Deep among duck and dusty nettle lay
Each ruin of a will; manors of mould
Grew into empires as a westering sun
Left the air chilly; not a sound disturbed
The autumn dusk except a stertorous snore
That over their drowned condition like a sea
Wept without grief.

THOUGHT

My recent company
Was worse than your three visions. Where I was,
The haunting ghosts were figures with no ground,
Areas of wide omission and vast regions
Of passive colour; higher than any squeak,
One note went on for ever; an embarrassed sum
Stuck on the stutter of a decimal,
And points almost coincident already
Approached so slowly they could never meet.
There nothing could be stated or constructed:
To Be was an archaic nuisance.

INTUITION

Look. There is someone in the garden.

FEELING

The garden is unchanged, the silence is unbroken
For she is still walking in her sleep of childhood:
Many before
Have wandered in, like her, then wandered out
Unconscious of their visit and unaltered,
The garden unchanged, the silence unbroken:
None may wake there but One who shall be woken.

THE ANGEL GABRIEL

Wake.

III

GABRIEL

Mary, in a dream of love
Playing as all children play,
For unsuspecting children may
Express in comic make-believe
The wish that later they will know
Is tragic and impossible;
Hear, child, what I am sent to tell:
Love wills your dream to happen, so
Love's will on earth may be, through you,
No longer a pretend but true.

MARY

What dancing joy would whirl
My ignorance away?
Light blazes out of the stone,
The taciturn water
Burst into music,
And warm wings throb within
The motionless rose:
What sudden rush of Power
Commands me to command?

GABRIEL

When Eve, in love with her own will,
Denied the will of Love and fell,
She turned the flesh Love knew so well
To knowledge of her love until
Both love and knowledge were of sin:
What her negation wounded, may
Your affirmation heal today;
Love's will requires your own, that in
The flesh whose love you do not know,
Love's knowledge into flesh may grow.

278

MARY

My flesh in terror and fire
Rejoices that the Word
Who utters the world out of nothing,
As a pledge of His word to love her
Against her will, and to turn
Her desperate longing to love,
Should ask to wear me,
From now to their wedding day,
For an engagement ring.

GABRIEL

Since Adam, being free to choose,
Chose to imagine he was free
To choose his own necessity,
Lost in his freedom, Man pursues
The shadow of his images:
Today the Unknown seeks the known;
What I am willed to ask, your own
Will has to answer; child, it lies
Within your power of choosing to
Conceive the Child who chooses you.

IV

SOLO AND CHORUS

Let number and weight rejoice
In this hour of their translation
Into conscious happiness:
For the whole in every part,
The truth at the proper centre
(*There's a Way. There's a Voice.*)
Of language and distress
Is recognized in her heart
Singing and dancing.

Let even the great rejoice.
Though buffeted by admirers
And arrogant as noon,
The rich and the lovely have seen
For an infinitesimal moment
(*There's a Way. There's a Voice.*)
In another's eye till their own
Reflection came between,
Singing and dancing.

Let even the small rejoice.
Though threatened from purple rostra
And dazed by the soldier's drum
Proclaiming total defeat,
The general loquacious Public
(*There's a Way. There's a Voice.*)
Have been puzzled and struck dumb,
Hearing in every street
Singing and dancing.

Let even the young rejoice.
Lovers at their betrayal
Weeping alone in the night,
Have fallen asleep as they heard,
Though too far off to be certain
(*There's a Way. There's a Voice.*)
They had not imagined it,
Sounds that made grief absurd,
Singing and dancing.

Let even the old rejoice.
The Bleak and the Dim, abandoned
By impulse and regret,
Are startled out of their lives;
For to footsteps long expected
(*There's a Way. There's a Voice.*)
Their ruins echo, yet
The Demolisher arrives
Singing and dancing.

The Temptation of St. Joseph

I

JOSEPH

My shoes were shined, my pants were cleaned and pressed,
And I was hurrying to meet
  My own true Love:
But a great crowd grew and grew
Till I could not push my way through,
  Because
A star had fallen down the street;
  When they saw who I was,
The police tried to do their best.

CHORUS [*off*]
Joseph, you have heard
What Mary says occurred;
Yes, it may be so.
Is it likely? No.

JOSEPH
The bar was gay, the lighting well-designed,
And I was sitting down to wait
  My own true Love:
A voice I'd heard before, I think,
Cried: 'This is on the House. I drink
  To him
Who does not know it is too late;'
  When I asked for the time,
Everyone was very kind.

CHORUS [*off*]
Mary may be pure,
But, Joseph, are you sure?
How is one to tell?
Suppose, for instance . . . Well . . .

JOSEPH
Through cracks, up ladders, into waters deep,
I squeezed, I climbed, I swam to save
  My own true Love:
Under a dead apple tree
I saw an ass; when it saw me
  It brayed;
A hermit sat in the mouth of a cave:
  When I asked him the way,
He pretended to be asleep.

CHORUS [*off*]
Maybe, maybe not.
But, Joseph, you know what
Your world, of course, will say
About you anyway.

JOSEPH
Where are you, Father, where?
Caught in the jealous trap
Of an empty house I hear
As I sit alone in the dark
Everything, everything,
The drip of the bathroom tap,
The creak of the sofa spring,
The wind in the air-shaft, all
Making the same remark
Stupidly, stupidly,
Over and over again.
Father, what have I done?
Answer me, Father, how
Can I answer the tactless wall
Or the pompous furniture now?
Answer them . . .

GABRIEL
    No, you must.

JOSEPH
How then am I to know,
Father, that you are just?
Give me one reason.

GABRIEL
    No.

JOSEPH
All I ask is one
Important and elegant proof

That what my Love had done
Was really at your will
And that your will is Love.

GABRIEL
No, you must believe;
Be silent, and sit still.

II
NARRATOR
    For the perpetual excuse
Of Adam for his fall—'My little Eve,
God bless her, did beguile me and I ate,'
    For his insistence on a nurse,
All service, breast, and lap, for giving Fate
Feminine gender to make girls believe
That they can save him, you must now atone,
    Joseph, in silence and alone;
While she who loves you makes you shake with fright,
Your love for her must tuck you up and kiss good night.

    For likening Love to war, for all
The pay-off lines of limericks in which
The weak resentful bar-fly shows his sting,
    For talking of their spiritual
Beauty to chorus-girls, for flattering
The features of old gorgons who are rich,
For the impudent grin and Irish charm
    That hides a cold will to do harm,
Today the roles are altered; you must be
The Weaker Sex whose passion is passivity.

    For those delicious memories
Cigars and sips of brandy can restore
To old dried boys, for gallantry that scrawls
    In idolatrous detail and size
A symbol of aggression on toilet walls,
For having reasoned—'Woman is naturally pure
Since she has no moustache,' for having said,
    'No woman has a business head,'
You must learn now that masculinity,
To Nature, is a non-essential luxury.

    Lest, finding it impossible
To judge its object now or throatily
Forgive it as eternal God forgives,
    Lust, tempted by this miracle
To more ingenious evil, should contrive
A heathen fetish from Virginity
To soothe the spiritual petulance
    Of worn-out rakes and maiden aunts,
Forgetting nothing and believing all,
You must behave as if this were not strange at all.

282

Without a change in look or word,
You both must act exactly as before;
Joseph and Mary shall be man and wife
   Just as if nothing had occurred.
There is one World of Nature and one Life;
Sin fractures the Vision, not the Fact; for
The Exceptional is always usual
   And the Usual exceptional.
To choose what is difficult all one's days
As if it were easy, that is faith. Joseph, praise.

III

SEMI-CHORUS

Joseph, Mary, pray for those
Misled by moonlight and the rose,
For all in our perplexity.
Lovers who hear a distant bell
That tolls from somewhere in their head
Across the valley of their dream—
'All those who love excessively
Foot or thigh or arm or face
Pursue a louche and fatuous fire
And stumble into Hell'—
Yet what can such foreboding seem
But intellectual talk
So long as bodies walk
An earth where Time and Space
Turn Heaven to a finite bed
And Love into desire?
Pray for us, enchanted with
The green Bohemia of that myth
Where knowledge of the flesh can take
The guilt of being born away,
Simultaneous passions make
One eternal chastity:
Pray for us romantics, pray.

BOYS' SEMI-CHORUS

Joseph, Mary, pray for us,
Independent embryos who,
Unconscious in another, do
Evil as each creature does
In every definite decision
To improve; for even in
The germ-cell's primary division
Innocence is lost and sin,
Already given as a fact,
Once more issues as an act.

SEMI-CHORUS

Joseph, Mary, pray for all
The proper and conventional
Of whom this world approves.

Pray for us whose married loves
Acquire so readily
The indolent fidelity
Of unaired beds, for us to whom
Domestic hatred can become
A habit-forming drug, whose will
To civil anarchy
Uses disease to disobey
And makes our private bodies ill.
O pray for our salvation
Who take the prudent way,
Believing we shall be exempted
From the general condemnation
Because our self-respect is tempted
To incest not adultery:
O pray for us, the bourgeoisie.

BOYS' SEMI-CHORUS

Joseph, Mary, pray
For us children as in play
Upon the nursery floor
We gradually explore
Our members till our jealous lives
Have worked through to a clear
But trivial idea
Of that whence each derives
A vague but massive feel
Of being individual.
O pray for our redemption; for
The will that occupies
Our sensual infancy
Already is mature
And could immediately
Beget upon our flesh far more
Expressions of its disbelief
Than we shall manage to conceive
In a long life of lies.

CHORUS

Blessed Woman,
Excellent Man,
Redeem for the dull the
Average Way,
That common ungifted
Natures may
Believe that their normal
Vision can
Walk to perfection.

The Summons

I
STAR OF THE NATIVITY

I am that star most dreaded by the wise,
For they are drawn against their will to me,
Yet read in my procession through the skies
The doom of orthodox sophrosyne:
I shall discard their major preservation,
All that they know so long as no one asks;
I shall deprive them of their minor tasks
In free and legal households of sensation,
Of money, picnics, beer, and sanitation.

Beware. All those who follow me are led
Onto that Glassy Mountain where are no
Footholds for logic, to that Bridge of Dread
Where knowledge but increases vertigo:
Those who pursue me take a twisting lane
To find themselves immediately alone
With savage water or unfeeling stone,
In labyrinths where they must entertain
Confusion, cripples, tigers, thunder, pain.

THE FIRST WISE MAN

To break down Her defences
    And profit from the vision
That plain men can predict through an
    Ascesis of their senses,
With rack and screw I put Nature through
    A thorough inquisition:
But She was so afraid that if I were disappointed
I should hurt Her more that Her answers were disjointed—
    I did. I didn't. I will. I won't.
She is just as big a liar, in fact, as we are.
    To discover how to be truthful now
    Is the reason I follow this star.

THE SECOND WISE MAN

My faith that in Time's constant
    Flow lay real assurance
Broke down on this analysis—
    At any given instant
All solids dissolve, no wheels revolve,
    And facts have no endurance—
And who knows if it is by design or pure inadvertence
That the Present destroys its inherited self-importance?
    With envy, terror, rage, regret,
We anticipate or remember but never are.
    To discover how to be living now
    Is the reason I follow this star.

THE THIRD WISE MAN

Observing how myopic
　　Is the Venus of the Soma,
The concept Ought would make, I thought,
　　Our passions philanthropic,
And rectify in the sensual eye
　　Both lens-flare and lens-coma:
But arriving at the Greatest Good by introspection
And counting the Greater Number, left no time for affection,
　　Laughter, kisses, squeezing, smiles:
And I learned why the learned are as despised as they are.
　　To discover how to be loving now
　　Is the reason I follow this star.

THE THREE WISE MEN

The weather has been awful,
　　The countryside is dreary,
Marsh, jungle, rock; and echoes mock,
　　Calling our hope unlawful;
But a silly song can help along
　　Yours ever and sincerely:
At least we know for certain that we are three old sinners,
That this journey is much too long, that we want our dinners,
　　And miss our wives, our books, our dogs,
But have only the vaguest idea why we are what we are.
　　To discover how to be human now
　　Is the reason we follow this star.

STAR OF THE NATIVITY

Descend into the fosse of Tribulation,
Take the cold hand of Terror for a guide;
Below you in its swirling desolation
Hear tortured Horror roaring for a bride:
O do not falter at the last request
But, as the huge deformed head rears to kill,
Answer its craving with a clear I Will;
Then wake, a child in the rose-garden, pressed
Happy and sobbing to your lover's breast.

II

NARRATOR

Now let the wife look up from her stove, the husband
Interrupt his work, the child put down its toy,
That His voice may be heard in our Just Society
　　Who under the sunlight
Of His calm, possessing the good earth, do well. Pray
Silence for Caesar: stand motionless and hear
In a concourse of body and concord of soul
　　His proclamation.

RECITATIVE

CITIZENS OF THE EMPIRE, GREETING. ALL MALE PERSONS WHO SHALL
HAVE ATTAINED THE AGE OF TWENTY-ONE YEARS OR OVER MUST

PROCEED IMMEDIATELY TO THE VILLAGE, TOWNSHIP, CITY, PRECINCT
OR OTHER LOCAL ADMINISTRATIVE AREA IN WHICH THEY WERE BORN
AND THERE REGISTER THEMSELVES AND THEIR DEPENDANTS IF ANY
WITH THE POLICE. WILFUL FAILURE TO COMPLY WITH THIS ORDER IS
PUNISHABLE BY CONFISCATION OF GOODS AND LOSS OF CIVIL RIGHTS.

NARRATOR
You have been listening to the voice of Caesar
Who overcame implacable Necessity
By His endurance and by His skill has subdued the
   Welter of Fortune.
It is meet, therefore, that, before dispersing
In pious equanimity to obey His orders,
With well-tuned instruments and grateful voices
   We should praise Caesar.

III
FUGAL-CHORUS
Great is Caesar: He has conquered Seven Kingdoms.
The First was the Kingdom of Abstract Idea:
Last night it was Tom, Dick and Harry; to-night it is S's with P's;
Instead of inflexions and accents
There are prepositions and word-order;
Instead of aboriginal objects excluding each other
There are specimens reiterating a type;
Instead of wood-nymphs and river-demons,
There is one unconditioned ground of Being.
Great is Caesar: God must be with Him.

Great is Caesar: He has conquered Seven Kingdoms.
The Second was the Kingdom of Natural Cause:
Last night it was Sixes and Sevens; to-night it is One and Two;
Instead of saying, 'Strange are the whims of the Strong,'
We say, 'Harsh is the Law but it is certain;'
Instead of building temples, we build laboratories;
Instead of offering sacrifices, we perform experiments;
Instead of reciting prayers, we note pointer-readings;
Our lives are no longer erratic but efficient.
Great is Caesar: God must be with Him.

Great is Caesar: He has conquered Seven Kingdoms.
The Third was the Kingdom of Infinite Number:
Last night it was Rule-of-Thumb, to-night it is To-a-T;
Instead of Quite-a-lot, there is Exactly-so-many;
Instead of Only-a-few, there is Just-these;
Instead of saying, 'You must wait until I have counted,'
We say, 'Here you are. You will find this answer correct;'
Instead of a nodding acquaintance with a few integers,
The Transcendentals are our personal friends.
Great is Caesar: God must be with Him.

Great is Caesar: He has conquered Seven Kingdoms.
The Fourth was the Kingdom of Credit Exchange:
Last night it was Tit-for-Tat, to-night it is C.O.D.;
When we have a surplus, we need not meet someone with a deficit;
When we have a deficit, we need not meet someone with a surplus;
Instead of heavy treasures, there are paper symbols of value;
Instead of Pay at Once, there is Pay when you can;
Instead of My Neighbour, there is Our Customers;
Instead of Country Fair, there is World Market.
Great is Caesar: God must be with Him.

Great is Caesar: He has conquered Seven Kingdoms.
The Fifth was the Kingdom of Inorganic Giants:
Last night it was Heave-Ho, to-night it is Whee-Spree;
When we want anything, They make it;
When we dislike anything, They change it;
When we want to go anywhere, They carry us;
When the Barbarian invades us, They raise immovable shields;
When we invade the Barbarian, They brandish irresistible swords;
Fate is no longer a fiat of Matter, but a freedom of Mind.
Great is Caesar: God must be with Him.

Great is Caesar: He has conquered Seven Kingdoms.
The Sixth was the Kingdom of Organic Dwarfs:
Last night it was Ouch-Ouch, to-night it is Yum-Yum;
When diseases waylay us, They strike them dead;
When worries intrude on us, They throw them out;
When pain accosts us, They save us from embarrassment;
When we feel like sheep, They make us lions;
When we feel like geldings, They make us stallions;
Spirit is no longer under Flesh, but on top.
Great is Caesar: God must be with Him.

Great is Caesar: He has conquered Seven Kingdoms.
The Seventh was the Kingdom of Popular Soul:
Last night it was Order-Order, to-night it is Hear-Hear;
When he says, You are happy, we laugh;
When he says, You are wretched, we cry;
When he says, It is true, everyone believes it;
When he says, It is false, no one believes it;
When he says, This is good, this is loved;
When he says, That is bad, that is hated.
Great is Caesar: God must be with Him.

IV
NARRATOR

These are stirring times for the editors of newspapers:
History is in the making; Mankind is on the march.
The longest aqueduct in the world is already
Under construction; the Committees on Fen-Drainage
And Soil-Conservation will issue very shortly
Their Joint Report; even the problems of Trade Cycles
And Spiralling Prices are regarded by the experts

As practically solved; and the recent restrictions
Upon aliens and free-thinking Jews are beginning
To have a salutary effect upon public morale.
True, the Western seas are still infested with pirates,
And the rising power of the Barbarian in the North
Is giving some cause for uneasiness; but we are fully
Alive to these dangers; we are rapidly arming; and both
Will be taken care of in due course: then, united
In a sense of common advantage and common right,
Our great Empire shall be secure for a thousand years.
   If we were never alone or always too busy,
Perhaps we might even believe what we know is not true:
But no one is taken in, at least not all of the time;
In our bath, or the subway, or the middle of the night,
We know very well we are not unlucky but evil,
That the dream of a Perfect State or No State at all,
To which we fly for refuge, is a part of our punishment.
   Let us therefore be contrite but without anxiety,
For Powers and Times are not gods but mortal gifts from God;
Let us acknowledge our defeats but without despair,
For all societies and epochs are transient details,
Transmitting an everlasting opportunity
That the Kingdom of Heaven may come, not in our present
And not in our future, but in the Fullness of Time.
Let us pray.

V

CHORALE

Our Father, whose creative Will
   Asked Being for us all,
Confirm it that Thy Primal Love
May weave in us the freedom of
The actually deficient on
   The justly actual.

Though written by Thy children with
   A smudged and crooked line,
Thy Word is ever legible,
Thy Meaning unequivocal,
And for Thy Goodness even sin
   Is valid as a sign.

Inflict Thy promises with each
   Occasion of distress,
That from our incoherence we
May learn to put our trust in Thee,
And brutal fact persuade us to
   Adventure, Art, and Peace.

The Vision of the Shepherds

I

THE FIRST SHEPHERD

The winter night requires our constant attention,
  Watching that water and good-will,
Warmth and well-being, may still be there in the morning.

THE SECOND SHEPHERD

For behind the spontaneous joy of life
There is always a mechanism to keep going,

THE THIRD SHEPHERD

And someone like us is always there.

THE FIRST SHEPHERD

We observe that those who assure us their education
  And money would do us such harm,
How real we are just as we are, and how they envy us,
  For it is the centreless tree
And the uncivilized robin who are the truly happy,
  Have done pretty well for themselves:

THE SECOND SHEPHERD

Nor can we help noticing how those who insist that
  We ought to stand up for our rights,
And how important we are, keep insisting also
  That it doesn't matter a bit
If one of us gets arrested or injured, for
  It is only our numbers that count.

THE THIRD SHEPHERD

In a way they are right,

THE FIRST SHEPHERD

                    But to behave like a cogwheel
When one knows one is no such thing,

THE SECOND SHEPHERD

Merely to add to a crowd with one's passionate body,
  Is not a virtue.

THE THIRD SHEPHERD

                    What is real
About us all is that each of us is waiting.

THE FIRST SHEPHERD

That is why we are able to bear
Ready-made clothes, second-hand art and opinions
  And being washed and ordered about;

THE SECOND SHEPHERD

That is why you should not take our conversation
  Too seriously, nor read too much

Into our songs;

THE THIRD SHEPHERD
Their purpose is mainly to keep us
From watching the clock all the time.

THE FIRST SHEPHERD
For, though we cannot say why, we know that something
    Will happen:

THE SECOND SHEPHERD
What we cannot say,

THE THIRD SHEPHERD
Except that it will not be a reporter's item
    Of unusual human interest;

THE FIRST SHEPHERD
That always means something unpleasant.

THE SECOND SHEPHERD
                                But one day or
The next we shall hear the Good News.

II
THE THREE SHEPHERDS
Levers nudge the aching wrist:
    'You are free
    Not to be,
    Why exist?'
Wheels a thousand times a minute
    Mutter, stutter,
'End the self you cannot mend,
Did you, friend, begin it?'
    And the streets
    Sniff at our defeats.
Then who is the Unknown
Who answers for our fear
As if it were His own,
So that we reply
Till the day we die:
'No, I don't know why,
But I'm glad I'm here'?

III
CHORUS OF ANGELS
Unto you a Child,
A Son is given.
Praising, proclaiming
The ingression of Love,
Earth's darkness invents
The blaze of Heaven,

291

And frigid silence
Meditates a song;
For great joy has filled
The narrow and the sad,
While the emphasis
Of the rough and big,
The abiding crag
And wandering wave,
Is on forgiveness:
Sing Glory to God
And good-will to men,
All, all, all of them.
Run to Bethlehem.

SHEPHERDS
Let us run to learn
How to love and run;
Let us run to Love.

CHORUS
Now all things living,
Domestic or wild,
With whom you must share
Light, water, and air,
And suffer and shake
In physical need,
The sullen limpet,
The exuberant weed,
The mischievous cat,
And the timid bird,
Are glad for your sake
As the new-born Word
Declares that the old
Authoritarian
Constraint is replaced
By His Covenant,
And a city based
On love and consent
Suggested to men,
All, all, all of them.
Run to Bethlehem.

SHEPHERDS
Let us run to learn
How to love and run;
Let us run to Love.

CHORUS
The primitive dead
Progress in your blood,
And generations
Of the unborn, all
Are leaping for joy
In your veins today

When the Many shall,
Once in your common
Certainty of this
Child's lovableness,
Resemble the One,
That after today
The children of men
May be certain that
The Father Abyss
Is affectionate
To all Its creatures,
All, all, all of them,
Run to Bethlehem.

At the Manger

I

MARY

O shut your bright eyes that mine must endanger
With their watchfulness; protected by its shade
Escape from my care: what can you discover
From my tender look but how to be afraid?
Love can but confirm the more it would deny.
  Close your bright eye.

Sleep. What have you learned from the womb that bore you
But an anxiety your Father cannot feel?
Sleep. What will the flesh that I gave do for you,
Or my mother love, but tempt you from His will?
Why was I chosen to teach His Son to weep?
  Little One, sleep.

Dream. In human dreams earth ascends to Heaven
Where no one need pray nor ever feel alone.
In your first few hours of life here, O have you
Chosen already what death must be your own?
How soon will you start on the Sorrowful Way?
  Dream while you may.

II

FIRST WISE MAN

Led by the light of an unusual star,
We hunted high and low.

SECOND WISE MAN

            Have travelled far,
For many days, a little group alone
With doubts, reproaches, boredom, the unknown.

THIRD WISE MAN

Through stifling gorges.

FIRST WISE MAN
          Over level lakes,

SECOND WISE MAN
Tundras intense and irresponsive seas.

THIRD WISE MAN
In vacant crowds and humming silences,

FIRST WISE MAN
By ruined arches and past modern shops,

SECOND WISE MAN
Counting the miles,

THIRD WISE MAN
          And the absurd mistakes.

THE THREE WISE MEN
O here and now our endless journey stops.

FIRST SHEPHERD
We never left the place where we were born,

SECOND SHEPHERD
Have only lived one day, but every day,

THIRD SHEPHERD
Have walked a thousand miles yet only worn
The grass between our work and home away.

FIRST SHEPHERD
Lonely we were though never left alone.

SECOND SHEPHERD
The solitude familiar to the poor
Is feeling that the family next door,
The way it talks, eats, dresses, loves, and hates,
Is indistinguishable from one's own.

THIRD SHEPHERD
Tonight for the first time the prison gates
Have opened.

FIRST SHEPHERD
          Music and sudden light

SECOND SHEPHERD
Have interrupted our routine tonight,

THIRD SHEPHERD
And swept the filth of habit from our hearts.

THE THREE SHEPHERDS
O here and now our endless journey starts.

WISE MEN
Our arrogant longing to attain the tomb,

SHEPHERDS
Our sullen wish to go back to the womb,

WISE MEN
To have no past,

SHEPHERDS
No future,

TUTTI
Is refused.
And yet, without our knowledge, Love has used
Our weakness as a guard and guide.
We bless

WISE MEN
Our lives' impatience.

SHEPHERDS
Our lives' laziness,

TUTTI
And bless each other's sin, exchanging here

WISE MEN
Exceptional conceit

SHEPHERDS
With average fear.

TUTTI
Released by Love from isolating wrong,
Let us for Love unite our various song,
Each with his gift according to his kind
Bringing this child his body and his mind.

III
WISE MEN
Child, at whose birth we would do obsequy
For our tall errors of imagination,
Redeem our talents with your little cry.

SHEPHERDS
Clinging like sheep to the earth for protection,
We have not ventured far in any direction:
    Wean, Child, our ageing flesh away
    From its childish way.

WISE MEN

Love is more serious than Philosophy
Who sees no humour in her observation
That Truth is knowing that we know we lie.

SHEPHERDS

When, to escape what our memories are thinking,
We go out at nights and stay up drinking,
  Stay then with our sick pride and mind
  The forgetful mind.

WISE MEN

Love does not will enraptured apathy;
Fate plays the passive role of dumb temptation
To wills where Love can doubt, affirm, deny.

SHEPHERDS

When, chafing at the rule of old offences,
We run away to the sea of the senses,
  On strange beds then O welcome home
  Our horror of home.

WISE MEN

Love knows of no somatic tyranny;
For homes are built for Love's accommodation
By bodies from the void they occupy.

SHEPHERDS

When, exhausting our wills with our evil courses,
We demand the good-will of cards and horses,
  Be then our lucky certainty
  Of uncertainty.

WISE MEN

Love does not fear substantial anarchy,
But vividly expresses obligation
With movement and in spontaneity.

SHEPHERDS

When, feeling the great boots of the rich on our faces,
We live in the hope of one day changing places,
  Be then the truth of our abuse
  That we abuse.

WISE MEN

The singular is not Love's enemy;
Love's possibilities of realization
Require an Otherness that can say *I*.

SHEPHERDS

When in dreams the beasts and cripples of resentment
Rampage and revel to our hearts' contentment,
  Be then the poetry of hate
  That replaces hate.

Not In but With our time Love's energy
Exhibits Love's immediate operation;
The choice to love is open till we die.

SHEPHERDS
O Living Love, by your birth we are able
Not only, like the ox and ass of the stable,
　To love with our live wills, but love,
　Knowing we love.

TUTTI
O Living Love replacing phantasy,
O Joy of life revealed in Love's creation;
Our mood of longing turns to indication:
Space is the Whom our loves are needed by,
Time is our choice of How to love and Why.

The Meditation of Simeon

SIMEON
　As long as the apple had not been entirely digested, as long as there remained the least understanding between Adam and the stars, rivers and horses with whom he had once known complete intimacy, as long as Eve could share in any way with the moods of the rose or the ambitions of the swallow, there was still a hope that the effects of the poison would wear off, that the exile from Paradise was only a bad dream, that the Fall had not occurred in fact.

CHORUS
When we woke, it was day; we went on weeping

SIMEON
　As long as there were any roads to amnesia and anaesthesia still to be explored, any rare wine or curiosity of cuisine as yet untested, any erotic variation as yet unimagined or unrealized, any method of torture as yet undevised, any style of conspicuous waste as yet unindulged, any eccentricity of mania or disease as yet unrepresented, there was still a hope that man had not been poisoned but transformed, that Paradise was not an eternal state from which he had been forever expelled, but a childish state which he had permanently outgrown, that the Fall had occurred by necessity.

CHORUS
We danced in the dark, but were not deceived.

SIMEON
　As long as there were any experiments still to be undertaken in restoring that order in which desire had once rejoiced to be reflected, any

code of equity and obligation upon which some society had not yet been founded, any species of property of which the value had not yet been appreciated, any talent that had not yet won private devotion and public honour, any rational concept of the Good or intuitive feeling for the Holy that had not yet found its precise and beautiful expression, any technique of contemplation or ritual of sacrifice and praise that had not yet been properly conducted, any faculty of mind or body that had not yet been thoroughly disciplined, there was still a hope that some antidote might be found, that the gates of Paradise had indeed slammed to, but with the exercise of a little patience and ingenuity could be unlocked, that the Fall had occurred by accident.

CHORUS

Lions came loping into the lighted city.

SIMEON

Before the Positive could manifest Itself specifically, it was necessary that nothing should be left that negation could remove; the emancipation of Time from Space had first to be complete, the Revolution of the Images, in which the memories rose up and cast into subjection the senses by Whom hitherto they had been enslaved, successful beyond their wildest dreams, the mirror in which the Soul expected to admire herself so perfectly polished that her natural consolation of vagueness should be utterly withdrawn.

CHORUS

We looked at our Shadow, and, Lo, it was lame.

SIMEON

Before the Infinite could manifest Itself in the finite, it was necessary that man should first have reached that point along his road to Knowledge where, just as it rises from the swamps of Confusion onto the sunny slopes of Objectivity, it forks in opposite directions towards the One and the Many; where, therefore, in order to proceed at all, he must decide which is Real and which only Appearance, yet at the same time cannot escape the knowledge that his choice is arbitrary and subjective.

CHORUS

Promising to meet, we parted forever.

SIMEON

Before the Unconditional could manifest Itself under the conditions of existence, it was necessary that man should first have reached the ultimate frontier of consciousness, the secular limit of memory beyond which there remained but one thing for him to know, his Original Sin, but of this it is impossible for him to become conscious because it is itself what conditions his will to knowledge. For as long as he was in Paradise he could not sin by any conscious intention or act: his as yet unfallen will could only rebel against the truth by taking flight into an unconscious lie; he could only eat of the Tree of Knowledge of Good and Evil by forgetting that its existence was a fiction of the Evil One, that there is only the Tree of Life.

CHORUS
The bravest drew back on the brink of the Abyss.

SIMEON

From the beginning until now God spoke through his prophets. The Word aroused the uncomprehending depths of their flesh to a witnessing fury, and their witness was this: that the Word should be made Flesh. Yet their witness could only be received as long as it was vaguely misunderstood, as long as it seemed either to be neither impossible nor necessary, or necessary but not impossible, or impossible but not necessary; and the prophecy could not therefore be fulfilled. For it could only be fulfilled when it was no longer possible to receive, because it was clearly understood as absurd. The Word could not be made Flesh until men had reached a state of absolute contradiction between clarity and despair in which they would have no choice but either to accept absolutely or to reject absolutely, yet in their choice there should be no element of luck, for they would be fully conscious of what they were accepting or rejecting.

CHORUS
The eternal spaces were congested and depraved.

SIMEON

But here and now the Word which is implicit in the Beginning and in the End is become immediately explicit, and that which hitherto we could only passively fear as the incomprehensible I AM, henceforth we may actively love with comprehension that THOU ART. Wherefore, having seen Him, not in some prophetic vision of what might be, but with the eyes of our own weakness as to what actually is, we are bold to say that we have seen our salvation.

CHORUS
Now and forever, we are not alone.

SIMEON

By the event of this birth the true significance of all other events is defined, for of every other occasion it can be said that it could have been different, but of this birth it is the case that it could in no way be other than it is. And by the existence of this Child, the proper value of all other existences is given, for of every other creature it can be said that it has extrinsic importance but of this Child it is the case that He is in no sense a symbol.

CHORUS
We have right to believe that we really exist.

SIMEON

By Him is dispelled the darkness wherein the fallen will cannot distinguish between temptation and sin, for in Him we become fully conscious of Necessity as our freedom to be tempted, and of Freedom as our necessity to have faith. And by Him is illuminated the time in which we execute those choices through which our freedom is realized or prevented, for the course of History is predictable in the degree to which

299

all men love themselves, and spontaneous in the degree to which each man loves God and through Him his neighbour.

CHORUS

The distresses of choice are our chance to be blessed.

SIMEON

Because in Him the Flesh is united to the Word without magical transformation, Imagination is redeemed from promiscuous fornication with her own images. The tragic conflict of Virtue with Necessity is no longer confined to the Exceptional Hero; for disaster is not the impact of a curse upon a few great families, but issues continually from the hubris of every tainted will. Every invalid is Roland defending the narrow pass against hopeless odds, every stenographer Brünnhilde refusing to renounce her lover's ring which came into existence through the renunciation of love.

Nor is the Ridiculous a species any longer of the Ugly; for since of themselves all men are without merit, all are ironically assisted to their comic bewilderment by the Grace of God. Every Cabinet Minister is the woodcutter's simple-minded son to whom the fishes and the crows are always whispering the whereabouts of the Dancing Water or the Singing Branch, every heiress the washerwoman's butter-fingered daughter on whose pillow the fairy keeps laying the herb that could cure the Prince's mysterious illness.

Nor is there any situation which is essentially more or less interesting than another. Every tea-table is a battlefield littered with old catastrophes and haunted by the vague ghosts of vast issues, every martyrdom an occasion for flip cracks and sententious oratory.

Because in Him all passions find a logical In-Order-That, by Him is the perpetual recurrence of Art assured.

CHORUS

Safe in His silence, our songs are at play.

SIMEON

Because in Him the Word is united to the Flesh without loss of perfection, Reason is redeemed from incestuous fixation on her own Logic, for the One and the Many are simultaneously revealed as real. So that we may no longer, with the Barbarians, deny the Unity, asserting that there are as many gods as there are creatures, nor, with the philosophers, deny the Multiplicity, asserting that God is One who has no need of friends and is indifferent to a World of Time and Quantity and Horror which He did not create, nor, with Israel, may we limit the co-inherence of the One and the Many to a special case, asserting that God is only concerned with and of concern to that People whom out of all that He created He has chosen for His own.

For the Truth is indeed One, without which is no salvation, but the possibilities of real knowledge are as many as are the creatures in the very real and most exciting universe that God creates with and for His love, and it is not Nature which is one public illusion, but we who have each our many private illusions about Nature.

Because in Him abstraction finds a passionate For-The-Sake-Of, by Him is the continuous development of Science assured.

Our lost Appearances are saved by His love.

SIMEON

And because of His visitation, we may no longer desire God as if He were lacking: our redemption is no longer a question of pursuit but of surrender to Him who is always and everywhere present. Therefore at every moment we pray that, following Him, we may depart from our anxiety into His peace.

CHORUS

Its errors forgiven, may our Vision come home.

The Massacre of the Innocents

I

HEROD

Because I am bewildered, because I must decide, because my decision must be in conformity with Nature and Necessity, let me honour those through whom my nature is by necessity what it is.

To Fortune—that I have become Tetrarch, that I have escaped assassination, that at sixty my head is clear and my digestion sound.

To my Father—for the means to gratify my love of travel and study.

To my Mother—for a straight nose.

To Eva, my coloured nurse—for regular habits.

To my brother, Sandy, who married a trapeze-artist and died of drink—for so refuting the position of the Hedonists.

To Mr. Stewart, nicknamed The Carp, who instructed me in the elements of geometry through which I came to perceive the errors of the tragic poets.

To Professor Lighthouse—for his lectures on The Peloponnesian War.

To the stranger on the boat to Sicily—for recommending to me Brown on Resolution.

To my secretary, Miss Button—for admitting that my speeches were inaudible.

There is no visible disorder. No crime—what could be more innocent than the birth of an artisan's child? Today has been one of those perfect winter days, cold, brilliant, and utterly still, when the bark of the shepherd's dog carries for miles, and the great wild mountains come up quite close to the city walls, and the mind feels intensely awake, and this evening as I stand at this window high up in the citadel there is nothing in the whole magnificent panorama of plain and mountains to indicate that the Empire is threatened by a danger more dreadful than any invasion of Tartars on racing camels or conspiracy of the Praetorian Guard.

Barges are unloading soil fertilizer at the river wharves. Soft drinks and sandwiches may be had in the inns at reasonable prices. Allotment gardening has become popular. The highway to the coast goes straight up over the mountains and the truck-drivers no longer carry guns. Things are beginning to take shape. It is a long time since anyone stole the park benches or murdered the swans. There are children in this province who have never seen a louse, shopkeepers who have never handled a counterfeit coin, women of forty who have never hidden in a ditch except for fun. Yes, in twenty years I have managed to do a little. Not enough, of course. There are villages only a few miles from here where they still believe in witches. There isn't a single town where a good bookshop would pay. One could count on the fingers of one hand the people capable of solving the problem of Achilles and the Tortoise. Still it is a beginning. In twenty years the darkness has been pushed back a few inches. And what, after all, is the whole Empire, with its few thousand square miles on which it is possible to lead the Rational Life, but a tiny patch of light compared with those immense areas of barbaric night that surround it on all sides, that incoherent wilderness of rage and terror, where Mongolian idiots are regarded as sacred and mothers who give birth to twins are instantly put to death, where malaria is treated by yelling, where warriors of superb courage obey the commands of hysterical female impersonators, where the best cuts of meat are reserved for the dead, where, if a white blackbird has been seen, no more work may be done that day, where it is firmly believed that the world was created by a giant with three heads or that the motions of the stars are controlled from the liver of a rogue elephant?

Yet even inside this little civilized patch itself, where, at the cost of heaven knows how much grief and bloodshed, it has been made unnecessary for anyone over the age of twelve to believe in fairies or that First Causes reside in mortal and finite objects, so many are still homesick for that disorder wherein every passion formerly enjoyed a frantic licence. Caesar flies to his hunting lodge pursued by ennui; in the faubourgs of the Capital, Society grows savage, corrupted by silks and scents, softened by sugar and hot water, made insolent by theatres and attractive slaves; and everywhere, including this province, new prophets spring up every day to sound the old barbaric note.

I have tried everything. I have prohibited the sale of crystals and ouija-boards; I have slapped a heavy tax on playing cards; the courts are empowered to sentence alchemists to hard labour in the mines; it is a statutory offence to turn tables or feel bumps. But nothing is really effective. How can I expect the masses to be sensible when, for instance, to my certain knowledge, the captain of my own guard wears an amulet against the Evil Eye, and the richest merchant in the city consults a medium over every important transaction?

Legislation is helpless against the wild prayer of longing that rises, day in, day out, from all these households under my protection: 'O God, put away justice and truth for we cannot understand them and do not want them. Eternity would bore us dreadfully. Leave Thy heavens and come down to our earth of waterclocks and hedges. Become our uncle. Look after Baby, amuse Grandfather, escort Madam to the Opera, help Willy with his home-work, introduce Muriel to a handsome naval officer. Be interesting and weak like us, and we will love you as we love ourselves.'

Reason is helpless, and now even the Poetic Compromise no longer works, all those lovely fairy tales in which Zeus, disguising himself as a swan or a bull or a shower of rain or what-have-you, lay with some beautiful woman and begot a hero. For the Public has grown too sophisticated. Under all the charming metaphors and symbols, it detects the stern command, 'Be and act heroically'; behind the myth of divine

302

origin, it senses the real human excellence that is a reproach to its own baseness. So, with a bellow of rage, it kicks Poetry downstairs and sends for Prophecy. 'Your sister has just insulted me. I asked for a God who should be as like me as possible. What use to me is a God whose divinity consists in doing difficult things that I cannot do or saying clever things that I cannot understand? The God I want and intend to get must be someone I can recognize immediately without having to wait and see what he says or does. There must be nothing in the least extraordinary about him. Produce him at once, please. I'm sick of waiting.'

Today, apparently, judging by the trio who came to see me this morning with an ecstatic grin on their scholarly faces, the job has been done. 'God has been born,' they cried, 'we have seen him ourselves. The World is saved. Nothing else matters.'

One needn't be much of a psychologist to realize that if this rumour is not stamped out now, in a few years it is capable of diseasing the whole Empire, and one doesn't have to be a prophet to predict the consequences if it should.

Reason will be replaced by Revelation. Instead of Rational Law, objective truths perceptible to any who will undergo the necessary intellectual discipline, and the same for all, Knowledge will degenerate into a riot of subjective visions—feelings in the solar plexus induced by undernourishment, angelic images generated by fevers or drugs, dream warnings inspired by the sound of falling water. Whole cosmogonies will be created out of some forgotten personal resentment, complete epics written in private languages, the daubs of school children ranked above the greatest masterpieces.

Idealism will be replaced by Materialism. Priapus will only have to move to a good address and call himself Eros to become the darling of middle-aged women. Life after death will be an eternal dinner party where all the guests are twenty years old. Diverted from its normal and wholesome outlet in patriotism and civic or family pride, the need of the materialistic Masses for some visible Idol to worship will be driven into totally unsocial channels where no education can reach it. Divine honours will be paid to silver tea-pots, shallow depressions in the earth, names on maps, domestic pets, ruined windmills, even in extreme cases, which will become increasingly common, to headaches, or malignant tumours, or four o'clock in the afternoon.

Justice will be replaced by Pity as the cardinal human virtue, and all fear of retribution will vanish. Every corner-boy will congratulate himself: 'I'm such a sinner that God had to come down in person to save me. I must be a devil of a fellow.' Every crook will argue: 'I like committing crimes. God likes forgiving them. Really the world is admirably arranged.' And the ambition of every young cop will be to secure a death-bed repentance. The New Aristocracy will consist exclusively of hermits, bums, and permanent invalids. The Rough Diamond, the Consumptive Whore, the bandit who is good to his mother, the epileptic girl who has a way with animals will be the heroes and heroines of the New Tragedy when the general, the statesman, and the philosopher have become the butt of every farce and satire.

Naturally this cannot be allowed to happen. Civilization must be saved even if this means sending for the military, as I suppose it does. How dreary. Why is it that in the end civilization always has to call in these professional tidiers to whom it is all one whether it be Pythagoras or a homicidal lunatic that they are instructed to exterminate. O dear, Why couldn't this wretched infant be born somewhere else? Why can't people be sensible? I don't want to be horrid. Why can't they see that the notion of a finite God is absurd? Because it is. And suppose, just for the sake of argument, that it isn't, that this story is true, that this child is in some inexplicable manner both God and Man, that he grows up, lives, and dies, without committing a single sin? Would that make life any better? On the contrary it would make it far, far worse. For it could only mean this: that once having shown them how, God would expect every man, whatever his fortune, to lead a sinless life in the flesh and on earth. Then indeed would the human race be plunged into madness and despair. And for me personally at this moment it would mean that God had given me the power to destroy Himself. I refuse to be taken in. He could not play such a horrible practical joke. Why should He dislike me so? I've worked like a slave. Ask anyone you like. I read all official dispatches without skipping. I've taken elocution lessons. I've hardly ever taken bribes. How dare He allow me to decide? I've tried to be good. I brush my teeth every night. I haven't had sex for a month. I object. I'm a liberal. I want everyone to be happy. I wish I had never been born.

II
SOLDIERS

When the Sex War ended with the slaughter of the Grandmothers,
They found a bachelor's baby suffocating under them;
Somebody called him George and that was the end of it:
  They hitched him up to the Army.
  George, you old debutante,
  How did you get in the Army?

In the Retreat from Reason he deserted on his rocking-horse
And lived on a fairy's kindness till he tired of kicking her;
He smashed her spectacles and stole her cheque-book and
    mackintosh
  Then cruised his way back to the Army.
  George, you old numero,
  How did you get in the Army?

Before the Diet of Sugar he was using razor-blades
And exited soon after with an allergy to maidenheads;
He discovered a cure of his own, but no one would patent it,
  So he showed up again in the Army.
  George, you old flybynight,
  How did you get in the Army?

When the Vice Crusades were over he was hired by some
    Muscovites
Prospecting for deodorants among the Eskimos;
He was caught by a common cold and condemned to the whiskey
    mines,
  But schemozzled back to the Army.
  George, you old Emperor,
  How did you get in the Army?

Since Peace was signed with Honour he's been minding his
    business;
But, whoops, here comes His Idleness, buttoning his uniform;
Just in tidy time to massacre the Innocents;
    He's come home to roost in the Army.
    George, you old matador,
    Welcome back to the Army.

III
RACHEL
On the Left are grinning dogs, peering down into a solitude too deep to fill
    with roses.
On the Right are sensible sheep, gazing up at a pride where no dream can
    grow.
Somewhere in these unending wastes of delirium is a lost child, speaking
    of Long Ago in the language of wounds.
Tomorrow, perhaps, he will come to himself in Heaven.
But here Grief turns her silence, neither in this direction, nor in that, nor
    for any reason.
And her coldness now is on the earth forever.

The Flight into Egypt

I
JOSEPH
Mirror, let us through the glass
No authority can pass.

MARY
Echo, if the strong should come,
Tell a white lie or be dumb.

VOICES OF THE DESERT
It was visitors' day at the vinegar works
In Tenderloin Town when I tore my time;
A sorrowful snapshot was my sinful wage:
Was that why you left me, elusive bones?
    Come to our bracing desert
    Where eternity is eventful,
      For the weather-glass
      Is set at Alas,
    The thermometer at Resentful.

MARY
The Kingdom of the Robbers lies
Between Time and our memories;

JOSEPH

Fugitives from Space must cross
The waste of the Anonymous.

VOICES OF THE DESERT

How should he figure my fear of the dark?
The moment he can he'll remember me,
The silly, he locked in the cellar for fun,
And his dear little doggie shall die in his arms.
  Come to our old-world desert
  Where everyone goes to pieces;
    You can pick up tears
    For souvenirs
  Or genuine diseases.

JOSEPH

Geysers and volcanoes give
Sudden comical relief;

MARY

And the vulture is a boon
On a dull hot afternoon.

VOICES OF THE DESERT

All Father's nightingales knew their place,
The gardens were loyal: look at them now.
The roads are so careless, the rivers so rude,
My studs have been stolen; I must speak to the sea.
  Come to our well-run desert
  Where anguish arrives by cable,
    And the deadly sins
    May be bought in tins
  With instructions on the label.

MARY

Skulls recurring every mile
Direct the thirsty to the Nile;

JOSEPH

And the jackal's eye at night
Forces Error to keep right.

VOICES OF THE DESERT

In the land of lilies I lost my wits,
Nude as a number all night I ran
With a ghost for a guest along green canals;
By the waters of waking I wept for the weeds.
  Come to our jolly desert
  Where even the dolls go whoring;
    Where cigarette-ends
    Become intimate friends,
  And it's always three in the morning.

JOSEPH AND MARY

Safe in Egypt we shall sigh
For lost insecurity;
Only when her terrors come
Does our flesh feel quite at home.

II

RECITATIVE

Fly, Holy Family, from our immediate rage,
That our future may be freed from our past; retrace
    The footsteps of law-giving
Moses, back through the sterile waste,

Down to the rotten kingdom of Egypt, the damp
Tired delta where in her season of glory our
    Forefathers sighed in bondage;
Abscond with the Child to the place

That their children dare not revisit, to the time
They do not care to remember; hide from our pride
    In our humiliation;
Fly from our death with our new life.

III

NARRATOR

Well, so that is that. Now we must dismantle the tree,
Putting the decorations back into their cardboard boxes—
Some have got broken—and carrying them up to the attic.
The holly and the mistletoe must be taken down and burnt,
And the children got ready for school. There are enough
Left-overs to do, warmed-up, for the rest of the week—
Not that we have much appetite, having drunk such a lot,
Stayed up so late, attempted—quite unsuccessfully—
To love all of our relatives, and in general
Grossly overestimated our powers. Once again
As in previous years we have seen the actual Vision and failed
To do more than entertain it as an agreeable
Possibility, once again we have sent Him away,
Begging though to remain His disobedient servant,
The promising child who cannot keep His word for long.
The Christmas Feast is already a fading memory,
And already the mind begins to be vaguely aware
Of an unpleasant whiff of apprehension at the thought
Of Lent and Good Friday which cannot, after all, now
Be very far off. But, for the time being, here we all are,
Back in the moderate Aristotelian city
Of darning and the Eight-Fifteen, where Euclid's geometry
And Newton's mechanics would account for our experience,
And the kitchen table exists because I scrub it.
It seems to have shrunk during the holidays. The streets
Are much narrower than we remembered; we had forgotten
The office was as depressing as this. To those who have seen

The Child, however dimly, however incredulously
The Time Being is, in a sense, the most trying time of all.
For the innocent children who whispered so excitedly
Outside the locked door where they knew the presents to be
Grew up when it opened. Now, recollecting that moment
We can repress the joy, but the guilt remains conscious;
Remembering the stable where for once in our lives
Everything became a You and nothing was an It.
And craving the sensation but ignoring the cause,
We look round for something, no matter what, to inhibit
Our self-reflection, and the obvious thing for that purpose
Would be some great suffering. So, once we have met the Son,
We are tempted ever after to pray to the Father:
'Lead us into temptation and evil for our sake'.
They will come, all right, don't worry; probably in a form
That we do not expect, and certainly with a force
More dreadful than we can imagine. In the meantime
There are bills to be paid, machines to keep in repair,
Irregular verbs to learn, the Time Being to redeem
From insignificance. The happy morning is over,
The night of agony still to come; the time is noon:
When the Spirit must practise his scales of rejoicing
Without even a hostile audience, and the Soul endure
A silence that is neither for nor against her faith
That God's Will will be done, that, in spite of her prayers,
God will cheat no one, not even the world of its triumph.

IV
CHORUS

He is the Way.
Follow Him through the Land of Unlikeness;
You will see rare beasts, and have unique adventures.

He is the Truth.
Seek Him in the Kingdom of Anxiety;
You will come to a great city that has expected your return for years.

He is the Life.
Love Him in the World of the Flesh;
And at your marriage all its occasions shall dance for joy.

October 1941–July 1942

Part VIII

The Sea and the Mirror

A Commentary on Shakespeare's *The Tempest*

TO JAMES AND TANIA STERN

And am I wrong to worship where
Faith cannot doubt nor Hope despair
Since my own soul can grant my prayer?
Speak, God of Visions, plead for me
And tell why I have chosen thee.
                    EMILY BRONTË

Preface

(*The* STAGE MANAGER *to the Critics*)

The aged catch their breath,
For the nonchalant couple go
Waltzing across the tightrope
As if there were no death
Or hope of falling down;
The wounded cry as the clown
Doubles his meaning, and O
How the dear little children laugh
When the drums roll and the lovely
Lady is sawn in half.

O what authority gives
Existence its surprise?
Science is happy to answer
That the ghosts who haunt our lives
Are handy with mirrors and wire,
That song and sugar and fire,
Courage and come-hither eyes
Have a genius for taking pains.
But how does one think up a habit?
Our wonder, our terror remains.

Art opens the fishiest eye
To the Flesh and the Devil who heat
The Chamber of Temptation
Where heroes roar and die.
We are wet with sympathy now;
Thanks for the evening; but how
Shall we satisfy when we meet,
Between Shall-I and I-Will,
The lion's mouth whose hunger
No metaphors can fill?

Well, who in his own backyard
Has not opened his heart to the smiling
Secret he cannot quote?
Which goes to show that the Bard
Was sober when he wrote
That this world of fact we love
Is unsubstantial stuff:
All the rest is silence
On the other side of the wall;
And the silence ripeness,
And the ripeness all.

Prospero to Ariel

Stay with me, Ariel, while I pack, and with your first free act
    Delight my leaving; share my resigning thoughts
As you have served my revelling wishes: then, brave spirit,
    Ages to you of song and daring, and to me
Briefly Milan, then earth. In all, things have turned out better
    Than I once expected or ever deserved;
I am glad that I did not recover my dukedom till
    I do not want it; I am glad that Miranda
No longer pays me any attention; I am glad I have freed you,
    So at last I can really believe I shall die.
For under your influence death is inconceivable:
    On walks through winter woods, a bird's dry carcass
Agitates the retina with novel images,
    A stranger's quiet collapse in a noisy street
Is the beginning of much lively speculation,
    And every time some dear flesh disappears
What is real is the arriving grief; thanks to your service,
    The lonely and unhappy are very much alive.

But now all these heavy books are no use to me any more, for
    Where I go, words carry no weight: it is best,
Then, I surrender their fascinating counsel
    To the silent dissolution of the sea
Which misuses nothing because it values nothing;
    Whereas man overvalues everything
Yet, when he learns the price is pegged to his valuation,
    Complains bitterly he is being ruined which, of course, he is.
So kings find it odd they should have a million subjects
    Yet share in the thoughts of none, and seducers
Are sincerely puzzled at being unable to love
    What they are able to possess; so, long ago,
In an open boat, I wept at giving a city,
    Common warmth and touching substance, for a gift
In dealing with shadows. If age, which is certainly
    Just as wicked as youth, look any wiser,
It is only that youth is still able to believe
    It will get away with anything, while age
Knows only too well that it has got away with nothing:
    The child runs out to play in the garden, convinced
That the furniture will go on with its thinking lesson,
    Who, fifty years later, if he plays at all,
Will first ask its kind permission to be excused.

    When I woke into my life, a sobbing dwarf
Whom giants served only as they pleased, I was not what I seemed;
    Beyond their busy backs I made a magic
To ride away from a father's imperfect justice,
    Take vengeance on the Romans for their grammar,
Usurp the popular earth and blot for ever
    The gross insult of being a mere one among many:

Now, Ariel, I am that I am, your late and lonely master,
   Who knows now what magic is:—the power to enchant
That comes from disillusion. What the books can teach one
   Is that most desires end up in stinking ponds,
But we have only to learn to sit still and give no orders,
   To make you offer us your echo and your mirror;
We have only to believe you, then you dare not lie;
   To ask for nothing, and at once from your calm eyes,
With their lucid proof of apprehension and disorder,
   All we are not stares back at what we are. For all things,
In your company, can be themselves: historic deeds
   Drop their hauteur and speak of shabby childhoods
When all they longed for was to join in the gang of doubts
   Who so tormented them; sullen diseases
Forget their dreadful appearance and make silly jokes;
   Thick-headed goodness for once is not a bore.
No one but you had sufficient audacity and eyesight
   To find those clearings where the shy humiliations
Gambol on sunny afternoons, the waterhole to which
   The scarred rogue sorrow comes quietly in the small hours:
And no one but you is reliably informative on hell;
   As you whistle and skip past, the poisonous
Resentments scuttle over your unrevolted feet,
   And even the uncontrollable vertigo,
Because it can scent no shame, is unobliged to strike.

      Could he but once see Nature as
         In truth she is for ever,
      What oncer would not fall in love?
      Hold up your mirror, boy, to do
         Your vulgar friends this favour:
      One peep, though, will be quite enough;
         To those who are not true,
      A statue with no figleaf has
         A pornographic flavour.

      Inform my hot heart straight away
         Its treasure loves another,
      But turn to neutral topics then,
      Such as the pictures in this room,
         Religion or the Weather;
      Pure scholarship in Where and When,
         How Often and With Whom,
      Is not for Passion that must play
         The Jolly Elder Brother.

      Be frank about our heathen foe,
         For Rome will be a goner
      If you soft-pedal the loud beast;
      Describe in plain four-letter words
         This dragon that's upon her:
      But should our beggars ask the cost,
         Just whistle like the birds;
      Dare even Pope or Caesar know
         The price of faith and honour?

Today I am free and no longer need your freedom:
You, I suppose, will be off now to look for likely victims;
    Crowds chasing ankles, lone men stalking glory,
Some feverish young rebel among amiable flowers
    In consultation with his handsome envy,
A punctual plump judge, a fly-weight hermit in a dream
    Of gardens that time is for ever outside—
To lead absurdly by their self-important noses.
    Are you malicious by nature? I don't know.
Perhaps only incapable of doing nothing or of
    Being by yourself, and, for all your wry faces
May secretly be anxious and miserable without
    A master to need you for the work you need.
Are all your tricks a test? If so, I hope you find, next time,
    Someone in whom you cannot spot the weakness
Through which you will corrupt him with your charm. Mine you did
    And me you have: thanks to us both, I have broken
Both of the promises I made as an apprentice:—
    To hate nothing and to ask nothing for its love.
All by myself I tempted Antonio into treason;
    However that could be cleared up; both of us know
That both were in the wrong, and neither need be sorry:
    But Caliban remains my impervious disgrace.
We did it, Ariel, between us; you found on me a wish
    For absolute devotion; result—his wreck
That sprawls in the weeds and will not be repaired:
    My dignity discouraged by a pupil's curse,
I shall go knowing and incompetent into my grave.

    The extravagant children, who lately swaggered
Out of the sea like gods, have, I think, been soundly hunted
    By their own devils into their human selves:
To all, then, but me, their pardons. Alonso's heaviness
    Is lost; and weak Sebastian will be patient
In future with his slothful conscience—after all, it pays;
    Stephano is contracted to his belly, a minor
But a prosperous kingdom; stale Trinculo receives,
    Gratis, a whole fresh repertoire of stories, and
Our younger generation its independent joy.
    Their eyes are big and blue with love; its lighting
Makes even us look new: yes, today it all looks so easy.
    Will Ferdinand be as fond of a Miranda
Familiar as a stocking? Will a Miranda who is
    No longer a silly lovesick little goose,
When Ferdinand and his brave world are her profession,
    Go into raptures over existing at all?
Probably I over-estimate their difficulties;
    Just the same, I am very glad I shall never
Be twenty and have to go through that business again,
    The hours of fuss and fury, the conceit, the expense.

Sing first that green remote Cockagne
  Where whiskey-rivers run,
And every gorgeous number may
  Be laid by anyone;
For medicine and rhetoric
  Lie mouldering on shelves,
While sad young dogs and stomach-aches
  Love no one but themselves.

Tell then of witty angels who
  Come only to the beasts,
Of Heirs Apparent who prefer
  Low dives to formal feasts;
For shameless Insecurity
  Prays for a boot to lick,
And many a sore bottom finds
  A sorer one to kick.

Wind up, though, on a moral note; —
  That Glory will go bang,
Schoolchildren shall co-operate,
  And honest rogues must hang;
Because our sound committee man
  Has murder in his heart:
But should you catch a living eye,
  Just wink as you depart.

Now our partnership is dissolved, I feel so peculiar:
  As if I had been on a drunk since I was born
And suddenly now, and for the first time, am cold sober,
  With all my unanswered wishes and unwashed days
Stacked up all round my life; as if through the ages I had dreamed
  About some tremendous journey I was taking,
Sketching imaginary landscapes, chasms and cities,
  Cold walls, hot spaces, wild mouths, defeated backs,
Jotting down fictional notes on secrets overheard
  In theatres and privies, banks and mountain inns,
And now, in my old age, I wake, and this journey really exists.
  And I have actually to take it, inch by inch,
Alone and on foot, without a cent in my pocket,
  Through a universe where time is not foreshortened,
No animals talk, and there is neither floating nor flying.

When I am safely home, oceans away in Milan, and
Realize once and for all I shall never see you again,
  Over there, maybe, it won't seem quite so dreadful
Not to be interesting any more, but an old man
  Just like other old men, with eyes that water
Easily in the wind, and a head that nods in the sunshine,
  Forgetful, maladroit, a little grubby,
And to like it. When the servants settle me into a chair
  In some well-sheltered corner of the garden,
And arrange my muffler and rugs, shall I ever be able
  To stop myself from telling them what I am doing, —

315

Sailing alone, out over seventy thousand fathoms—?
  Yet if I speak, I shall sink without a sound
Into unmeaning abysses. Can I learn to suffer
  Without saying something ironic or funny
On suffering? I never suspected the way of truth
  Was a way of silence where affectionate chat
Is but a robbers' ambush and even good music
  In shocking taste; and you, of course, never told me.
If I peg away at it honestly every moment,
  And have luck, perhaps by the time death pounces
His stumping question, I shall just be getting to know
  The difference between moonshine and daylight. . . .
I see you starting to fidget. I forgot. To you
  That doesn't matter. My dear, here comes Gonzalo
With a solemn face to fetch me. O Ariel, Ariel,
  How I shall miss you. Enjoy your element. Good-bye.

                    Sing, Ariel, sing,
                    Sweetly, dangerously
                    Out of the sour
                    And shiftless water,
                    Lucidly out
                    Of the dozing tree,
                    Entrancing, rebuking
                    The raging heart
                    With a smoother song
                    Than this rough world,
                    Unfeeling god.

                    O brilliantly, lightly,
                    Of separation,
                    Of bodies and death,
                    Unanxious one, sing
                    To man, meaning me,
                    As now, meaning always,
                    In love or out,
                    Whatever that mean,
                    Trembling he takes
                    The silent passage
                    Into discomfort.

The Supporting Cast, Sotto Voce

ANTONIO

As all the pigs have turned back into men
And the sky is auspicious and the sea
Calm as a clock, we can all go home again.

Yes, it undoubtedly looks as if we
Could take life as easily now as tales
Write ever-after: not only are the

Two heads silhouetted against the sails
—And kissing, of course—well-built, but the lean
Fool is quite a person, the fingernails

Of the dear old butler for once quite clean,
And the royal passengers quite as good
As rustics, perhaps better, for they mean

What they say, without, as a rustic would,
Casting reflections on the courtly crew.
Yes, Brother Prospero, your grouping could

Not be more effective: given a few
Incomplete objects and a nice warm day,
What a lot a little music can do.

Dotted about the deck they doze or play,
Your loyal subjects all, grateful enough
To know their place and believe what you say.

Antonio, sweet brother, has to laugh.
How easy you have made it to refuse
Peace to your greatness! Break your wand in half,

The fragments will join; burn your books or lose
Them in the sea, they will soon reappear,
Not even damaged: as long as I choose

To wear my fashion, whatever you wear
Is a magic robe; while I stand outside
Your circle, the will to charm is still there.

As I exist so you shall be denied,
Forced to remain our melancholy mentor,
The grown-up man, the adult in his pride,

Never have time to curl up at the centre
Time turns on when completely reconciled,
Never become and therefore never enter
The green occluded pasture as a child.

Your all is partial, Prospero;
      My will is all my own:
Your need to love shall never know
Me: I am I, Antonio,
      By choice myself alone.

FERDINAND

Flesh, fair, unique, and you, warm secret that my kiss
Follows into meaning Miranda, solitude
Where my omissions are, still possible, still good,
Dear Other at all times, retained as I do this,

From moment to moment as you enrich them so
Inherit me, my cause, as I would cause you now
With mine your sudden joy, two wonders as one vow
Pre-empting all, here, there, for ever, long ago.

I would smile at no other promise than touch, taste, sight,
Were there not, my enough, my exaltation, to bless
As world is offered world, as I hear it tonight

Pleading with ours for us, another tenderness
That neither without either could or would possess,
The Right Required Time, The Real Right Place, O Light.

One bed is empty, Prospero,
      My person is my own;
Hot Ferdinand will never know
The flame with which Antonio
      Burns in the dark alone.

STEPHANO

Embrace me, belly, like a bride;
Dear daughter, for the weight you drew
From humble pie and swallowed pride,
Believe the boast in which you grew:
Where mind meets matter, both should woo;
Together let us learn that game
The high play better than the blue:
A lost thing looks for a lost name.

Behind your skirts your son must hide
When disappointments bark and boo;
Brush my heroic ghosts aside,
Wise nanny, with a vulgar pooh:
Exchanging cravings we pursue
Alternately a single aim:
Between the bottle and the 'loo'
A lost thing looks for a lost name.

Though in the long run satisfied,
The will of one by being two
At every moment is denied;
Exhausted glasses wonder who

Is self and sovereign, I or You?
We cannot both be what we claim,
The real Stephano—Which is true?
A lost thing looks for a lost name.

Child? Mother? Either grief will do;
The need for pardon is the same,
The contradiction is not new:
A lost thing looks for a lost name.

One glass is untouched, Prospero,
  My nature is my own;
Inert Stephano does not know
The feast at which Antonio
  Toasts One and One alone.

GONZALO

Evening, grave, immense, and clear,
Overlook our ship whose wake
Lingers undistorted on
Sea and silence; I look back
For the last time as the sun
Sets behind that island where
All our loves were altered: yes,
My prediction came to pass,
Yet I am not justified,
And I weep but not with pride.
Not in me the credit for
Words I uttered long ago
Whose glad meaning I betrayed;
Truths today admitted, owe
Nothing to the councillor
In whose booming eloquence
Honesty became untrue.
Am I not Gonzalo who
By his self-reflection made
Consolation an offence?

There was nothing to explain:
Had I trusted the Absurd
And straightforward note by note
Sung exactly what I heard,
Such immediate delight
Would have taken there and then
Our common welkin by surprise,
All would have begun to dance
Jigs of self-deliverance.
It was I prevented this,
Jealous of my native ear,
Mine the art which made the song
Sound ridiculous and wrong,
I whose interference broke
The gallop into jog-trot prose
And by speculation froze

319

Vision into an idea,
Irony into a joke,
Till I stood convicted of
Doubt and insufficient love.

Farewell, dear island of our wreck:
All have been restored to health,
All have seen the Commonwealth,
There is nothing to forgive.
Since a storm's decision gave
His subjective passion back
To a meditative man,
Even reminiscence can
Comfort ambient troubles like
Some ruined tower by the sea
Whence boyhoods growing and afraid
Learn a formula they need
In solving their mortality,
Even rusting flesh can be
A simple locus now, a bell
The Already There can lay
Hands on if at any time
It should feel inclined to say
To the lonely—'Here I am',
To the anxious—'All is well'.

One tongue is silent, Prospero,
   My language is my own;
Decayed Gonzalo does not know
The shadow that Antonio
   Talks to, at noon, alone.

ADRIAN *and* FRANCISCO
Good little sunbeams must learn to fly,
But it's madly ungay when the goldfish die.

One act is censored, Prospero,
   My audience is my own;
Nor Adrian nor Francisco know
The drama that Antonio
   Plays in his head alone.

ALONSO
Dear Son, when the warm multitudes cry,
Ascend your throne majestically,
But keep in mind the waters where fish
See sceptres descending with no wish
To touch them; sit regal and erect,
But imagine the sands where a crown
Has the status of a broken-down
Sofa or mutilated statue:
Remember as bells and cannon boom
The cold deep that does not envy you,
The sunburnt superficial kingdom
Where a king is an object.

Expect no help from others, for who
Talk sense to princes or refer to
The scorpion in official speeches
As they unveil some granite Progress
Leading a child and holding a bunch
Of lilies? In their Royal Zoos the
Shark and the octopus are tactfully
Omitted; synchronized clocks march on
Within their powers: without, remain
The ocean flats where no subscription
Concerts are given, the desert plain
Where there is nothing for lunch.

Only your darkness can tell you what
A prince's ornate mirror dare not,
Which you should fear more—the sea in which
A tyrant sinks entangled in rich
Robes while a mistress turns a white back
Upon his splutter, or the desert
Where an emperor stands in his shirt
While his diary is read by sneering
Beggars, and far off he notices
A lean horror flapping and hopping
Toward him with inhuman swiftness:
Learn from your dreams what you lack,

For as your fears are, so must you hope.
The Way of Justice is a tightrope
Where no prince is safe for one instant
Unless he trust his embarrassment,
As in his left ear the siren sings
Meltingly of water and a night
Where all flesh had peace, and on his right
The efreet offers a brilliant void
Where his mind could be perfectly clear
And all his limitations destroyed:
Many young princes soon disappear
To join all the unjust kings.

So, if you prosper, suspect those bright
Mornings when you whistle with a light
Heart. You are loved; you have never seen
The harbour so still, the park so green,
So many well-fed pigeons upon
Cupolas and triumphal arches,
So many stags and slender ladies
Beside the canals. Remember when
Your climate seems a permanent home
For marvellous creatures and great men,
What griefs and convulsions startled Rome,
Ecbatana, Babylon.

How narrow the space, how slight the chance
For civil pattern and importance
Between the watery vagueness and
The triviality of the sand,
How soon the lively trip is over
From loose craving to sharp aversion,
Aimless jelly to paralysed bone:
At the end of each successful day
Remember that the fire and the ice
Are never more than one step away
From the temperate city; it is
But a moment to either.

But should you fail to keep your kingdom
And, like your father before you, come
Where thought accuses and feeling mocks,
Believe your pain: praise the scorching rocks
For their desiccation of your lust,
Thank the bitter treatment of the tide
For its dissolution of your pride,
That the whirlwind may arrange your will
And the deluge release it to find
The spring in the desert, the fruitful
Island in the sea, where flesh and mind
Are delivered from mistrust.

Blue the sky beyond her humming sail
As I sit today by our ship's rail
Watching exuberant porpoises
Escort us homeward and writing this
For you to open when I am gone:
Read it, Ferdinand, with the blessing
Of Alonso, your father, once King
Of Naples, now ready to welcome
Death, but rejoicing in a new love,
A new peace, having heard the solemn
Music strike and seen the statue move
To forgive our illusion.

> One crown is lacking, Prospero,
>   My empire is my own;
> Dying Alonso does not know
> The diadem Antonio
>   Wears in his world alone.

MASTER *and* BOATSWAIN
At Dirty Dick's and Sloppy Joe's
  We drank our liquor straight,
Some went upstairs with Margery,
  And some, alas, with Kate;
And two by two like cat and mouse
The homeless played at keeping house.

There Wealthy Meg, the Sailor's Friend,
  And Marion, cow-eyed,
Opened their arms to me but I
  Refused to step inside;
I was not looking for a cage
In which to mope in my old age.

The nightingales are sobbing in
  The orchards of our mothers,
And hearts that we broke long ago
  Have long been breaking others;
Tears are round, the sea is deep:
Roll them overboard and sleep.

    One gaze points elsewhere, Prospero,
      My compass is my own;
   Nostalgic sailors do not know
   The waters where Antonio
      Sails on and on alone.

SEBASTIAN

My rioters all disappear, my dream
Where Prudence flirted with a naked sword,
Securely vicious, crumbles; it is day;
Nothing has happened; we are all alive:
I am Sebastian, wicked still, my proof
Of mercy that I wake without a crown.

What sadness signalled to our children's day
Where each believed all wishes wear a crown
And anything pretended is alive,
That one by one we plunged into that dream
Of solitude and silence where no sword
Will ever play once it is called a proof?

The arrant jewel singing in his crown
Persuaded me my brother was a dream
I should not love because I had no proof,
Yet all my honesty assumed a sword;
To think his death I thought myself alive
And stalked infected through the blooming day.

The lie of Nothing is to promise proof
To any shadow that there is no day
Which cannot be extinguished with some sword,
To want and weakness that the ancient crown
Envies the childish head, murder a dream
Wrong only while its victim is alive.

O blessed be bleak Exposure on whose sword,
Caught unawares, we prick ourselves alive!
Shake Failure's bruising fist! Who else would crown
Abominable error with a proof?
I smile because I tremble, glad today
To be ashamed, not anxious, not a dream.

Children are playing, brothers are alive,
And not a heart or stomach asks for proof
That all this dearness is no lovers' dream;
Just Now is what it might be every day,
Right Here is absolute and needs no crown,
Ermine or trumpets, protocol or sword.

In dream all sins are easy, but by day
It is defeat gives proof we are alive;
The sword we suffer is the guarded crown.

One face cries nothing, Prospero,
  My conscience is my own;
Pallid Sebastian does not know
The dream in which Antonio
  Fights the white bull alone.

TRINCULO

Mechanic, merchant, king,
Are warmed by the cold clown
Whose head is in the clouds
And never can get down.

Into a solitude
Undreamed of by their fat
Quick dreams have lifted me;
The north wind steals my hat.

On clear days I can see
Green acres far below,
And the red roof where I
Was Little Trinculo.

There lies that solid world
These hands can never reach;
My history, my love,
Is but a choice of speech.

A terror shakes my tree,
A flock of words fly out,
Whereat a laughter shakes
The busy and devout.

Wild images, come down
Out of your freezing sky,
That I, like shorter men,
May get my joke and die.

One note is jarring, Prospero,
  My humour is my own;
Tense Trinculo will never know
The paradox Antonio
  Laughs at, in woods, alone.

MIRANDA

My Dear One is mine as mirrors are lonely,
As the poor and sad are real to the good king,
And the high green hill sits always by the sea.

Up jumped the Black Man behind the elder tree,
Turned a somersault and ran away waving;
My Dear One is mine as mirrors are lonely.

The Witch gave a squawk; her venomous body
Melted into light as water leaves a spring,
And the high green hill sits always by the sea.

At the crossroads, too, the Ancient prayed for me;
Down his wasted cheeks tears of joy were running:
My Dear One is mine as mirrors are lonely.

He kissed me awake, and no one was sorry;
The sun shone on sails, eyes, pebbles, anything,
And the high green hill sits always by the sea.

So, to remember our changing garden, we
Are linked as children in a circle dancing:
My Dear One is mine as mirrors are lonely,
And the high green hill sits always by the sea.

One link is missing, Prospero,
My magic is my own;
Happy Miranda does not know
The figure that Antonio,
The Only One, Creation's O
Dances for Death alone.

III

Caliban to the Audience

If now, having dismissed your hired impersonators with verdicts ranging
from the laudatory orchid to the disgusted and disgusting egg, you ask
and, of course, notwithstanding the conscious fact of his irrevocable
absence, you instinctively *do* ask for our so good, so great, so dead author
to stand before the finally lowered curtain and take his shyly responsible
bow for this, his latest, ripest production, it is I—my reluctance is, I can
assure you, co-equal with your dismay who will always loom thus
wretchedly into your confused picture, for, in default of the all-wise, all-
explaining master you would speak *to*, who else at least can, who else
indeed must respond to your bewildered cry, but its very echo, the begged
question you would speak to him *about*.

*   *   *

We must own [*for the present I speak your echo*] to a nervous perplexity not unmixed, frankly, with downright resentment. How *can* we grant the indulgence for which in his epilogue your personified type of the creative so lamely, tamely pleaded? Imprisoned, by you, in the mood doubtful, loaded, by you, with distressing embarrassments, we are, we submit, in no position to set *anyone* free.

Our native Muse, heaven knows and heaven be praised, is not exclusive. Whether out of the innocence of a childlike heart to whom all things are pure, or with the serenity of a status so majestic that the mere keeping up of tones and appearances, the suburban wonder as to what the strait-laced Unities might possibly think, or sad sour Probability possibly say, are questions for which she doesn't because she needn't, she hasn't in her lofty maturity any longer, to care a rap, she invites, dear generous-hearted creature that she is, just *tout le monde* to drop in at any time so that her famous, memorable, sought-after evenings present to the speculative eye an ever-shining, never-tarnished proof of her amazing unheard-of power to combine and happily contrast, to make *every* shade of the social and moral palette contribute to the general richness, of the skill, unapproached and unattempted by Grecian aunt or Gallic sister, with which she can skate full tilt toward the forbidden incoherence and then, in the last split second, on the shuddering edge of the bohemian standardless abyss, effect her breathtaking triumphant turn.

No timid segregation by rank or taste for her, no prudent listing into those who will, who might, who certainly would not get on, no nicely graded scale of invitations to heroic formal Tuesdays, young comic Thursdays, al fresco farcical Saturdays. No, the real, the only, test of the theatrical as of the gastronomic, her practice confidently wagers, is the mixed perfected brew.

As he looks in on her, so marvellously at home with all her cosy swarm about her, what accents will not assault the new arrival's ear, the magnificent tropes of tragic defiance and despair, the repartee of the high humour, the pun of the very low, cultured drawl and manly illiterate bellow, yet all of them gratefully doing their huge or tiny best to make the party go?

And if, assured by her smiling wave that of course he may, he should presently set out to explore her vast and rambling mansion, to do honour to its dear odd geniuses of local convenience and proportion, its multiplied deities of mysterious stair and interesting alcove, not one of the laughing groups and engrossed warmed couples that he keeps 'surprising'—the never-ending surprise for him is that he doesn't seem to—but affords some sharper instance of relations he would have been the last to guess at, choleric prince at his ease with lymphatic butler, moist hand taking so to dry, youth getting on quite famously with stingy cold old age, some stranger vision of the large loud liberty violently rocking yet never, he is persuaded, finally upsetting the jolly crowded boat.

What, he may well ask, has the gracious goddess done to all these people that, at her most casual hint, they should so trustingly, so immediately take off those heavy habits one thinks of them as having for their health and happiness day and night to wear, without in this unfamiliar unbuttoned state—the notable absence of the slightest shiver or not-quite-inhibited sneeze is indication positive—for a second feeling the draught? Is there, could there be, *any* miraculous suspension of the wearily historic, the dingily geographic, the dully drearily sensible beyond her faith, her charm, her love, to command? Yes, there could be, yes, alas, indeed yes, O there is, right here, right now before us, the situation present.

How *could* you, you who are one of the oldest habitués at these delightful functions, one, possibly the closest, of her trusted inner circle, how could you be guilty of the incredible unpardonable treachery of bringing along the one creature, as you above all men must have known, whom she cannot and will not under any circumstances stand, the solitary exception she is not at any hour of the day or night at home to, the unique case that her attendant spirits have absolute instructions never, neither at the front door nor at the back, to admit?

At Him and at Him only does she draw the line, not because there are any limits to her sympathy but precisely because there are none. Just because of all she is and all she means to be, she cannot conceivably tolerate in her presence the represented principle of *not* sympathizing, *not* associating, *not* amusing, the only child of her Awful Enemy, the rival whose real name she will never sully her lips with—'that envious witch' is sign sufficient—who does not rule but defiantly is the unrectored chaos.

All along and only too well she has known what would happen if, by any careless mischance—of conscious malice she never dreamed till now—He should ever manage to get in. She foresaw what He would do to the conversation, lying in wait for its vision of private love or public justice to warm to an Egyptian brilliance and then with some fishlike odour or *bruit insolite* snatching the visionaries back tongue-tied and blushing to the here and now; she foresaw what He would do to the arrangements, breaking, by a refusal to keep in step, the excellent order of the dancing ring, and ruining supper by knocking over the loaded appetising tray; worst of all, she foresaw, she dreaded, what He would end up by doing to her, that, not content with upsetting her guests, with spoiling their fun, His progress from outrage to outrage would not relent before the gross climax of His making, horror unspeakable, a pass at her virgin self.

Let us suppose, even, that in your eyes she is by no means as we have always fondly imagined, your dear friend, that what we have just witnessed was not what it seemed to us, the inexplicable betrayal of a life-long sacred loyalty, but your long-premeditated just revenge, the final evening up of some ancient never-forgotten score, then even so, why make us suffer who have never, in all conscience, done you harm? Surely the theatrical relation, no less than the marital is governed by the sanely decent general law that, before visitors, in front of the children or the servants, there shall be no indiscreet revelation of animosity, no 'scenes', that, no matter to what intolerable degrees of internal temperature and pressure restraint may raise both the injured and the guilty, nevertheless such restraint is applied to tones and topics, the exhibited picture must be still as always the calm and smiling one the most malicious observer can see nothing wrong with, and not until the last of those whom manifested anger or mistrust would embarrass or amuse or not be good for have gone away or out or up, is the voice raised, the table thumped, the suspicious letter snatched at or the outrageous bill furiously waved.

For we, after all—you cannot have forgotten this—are strangers to her. We have never claimed her acquaintance, knowing as well as she that we do not and never could belong on her side of the curtain. All we have ever asked for is that for a few hours the curtain should be left undrawn, so as to allow our humble ragged selves the privilege of craning and gaping at the splendid goings-on inside. We most emphatically do *not* ask that she should speak to us, or try to understand us; on the contrary our one desire has always been that she should preserve for ever her old high strangeness, for what delights us about her world is just that it neither is nor possibly could become one in which we could breathe or behave, that in her house the right of innocent passage should remain so universal that the same neutral space accommodates the conspirator and his victim; the generals of both armies, the chorus of patriots and the choir of nuns, palace and farmyard, cathedral and smugglers' cave, that time should never revert to that intransigent element we are so ineluctably and only too familiarly in, but remain the passive good-natured creature she and her friends can by common consent do anything they like with—(it is not surprising that they should take advantage of their strange power and so frequently skip hours and days and even years: the dramatic mystery is that they should always so unanimously agree upon exactly how many hours and days and years to skip)—that upon their special constitutions the moral law should continue to operate so exactly that the timid not only deserve but actually win the fair, and it is the socially and physically unemphatic David who lays low the gorilla-chested Goliath with one well-aimed custard pie, that in their blessed climate, the manifestation of the inner life should always remain so easy and habitual that a sudden eruption of musical and metaphorical power is instantly recognized as standing for grief and disgust, an elegant *contrapposto* for violent death, and that consequently the picture which they in there present to us out here is always that of the perfectly tidiable case of disorder, the beautiful and serious problem exquisitely set without a single superfluous datum and insoluble with less, the expert landing of all the passengers with all their luggage safe and sound in the best of health and spirits and without so much as a scratch or a bruise.

Into that world of freedom without anxiety, sincerity without loss of vigour, feeling that loosens rather than ties the tongue, we are not, we reiterate, so blinded by presumption to our proper status and interest as to expect or even wish at any time to enter, far less to dwell there.

Must we—it seems oddly that we must—remind you that our existence does not, like hers, enjoy an infinitely indicative mood, an eternally present tense, a limitlessly active voice, for in our shambling, slovenly makeshift world any two persons, whether domestic first or neighbourly second, require and necessarily presuppose in both their numbers and in all their cases, the whole inflected gamut of an alien third, since, without a despised or dreaded Them to turn the back *on*, there could be no intimate or affectionate Us to turn the eye *to*; that, *chez nous*, space is never the whole uninhibited circle but always some segment, its eminent domain upheld by two co-ordinates. There always has been and always will be not only the vertical boundary, the river on this side of which initiative and honesty stroll arm in arm wearing sensible clothes, and beyond which is a savage elsewhere swarming with contagious diseases, but also its horizontal counterpart, the railroad above which houses stand in their own grounds, each equipped with a garage and a beautiful woman, sometimes with several, and below which huddled shacks provide a squeezing shelter to collarless herds who eat blancmange and have never said anything witty. Make the case as special as you please; take the tamest congregation or the wildest faction; take, say, a college. What river and railroad did for the grosser instance, lawn and corridor do for the more refined, dividing the tender who value from the tough who measure, the superstitious who still sacrifice to causation from the heretics who have already reduced the worship of truth to bare description, and so creating the academic fields to be guarded with umbrella and learned periodical against the trespass of any unqualified stranger not a whit less jealously than the game-preserve is protected from the poacher by the unamiable shot-gun. For without these prohibitive frontiers we should never know who we were or what we wanted. It is they who donate to neighbourhood all its accuracy and vehemence. It is thanks to them that we do know with whom to associate, make love, exchange recipes and jokes, go mountain climbing or sit side by side fishing from piers. It is thanks to them, too, that we know against whom to rebel. We *can* shock our parents by visiting the dives below the railroad tracks, we *can* amuse ourselves on what would otherwise have been a very dull evening indeed, in plotting to seize the post office across the river.

Of course, these several private regions must together comprise one public whole—we would never deny that logic and instinct require that. Of course, We and They are united in the candid glare of the same commercial hope by day, and the soft refulgence of the same erotic nostalgia by night but—and this is our point—without our privacies of situation, our local idioms of triumph and mishap, our different doctrines concerning the transubstantiation of the larger pinker bun on the terrestrial dish for which the mature sense may reasonably water and the adult fingers furtively or unabashedly go for, our specific choices of which hill it would be romantic to fly away over or what sea it would be exciting to run away to, our peculiar visions of the absolute stranger with a spontaneous longing for the lost who will adopt our misery not out of desire but pure compassion, without, in short, our devoted pungent expression of the partial and contrasted, the Whole would have no importance and its Day and Night no interest.

So, too, with Time who, in our auditorium, is not her dear old buffer so anxious to please everybody, but a prim magistrate whose court never adjourns, and from whose decisions, as he laconically sentences one to loss of hair and talent, another to seven days' chastity, and a third to boredom for life, there is no appeal. We should not be sitting here now, washed, warm, well-fed, in seats we have paid for, unless there were others who are not here; our liveliness and good-humour, such as they are, are those of survivors, conscious that there are others who have not been so fortunate, others who did not succeed in navigating the narrow passage or to whom the natives were not friendly, others whose streets were chosen by the explosion or through whose country the famine turned aside from ours to go, others who failed to repel the invasion of bacteria or to crush the insurrection of their bowels, others who lost their suit against their parents or were ruined by wishes they could not adjust or murdered by resentments they could not control; aware of some who were better and bigger but from whom, only the other day, Fortune withdrew her hand in sudden disgust, now nervously playing chess with drunken sea-captains in sordid cafés on the equator or the Arctic Circle, or lying, only a few blocks away, strapped and screaming on iron beds or dropping to naked pieces in damp graves. And shouldn't you too, dear master, reflect—forgive us for mentioning it—that we might very well not have been attending a production of yours this evening, had not some other and maybe—who can tell?—brighter talent married a barmaid or turned religious and shy or gone down in a liner with all his manuscripts, the loss recorded only in the corner of some country newspaper below A Poultry Lover's Jottings?

You yourself, we seem to remember, have spoken of the conjured spectacle as 'a mirror held up to nature', a phrase misleading in its aphoristic sweep but indicative at least of one aspect of the relation between the real and the imagined, their mutual reversal of value, for isn't the essential artistic strangeness to which your citation of the sinisterly biassed image would point just this: that on the far side of the mirror the general will to compose, to form at all costs a felicitous pattern becomes the *necessary cause* of any particular effort to live or act or love or triumph or vary, instead of being as, in so far as it emerges at all, it is on this side, their *accidental effect*?

Does Ariel—to nominate the spirit of reflection in your terms—call for manifestation? Then neither modesty nor fear of reprisals excuses the one so called on from publicly confessing that she cheated at croquet or that he committed incest in a dream. Does He demand concealment? Then their nearest and dearest must be deceived by disguises of sex and age which anywhere else would at once attract the attention of the police or the derisive whistle of the awful schoolboy. That is the price asked, and how promptly and gladly paid, for universal reconciliation and peace, for the privilege of all galloping together past the finishing post neck and neck.

How then, we continue to wonder, knowing all this, could you act as if you did not, as if you did not realize that the embarrassing compresence of the absolutely natural, incorrigibly right-handed, and, to any request for co-operation, utterly negative, with the enthusiastically self-effacing would be a simultaneous violation of both worlds, as if you were not perfectly well aware that the magical musical condition, the orphic spell that turns the fierce dumb greedy beasts into grateful guides and oracles who will gladly take one anywhere and tell one everything free of charge, is precisely and simply that of his finite immediate note *not*, under any circumstances, being struck, of its not being tentatively whispered, far less positively banged.

Are we not bound to conclude, then, that, whatever snub to the poetic you may have intended incidentally to administer, your profounder motive in so introducing Him to them among whom, because He doesn't belong, He couldn't appear as anything but His distorted parody, a deformed and savage slave, was to deal a mortal face-slapping insult to us among whom He does and is, moreover, all grossness turned to glory, no less a person than the nude august elated archer of our heaven, the darling single son of Her who, in her right milieu, is certainly no witch but the most sensible of all the gods, whose influence is as sound as it is pandemic, on the race-track no less than in the sleeping cars of the Orient Express, our great white Queen of Love herself?

But even that is not the worst we suspect you of. If your words have not buttered any parsnips, neither have they broken any bones.

He, after all, can come back to us now to be comforted and respected, perhaps, after the experience of finding Himself for a few hours and for the first time in His life not wanted, more fully and freshly appreciative of our affection than He has always been in the past; as for His dear mother, She is far too grand and far too busy to hear or care what you say or think. If only we were certain that your malice was confined to the verbal affront, we should long ago have demanded our money back and gone whistling home to bed. Alas, in addition to resenting what you have openly said, we fear even more what you may secretly have done. Is it possible that, not content with inveigling Caliban into Ariel's kingdom, you have also let loose Ariel in Caliban's? We note with alarm that when the other members of the final tableau were dismissed, He was not returned to His arboreal confinement as He should have been. Where is He now? For if the intrusion of the real has disconcerted and incommoded the poetic, that is a mere bagatelle compared to the damage which the poetic would inflict if it ever succeeded in intruding upon the real. We want no Ariel here, breaking down our picket fences in the name of fraternity, seducing our wives in the name of romance, and robbing us of our sacred pecuniary deposits in the name of justice. Where is Ariel? What have you done with Him? For we won't, we daren't leave until you give us a satisfactory answer.

*   *   *

Such (*let me cease to play your echo and return to my officially natural role*)—such are your questions, are they not, but before I try to deal with them, I must ask for your patience, while I deliver a special message for our late author to those few among you, if indeed there be any—I have certainly heard no comment yet from them—who have come here, not to be entertained but to learn; that is, to any gay apprentice in the magical art who may have chosen this specimen of the prestidigitatory genus to study this evening in the hope of grasping more clearly just how the artistic contraption works, of observing some fresh detail in the complex process by which the heady wine of amusement is distilled from the grape of composition. The rest of you I must beg for a little while to sit back and relax as the remarks I have now to make do not concern you; your turn will follow later.

*   *   *

So, strange young man,—it is at his command, remember, that I say this to you; whether I agree with it or not is neither here nor there—you have decided on the conjurer's profession. Somewhere, in the middle of a salt marsh or at the bottom of a kitchen garden or on the top of a bus, you heard imprisoned Ariel call for help, and it is now a liberator's face that congratulates you from your shaving mirror every morning. As you walk the cold streets hatless, or sit over coffee and doughnuts in the corner of a cheap restaurant, your secret has already set you apart from the howling merchants and transacting multitudes to watch with fascinated distaste the bellowing barging banging passage of the awkward profit-seeking elbow, the dazed eye of the gregarious acquisitive condition. Lying awake at night in your single bed you are conscious of a power by which you will survive the wallpaper of your boardinghouse or the expensive bourgeois horrors of your home. Yes, Ariel is grateful; He does come when you call, He does tell you all the gossip He overhears on the stairs, all the goings-on He observes through the keyhole; He really is willing to arrange anything you care to ask for, and you are rapidly finding out the right orders to give—who should be killed in the hunting accident, which couple to send into the cast-iron shelter, what scent will arouse a Norwegian engineer, how to get the young hero from the country lawyer's office to the Princess' reception, when to mislay the letter, where the cabinet minister should be reminded of his mother, why the dishonest valet must be a martyr to indigestion but immune from the common cold.

As the gay productive months slip by, in spite of fretful discouraged days, of awkward moments of misunderstanding or rather, seen retrospectively as happily cleared up and got over, verily because of them, you are definitely getting the hang of this, at first so novel and bewildering, relationship between magician and familiar, whose duty it is to sustain your infinite conceptual appetite with vivid concrete experiences. And, as the months turn into years, your wonder-working romance into an economic habit, the encountered case of good or evil in our wide world of property and boredom which leaves you confessedly and unsympathetically at a loss, the aberrant phase in the whole human cycle of ecstasy and exhaustion with which you are imperfectly familiar, become increasingly rare. No perception however *petite*, no notion however subtle, escapes your attention or baffles your understanding: on entering any room you immediately distinguish the wasters who throw away their fruit half-eaten from the preservers who bottle all the summer; as the passengers file down the ship's gangway you unerringly guess which suitcase contains indecent novels; a five-minute chat about the weather or the coming elections is all you require to diagnose any distemper, however self-assured, for by then your eye has already spotted the tremor of the lips in that infinitesimal moment while the lie was getting its balance, your ear already picked up the heart's low whimper which the capering legs were determined to stifle, your nose detected on love's breath the trace of ennui which foretells his early death, or the despair just starting to smoulder at the base of the scholar's brain which years hence will suddenly blow it up with one appalling laugh: in every case you can prescribe the saving treatment called for, knowing at once when it may be gentle and remedial, when all that is needed is soft music and a pretty girl, and when it must be drastic and surgical, when nothing will do any good but political disgrace or financial and erotic failure. If I seem to attribute these powers to you when the eyes, the ears, the nose, the putting two and two together are, of course, all His, and yours only the primitive wish to know, it is a rhetorical habit I have caught from your, in the main juvenile and feminine, admirers whose naïve unawareness of whom they ought properly to thank and praise you see no point in, for mere accuracy's stuffy sake, correcting.

Anyway, the partnership is a brilliant success. On you go together to ever greater and faster triumphs; ever more major grows the accumulated work, ever more masterly the manner, sound even at its pale sententious worst, and at its best the rich red personal flower of the grave and grand, until one day which you can never either at the time or later identify exactly, your strange fever reaches its crisis and from now on begins, ever so slowly, maybe to subside. At first you cannot tell what or why is the matter; you have only a vague feeling that it is no longer between you so smooth and sweet as it used to be. Sour silences appear, at first only for an occasional moment, but progressively more frequently and more prolonged, curdled moods in which you cannot for the life of you think of any request to make, and His dumb standing around, waiting for orders gets inexplicably but maddeningly on your nerves, until presently, to your amazement, you hear yourself asking Him if He wouldn't like a vacation and are shocked by your feeling of intense disappointment when He who has always hitherto so immediately and recklessly taken your slightest hint, says gauchely 'No'. So it goes on from exasperated bad to desperate worst until you realize in despair that there is nothing for it but you two to part. Collecting all your strength for the distasteful task, you finally manage to stammer or shout 'You are free. Good-bye', but to your dismay He whose obedience through all the enchanted years has never been less than perfect, now refuses to budge. Striding up to Him in fury, you glare into His unblinking eyes and stop dead, transfixed with horror at seeing reflected there, not what you had always expected to see, a conqueror smiling at a conqueror, both promising mountains and marvels, but a gibbering fist-clenched creature with which you are all too unfamiliar, for this is the first time indeed that you have met the only subject that you have, who is not a dream amenable to magic but the all too solid flesh you must acknowledge as your own; at last you have come face to face with me, and are appalled to learn how far I am from being, in any sense, your dish; how completely lacking in that poise and calm and all-forgiving because all-understanding good nature which to the critical eye is so wonderfully and domestically present on every page of your published inventions.

But where, may I ask, should I have acquired them, when, like a society mother who, although she is, of course, as she tells everyone, absolutely *devoted* to her child, simply *cannot* leave the dinner table just now and really *must* be in Le Touquet tomorrow, and so leaves him in charge of servants she doesn't know or boarding schools she has never seen, you have never in all these years taken the faintest personal interest in me? 'Oh!' you protestingly gasp, 'but how can you say such a thing, after I've toiled and moiled and worked my fingers to the bone, trying to give you a good home, after all the hours I've spent planning wholesome nourishing meals for you, after all the things I've gone without so that you should have swimming lessons and piano lessons and a new bicycle. Have I ever let you go out in summer without your sun hat, or come in in winter without feeling your stockings and insisting, if they were the least bit damp, on your changing them at once? Haven't you always been allowed to do everything, in reason, that you liked?'

Exactly: even deliberate ill-treatment would have been less unkind. Gallows and battlefields are, after all, no less places of mutual concern than sofa and bridal-bed; the dashing flirtations of fighter pilots and the coy tactics of twirled moustache and fluttered fan, the gasping mudcaked wooing of the coarsest foes and the reverent rage of the highest-powered romance, the lover's nip and the grip of the torturer's tongs are all,—ask Ariel,—variants of one common type, the bracket within which life and death with such passionate gusto cohabit, to be distinguished solely by the plus or minus sign which stands before them, signs which He is able at any time and in either direction to switch, but the one exception, the sum no magic of His can ever transmute, is the indifferent zero. Had you tried to destroy me, had we wrestled through long dark hours, we might by daybreak have learnt something from each other; in some panting pause to recover breath for further more savage blows or in the moment before your death or mine, we might both have heard together that music which explains and pardons all.

Had you, on the other hand, really left me alone to go my whole free-wheeling way to disorder, to be drunk every day before lunch, to jump stark naked from bed to bed, to have a fit every week or a major operation every other year, to forge checks or water the widow's stock, I might, after countless skids and punctures, have come by the bumpy third-class road of guilt and remorse smack into that very same truth which you were meanwhile admiring from your distant comfortable veranda but would never point out to me.

Such genuine escapades, though, might have disturbed the master at

333

his meditations and even involved him in trouble with the police. The strains of oats, therefore, that you prudently permitted me to sow were each and all of an unmitigatedly minor wildness: a quick cold clasp now and then in some *louche* hotel to calm me down while you got on with the so thorough documentation of your great unhappy love for one who by being bad or dead or married provided you with the Good Right Subject that would never cease to bristle with importance; one bout of flu per winter, an occasional twinge of toothache, and enough tobacco to keep me in a good temper while you composed your melting eclogues of rustic piety; licence to break my shoelaces, spill soup on my tie, burn cigarette holes in the tablecloth, lose letters and borrowed books, and generally keep myself busy while you polished to a perfection your lyric praises of the more candid, more luxurious world to come.

Can you wonder then, when, as was bound to happen sooner or later, your charms, because they no longer amuse you, have cracked and your spirits, because you are tired of giving orders, have ceased to obey, and you are left alone with me, the dark thing you could never abide to be with, if I do not yield you kind answer or admire you for the achievements I was never allowed to profit from, if I resent hearing you speak of your neglect of me as your 'exile', of the pains you never took with me as 'all lost'?

But why continue? From now on we shall have, as we both know only too well, no company but each other's, and if I have had, as I consider, a good deal to put up with from you, I must own that, after all, I am not just the person I would have chosen for a life companion myself; so the only chance, which in any case is slim enough, of my getting a tolerably new master and you a tolerably new man, lies in our both learning, if possible and as soon as possible, to forgive and forget the past, and to keep our respective hopes for the future, within moderate, very moderate, limits.

*   *   *

And now at last it is you, assorted, consorted specimens of the general popular type, the major flock who have trotted trustingly hither but found, you reproachfully baah, no grazing, that I turn to and address on behalf of Ariel and myself. To your questions I shall attempt no direct reply, for the mere fact that you have been able so anxiously to put them is in itself sufficient proof that you possess their answers. All your clamour signifies is this: that your first big crisis, the breaking of the childish spell in which, so long as it enclosed you, there was, for you, no mirror, no magic, for everything that happened was a miracle—it was just as extraordinary for a chair to be a chair as for it to turn into a horse; it was no more absurd that the girding on of coal-scuttle and poker should transform you into noble Hector than that you should have a father and mother who called you Tommy—and it was therefore only necessary for you to presuppose one genius, one unrivalled I to wish these wonders in all their endless plenitude and novelty to be, is, in relation to your present, behind, that your singular transparent globes of enchantment have shattered one by one, and you have now all come together in the larger colder emptier room on this side of the mirror which *does* force your eyes to recognize and reckon with the two of us, your ears to detect the irreconcilable difference between my reiterated affirmation of what your furnished   circumstances   categorically   are,   and   His   successive propositions as to everything else which they conditionally might be. You have, as I say, taken your first step.

The Journey of life—the down-at-heels disillusioned figure can still put its characterization across—is infinitely long and its possible destinations infinitely distant from one another, but the time spent in actual travel is infinitesimally small. The hours the traveller measures are those in which he is at rest between the three or four decisive instants of transportation which are all he needs and all he gets to carry him the whole of his way; the scenery he observes is the view, gorgeous or drab, he glimpses from platform and siding; the incidents he thrills or blushes to remember take place in waiting and washrooms, ticket queues and parcels offices: it is in those promiscuous places of random association, in that air of anticipatory fidget, that he makes friends and enemies, that he promises, confesses, kisses, and betrays until, either because it is the one he has been expecting, or because, losing his temper, he has vowed to take the first to come along, or because he has been given a free ticket, or simply by misdirection or mistake, a train arrives which he does get into: it whistles—at least he thinks afterwards he remembers it whistling—but before he can blink, it has come to a standstill again and there he stands clutching his battered bags, surrounded by entirely strange smells and noises—yet in their smelliness and noisiness how familiar—one vast important stretch the nearer Nowhere, that still smashed terminus at which he will, in due course, be deposited, seedy and by himself.

Yes, you have made a definite start; you *have* left your homes way back in the farming provinces or way out in the suburban tundras, but whether you have been hanging around for years or have barely and breathlessly got here on one of those locals which keep arriving minute after minute, this is still only the main depot, the Grandly Average Place from which at odd hours the expresses leave seriously and sombrely for Somewhere, and where it is still possible for me to posit the suggestion that you go no farther. You will never, after all, feel better than in your present shaved and breakfasted state which there are restaurants and barber shops here indefinitely to preserve; you will never feel more secure than you do now in your knowledge that you *have* your ticket, your passport *is* in order, you have *not* forgotten to pack your pyjamas and an extra clean shirt; you will never have the same opportunity of learning about *all* the holy delectable spots of current or historic interest—an insistence on reaching *one* will necessarily exclude the others—than you have in these bepostered halls; you will never meet a jollier, more various crowd than you see around you here, sharing with you the throbbing, suppressed excitement of those to whom the exciting thing is still, perhaps, to happen. But once you leave, no matter in which direction, your next stop will be far outside this land of habit that so democratically stands up for your right to stagestruck hope, and well inside one of those, all equally foreign, uncomfortable and despotic, certainties of failure or success. Here at least I, and Ariel too, are free to warn you not, should we meet again there, to speak to either of us, not to engage either of us as your guide, but there we shall no longer be able to refuse you; then, unfortunately for you, we shall be compelled to say nothing and obey your fatal foolish commands. Here, whether you listen to me or not, and it's highly improbable that you will, I can at least warn you what will happen if at our next meeting you should insist—and that is all too probable—on putting one of us in charge.

*   *   *

'Release us,' you will beg, then, supposing it is I whom you make for,—oh how awfully uniform, once one translates them out of your private lingoes of expression, all your sorrows are and how awfully well I know them—'release us from our minor roles. Carry me back, Master, to the cathedral town where the canons run through the water meadows with butterfly nets and the old women keep sweet-shops in the cobbled side streets, or back to the upland mill town (gunpowder and plush) with its grope-movie and its poolroom lit by gas, carry me back to the days before my wife had put on weight, back to the years when beer was cheap and the rivers really froze in winter. Pity me, Captain, pity a poor old stranded sea-salt whom an unlucky voyage has wrecked on the desolate mahogany coast of this bar with nothing left him but his big moustache. Give me my passage home, let me see that harbour once again just as it was before I learned the bad words. Patriarchs wiser than Abraham mended their nets on the modest wharf; white and wonderful beings undressed on the sand-dunes; sunset glittered on the plate-glass windows of the Marine Biological Station; far off on the extreme horizon a whale spouted. Look, Uncle, look. They have broken my glasses and I have lost my silver whistle. Pick me up, Uncle, let little Johnny ride away on your massive shoulders to recover his green kingdom, where the steam rollers are as friendly as the farm dogs and it would never become necessary to look over one's left shoulder or clench one's right fist in one's pocket. You cannot miss it. Blackcurrant bushes hide the ruined opera house where badgers are said to breed in great numbers; an old horse-tramway winds away westward through suave foothills crowned with stone circles—follow it and by nightfall one would come to a large good-natured waterwheel—to the north, beyond a forest inhabited by charcoal burners, one can see the Devil's Bedposts quite distinctly, to the east the museum where for sixpence one can touch the ivory chessmen. O Cupid, Cupid, howls the whole dim chorus, take us home. We have never felt really well in this climate of distinct ideas; we have never been able to follow the regulations properly; Business, Science, Religion, Art, and all the other fictitious immortal persons who matter here have, frankly, not been very kind. We're so, so tired, the rewarding soup is stone cold, and over our blue wonders the grass grew long ago. O take us home with you, strong and swelling One, home to your promiscuous pastures where the minotaur of authority is just a roly-poly ruminant and nothing is at stake, those purring sites and amusing vistas where the fluctuating arabesques of sound, the continuous eruption of colours and scents, the whole rich incoherence of a nature made up of gaps and asymmetrical events plead beautifully and bravely for our undistress.'

And in that very moment when you so cry for deliverance from any and every anxious possibility, I shall have no option but to be faithful to my oath of service and instantly transport you, not indeed to any cathedral town or mill town or harbour or hillside or jungle or other specific Eden which your memory necessarily but falsely conceives of as the ultimately liberal condition, which in point of fact you have never known yet, but directly to that downright state itself. Here you are. This is it. Directly overhead a full moon casts a circle of dazzling light without any penumbra, exactly circumscribing its desolation in which every object is extraordinarily still and sharp. Cones of extinct volcanos rise up abruptly from the lava plateau fissured by chasms and pitted with hot springs from which steam rises without interruption straight up into the windless rarefied atmosphere. Here and there a geyser erupts without warning, spouts furiously for a few seconds and as suddenly subsides. Here, where the possessive note is utterly silent and all events are tautological repetitions and no decision will ever alter the secular stagnation, at long last you are, as you have asked to be, the only subject. Who, When, Why, the poor tired little historic questions fall wilting into a hush of utter failure. Your tears splash down upon clinkers which will never be persuaded to recognize a neighbour and there is really and truly no one to appear with tea and help. You have indeed come all the way to the end of your bachelor's journey where Liberty stands with her hands behind her back, not caring, not minding *anything*. Confronted by a straight and snubbing stare to which mythology is bosh, surrounded by an infinite passivity and purely arithmetical disorder which is only open to perception, and with nowhere to go on to, your existence is indeed free at last to choose its own meaning, that is, to plunge headlong into despair and fall through silence fathomless and dry, all fact your single drop, all value your pure alas.

*　　*　　*

But what of that other, smaller but doubtless finer group among you, important persons at the top of the ladder, exhausted lions of the season, local authorities with their tense tired faces, elderly hermits of both sexes living gloomily in the delta of a great fortune, whose *amour propre* prefers to turn for help to my more spiritual colleague?

'O yes,' you will sigh, 'we have had what once we would have called success. I moved the vices out of the city into a chain of reconditioned lighthouses. I introduced statistical methods into the Liberal Arts. I revived the country dances and installed electric stoves in the mountain cottages. I saved democracy by buying steel. I gave the caesura its freedom. But this world is no better and it is now quite clear to us that there is nothing to be done with such a ship of fools, adrift on a sugarloaf sea in which it is going very soon and suitably to founder. Deliver us, dear Spirit, from the tantrums of our telephones and the whispers of our secretaries conspiring against Man; deliver us from these helpless agglomerations of dishevelled creatures with their bed-wetting, vomiting, weeping bodies, their giggling, fugitive, disappointing hearts, and scrawling, blotted, misspelt minds, to whom we have so foolishly tried to bring the light they did not want; deliver us from all the litter of *billets-doux*, empty beer bottles, laundry lists, directives, promissory notes and broken toys, the terrible mess that this particularized life, which we have so futilely attempted to tidy, sullenly insists on leaving behind it; translate us, bright Angel, from this hell of inert and ailing matter, growing steadily senile in a time for ever immature, to that blessed realm, so far above the twelve impertinent winds and the four unreliable seasons, that Heaven of the Really General Case where, tortured no longer by three dimensions and immune from temporal vertigo, Life turns into Light, absorbed for good into the permanently stationary, completely self-sufficient, absolutely reasonable One.'

Obliged by the terms of His contract to gratify this other request of yours, the wish for freedom to transcend *any* condition, for direct unentailed power without *any*, however secretly immanent, obligation to inherit or transmit, what can poor shoulder-shrugging Ariel do but lead you forthwith into a nightmare which has all the wealth of exciting action and all the emotional poverty of an adventure story for boys, a

337

state of perpetual emergency and everlasting improvisation where all is need and change.

All the phenomena of an empirically ordinary world are given. Extended objects appear to which events happen—old men catch dreadful coughs, little girls get their arms twisted, flames run whooping through woods, round a river bend, as harmless looking as a dirty old bearskin rug, comes the gliding fury of a town-effacing wave, but these are merely elements in an allegorical landscape to which mathematical measurement and phenomenological analysis have no relevance.

All the voluntary movements are possible—crawling through flues and old sewers, sauntering past shop-fronts, tiptoeing through quicksands and mined areas, running through derelict factories and across empty plains, jumping over brooks, diving into pools or swimming along between banks of roses, pulling at manholes or pushing at revolving doors, clinging to rotten balustrades, sucking at straws or wounds; all the modes of transport, letters, oxcarts, canoes, hansom cabs, trains, trolleys, cars, aeroplanes, balloons, are available, but any sense of direction, any knowledge of where on earth one has come from or where on earth one is going to is completely absent.

Religion and culture seem to be represented by a catholic belief that something is lacking which must be found, but as to what that something is, the keys of heaven, the missing heir, genius, the smells of childhood, or a sense of humour, why it is lacking, whether it has been deliberately stolen, or accidentally lost or just hidden for a lark, and who is responsible, our ancestors, ourselves, the social structure, or mysterious wicked powers, there are as many faiths as there are searchers, and clues can be found behind every clock, under every stone, and in every hollow tree to support all of them.

Again, other selves undoubtedly exist, but though everyone's pocket is bulging with birth certificates, insurance policies, passports and letters of credit, there is no way of proving whether they are genuine or planted or forged, so that no one knows whether another is his friend disguised as an enemy or his enemy disguised as a friend (there is probably no one whose real name is Brown), or whether the police who here as elsewhere are grimly busy, are crushing a criminal revolt or upholding a vicious tyranny, any more than he knows whether he himself is a victim of the theft, or the thief, or a rival thief, a professionally interested detective or a professionally impartial journalist.

Even the circumstances of the tender passion, the long-distance calls, the assignation at the aquarium, the farewell embrace under the fish-tail burner on the landing, are continually present, but since, each time it goes through its performance, it never knows whether it is saving a life, or obtaining secret information, or forgetting or spiting its real love, the heart feels nothing but a dull percussion of conceptual forboding. Everything, in short, suggests Mind but, surrounded by an infinite extension of the adolescent difficulty, a rising of the subjective and subjunctive to ever steeper, stormier heights, the panting frozen expressive gift has collapsed under the strain of its communicative anxiety, and contributes nothing by way of meaning but a series of staccato barks or a delirious gush of glossolalia.

And from this nightmare of public solitude, this everlasting Not Yet, what relief have you but in an ever giddier collective gallop, with bisson eye and bevel course, toward the grey horizon of the bleaker vision, what landmarks but the four dead rivers, the Joyless, the Flaming, the

Mournful, and the Swamp of Tears, what goal but the Black Stone on which the bones are cracked, for only there in its cry of agony can your existence find at last an unequivocal meaning and your refusal to be yourself become a serious despair, the love nothing, the fear all?

*   *   *

Such are the alternative routes, the facile glad-handed highway or the virtuous averted track, by which the human effort to make its own fortune arrives all eager at its abruptly dreadful end. I have tried—the opportunity was not to be neglected—to raise the admonitory forefinger, to ring the alarming bell, but with so little confidence of producing the right result, so certain that the open eye and attentive ear will always interpret any sight and any sound to their advantage, every rebuff as a consolation, every prohibition as a rescue—that is what they open and attend for—that I find myself almost hoping, for your sake, that I have had the futile honour of addressing the blind and the deaf.

Having learnt his language, I begin to feel something of the serio-comic embarrassment of the dedicated dramatist, who, in representing to you your condition of estrangement from the truth, is doomed to fail the more he succeeds, for the more truthfully he paints the condition, the less clearly can he indicate the truth from which it is estranged, the brighter his revelation of the truth in its order, its justice, its joy, the fainter shows his picture of your actual condition in all its drabness and sham, and, worse still, the more sharply he defines the estrangement itself—and, ultimately, what other aim and justification has he, what else exactly *is* the artistic gift which he is forbidden to hide, if not to make you unforgettably conscious of the ungarnished offended gap between what you so questionably are and what you are commanded without any question to become, of the unqualified No that opposes your every step in any direction?—the more he must strengthen your delusion that an awareness of the gap is in itself a bridge, your interest in your imprisonment a release, so that, far from your being led by him to contrition and surrender, the regarding of your defects in his mirror, your dialogue, using his words, with yourself about yourself, becomes the one activity which never, like devouring or collecting or spending, lets you down, the one game which can be guaranteed, whatever the company, to catch on, a madness of which you can only be cured by some shock quite outside his control, an unpredictable misting over of his glass or an absurd misprint in his text.

Our unfortunate dramatist, therefore, is placed in the unseemly predicament of having to give all his passion, all his skill, all his time to the task of 'doing' life—consciously to give anything less than all would be a gross betrayal of his gift and an unpardonable presumption—as if it lay in *his* power to solve this dilemma—yet of having at the same time to hope that some unforeseen mishap will intervene to ruin his effect, without, however, obliterating your disappointment, the expectation aroused by him that there was an effect to ruin, that, if the smiling interest never did arrive, it must, through no fault of its own, have got stuck somewhere; that, exhausted, ravenous, delayed by fog, mobbed and mauled by a thousand irrelevancies, it has, nevertheless, not forgotten its promise but is still trying desperately to get a connection.

Beating about for some large loose image to define the original drama which aroused his imitative passion, the first performance in which the players were their own audience, the worldly stage on which their behaving flesh was really sore and sorry—for the floods of tears were not caused by onions, the deformities and wounds did not come off after a good wash, the self-stabbed heroine could not pick herself up again to make a gracious bow nor her seducer go demurely home to his plain and middle-aged spouse—the fancy immediately flushed is of the greatest grandest opera rendered by a very provincial touring company indeed.

Our performance—for Ariel and I are, you know this now, just as deeply involved as any of you—which we were obliged, all of us, to go on with and sit through right to the final dissonant chord, has been so indescribably inexcusably awful. Sweating and shivering in our moth-eaten ill-fitting stock costumes which with only a change of hat and re-arrangement of safety-pins, had to do for the *Landsknecht* and the Parisian art-student, bumping into, now a rippling palace, now a primeval forest full of holes, at cross purposes with the scraping bleating orchestra we could scarcely hear, for half the instruments were missing and the cottage piano which was filling-out must have stood for too many years in some damp parlour, we floundered on from fiasco to fiasco, the schmalz tenor never quite able at his big moments to get right up nor the ham bass right down, the stud contralto gargling through her maternal grief, the ravished coloratura trilling madly off-key and the re-united lovers half a bar apart, the knock-kneed armies shuffling limply through their bloody battles, the unearthly harvesters hysterically entangled in their honest fugato.

Now it is over. No, we have not dreamt it. Here we really stand, down stage with red faces and no applause; no effect, however simple, no piece of business, however unimportant, came off; there was not a single aspect of our whole production, not even the huge stuffed bird of happiness, for which a kind word could, however patronizingly, be said.

Yet, at this very moment when we do at last see ourselves as we are, neither cosy nor playful, but swaying out on the ultimate wind-whipped cornice that overhangs the unabiding void—we have never stood anywhere else,—when our reasons are silenced by the heavy huge derision,—There is nothing to say. There never has been,—and our wills chuck in their hands—There is no way out. There never was,—it is at this moment that for the first time in our lives we hear, not the sounds which, as born actors, we have hitherto condescended to use as an excellent vehicle for displaying our personalities and looks, but the real Word which is our only *raison d'être*. Not that we have improved; everything, the massacres, the whippings, the lies, the twaddle, and all their carbon copies are still present, more obviously than ever; nothing has been reconstructed; our shame, our fear, our incorrigible staginess, all wish and no resolve, are still, and more intensely than ever, all we have: only now it is not in spite of them but with them that we are blessed by that Wholly Other Life from which we are separated by an essential emphatic gulf of which our contrived fissures of mirror and proscenium arch—we understand them at last—are feebly figurative signs, so that all our meanings are reversed and it is precisely in its negative image of Judgment that we can positively envisage Mercy; it is just here, among the ruins and the bones, that we may rejoice in the perfected Work which is not ours. Its great coherences stand out through our secular blur in all their overwhelmingly righteous obligation; its voice speaks through our muffling banks of artificial flowers and unflinchingly delivers its authentic molar pardon; its spaces greet us with all their grand old prospect of wonder and width; the working charm is the full bloom of the unbothered state; the sounded note is the restored relation.

Postscript

(ARIEL *to Caliban. Echo by the* PROMPTER)

Weep no more but pity me,
Fleet persistent shadow cast
By your lameness, caught at last,
Helplessly in love with you,
Elegance, art, fascination,
  Fascinated by
  Drab mortality;
Spare me a humiliation,
  To your faults be true:
I can sing as you reply
                    . . . I

Wish for nothing lest you mar
The perfection in these eyes
Whose entire devotion lies
At the mercy of your will;
Tempt not your sworn comrade,—only
  As I am can I
  Love you as you are—
For my company be lonely
  For my health be ill:
I will sing if you will cry
                    . . . I

Never hope to say farewell,
For our lethargy is such
Heaven's kindness cannot touch
Nor earth's frankly brutal drum;
This was long ago decided,
  Both of us know why,
  Can, alas, foretell,
When our falsehoods are divided,
  What we shall become,
One evaporating sigh
                    . . . I

August 1942–February 1944

Part IX

The Age of Anxiety

A Baroque Eclogue

TO JOHN BETJEMAN

Lacrimosa dies illa
Qua resurget ex favilla
Iudicandus homo reus
THOMAS A CELANO (?)
Dies Irae

Part IX

The Age of Anxiety

A Baroque Eclogue

PART ONE

Prologue

Now the day is over,
Night is drawing nigh,
Shadows of the evening
Steal across the sky.
            S. BARING-GOULD

When the historical process breaks down and armies organize with their embossed debates the ensuing void which they can never consecrate, when necessity is associated with horror and freedom with boredom, then it looks good to the bar business.

In times of peace there are always a number of persons who wake up each morning excited by the prospect of another day of interesting and difficult work, or happily certain that the one with whom they shared their bed last night will be sharing it with them again the next, and who, in consequence, must be written off by the proprietor as a lost market. Not that he need worry. There will always be enough lonelies and enough failures who need desperately what he has to offer—namely, an unprejudiced space in which nothing particular ever happens, and a choice of physiological aids to the imagination whereby each may appropriate it for his or her private world of repentant felicitous forms, heavy expensive objects or avenging flames and floods—to guarantee him a handsome profit still.

But in wartime, when everybody is reduced to the anxious status of a shady character or a displaced person, when even the most prudent become worshippers of chance, and when, in comparison to the universal disorder of the world outside, his Bohemia seems as cosy and respectable as a suburban villa, he can count on making his fortune.

Looking up from his drink, QUANT caught the familiar eye of his reflection in the mirror behind the bar and wondered why he was still so interested in that tired old widower who would never be more now than a clerk in a shipping office near the Battery.

More, that is, as a public figure: for as so often happens in the modern world—and how much restlessness, envy and self-contempt it causes—there was no one-to-one correspondence between his social or economic position and his private mental life. He had come to America at the age of six when his father, implicated somehow in the shooting of a landlord, had had to leave Ireland in a hurry, and, from time to time, images, some highly-colored, some violent, derived from a life he could not remember, would enter unexpectedly and incomprehensibly into his dreams. Then, again, in early manhood, when unemployed during a depression, he had spent many hours one winter in the Public Library reading for the most part—he could not have told you why—books on Mythology. The knowledge gained at that time had ever since lain oddly around in a corner of his mind like luggage left long ago in an emergency by some acquaintance and never reclaimed.

Watching the bubbles rise in his glass, MALIN was glad to forget for his few days of leave the uniform of the Canadian Air Force he was wearing and the life it represented, at once disjointed and mechanical, alternately exhausting and idle, of a Medical Intelligence officer; trying to recapture the old atmosphere of laboratory and lecture hall, he returned with pleasure to his real interest.

Lighting a cigarette, ROSETTA, too, ignored her surroundings but with less ease. Yes, she made lots of money—she was a buyer for a big department store and did it very well—and that was a great deal, for, like anyone who has ever been so, she had a sensible horror of being poor. Yes, America was the best place on earth to come to if you had to earn your living, but did it have to be so big and empty and noisy and messy? Why could she not have been rich? Yes, though she was not as young as she looked, there were plenty of men who either were deceived or preferred a girl who might be experienced—which indeed she was. But why were the men one liked not the sort who proposed marriage and the men who proposed marriage not the sort one liked? So she returned now to her favorite day-dream in which she indulged whenever she got a little high—which was rather too often—and conjured up, detail by detail, one of those landscapes familiar to all readers of English detective stories, those lovely innocent countrysides inhabited by charming eccentrics with independent means and amusing hobbies to whom, until the sudden intrusion of a horrid corpse onto the tennis court or into the greenhouse, work and law and guilt are just literary words.

EMBLE, on the other hand, put down his empty glass and looked about him as if he hoped to read in all those faces the answer to his own disquiet. Having enlisted in the Navy during his sophomore year at a Mid-Western university, he suffered from that anxiety about himself and his future which haunts, like a bad smell, the minds of most young men, though most of them are under the illusion that their lack of confidence is a unique and shameful fear which, if confessed, would make them an object of derision to their normal contemporaries. Accordingly, they watch others with a covert but passionate curiosity. What makes them tick? What would it feel like to be a success? Here is someone who is nobody in particular, there even an obvious failure, yet they do not seem to mind. How is that possible? What is their secret?

In certain cases—his was one—this general unease of youth is only aggravated by what would appear to alleviate it, a grace of person which grants them, without effort on their part, a succession of sexual triumphs. For then the longing for success, the doubt of ever being able to achieve the kinds of success which have to be earned, and the certainty of being able to have at this moment a kind which does not, play dangerously into each other's hands.

So, fully conscious of the attraction of his uniform to both sexes, he looked round him, slightly contemptuous when he caught an admiring glance, and slightly piqued when he did not.

It was the night of All Souls.

QUANT was thinking:
> My deuce, my double, my dear image,
> Is it lively there, that land of glass
> Where song is a grimace, sound logic
> A suite of gestures? You seem amused.
> How well and witty when you wake up,
> How glad and good when you go to bed,
> Do you feel, my friend? What flavor has
> That liquor you lift with your left hand;

Is it cold by contrast, cool as this
For a soiled soul; does your self like mine
Taste of untruth? Tell me, what are you
Hiding in your heart, some angel face,
Some shadowy she who shares in my absence,
Enjoys my jokes? I'm jealous, surely,
Nicer myself (though not as honest),
The marked man of romantic thrillers
Whose brow bears the brand of a winter
No priest can explain, the poet disguised,
Thinking over things in thieves' kitchens,
Wanted by the waste, whom women's love
Or his own silhouette might all too soon
Betray to its tortures. I'll track you down,
I'll make you confess how much you know who
View my vices with a valet's slight
But shameless shrug, the *Schadenfreude*
Of cooks at keyholes. Old comrade, tell me
The lie of my lifetime but look me up in
Your good graces; agree to be friends
Till our deaths differ; drink, strange future,
To your neighbor now.

MALIN was thinking:

                                 No chimpanzee
Thinks it thinks. Things are divisible,
Creatures are not. In chaos all bodies
Would differ in weight. Dogs can learn to
Fear the future. The faceless machine
Lacks a surround. The laws of science have
Never explained why novelty always
Arrives to enrich (though the wrong question
Initiates nothing). Nature rewards
Perilous leaps. The prudent atom
Simply insists upon its safety now,
Security at all costs; the calm plant
Masters matter then submits to itself,
Busy but not brave; the beast assures
A stabler status to stolen flesh,
Assists though it enslaves: singular then
Is the human way; for the ego is a dream
Till a neighbor's need by name create it;
Man has no mean; his mirrors distort;
His greenest arcadias have ghosts too;
His utopias tempt to eternal youth
Or self-slaughter.

ROSETTA was thinking:

                           From Seager's Folly
We beheld what was ours. Undulant land
Rose layer by layer till at last the sea
Far away flashed; from fretted uplands
That lay to the north, from limestone heights
Incisive rains had dissected well,

For down each dale industrious there ran
A paternoster of ponds and mills,
Came sweet waters, assembling quietly
By a clear congress of accordant streams
A mild river that moseyed at will
Through parks and ploughland, purring southward
In a wide valley. Wolds on each side
Came dawdling downwards in double curves,
Mellow, mature, to meadowlands and
Sedentary orchards, settled places
Crowded with lives; fat cattle brooded
In the shade of great oaks, sheep grazed in
The ancient hollows of meander scars and
Long-legged ladies with little-legged dogs
Lolled with their lovers by lapsing brooks.
A couth region: consonant, lofty,
Volatile vault and vagrant buttress
Showed their shapeliness; with assured ease,
Proud on that plain, St. Peter Acorn,
St. Dill-in-the-Deep, St. Dust, St. Alb,
St. Bee-le-bone, St. Botolph-the-less,
High gothic growths in a grecian space,
Lorded over each leafy parish
Where country curates in cold bedrooms
Dreamed of deaneries till at day-break
The rector's rooks with relish described
Their stinted station.

EMBLE was thinking:
                              Estranged, aloof,
They brood over being till the bars close,
The malcontented who might have been
The creative odd ones the average need
To suggest new goals. Self-judged they sit,
Sad haunters of Perhaps who after years
To grasp and gaze in get no further
Than their first beholding, phantoms who try
Through much drink by magic to restore
The primitive pact with pure feeling,
Their flesh as it felt before sex was
(The archaic calm without cultural sin
Which her Adam is till his Eve does),
Eyeing the door, for ever expecting
Night after night the Nameless One, the
Smiling sea-god who shall safely land
Shy and broad-shouldered on the shore at last,
Enthusiastic, of their convenient
And dangerous dream; while days away, in
Prairie places where no person asks
What is suffered in ships, small tradesmen,
Wry relatives on rocking-chairs in
Moss-grown mansions, mothers whose causes
For right and wrong are unreal to them,
Grieve vaguely over theirs: their vision shrinks

As their dreams darken; with dulling voice
Each calls across a colder water,
Tense, optative, interrogating
Some sighing several who sadly fades.

But now the radio, suddenly breaking in with its banal noises upon their separate senses of themselves, by compelling them to pay attention to a common world of great slaughter and much sorrow, began, without their knowledge, to draw these four strangers closer to each other. For in response to its official doctored message:

Now the news. Night raids on
Five cities. Fires started.
Pressure applied by pincer movement
In threatening thrust. Third Division
Enlarges beachhead. Lucky charm
Saves sniper. Sabotage hinted
In steel-mill stoppage. Strong point held
By fanatical Nazis. Canal crossed
By heroic marines. Rochester barber
Fools foe. Finns ignore
Peace feeler. Pope condemns
Axis excesses. Underground
Blows up bridge. Thibetan prayer-wheels
Revolve for victory. Vital crossroads
Taken by tanks. Trend to the left
Forecast by Congressman. Cruiser sunk
In Valdivian Deep. Doomed sailors
Play poker. Reporter killed.

MALIN thought:
Untalkative and tense, we took off
Anxious into air; our instruments glowed,
Dials in darkness, for dawn was not yet;
Pulses pounded; we approached our target,
Conscious in common of our closed Here
And of Them out There, thinking of Us
In a different dream, for we die in theirs
Who kill in ours and become fathers,
Not twisting tracks their trigger hands are
Given goals by; we began our run;
Death and damage darted at our will,
Bullets were about, blazing anger
Lunged from below, but we laid our eggs
Neatly in their nest, a nice deposit,
Hatched in an instant; houses flamed in
Shuddering sheets as we shed our big
Tears on their town: we turned to come back,
But at high altitudes, hostile brains
Waited in the west, a wily flock
Vowed to vengeance in the vast morning,
—A mild morning where no marriage was,
And gravity a god greater than love—
Fierce interferers. We fought them off

349

But paid a price; there was pain for some.
'Why have They killed me?' wondered our Bert, our
Greenhouse gunner, forgot our answer,
Then was not with us. We watched others
Drop into death; dully we mourned each
Flare as it fell with a friend's lifetime,
While we hurried on to our home bases
To the safe smells and a sacrament
Of tea with toast. At twenty to eight I
Stepped onto grass, still with the living,
While far and near a fioritura
Of brooks and blackbirds bravely struck the
International note with no sense
Of historic truth, of time meaning
Once and for all, and my watch stuttered:—
Many have perished; more will.

And QUANT thought:
All war's woes I can well imagine.
Gun-barrels glint, gathered in ambush,
Mayhem among mountains; minerals break
In by order on intimate groups of
Tender tissues; at their tough visit
Flesh flusters that was so fluent till now,
Stammers some nonsense, stops and sits down,
Apathetic to all this. Thousands lie in
Ruins by roads, irrational in woods,
Insensitive upon snow-bound plains,
Or littered lifeless along low coasts
Where shingle shuffles as shambling waves
Feebly fiddle in the fading light
With bloated bodies, beached among groynes,
Male no longer, unmotivated,
Have-beens without hopes: Earth takes charge of,
Soil accepts for a serious purpose
The jettisoned blood of jokes and dreams,
Making buds from bone, from brains the good
Vague vegetable; survivors play
Cards in kitchens while candles flicker
And in blood-spattered barns bandaged men,
Their poor hands in a panic of need
Groping weakly for a gun-butt or
A friendly fist, are fetched off darkling.
Many have perished; more will.

And EMBLE thought:
High were those headlands; the eagles promised
Life without lawyers. Our long convoy
Turned away northward as tireless gulls
Wove over water webs of brightness
And sad sound. The insensible ocean,
Miles without mind, moaned all around our
Limited laughter, and below our songs
Were deaf deeps, denes of unaffection,

Their chill unchanging, chines where only
The whale is warm, their wildness haunted
By metal fauna moved by reason
To hunt not in hunger but for hate's sake,
Stalking our steamers. Strained with gazing
Our eyes ached, and our ears as we slept
Kept their care for the crash that would turn
Our fears into fact. In the fourth watch
A torpedo struck on the port bow:
The blast killed many; the burning oil
Suffocated some; some in lifebelts
Floated upright till they froze to death;
The younger swam but the yielding waves
Denied help; they were not supported,
They swallowed and sank, ceased thereafter
To appear in public; exposed to snap
Verdicts of sharks, to vague inquiries
Of amoeboid monsters, mobbed by slight
Unfriendly fry, refused persistence.
They are nothing now but names assigned to
Anguish in others, areas of grief.
Many have perished; more will.

ROSETTA thought:
I see in my mind a besieged island,
That island in arms where my home once was.
Round green gardens, down grooves between white
Hawthorne-hedges, long hospital trains
Smoothly slide with their sensitized freight
Of mangled men, moving them homeward
In pain through pastures. In a packed hall
Two vicious rivals, two virtuosos
Appear on one platform and play duets
To war-orphans and widowed ladies,
Grieving in gloves; while to grosser ears
In clubs and cabarets crooners wail
Some *miserere* modern enough
In its thorough thinness. I think too of
The conquered condition, countries where
Arrogant officers, armed in cars,
Go roaring down roads on the wrong side,
Courts martial meet at midnight with drums,
And pudgy persons pace unsmiling
The quays and stations or cruise the nights
In vans for victims, to investigate
In sound-proof cells the Sense of Honor,
While in turkish baths with towels round them
Imperilled plotters plan in outline
Definitions and norms for new lives,
Half-truths for their times. As tense as these,
Four who are famous confer in a *schloss*
At night on nations. They are not equal:
Three stand thoughtful on a thick carpet
Awaiting the Fourth who wills they shall

351

Till, suddenly entering through a side-door,
Quick, quiet, unquestionable as death,
Grief or guilt, he greets them and sits down,
Lord of this life. He looks natural,
He smiles well, he smells of the future,
Odorless ages, an ordered world
Of planned pleasures and passport-control,
Sentry-go, sedatives, soft drinks and
Managed money, a moral planet
Tamed by terror: his telegram sets
Grey masses moving as the mud dries.
Many have perished; more will.

And when in conclusion the instrument said:

Buy a bond. Blood saves lives.
Donate now. Name this station.

they could no longer keep these thoughts to themselves, but turning
towards each other on their high wooden stools, became acquainted.

ROSETTA spoke first:
Numbers and nightmares have news value.

Then MALIN:
A crime has occurred, accusing all.

Then QUANT:
The world needs a wash and a week's rest.

To which EMBLE said:
Better this than barbarian misrule.
History tells more often than not
Of wickedness with will, wisdom but
An interjection without a verb,
And the godless growing like green cedars
On righteous ruins. The reticent earth,
Exposed by the spade, speaks its warning
With successive layers of sacked temples
And dead civilians. They dwelt at ease
In their sown centres, sunny their minds,
Fine their features; their flesh was carried
On beautiful bones; they bore themselves
Lightly through life; they loved their children
And entertained with all their senses
A world of detail. Wave and pebble,
Boar and butterfly, birch and carp, they
Painted as persons, portraits that seem
Neighbours with names; one knows from them what
A leaf must feel. By lakes at twilight
They sang of swans and separations,
Mild, unmilitant, as the moon rose
And reeds rustled; ritual appointed
Tastes and textures; their touch preferred the
Spectrum of scents to Spartan morals,
Art to action. But, unexpected, as

Bells babbled in a blossoming month,
Near-sighted scholars on canal paths
Defined their terms, and fans made public
The hopes of young hearts, out of the north, from
Black tundras, from basalt and lichen,
Peripheral people, rancid ones
Stocky on horses, stomachs in need of
Game and grazing, by grass corridors
Coursed down on their concatenation
Of smiling cities. Swords and arrows
Accosted their calm; their climate knew
Fire and fear; they fell, they bled, not an
Eye was left open; all disappeared:
Utter oblivion they had after that.

MALIN said:
But the new barbarian is no uncouth
Desert-dweller; he does not emerge
From fir forests; factories bred him;
Corporate companies, college towns
Mothered his mind, and many journals
Backed his beliefs. He was born here. The
Bravura of revolvers in vogue now
And the cult of death are quite at home
Inside the city.

QUANT said:
The soldiers' fear
And the shots will cease in a short while,
More ruined regions surrender to less,
Prominent persons be put to death
For mass-murder, and what moves us now,
The defence of friends against foes' hate,
Be over for ever. Then, after that,
What shall we will? Why shall we practise
Vice or virtue when victory comes?
The celebrations are suddenly hushed,
The coarse crowds uncomfortably still,
Form, arm-in-arm now, behind the festooned
Conqueror's car there come his heirs, the
Public hangman, the private wastrel.

ROSETTA said:
Lies and lethargies police the world
In its periods of peace. What pain taught
Is soon forgotten; we celebrate
What ought to happen as if it were done,
Are blinded by our boasts. Then back they come,
The fears that we fear. We fall asleep
Only to meet the idiot children of
Our revels and wrongs; farouche they appear,
Reluctant look-behinds, loitering through
The mooing gate, menacing or smiling,
Nocturnal trivia, torts and dramas,

353

Wrecks, arrivals, rose-bushes, armies,
Leopards and laughs, alarming growths of
Moulds and monsters on memories stuffed
With dead men's doodles, dossiers written
In lost lingos, too long an account
To take out in trade, no time either,
Since we wake up. We are warm, our active
Universe is young; yet we shiver:
For athwart our thinking the threat looms,
Huge and awful as the hump of Saturn
Over modest Mimas, of more deaths
And worse wars, a winter of distaste
To last a lifetime. Our lips are dry, our
Knees numb; the enormous disappointment
With a smiling sigh softly flings her
Indolent apron over our lives
And sits down on our day. Damning us,
On our present purpose the past weighs
Heavy as alps, for the absent are never
Mislaid or lost: as lawyers define
The grammar of our grief, their ghosts rise,
Hanged or headless, hosts who disputed
With good governors, their guilty flesh
Racked and raving but unreconciled,
The punished people to pass sentence
On the jolly and just; and, joining these
Come worse warlocks, the wailing infants
Who know now they will never be born,
Refused a future. Our failings give
Their resentment seizin; our Zion is
A doomed Sodom dancing its heart out
To treacly tunes, a tired Gomorrah
Infatuated with her former self
Whose dear dreams though they dominate still
Are formal facts which refresh no more.

They fell silent and immediately became conscious again of the radio,
now blandly inexorably bringing to all John Doakes and G.I. Joes tidings
of great joy and saying

Definitely different. Has that democratic
Extra elegance. Easy to clean.
Will gladden grand-dad and your girl friend.
Lasts a lifetime. Leaves no odor.
American made. A modern product
Of nerve and know-how with a new thrill.
Patriotic to own. Is on its way
In a patent package. Pays to investigate.
Serves through science. Has something added
By skilled Scotchmen. Exclusively used
By upper classmen and Uncle Sam.
Tops in tests by teenagers.
Just ask for it always.

Matter and manner set their teeth on edge, especially MALIN's who felt
like talking. So he ordered a round of drinks, then said:

> Here we sit
> Our bodies bound to these bar-room lights,
> The night's odours, the noise of the El on
> Third Avenue, but our thoughts are free . . .
> Where shall they wander? To the wild past
> When, beaten back, banished to their cirques
> The horse-shoe glaciers curled up and died,
> And cold-blooded through conifers slouched
> Fumbling amphibians; forward into
> Tidy utopias of eternal spring,
> Vitamins, villas, visas for dogs
> And art for all; or up and down through
> Those hidden worlds of alien sizes
> Which lenses elicit?

But EMBLE objected:
> Muster no monsters, I'll meeken my own.

So did ROSETTA:
> You may wish till you waste, I'll want here.

So did QUANT:
> Too blank the blink of these blind heavens.

MALIN suggested:
> Let us then
> Consider rather the incessant Now of
> The traveller through time, his tired mind
> Biased towards bigness since his body must,
> Exaggerate to exist, possessed by hope,
> Acquisitive, in quest of his own
> Absconded self yet scared to find it
> As he bumbles by from birth to death
> Menaced by madness; whose mode of being,
> Bashful or braggart, is to be at once
> Outside and inside his own demand
> For personal pattern. His pure I
> Must give account of and greet his Me,
> That field of force where he feels he thinks,
> His past present, presupposing death,
> Must ask what he is in order to be
> And make meaning by omission and stress,
> Avid of elseness. All that exists
> Matters to man; he minds what happens
> And feels he is at fault, a fallen soul
> With power to place, to explain every
> What in his world but why he is neither
> God nor good, this guilt the insoluble
> Final fact, infusing his private
> Nexus of needs, his noted aims with
> Incomprehensible comprehensive dread

At not being what he knows that before
This world was he was willed to become.

QUANT approved:
Set him to song, the surly old dodger.

So did EMBLE:
Relate his lies to his longings for truth.

So did ROSETTA:
Question his crimes till his clues confess.

The radio attempted to interrupt by remarking

And now Captain Kidd in his Quiz Programme
HOW ALERT ARE YOU

But QUANT pointed a finger at it and it stopped immediately. He said:

Listen, Box,
And keep quiet. Listen courteously to us
Four reformers who have founded—why not?—
The Gung-Ho Group, the Ganymede Club
For homesick young angels, the Arctic League
Of Tropical Fish, the Tomboy Fund
For Blushing Brides and the Bide-a-wees
Of Sans-Souci, assembled again
For a Think-Fest: Our theme tonight is
HOMO ABYSSUS OCCIDENTALIS
or
A CURIOUS CASE OF COLD FEET
or
SEVEN SELFISH SUPPERLESS AGES

And now, at ROSETTA's suggestion, they left their bar-stools and moved
to the quieter intimacy of a booth. Drinks were ordered and the
discussion began.

PART TWO

The Seven Ages

A sick toss'd vessel, dashing on each thing;
Nay, his own shelf:
My God, I mean myself.
GEORGE HERBERT *Miserie*

MALIN began:
> Behold the infant, helpless in cradle and
> Righteous still, yet already there is
> Dread in his dreams at the deed of which
> He knows nothing but knows he can do,
> The gulf before him with guilt beyond,
> Whatever that is, whatever why
> Forbids his bound; till that ban tempts him;
> He jumps and is judged: he joins mankind,
> The fallen families, freedom lost,
> Love become Law. Now he looks at grown-ups
> With conscious care, and calculates on
> The effect of a frown or filial smile,
> Accuses with a cough, claims pity
> With scratched knees, skilfully avenges
> Pains and punishments on puny insects,
> Grows into a grin, and gladly shares his
> Small secret with the supplicating
> Instant present. His emptiness finds
> Its joy in a gang and is joined to others
> By crimes in common. Clumsy and alarmed,
> As the blind bat obeys the warnings
> Of its own echoes, his inner life
> Is a zig-zag, a bizarre dance of
> Feelings through facts, a foiled one learning
> Shyness and shame, a shadowed flier.

QUANT said:
> O
> Secret meetings at the slaughter-house
> With nickels and knives, initiations
> Behind the billboards. Then the hammerpond looked
> So green and grim, yet graciously its dank
> Water made us welcome—once in, we
> Swam without swearing. The smelting mill
> We broke into had a big chimney
> And huge engines; holding our breath, we
> Lighted matches and looked at the gears,
> The cruel cogwheels, the crank's absolute
> Veto on pleasure. In a vacant lot
> We built a bonfire and burned alive
> Some stolen tires. How strong and good one
> Felt at first, how fagged coming home through
> The urban evening. Heavy like us

Sank the gas-tanks—it was supper time.
In hot houses helpless babies and
Telephones gabbled untidy cries,
And on embankments black with burnt grass
Shambling freight-trains were shunted away
Past crimson clouds.

EMBLE said:

My cousins were both
Strong and stupid: they stole my candy,
They tied me to a tree, they twisted my arms,
Called me crybaby. 'Take care,' I sobbed,
'I could hold up my hand and hot water
Would come down on your drought and drown you all
In your big boots.' In our back garden
One dark afternoon I dug quite a hole
Planning to vanish.

ROSETTA said:

On picnic days
My dearest doll was deaf and spoke in
Grunts like grandfather. God understood
If we washed our necks he wasn't ever
To look in the loft where the Lamps were
And the Holy Hook. In the housekeeper's room there
Was currant cake and calves-foot jelly
As we did our sums while down below,
Tall in tweeds on the terrace gravel,
Father and his friends reformed régimes,
Monies and monarchs, and mother wrote
Swift and sure in the silk-hung saloon
Her large round letters. Along the esker,
Following a fox with our fingers crossed
Or after the ogre in Indian file,
We stole with our sticks through a still world of
Hilarious light, our lives united
Like fruit in a bowl, befriended by
The supple silence, incited by
Our shortened shadows.

MALIN went on to the Second Age:

With shaving comes
An hour when he halts, hearing the crescent
Roar of hazard, and realizes first
He has laid his life-bet with a lying self
Who wins or welches. Thus woken, he is
Amused no more by a merely given
Felt fact, the facile emergence of
Thought with thing, but, threatened from all sides,
Embarrassed by his body's bald statements,
His sacred soul obscenely tickled
And bellowed at by a blatant Without,
A dog by daylight, in dreams a lamb
Whom the nightmare ejects nude into

A ball of princes too big to feel
Disturbed by his distress, he starts off now,
Poor, unprepared, on his pilgrimage
To find his friends, the far-off *élite*,
And, knowing no one, a nameless young man,
Pictures as he plods his promised chair
In their small circle secret to those
With no analogies, unique persons,
The originals' ring, the round table
Of master minds. Mountains he loves now,
Piers and promontories, places where
Evening brings him all that grandeur
Of scope and scale which the sky is believed
To promise or recall, pacing by
In a sunset trance of self-pity,
While his toy tears with a touching grace
Like little balloons sail lonely away
To dusk and death.

QUANT said:
                    With diamonds to offer,
A cleaned tycoon in a cooled office,
I smiled at a siren with six breasts,
Leaning on leather, looking up at
Her righteous robber, her Robin Hood,
Her plump prince. All the public could see
Was a bus-boy brushing a table,
Sullen and slight.

ROSETTA said:
                    In my sixteenth year
Before sleeping I fancied nightly
The house on the headland I would own one day.
Its long windows overlooked the sea
And its turf terrace topped a sunny
Sequestered cove. A corkscrew staircase
From a green gate in the garden wall
Descended the cliff, the sole entrance
To my beach where bathers basked beside
The watchet waves. Though One was special,
All forms were friends who freely told their
Secrets to me; but, safe in my purse
I kept the key to the closet where
A sliding panel concealed the lift,
Known to none, which at night would take me
Down through the dark to my dock below,
A chamber chiselled in the chalk hill,
Private and perfect; thence, putting forth
Alone in my launch through a low tunnel
Out to the ocean, while all others slept,
Smiling and singing I sailed till dawn,
Happy, hatless.

EMBLE said:
After a dreadful
Row with father, I ran with burning
Cheeks to the pasture and chopped wood, my
Stomach like a stone. I strode that night
Through wicked dreams: waking, I skipped to
The shower and sang, ashamed to recall
With whom or how; the hiss of the water
Composed the tune, I supplied the words
For a fine dirge which fifty years hence
Massed choirs would sing as my coffin passed,
Grieved for and great on a gun-carriage.

MALIN went on, spoke of the Third Age:
Such pictures fade as his path is blocked
By Others from Elsewhere, alien bodies
Whose figures fasten on his free thoughts,
Ciphers and symbols secret to his flesh,
Uniquely near, needing his torments,
His lonely life, and he learns what real
Images are; that, however violent
Their wish to be one, that wild promise
Cannot be kept, their case is double;
For each now of need ignores the other as
By rival routes of recognition
Diminutive names that midnight hears
Intersect upon their instant way
To solid solitudes, and selves cross
Back to bodies, both insisting each
Proximate place a pertinent thing.
So, learning to love, at length he is taught
To know he does not.

QUANT said:
Since the neighbors did,
With a multitude I made the long
Visitors' voyage to Venus Island,
Elated as they, landed upon
The savage shore where old swains lay wrecked
Unfit for her fable, followed up
The basalt stairway bandying jokes with
The thoughtless throng, but then, avoiding
The great gate where she gives all pilgrims
Her local wine, I legged it over
A concrete wall, was cold sober as,
Pushing through brambles, I peeked out at
Her fascination. Frogs were shooting
Craps in a corner; cupids on stilts,
Their beautiful bottoms breaking wind,
Hunted hares with hurricane lanterns
Through woods on one side, while on the other,
Shining out through shivering poplars,
Stood a brick bath-house where burghers mixed
With light-fingered ladies and louche trade,

Dancing in serpents and daisy chains
To mad music. In the mid-distance
On deal chairs sat a dozen decayed
Gentlewomen with dejected backs
And raw fingers morosely stitching
Red flannel scivvies for heroic herms.
Primroses, peacocks and peachtrees made
A fair foreground but fairer there, with
An early Madonna's oval face
And lissom limbs, delighting that whole
Degraded glen, the Goddess herself
Presided smiling; a saucy wind,
Plucking from her thigh her pink wrapper
Of crêpe-de-chine, disclosed a very
Indolent ulcer.

ROSETTA said nothing but, placing a nickel in the Wallomatic, selected
a sad little tune *The Case is Closed* (*Tchaikovsky-Fink*) and sang to it softly:

Deep in my dark the dream shines
Yes, of you, you dear always;
My cause to cry, cold but my
Story still, still my music.

Mild rose the moon, moving through our
Naked nights: tonight it rains;
Black umbrellas blossom out;
Gone the gold, my golden ball.

Heavy these hands. I believed
That pleased pause, your pause was me
To love alone till life's end:
I thought this; this was not true.

You touched, you took. Tears fall. O
Fair my far, when far ago
Like waterwheels wishes spun
Radiant robes: but the robes tore.

EMBLE did likewise but his choice was a hot number, *Bugs in the Bed* by
Bog Myrtle & Her Two-Timers. He sang gaily:

His Queen was forward, Her King was shy;
He hoped for Her Heart but He overbid;
When She ducked His Diamond down They went.

In Smuggler's Cove He smelt near Him
Her musical mermaids; She met His angels
In Locksmith's Lane, the little dears.

He said to Her: 'You're a hazy truth;'
She said to Him: 'You're a shining lie;'
Each went to a washroom and wept much.

The public applauded and the poets drew
A moral for marriage: 'The moths will get you
If the wolves won't, so why not now?'

The consequence was Both claimed the insurance
And the furniture gave what-for to Their elbows.
A reason for One, a risk on the Pair.

MALIN went on, spoke of the Fourth Age:
      Now unreckoned with, rough, his road descends
      From the haughty and high, the humorless places
      His dreams would prefer, and drops him till,
      As his forefathers did, he finds out
      Where his world lies. By the water's edge,
      The unthinking flood, down there, yes, is his
      Proper place, the polychrome Oval
      With its kleig lights and crowd engineers,
      The mutable circus where mobs rule
      The arena with roars, the real world of
      Theology and horses, our home because
      In that doubt-condemning dual kingdom
      Signs and insignia decide our cause,
      Fanatics of the Egg or Knights sworn to
      Die for the Dolphin, and our deeds wear
      Heretic green or orthodox blue,
      Safe and certain.

ROSETTA said:
                      Too soon we embrace that
      Impermanent appetitive flux,
      Humorous and hard, which adults fear
      Is real and right, the irreverent place,
      The clown's cosmos.

EMBLE said:
                    Who is comforted by it?
      Pent in the packed compulsory ring
      Round father's frown each *famus* waits his
      Day to dominate. Here a dean sits
      Making bedroom eyes at a beef steak,
      As wholly oral as the avid creatures
      Of the celibate sea; there, sly and wise
      Commuters mimic the Middle Way,
      Trudging on time to a tidy fortune.
      (A senator said: 'From swimming-hole
      To board-meeting is a big distance.')
      Financiers on knolls, noses pointing
      East towards oil fields, inhale the surplus
      Their bowels boast of, while boys and girls, their
      Hot hearts covered over with marriage
      To tyrant functions, turn by degrees
      To cold fish, though, precarious on the
      Fringes of their feeling, a fuzzy hope
      Persists somehow that sometime all this

Will walk away, and a wish gestates
For explosive pain, a punishing
Demanded moment of mortal change,
The Night of the Knock when none shall sleep,
The Absolute Instant.

QUANT said:
                              It is here, now.
For the huge wild beast of the Unexpected
Leaps on the lax recollecting back;
Unknown to him, binoculars follow
The leaping lad; lightning at noonday
Swiftly stooping to the summer-house
Engraves its disgust on engrossed flesh,
And at tea-times through tall french windows
Hurtle anonymous hostile stones.
No soul is safe. Let slight infection
Disturb a trifle some tiny gland,
And Caustic Keith grows kind and silly
Or Dainty Daisy dirties herself.
We are mocked by unmeaning; among us fall
Aimless arrows, hurting at random
As we plan to pain.

MALIN went on, spoke of the Fifth Age:
                              In peace or war,
Married or single, he muddles on,
Offending, fumbling, falling over,
And then, rather suddenly, there he is
Standing up, an astonished victor
Gliding over the good glib waters
Of the social harbor to set foot
On its welcoming shore where at last
Recognition surrounds his days with
Her felicitous light. He likes that;
He fairly blooms; his fever almost
Relaxes its hold. He learns to speak
Softer and slower, not to seem so eager;
His body acquires the blander motions
Of the approved state. His positive glow
Of fiscal health affects that unseen
Just judge, that Generalized Other
To whom he thinks and is understood by,
Who grows less gruff as if gravely impressed
By his evident air of having now
Really arrived, bereaved of every
Low relation.

EMBLE said:
                              Why leave out the worst
Pang of youth? The princes of fiction,
Who ride through risks to rescue their loves,
Know their business, are not really
As young as they look. To be young means

To be all on edge, to be held waiting in
A packed lounge for a Personal Call
From Long Distance, for the low voice that
Defines one's future. The fears we know
Are of not knowing. Will nightfall bring us
Some awful order—Keep a hardware store
In a small town. . . . Teach science for life to
Progressive girls—? It is getting late.
Shall we ever be asked for? Are we simply
Not wanted at all?

QUANT said:
                        Well, you will soon
Not bother but acknowledge yourself
As market-made, a commodity
Whose value varies, a vendor who has
To obey his buyer, will embrace moreover
The problems put you by opposing time,
The fight with work, the feud of marriage,
Whose detonating details day and night
Invest your breathing and veto sleep,
As their own answers, like others find
The train-ride between your two natures,
The morning-evening moment when
You are free to reflect on your faults still,
Is an awkward hiatus, is indeed
The real risk to be read away with
Print and pictures, reports of what should
Never have happened, will no longer
Expect more pattern, more purpose than
Your finite fate.

ROSETTA said:
                        I refuse to accept
Your plain place, your unprivileged time.
No. No. I shall not apologize
Nor retire contempt for this tawdry age.
The juke-box jives rejoicing madly
As life after life lapses out of
Its essential self and sinks into
One press-applauded public untruth
And, massed to its music, all march in step
Led by that liar, the lukewarm Spirit
Of the Escalator, ever timely,
His whims their will, away from freedom
To a locker-room life at low tension,
Abnormal none, anonymous hosts
Driven like Danaids by drill sergeants
To ply well-paid repetitive tasks
(Dowdy they'll die who have so dimly lived)
In cosy crowds. Till the caring poet,
Child of his chamber, chooses rightly
His pleased picture of pure solitudes
Where gusts gamble over gaunt areas

Frozen and futile but far enough
From vile civilities vouched for by
Statisticians, this stupid world where
Gadgets are gods and we go on talking,
Many about much, but remain alone,
Alive but alone, belonging—where?—
Unattached as tumbleweed. Time flies.

QUANT said:
No, Time returns, a continuous Now
As the clock counts. The captain sober
Gulps his beer as the galley-boy drunk
Gives away his water; William East is
Entering Olive as Alfred West
Is leaving Elaine; Lucky McGuire
Divides the spoil as Vacuous Molly
Joins in the joke; Justice van Diemen
Foresees the day when the slaves rise and
Ragamuffins roll around the block
His cone-shaped skull, while Convict 90
Remembers his mother. We move on
As the wheel wills; one revolution
Registers all things, the rise and fall
In pay and prices, peregrinations
Of lies and loves, colossal bangs and
Their sequential quiets in quick order.
And who runs may read written on walls
Eternal truths: 'Teddy Peterson
Never washes.' 'I'm not your father
You slobbering Swede.' 'Sulky Moses
Has bees in his bush.' 'Betty is thinner
But Connie lays.'—Who closes his eyes
Sees the blonde vistas bathed in sunlight,
The temples, tombs, and terminal god,
Tall by a torrent, the etruscan landscape
Of Man's Memory. His myths of Being
Are there always. In that unchanging
Lucid lake where he looks for ever
Narcissus sees the sensitive face
He's too intelligent to trust or like,
Pleading his pardon. Polyphemus
Curses his cave or, catching a nymph,
Begs for brotherhood with a big stick,
Hobbledehoy and helpless. Kind Orpheus lies
Violently slain on the virid bank,
That smooth sward where he sinned against kind,
And, wild by the water, women stone
The broken torso but the bloody head,
In the far distance, floating away
Down the steady stream, still opening
Its charming mouth, goes chanting on in
Fortissimo tones, a tenor lyre
Dinning the doom into a deaf Nature
Of her loose chaos. For Long-Ago has been

Ever-After since Ur-Papa gave
The Primal Yawn that expressed all things
(In His Boredom their beings) and brought forth
The wit of this world. One-Eye's mistake
Is sorry He spoke.

MALIN went on, spoke of the Sixth Age:
                    Our subject has changed.
He looks far from well; he has fattened on
His public perch; takes pills for vigor
And sound sleep, and sees in his mirror
The jawing genius of a jackass age,
A rich bore. When he recollects his
Designed life, the presented pomp is
A case of chaos, a constituted
Famine of effect. Feverish in
Their bony building his brain cells keep
Their hectic still, but his heart transfixed
By the ice-splinter of an ingrown tear,
Comatose in her cave, cares little
What the senses say; at the same time,
Dedicated, clandestine under
The guilt and grime of a great career,
The bruise of his boyhood is as blue still,
Horrid and hurting, hostile to his life
As a praised person. He pines for some
Nameless Eden where he never was
But where in his wishes once again
On hallowed acres, without a stitch
Of achievement on, the children play
Nor care how comely they couldn't be
Since they needn't know they're not happy.

QUANT said:
          So do the ignored. In the soft-footed
Hours of darkness when elevators
Raise blondes aloft to bachelor suites
And the night-nurse notices a change
In the patient's breathing, and Pride lies
Awake in himself too weak to stir
As Shame and Regret shove into his their
Inflamed faces, we failures inquire
For the treasure also. I too have shed
The tears of parting at Traitor's Halt
Where comforts finished and kind but dull,
In low landaus and electric broughams,
Through wrought-iron gates, down rhododendron
Avenues they came, Sir Ambrose Touch,
Fat Lady Feel, Professor Howling,
Doctor Dort, dear Mrs. Pollybore,
And the Scarsdale boy with a school friend
To see us off. (But someone important,
Alas, was not there.) Some laughed of course.
Ha-ha, ha-ha, cried Hairy Mary

The lighthouse lady, little Miss Odd,
And Will Walton the watercress man,
And pointed northward. Repellent there
A storm was brewing, but we started out
In carpet-slippers by candlelight
Through Wastewood in the wane of the year,
Past Torture Tower and Twisting Ovens,
Their ruins ruled by the arrested insect
And abortive bird. In the bleak dawn
We reached Red River; on Wrynose Weir
Lay a dead salmon; when the dogs got wind
They turned tail. We talked very little;
Thunder thudded; on the thirteenth day
Our diseased guide deserted with all
The milk chocolate. Emerging from
Forest to foothills, our fears increased,
For roads grew rougher and ridges were
Congested with gibbets. We had just reached
The monastery bridge; the mist cleared;
I got one glimpse of the granite walls
And the glaciers guarding the Good Place.
(A giant jawbone jutted from that ice;
Condors on those crags coldly observed our
Helpless anguish.) My hands in my pockets,
Whistling ruefully I wandered back
By Maiden Moor and Mockbeggar Lane
To Nettlenaze where nightingales sang
Of my own evil.

ROSETTA said:
                    Yet holy are the dolls
Who, junior for ever, just begin
Their open lives in absolute space,
Are simply themselves, deceiving none,
Their clothes creatures, so clearly expressing,
Tearless, timeless, the paternal world
Of pillars and parks. O Primal Age
When we danced deisal, our dream-wishes
Vert and volant, unvetoed our song.
For crows brought cups of cold water to
Ewes that were with young; unicorn herds
Galumphed through lilies; little mice played
With great cock-a-hoop cats; courteous griffins
Waltzed with wyverns, and the wild horses
Drew nigh their neighbors and neighed with joy,
All feasting with friends. What faded you
To this drab dusk? O the drains are clogged,
Rain-rusted, the roofs of the privies
Have fallen in, the flag is covered
With stale stains and the stable-clock face
Mottled with moss. Mocking blows the wind
Into my mouth. O but they've left me.
I wronged. Then they ran. I'm running down.

Wafna. Wafna. Who's to wind me now
In this lost land?

EMBLE said:
                              I've lost the key to
The garden gate. How green it was there,
How large long ago when I looked out,
Excited by sand, the sad glitter
Of desert dreck, not dreaming I saw
My future home. It foils my magic:
Right is the ritual but wrong the time,
The place improper.

QUANT said:
                              Reproaches come,
Emanating from some hidden centre,
Cold radiations directed at us
In waves unawares, and we are shaken
By a sceptical sigh from a scotch fir,
The Accuser crying in a cocktail glass.

Someone had put on the juke box a silly number *With That Thing* as
played by *The Three Snorts*, and to this he sang:

Let me sell you a song, the most side-splitting tale
Since old Chaos caught young Cosmos bending
With his back bare and his braces down,
Homo Vulgaris, the Asterisk Man.

He burned all his boats and both pink ends
Of his crowing candle, cooked his goose-flesh,
Jumped his bailiwick, jilted his heirs
And pickled his piper, the Approximate Man.

With his knees to the north and the night in his stride
He advanced on the parlors, then vanished upstairs
As a bath-tub admiral to bark commands
At his ten hammer toes, the Transient Man.

Once in his while his wit erupted
One pure little puff, one pretty idea;
A fumerole since, he has fizzled a cloud
Of gossip and gas, the Guttering Man.

Soon his soul will be sent up to Secret Inks,
His body be bought by the Breakdown Gang;
It's time for the Ticklers to take him away
In a closed cab, the Camouflage Man.

So look for a laundress to lay him out cold,
A fanciful fairy to fashion his tomb
In Rest-room Roman; get ready to pray
In a wheel-chair voice for the Watery Man.

MALIN went on once more, spoke of the Seventh Age:
    His last chapter has little to say.
    He grows backward with gradual loss of
    Muscular tone and mental quickness:
    He lies down; he looks through the window
    Ailing at autumn, asks a sign but
    The afternoons are inert, none come to
    Quit his quarrel or quicken the long
    Years of yawning and he yearns only
    For total extinction. He is tired out;
    His last illusions have lost patience
    With the human enterprise. The end comes: he
    Joins the majority, the jaw-dropped
    Mildewed mob and is modest at last.
    There his case rests: let who can disprove.

So their discussion concluded. MALIN excused himself and went to the men's room. QUANT went to the bar to fetch more drinks. ROSETTA and EMBLE sat silent, occupied with memories of a distant or recent, a real or imaginary past.

ROSETTA was thinking:
    There was Lord Lugar at Lighthazels,
    Violent-tempered; he voted against
    The Banking Bill. At Brothers Intake
    Sir William Wand; his Water Treaty
    Enriched Arabia. At Rotherhope
    General Locke, a genial man who
    Kept cormorants. At Craven Ladies
    Old Tillingham-Trench; he had two passions,
    Women and walking-sticks. At Wheels Rake,
    In his low library loving Greek
    Bishop Bottrel; he came back from the East
    With a fat notebook full of antique
    Liturgies and laws, long-forgotten
    Christian creeds occluded within a
    Feldspar fortress. Fay was his daughter;
    A truant mutation, she took up art,
    Carved in crystal, became the friend of
    Green-eyed Gelert the great dressmaker,
    And died in Rome. There was Dr Sykes
    At Mugglers Mound; his monograph on
    The chronic cough is a classic still;
    He was loved by all. At Lantern Byepew
    Susan O'Rourke, a sensitive who
    Prayed for the plants. They have perished now; their
    Level lawns and logical vistas
    Are obliterated; their big stone
    Houses are shut. Ease is rejected,
    Poor and penalized the private state.

EMBLE was thinking:

        I have friends already, faces I know
        In that calm crowd, wearing clothes like mine,
        Who have settled down, accepted at once,
        Contemporary with Trojan Knights
        And Bronze-Age bagmen; Bud and Whitey
        And Clifford Monahan and Clem Lifschutz,
        Dicky Lamb, Dominic Moreno,
        Svensson, Seidel: they seem already
        Like anyone else. Must I end like that?

Waiting to be served, QUANT caught sight of himself again in the bar mirror and thought:

        Ingenious George reached his journey's end
        Killed by a cop in a comfort station,
        Dan dropped dead at his dinner table,
        Mrs O'Malley with Miss De Young
        Wandered away into wild places
        Where desert dogs reduced their status
        To squandered bones, and it's scared you look,
        Dear friend of a friend, to face me now.
        How limply you've aged, how loose you stand
        A frog in your fork, my far-away
        Primrose prince, but a passenger here
        Retreating to his tent. Whose trump hails your
        Shenanigans now? Kneel to your bones
        And cuddle your cough. Your castle's down.
        It rains as you run, rusts where you lie.
        Beware my weakness. Worse will follow.
        The Blue Little Boys should blow their horns
        Louder and longer, for the lost sheep
        Are nibbling nightshade. But never mind . . .

MALIN returned and QUANT brought back drinks to the table. Then raising his glass to ROSETTA, QUANT said:

        Come, peregrine nymph, display your warm
        Euphoric flanks in their full glory
        Of liberal life; with luscious note
        Smoothly sing the softer data of an
        Unyielding universe, youth, money,
        Liquor and love; delight your shepherds
        For crazed we come and coarsened we go
        Our wobbling way: there's a white silence
        Of antiseptics and instruments
        At both ends, but a babble between
        And a shame surely. O show us the route
        Into hope and health; give each the required
        Pass to appease the superior archons;
        Be our good guide.

To which ROSETTA answered:

                    What gift of direction
         Is entrusted to me to take charge
         Of an expedition any may
         Suggest or join? For the journey homeward
         Arriving by roads already known
         At sites and sounds one has sensed before,
         The knowledge needed is not special,
         The sole essential a sad unrest
         Which no life can lack. Long is the way
         Of the Seven Stages, slow the going,
         And few, maybe, are faithful to the end,
         But all start out with the hope of success,
         Arm in arm with their opposite type
         Like dashing Adonis dressed to kill
         And worn Wat with his walrus moustache,
         Or one by one like Wandering Jews,
         Bullet-headed bandit, broad churchman,
         Lobbyist, legatee, loud virago,
         Uncle and aunt and alien cousin,
         Mute or maddening through the Maze of Time,
         Seek its centre, desiring like us
         The Quiet Kingdom. Comfort your wills then
         With hungry hopes; to this indagation
         Allay your longings: may our luck find the
         Regressive road to Grandmother's House.

As everyone knows, many people reveal in a state of semi-intoxication capacities which are quite beyond them when they are sober: the shy talk easily and brilliantly to total strangers, the stammerers get through complicated sentences without a hitch, the unathletic is translated into a weight-lifter or a sprinter, the prosaic show an intuitive grasp of myth and symbol. A less noted and a more significant phenomenon, however, is the way in which our faith in the existence of other selves, normally rather wobbly, is greatly strengthened and receives, perhaps precisely because, for once, doubt is so completely overcome, the most startling justifications. For it can happen, if circumstances are otherwise propitious, that members of a group in this condition establish a rapport in which communication of thoughts and feelings is so accurate and instantaneous, that they appear to function as a single organism.

So it was now as they sought that state of prehistoric happiness which, by human beings, can only be imagined in terms of a landscape bearing a symbolic resemblance to the human body. The more completely these four forgot their surroundings and lost their sense of time, the more sensitively aware of each other they became, until they achieved in their dream that rare community which is otherwise only attained in states of extreme wakefulness. But this did not happen all at once.

PART THREE

The Seven Stages

O Patria, patria! Quanto mi costi!
A. GHISLANZONI *Aida*

At first all is dark and each walks alone. What they share is only the feeling of remoteness and desertion, of having marched for miles and miles, of having lost their bearings, of a restless urge to find water. Gradually for each in turn the darkness begins to dissolve and their vision to take shape.

QUANT is the first to see anything. He says:

> Groping through fog, I begin to hear
> A salt lake lapping:
> Dotterels and dunlins on its dark shores
> Scurry this way and that.

Now ROSETTA perceives clearly and says:

> In the centre of a sad plain
> Without forests or footpaths,
> Rimmed with rushes and moss
> I see a tacit tarn.
>
> Some oddling angler in summer
> May visit the spot, or a spy
> Come here to cache a stolen
> Map or meet a rival.
>
> But who remarks the beehive mounds,
> Graves of creatures who cooked
> And wanted to be worshipped and perhaps
> Were the first to feel our sorrow?

And now MALIN:

> How still it is; our horses
> Have moved into the shade, our mothers
> Have followed their migrating gardens.
>
> Curlews on kettle moraines
> Foretell the end of time,
> The doom of paradox.
>
> But lovelorn sighs ascend
> From wretched greedy regions
> Which cannot include themselves;
>
> And the freckled orphan flinging
> Ducks and drakes at a pond
> Stops looking for stones,

And wishes he were a steamboat,
Or Lugalzaggisi, the loud
Tyrant of Erech and Umma.

And last EMBLE:
The earth looks woeful and wet;
On the raw horizon regiments pass
Tense against twilight, tired beneath
Their corresponsive spears.

Slogging on through slush
By broken bridges and burnt hamlets
Where the starving stand, staring past them
At remote inedible hills.

And now, though separate still, they begin to advance from their
several starting-points into the same mountainous district. ROSETTA
says:

Now peaks oppose to the ploughman's march
Their twin confederate forms,
In a warm weather, white with lilies,
Evergreen for grazing.

Smooth the surfaces, sweeping the curves
Of these comely frolic clouds,
Where the great go to forget themselves,
The beautiful and boon to die.

QUANT says:
Lights are moving
On domed hills
Where little monks
Get up in the dark.

Though wild volcanoes
Growl in their sleep
At a green world,
Inside their cloisters

They sit, translating
A vision into
The vulgar lingo
Of armed cities,

Where brides arrive
Through great doors
And robbers' bones
Dangle from gallows.

EMBLE says:
Bending forward
With stern faces,
Pilgrims puff

Up the steep bank
In huge hats.

Shouting, I run
In the other direction,
Cheerful, unchaste,
With open shirt
And tinkling guitar.

MALIN says:
    Looming over my head
    Mountains menace my life,
    But on either hand, let down
    From U-valleys like yarn,
    Waterfalls all the way
    Quietly encourage me on.

And now one by one they enter the same valley and begin to ascend the same steep pass. ROSETTA is in front, then EMBLE, then MALIN and QUANT last.

ROSETTA says:
    These hills may be hollow; I've a horror of dwarfs
    And a streaming cold.

EMBLE says:
              This stony pass
    Is bad for my back. My boots are too small
    My haversack too heavy. I hate my knees
    But like my legs.

MALIN says:
              The less I feel
    The more I mind. I should meet death
    With great regret.

QUANT says:
              Thank God I was warned
    To bring an umbrella and had bribes enough
    For the red-haired rascals, for the reservoir guard
    A celluloid sandwich, and silk eggs
    For the lead smelters; for Lizzie O'Flynn,
    The capering cowgirl with clay on her hands,
    Tasty truffles in utopian jars,
    And dungarees with Danish buttons
    For Shilly and Shally the shepherd kings.

Now ROSETTA says:
    The ground's aggression is growing less.
    The clouds are clearing.

EMBLE says:
              My cape is dry.
    I can reckon correctly.

MALIN says:

                                  My real intentions
            Are nicer now.

      And QUANT says:

                              I'm nearing the top.
            When I hear what I'm up to, how I shall laugh.

   And so, on a treeless watershed, at the tumbledown Mariners Tavern
(which is miles inland) the four assemble, having completed the first
stage of their journey. They look about them, and everything seems
somehow familiar. EMBLE says:

            The railroads like the rivers run for the most part
                East and west, and from here
            On a clear day both coasts are visible
                And the long piers of their ports.
            To the south one sees the sawtooth range
                Our nickel and copper come from,
            And beyond it the Barrens used for Army
                Manœuvres; while to the north
            A brown blur of buildings marks
                Some sacred or secular town.

      MALIN says:

            Every evening the oddest collection
                Of characters crowd this inn:
            Here a face from a farm, its frankness yearning
                For corruption and riches; there
            A gaunt gospel whom grinning miners
                Will stone to death by a dolmen;
            Heroes confess to whores, detectives
                Chat or play chess with thieves.

      QUANT says:

            And one finds it hard to fall asleep here.
                Lying awake and listening
            To the creak of new creeds on the kitchen stairs
                Or the sob of a dream next door,
            (By pass and port they percolated,
                By friendships and official channels)
            Gentler grows the heart, gentler and much
                Less certain it will succeed.

   But ROSETTA says impatiently:

            Questioned by these crossroads our common hope
            Replies we must part; in pairs proceed
            By bicycle, barge, or bumbling local,
            As vagabonds or in wagon-lits,
            On weedy waters, up winding lanes,
            Down rational roads the Romans built,
            Over or into, under or round
            Mosses dismal or mountains sudden,
            Farmlands or fenlands or factory towns,

Left and right till the loop be complete
And we meet once more.

EMBLE whispers to himself:
                              Do I mind with whom?
           Yes, a great deal.

And MALIN:
                         In youth I would have cared,
           But not now.

And QUANT:
                    I know what will happen,
           Am sincerely sorry.

   They divide thus, youth with youth and age with age. To the left go
ROSETTA and EMBLE, to the right QUANT and MALIN, these on foot, those
by car, moving outwards in opposite directions from the high heartland
to the maritime plains.

           EMBLE says:
                As I pull on my gloves and prepare
                For another day-long drive,
                The landscape is full of life:
                Nieces of millionaires
                Twitter on terraces,
                Peasant wives are pounding
                Linen on stones by a stream,
                And a doctor's silk hat dances
                On top of a hedge as he hurries
                Along a sunken lane.

                All these and theirs are at home,
                May love or hate their age
                And the beds they are built to fit;
                Only I have no work
                But my endless journey, its joy
                The whirr of wheels, the hiss
                As moonlit miles flash by,
                Its grief the glimpse of a face
                Whose unique beauty cannot
                Be asked to alter with me.

                Or must everyone see himself
                As I, as the pilgrim prince
                Whose life belongs to his quest
                For the Truth, the tall princess,
                The buried gold or the Grail,
                The important thought-of Thing
                Which is never here and now
                Like this world through which he goes
                That all the others appear
                To possess the secret of?

QUANT says:
> Between pollarded poplars
> This rural road
> Ambles downhill
> In search of the sea.
>
> Nothing, neither
> The farms nor the flowers,
> The cows nor the clouds,
> Look restive or wrong.
>
> Then why without warning,
> In my old age,
> My duty done,
> Do I change to a child,
>
> And shake with shame,
> Afraid of Father,
> Demanding Mother's
> Forgiveness again?

ROSETTA says:
> The light collaborates with a land of ease,
>   And rivers meander at random
> Through meadowsweet massed on moist pastures,
>   Past decrepit palaces
> Where, brim from belvederes, bred for riding
>   And graceful dancing, gaze
> Fine old families who fear dishonour.
>
> But modern on the margin of marshy ground
>   Glitter the glassier homes
> Of more practical people with plainer minds,
>   And along the vacationer's coast,
> Distributed between its hotels and casinos,
>   Ex-monarchs remember a past
> Of wars and waltzes as they wait for death.

MALIN says:
> Though dunes still hide from the eye
>   The shining shore,
> Already by a certain exciting
>   Kind of discomfort
> I know the ocean near.
>
> For wind and whining gull
>   Are saying something,
> Or trying to say, about time
>   And the anxious heart
> Which a matter-snob would dismiss.

So, arriving two and two at the rival ports, they complete the second stage of their journey.

ROSETTA says:

    These ancient harbors are hailed by the morning
      Light that untidies
    Warehouses and wharves and wilder rocks
      Where intolerant lives
    Fight and feed in the fucoid thickets
      Of popular pools.

EMBLE says:

    Reflected fleets, feeling in awe
      Of their sheltered lagoons,
    Stand still, a steady congregation
      Of gigantic shadows;
    Derricks on these docks adore in silence
      The noon they denote.

MALIN says:

    Quiet falls the dusk at this queasy juncture
      Of water and earth,
    And lamps are lit on the long esplanade;
      Urgent whispers
    Promise peace, and impatience shakes
      Ephemeral flesh.

And QUANT says:

    As, far from furniture and formal gardens
      The desperate spirit
    Thinks of its end in the third person,
      As a speck drowning
    In those wanton mansions where the whales take
      Their huge fruitions.

But here they may not linger long. EMBLE says to ROSETTA:

    A private plane, its propeller tied
    With red ribbons is ready waiting
    To take us to town.

MALIN says to QUANT:

              A train whistles
    For the last time. We must leave at once.

And so by air, by rail, they turn inland again towards a common goal.

QUANT says:

    Autumn has come early; evening falls;
    Our train is traversing at top speed
    A pallid province of puddles and stumps
    Where helpless objects, an orphaned quarry,
    A waif of a works, a widowed engine,
    For a sorry second sigh and are gone
    As we race through the rain with rattling windows
    Bound for a borough all bankers revere.

ROSETTA says:
>Lulled by an engine's hum,
>Our insulated lives
>Go floating freely through
>Space in a metal spore.
>
>White hangs the waning moon,
>A scruple on the sky,
>And constellations crowd
>Our neighborhood the night.

QUANT says:
>In the smoking cars all seats are taken
>By melancholics mewed in their dumps,
>Elegant old-school ex-lieutenants
>Cashiered for shuddering, short blowhards,
>Thwarted geniuses in threadbare coats,
>Once well-to-do's at their wits' end,
>And underpaid agents of underground powers
>The faded and failing in flight towards town.

ROSETTA says:
>Just visible but vague,
>Way down below us lies
>The world of hares and hounds,
>Open to our contempt.
>
>Escaping by our skill
>Its public prison, we
>Could love ourselves and live
>In just anarchic joy.

QUANT says:
>The parlor cars and Pullmans are packed also
>With scented assassins, salad-eaters
>Who murder on milk, merry expressives,
>Pert pyknics with pumpkin heads,
>Clever cardinals with clammy hands,
>Jolly logicians with juvenile books,
>Farmers, philistines, *filles-de-joie*,
>The successful smilers the city can use.

ROSETTA says:
>What fear of freedom then
>Causes our clasping hands
>To make in miniature
>That earth anew, and now
>
>By choice instead of chance
>To suffer from the same
>Attraction and untruth,
>Suspicion and respect?

QUANT says:
What mad oracle could have made us believe
The capital will be kind when the country is not,
And value our vanities, provide our souls
With play and pasture and permanent water?

They lose altitude, they slow down, they arrive at the city, having completed the third stage of the journey, and are united once more, greet each other.

EMBLE says:
Here we are.

MALIN says:
As we hoped we have come
Together again.

ROSETTA says:
I am glad, I think.
It is fun to be four.

QUANT says:
The flushed animations
Of crowds and couples look comic to friends.

They look about them with great curiosity. Then MALIN says:

The scene has all the signs of a facetious culture,
Publishing houses, pawnshops and pay-toilets;
August and Graeco-Roman are the granite temples
Of the medicine men whose magic keeps this body
Politic free from fevers,
Cancer and constipation.

The rooms near the railroad-station are rented mainly
By the criminally inclined; the Castle is open on Sundays;
There are parks for plump and playgrounds for pasty children;
The police must be large, but little men are hired to
Service the subterranean
Miles of dendritic drainage.

A married tribe commutes, mild from suburbia,
Whom ritual rules protect against raids by the nomad
Misfortunes they fear; for they flinch in their dreams at the
scratch
Of coarse pecuniary claws, at crying images,
Petulant, thin, reproachful,
Destitute shades of dear ones.

Well, here I am but how, how, asks the visitor,
Strolling through the strange streets, can I start to discover
The fashionable feminine fret, or the form of insult
Minded most by the men? In what myth do their sages
Locate the cause of evil?
How are these people punished?

380

How, above all, will they end? By any natural
Fascination of frost or flood, or from the artful
Obliterating bang whereby God's rebellious image
After thousands of thankless years spent in thinking about it,
     Finally finds a solid
      Proof of its independence?

Now a trolley car comes, going northward. They take it. EMBLE says:
    This tortuous route through town
    Was planned, it seems, to serve
    Its institutions; for we halt
    With a jerk at the Gothic gates
    Of the Women's Prison, the whitewashed
    Hexagonal Orphanage for
    Doomed Children, the driveway,
    Bordered with trees in tubs
    Of the Orthopædic Hospital,
    And are crowded by the close relatives
    Of suffering, who sit upright
    With little offerings on their laps
    Of candy, magazines, comics,
    Avoiding each other's eyes,
    Shy of a rival shame.

    Slums are replaced by suburbs,
    Suburbs by tennis-courts, tennis-courts
    By greenhouses and vegetable gardens.
    The penultimate stop is the State
    Asylum, a large Palladian
    Edifice in acres of grounds
    Surrounded by iron railings;
    And now there is no one left
    For the final run through fields
    But ourselves whose diseases as yet
    Are undiagnosed, and the driver
    Who is anxious to get home to his tea.

    The buttercups glitter; our bell
    Clangs loudly; and the lark's
    Song is swallowed up in
    The blazing blue: we are set
    Down and do not care
    Very much but wonder why.

Now they see before them, standing, half hidden by trees, on a little
insurrection of red sandstone above a coiling river, the big house which
marks the end of their journey's fourth stage. ROSETTA is enthusiastic
and runs forward saying:

    In I shall go, out I shall look.

But the others are tired and MALIN says:

    Very well, we will wait, watch from outside.

QUANT says:
        A scholarly old scoundrel,
  Whose fortune was founded on the follies of others,
     Built it for his young bride.
  She died in childbed; he died on the gallows;
     The property passed to the Crown.

     The façade has a lifeless look,
  For no one uses the enormous ballroom;
     But in book-lined rooms at the back
  Committees meet, and many strange
     Decisions are secretly taken.

     High up in the East Tower,
  A pale-faced widow looks pensively down
     At the terrace outside where the snow
  Flutters and flurries round the formal heads
     Of statues that stare at the park.

     And the guards at the front gate
  Change with the seasons; in cheerful Spring
     How engaging their glances; but how
  Morose in Fall: ruined kitchen-maids
     Blubber behind the bushes.

ROSETTA returns, more slowly than she left. EMBLE asks:

  Well, how was it? What did you see?

ROSETTA answers:
     Opera glasses on the ormolu table,
     Frock-coated father framed on the wall
     In a bath-chair facing a big bow-window,
     With valley and village invitingly spread,
          I got what is going on.

     At the bend of the Bourne where the brambles grow thickest
     Major Mott joins Millicent Rusk;
     Discreetly the kingfisher keeps his distance
     But an old cob swan looks on as they
          Commit the sanguine sin.

     Heavy the orchards; there's Alison pinching
     Her baby brother, Bobby and Dick
     Frying a frog with their father's reading-glass,
     Conrad and Kay in the carpentry shed
          Where they've no business to be.

     Cold are the clays of Kibroth-Hattaavah,
     Babel's urbanities buried in sand,
     Red the geraniums in the rectory garden
     Where the present incumbent reads Plato in French
          And has lost his belief in Hell.

From the gravel-pits in Groaning Hollow
To the monkey-puzzle on Murderer's Hill,
From the Wellington Arms to the white steam laundry,
The significant note is nature's cry
    Of long-divided love.

I have watched through a window a World that is fallen,
The mating and malice of men and beasts,
The corporate greed of quiet vegetation,
And the homesick little obstinate sobs
    Of things thrown into being.

I would gladly forget; let us go quickly.

EMBLE said:
    Yonder, look, is a yew avenue,
    A mossy mile. For amusement's sake
    Let us run a race till we reach the end.

This, willing or unwilling, they start to do and, as they run, their rival natures, by art comparing and compared, reveal themselves. Thus MALIN mutters:

    'Alas,' say my legs, 'if we lose it will be
    A sign you have sinned.'

And QUANT:
                The safest place
    Is the more or less middling: the mean average
    Is not noticed.

And EMBLE:
            How nice it feels
    To be out ahead: I'm always lucky
    But must remember how modest to look.

And ROSETTA:
    Let them call; I don't care. I shall keep them waiting.
    They ought to have helped me. I can't hope to be first
    So let me be last.

In this manner, sooner or later they come to the crumbling lichen-covered wall of the forgotten graveyard which marks the end of the fifth stage of their journey. At their feet lies a fallen wooden sign, bearing in faded letters the warning:

No Entrance Here Without a Subject

and underneath this, in smaller, barely decipherable script, some verses which EMBLE starts to read aloud:

    Stranger, this still
    Museum exhibits
    The results of life:
    Thoughtfully, therefore,

Peer as you pass
These cases clouded
By vetch and eyebright
And viper's bugloss
At each little collection
Loosely arranged
Of dated dust.

Here it is holy,
Here at last
In mute marble
The Master closed
His splendid period;
A spot haunted
By goat-faced grasshoppers
And gangling boys
Taunted by talents
Which tell them more
Than their flesh can feel.

Here impulse loses
Its impetus: thus
Far and no farther
Their legs, resolutions
And longings carried
The big, the ambitious,
The beautiful; all
Stopped in mid-stride
At this straggling border
Where wildflowers begin
And wealth ends.

Yet around their rest
Flittermice, finches
And flies restore
Their lost milieu;
An inconsequential
Host of pert
Occasional creatures,
Blindly, playfully,
Bridging death's
Eternal gap
With quotidian joy.

MALIN sighs and says what they are all thinking but wish they were not.

Again we must digress, go by different
Paths in pairs to explore the land.

Knowing they will never be able to agree as to who shall accompany
whom, they cast lots and so it falls out that ROSETTA is to go with QUANT
and EMBLE with MALIN. Two are disappointed, two are disturbed.

QUANT mutters:
      This bodes badly.

And MALIN:
            So be it. Who knows
      If we wish what we will?

And ROSETTA:
              Will you forget
      If you know that I won't?

And EMBLE:
              Will your need be me?

They depart now, MALIN and EMBLE westward on bicycles, QUANT and ROSETTA eastward by boat, sad through fair scenes, thinking of another and talking to themselves.

MALIN says:
      As we cycle silent through a serious land
      For hens and horses, my hunger for a live
      Person to father impassions my sense
      Of this boy's beauty in battle with time.

      These old-world hamlets and haphazard lanes
      Are perilous places; how plausible here
      All arcadian cults of carnal perfection,
      How intoxicating the platonic myth.

EMBLE says:
      Pleasant my companion but I pine for another.

QUANT says:
      Our canoe makes no noise; monotonous
      Ramparts of reeds surround our navigation;
      The waterway winds as it wants through the hush:
      O fortunate fluid her fingers caress.

      Welcome her, world; sedge-warblers, betray your
      Hiding places with song; and eddy, butterflies,
      In frivolous flights about that fair head:
      How apt your homage to her innocent disdain.

ROSETTA says:
      The figure I prefer is far away.

MALIN says:
      To know nature is not enough for the ego;
      The aim of its eros is to create a soul,
      The start of its magic is stolen flesh.

QUANT says:
      Let nature unite us whose needs belong to
      Separate systems that make no sense to each other:
      She is not my sister and I am not her friend.

EMBLE says:

    Unequal our happiness: his is greater.

ROSETTA says:

    Lovelier would this look if my love were with me.

MALIN says:

    Girlishly glad that my glance is not chaste,
    He wants me to want what he would refuse:
    For sons have this desire for a slave also.

QUANT says:

    Both graves of the stream are agog as here
    Comes a bride for a bridegroom in a boat ferried
    By a dying man dreaming of a daughter-wife.

Now they arrive, two and two, east and west, at the hermetic gardens and the sixth stage of their journey is completed. They gaze about them entranced at the massive mildness of these survivals from an age of cypresses and cisterns.

ROSETTA says:

    How tempting to trespass in these Italian gardens
    With their smirk ouches and sweet-smelling borders,
      To lean on the low
    Parapet of some pursive fountain
    And drowse through the unctuous day.

EMBLE says:

    There are special perspectives for speculation,
    Random rose-walks, and rustic bridges
      Over neat canals;
    A miniature railroad with mossy halts
      Wambles through wanton groves.

QUANT says:

    Yet this is a theatre where thought becomes act
    And beside a sundial, in the silent umbrage
      Of some dark daedal,
    The ruined rebel is recreated
      And chooses a chosen self.

    From lawns and relievos the leisure makes
    Its uncomfortable claim and, caught off its guard,
      His hardened heart
    Consents to suffer, and the sudden instant
      Touches his time at last.

MALIN says:

    Tense on the parterre, he takes the hero's
    Leap into love; then, unlatching the wicket
      Gate he goes:
    The plains of his triumph appear empty,
      But now among their motionless

Avenues and urns with extra élan
Faster revolves the invisible corps
    Of pirouetting angels,
And a chronic chorus of cascades and birds
    Cuts loose in a wild cabaletta.

Presently the extraordinary charm of these gardens begins to work upon them also. It seems an accusation. They become uneasy and unwell.

EMBLE says:
        I would stay to be saved but the stillness here
        Reminds me too much of my mother's grief;
        It scorns and scares me.

QUANT says:
                            My excuses throb
        Louder and lamer.

ROSETTA says:
                        The long shadows
        Disapprove of my person.

MALIN says:
                            Reproached by the doves,
        My groin groans.

ROSETTA:
                            I've got a headache,
        And my nose is inflamed.

QUANT:
                            My knees are stiff.

EMBLE:
        My teeth need attention.

Then QUANT says:
                        Who will trust me now,
        Who with broad jokes have bored my children
        And, warm by my wife, have wished her dead
        Yet turned her over, who have told strangers
        Of the cars and castles that accrued with the fortune
        I might have made?

And EMBLE says:
                        My mortal body
        Has sinned on sofas; assigning to each
        Points for pleasure, I have pencilled on envelopes
        Lists of my loves.

And ROSETTA says:
                        Alas for my sneers
        At the poor and plain: I must pay for thinking
        Failure funny.

387

And MALIN says:

> I have felt too good
> At being better than the best of my colleagues:
> Walking by water, have worked out smiling
> Deadly reviews. My deeds forbid me
> To linger longer. I'll leave my friend,
> Be sorry by myself.

Then EMBLE again:

> I must slip off
> To the woods to worry.

Then ROSETTA:

> I want to retire
> To some private place and pray to be made
> A good girl.

And then QUANT:

> I must go away
> With my terrors until I have taught them to sing.

So one by one they plunge into the labyrinthine forest and vanish down solitary paths, with no guide but their sorrows, no companion but their own voices. Their ways cross and recross yet never once do they meet though now and then one catches somewhere not far off a brief snatch of another's song. Thus QUANT's voice is heard singing:

> A vagrant veteran I,
> Discharged with grizzled chin,
> Sans youth or use, sans uniform,
> A tiger turned an ass.

Then MALIN's:

> These branches deaf and dumb
> Were woeful suitors once;
> Mourning unmanned, and moping turned
> Their sullen souls to wood.

Then ROSETTA's:

> My dress is torn, my tears
> Are running as I run
> Through forests far from father's eye
> To look for a true love.

Then EMBLE's:

> My mother weeps for me
> Who disappeared at play
> From home and hope like all who chase
> The blue elusive bird.

Now QUANT's again:

> Through gloomy woods I go
> Ex-demigod; the damp
> Awakes my wound; I want my tea
> But needed am of none.

Now EMBLE'S:
>More faint, more far away
>The huntsman's social horn
>Calls through the cold uncanny woods
>And nearer draws the night.

Now ROSETTA'S:
>Dear God, regard thy child;
>Repugn or pacify
>All furry forms and fangs that lurk
>Within this horrid shade.

Now MALIN'S:
>Their given names forgot,
>Mere species of despair,
>On whims of wind their wills depend,
>On temperatures their mood.

And yet once more QUANT'S:
>So, whistling as I walk
>Through brake and copse, I keep
>A lookout for the Limping One
>Who buys abandoned souls.

Obedient to their own mysterious laws of direction, their twisting paths converge, approach their several voices, and collect the four for a startled reunion at the forest's edge. They stare at what they see.

QUANT says:
>The climate of enclosure, the cool forest
>>Break off abruptly:
>Giddy with the glare and ungoverned heat,
>>We stop astonished,
>Interdicted by desert, its dryness edged
>>By a scanty scrub
>Of Joshua trees and giant cacti;
>>Then, vacant of value,
>Incoherent and infamous sands,
>>Rainless regions
>Swarming with serpents, ancestral wastes,
>>Lands beyond love.

Now, with only the last half of the seventh stage to go to finish their journey, for the first time fear and doubt dismay them. Is triumph possible? If so, are they chosen? Is triumph worth it? If so, are they worthy?

MALIN says:
>Boring and bare of shade,
>Devoid of souvenirs and voices,
>It takes will to cross this waste

>Which is really empty: the mirage
>Need not be tasty to tempt;
>For the senses arouse themselves,

389

And an image of humpbacked girls
Or plates of roasted rats
Can make the mouth water.

With nothing to know about,
The mind reflects on its movements
And so doubles any distance.

Even if we had time
To read through all the wrinkled
Reports of explorers who claim

That hidden arrant streams
Chuckle through this chapped land
In profound and meagre fissures,

Or that this desert is dotted with
Oases where acrobats dwell
Who make unbelievable leaps,

We should never have proof they were not
Deceiving us. For the only certain
Truth is that they returned,

And that we cannot be deaf to the question:
'Do I love this world so well
That I have to know how it ends?'

EMBLE says:
As yet the young hero's
Brow is unkissed by battle,
But he knows how necessary
Is his defiance of fate
And, serene already, he sails
Down the gorge between the august
Faces carved in the cliffs
Towards the lordship of the world.

And the gentle majority are not
Afraid either, but, owl-like
And sedate in their glass globes
The wedded couples wave
At the bandits racing by
With affection, and the learned relax
On pinguid plains among
A swarm of flying flowers.

But otherwise is it with the play
Of the child whom chance decrees
To say what all men suffer:
For he wishes against his will
To be lost, and his fear leads him
To dales of driving rain
Where peasants with penthouse eyebrows
Sullenly guard the sluices.

And his steps follow the stream
Past rusting apparatus
To its gloomy beginning, the original
Chasm where brambles block
The entrance to the underworld;
There the silence blesses his sorrow,
And holy to his dread is that dark
Which will neither promise nor explain.

ROSETTA says:
    Are our dreams indicative? Does it exist,
      That last landscape
Of gloom and glaciers and great storms
Where, cold into chasms, cataracts
      Topple, and torrents
Through rocky ruptures rage for ever
In a winter twilight watched by ravens,
      Birds on basalt,
And shadows of ships long-shattered lie,
Preserved disasters, in the solid ice
      Of frowning fjords?
Does the Moon's message mean what it says:
'In that oldest and most hidden of all places
      Number is unknown?'
Can lying lovers believe their bones'
      Unshaken assurance
That all the elegance, all the promise
Of the world they wish is waiting there?

Even while she is still speaking, their fears are confirmed, their hopes denied. For the world from which their journey has been one long flight rises up before them now as if the whole time it had been hiding in ambush, only waiting for the worst moment to reappear to its fugitives in all the majesty of its perpetual fury.

QUANT says:
    My shoulders shiver. A shadow chills me
    As thunderheads threaten the sun.

MALIN says:
    Righteous wrath is raising its hands
    To strike and destroy.

EMBLE says:
              Storm invades
    The Euclidean calm. The clouds explode.
    The scene dissolves, is succeeded by
    A grinning gap, a growth of nothing
    Pervaded by vagueness.

ROSETTA says:
             Violent winds
    Tear us apart. Terror scatters us
    To the four coigns. Faintly our sounds

Echo each other, unrelated
Groans of grief at a great distance.

QUANT says:

In the wild West they are whipping each other.

EMBLE says:

In the hungry East they are eating their books.

ROSETTA says:

In the numb North there are no more cradles.

MALIN says:

The sullen South has been set on fire.

EMBLE says:

Dull through the darkness, indifferent tongues
From bombed buildings, from blacked-out towns,
Camps and cockpits, from cold trenches,
Submarines and cells, recite in unison
A common creed, declaring their weak
Faith in confusion. The floods are rising;
Rain ruins on the routed fragments
Of all the armies; indistinct
Are friend and foe, one flux of bodies
Miles from mother, marriage, or any
Workable world.

QUANT says:

           The wall is fallen
That Balbus built, and back they come
The Dark Ones to dwell in the statues,
Manias in marble, messengers from
The Nothing who nothings. Night descends;
Through thickening darkness thin uneases,
Ravenous unreals, perambulate
Our paths and pickles.

MALIN says:

           The primary colors
Are all mixed up; the whole numbers
Have broken down, the big situations
Ceased to excite.

ROSETTA says:

           Sick of time,
Long Ada and her Eleven Daughters,
The standing stones, stagger, disrupt
Their petrified polka on Pillicock Mound;
The chefs and shepherds have shot themselves,
The dowagers dropped in their Dutch gardens,
The battle-axe and the bosomed war-horse
Swept grand to their graves. Graven on all things,
Inscribed on skies, escarpments, trees,

Notepaper, neckties, napkin rings,
Brickwalls and barns, or branded into
The livid limbs of lambs and men,
Is the same symbol, the signature
Of reluctant allegiance to a lost cause.

MALIN says:
Our ideas have got drunk and drop their H's.

EMBLE:
We err what we are as if we were not.

ROSETTA:
The honest and holy are hissed at the races.

QUANT:
God's in his greenhouse, his geese in the world.

Saying this, they woke up and recognized where they sat and who they were. The darkness which had invaded their dream was explained, for it was closing time and the bartender was turning off the lights. What they had just dreamed they could no longer recall exactly, but when EMBLE and ROSETTA looked at each other, they were conscious of some sweet shared secret which it might be dangerous to remember too well. Perhaps it was this which prompted ROSETTA to suggest that they all come back to her apartment for a snack and a nightcap for, when they accepted, she realized that she had been expecting QUANT and MALIN to decline. But it was too late now. They were out in the street already and EMBLE had hailed a cab.

PART FOUR

The Dirge

His mighty work for the nation,
Strengthening peace and securing union,
Always at it since on the throne,
Has saved the country more than one billion.
BROADSHEET on the death of King Edward VII

As they drove through the half-lit almost empty streets, the effect of their dream had not yet worn off but persisted as a mutual mood of discouragement. Whether they thought of Nature, of her unending stream of irrelevant events without composition or centre, her reckless waste of value, her alternate looks of idiotic inertia and insane ferocity, or whether they thought of Man, of the torpor of his spirit, the indigent dryness of his soul, his bottomless credulity, his perverse preference for the meretricious or the insipid—it seemed impossible to them that either

393

could have survived so long had not some semi-divine stranger with superhuman powers, some Gilgamesh or Napoleon, some Solon or Sherlock Holmes, appeared from time to time to rescue both, for a brief bright instant, from their egregious destructive blunders. And for such a great one who, long or lately, has always died or disappeared, they now lamented thus.

> Sob, heavy world,
> Sob as you spin
> Mantled in mist, remote from the happy:
> The washerwomen have wailed all night,
> The disconsolate clocks are crying together,
> And the bells toll and toll
> For tall Agrippa who touched the sky:
> Shut is that shining eye
> Which enlightened the lampless and lifted up
> The flat and foundering, reformed the weeds
> Into civil cereals and sobered the bulls;
> Away the cylinder seal,
> The didactic digit and dreaded voice
> Which imposed peace on the pullulating
> Primordial mess. Mourn for him now,
> Our lost dad,
> Our colossal father.

> For seven cycles
> For seven years
> Past vice and virtue, surviving both,
> Through pluvial periods, paroxysms
> Of wind and wet, through whirlpools of heat,
> And comas of deadly cold,
> On an old white horse, an ugly nag,
> In his faithful youth he followed
> The black ball as it bowled downhill
> On the spotted spirit's spiral journey,
> Its purgative path to that point of rest
> Where longing leaves it, and saw
> Shimmering in the shade the shrine of gold,
> The magical marvel no man dare touch,
> Between the towers the tree of life
> And the well of wishes
> The waters of joy.

> Then he harrowed hell,
> Healed the abyss
> Of torpid instinct and trifling flux,
> Laundered it, lighted it, made it lovable with
> Cathedrals and theories; thanks to him
> Brisker smells abet us,
> Cleaner clouds accost our vision
> And honest sounds our ears.
> For he ignored the Nightmares and annexed their ranges,
> Put the clawing Chimaeras in cold storage,
> Berated the Riddle till it roared and fled,

Won the Battle of Whispers,
Stopped the Stupids, stormed into
The Fumblers' Forts, confined the Sulky
To their drab ditches and drove the Crashing
      Bores to their bogs,
      Their beastly moor.

In the high heavens,
      The ageless places,
The gods are wringing their great worn hands
For their watchman is away, their world-engine
Creaking and cracking. Conjured no more
      By his master music to wed
Their truths to times, the Eternal Objects
      Drift about in a daze:
O the lepers are loose in Lombard Street,
The rents are rising in the river basins,
The insects are angry. Who will dust
      The cobwebbed kingdoms now?
For our lawgiver lies below his people,
Bigger bones of a better kind,
Unwarped by their weight, as white limestone
      Under green grass,
      The grass that fades.

But now the cab stopped at ROSETTA's apartment house. As they went up in the elevator, they were silent but each was making a secret resolve to banish such gloomy reflection and become, or at least appear, carefree and cheerful.

PART FIVE

The Masque

'Oh, Heaven help me,' she prayed, 'to be decorative and to do right.'
RONALD FIRBANK *The Flower beneath the Foot*

Rosetta had shown the men where everything was and, as they trotted between the kitchen and the living room, cutting sandwiches and fixing drinks, all felt that it was time something exciting happened and decided to do their best to see that it did. Had they been perfectly honest with themselves, they would have had to admit that they were tired and wanted to go home alone to bed. That they were not was in part due, of course, to vanity, the fear of getting too old to want fun or too ugly to get it, but also to unselfishness, the fear of spoiling the fun for others. Besides, only animals who are below civilization and the angels who are beyond it can be sincere. Human beings are, necessarily, actors who cannot become something before they have first pretended to be it; and

395

they can be divided, not into the hypocritical and the sincere, but into the sane who known they are acting and the mad who do not. So it was now as ROSETTA switched on the radio which said:

> *Music past midnight. For men in the armed*
> *Forces on furlough and their feminine consorts,*
> *For war-workers and women in labor,*
> *For Bohemian artists and owls of the night,*
> *We present a series of savage selections*
> *By brutal bands from bestial tribes,*
> *The Quaraquorams and the Quaromanlics,*
> *The Arsocids and the Alonites,*
> *The Ghuzz, the Guptas, the gloomy Krimchaks,*
> *The Timurids and Torguts, with terrible cries*
> *Will drag you off to their dream retreats*
> *To dance with your deaths till the dykes collapse.*

EMBLE asked ROSETTA to dance. The others sat watching. QUANT waved his cigar in time to the music and sang a verse from an old prospector's ballad.

> When Laura lay on her ledger side
> And nicely threw her north cheek up,
> How pleasing the plight of her promising grove
> And how rich the random I reached with a rise.

Whereupon MALIN sang a verse of a folksong from a Fen District.

> When in wan hope I wandered away and alone,
> How brag were the birds, how buxom the sky,
> But sad were the sallows and slow were the brooks
> And how dismal that day when I danced with my dear.

Moving well together to the music, ROSETTA and EMBLE were becoming obviously attracted to each other. In times of war even the crudest kind of positive affection between persons seems extraordinarily beautiful, a noble symbol of the peace and forgiveness of which the whole world stands so desperately in need. So to dancers and spectators alike, this quite casual attraction seemed and was of immense importance.

ROSETTA and EMBLE sang together:

> Hushed is the lake of hawks
> Bright with our excitement,
> And all the sky of skulls
> Glows with scarlet roses;
> The melter of men and salt
> Admires the drinker of iron:
> Bold banners of meaning
> Blaze o'er the host of days.

MALIN has been building a little altar of sandwiches. Now he placed an olive upon it and invoked the Queen of love.

Hasten earthward, Heavenly Venus,
Mistress of motion, Mother of loves,
A signal from whom excites time to
Confused outbursts, filling spaces with
Lights and leaves. In pelagic meadows
The plankton open their parachutes;
The mountains are amused; mobs of birds
Shout at fat shopkeepers—'Shucks! We are free.
Imitate us'—and out of the blue
Come bright boys with bells on their ankles
To tease with roses Cartesian monks
Till their heads ache, geometers vexed by
Irrelevant reds. May your right hand,
Lightly alighting on their longing flesh,
Promise this pair what their prayers demand,
Bliss in both, born of each other, a
Double dearness; let their dreams descend
Into concrete conduct. Claim your own.

ROSETTA and EMBLE had stopped dancing and sat down on the couch.
Now he put his arm around her and said:

Enter my aim from all directions, O
Special spirit whose expressions are
My carnal care, my consolation:
Be many or one. Meet me by chance on
Credulous coasts where cults intersect
Or join as arranged by the Giants' Graves,
Titanic tombs which at twilight bring
Greetings from the great misguided dead;
Hide from, haunt me, on hills to be seen
Far away through the forelegs of mares;
Stay till I come in the startling light
When the tunnel turns to teach surprise,
Or face me and fight for a final stand
With a brave blade in your buffer states,
My visible verb, my very dear,
Till I die, darling.

ROSETTA laid her head on his shoulder and said:

O the deep roots
Of the cross-roads yew, calm for so long,
Have felt you afar and faintly begin
To tingle now. What twitters there'll be in
The brook bushes at the bright sound of
Your bicycle bell. What barking then
As you stride the stiles to startle one
Great cry in the kitchen when you come home,
My doom, my darling.

They kissed. Then EMBLE said:

            Till death divide
May the Four Faces Feeling can make
Assent to our sighs.

She said:

            The snap of the Three
Grim Spinning Sisters' Spectacle Case
Uphold our honors.

He said:

            The Heavenly Twins
Guard our togetherness from ghostly ills.

She said:

            The Outer Owner, that Oldest One whom
This world is with, be witness to our vows.

Which vows they now alternately swore.

            If you blush, I'll build breakwaters.
            When you're tired, I'll tidy your table.
            If you cry, I'll climb crags.
            When you're sick, I'll sit at your side.
            If you frown, I'll fence fields.
            When you're ashamed, I'll shine your shoes.
            If you laugh, I'll liberate lands.
            When you're depressed, I'll play you the piano.
            If you sigh, I'll sack cities.
            When you're unlucky, I'll launder your linen.
            If you sing, I'll save souls.
            When you're hurt, I'll hold your hand.
            If you smile, I'll smelt silver.
            When you're afraid, I'll fetch you food.
            If you talk, I'll track down trolls.
            When you're on edge, I'll empty your ash-tray.
            If you whisper, I'll wage wars.
            When you're cross, I'll clean your coat.
            If you whistle, I'll water wastes.
            When you're bored, I'll bathe your brows.

    Again they embraced. QUANT poured out the dregs of the glass on the
carpet as a libation and invoked the local spirits:

            Ye little larvae, lords of the household,
            Potty, P-P, Peppermill, Lampshade,
            Funnybone, Faucet, Face-in-the-wall,
            Head-over-heels and Upsy-daisy
            And Collywobbles and Cupboard-Love,
            Be good, little gods, and guard these lives,
            Innocent be all your indiscretions,
            That no paranoic notion obsess
            Nor dazing dump bedevil their minds
            With faceless fears; no filter-passing
            Virus invade; no invisible germ,

Transgressing rash or gadding tumor
Attack their tissues; nor, taking by
Spiteful surprise, conspiring objects
With slip or sharpness or sly fracture
Menace or mangle the morbid flesh
Of our king and queen.

Now, turning to ROSETTA, MALIN said:

                    O clear Princess,
Learn from your hero his love of play,
Cherish his childishness, choose in him
Your task and toy, your betrayer also
Who gives gladly but forgets as soon
What and why, for the world he is true to
Is his own creation; to act like father,
And beget like God a gayer echo,
An unserious self, is the sole thought
Of this bragging boy. Be to him always
The mother-moment which makes him dream
He is lord of time. Belong to his journey:
O rest on his rock in your red dress,
His youth and future.

Then, turning to EMBLE, he said:
                    And you, bright Prince,
Invent your steps, go variously about
Her pleasant places, disposed to joy;
O stiffly stand, a staid monadnock,
On her peneplain; placidly graze
On her outwash apron, her own steed;
Dance, a wild deer, in her dark thickets;
Run, a river, all relish through her vales.

Alcohol, lust, fatigue, and the longing to be good, had by now induced in
them all a euphoric state in which it seemed as if it were only some
trifling and easily rectifiable error, improper diet, inadequate schooling,
or an outmoded moral code which was keeping mankind from the
millennial Earthly Paradise. Just a little more effort, perhaps merely the
discovery of the right terms in which to describe it, and surely absolute
pleasure must immediately descend upon the astonished armies of this
world and abolish for ever all their hate and suffering. So, such effort as at
that moment they could, they made. ROSETTA cried:

Let brazen bands abrupt their din and
Song grow civil, for the siege is raised.
The mad gym-mistress, made to resign,
Can pinch no more.

EMBLE cried:
                    Deprived of their files,
The vice-squads cavort in the mountains,
The Visa-Division vouch for all.

Then ROSETTA:

> The shops which displayed shining weapons
> And crime-stories carry delicate
> Pastoral poems and porcelain groups.

Then EMBLE:

> Nor money, magic, nor martial law,
> Hardness of heart nor hocus-pocus
> Are needed now on the novel earth.

ROSETTA:

> Nor terrors, tides, contagion longer
> Lustrate her stables: their strictures yield
> To play and peace.

EMBLE:

> Where pampered opulent
> Grudges governed, the Graces shall dance
> In excellent order with hands linked.

ROSETTA:

> Where, cold and cruel, critical faces
> Watched from windows, shall wanton putti
> Loose floods of flowers.

EMBLE:

> Where frontier sentries
> Stood so glumly on guard, young girls shall pass
> Trespassing in extravagant clothes.

ROSETTA:

> Where plains winced as punishing engines
> Raised woeful welts, tall windmills shall pat
> The flexible air and fan good cows.

EMBLE:

> Where hunted hundreds helplessly drowned,
> Rose-cheeked riders shall rein their horses
> To smile at swans.

The others joined in chorus. MALIN cried:

> It is safe to endure:
> Each flat defect has found its solid
> Gift to shadow, each goal its unique
> Longing to lure, relatedness its
> Invariant base, since Venus has now
> Agreed so gladly to guarantee
> Plenty of water to the plants this year,
> Aid to the beasts, to all human demands
> Full satisfaction with fresh structures
> For crucial regions.

QUANT cried:

                                A kind word and
                A fatherly peak not far away
                For city orphans.

Then ROSETTA again:

                                Synchronized watches
                And a long lane with a lot of twists
                For both sexes.

And EMBLE:

                                Barns and shrubberies
                For game-playing gangs.

QUANT:

                                        Grates full of logs and
                Hinterland homes for old proconsuls
                And pensioned pairs.

EMBLE:

                                        Places of silence
                For real readers.

ROSETTA:

                                A room with a view
                For a shut-in soul.

MALIN:

                                A shady walk
                There and back for a thinker or two.

EMBLE:

                A gentle jaunt for dejected nerves
                Over warm waters.

ROSETTA:

                                A wild party
                Every night for the outgoing classes.

MALIN:

                A long soliloquy to learn by heart
                For the verbal type.

QUANT:

                                Vast museums
                For the acquisitive kind to keep tidy.

MALIN:

                Spigots to open for the spendthrift lot,
                And choke-pear choices for champion wills.

    MALIN caught QUANT's eye and they rose to take their leave. As they
were getting their hats and coats, QUANT sang:

O gifted ghosts, be gone now to affirm
Your dedication; dwell in your choice:
   Venus with grace preventing
Requires what she may quicken.

Royal with roses be your resting place,
Balmy the airways, blue the welkin that
   Attend your time of passage,
   And easy seas assist you.

MALIN sang:
   Redeem with a clear
   Configuration
   Of routes and goals
   The ages of anguish,
   All griefs endured
   At the feet of appalling
   Fortresses; may
   Your present motions
   Satisfy all
   Their antecedents.

ROSETTA went with them to the elevator. As they waited in the corridor for it to come up, QUANT went on singing:

   Wonder warm you with its wisdom now,
   Genial joy rejuvenate your days,
     A light of self-translation,
     A blessed interior brightness,

   Animate also your object world
   Till its pure profiles appear again,
     Losing their latter vagueness,
     In the sharp shapes of childhood.

So did MALIN as they entered the elevator:

   Plumed and potent
   Go forth, fulfil
   A happy future
   And occupy that
   Permanent kingdom
   Parameters rule,
   Loved by infinite
   Populations
   Of possible cases:
   Away. Farewell.

Then they sank from her sight. When she got back to her apartment, she found that EMBLE had gone into her bedroom and passed out. She looked down at him, half sadly, half relieved, and thought thus:

   Blind on the bride-bed, the bridegroom snores,
   Too aloof to love. Did you lose your nerve

And cloud your conscience because I wasn't
Your dish really? You danced so bravely
Till I wished I were. Will you remain
Such a pleasant prince? Probably not.
But you're handsome, aren't you? even now
A kingly corpse. I'll coffin you up till
You rule again. Rest for us both and
Dream, dear one. I'll be dressed when you wake
To get coffee. You'll be glad you didn't
While your headache lasts, and I won't shine
In the sobering sun. We're so apart
When our ways have crossed and our words touched
On Babylon's banks. You'll build here, be
Satisfied soon, while I sit waiting
On my light luggage to leave if called
For some new exile, with enough clothes
But no merry maypole. Make your home
With some glowing girl; forget with her what
Happens also. If ever you see
A fuss forming in the far distance,
Lots of police, and a little group
In terrible trouble, don't try to help;
They'd make you mock and you might be ashamed.
As long as you live may your lying be
Poetic only. I'd hate you to think
How gentile you feel when you join in
The rowdy cries at Rimmon's party;
'—Fasten your figleaf, the Fleet is in.
Caesar is sitting in solemn thought,
Do not disturb. I'm dying tonight with
The tragic poets—' for you'll trust them all,
Be at home in there where a host of creatures,
Shot or squashed, have insured good-luck to
Their bandit bodies, blond mausoleums
Of the inner life. How could I share their
Light elations who belong after
Such hopes end? So be off to the game, dear,
And moot your mischief, I'll mind the shop.
You'll never notice what's not for sale
To charming children. Don't choose to ask me.
You're too late to believe. Your lie is showing,
Your creed is creased. But have Christian luck.
Your Jesus has wept; you may joke now,
Be spick and span, spell out the bumptious
Morals on monuments, mind your poise
And take up your cues, attract Who's-Who,
Ignore What's-Not. Niceness is all and
The rest bores. I'm too rude a question.
You'd learn to loathe, your legs forget their
Store of proverbs, the staircase wit of
The sleep-walker. You'd slip and blame me
When you came to, and couldn't accept
Our anxious hope with no household god or
Harpist's Haven for hearty climbers.

So fluke through unflustered with full marks in
House-geography: let history be.
Time is our trade, to be tense our gift
Whose woe is our weight; for we are His Chosen,
His ragged remnant with our ripe flesh
And our hats on, sent out of the room
By their dying grandees and doleful slaves,
Kicked in corridors and cold-shouldered
At toll-bridges, teased upon the stage,
Snubbed at sea, to seep through boundaries,
Diffuse like firearms through frightened lands,
Transpose our plight like a poignant theme
Into twenty tongues, time-tormented
But His People still. We'll point for Him,
Be as obvious always if He won't show
To threaten their thinking in their way,
Nor His strong arm that stood no nonsense,
Fly, let's face it, to defend us now
When bruised or broiled our bodies are chucked
Like cracked crocks onto kitchen middens
In the time He takes. We'll trust. He'll slay
If His Wisdom will. He won't alter
Nor fake one fact. Though I fly to Wall Street
Or Publisher's Row, or pass out, or
Submerge in music, or marry well,
Marooned on riches, He'll be right there
With His Eye upon me. Should I hide away
My secret sins in consulting rooms,
My fears are before Him; He'll find all,
Ignore nothing. He'll never let me
Conceal from Him the semi-detached
Brick villa in Laburnum Crescent,
The poky parlor, the pink bows on
The landing-curtains, or the lawn-mower
That wouldn't work, for He won't pretend to
Forget how I began, nor grant belief
In the mythical scenes I make up
Of a home like theirs, the Innocent Place where
His Law can't look, the leaves are so thick.
I've made their magic but their Momma Earth
Is His stone still, and their stately groves,
Though I wished to worship, His wood to me.
More boys like this one may embrace me yet
I shan't find shelter, I shan't be at peace
Till I really take your restless hands,
My poor fat father. How appalling was
Your taste in ties. How you tried to have fun,
You so longed to be liked. You lied so,
Didn't you, dad? When the doll never came,
When mother was sick and the maid laughed.
—Yes, I heard you in the attic. At her grave you
Wept and wilted. Was that why you chose
So blatant a voice, such button eyes
To play house with you then? Did you ever love

Stepmother Stupid? You'd a strange look,
Sad as the sea, when she searched your clothes.
Don't be cruel and cry. I couldn't stay to
Be your baby. We both were asking
For a warmth there wasn't, and then wouldn't write.
We mustn't, must we? Moses will scold if
We're not all there for the next meeting
At some brackish well or broken arch,
Tired as we are. We must try to get on
Though mobs run amok and markets fall,
Though lights burn late at police stations,
Though passports expire and ports are watched,
Though thousands tumble. Must their blue glare
Outlast the lions? Who'll be left to see it
Disconcerted? I'll be dumb before .
The barracks burn and boisterous Pharaoh
Grow ashamed and shy. *Sh'ma' Yisra'el.*
'^adonai '^elohenu, '^adonai 'echad.

PART SIX

Epilogue

Some natural tears they drop'd, but wip'd them soon;
The world was all before them, where to choose . . .
JOHN MILTON *Paradise Lost*

Meanwhile in the street outside, QUANT and MALIN, after expressing their mutual pleasure at having met, after exchanging addresses and promising to look each other up some time, had parted and immediately forgotten each other's existence. Now MALIN was travelling southward by subway while QUANT was walking eastward, each to his own place. Dawn had begun to break.

Walking through the streets, QUANT sang to himself an impromptu ballad:

When the Victory Powers convened at Byzantium,
The shiners declined to show their faces,
And the ambiences of heaven uttered a plethora
Of admonitory monsters which dismayed the illiterate.

Sitting in the train, MALIN thought:

Age softens the sense of defeat
As well as the will to success,
Till the unchangeable losses of childhood,
The forbidden affections rebel
No more; so now in the mornings

405

I wake, neither warned nor refreshed,
From dreams without daring, a series
Of vaguely disquieting adventures
Which never end in horror,
Grief or forgiving embraces.

QUANT sang:

But peace was promised by the public hepatoscopists
As the Ministers met to remodel the Commonwealth
In what was formerly the Museum of Fashion and
                                        Handicrafts,
While husky spectres haunted the corridors.

MALIN thought:

Do we learn from the past? The police,
The dress-designers, etc.,
Who manage the mirrors, say—No.
A hundred centuries hence
The gross and aggressive will still
Be putting their trust in a patron
Saint or a family fortress,
The seedy be taking the same
Old treatments for tedium vitae,
Religion, Politics, Love.

QUANT sang:

The Laurentian Landshield was ruthlessly gerrymandered,
And there was a terrible tussle over the Tethys Ocean;
Commentators broadcast by the courtesy of a
                                        shaving-cream
Blow by blow the whole debate on the Peninsulas.

MALIN thought:

Both professor and prophet depress,
For vision and longer view
Agree in predicting a day
Of convulsion and vast evil,
When the Cold Societies clash
Or the mosses are set in motion
To overrun the earth,
And the great brain which began
With lucid dialectics
Ends in a horrid madness.

QUANT sang:

But there were some sensible settlements in the
                                        sub-committees:
The Duodecimal System was adopted unanimously,
The price of obsidian pegged for a decade,
Technicians sent north to get nitrogen from the ice-cap.

MALIN thought:

Yet the noble despair of the poets
Is nothing of the sort; it is silly

To refuse the tasks of time
And, overlooking our lives,
Cry—'Miserable wicked me,
How interesting I am.'
We would rather be ruined than changed,
We would rather die in our dread
Than climb the cross of the moment
And let our illusions die.

QUANT sang:
Outside these decisions the cycle of Nature
Revolved as usual, and voluble sages
Preached from park-benches to passing fornicators
A Confucian faith in the Functional Society.

MALIN thought:
We're quite in the dark: we do not
Know the connection between
The clock we are bound to obey
And the miracle we must not despair of;
We simply cannot conceive
With any feelings we have
How the raging lion is to lime
With the yearning unicorn;
Nor shall we, till total shipwreck
Deprive us of our persons.

QUANT had now reached the house where he lived and, as he started to climb the steps of his stoop, he tripped and almost fell. At which he said:

Why, Miss *ME*, what's the matter? *Must* you go woolgathering?
Once I was your wonder. How short-winded you've gotten.
Come, Tinklebell, trot. Let's pretend you're a thoroughbred.
Over the hill now into Abraham's Bosom.

So saying, he opened his front door and disappeared. But MALIN's journey was still not done. He was thinking:

For the new locus is never
Hidden inside the old one
Where Reason could rout it out,
Nor guarded by dragons in distant
Mountains where Imagination
Could explore it; the place of birth
Is too obvious and near to notice,
Some dull dogpatch a stone's throw
Outside the walls, reserved
For the eyes of faith to find.

Now the train came out onto the Manhattan Bridge. The sun had risen. The East River glittered. It would be a bright clear day for work and for war.

MALIN thought:
>   For the others, like me, there is only the flash
>   Of negative knowledge, the night when, drunk, one
>   Staggers to the bathroom and stares in the glass
>   To meet one's madness, when what mother said seems
>   Such darling rubbish and the decent advice
>   Of the liberal weeklies as lost an art
>   As peasant pottery, for plainly it is not
>   To the Cross or to *Clarté* or to Common Sense
>   Our passions pray but to primitive totems
>   As absurd as they are savage; science or no science,
>   It is Bacchus or the Great Boyg or Baal-Peor,
>   Fortune's Ferris-wheel or the physical sound
>   Of our own names which they actually adore as their
>   Ground and goal. Yet the grossest of our dreams is
>   No worse than our worship which for the most part
>   Is so much galimatias to get out of
>   Knowing our neighbor, all the needs and conceits of
>   The poor muddled maddened mundane animal
>   Who is hostess to us all, for each contributes his
>   Personal panic, his predatory note
>   To her gregarious grunt as she gropes in the dark
>   For her lost lollypop. We belong to our kind,
>   Are judged as we judge, for all gestures of time
>   And all species of space respond in our own
>   Contradictory dialect, the double talk
>   Of ambiguous bodies, born like us to that
>   Natural neighborhood which denial itself
>   Like a friend confirms; they reflect our status,
>   Temporals pleading for eternal life with
>   The infinite impetus of anxious spirits,
>   Finite in fact yet refusing to be real,
>   Wanting our own way, unwilling to say Yes
>   To the Self-So which is the same at all times,
>   That Always-Opposite which is the whole subject
>   Of our not-knowing, yet from no necessity
>   Condescended to exist and to suffer death
>   And, scorned on a scaffold, ensconced in His life
>   The human household. In our anguish we struggle
>   To elude Him, to lie to Him, yet His love observes
>   His appalling promise; His predilection
>   As we wander and weep is with us to the end,
>   Minding our meanings, our least matter dear to Him,
>   His Good ingressant on our gross occasions
>   Envisages our advance, valuing for us
>   Though our bodies too blind or too bored to examine
>   What sorts excite them are slain interjecting
>   Their childish Ows and, in choosing how many
>   And how much they will love, our minds insist on
>   Their own disorder as their own punishment,
>   His Question disqualifies our quick senses,
>   His Truth makes our theories historical sins,
>   It is where we are wounded that is when He speaks
>   Our creaturely cry, concluding His children

In their mad unbelief to have mercy on them all
As they wait unawares for His World to come.

So thinking, he returned to duty, reclaimed by the actual world where time is real and in which, therefore, poetry can take no interest.

Facing another long day of servitude to wilful authority and blind accident, creation lay in pain and earnest, once more reprieved from self-destruction, its adoption, as usual, postponed.

July 1944–November 1946

Part X

1948–1957

In Transit

Let out where two fears intersect, a point selected
    Jointly by general staffs and engineers,
In a wet land, facing rough oceans, never invaded
    By Caesars or a cartesian doubt, I stand,
Pale, half asleep, inhaling its new fresh air that smells
    So strongly of soil and grass, of toil and gender,
But not for long: a professional friend is at hand
    Who smiling leads us indoors; we follow in file,

Obeying that fond peremptory tone reserved for those
    Nervously sick and children one cannot trust,
Who might be tempted by ponds or learn some disgusting
    Trick from a ragamuffin. Through modern panes
I admire a limestone hill I have no permission to climb
    And the pearly clouds of a sunset that seems
Oddly early to me: maybe an ambitious lad stares back,
    Dreaming of elsewhere and our godlike freedom.

Somewhere are places where we have really been, dear spaces
    Of our deeds and faces, scenes we remember
As unchanging because there we changed, where shops have names,
    Dogs bark in the dark at a stranger's footfall
And crops grow ripe and cattle fatten under the kind
    Protection of a godling or goddessling
Whose affection has been assigned them, to heed their needs and
    Plead in heaven the special case of their place.

Somewhere, too, unique for each, his frontier dividing
    Past from future, reached and crossed without warning:
That bridge where an ageing destroyer takes his last salute,
    In his rear all rivals fawning, in cages
Or dead, ahead a field of wrath; and that narrow pass where,
    Late from a sullen childhood, a fresh creator
Yields, glowing, to a boyish rapture, wild gothic peaks above him,
    Below, Italian sunshine, Italian flesh.

But here we are nowhere, unrelated to day or to Mother
    Earth in love or in hate; our occupation
Leaves no trace on this place or each other who do not
    Meet in its mere enclosure but are exposed
As objects for speculation, aggressive creatures
    On their way to their prey but now quite docile,
Told to wait and controlled by a voice that from time to time calls
    Some class of souls to foregather at the gate.

It calls me again to our plane and soon we are floating above
    A possessed congested surface, a world: down there
Motives and natural processes are stirred by spring
    And wrongs and graves grow greenly; slaves in quarries

Against their wills feel the will to live renewed by the song
   Of a loose bird, maculate cities are spared
Through the prayers of illiterate saints, and an ancient
   Feud re-opens with the debacle of a river.

1950

In Praise of Limestone

If it form the one landscape that we, the inconstant ones,
   Are consistently homesick for, this is chiefly
Because it dissolves in water. Mark these rounded slopes
   With their surface fragrance of thyme and, beneath,
A secret system of caves and conduits; hear the springs
   That spurt out everywhere with a chuckle,
Each filling a private pool for its fish and carving
   Its own little ravine whose cliffs entertain
The butterfly and the lizard; examine this region
   Of short distances and definite places:
What could be more like Mother or a fitter background
   For her son, the flirtatious male who lounges
Against a rock in the sunlight, never doubting
   That for all his faults he is loved; whose works are but
Extensions of his power to charm? From weathered outcrop
   To hill-top temple, from appearing waters to
Conspicuous fountains, from a wild to a formal vineyard,
   Are ingenious but short steps that a child's wish
To receive more attention than his brothers, whether
   By pleasing or teasing, can easily take.

Watch, then, the band of rivals as they climb up and down
   Their steep stone gennels in twos and threes, at times
Arm in arm, but never, thank God, in step; or engaged
   On the shady side of a square at midday in
Voluble discourse, knowing each other too well to think
   There are any important secrets, unable
To conceive a god whose temper-tantrums are moral
   And not to be pacified by a clever line
Or a good lay: for, accustomed to a stone that responds,
   They have never had to veil their faces in awe
Of a crater whose blazing fury could not be fixed;
   Adjusted to the local needs of valleys
Where everything can be touched or reached by walking,
   Their eyes have never looked into infinite space
Through the lattice-work of a nomad's comb; born lucky,
   Their legs have never encountered the fungi
And insects of the jungle, the monstrous forms and lives
   With which we have nothing, we like to hope, in common.
So, when one of them goes to the bad, the way his mind works
   Remains comprehensible: to become a pimp
Or deal in fake jewellery or ruin a fine tenor voice
   For effects that bring down the house, could happen to all
But the best and the worst of us . . .
                    That is why, I suppose,

The best and worst never stayed here long but sought
Immoderate soils where the beauty was not so external,
　　The light less public and the meaning of life
Something more than a mad camp. 'Come!' cried the granite wastes,
　　'How evasive is your humour, how accidental
Your kindest kiss, how permanent is death.' (Saints-to-be
　　Slipped away sighing.) 'Come!' purred the clays and gravels,
'On our plains there is room for armies to drill; rivers
　　Wait to be tamed and slaves to construct you a tomb
In the grand manner: soft as the earth is mankind and both
　　Need to be altered.' (Intendant Caesars rose and
Left, slamming the door.) But the really reckless were fetched
　　By an older colder voice, the oceanic whisper:
'I am the solitude that asks and promises nothing;
　　That is how I shall set you free. There is no love;
There are only the various envies, all of them sad.'

They were right, my dear, all those voices were right
And still are; this land is not the sweet home that it looks,
　　Nor its peace the historical calm of a site
Where something was settled once and for all: A backward
　　And dilapidated province, connected
To the big busy world by a tunnel, with a certain
　　Seedy appeal, is that all it is now? Not quite:
It has a worldly duty which in spite of itself
　　It does not neglect, but calls into question
All the Great Powers assume; it disturbs our rights. The poet,
　　Admired for his earnest habit of calling
The sun the sun, his mind Puzzle, is made uneasy
　　By these marble statues which so obviously doubt
His antimythological myth; and these gamins,
　　Pursuing the scientist down the tiled colonnade
With such lively offers, rebuke his concern for Nature's
　　Remotest aspects: I, too, am reproached, for what
And how much you know. Not to lose time, not to get caught,
　　Not to be left behind, not, please! to resemble
The beasts who repeat themselves, or a thing like water
　　Or stone whose conduct can be predicted, these
Are our Common Prayer, whose greatest comfort is music
　　Which can be made anywhere, is invisible,
And does not smell. In so far as we have to look forward
　　To death as a fact, no doubt we are right: But if
Sins can be forgiven, if bodies rise from the dead,
　　These modifications of matter into
Innocent athletes and gesticulating fountains,
　　Made solely for pleasure, make a further point:
The blessed will not care what angle they are regarded from,
　　Having nothing to hide. Dear, I know nothing of
Either, but when I try to imagine a faultless love
　　Or the life to come, what I hear is the murmur
Of underground streams, what I see is a limestone landscape.
                                                        May 1948

Ischia
(for Brian Howard)

There is a time to admit how much the sword decides,
with flourishing horns to salute the conqueror,
    impassive, cloaked and great on
  horseback under his faffling flag.

Changes of heart should also occasion song, like his
who, turning back from the crusaders' harbour, broke
    with our aggressive habit
  once and for all and was the first

to see all penniless creatures as our siblings. Then
at all times it is good to praise the shining earth,
    dear to us whether we choose our
  duty or do something horrible.

Dearest to each his birthplace; but to recall a green
valley where mushrooms fatten in the summer nights
    and silvered willows copy
  the circumflexions of the stream

is not my gladness today: I am presently moved
by sun-drenched Parthenopea, my thanks are for you,
    Ischia, to whom a fair wind has
  brought me rejoicing with dear friends

from soiled productive cities. How well you correct
our injured eyes, how gently you train us to see
    things and men in perspective
  underneath your uniform light.

Noble are the plans of the shirt-sleeved engineer,
but luck, you say, does more. What design could have washed
    with such delicate yellows
  and pinks and greens your fishing ports

that lean against ample Epomeo, holding on
to the rigid folds of her skirts? The boiling springs
    which betray her secret fever,
  make limber the gout-stiffened joint

and improve the venereal act; your ambient peace
in any case is a cure for, ceasing to think
    of a way to get on, we
  learn to simply wander about

by twisting paths which at any moment reveal
some vista as an absolute goal; eastward, perhaps,
    suddenly there, Vesuvius,
  looming across the bright bland bay

like a massive family pudding, or, around
a southern point, sheer-sided Capri who by herself
    defends the cult of Pleasure,
  a jealous, sometimes a cruel, god.

Always with some cool space or shaded surface, too,
you offer a reason to sit down; tasting what bees
    from the blossoming chestnut
  or short but shapely dark-haired men

from the aragonian grape distil, your amber wine,
your coffee-coloured honey, we believe that our
    lives are as welcome to us as
  loud explosions are to your saints.

Not that you lie about pain or pretend that a time
of darkness and outcry will not come back; upon
    your quays, reminding the happy
  stranger that all is never well,

sometimes a donkey breaks out into a choking wail
of utter protest at what is the case or his
    master sighs for a Brooklyn
  where shirts are silk and pants are new,

far from tall Restituta's all-too-watchful eye,
whose annual patronage, they say, is bought with blood.
    That, blessed and formidable
  Lady, we hope is not true; but, since

nothing is free, whatever you charge shall be paid,
that these days of exotic splendour may stand out
    in each lifetime like marble
  mileposts in an alluvial land.

                            June 1948

Under Sirius

Yes, these are the dog-days, Fortunatus:
    The heather lies limp and dead
  On the mountain, the battering torrent
    Shrunk to a soodling thread;
Rusty the spears of the legion, unshaven its captain,
    Vacant the scholar's brain
    Under his great hat,
  Drug though She may, the Sybil utters
    A gush of table-chat.

And you yourself with a head-cold and upset stomach,
    Lying in bed till noon,
  Your bills unpaid, your much advertised
    Epic not yet begun,

Are a sufferer too. All day, you tell us, you wish
    Some earthquake would astonish,
    Or the wind of the Comforter's wing
Unlock the prisons and translate
    The slipshod gathering.

And last night, you say, you dreamed of that bright blue morning,
    The hawthorn hedges in bloom,
When, serene in their ivory vessels,
    The three wise Maries come,
Sossing through seamless waters, piloted in
    By sea-horse and fluent dolphin:
    Ah! how the cannons roar,
How jocular the bells as They
    Indulge the peccant shore.

It is natural to hope and pious, of course, to believe
    That all in the end shall be well,
But first of all, remember,
    So the Sacred Books foretell,
The rotten fruit shall be shaken. Would your hope make sense
    If today were that moment of silence,
    Before it break and drown,
When the insurrected eagre hangs
    Over the sleeping town?

How will you look and what will you do when the basalt
    Tombs of the sorcerers shatter
And their guardian megalopods
    Come after you pitter-patter?
How will you answer when from their qualming spring
    The immortal nymphs fly shrieking,
    And out of the open sky
The pantocratic riddle breaks—
    'Who are you and why?'

For when in a carol under the apple-trees
    The reborn featly dance,
There will also, Fortunatus,
    Be those who refused their chance,
Now pottering shades, querulous beside the salt-pits,
    And mawkish in their wits,
    To whom these dull dog-days
Between event seem crowned with olive
    And golden with self-praise.

1949

Cattivo Tempo

Sirocco brings the minor devils:
A slamming of doors
At four in the morning
Announces they are back,
Grown insolent and fat
On cheesy literature
And corny dramas,
Nibbar, demon
Of ga-ga and bêtise,
Tubervillus, demon
Of gossip and spite.

Nibbar to the writing-room
Plausibly to whisper
The nearly fine,
The almost true;
Beware of him, poet,
Lest, reading over
Your shoulder, he find
What makes him glad,
The manner arch,
The meaning blurred,
The poem bad.

Tubervillus to the dining-room
Intently to listen,
Waiting his cue;
Beware of him, friends,
Lest the talk at his prompting
Take the wrong turning,
The unbated tongue
In mischief blurt
The half-home-truth,
The fun turn ugly,
The jokes hurt.

Do not underrate them; merely
To tear up the poem,
To shut the mouth
Will defeat neither:
To have got you alone
Self-confined to your bedroom
Manufacturing there
From lewdness or self-care
Some whining unmanaged
Imp of your own,
That too is their triumph.

The proper riposte is to bore them;
To scurry the dull pen
Through dull correspondence,
To wag the sharp tongue
In pigeon Italian,
Asking the socialist
Barber to guess
Or the monarchist fisherman to tell
When the wind will change,
Outwitting hell
With human obviousness.

1949

Hunting Season

A shot: from crag to crag
    The tell-tale echoes trundle;
Some feathered he-or-she
    Is now a lifeless bundle
And, proud into a kitchen, some
Example of our tribe will come.

Down in the startled valley
    Two lovers break apart:
He hears the roaring oven
    Of a witch's heart;
Behind his murmurs of her name
She sees a marksman taking aim.

Reminded of the hour
    And that his chair is hard,
A deathless verse half done,
    One interrupted bard
Postpones his dying with a dish
Of several suffocated fish.

1952

Fleet Visit

The sailors come ashore
Out of their hollow ships,
Mild-looking middle-class boys
Who read the comic strips;
One baseball game is more
To them than fifty Troys.

They look a bit lost, set down
In this unamerican place
Where natives pass with laws
And futures of their own;
They are not here because
But only just-in-case.

420

The whore and ne'er-do-well
Who pester them with junk
In their grubby ways at least
Are serving the Social Beast;
They neither make nor sell—
No wonder they get drunk.

But their ships on the vehement blue
Of this harbor actually gain
From having nothing to do;
Without a human will
To tell them whom to kill
Their structures are humane

And, far from looking lost,
Look as if they were meant
To be pure abstract design
By some master of pattern and line,
Certainly worth every cent
Of the billions they must have cost.

1951

An Island Cemetery

This graveyard with its umbrella pines
Is inferior in status to the vines
And, though new guests keep crowding in,
Must stay the size it's always been.

Where men are many, acres few,
The dead must be cultivated too,
Like seeds in any farmer's field
Are planted for the bones they yield.

It takes about eighteen months for one
To ripen into a skeleton,
To be washed, folded, packed in a small
Niche hollowed out of the cemetery wall.

Curiosity made me stop
While sextons were digging up a crop:
Bards have taken it too amiss
That Alexanders come to this.

Wherever our personalities go
(And, to tell the truth, we do not know),
The solid structures they leave behind
Are no discredit to our kind.

Mourners may miss, and they do, a face,
But at least they cannot detect a trace
Of those fish-like hungers, mammalian heats,
That kin our flesh to the coarser meats.

And who would be ashamed to own
To a patience that we share with stone,
This underlying thing in us
Which never at any time made a fuss?

Considering what our motives are,
We ought to thank our lucky star
That Love must ride to reach his ends
A mount which has no need of friends.

? 1956

Not in Baedeker

There were lead-mines here before the Romans
(Is there a once that is not already?),
Then mines made the manor a looming name
In bridal portions and disputed wills
(Once it changed owners during a card-game),
Then with the coming of the steam-engine
Their heyday arrived (An Early Victorian
Traveller has left us a description:
The removal of the ore, he writes, bless him,
*Leaves a horrid gulph. The wild scene is worthy
Of the pencil of Salvator Rosa.
The eye is awe-struck at the extraordinary
Richness of the deposits and the vast
Scale of the operations.*), and then, then on
A certain day (whether of time or rock
A lot is only so much and what ends
Ends at a definite moment) there came
Their last day, the day of the last lump, the actual
Day, now vaguely years, say sixty, ago,
When engines and all stopped. Today it would take
A geologist's look to guess that these hills
Provided roofs for some great cathedrals
(One irrevocably damaged by bombs)
And waterproof linings for the coffins
Of statesmen and actresses (all replaced),
Nor could one possibly (because of the odd
Breeding-habits of money, its even
Odder nomadic mania) discover
Where and to whom the more than one large fortune
Made here has got to now. A certain place
Has gone back to being (what most of the earth is
Most of the time) in the country somewhere.

Man still however (to discourage any
Romantic glooming over the Universe
Or any one marriage of work and love)
Exists on these uplands and the present
Is not uncheerful: so-so sheep are raised
And sphagnum moss (in the Latin countries
Still used in the treatment of gunshot wounds)

422

Collected; even the past is not dead
But revives annually on the festival
(Which occurs in the month of the willow)
Of St. Cobalt whose saturnine image,
Crude but certainly medieval is borne
In gay procession around the parish,
Halting at each of the now filled-in shafts
To the shrill chants of little girls in white
And the sneers of the local bus-driver
(Who greases his hair and dreams of halting
For a mysterious well-dressed passenger
Who offers at once to take him to the States).
Indeed, in its own quiet way, the place can strike
Most if not all of the historical notes
Even (what place can not?) the accidental:
One September Thursday two English cyclists
Stopped here for a *fine* and afterwards strolled
Along the no longer polluted stream
As far as the Shot Tower (indirectly
Responsible in its day for the deaths
Of goodness knows how many grouse, wild duck
And magnificent stags) where the younger
(Whose promise one might have guessed even then
Would come to nothing), using a rotting
Rickety gallery for a lectern,
To amuse his friend gave an imitation
Of a clergyman with a cleft palate.

1949

Ode to Gaea

From this new culture of the air we finally see,
far-shining in excellence, what our Mother, the
          nicest daughter of Chaos, would
       admire could she look in a glass,

and what, in her eyes, is natural: it is the old
grand style of gesture we watch as, heavy with cold,
          the top-waters of all her
       northern seas take their vernal plunge,

and suddenly her desolations, salt as blood,
prolix yet terse, are glamorously carpeted
          with great swatches of plankton,
       delicious spreads of nourishment,

while, in her realm of solids, lively dots expand,
companionship becomes an unstaid passion and
          leaves by the mile hide tons of
       pied pebbles that will soon be birds.

Now that we know how she looks, she seems more mysterious
than when, in her *partibus infidelibus*,
      we painted sizzling dragons
    and wizards reading upside down,

but less approachable: where she joins girl's-ear lakes
to bird's-foot deltas with lead-blue squiggles she makes,
      surely, a value judgment,
    'of pure things Water is the best,'

but how does she rank wheelwrights? One doubts if she knows
which sub-species of folly is peculiar to those
      pretty molehills, where on that
    pocket-handkerchief of a plain

the syntax changes: peering down sleepily at
a crenellated shore, the tired old diplomat
      becomes embarrassed—Should he
    smile for 'our great good ally', scowl

at 'that vast and detestable empire' or choose
the sneer reserved for certain Southern countries 'whose
      status and moral climate
    we have no desire, sir, to emulate'?

But why we should feel neglected on mountain drives,
unpopular in woods, is quite clear; the older lives
      have no wish to be stood in
    rows or at right angles: below,

straight as its railroads, cutting diagonally across
a positivist republic, two lines of moss
      show where the Devil's Causeway
    drew pilgrims thirteen gods ago,

and on this eve of whispers and tapped telephones
before the Ninth Catastrophe, square corner-stones
      still distinguish a fortress
    of the High Kings from untutored rock.

Tempting to mortals is the fancy of half-concerned
Gods in the sky, of a bored Thunderer who turned
      from the Troy-centred grief to
    watch the Hippemolgoi drink their milk,

and how plausible from his look-point: we may well
shake a weak fist one day at this vision, but the spell
      of high places will haunt us
    long after our jaunt has declined,

as soon it must, to the hard ground. Where six foot is tall,
good-manners will ask easy riddles like 'Why are all
      the rowdiest marches and the
    most venomous iambics composed

by lame clergymen?', will tell no tales which end in worse
disaster than that of the tipsy poet who cursed
      a baby for whom later
    he came to sigh. So we were taught

before the Greater Engines came and the police
who go with them, when the long rivers ran through peace
      and the holy laws of Speech were
    held in awe, even by evil tongues,

and manners, maybe, will stand us in better stead,
down there, than a kantian conscience. From overhead
      much harm is discernible,
    farms unroofed and harbor-works wrecked

in the Second Assault; frank to an ungrieving sky
as still they look, too many fertilities lie
      in dread of the tormentor's
    fondling finger, and in the few

that still have poky shops and audiences of one,
many are overweight, the pious peasant's only son,
      goading their crumpled faces
    down innocence-corrupting roads,

dreams of cities where his cows are whores. When the wise
wilt in the glare of the Shadow, the stern advise
      tribute, and the large-hearted
    already talk Its gibberish,

perhaps a last stand in the passes will be made
by those whose Valhalla would be hearing verse by Praed
      or arias by Rossini
    between two entrées by Carême.

We hope so. But who on Cupid's Coming would care to bet?
More than one World's Bane has been scotched before this, yet
      Justice during his *Te Deum*
    slipped away sighing from the hero's pew,

and Earth, till the end, will be Herself. She has never been moved
except by Amphion, and orators have not improved
      since misled Athens perished
    upon Sicilian marble: what,

to Her, the real one, can our good landscapes be but lies,
those woods where tigers chum with deer and no root dies,
      that tideless bay where children
    play Bishop on a golden shore?

                       August 1954

Bucolics

1. WINDS
(for Alexis Leger)

Deep, deep below our violences,
Quite still, lie our First Dad, his watch
  And many little maids,
But the boneless winds that blow
  Round law-court and temple
Recall to Metropolis
  That Pliocene Friday when,
At His holy insufflation
  (Had He picked a teleost
Or an arthropod to inspire,
  Would our death also have come?)
One bubble-brained creature said—
  'I am loved, therefore I am'—:
And well by now might the lion
  Be lying down with the kid,
Had he stuck to that logic.

Winds make weather; weather
Is what nasty people are
  Nasty about and the nice
Show a common joy in observing:
  When I seek an image
For our Authentic City
  (Across what brigs of dread,
Down what gloomy galleries,
  Must we stagger or crawl
Before we may cry—O look!?),
  I see old men in hall-ways
Tapping their barometers,
  Or a lawn over which
The first thing after breakfast,
  A paterfamilias
Hurries to inspect his rain-gauge.

Goddess of winds and wisdom,
  When, on some windless day
Of dejection, unable
  To name or to structure,
Your poet with bodily tics,
  Scratching, tapping his teeth,
Tugging the lobe of an ear,
  Unconsciously invokes You,
Show Your good nature, allow
  Rooster or whistling maid
To fetch him Arthur O'Bower;
  Then, if moon-faced Nonsense,
That erudite forger, stalk
  Through the seven kingdoms,

Set Your poplars a-shiver
   To warn Your clerk lest he
Die like an Old Believer
   For some spurious reading:
And in all winds, no matter
   Which of Your twelve he may hear,
Equinox gales at midnight
   Howling through marram grass,
Or a faint susurration
   Of pines on a cloudless
Afternoon in midsummer,
   Let him feel You present,
That every verbal rite
   May be fittingly done,
And done in anamnesis
   Of what is excellent
Yet a visible creature,
   Earth, Sky, a few dear names.

September 1953

2. WOODS
(for Nicolas Nabokov)

Sylvan meant savage in those primal woods
Piero di Cosimo so loved to draw,
Where nudes, bears, lions, sows with women's heads,
Mounted and murdered and ate each other raw,
Nor thought the lightning-kindled bush to tame
But, flabbergasted, fled the useful flame.

Reduced to patches, owned by hunting squires,
Of villages with ovens and a stocks,
They whispered still of most unsocial fires,
Though Crown and Mitre warned their silly flocks
The pasture's humdrum rhythms to approve
And to abhor the licence of the grove.

Guilty intention still looks for a hotel
That wants no details and surrenders none;
A wood is that, and throws in charm as well,
And many a semi-innocent, undone,
Has blamed its nightingales who round the deed
Sang with such sweetness of a happy greed.

Those birds, of course, did nothing of the sort,
And, as for sylvan nature, if you take
A snapshot at a picnic, O how short
And lower-ordersy the Gang will look
By those vast lives that never took another
And are not scared of gods, ghosts, or stepmother.

Among these coffins of its by-and-by
The Public can (it cannot on a coast)
Bridle its skirt-and-bargain-chasing eye,
And where should an austere philologist
Relax but in the very world of shade
From which the matter of his field was made.

Old sounds re-educate an ear grown coarse,
As Pan's green father suddenly raps out
A burst of undecipherable Morse,
And cuckoos mock in Welsh, and doves create
In rustic English over all they do
To rear their modern family of two.

Now here, now there, some loosened element,
A fruit in vigor or a dying leaf,
Utters its private idiom for descent,
And late man, listening through his latter grief,
Hears, close or far, the oldest of his joys,
Exactly as it was, the water noise.

A well-kempt forest begs Our Lady's grace;
Someone is not disgusted, or at least
Is laying bets upon the human race
Retaining enough decency to last;
The trees encountered on a country stroll
Reveal a lot about a country's soul.

A small grove massacred to the last ash,
An oak with heart-rot, give away the show:
This great society is going smash;
They cannot fool us with how fast they go,
How much they cost each other and the gods.
A culture is no better than its woods.

August 1952

3. MOUNTAINS
(for Hedwig Petzold)

I know a retired dentist who only paints mountains,
  But the Masters rarely care
That much, who sketch them in beyond a holy face
  Or a highly dangerous chair;
While a normal eye perceives them as a wall
Between worse and better, like a child, scolded in France,
Who wishes he were crying on the Italian side of the Alps:
  Caesar does not rejoice when high ground
    Makes a darker map,
  Nor does Madam. Why should they? A serious being
    Cries out for a gap.

428

And it is curious how often in steep places
    You meet someone short who frowns,
A type you catch beheading daisies with a stick:
    Small crooks flourish in big towns,
But perfect monsters—remember Dracula—
Are bred on crags in castles. Those unsmiling parties,
Clumping off at dawn in the gear of their mystery
        For points up, are a bit alarming;
            They have the balance, nerve,
And habit of the Spiritual, but what God
        Does their Order serve?

A civil man is a citizen. Am I
    To see in the Lake District, then,
Another bourgeois invention like the piano?
    Well, I won't. How can I, when
I wish I stood now on a platform at Penrith,
Zurich, or any junction at which you leave the express
For a local that swerves off soon into a cutting? Soon
        Tunnels begin, red farms disappear,
            Hedges turn to walls,
Cows become sheep, you smell peat or pinewood, you hear
        Your first waterfalls,

And what looked like a wall turns out to be a world
    With measurements of its own
And a style of gossip. To manage the Flesh,
    When angels of ice and stone
Stand over her day and night who make it so plain
They detest any kind of growth, does not encourage
Euphemisms for the effort: here wayside crucifixes
        Bear witness to a physical outrage,
            And serenades too
Stick to bare fact: 'O my girl has a goitre,
        I've a hole in my shoe!'

Dour. Still, a fine refuge. That boy behind his goats
    Has the round skull of a clan
That fled with bronze before a tougher metal,
    And that quiet old gentleman
With a cheap room at the Black Eagle used to own
Three papers but is not received in Society now:
These farms can always see a panting government coming;
        I'm nordic myself, but even so
            I'd much rather stay
Where the nearest person who could have me hung is
        Some ridges away.

To be sitting in privacy, like a cat
    On the warm roof of a loft,
Where the high-spirited son of some gloomy tarn
    Comes sprinting down through a green croft,
Bright with flowers laid out in exquisite splodges

Like a Chinese poem, while, near enough, a real darling
Is cooking a delicious lunch, would keep me happy for
    What? Five minutes? For an uncatlike
      Creature who has gone wrong,
  Five minutes on even the nicest mountain
     Are awfully long.

? July 1952

4. LAKES
(for Isaiah Berlin)

A lake allows an average father, walking slowly,
  To circumvent it in an afternoon,
And any healthy mother to halloo the children
  Back to her bedtime from their games across:
(Anything bigger than that, like Michigan or Baikal,
  Though potable, is an 'estranging sea').

Lake-folk require no fiend to keep them on their toes;
  They leave aggression to ill-bred romantics
Who duel with their shadows over blasted heaths:
  A month in a lacustrine atmosphere
Would find the fluvial rivals waltzing not exchanging
  The rhyming insults of their great-great-uncles.

No wonder Christendom did not get really started
  Till, scarred by torture, white from caves and jails,
Her pensive chiefs converged on the Ascanian Lake
  And by that stork-infested shore invented
The life of Godhead, making catholic the figure
  Of three small fishes in a triangle.

Sly Foreign Ministers should always meet beside one,
  For, whether they walk widdershins or deasil,
The path will yoke their shoulders to one liquid centre
  Like two old donkeys pumping as they plod;
Such physical compassion may not guarantee
  A marriage for their armies, but it helps.

Only a very wicked or conceited man,
  About to sink somewhere in mid-Atlantic,
Could think Poseidon's frown was meant for him in person,
  But it is only human to believe
The little lady of the glacier lake has fallen
  In love with the rare bather whom she drowns.

The drinking water of the city where one panics
  At nothing noticing how real one is
May come from reservoirs whose guards are all too conscious
  Of being followed: Webster's cardinal
Saw in a fish-pool something horrid with a hay-rake;
  I know a Sussex hammer-pond like that.

A haunted lake is sick, though; normally, they doctor
  Our tactile fevers with a visual world
Where beaks are dumb like boughs and faces calm like houses;
  The water-scorpion finds it quite unticklish,
And, if it shudder slightly when caressed by boats,
  It never asks for water or a loan.

Liking one's Nature, as lake-lovers do, benign
  Goes with a wish for savage dogs and man-traps:
One Fall, one dispossession, is enough, I'm sorry;
  Why should I give Lake Eden to the Nation
Just because every mortal Jack and Jill has been
  The genius of some amniotic mere?

It is unlikely I shall ever keep a swan
  Or build a tower on any small tombolo,
But that's not going to stop me wondering what sort
  Of lake I would decide on if I should.
Moraine, pot, oxbow, glint, sink, crater, piedmont, dimple . . .?
  Just reeling off their names is ever so comfy.

1952

5. ISLANDS
(for Giovanni Maresca)

Old saints on millstones float with cats
  To islands out at sea
Whereon no female pelvis can
  Threaten their agape.

Beyond the long arm of the Law,
  Close to a shipping road,
Pirates in their island lairs
  Observe the pirate code.

Obsession with security
  In Sovereigns prevails;
His Highness and The People both
  Pick islands for their jails.

Once, where detected worldlings now
  Do penitential jobs,
Exterminated species played
  Who had not read their Hobbes.

His continental damage done,
  Laid on an island shelf,
Napoleon has five years more
  To talk about himself.

How fascinating is that class
  Whose only member is Me!
Sappho, Tiberius and I
  Hold forth beside the sea.

What is cosier than the shore
   Of a lake turned inside out?
How do all these other people
   Dare to be about?

In democratic nudity
   Their sexes lie; except
By age or weight you could not tell
   The keeping from the kept.

They go, she goes, thou goest, I go
   To a mainland livelihood:
Farmer and fisherman complain
   The other has it good.   *? September 1953*

6. PLAINS
(for Wendell Johnson)

I can imagine quite easily ending up
   In a decaying port on a desolate coast,
Cadging drinks from the unwary, a quarrelsome,
   Disreputable old man; I can picture
A second childhood in a valley, scribbling
   Reams of edifying and unreadable verse;
But I cannot see a plain without a shudder:
   'O God, please, please, don't ever make me live there!'

It's horrible to think what peaks come down to,
   That pecking rain and squelching glacier defeat
Tall pomps of stone where goddesses lay sleeping,
   Dreaming of being woken by some chisel's kiss,
That what those blind brutes leave when they are through is nothing
   But a mere substance, a clay that meekly takes
The potter's cuff, a gravel that as concrete
   Will unsex any space which it encloses.

And think of growing where all elsewheres are equal!
   So long as there's a hill-ridge somewhere the dreamer
Can place his land of marvels; in poor valleys
   Orphans can head downstream to seek a million:
Here nothing points; to choose between Art and Science
   An embryo genius would have to spin a stick.
What could these farms do if set loose but drift like clouds,
   What goal of unrest is there but the Navy?

Romance? Not in this weather. Ovid's charmer
   Who leads the quadrilles in Arcady, boy-lord
Of hearts who can call their Yes and No their own,
   Would, madcap that he is, soon die of cold or sunstroke:
These lives are in firmer hands; that old grim She
   Who makes the blind dates for the hatless genera
Creates their country matters. (Woe to the child-bed,
   Woe to the strawberries if She's in Her moods!)

432

And on these attend, greedy as fowl and harsher
   Than any climate, Caesar with all his They.
If a tax-collector disappear in the hills,
   If, now and then, a keeper is shot in the forest,
No thunder follows, but where roads run level,
   How swift to the point of protest strides the crown.
It hangs, it flogs, it fines, it goes. There is drink.
   There are wives to beat. But Zeus is with the strong,

Born as a rule in some small place (an island,
   Quite often, where a smart lad can spot the bluff
Whence cannon would put the harbor at his mercy),
   Though it is here they chamber with Clio. At this brook
The Christian cross-bow stopped the Heathen scimitar;
   Here is a windmill whence an emperor saw
His right wing crumple; across these cabbage fields
   A pretender's Light Horse made their final charge.

If I were a plainsman I should hate us all,
   From the mechanic rioting for a cheap loaf
To the fastidious palate, hate the painter
   Who steals my wrinkles for his Twelve Apostles,
Hate the priest who cannot even make it shower.
   What could I smile at as I trudged behind my harrow
But bloodshot images of rivers howling,
   Marbles in panic, and Don't-Care made to care?

As it is, though, I know them personally
   Only as a landscape common to two nightmares:
Across them, spotted by spiders from afar,
   I have tried to run, knowing there was no hiding and no help;
On them, in brilliant moonlight, I have lost my way
   And stood without a shadow at the dead centre
Of an abominable desolation,
   Like Tarquin ravished by his post-coital sadness.

Which goes to show I've reason to be frightened
   Not of plains, of course, but of me. I should like
—Who wouldn't?—to shoot beautifully and be obeyed
   (I should also like to own a cave with two exits);
I wish I weren't so silly. Though I can't pretend
   To think these flats poetic, it's as well at times
To be reminded that nothing is lovely,
   Not even in poetry, which is not the case.

? July 1953

7. STREAMS
(for *Elizabeth Drew*)

Dear water, clear water, playful in all your streams,
  as you dash or loiter through life who does not love
    to sit beside you, to hear you and see you,
  pure being, perfect in music and movement?

Air is boastful at times, earth slovenly, fire rude,
but you in your bearing are always immaculate,
      the most well-spoken of all the older
   servants in the household of Mrs. Nature.

Nobody suspects you of mocking him, for you still
use the same vocables you were using the day
      before that unexpected row which
   downed every hod on half-finished Babel,

and still talk to yourself: nowhere are you disliked;
arching your torso, you dive from a basalt sill,
      canter across white chalk, slog forward
   through red marls, the aboriginal pilgrim,

at home in all sections, but for whom we should be
idolaters of a single rock, kept apart
      by our landscapes, excluding as alien
   the tales and diets of all other strata.

How could we love the absent one if you did not keep
coming from a distance, or quite directly assist,
      as when past Iseult's tower you floated
   the willow pash-notes of wanted Tristram?

And *Homo Ludens*, surely, is your child, who make
fun of our feuds by opposing identical banks,
      transferring the loam from Huppim
   to Muppim and back each time you crankle.

Growth cannot add to your song: as unchristened brooks
already you whisper to ants what, as Brahma's son,
      descending his titanic staircase
   into Assam, to Himalayan bears you thunder.

And not even man can spoil you: his company
coarsens roses and dogs but, should he herd you through a sluice
      to toil at a turbine, or keep you
   leaping in gardens for his amusement,

innocent still is your outcry, water, and there
even, to his soiled heart raging at what it is,
      tells of a sort of world, quite other,
   altogether different from this one

with its envies and passports, a polis like that
to which, in the name of scholars everywhere,
      Gaston Paris pledged his allegiance
   as Bismarck's siege-guns came within earshot.

Lately, in that dale of all Yorkshire's the loveliest,
where, off its fell-side helter-skelter, Kisdon Beck
      jumps into Swale with a boyish shouting,
   sprawled out on grass, I dozed for a second,

434

and found myself following a croquet tournament
in a calm enclosure, with thrushes popular:
    of all the players in that cool valley
    the best with the mallet was my darling.

While, on the wolds that begirdled it, wild old men
hunted with spades and hammers, monomaniac each,
    for a megalith or a fossil,
    and bird-watchers crept through mossy beech-woods.

Suddenly, over the lawn we started to run
for, lo, through the trees, in a cream and golden coach
    drawn by two baby locomotives,
    the god of mortal doting approached us,

flanked by his bodyguard, those hairy armigers in green
who laugh at thunderstorms and weep at a blue sky:
    He thanked us for our cheers of homage,
    and promised X and Y a passion undying.

With a wave of his torch he commanded a dance;
so round in a ring we flew, my dear on my right,
    when I awoke. But fortunate seemed that
    day because of my dream and enlightened,

and dearer, water, than ever your voice, as if
glad—though goodness knows why—to run with the human race,
    wishing, I thought, the least of men their
    figures of splendor, their holy places.

? July 1953

Shorts

IN MEMORIAM L. K.-A. 1950–1952

At peace under this mandarin, sleep, Lucina,
Blue-eyed Queen of white cats: for you the Ischian wave shall weep
When we who now miss you are American dust, and steep
Epomeo in peace and war augustly a grave-watch keep.

October 1953

*   *   *

EPITAPH FOR THE UNKNOWN SOLDIER

To save your world, you asked this man to die:
Would this man, could he see you now, ask why?

October 1953

*   *   *

O where would those choleric boys,
Our political orators be,
Were one to deprive them of all
Their igneous figures of speech,
If, instead of stamping out flames
Or consuming stubble with fire,
They could only shut out a draught
Or let in a little fresh air?

September 1953

* * *

Behold the manly mesomorph
Showing his bulging biceps off,
Whom social workers love to touch,
Though the loveliest girls do not care for him much.

Pretty to watch with bat or ball,
An Achilles, too, in a bar-room brawl,
But in the ditch of hopeless odds,
The hour of desertion by brass and gods,

Not a hero. It is the pink-and-white,
Fastidious, almost girlish, in the night
When the proud-arsed broad-shouldered break and run,
Who covers their retreat, dies at his gun.

1950

* * *

Give me a doctor, partridge-plump,
Short in the leg and broad in the rump,
An endomorph with gentle hands,
Who'll never make absurd demands
That I abandon all my vices,
Nor pull a long face in a crisis,
But with a twinkle in his eye
Will tell me that I have to die.

1950

* * *

Fair is Middle-Earth nor changes, though to Age,
Raging at his uncomeliness,
Her wine turn sour, her bread tasteless.

1954

* * *

A Young Person came out of the mists,
Who had the most beautiful wrists:
   A scandal occurred
   Which has long been interred,
But the legend about them persists.

? 1950

* * *

As the poets have mournfully sung,
Death takes the innocent young,
  The rolling in money,
  The screamingly funny,
And those who are very well hung.

? 1950

*   *   *

Guard, Civility, with guns
Your modes and your declensions:
Any lout can spear with ease
Singular Archimedes.

1954

*   *   *

Bull-roarers cannot keep up the annual rain,
The water-table of a once green champaign
Sinks, will keep on sinking: but why complain? Against odds,
Methods of dry-farming shall still produce grain.

1959

*   *   *

From bad lands where eggs are small and dear,
Climbing to worse by a stonier
Track, when all are spent we hear it:—the right song
For the wrong time of year.

1954

Five Songs

I

Deftly, admiral, cast your fly
  Into the slow deep hover,
Till the wise old trout mistake and die;
  Salt are the deeps that cover
  The glittering fleets you led,
    White is your head.

Read on, ambassador, engrossed
  In your favourite Stendhal;
The Outer Provinces are lost,
  Unshaven horsemen swill
  The great wines of the Chateaux
    Where you danced long ago.

Do not turn, do not lift your eyes
  Toward the still pair standing
On the bridge between your properties,
  Indifferent to your minding:
  In its glory, in its power,
    This is their hour.

437

Nothing your strength, your skill, could do
   Can alter their embrace
Or dispersuade the Furies who
   At the appointed place
With claw and dreadful brow
   Wait for them now.

                               June 1948

II

The Emperor's favorite concubine
   Was in the Eunuch's pay,
The Wardens of the Marches turned
   Their spears the other way;
The vases crack, the ladies die,
   The Oracles are wrong:
We suck our thumbs or sleep; the show
   Is gamey and too long.

But—Music Ho!—at last it comes,
   The Transformation Scene:
A rather scruffy-looking god
   Descends in a machine
And, gabbling off his rustic rhymes,
   Misplacing one or two,
Commands the prisoners to walk,
   The enemies to screw.

                               May 1948

III

A starling and a willow-wren
   On a may-tree by a weir
Saw them meet and heard him say:
   'Dearest of my dear,
More lively than these waters chortling
   As they leap the dam,
My sweetest duck, my precious goose,
   My white lascivious lamb.'
With a smile she listened to him,
   Talking to her there:
What does he want? said the willow-wren;
   Much too much, said the stare.

'Forgive these loves who dwell in me,
   These brats of greed and fear,
The honking bottom-pinching clown,
   The snivelling sonneteer,
That so, between us, even these,
   Who till the grave are mine,
For all they fall so short of may,
   Dear heart, be still a sign.'
With a smile she closed her eyes,
   Silent she lay there:
Does he mean what he says? said the willow-wren;
   Some of it, said the stare.

'Hark! Wild Robin winds his horn
    And, as his notes require,
Now our laughter-loving spirits
    Must in awe retire
And let their kinder partners,
    Speechless with desire,
Go in their holy selfishness,
    Unfunny to the fire.'
Smiling, silently she threw
    Her arms about him there:
Is it only that? said the willow-wren;
    It's that as well, said the stare.

Waking in her arms he cried,
    Utterly content:
'I have heard the high good noises,
    Promoted for an instant,
Stood upon the shining outskirts
    Of that Joy I thank
For you, my dog and every goody.'
    There on the grass bank
She laughed, he laughed, they laughed together,
    Then they ate and drank:
Did he know what he meant? said the willow-wren—
    God only knows, said the stare.

                                        1953

                    IV
'When rites and melodies begin
    To alter modes and times,
And timid bar-flies boast aloud
    Of uncommitted crimes,
And leading families are proud
    To dine with their black sheep,
What promises, what discipline,
    If any, will Love keep?'
    So roared Fire on their right:
        But Tamino and Pamina
        Walked past its rage,
    Sighing O, sighing O,
In timeless fermatas of awe and delight
    (Innocent? Yes. Ignorant? No.)
        Down the grim passage.

'When stinking Chaos lifts the latch,
    And Grotte backward spins,
And Helen's nose becomes a beak,
    And cats and dogs grow chins,
And daisies claw and pebbles shriek,
    And Form and Color part,
What swarming hatreds then will hatch
    Out of Love's riven heart?'
        So hissed Water on their left:
            But Pamina and Tamino

Opposed its spite,
With his worship, with her sweetness—
O look now! See how they emerge from the cleft
(Frightened? No. Happy? Yes.)
Out into sunlight.

August 1953

V

Make this night loveable,
Moon, and with eye single
Looking down from up there
Bless me, One especial
And friends everywhere.

With a cloudless brightness
Surround our absences;
Innocent be our sleeps,
Watched by great still spaces,
White hills, glittering deeps.

Parted by circumstance,
Grant each your indulgence
That we may meet in dreams
For talk, for dalliance,
By warm hearths, by cool streams.

Shine lest tonight any,
In the dark suddenly,
Wake alone in a bed
To hear his own fury
Wishing his love were dead.

October 1953

Three Occasional Poems

I. TO T. S. ELIOT ON HIS SIXTIETH BIRTHDAY
(1948)

When things began to happen to our favourite spot,
a key missing, a library bust defaced,
    then on the tennis-court one morning,
outrageous, the bloody corpse, and always,

blank day after day, the unheard-of drought, it was you
who, not speechless from shock but finding the right
    language for thirst and fear, did much to
prevent a panic. It is the crime that

counts, you will say. We know, but would gratefully add,
to-day as we wait for the Law to take its course
    (and which of us shall escape whipping?),
that your sixty years have not been wasted.

May 1948

II. METALOGUE TO THE MAGIC FLUTE

(Lines composed in commemoration of the Mozart Bicentenary, 1956.
To be spoken by the singer playing the role of Sarastro.)

Relax, Maestro, put your baton down:
Only the fogiest of the old will frown
If you the trials of the PRINCE prorogue
To let SARASTRO speak this Metalogue,
A form acceptable to us, although
Unclassed by ARISTOTLE or BOILEAU.
No modern audience finds it incorrect,
For interruption is what we expect
Since that new god, the Paid Announcer, rose,
Who with his quasi-Ossianic prose
Cuts in upon the lovers, halts the band,
To name a sponsor or to praise a brand.
Not that I have a product to describe
That you could wear or cook with or imbibe;
You cannot hoard or waste a work of art:
I come to praise but not to sell MOZART,
Who came into this world of war and woe
At Salzburg just two centuries ago,
When kings were many and machines were few
And open Atheism something new.
(It makes a servantless New Yorker sore
To think sheer Genius had to stand before
A mere Archbishop with uncovered head:
But MOZART never had to make his bed.)

The history of Music as of Man
Will not go cancrizans, and no ear can
Recall what, when the Archduke FRANCIS reigned,
Was heard by ears whose treasure-hoard contained
A *Flute* already but as yet no *Ring*;
Each age has its own mode of listening.
We know the MOZART of our fathers' time
Was gay, rococo, sweet, but not sublime,
A Viennese Italian; that is changed
Since music critics learned to feel 'estranged';
Now it's the Germans he is classed amongst.
A *Geist* whose music was composed from *Angst*,
At International Festivals enjoys
An equal status with the Twelve-Tone Boys;
He awes the lovely and the very rich,
And even those *Divertimenti* which
He wrote to play while bottles were uncorked,
Milord chewed noisily, Milady talked,
Are heard in solemn silence, score on knees,
Like quartets by the deafest of the B's.
What next? One can no more imagine how,
In concert halls two hundred years from now,
When the mozartian sound-waves move the air,
The cognoscenti will be moved, than dare
Predict how high orchestral pitch will go,

441

How many tones will constitute a row,
The tempo at which regimented feet
Will march about the Moon, the form of Suite
For Piano in a Post-Atomic Age,
Prepared by some contemporary CAGE.

An opera composer may be vexed
By later umbrage taken at his text:
⎧ Even MACAULAY's schoolboy knows to-day
⎨ What ROBERT GRAVES or MARGARET MEAD would say
⎩ About the status of the sexes in this play,
Writ in that era of barbaric dark
'Twixt Modern Mom and Bronze-Age Matriarch.
Where now the Roman Fathers and their creed?
'Ah, where' sighs MR. MITTY, 'where indeed?',
And glances sideways at his vital spouse
Whose rigid jaw-line and contracted brows
Express her scorn and utter detestation
For Roman views of Female Education.

In Nineteen-Fifty-Six we find the QUEEN
A highly-paid and most efficient Dean
(Who, as we all know, really runs the College),
SARASTRO, tolerated for his knowledge,
Teaching the History of Ancient Myth
At BRYN MAWR, VASSAR, BENNINGTON or SMITH;
PAMINA may a *Time* researcher be
To let TAMINO take his Ph.D.,
Acquiring manly wisdom as he wishes
While changing diapers and doing dishes;
Sweet PAPAGENA, when she's time to spare,
Listens to MOZART operas on the air,
Though PAPAGENO, we are sad to feel,
Prefers the juke-box to the glockenspiel,
And how is—what was easy in the past—
A democratic villain to be cast?
MONOSTATOS must make his bad impression
Without a race, religion or profession.

A work that lasts two hundred years is tough,
And operas, God knows, must stand enough:
What greatness made small vanities abuse.
What must they not endure? The Diva whose
Fioriture and climactic note
The silly old composer never wrote,
Conductor X, that over-rated bore
Who alters tempi and who cuts the score,
Director Y who with ingenious wit
Places his wretched singers in the pit
While dancers mime their roles, Z the Designer
Who sets the whole thing on an ocean liner,
The girls in shorts, the men in yachting caps;
Yet Genius triumphs over all mishaps,
Survives a greater obstacle than these,

Translation into foreign Operese
(English sopranos are condemned to *languish*
Because our tenors have to hide their *anguish*);
It soothes the Frank, it stimulates the Greek:
Genius surpasses all things, even Chic.
We who know nothing—which is just as well—
About the future, can, at least, foretell,
Whether they live in air-borne nylon cubes,
Practise group-marriage or are fed through tubes,
That crowds two centuries from now will press
(Absurd their hair, ridiculous their dress)
And pay in currencies, however weird,
To hear Sarastro booming through his beard,
Sharp connoisseurs approve if it is clean
The F in alt of the Nocturnal Queen,
Some uncouth creature from the Bronx amaze
Park Avenue by knowing all the K's.

How seemly, then, to celebrate the birth
Of one who did no harm to our poor earth,
Created masterpieces by the dozen,
Indulged in toilet humor with his cousin,
And had a pauper's funeral in the rain,
The like of whom we shall not see again:
How comely, also, to forgive; we should,
As Mozart, were he living, surely would,
Remember kindly Salieri's shade,
Accused of murder and his works unplayed,
Nor, while we praise the dead, should we forget
We have Stravinsky—bless him!—with us yet.
{ *Basta!* Maestro, make your minions play!
{ In all hearts, as in our finale, may
{ Reason & Love be crowned, assume their rightful sway.

1955

III

*Lines addressed to Dr. Claude Jenkins, Canon of Christ Church, Oxford, on
the occasion of his Eightieth Birthday. (May 26th, 1957)*

Let both our Common Rooms combine to cheer
This day when you complete your eightieth year,
The tribes who study and the sporting clan
Applaud the scholar and approve the man,
While, in cold Mercury, complacent fish
From well-fed tummies belch a birthday wish.
Long may you see a congregation sit
Enraptured by your piety and wit,
{ At many a luncheon feed us from your store
{ Of curious fact and anecdotal lore
{ (Why! even Little knows but little more):
And when at last your eager soul shall fly
(As do all Canons of the House) on high,
May you find all things to your liking there,
A warmer Canonry await you where

443

Nor dry-rot shall corrupt, nor moisture rust,
Nor froward CENSOR dare break in to dust,
Celestial rooms where you may talk with men
Like ST. AUGUSTINE, DUCHESNE, ORIGEN,
While Seraphim purvey immortal snuff,
More pungent than our mere sub-lunar stuff,
Baroquish Cherubim cry:—'Glory, Laud,
Eternal Honour to our DR. CLAUDE!'

1957

Their Lonely Betters

As I listened from a beach-chair in the shade
To all the noises that my garden made,
It seemed to me only proper that words
Should be withheld from vegetables and birds.

A robin with no Christian name ran through
The Robin-Anthem which was all it knew,
And rustling flowers for some third party waited
To say which pairs, if any, should get mated.

Not one of them was capable of lying,
There was not one which knew that it was dying
Or could have with a rhythm or a rhyme
Assumed responsibility for time.

Let them leave language to their lonely betters
Who count some days and long for certain letters;
We, too, make noises when we laugh or weep:
Words are for those with promises to keep.

1950

First Things First

Woken, I lay in the arms of my own warmth and listened
To a storm enjoying its storminess in the winter dark
Till my ear, as it can when half-asleep or half-sober,
Set to work to unscramble that interjectory uproar,
Construing its airy vowels and watery consonants
Into a love-speech indicative of a Proper Name.

Scarcely the tongue I should have chosen, yet, as well
As harshness and clumsiness would allow, it spoke in your praise,
Kenning you a god-child of the Moon and the West Wind
With power to tame both real and imaginary monsters,
Likening your poise of being to an upland county,
Here green on purpose, there pure blue for luck.

Loud though it was, alone as it certainly found me,
It reconstructed a day of peculiar silence
When a sneeze could be heard a mile off, and had me walking

444

On a headland of lava beside you, the occasion as ageless
As the stare of any rose, your presence exactly
So once, so valuable, so there, so now.

This, moreover, at an hour when only too often
A smirking devil annoys me in beautiful English,
Predicting a world where every sacred location
Is a sand-buried site all cultured Texans do,
Misinformed and thoroughly fleeced by their guides,
And gentle hearts are extinct like Hegelian Bishops.

Grateful, I slept till a morning that would not say
How much it believed of what I said the storm had said
But quietly drew my attention to what had been done
—So many cubic metres the more in my cistern
Against a leonine summer—, putting first things first:
Thousands have lived without love, not one without water.

? 1957

The More Loving One

Looking up at the stars, I know quite well
That, for all they care, I can go to hell,
But on earth indifference is the least
We have to dread from man or beast.

How should we like it were stars to burn
With a passion for us we could not return?
If equal affection cannot be,
Let the more loving one be me.

Admirer as I think I am
Of stars that do not give a damn,
I cannot, now I see them, say
I missed one terribly all day.

Were all stars to disappear or die,
I should learn to look at an empty sky
And feel its total dark sublime,
Though this might take me a little time.

1957

A Permanent Way

Self-drivers may curse their luck,
Stuck on new-fangled trails,
But the good old train will jog
To the dogma of its rails,

And steam so straight ahead
That I cannot be led astray
By tempting scenes which occur
Along any permanent way.

445

Intriguing dales escape
Into hills of the shape I like,
Though, were I actually put
Where a foot-path leaves the pike

For some steep romantic spot,
I should ask what chance there is
Of at least a ten-dollar cheque
Or a family peck of a kiss:

But, forcibly held to my tracks,
I can safely relax and dream
Of a love and a livelihood
To fit that wood or stream;

And what could be greater fun,
Once one has chosen and paid,
Than the inexpensive delight
Of a choice one might have made?

1954

Nocturne

Appearing unannounced, the moon
Avoids a mountain's jagged prongs
And sweeps into the open sky
Like one who knows where she belongs.

To me, immediately, my heart:
'Adore Her, Mother, Virgin, Muse,
A Face worth watching Who can make
Or break you as Her fancy choose.'

At which the reflex of my mind:
'You will not tell me, I presume,
That bunch of barren craters care
Who sleeps with or who tortures whom.'

Tonight, like umpteen other nights,
The baser frankness wins of course,
My tougher mind which dares admit
That both are worshippers of force.

Granted what both of them believe,
The Goddess, clearly, has to go,
Whose majesty is but the mask
That hides a faceless dynamo;

And neither of my natures can
Complain if I should be reduced
To a small functionary whose dreams
Are vast, unscrupulous, confused.

Supposing, though, my face is real
And not a myth or a machine,
The moon should look like x and wear
Features I've actually seen,

My neighbor's face, a face as such,
Neither a status nor a sex,
Constant for me no matter what
The value I assign to x;

That gushing lady, possibly,
Who brought some verses of her own,
That hang-dog who keeps coming back
For just a temporary loan;

A counter-image, anyway,
To balance with its lack of weight
My world, the private motor-car
And all the engines of the State.

? 1951

Precious Five

Be patient, solemn nose,
Serve in a world of prose
The present moment well,
Nor surlily contrast
Its brash ill-mannered smell
With grand scents of the past.
That calm enchanted wood,
That grave world where you stood
So gravely at its middle,
Its oracle and riddle,
Has all been altered; now
In anxious times you serve
As bridge from mouth to brow,
An asymmetric curve
Thrust outward from a face
Time-conscious into space,
Whose oddness may provoke
To a mind-saving joke
A mind that would it were
An apathetic sphere:
Point, then, for honor's sake
Up the storm-beaten slope
From memory to hope
The way you cannot take.

Be modest, lively ears,
Spoiled darlings of a stage
Where any caper cheers
The paranoiac mind
Of this undisciplined

447

And concert-going age,
So lacking in conviction
It cannot take pure fiction,
And what it wants from you
Are rumors partly true;
Before you catch its sickness
Submit your lucky quickness
And levity to rule,
Go back again to school,
Drudge patiently until
No whisper is too much
And your precision such
At any sound that all
Seem natural, not one
Fantastic or banal,
And then do what you will:
Dance with angelic grace,
In ecstasy and fun,
The luck you cannot place.

Be civil, hands; on you
Although you cannot read
Is written what you do
And blows you struck so blindly
In temper or in greed,
Your tricks of long ago,
Eyes, kindly or unkindly,
Unknown to you will know.
Revere those hairy wrists
And leg-of-mutton fists
Which pulverised the trolls
And carved deep Donts in stone,
Great hands which under knolls
Are now disjointed bone,
But what has been has been;
A tight arthritic claw
Or aldermanic paw
Waving about in praise
Of those homeric days
Is impious and obscene:
Grow, hands, into those living
Hands which true hands should be
By making and by giving
To hands you cannot see.

Look, naked eyes, look straight
At all eyes but your own
Lest in a tête-à-tête
Of glances double-crossed,
Both knowing and both known,
Your nakedness be lost;
Rove curiously about
But look from inside out,
Compare two eyes you meet

By dozens on the street,
One shameless, one ashamed,
Too lifeless to be blamed,
With eyes met now and then
Looking from living men,
Which in petrarchan fashion
Play opposite the heart,
Their humor to her passion,
Her nature to their art,
For mutual undeceiving;
True seeing is believing
(What sight can never prove)
There is a world to see:
Look outward, eyes, and love
Those eyes you cannot be.

Praise, tongue, the Earthly Muse
By number and by name
In any style you choose,
For nimble tongues and lame
Have both found favor; praise
Her port and sudden ways,
Now fish-wife and now queen,
Her reason and unreason:
Though freed from that machine,
Praise Her revolving wheel
Of appetite and season
In honor of Another,
The old self you become
At any drink or meal,
That animal of taste,
And of his twin, your brother,
Unlettered, savage, dumb,
Down there below the waist:
Although your style be fumbling,
Half stutter and half song,
Give thanks however bumbling,
Telling for Her dear sake
To whom all styles belong
The truth She cannot make.

Be happy, precious five,
So long as I'm alive
Nor try to ask me what
You should be happy for;
Think, if it helps, of love
Or alcohol or gold,
But do as you are told.
I could (which you cannot)
Find reasons fast enough
To face the sky and roar
In anger and despair
At what is going on,
Demanding that it name

Whoever is to blame:
The sky would only wait
Till all my breath was gone
And then reiterate
As if I wasn't there
That singular command
I do not understand,
Bless what there is for being,
Which has to be obeyed, for
What else am I made for,
Agreeing or disagreeing?

1950

Memorial for the City
(In Memoriam Charles Williams, d. April 1945)

*In the self-same point that our soul is made sensual, in the self-same point is
the City of God ordained to him from without beginning.*

JULIANA OF NORWICH

I

The eyes of the crow and the eye of the camera open
Onto Homer's world, not ours. First and last
They magnify earth, the abiding
Mother of gods and men; if they notice either
It is only in passing: gods behave, men die,
Both feel in their own small way, but She
Does nothing and does not care.
She alone is seriously there.

The crow on the crematorium chimney
And the camera roving the battle
Record a space where time has no place.
On the right a village is burning, in a market-town to the left
The soldiers fire, the mayor bursts into tears,
The captives are led away, while far in the distance
A tanker sinks into a dedolant sea.
That is the way things happen; for ever and ever
Plum-blossom falls on the dead, the roar of the waterfall covers
The cries of the whipped and the sighs of the lovers
And the hard bright light composes
A meaningless moment into an eternal fact
Which a whistling messenger disappears with into a defile:
One enjoys glory, one endures shame;
He may, she must. There is no one to blame.

The steady eyes of the crow and the camera's candid eye
See as honestly as they know how, but they lie.
The crime of life is not time. Even now, in this night
Among the ruins of the Post-Vergilian City
Where our past is a chaos of graves and the barbed-wire
    stretches ahead
Into our future till it is lost to sight,

450

Our grief is not Greek: As we bury our dead
We know without knowing there is reason for what we bear,
That our hurt is not a desertion, that we are to pity
Neither ourselves nor our city;
Whoever the searchlights catch, whatever the loudspeakers blare,
We are not to despair.

II

Alone in a room Pope Gregory whispered his name
  While the Emperor shone on a centreless world
From wherever he happened to be; the New City rose
  Upon their opposition, the yes and no
Of a rival allegiance; the sword, the local lord
  Were not all; there was home and Rome;
Fear of the stranger was lost on the way to the shrine.

The facts, the acts of the City bore a double meaning:
  Limbs became hymns; embraces expressed in jest
A more permanent tie; infidel faces replaced
  The family foe in the choleric's nightmare;
The children of water parodied in their postures
  The infinite patience of heaven;
Those born under Saturn felt the gloom of the day of doom.

Scribes and innkeepers prospered; suspicious tribes combined
  To rescue Jerusalem from a dull god,
And disciplined logicians fought to recover thought
  From the eccentricities of the private brain
For the Sane City; framed in her windows, orchards, ports,
  Wild beasts, deep rivers and dry rocks
Lay nursed on the smile of a merciful Madonna.

In a sandy province Luther denounced as obscene
  The machine that so smoothly forgave and saved
If paid; he announced to the Sinful City a grinning gap
  No rite could cross; he abased her before the Grace:
Henceforth division was also to be her condition;
  Her conclusions were to include doubt,
Her loves were to bear with her fear; insecure, she endured.

Saints tamed, poets acclaimed the raging herod of the will;
  The groundlings wept as on a secular stage
The grand and the bad went to ruin in thundering verse;
  Sundered by reason and treason the City
Found invisible ground for concord in measured sound,
  While wood and stone learned the shameless
Games of man, to flatter, to show off, be pompous, to romp.

Nature was put to the Question in the Prince's name;
  She confessed, what he wished to hear, that she had no soul;
Between his scaffold and her coldness the restrained style,
  The ironic smile became the worldly and devout,
Civility a city grown rich: in his own snob way
  The unarmed gentleman did his job
As a judge to her children, as a father to her forests.

In a national capital Mirabeau and his set
   Attacked mystery; the packed galleries roared
And history marched to the drums of a clear idea,
   The aim of the Rational City, quick to admire,
Quick to tire: she used up Napoleon and threw him away;
   Her pallid affected heroes
Began their hectic quest for the prelapsarian man.

The deserts were dangerous, the waters rough, their clothes
   Absurd but, changing their Beatrices often,
Sleeping little, they pushed on, raised the flag of the Word
   Upon lawless spots denied or forgotten
By the fear or the pride of the Glittering City;
   Guided by hated parental shades,
They invaded and harrowed the hell of her natural self.

Chimeras mauled them, they wasted away with the spleen,
   Suicide picked them off; sunk off Cape Consumption,
Lost on the Tosspot Seas, wrecked on the Gibbering Isles
   Or trapped in the ice of despair at the Soul's Pole,
They died, unfinished, alone; but now the forbidden,
   The hidden, the wild outside were known:
Faithful without faith, they died for the Conscious City.

III
   Across the square,
Between the burnt-out Law Courts and Police Headquarters,
Past the Cathedral far too damaged to repair,
Around the Grand Hotel patched up to hold reporters,
   Near huts of some Emergency Committee,
   The barbed wire runs through the abolished City.

   Across the plains,
Between two hills, two villages, two trees, two friends,
The barbed wire runs which neither argues nor explains
But, where it likes, a place, a path, a railroad ends,
   The humor, the cuisine, the rites, the taste,
   The pattern of the City, are erased.

   Across our sleep
The barbed wire also runs: It trips us so we fall
And white ships sail without us though the others weep,
It makes our sorry fig-leaf at the Sneerers' Ball,
   It ties the smiler to the double bed,
   It keeps on growing from the witch's head.

   Behind the wire
Which is behind the mirror, our Image is the same
Awake or dreaming: It has no image to admire,
No age, no sex, no memory, no creed, no name,
   It can be counted, multiplied, employed
   In any place, at any time destroyed.

Is It our friend?
No; that is our hope; that we weep and It does not grieve,
That for It the wire and the ruins are not the end:
This is the flesh we are but never would believe,
    The flesh we die but it is death to pity;
    This is Adam waiting for His City.

Let Our Weakness speak

IV

Without me Adam would have fallen irrevocably with Lucifer; he would
    never have been able to cry *O felix culpa.*
It was I who suggested his theft to Prometheus; my frailty cost Adonis
    his life.
I heard Orpheus sing; I was not quite as moved as they say.
I was not taken in by the sheep's-eyes of Narcissus; I was angry with
    Psyche when she struck a light.
I was in Hector's confidence; so far as it went.
Had he listened to me Oedipus would never have left Corinth; I cast no
    vote at the trial of Orestes.
I fell asleep when Diotima spoke of love; I was not responsible for the
    monsters which tempted St. Anthony.
To me the Saviour permitted His Fifth Word from the cross; to be a
    stumbling-block to the stoics.
I was the unwelcome third at the meetings of Tristan with Isolda; they
    tried to poison me.
I rode with Galahad on his Quest for the San Graal; without
    understanding I kept his vow.
I was the just impediment to the marriage of Faustus with Helen; I
    know a ghost when I see one.
With Hamlet I had no patience; but I forgave Don Quixote all for his
    admission in the cart.
I was the missing entry in Don Giovanni's list; for which he could never
    account.
I assisted Figaro the Barber in all his intrigues; when Prince Tamino
    arrived at wisdom I too obtained my reward.
I was innocent of the sin of the Ancient Mariner; time after time I
    warned Captain Ahab to accept happiness.
As for Metropolis, that too-great city; her delusions are not mine.
Her speeches impress me little, her statistics less; to all who dwell on
    the public side of her mirrors, resentments and no peace.
At the place of my passion her photographers are gathered together;
    but I shall rise again to hear her judged.

June 1949

453

The Shield of Achilles

> She looked over his shoulder
>   For vines and olive trees,
> Marble well-governed cities
>   And ships upon untamed seas,
> But there on the shining metal
>   His hands had put instead
> An artificial wilderness
>   And a sky like lead.

A plain without a feature, bare and brown,
  No blade of grass, no sign of neighborhood,
Nothing to eat and nowhere to sit down,
  Yet, congregated on its blankness, stood
  An unintelligible multitude,
A million eyes, a million boots in line,
Without expression, waiting for a sign.

Out of the air a voice without a face
  Proved by statistics that some cause was just
In tones as dry and level as the place:
  No one was cheered and nothing was discussed;
  Column by column in a cloud of dust
They marched away enduring a belief
Whose logic brought them, somewhere else, to grief.

> She looked over his shoulder
>   For ritual pieties,
> White flower-garlanded heifers,
>   Libation and sacrifice,
> But there on the shining metal
>   Where the altar should have been,
> She saw by his flickering forge-light
>   Quite another scene.

Barbed wire enclosed an arbitrary spot
  Where bored officials lounged (one cracked a joke)
And sentries sweated for the day was hot:
  A crowd of ordinary decent folk
  Watched from without and neither moved nor spoke
As three pale figures were led forth and bound
To three posts driven upright in the ground.

The mass and majesty of this world, all
  That carries weight and always weighs the same
Lay in the hands of others; they were small
  And could not hope for help and no help came:
  What their foes liked to do was done, their shame
Was all the worst could wish; they lost their pride
And died as men before their bodies died.

She looked over his shoulder
   For athletes at their games,
Men and women in a dance
   Moving their sweet limbs
Quick, quick, to music,
   But there on the shining shield
His hands had set no dancing-floor
   But a weed-choked field.

A ragged urchin, aimless and alone,
  Loitered about that vacancy; a bird
Flew up to safety from his well-aimed stone:
  That girls are raped, that two boys knife a third,
  Were axioms to him, who'd never heard
Of any world where promises were kept,
Or one could weep because another wept.

   The thin-lipped armorer,
      Hephaestos, hobbled away,
   Thetis of the shining breasts
      Cried out in dismay
   At what the god had wrought
      To please her son, the strong
   Iron-hearted man-slaying Achilles
      Who would not live long.

1952

Secondary Epic

No, Virgil, no:
Not even the first of the Romans can learn
His Roman history in the future tense,
Not even to serve your political turn;
Hindsight as foresight makes no sense.

How was your shield-making god to explain
Why his masterpiece, his grand panorama
Of scenes from the coming historical drama
Of an unborn nation, war after war,
All the birthdays needed to pre-ordain
The Octavius the world was waiting for,
Should so abruptly, mysteriously stop,
What cause could he show why he didn't foresee
The future beyond 31 B.C.,
Why a curtain of darkness should finally drop
On Carians, Morini, Gelonians with quivers,
Converging Romeward in abject file,
Euphrates, Araxes and similar rivers
Learning to flow in a latinate style,
And Caesar be left where prophecy ends,
Inspecting troops and gifts for ever?
Wouldn't Aeneas have asked:—'What next?
After this triumph, what portends?'

As rhetoric your device was too clever:
It lets us imagine a continuation
To your Eighth Book, an interpolation,
Scrawled at the side of a tattered text
In a decadent script, the composition
Of a down-at-heels refugee rhetorician
With an empty belly, seeking employment,
Cooked up in haste for the drunken enjoyment
Of some blond princeling whom loot had inclined
To believe that Providence had assigned
To blonds the task of improving mankind.

...Now Mainz appears and starry New Year's Eve
As two-horned Rhine throws off the Latin yoke
To bear the Vandal on his frozen back;
Lo! Danube, now congenial to the Goth,
News not unwelcome to Teutonic shades
And all lamenting beyond Acheron
Demolished Carthage or a plundered Greece:
And now Juturna leaves the river-bed
Of her embittered grievance—loud her song,
Immoderate her joy—for word has come
Of treachery at the Salarian Gate.
Alaric has avenged Turnus. . . .

No, Virgil, no:
Behind your verse so masterfully made
We hear the weeping of a Muse betrayed.
Your Anchises isn't convincing at all:
It's asking too much of us to be told
A shade so long-sighted, a father who knows
That Romulus will build a wall,
Augustus found an Age of Gold,
And is trying to teach a dutiful son
The love of what will be in the long run,
Would mention them both but not disclose
(Surely, no prophet could afford to miss,
No man of destiny fail to enjoy
So clear a proof of Providence as this.)
The names predestined for the Catholic boy
Whom Arian Odovacer will depose.

? 1959

Makers of History

Serious historians care for coins and weapons,
Not those re-iterations of one self-importance
By whom they date them,
Knowing that clerks could soon compose a model
As manly as any of whom schoolmasters tell
Their yawning pupils,

With might-be maps of might-have-been campaigns,
Showing in colour the obediences
Before and after,
Quotes from four-letter pep-talks to the troops
And polysyllabic reasons to a Senate
For breaking treaties.

Simple to add how Greatness, incognito,
Admired plain-spoken comment on itself
By Honest John,
And simpler still the phobia, the perversion,
Such curiosa as tease humanistic
Unpolitical palates.

How justly legend melts them into one
Composite demi-god, prodigious worker,
Deflecting rivers,
Walling in cities with his two bare hands,
The burly slave of ritual and a martyr
To Numerology.

With twelve twin brothers, three wives, seven sons,
Five weeks a year he puts on petticoats,
Stung mortally
During a nine-day tussle with King Scorpion,
Dies in the thirteenth month, becomes immortal
As a constellation.

Clio loves those who bred them better horses,
Found answers to their questions, made their things,
Even those fulsome
Bards they hoarded: but these mere commanders,
Like boys in pimple-time, like girls at awkward ages,
What did they do but wish?

1955

T the Great

Begot like other children, he
Was known among his kin as T,

A name, like those we never hear of,
Which nobody yet walked in fear of.

One morning when the West awoke,
The rising sun was veiled in smoke,

And fugitives, their horse-hooves drumming,
Cried:—'Death is on you! T is coming!'

For a considerable season
The name T was sufficient reason

457

To raise the question (Who can drop it?):
'If God exists, why can't He stop it?',

A synonym in a whole armful
Of languages for what is harmful.

Those, even, who had borne no loss themselves,
If T was spoken of, would cross themselves,

And after he was dead, his traces
Were visible for years—in faces

That wore expressions of alas on them,
And plains without a blade of grass on them.

(Some regions, travellers avow,
Have not recovered even now.)

As earth was starting to breathe freely,
Out of the North, efficient, steely,

Reminding life that hope is vanity,
Came N to bring her back to sanity,

And T was pushed off to the nursery
Before his hundredth anniversary

To play the bogey-man that comes
To naughty boys who suck their thumbs.

After some military success
N died (to be replaced by S)

And took T's job as Kid Detective,
Leaving him wholly ineffective.

For all the harm, and it was quite a lot, he did,
The public could not care less what he did.

(Some scholar cares, we may presume,
But in a Senior Common Room

It is unpopular to throw about
Matters your colleagues do not know about.)

Though T cannot win Clio's cup again,
From time to time the name crops up again,

E.g., as a crossword anagram:
11 Down—A NUBILE TRAM.

1959

The Managers

In the bad old days it was not so bad:
   The top of the ladder
Was an amusing place to sit; success
   Meant quite a lot—leisure
And huge meals, more palaces filled with more
   Objects, books, girls, horses
Than one would ever get round to, and to be
   Carried uphill while seeing
Others walk. To rule was a pleasure when
   One wrote a death-sentence
On the back of the Ace of Spades and played on
   With a new deck. Honours
Are not so physical or jolly now,
   For the species of Powers
We are used to are not like that. Could one of them
   Be said to resemble
The Tragic Hero, the Platonic Saint,
   Or would any painter
Portray one rising triumphant from a lake
   On a dolphin, naked,
Protected by an umbrella of cherubs? Can
   They so much as manage
To behave like genuine Caesars when alone
   Or drinking with cronies,
To let their hair down and be frank about
   The world? It is doubtful.
The last word on how we may live or die
   Rests today with such quiet
Men, working too hard in rooms that are too big,
   Reducing to figures
What is the matter, what is to be done.
   A neat little luncheon
Of sandwiches is brought to each on a tray,
   Nourishment they are able
To take with one hand without looking up
   From papers a couple
Of secretaries are needed to file,
   From problems no smiling
Can dismiss. The typewriters never stop
   But whirr like grasshoppers
In the silent siesta heat as, frivolous
   Across their discussions,
From woods unaltered by our wars and our vows
   There drift the scents of flowers
And the songs of birds who will never vote
   Or bother to notice
Those distinguishing marks a lover sees
   By instinct and policemen
Can be trained to observe. Far into the night
   Their windows burn brightly
And, behind their backs bent over some report,
   On every quarter,

For ever like a god or a disease
   There on the earth the reason
In all its aspects why they are tired, the weak,
   The inattentive, seeking
Someone to blame. If, to recuperate
   They go a-playing, their greatness
Encounters the bow of the chef or the glance
   Of the ballet-dancer
Who cannot be ruined by any master's fall.
   To rule must be a calling,
It seems, like surgery or sculpture; the fun
   Neither love nor money
But taking necessary risks, the test
   Of one's skill, the question,
If difficult, their own reward. But then
   Perhaps one should mention
Also what must be a comfort as they guess
   In times like the present
When guesses can prove so fatally wrong,
   The fact of belonging
To the very select indeed, to those
   For whom, just supposing
They do, there will be places on the last
   Plane out of disaster.
No; no one is really sorry for their
   Heavy gait and careworn
Look, nor would they thank you if you said you were.

June 1948

The Epigoni

No use invoking Apollo in a case like theirs;
The pleasure-loving gods had died in their chairs
And would not get up again, one of them, ever,
Though guttural tribes had crossed the Great River,
Roasting their dead and with no name for the yew;
No good expecting long-legged ancestors to
Return with long swords from pelagic paradises
(They would be left to their own devices,
Supposing they had some); no point pretending
One didn't foresee the probable ending
As dog-food, or landless, submerged, a slave:
Meanwhile, how should a cultured gentleman behave?

It would have been an excusable failing
Had they broken out into womanish wailing
Or, dramatising their doom, held forth
In sonorous clap-trap about death;
To their credit, a reader will only perceive
That the language they loved was coming to grief,
Expiring in preposterous mechanical tricks,
Epanaleptics, rhopalics, anacyclic acrostics:
To their lasting honor, the stuff they wrote

Can safely be spanked in a scholar's foot-note,
Called shallow by a mechanised generation to whom
Haphazard oracular grunts are profound wisdom.

1955

Bathtub Thoughts
(c. 500–c. 1950)

Hail, future friend, whose present I
With gratitude now prophesy,
Kind first to whom it shall occur
My past existence to infer.
Brief salutation best beseems
Two nameless ordinal extremes:
Hail and farewell! Chance only knows
The length of our respective rows,
But our numeric bond is such
As gods nor love nor death can touch.

So thought, I thought, the last Romano-Briton
To take his last hot bath.

1955

The Old Man's Road

Across the Great Schism, through our whole landscape,
Ignoring God's Vicar and God's Ape,

Under their noses, unsuspected,
The Old Man's Road runs as it did

When a light subsoil, a simple ore
Were still in vogue: true to His wherefore,

By stiles, gates, hedge-gaps it goes
Over ploughland, woodland, cow meadows,

Past shrines to a cosmological myth
No heretic to-day would be caught dead with,

Near hill-top rings that were so safe then,
Now stormed easily by small children

(Shepherds use bits in the high mountains,
Hamlets take stretches for Lovers' Lanes),

Then through cities threads its odd way,
Now without gutters, a Thieves' Alley,

Now with green lamp-posts and white curb,
The smart Crescent of a high-toned suburb,

Giving wide berth to an old Cathedral,
Running smack through a new Town Hall,

Unlookable for, by logic, by guess:
Yet some strike it, and are struck fearless.

No life can know it, but no life
That sticks to this course can be made captive,

And who wander with it are not stopped at
Borders by guards of some Theocrat,

Crossing the pass so almost where
His searchlight squints but no closer

(And no further where it might by chance):
So in summer sometimes, without hindrance,

Apotropaically scowling, a tinker
Shuffles past, in the waning year

Potters a coleopterist, poking
Through yellow leaves, and a youth in spring

Trots by after a new excitement,
His true self, hot on the scent.

The Old Man leaves his Road to those
Who love it no less since it lost purpose,

Who never ask what History is up to,
So cannot act as if they knew:

Assuming a freedom its Powers deny,
Denying its Powers, they pass freely.

1955

The History of Science

All fables of adventure stress
The need for courtesy and kindness:
Without the Helpers none can win
The flaxen-haired Princess.

They look the ones in need of aid,
Yet, thanks to them, the gentle-hearted
Third Brother beds the woken Queen,
While seniors who made

Cantankerous replies to crones
And dogs who begged to share their rations,
Must expiate their pride as daws
Or wind-swept bachelor stones.

Few of a sequel, though, have heard:
Uneasy pedagogues have censored
All written reference to a brother
Younger than the Third.

Soft-spoken as New Moon this Fourth,
A Sun of gifts to all he met with,
But when advised 'Go South a while!'
Smiled 'Thank You!' and turned North,

Trusting some map in his own head,
So never reached the goal intended
(His map, of course, was out) but blundered
On a wonderful instead,

A tower not circular but square,
A treasure not of gold but silver:
He kissed a shorter Sleeper's hand
And stroked her raven hair.

Dare sound Authority confess
That one can err his way to riches,
Win glory by mistake, his dear
Through sheer wrong-headedness?

1955

The History of Truth

In that ago when being was believing,
Truth was the most of many credibles,
More first, more always, than a bat-winged lion,
A fish-tailed dog or eagle-headed fish,
The least like mortals, doubted by their deaths.

Truth was their model as they strove to build
A world of lasting objects to believe in,
Without believing earthenware and legend,
Archway and song, were truthful or untruthful:
The Truth was there already to be true.

This while when, practical like paper-dishes,
Truth is convertible to kilowatts,
Our last to do by is an anti-model,
Some untruth anyone can give the lie to,
A nothing no one need believe is there.

? 1958

Homage to Clio

Our hill has made its submission and the green
    Swept on into the north: around me,
From morning to night, flowers duel incessantly,
    Colour against colour, in combats

463

Which they all win, and at any hour from some point else
     May come another tribal outcry
Of a new generation of birds who chirp,
     Not for effect but because chirping

Is the thing to do. More lives than I perceive
     Are aware of mine this May morning
As I sit reading a book, sharper senses
     Keep watch on an inedible patch

Of unsatisfactory smell, unsafe as
     So many areas are: to observation
My book is dead, and by observations they live
     In space, as unaware of silence

As Provocative Aphrodite or her twin,
     Virago Artemis, the Tall Sisters
Whose subjects they are. That is why, in their Dual Realm,
     Banalities can be beautiful,

Why nothing is too big or too small or the wrong
     Colour, and the roar of an earthquake
Rearranging the whispers of streams a loud sound
     Not a din: but we, at haphazard

And unseasonably, are brought face to face
     By ones, Clio, with your silence. After that
Nothing is easy. We may dream as we wish
     Of phallic pillar or navel-stone

With twelve nymphs twirling about it, but pictures
     Are no help: your silence already is there
Between us and any magical centre
     Where things are taken in hand. Besides,

Are we so sorry? Woken at sun-up to hear
     A cock pronouncing himself himself
Though all his sons had been castrated and eaten,
     I was glad I could be unhappy: if

I don't know how I shall manage, at least I know
     The beast-with-two-backs may be a species
Evenly distributed but Mum and Dad
     Were not two other people. To visit

The grave of a friend, to make an ugly scene,
     To count the loves one has grown out of,
Is not nice, but to chirp like a tearless bird,
     As though no one dies in particular

And gossip were never true, unthinkable:
     If it were, forgiveness would be no use,
One-eye-for-one would be just and the innocent
     Would not have to suffer. Artemis,

Aphrodite, are Major Powers and all wise
    Castellans will mind their p's and q's,
But it is you, who never have spoken up,
    Madonna of silences, to whom we turn

When we have lost control, your eyes, Clio, into which
    We look for recognition after
We have been found out. How shall I describe you? They
    Can be represented in granite

(One guesses at once from the perfect buttocks,
    The flawless mouth too grand to have corners,
Whom the colossus must be), but what icon
    Have the arts for you, who look like any

Girl one has not noticed and show no special
    Affinity with a beast? I have seen
Your photo, I think, in the papers, nursing
    A baby or mourning a corpse: each time

You had nothing to say and did not, one could see,
    Observe where you were, Muse of the unique
Historical fact, defending with silence
    Some world of your beholding, a silence

No explosion can conquer but a lover's Yes
    Has been known to fill. So few of the Big
Ever listen: that is why you have a great host
    Of superfluous screams to care for and

Why, up and down like the Duke of Cumberland,
    Or round and round like the Laxey Wheel,
The Short, The Bald, The Pious, The Stammerer went,
    As the children of Artemis go,

Not yours. Lives that obey you move like music,
    Becoming now what they only can be once,
Making of silence decisive sound: it sounds
    Easy, but one must find the time. Clio,

Muse of Time, but for whose merciful silence
    Only the first step would count and that
Would always be murder, whose kindness never
    Is taken in, forgive our noises

And teach us our recollections: to throw away
    The tiniest fault of someone we love
Is out of the question, says Aphrodite,
    Who should know, yet one has known people

Who have done just that. Approachable as you seem,
    I dare not ask you if you bless the poets,
For you do not look as if you ever read them,
    Nor can I see a reason why you should.

                                                    1955

The Love Feast

In an upper room at midnight
See us gathered on behalf
Of love according to the gospel
Of the radio-phonograph.

Lou is telling Anne what Molly
Said to Mark behind her back;
Jack likes Jill who worships George
Who has the hots for Jack.

Catechumens make their entrance;
Steep enthusiastic eyes
Flicker after tits and baskets;
Someone vomits; someone cries.

Willy cannot bear his father,
Lilian is afraid of kids;
The Love that rules the sun and stars
Permits what He forbids.

Adrian's pleasure-loving dachshund
In a sinner's lap lies curled;
Drunken absent-minded fingers
Pat a sinless world.

Who is Jenny lying to
In her call, Collect, to Rome?
The Love that made her out of nothing
Tells me to go home.

But that Miss Number in the corner
Playing hard to get. . . .
I am sorry I'm not sorry . . .
Make me chaste, Lord, but not yet.

May 1948

The Chimeras

Absence of heart—as in public buildings—
Absence of mind—as in public speeches—
Absence of worth—as in goods intended for the public,

Are telltale signs that a chimera has just dined
On someone else; of him, poor foolish fellow,
Not a scrap is left, not even his name.

Indescribable—being neither this nor that—
Uncountable—being any number—
Unreal—being anything but what they are,

466

And ugly customers for someone to encounter,
It is our fault entirely if we do:
They cannot touch us; it is we who will touch them.

Curious from wantonness—to see what they are like—
Cruel from fear—to put a stop to them—
Incredulous from conceit—to prove they cannot be—

We prod or kick or measure and are lost:
The stronger we are the sooner all is over;
It is our strength with which they gobble us up.

If someone, being chaste, brave, humble,
Get by them safely, he is still in danger,
With pity remembering what once they were,

Of turning back to help them. Don't.
What they were once was what they would not be;
Not liking what they are not is what now they are.

No one can help them; walk on, keep on walking,
And do not let your goodness self-deceive you:
It is good that they are but not that they are thus.

1950

Merax & Mullin

There is one devil in the lexicon
Who waits for those who would unwish themselves
Yet blow a trumpet,
To fill their voids of insufficiency
With pejorative noises.

In timid, gouty, bastard, cuckolded fingers
How swift, so prompted, fly polemic pens,
Scoring the foolscap
With bestial engagements quite unknown
To Natural History,

And when superior devils start a war,
How soon the home-sick ranks in either army
Credit his cosmos,
Where officers, machinery, abstractions
Are sexually aberrant.

There is an even nastier, more deadly,
Philological imp,
Who with endearing diminutives eggs on
Laodicean lovers till they swear
Undying love.

1955

Limbo Culture

The tribes of Limbo, travellers report,
On first encounter seem much like ourselves;
They keep their houses practically clean,
Their watches round about a standard time,
They serve you almost appetising meals:
But no one says he saw a Limbo child.

The language spoken by the tribes of Limbo
Has many words far subtler than our own
To indicate how much, how little, something
Is pretty closely or not quite the case,
But none you could translate by *Yes* or *No*,
Nor do its pronouns distinguish between Persons.

In tales related by the tribes of Limbo,
Dragon and Knight set to with fang and sword
But miss their rival always by a hair's-breadth,
Old Crone and Stripling pass a crucial point,
She seconds early and He seconds late,
A magic purse mistakes the legal tender:

'And so,' runs their concluding formula,
'Prince and Princess are nearly married still.'
Why this concern, so marked in Limbo culture,
This love for inexactness? Could it be
A Limbo tribesman only loves himself?
For that, we know, cannot be done exactly.

1957

There Will Be No Peace

Though mild clear weather
Smile again on the shire of your esteem
And its colours come back, the storm has changed you:
  You will not forget, ever,
The darkness blotting out hope, the gale
  Prophesying your downfall.

You must live with your knowledge.
Way back, beyond, outside of you are others,
In moonless absences you never heard of,
  Who have certainly heard of you,
Beings of unknown number and gender:
  And they do not like you.

What have you done to them?
Nothing? Nothing is not an answer:
You will come to believe—how can you help it?—
  That you did, you did do something;
You will find yourself wishing you could make them laugh,
  You will long for their friendship.

468

There will be no peace.
Fight back, then, with such courage as you have
And every unchivalrous dodge you know of,
    Clear in your conscience on this:
Their cause, if they had one, is nothing to them now;
    They hate for hate's sake.

1956

A Household

When, to disarm suspicious minds at lunch
Before coming to the point, or at golf,
The bargain driven, to soothe hurt feelings,

He talks about his home, he never speaks
(A reticence for which they all admire him)
Of his bride so worshipped and so early lost,

But proudly tells of that young scamp his heir,
Of black eyes given and received, thrashings
Endured without a sound to save a chum;

Or calls their spotted maleness to revere
His saintly mother, calm and kind and wise,
A grand old lady pouring out the tea.

Whom, though, has he ever asked for the week-end?
Out to his country mansion in the evening,
Another merger signed, he drives alone:

To be avoided by a miserable runt
Who wets his bed and cannot throw or whistle,
A tell-tale, a crybaby, a failure;

To the revilings of a slatternly hag
Who caches bottles in her mattress, spits
And shouts obscenities from the landing;

Worse, to find both in an unholy alliance,
Youth stealing Age the liquor-cupboard key,
Age teaching Youth to lie with a straight face.

Disgraces to keep hidden from the world
Where rivals, envying his energy and brains
And with rattling skeletons of their own,

Would see in him the villain of this household,
Whose bull-voice scared a sensitive young child,
Whose coldness drove a doting parent mad.

Besides (which might explain why he has neither
Altered his will nor called the doctor in),
He half believes, call it a superstition,

469

It is for his sake that they hate and fear him:
Should they unmask and show themselves worth loving,
Loving and sane and manly, he would die.

1948

'The Truest Poetry is the Most Feigning'
(for Edgar Wind)

By all means sing of love but, if you do,
Please make a rare old proper hullabaloo:
When ladies ask *How much do you love me?*
The Christian answer is *così-così*;
But poets are not celibate divines:
Had Dante said so, who would read his lines?
Be subtle, various, ornamental, clever,
And do not listen to those critics ever
Whose crude provincial gullets crave in books
Plain cooking made still plainer by plain cooks,
As though the Muse preferred her half-wit sons;
Good poets have a weakness for bad puns.

Suppose your Beatrice be, as usual, late,
And you would tell us how it feels to wait,
You're free to think, what may be even true,
You're so in love that one hour seems like two,
But write—*As I sat waiting for her call,*
Each second longer darker seemed than all
(Something like this but more elaborate still)
Those raining centuries it took to fill
That quarry whence Endymion's Love was torn;
From such ingenious fibs are poems born.
Then, should she leave you for some other guy,
Or ruin you with debts, or go and die,
No metaphor, remember, can express
A real historical unhappiness;
Your tears have value if they make us gay;
O Happy Grief! is all sad verse can say.

The living girl's your business (some odd sorts
Have been an inspiration to men's thoughts):
Yours may be old enough to be your mother,
Or have one leg that's shorter than the other,
Or play Lacrosse or do the Modern Dance,
To you that's destiny, to us it's chance;
We cannot love your love till she take on,
Through you, the wonders of a paragon.
Sing her triumphant passage to our land,
The sun her footstool, the moon in her right hand,
And seven planets blazing in her hair,
Queen of the Night and Empress of the Air;
Tell how her fleet by nine king swans is led,
Wild geese write magic letters overhead
And hippocampi follow in her wake

With Amphisboene, gentle for her sake;
Sing her descent on the exulting shore
To bless the vines and put an end to war.

If half-way through such praises of your dear,
Riot and shooting fill the streets with fear,
And overnight as in some terror dream
Poets are suspect with the New Regime,
Stick at your desk and hold your panic in,
What you are writing may still save your skin:
Re-sex the pronouns, add a few details,
And, lo, a panegyric ode which hails
(How is the Censor, bless his heart, to know?)
The new pot-bellied Generalissimo.
Some epithets, of course, like *lily-breasted*
Need modifying to, say, *lion-chested*,
A title *Goddess of wry-necks and wrens*
To *Great Reticulator of the fens*,
But in an hour your poem qualifies
For a State pension or His annual prize,
And you will die in bed (which He will not:
That public nuisance will be hanged or shot).
Though honest Iagos, true to form, will write
Shame! in your margins, *Toady! Hypocrite!*,
True hearts, clear heads will hear the note of glory
And put inverted commas round the story,
Thinking—*Old Sly-boots! We shall never know
Her name or nature. Well, it's better so.*

For given Man, by birth, by education,
Imago Dei who forgot his station,
The self-made creature who himself unmakes,
The only creature ever made who fakes,
With no more nature in his loving smile
Than in his theories of a natural style,
What but tall tales, the luck of verbal playing,
Can trick his lying nature into saying
That love, or truth in any serious sense,
Like orthodoxy, is a reticence?

                                    ? September 1953

We Too Had Known Golden Hours

We, too, had known golden hours
When body and soul were in tune,
Had danced with our true loves
By the light of a full moon,
And sat with the wise and good
As tongues grew witty and gay
Over some noble dish
Out of Escoffier;
Had felt the intrusive glory
Which tears reserve apart,

And would in the old grand manner
Have sung from a resonant heart.
But, pawed-at and gossiped-over
By the promiscuous crowd,
Concocted by editors
Into spells to befuddle the crowd,
All words like Peace and Love,
All sane affirmative speech,
Had been soiled, profaned, debased
To a horrid mechanical screech.
No civil style survived
That pandaemonium
But the wry, the sotto-voce,
Ironic and monochrome:
And where should we find shelter
For joy or mere content
When little was left standing
But the suburb of dissent?

? 1950

Secrets

That we are always glad
When the Ugly Princess, parting the bushes
To find out why the woodcutter's children are happy,
Disturbs a hornets' nest, that we feel no pity
When the informer is trapped by the gang in a steam-room,
That we howl with joy
When the short-sighted Professor of Icelandic
Pronounces the Greek inscription
A Runic riddle which he then translates:

Denouncing by proxy our commonest fault as our worst;
That, waiting in his room for a friend,
We start so soon to turn over his letters,
That with such assurance we repeat as our own
Another's story, that, dear me, how often
We kiss in order to tell,
Defines precisely what we mean by love:—
To share a secret.

The joke, which we seldom see, is on us;
For only true hearts know how little it matters
What the secret is they keep:
An old, a new, a blue, a borrowed something,
Anything will do for children
Made in God's image and therefore
Not like the others, not like our dear dumb friends
Who, poor things, have nothing to hide,
Not, thank God, like our Father either
From whom no secrets are hid.

1949

Numbers and Faces

The Kingdom of Number is all boundaries
Which may be beautiful and must be true;
To ask if it is big or small proclaims one
The sort of lover who should stick to faces.

Lovers of small numbers go benignly potty,
Believe all tales are thirteen chapters long,
Have animal doubles, carry pentagrams,
Are Millerites, Baconians, Flat-Earth-Men.

Lovers of big numbers go horridly mad,
Would have the Swiss abolished, all of us
Well purged, somatotyped, baptised, taught baseball:
They empty bars, spoil parties, run for Congress.

True, between faces almost any number
Might come in handy, and One is always real;
But which could any face call good, for calling
Infinity a number does not make it one.

1950

Objects

All that which lies outside our sort of why,
Those wordless creatures who are there as well,
Remote from mourning yet in sight and cry,
Make time more golden than we meant to tell.

Tearless, their surfaces appear as deep
As any longing we believe we had;
If shapes can so to their own edges keep,
No separation proves a being bad.

There is less grief than wonder on the whole,
Even at sunset, though of course we care
Each time the same old shadow falls across

One Person who is not: somewhere, a soul,
Light in her bestial substance, well aware,
Extols the silence of how soon a loss.

1956

Words

A sentence uttered makes a world appear
Where all things happen as it says they do;
We doubt the speaker, not the tongue we hear:
Words have no word for words that are not true.

Syntactically, though, it must be clear;
One cannot change the subject half-way through,
Nor alter tenses to appease the ear:
Arcadian tales are hard-luck stories too.

But should we want to gossip all the time,
Were fact not fiction for us at its best,
Or find a charm in syllables that rhyme,

Were not our fate by verbal chance expressed,
As rustics in a ring-dance pantomime
The Knight at some lone cross-roads of his quest?

? 1956

The Song

So large a morning so itself to lean
Over so many and such little hills
All at rest in roundness and rigs of green
Can cope with a rebellious wing that wills
To better its obedient double quite
As daring in the lap of any lake
The wind from which ascension puts to flight
Tribes of a beauty which no care can break.

Climbing to song it hopes to make amends
For whiteness drabbed for glory said away
And be immortal after but because
Light upon a valley where its love was
So lacks all picture of reproach it ends
Denying what it started up to say.

1956

One Circumlocution

Sometimes we see astonishingly clearly
The out-there-now we are already in;
Now that is not what we are here-for really.

All its to-do is bound to re-occur,
Is nothing therefore that we need to say;
How then to make its compromise refer

To what could not be otherwise instead
And has its being as its own to be,
The once-for-all that is not seen nor said?

Tell for the power how to thunderclaps
The graves flew open, the rivers ran up-hill;
Such staged importance is at most perhaps.

Speak well of moonlight on a winding stair,
Of light-boned children under great green oaks:
The wonder, yes, but death should not be there.

One circumlocution as used as any
Depends, it seems, upon the joke of rhyme
For the pure joy; else why should so many

Poems which make us cry direct us to
Ourselves at our least apt, least kind, least true,
Where a blank I loves blankly a blank You?

April 1949

Horae Canonicae

'Immolatus vicerit'

1. PRIME

Simultaneously, as soundlessly,
  Spontaneously, suddenly
As, at the vaunt of the dawn, the kind
  Gates of the body fly open
To its world beyond, the gates of the mind,
  The horn gate and the ivory gate
Swing to, swing shut, instantaneously
  Quell the nocturnal rummage
Of its rebellious fronde, ill-favored,
  Ill-natured and second-rate,
Disenfranchised, widowed and orphaned
  By an historical mistake:
Recalled from the shades to be a seeing being,
  From absence to be on display,
Without a name or history I wake
  Between my body and the day.

Holy this moment, wholly in the right,
  As, in complete obedience
To the light's laconic outcry, next
  As a sheet, near as a wall,
Out there as a mountain's poise of stone,
  The world is present, about,
And I know that I am, here, not alone
  But with a world and rejoice
Unvexed, for the will has still to claim
  This adjacent arm as my own,
The memory to name me, resume
  Its routine of praise and blame,
And smiling to me is this instant while
  Still the day is intact, and I
The Adam sinless in our beginning,
  Adam still previous to any act.

475

I draw breath; that is of course to wish
    No matter what, to be wise,
To be different, to die and the cost,
    No matter how, is Paradise
Lost of course and myself owing a death:
    The eager ridge, the steady sea,
The flat roofs of the fishing village
    Still asleep in its bunny,
Though as fresh and sunny still, are not friends
    But things to hand, this ready flesh
No honest equal, but my accomplice now,
    My assassin to be, and my name
Stands for my historical share of care
    For a lying self-made city,
Afraid of our living task, the dying
    Which the coming day will ask.

1949

2. TERCE

After shaking paws with his dog
(Whose bark would tell the world that he is always kind),
    The hangman sets off briskly over the heath;
He does not know yet who will be provided
    To do the high works of Justice with:
Gently closing the door of his wife's bedroom
    (Today she has one of her headaches),
With a sigh the judge descends his marble stair;
    He does not know by what sentence
He will apply on earth the Law that rules the stars:
    And the poet, taking a breather
Round his garden before starting his eclogue,
    Does not know whose Truth he will tell.

Sprites of hearth and store-room, godlings
Of professional mysteries, the Big Ones
    Who can annihilate a city
Cannot be bothered with this moment: we are left,
    Each to his secret cult. Now each of us
Prays to an image of his image of himself:
    'Let me get through this coming day
Without a dressing down from a superior,
    Being worsted in a repartee,
Or behaving like an ass in front of the girls;
    Let something exciting happen,
Let me find a lucky coin on a sidewalk,
    Let me hear a new funny story.'

At this hour we all might be anyone:
It is only our victim who is without a wish,
    Who knows already (that is what
We can never forgive. If he knows the answers,
    Then why are we here, why is there even dust?),
Knows already that, in fact, our prayers are heard,

That not one of us will slip up,
That the machinery of our world will function
   Without a hitch, that today, for once,
There will be no squabbling on Mount Olympus,
   No Chthonian mutters of unrest,
But no other miracle, knows that by sundown
   We shall have had a good Friday.

October 1953

3. SEXT

I

You need not see what someone is doing
to know if it is his vocation,

you have only to watch his eyes:
a cook mixing a sauce, a surgeon

making a primary incision,
a clerk completing a bill of lading,

wear the same rapt expression,
forgetting themselves in a function.

How beautiful it is,
that eye-on-the-object look.

To ignore the appetitive goddesses,
to desert the formidable shrines

of Rhea, Aphrodite, Demeter, Diana,
to pray instead to St. Phocas,

St. Barbara, San Saturnino,
or whoever one's patron is,

that one may be worthy of their mystery,
what a prodigious step to have taken.

There should be monuments, there should be odes,
to the nameless heroes who took it first,

to the first flaker of flints
who forgot his dinner,

the first collector of sea-shells
to remain celibate.

Where should we be but for them?
Feral still, un-housetrained, still

wandering through forests without
a consonant to our names,

slaves of Dame Kind, lacking
all notion of a city,

and, at this noon, for this death,
there would be no agents.

II

You need not hear what orders he is giving
to know if someone has authority,

you have only to watch his mouth:
when a besieging general sees

a city wall breached by his troops,
when a bacteriologist

realizes in a flash what was wrong
with his hypothesis, when,

from a glance at the jury, the prosecutor
knows the defendant will hang,

their lips and the lines around them
relax, assuming an expression

not of simple pleasure at getting
their own sweet way but of satisfaction

at being right, an incarnation
of *Fortitudo, Justicia, Nous*.

You may not like them much
(who does?) but we owe them

basilicas, divas,
dictionaries, pastoral verse,

the courtesies of the city:
without these judicial mouths

(which belong for the most part
to very great scoundrels)

how squalid existence would be,
tethered for life to some hut village,

afraid of the local snake
or the local ford demon,

speaking the local patois
of some three hundred words

(think of the family squabbles and the
poison-pens, think of the inbreeding),

478

and, at this noon, there would be no authority
to command this death.

III

Anywhere you like, somewhere
on broad-chested life-giving Earth,

anywhere between her thirstlands
and undrinkable Ocean,

the crowd stands perfectly still,
its eyes (which seem one) and its mouths

(which seem infinitely many)
expressionless, perfectly blank.

The crowd does not see (what everyone sees)
a boxing match, a train wreck,

a battleship being launched,
does not wonder (as everyone wonders)

who will win, what flag she will fly,
how many will be burned alive,

is never distracted
(as everyone is always distracted)

by a barking dog, a smell of fish,
a mosquito on a bald head:

the crowd sees only one thing
(which only the crowd can see),

an epiphany of that
which does whatever is done.

Whatever god a person believes in,
in whatever way he believes

(no two are exactly alike),
as one of the crowd he believes

and only believes in that
in which there is only one way of believing.

Few people accept each other and most
will never do anything properly,

but the crowd rejects no one, joining the crowd
is the only thing all men can do.

Only because of that can we say
all men are our brothers,

superior, because of that,
to the social exoskeletons: When

have they ever ignored their queens,
for one second stopped work

on their provincial cities, to worship
The Prince of this world like us,

at this noon, on this hill,
in the occasion of this dying?

? 1954

4. NONES

What we know to be not possible,
   Though time after time foretold
By wild hermits, by shaman and sybil
   Gibbering in their trances,
Or revealed to a child in some chance rhyme
   Like *will* and *kill*, comes to pass
Before we realize it. We are surprised
   At the ease and speed of our deed
And uneasy: It is barely three,
   Mid-afternoon, yet the blood
Of our sacrifice is already
   Dry on the grass; we are not prepared
For silence so sudden and so soon;
   The day is too hot, too bright, too still,
Too ever, the dead remains too nothing.
   What shall we do till nightfall?

The wind has dropped and we have lost our public.
   The faceless many who always
Collect when any world is to be wrecked,
   Blown up, burnt down, cracked open,
Felled, sawn in two, hacked through, torn apart,
   Have all melted away. Not one
Of these who in the shade of walls and trees
   Lie sprawled now, calmly sleeping,
Harmless as sheep, can remember why
   He shouted or what about
So loudly in the sunshine this morning;
   All if challenged would reply
—'It was a monster with one red eye,
   A crowd that saw him die, not I.'—
The hangman has gone to wash, the soldiers to eat:
   We are left alone with our feat.

The Madonna with the green woodpecker,
   The Madonna of the fig-tree,
The Madonna beside the yellow dam,
   Turn their kind faces from us
And our projects under construction,

Look only in one direction,
   Fix their gaze on our completed work:
      Pile-driver, concrete-mixer,
Crane and pick-axe wait to be used again,
      But how can we repeat this?
Outliving our act, we stand where we are,
      As disregarded as some
Discarded artifact of our own,
      Like torn gloves, rusted kettles,
Abandoned branch-lines, worn lop-sided
      Grindstones buried in nettles.

This mutilated flesh, our victim,
      Explains too nakedly, too well,
The spell of the asparagus garden,
      The aim of our chalk-pit game; stamps,
Birds' eggs are not the same, behind the wonder
      Of tow-paths and sunken lanes,
Behind the rapture on the spiral stair,
      We shall always now be aware
Of the deed into which they lead, under
      The mock chase and mock capture,
The racing and tussling and splashing,
      The panting and the laughter,
Be listening for the cry and stillness
      To follow after: wherever
The sun shines, brooks run, books are written,
      There will also be this death.

Soon cool tramontana will stir the leaves,
      The shops will re-open at four,
The empty blue bus in the empty pink square
      Fill up and depart: we have time
To misrepresent, excuse, deny,
      Mythify, use this event
While, under a hotel bed, in prison,
      Down wrong turnings, its meaning
Waits for our lives. Sooner than we would choose
      Bread will melt, water will burn,
And the great quell begin, Abaddon
      Set up his triple gallows
At our seven gates, fat Belial make
      Our wives waltz naked; meanwhile
It would be best to go home, if we have a home,
      In any case good to rest.

That our dreaming wills may seem to escape
      This dead calm, wander instead
On knife edges, on black and white squares,
      Across moss, baize, velvet, boards,
Over cracks and hillocks, in mazes
      Of string and penitent cones,
Down granite ramps and damp passages,
      Through gates that will not relatch

And doors marked *Private*, pursued by Moors
    And watched by latent robbers,
To hostile villages at the heads of fjords,
    To dark chateaux where wind sobs
In the pine-trees and telephones ring,
    Inviting trouble, to a room,
Lit by one weak bulb, where our Double sits
    Writing and does not look up.

That, while we are thus away, our own wronged flesh
    May work undisturbed, restoring
The order we try to destroy, the rhythm
    We spoil out of spite: valves close
And open exactly, glands secrete,
    Vessels contract and expand
At the right moment, essential fluids
    Flow to renew exhausted cells,
Not knowing quite what has happened, but awed
    By death like all the creatures
Now watching this spot, like the hawk looking down
    Without blinking, the smug hens
Passing close by in their pecking order,
    The bug whose view is balked by grass,
Or the deer who shyly from afar
    Peer through chinks in the forest.

1950

5. VESPERS

If the hill overlooking our city has always been known as Adam's Grave, only at dusk can you see the recumbent giant, his head turned to the west, his right arm resting for ever on Eve's haunch,

can you learn, from the way he looks up at the scandalous pair, what a citizen really thinks of his citizenship,

just as now you can hear in a drunkard's caterwaul his rebel sorrows crying for a parental discipline, in lustful eyes perceive a disconsolate soul,

scanning with desperation all passing limbs for some vestige of her faceless angel who in that long ago when wishing was a help mounted her once and vanished:

For Sun and Moon supply their conforming masks, but in this hour of civil twilight all must wear their own faces.

And it is now that our two paths cross.

Both simultaneously recognise his Anti-type: that I am an Arcadian, that he is a Utopian.

He notes, with contempt, my Aquarian belly: I note, with alarm, his Scorpion's mouth.

482

He would like to see me cleaning latrines: I would like to see him removed to some other planet.

Neither speaks. What experience could we possibly share?

Glancing at a lampshade in a store window, I observe it is too hideous for anyone in their senses to buy: He observes it is too expensive for a peasant to buy.

Passing a slum child with rickets, I look the other way: He looks the other way if he passes a chubby one.

I hope our senators will behave like saints, provided they don't reform me: He hopes they will behave like *baritoni cattivi*, and, when lights burn late in the Citadel,

I (who have never seen the inside of a police station) am shocked and think, 'Were the city as free as they say, after sundown all her bureaus would be huge black stones.':

He (who has been beaten up several times) is not shocked at all but thinks, 'One fine night our boys will be working up there.'

You can see, then, why, between my Eden and his New Jerusalem, no treaty is negotiable.

In my Eden a person who dislikes Bellini has the good manners not to get born: In his New Jerusalem a person who dislikes work will be very sorry he was born.

In my Eden we have a few beam-engines, saddle-tank locomotives, overshot waterwheels and other beautiful pieces of obsolete machinery to play with: In his New Jerusalem even chefs will be cucumber-cool machine minders.

In my Eden our only source of political news is gossip: In his New Jerusalem there will be a special daily in simplified spelling for non-verbal types.

In my Eden each observes his compulsive rituals and superstitious tabus but we have no morals: In his New Jerusalem the temples will be empty but all will practise the rational virtues.

One reason for his contempt is that I have only to close my eyes, cross the iron footbridge to the tow-path, take the barge through the short brick tunnel and

there I stand in Eden again, welcomed back by the krum-horns, doppions, sordumes of jolly miners and a bob major from the Cathedral (romanesque) of St. Sophie (*Die Kalte*):

One reason for my alarm is that, when he closes his eyes, he arrives, not in New Jerusalem, but on some august day of outrage when hellikins cavort through ruined drawing-rooms and fishwives intervene in the Chamber or

some autumn night of delations and noyades, when the unrepentant
thieves (including me) are sequestered and those he hates shall hate
themselves instead.

So with a passing glance we take the other's posture. Already our steps
recede, heading, incorrigible each, towards his kind of meal and evening.

Was it (as it must look to any god of cross-roads) simply a fortuitous
intersection of life-paths, loyal to different fibs?

Or also a rendezvous between two accomplices who, in spite of
themselves, cannot resist meeting

to remind the other (do both, at bottom, desire truth?) of that half of
their secret which he would most like to forget,

forcing us both, for a fraction of a second, to remember our victim (but
for him I could forget the blood, but for me he could forget the innocence),

on whose immolation (call him Abel, Remus, whom you will, it is one
Sin Offering) arcadias, utopias, our dear old bag of a democracy are alike
founded:

For without a cement of blood (it must be human, it must be innocent)
no secular wall will safely stand.

? 1954

6. COMPLINE

Now, as desire and the things desired
    Cease to require attention,
As, seizing its chance, the body escapes,
    Section by section, to join
Plants in their chaster peace which is more
    To its real taste, now a day is its past,
Its last deed and feeling in, should come
    The instant of recollection
When the whole thing makes sense: it comes, but all
    I recall are doors banging,
Two housewives scolding, an old man gobbling,
    A child's wild look of envy,
Actions, words, that could fit any tale,
    And I fail to see either plot
Or meaning; I cannot remember
    A thing between noon and three.

Nothing is with me now but a sound,
    A heart's rhythm, a sense of stars
Leisurely walking around, and both
    Talk a language of motion
I can measure but not read: maybe
    My heart is confessing her part
In what happened to us from noon till three,
    That constellations indeed

484

Sing of some hilarity beyond
   All liking and happening,
But, knowing I neither know what they know
   Nor what I ought to know, scorning
All vain fornications of fancy,
   Now let me, blessing them both
For the sweetness of their cassations,
   Accept our separations.

A stride from now will take me into dream,
   Leave me, without a status,
Among its unwashed tribes of wishes
   Who have no dances and no jokes
But a magic cult to propitiate
   What happens from noon till three,
Odd rites which they hide from me—should I chance,
   Say, on youths in an oak-wood
Insulting a white deer, bribes nor threats
   Will get them to blab—and then,
Past untruth is one step to nothing, .
   For the end, for me as for cities,
Is total absence: what comes to be
   Must go back into non-being
For the sake of the equity, the rhythm
   Past measure or comprehending.

Can poets (can men in television)
   Be saved? It is not easy
To believe in unknowable justice
   Or pray in the name of a love
Whose name one's forgotten: *libera*
   Me, libera U (dear C)
And all poor s-o-b's who never
   Do anything properly, spare
Us in the youngest day when all are
   Shaken awake, facts are facts,
(And I shall know exactly what happened
   Today between noon and three)
That we, too, may come to the picnic
   With nothing to hide, join the dance
As it moves in perichoresis,
   Turns about the abiding tree.

? 1954

7. LAUDS

Among the leaves the small birds sing;
The crow of the cock commands awaking:
In solitude, for company.

Bright shines the sun on creatures mortal;
Men of their neighbors become sensible:
In solitude, for company.

The crow of the cock commands awaking;
Already the mass-bell goes dong-ding:
In solitude, for company.

Men of their neighbors become sensible;
God bless the Realm, God bless the People:
In solitude, for company.

Already the mass-bell goes dong-ding;
The dripping mill-wheel is again turning:
In solitude, for company.

God bless the Realm, God bless the People;
God bless this green world temporal:
In solitude, for company.

The dripping mill-wheel is again turning;
Among the leaves the small birds sing:
In solitude, for company.

? 1952

Good-Bye to the Mezzogiorno
(for Carlo Izzo)

Out of a gothic North, the pallid children
    Of a potato, beer-or-whisky
Guilt culture, we behave like our fathers and come
    Southward into a sunburnt otherwhere

Of vineyards, baroque, *la bella figura*,
    To these feminine townships where men
Are males, and siblings untrained in a ruthless
    Verbal in-fighting as it is taught

In Protestant rectories upon drizzling
    Sunday afternoons—no more as unwashed
Barbarians out for gold, nor as profiteers
    Hot for Old Masters, but for plunder

Nevertheless—some believing *amore*
    Is better down South and much cheaper
(Which is doubtful), some persuaded exposure
    To strong sunlight is lethal to germs

(Which is patently false) and others, like me,
    In middle-age hoping to twig from
What we are not what we might be next, a question
    The South seems never to raise. Perhaps

A tongue in which Nestor and Apemantus,
    Don Ottavio and Don Giovanni make
Equally beautiful sounds is unequipped
    To frame it, or perhaps in this heat

486

It is nonsense: the Myth of an Open Road
   Which runs past the orchard gate and beckons
Three brothers in turn to set out over the hills
   And far away, is an invention

Of a climate where it is a pleasure to walk
   And a landscape less populated
Than this one. Even so, to us it looks very odd
   Never to see an only child engrossed

In a game it has made up, a pair of friends
   Making fun in a private lingo,
Or a body sauntering by himself who is not
   Wanting, even as it perplexes

Our ears when cats are called *Cat* and dogs either
   Lupo, Nero or *Bobby*. Their dining
Puts us to shame: we can only envy a people
   So frugal by nature it costs them

No effort not to guzzle and swill. Yet (if I
   Read their faces rightly after ten years)
They are without hope. The Greeks used to call the Sun
   He-who-smites-from-afar, and from here, where

Shadows are dagger-edged, the daily ocean blue,
   I can see what they meant: his unwinking
Outrageous eye laughs to scorn any notion
   Of change or escape, and a silent

Ex-volcano, without a stream or a bird,
   Echoes that laugh. This could be a reason
Why they take the silencers off their Vespas,
   Turn their radios up to full volume,

And a minim saint can expect rockets—noise
   As a counter-magic, a way of saying
Boo to the Three Sisters: 'Mortal we may be,
   But we are still here!'—might cause them to hanker

After proximities—in streets packed solid
   With human flesh, their souls feel immune
To all metaphysical threats. We are rather shocked,
   But we need shocking: to accept space, to own

That surfaces need not be superficial
   Nor gestures vulgar, cannot really
Be taught within earshot of running water
   Or in sight of a cloud. As pupils

We are not bad, but hopeless as tutors: Goethe,
   Tapping homeric hexameters
On the shoulder-blade of a Roman girl, is
   (I wish it were someone else) the figure

Of all our stamp: no doubt he treated her well,
   But one would draw the line at calling
The Helena begotten on that occasion,
   Queen of his Second *Walpurgisnacht*,

Her baby: between those who mean by a life a
   Bildungsroman and those to whom living
Means to-be-visible-now, there yawns a gulf
   Embraces cannot bridge. If we try

To 'go southern', we spoil in no time, we grow
   Flabby, dingily lecherous, and
Forget to pay bills: that no one has heard of them
   Taking the Pledge or turning to Yoga

Is a comforting thought—in that case, for all
   The spiritual loot we tuck away,
We do them no harm—and entitles us, I think
   To one little scream at *A piacere*,

Not two. Go I must, but I go grateful (even
   To a certain *Monte*) and invoking
My sacred meridian names, *Vico, Verga,*
   Pirandello, Bernini, Bellini,

To bless this region, its vendages, and those
   Who call it home: though one cannot always
Remember exactly why one has been happy,
   There is no forgetting that one was.

September 1958

Part XI

Dichtung und Wahrheit

<small>(AN UNWRITTEN POEM)</small>

I

Expecting your arrival tomorrow, I find myself thinking *I love You:* then comes the thought—*I should like to write a poem which would express exactly what I mean when I think these words.*

II

Of any poem written by someone else, my first demand is that it be good (who wrote it is of secondary importance); of any poem written by myself, my first demand is that it be genuine, recognizable, like my handwriting, as having been written, for better or worse, by me. (When it comes to his own poems, a poet's preferences and those of his readers often overlap but seldom coincide.)

III

But this poem which I should now like to write would not only have to be good and genuine: if it is to satisfy me, it must also be true.

I read a poem by someone else in which he bids a tearful farewell to his beloved: the poem is good (it moves me as other good poems do) and genuine (I recognize the poet's 'handwriting'). Then I learn from a biography that, at the time he wrote it, the poet was sick to death of the girl but pretended to weep in order to avoid hurt feelings and a scene. Does this information affect my appreciation of his poem? Not in the least: I never knew him personally and his private life is no business of mine. Would it affect my appreciation if I had written the poem myself? I hope so.

IV

It would not be enough that I should believe that what I had written was true: to satisfy me, the truth of this poem must be self-evident. It would have to be written, for example, in such a way that no reader could misread *I love You* as 'I love you.'

V

If I were a composer, I believe I could produce a piece of music which would express to a listener what I mean when I think the word *love,* but it would be impossible for me to compose it in such a way that he would know that this love was felt for *You* (not for God, or my mother, or the decimal system). The language of music is, as it were, intransitive, and it is just this intransitivity which makes it meaningless for a listener to ask: 'Does the composer really mean what he says, or is he only pretending?'

VI

If I were a painter, I believe I could paint a portrait that would express to an onlooker what I mean when I think the word *You* (beautiful, lovable, etc.), but it would be impossible for me to paint it in such a way that he would know that *I* loved You. The language of painting lacks, as it were, the Active Voice, and it is just this objectivity which makes it meaningless for an onlooker to ask: 'Is this really a portrait of *N* (not of a young boy, a judge or a locomotive in disguise)?'

VII

The 'symboliste' attempt to make poetry as intransitive as music can get no further than the narcissistic reflexive—'I love Myself'; the attempt to make poetry as objective as painting can get no further than the single comparison 'A is like B,' 'C is like D,' 'E is like F'. . . No 'imagist' poem can be more than a few words long.

VIII

As an artistic language, Speech has many advantages—three persons, three tenses (Music and Painting have only the Present Tense), both the active and the passive voice—but it has one serious defect: it lacks the Indicative Mood. All its statements are in the subjunctive and only possibly true until verified (which is not always possible) by non-verbal evidence.

IX

First I write *I was born in York;* then, *I was born in New York:* to discover which statement is true and which false, it is no use studying my handwriting.

X

I can imagine a forger clever enough to imitate another's signature so exactly that a handwriting expert would swear in court that it was genuine, but I cannot imagine a forger so clever that he could imitate his own signature inexactly enough to make a handwriting expert swear that it was a forgery. (Or is it only that I cannot imagine the circumstances in which anyone could want to do such a thing?)

XI

In the old days, a poet normally wrote in the third person, and his normal subject was the deeds of others. The use of the first person he reserved for invoking the Muse or reminding his Prince that it was payday; even then, he spoke, not as himself, but in his professional capacity as a bard.

XII

So long as a poet speaks of the deeds of others, his poem may be bad but it cannot be untrue, even if the deeds are legendary, not historical fact. When, in the old days, a poet told how a stripling of nine stone challenged to mortal combat a firedrake weighing twenty tons, or how a rascal stole the Bishop's horse, cuckolded the Grand Vizier and escaped from jail disguised as a washerwoman, it never occurred to anyone in his audience to think: 'Well, his verses may be all very fine or funny, but was the warrior as brave or the rogue as cunning as he says?': their deeds made common sense of his syllabic spell.

XIII

So long as he speaks of the deeds of others, a poet has no difficulty in deciding what style of speech to adopt: a heroic deed calls for a 'high' style, a deed of comic cunning for a 'low' style, etc.

But suppose there had been no Homer so that Hector and Achilles were forced to write the *Iliad* themselves in the first person. If what they wrote were in all other respects the poem we know, should we not think: 'Genuine heroes do not speak about their deeds in this grand way. These fellows must be play-acting.' But, if it is inappropriate for a hero to speak of his own deeds in a grand style, in what style may he appropriately speak? A Comic? Shall we not then suspect him of false modesty?

XIV

The poetic dramatist makes his characters speak in the first person and, very often, in a high style. Why does this not disturb us? (Doesn't it, though?) Is it because we know that the dramatist who wrote their speeches was not talking about himself, and that the actors who deliver them are only play-acting? Can inverted commas make acceptable what without them would disturb?

XV

It is easy for a poet to speak truthfully of brave warriors and cunning rascals because courage and cunning have deeds of their own by which they manifest their character. But how is he to speak truthfully of lovers? Love has no deed of its own: it has to borrow the act of kind which, in itself, is not a deed but a form of behavior (not a *human* deed, that is. One can, if one likes, call it a deed of Aphrodite's or Frau Minne's or Dame Kind's).

XVI

One deed ascribed to Hercules was 'making love' with fifty virgins in the course of a single night: one might on that account say that Hercules was beloved of Aphrodite, but one would not call him a lover.

XVII

Which is Tristan? Which Don Giovanni? No Peeping Tom can tell.

XVIII

It is easy for a poet to hymn the benevolent deeds of Aphrodite (filling his song with charming pictures like the courtship ritual of the Great Crested Grebe or the curious behavior of the male stickleback, and then all those jolly nymphs and shepherds loving away like mad while empires rise and fall) provided that he thinks of her as directing the lives of creatures (even human beings) *in general*. But what is her role when it is a matter of love between two people with proper names who speak in the first and second person? When I say *I love You*, I admit, naturally, that I owe to Aphrodite the general possibility of loving, but that *I* should love *You* is, I claim, my decision (or Your command) not hers. Or so, at least, I shall claim when I am happily in love: should I find myself unhappily in love (reason, conscience, my friends warn me that my love threatens my health, pocket and spiritual salvation, nevertheless I remain attached), then I may very well hold Aphrodite responsible and regard myself as her helpless victim. So, when a poet wishes to speak of the role of Aphrodite in a personal relation, he usually sees her as a malevolent Goddess: it is not of happy marriages that he tells, but of tragic and mutually destructive affairs.

XIX

The unhappy lover who commits suicide does not kill himself for love but in spite of it: to prove to Aphrodite that he is still a freeman, capable of a human deed, not her slave, reduced to mere behavior.

XX

Without personal love the act of kind cannot be a deed, but it can be a social event. A poet, commissioned to write an epithalamium, must know the names and social status of the bride and bridegroom before he can decide upon the style of diction and imagery appropriate to the occasion. (Is it for a royal or a rustic wedding?) But he will never ask: 'Are the bride and bridegroom in love?': for that is irrelevant to a social event. Rumors may reach him that the Prince and Princess cannot bear each other but must marry for dynastic reasons, or that the union of Jack and Jill is really the mating of two herds of cattle, but such gossip will have no influence upon what he writes. That is why it is possible for an epithalamium to be commissioned.

XXI

The poets tell us of heroic deeds done for love: the lover goes to the ends of the earth to fetch the Water of Life, he slays ogres and dragons, he scales a glass mountain, etc., and his final reward is the hand and heart of the girl he loves (who is usually a Princess). But all this is in the social realm, not the personal. It is quite in order that the girl's parents (or public opinion) should say: 'Such-and-such a quality is essential in a son-in-law (or a king),' and insist that every suitor submit to whatever test, be it scaling a glass mountain or translating a passage of Thucydides unseen, will show whether he possesses it or not: and any suitor who passes the test successfully has the right to demand their consent to the match. But no test is conceivable which would make the girl herself say: 'I could not love any suitor who fails it, but I shall love the suitor, whoever he may be, who passes it'; nor is any deed conceivable which would give a suitor the right to demand her love.

Suppose, too, that she doubt the quality of his affection (Is he only after her body or her money?), then no deed of his, however heroic, can reassure her; in relation to her personally, all it can prove is that his motive, noble or base, is strong enough to make him submit to the Test.

XXII

To give another a present is a deed of generosity, and the epic poet spends almost as much time describing the gifts his heroes exchange and the feasts they give as he spends describing their deeds in battle, for the epic hero is expected to be as generous as he is brave. The degree of generosity is verified by the market value of the gift: the poet has only to tell us the size of the rubies and emeralds set in the scabbard, or the number of sheep and oxen consumed at the feast. But how is a poet to speak convincingly of gifts made for love ('I will give you the Keys of Heaven,' etc.)? The market value of a personal gift is irrelevant. The lover tries to choose what, from his knowledge of his beloved's tastes, he believes she would like most to receive at the moment (and receive from him): this might be a Cadillac, but it might equally well be a comic postcard. If he is a would-be seducer, hoping to buy, or she a would-be prostitute, hoping to sell, then, of course, the market value is very relevant. (Not invariably: his intended victim might be a very rich girl whose sole interest in life was collecting comic postcards.)

XXIII

The anonymous gift is a deed of charity, but we are speaking of *eros*, not of *agape*. It is as much of the essence of erotic love that it should desire to disclose itself to one other, as it is of the essence of charity that it should desire to conceal itself from all. Under certain circumstances, a lover may try to conceal his love (he is a hunchback, the girl is his own sister, etc.) but it is not as a lover that he tries to conceal it; and if he were then to send her gifts anonymously, would not this betray a hope, conscious or unconscious, of arousing her curiosity to the point where she would take steps to discover his identity?

XXIV

When his affair with Criseyde was going nicely, Troilus became an even fiercer warrior than before—'Save Ector most ydred of any wight'—but a gentler sportsman—'The smale bestes leet he gon biside.' And we certainly sometimes say of an acquaintance who claims to have fallen in love: 'It must be true this time. He used to be so malicious about everybody but now, since he met N, he never utters an unkind word.' But it is impossible to imagine a lover himself saying: 'It must be true that I love N because I am so much nicer now than I was before we met.' (It is, perhaps, just possible to imagine him saying: 'I believe that N must really love me because she has made me so much nicer.')

XXV

In any case, this poem I should like to write is not concerned with the proposition 'He loves Her' (where He and She could be fictitious persons whose characters and history the poet is free to idealize as much as he choose), but with my proposition *I love You* (where *I* and *You* are persons whose existence and histories could be verified by a private detective).

XXVI

It is a grammatical convention of the English language that a speaker should refer to himself as 'I' and to the person he is addressing as 'You,' but there are many situations in which a different convention would serve equally well. It might be the rule, for example, when making polite conversation with strangers or when addressing public officials, to use the third person: 'Mr. Smith likes cats, doesn't Miss Jones?'; 'Can the honorable conductor tell the humble passenger when this train leaves?' There are many situations, that is to say, in which the use of the pronoun 'I' and 'You' is not accompanied by the I-feeling or the You-feeling.

XXVII

The I-feeling: a feeling of being-responsible-for. (It cannot accompany a verb in the passive.) I wake in the morning with a violent headache and cry *Ouch!* This cry is involuntary and devoid of I-feeling. Then I think: 'I have a hangover'; some I-feeling accompanies this thought—the act of locating and identifying the headache is mine—but very little. Then I think: 'I drank too much last night.' Now the I-feeling is much stronger: I could have drunk less. A headache has become *my* hangover, an incident in my personal history. (I cannot identify my hangover by pointing to my head and groaning, for what makes it mine is my past act and I cannot point to myself yesterday.)

XXVIII

The You-feeling: a feeling of attributing-responsibility-to. If, when I think *You are beautiful*, this thought is accompanied by the You-feeling, I mean that I hold you responsible, in part at least, for your physical appearance; it is not merely due to a lucky combination of genes.

XXIX

Common to both the I- and the You-feeling: a feeling of being-in-the-middle-of-a-story. I cannot think *I love You* without including the thoughts *I have already loved You* (if only for a moment) and *I shall still love You* (if only for a moment). If therefore, I attempt, as I should like to do in this poem, to express what I mean by this thought, I turn myself into a historian, faced with a historian's problems. Of the documents at my disposal (memories of myself, of You, of what I have heard on the subject of love), some have probably been doctored, some may even be downright forgeries; where I have no documents, I cannot tell if this is because they never existed or because they have been lost or hidden and, if so, what difference it would make to my historical picture if they could be recovered. Even were I gifted with total recall, I should still be faced with the task of interpreting them and assessing their relative importance.

XXX

Autobiographers are just like other historians: some are Whigs, some Tories, some Geistesgeschichtswissenschaftler, some Feuilletonistes, etc. (I should like to believe that I think *I love You* more as De Tocqueville might have thought it than De Maistre.)

XXXI

The most difficult problem in personal knowledge, whether of oneself or of others, is the problem of guessing when to think as a historian and when to think as an anthropologist. (It is relatively easy to guess when one should think as a physician.)

XXXII

Who am I? (Was ist denn eigentlich mit mir geschehen?) Several answers are plausible, but there can no more be one definitive answer than there can be one definitive history of the Thirty Years' War.

XXXIII

Alas, it is as impossible that my answer to the question *Who are You?* and your answer to the question 'Who am I?' should be the same as that either of them should be exactly and completely true. But if they are not the same, and neither is quite true, then my assertion *I love You* cannot be quite true either.

XXXIV

'I love you'; 'Je t'aime'; 'Ich liebe Dich'; 'Io t'amo'... there is no language on earth into which this phrase cannot be exactly translated, on condition that, for what is meant by it, speech is unnecessary, so long as, instead of opening his mouth, the speaker might equally well point a finger first at himself, then at 'You' and follow this up with a gesture in imitation of the act of 'making love.'

Under these conditions the phrase is devoid both of I-feeling and You-feeling; 'I' means 'this' member of the human race (not my drinking companion or the bartender), 'You' means 'that' member of the human race (not the cripple to your left, the baby to your right or the old crone behind you) and 'love' identifies 'which' physical need I am at this moment the passive victim of (I am not asking you the way to a good restaurant or the nearest W.C.).

XXXV

If we were total strangers (so that the possibility of a You-feeling on either side were excluded) and, accosting you in the street, I were to say *I love You*, you would not only understand exactly what I was saying but also have no doubt that I meant it; you would never think: 'Is this man deceiving himself or lying to me?' (Of course, you might be wrong: I might be accosting you in order to win a bet or make someone else jealous.)

But we are not strangers and that is not what I mean (or not all that I mean).

Whatever I may mean could not be equally well conveyed by gestures but can be expressed, if at all, in speech (that is why I wish to write this poem), and wherever speech is necessary, lying and self-deception are both possible.

XXXVI

I can pretend to others that I am not hungry when I am (I feel ashamed to admit I cannot afford a decent meal) or that I am hungry when I am not (my hostess's feelings will be hurt if I don't eat): But— *Am I hungry or not? How hungry?* It is difficult to imagine being uncertain or self-deceived as to the true answer.

XXXVII

I am slightly hungry; I am very hungry; I am starving: it is clear that I am speaking of three degrees of the same appetite. *I love You a bit; I love You a lot; I love You madly:* Am I still speaking of different degrees? Or of different kinds?

XXXVIII

Do I love You? I could answer *No* with a certainty that I was speaking the truth on condition that you were someone in whom I took so little interest that it would never occur to me to ask myself the question; but there is no condition which would allow me to answer *Yes* with certainty. Indeed, I am inclined to believe that the more closely my feelings might approximate to the feeling which would make *Yes* the true answer, the more doubtful I should become. (Were you to ask: 'Do you love me?' I should be readier, I believe, to answer *Yes*, if I knew this to be a lie.)

XXXIX

Can I imagine I love when in fact I do not? Certainly. Can I imagine that I do not hate when in fact I do? Certainly. Can I imagine I *only* hate when in fact I both hate *and* love? Yes, that is possible too. But could I imagine that I hated when in fact I did not? Under what circumstances would I have a motive for deceiving myself about this?

XL

Romantic Love: I do not need to have experienced this myself to give a fairly accurate description, since for centuries the notion has been one of the main obsessions of Western Culture. Could I imagine its counternotion—Romantic Hate? What would be its conventions? Its vocabulary? What would a culture be like in which this notion was as much an obsession as that of Romantic Love is in our own? Supposing I were to experience it myself, should I be able to recognize it as Romantic Hate?

XLI

Hatred tends to exclude from consciousness every thought except that of the Hated One; but love tends to enlarge consciousness; the thought of the Beloved acts like a magnet, surrounding itself with other thoughts. Is this one reason why a happy love poem is rarely so convincing as an unhappy one: the happy lover seems continually to be forgetting his beloved to think about the universe?

XLII

Of the many (far too many) love poems written in the first person which I have read, the most convincing were, either the fa-la-la's of a good-natured sensuality which made no pretense at serious love, or howls of grief because the beloved had died and was no longer capable of love, or roars of disapproval because she loved another or nobody but herself; the least convincing were those in which the poet claimed to be in earnest, yet had no complaint to make.

XLIII

A soldier in battle who knows his Homer well may take the deeds of Hector and Achilles (which are possibly fictitious) as a model and thereby be inspired to fight bravely himself. But a would-be lover who knows his Petrarch well cannot thereby be inspired to love: if he takes the sentiments expressed by Petrarch (who was certainly a real person) as a model and attempts to imitate them, then he ceases to be a lover and becomes an actor playing the role of the poet Petrarch.

XLIV

Many poets have attempted to describe the experience of Romantic Love as distinct from vulgar desire. (*Suddenly abashed, I should like to say, aware of having irreverently blundered, like a chattering monkey or an unwashed stableboy, into a Sovereign Presence, tongue-tied, trembling, afraid to stay yet loath to go, for here, if anywhere, it is good to be...*) But has one not had similar experiences (of a numinous encounter) in non-human contexts? (I remember coming unexpectedly upon a derelict iron foundry in the Harz Mountains.) What makes the difference in the human context? Vulgar desire?

XLV

I should like to believe that it is some evidence of love when I can truthfully say: *Desire, even in its wildest tantrums, can neither persuade me it is love nor stop me wishing it were.*

XLVI

'My Love,' says the poet, 'is more wonderful, more beautiful, more to be desired than...'—there follows a list of admirable natural objects and human artifacts—(*more wonderful, I should like to say, than Swaledale or the coast of North-West Iceland, more beautiful than a badger, a sea-horse or a turbine built by Gilkes & Co. of Kendal, more to be desired than cold toast for breakfast or unlimited hot water...*)

What do such comparisons provide? Certainly not a description by which *You* could be distinguished from a hundred possible rivals of a similar type.

XLVII

'The One I worship has more soul than other folks. . . .' (*Much funnier*, I should like to say.) To be accurate, should not the poet have written... 'than any I have met so far'?

XLVIII

'I will love You forever,' swears the poet. I find this easy to swear too. *I will love You at 4:15* P.M. *next Tuesday:* is that still as easy?

XLIX

'I will love You whatever happens, even though...'—there follows a list of catastrophic miracles—(*even though*, I should like to say, *all the stones of Balbek split into exact quarters, the rooks of Repton utter dire prophecies in Greek and the Windrush bellow imprecations in Hebrew, Time run boustrophedon and Paris and Vienna thrice be lit again by gas. . . .*)

Do I believe that these events might conceivably occur during my lifetime? If not, what have I promised? *I will love You whatever happens, even though You put on twenty pounds or become afflicted with a mustache:* dare I promise that?

L

This poem I wished to write was to have expressed exactly what I mean when I think the words *I love You*, but I cannot know exactly what I mean; it was to have been self-evidently true, but words cannot verify themselves. So this poem will remain unwritten. That doesn't matter. Tomorrow You will be arriving; if I were writing a novel in which both of us were characters, I know exactly how I should greet You at the station: *adoration in the eye; on the tongue banter and bawdry.* But who knows exactly how I *shall* greet You? Dame Kind? Now, that's an idea. Couldn't one write a poem (slightly unpleasant, perhaps) about Her?

1959

Part XII

1958–1971

Dame Kind

Steatopygous, sow-dugged
           and owl-headed,
To Whom—Whom else?—the first innocent blood
           was formally shed
By a chinned mammal that hard times
           had turned carnivore,
From Whom his first promiscuous orgy
           begged a downpour
To speed the body-building cereals
           of a warmer age:
Now who put *us*, we should like to know,
           in *Her* manage?

Strait-laced She never was
           and has not grown more so
Since the skeptical academies got wind
           of the *Chi-Rho*;
St. Cuckoo's wooden church for Her
           where on Green Sundays
Bald hermits celebrate a wordless
           cult in Her praise:
So pocket your fifty sonnets, Bud;
           tell Her a myth
Of unpunishable gods and all the girls
           they interfered with.

Haven't we spotted Her Picked Winners
           whom She cossets, ramparts
And does the handsome by? Didn't the darlings
           have cold hearts?
. . . ONE BOMB WOULD BE ENOUGH. . . . Now look
           who's thinking gruesome!
Brother, you're worse than a lonesome Peeper
           or a He-Virgin
Who nightly abhors the Primal Scene
           in medical Latin:
She mayn't be all She might be but
           She *is* our Mum.

You can't tell *us* your hypochondriac
           Blue-Stocking from Provence
Who makes the clockwork arcadies go round
           is worth twopence;
You won't find a steady in *that* museum
           unless you prefer
Tea with a shapeless angel to bedtime
           with a lovely monster:
Before you catch it for your mim look
           and gnostic chirrup,
Ask the Kind Lady who fitted you out
           to fix you up.

Supposing even (through misdirections
                        or your own mischief)
You do land in that anomalous duchy,
                        Her remotest fief,
Where four eyes encounter in two
                        one mirror perilous
As the clear rock basin that stultified
                        frigid Narcissus,
Where tongues stammer on a First name,
                        bereft of guile,
And common snub-nosed creatures are abashed
                        at a face in profile,

Even there, as your blushes invoke its Guardian
                        (whose true invocable
Name is singular for each true heart
                        and false to tell)
To sacre your courtship ritual so
                        it deserves a music
More solemn than the he-hawing
                        of a salesman's limerick,
Do a bow to the Coarse Old Party that wrought you
                        an alderliefest
Of the same verbose and sentient kidney,
                        grateful not least

For all the dirty work She did.
                        How many hundreds
Of lawful, unlawful, both equally
                        loveless beds,
Of lying endearments, crooked questions,
                        crookeder answers,
Of bawling matches, sarcastic silences,
                        megrims, tears,
How much half-witted horseplay and sheer
                        bloody misrule
It took to bring you two together
                        both on schedule?

1959

Reflections in a Forest

Within a shadowland of trees
Whose lives are so uprightly led
In nude august communities,
To move about seems underbred

And common any taste for words;
When, thoughtlessly, they took to song,
Whatever one may think of birds,
The example that they set was wrong.

504

In keeping still, in staying slow,
For posture and for social ease,
How much these living statues owe
Their scent-and-color languages.

For who can quarrel without terms
For Not or Never, who can raise
Objections when what one affirms
Is necessarily the case?

But trees are trees, an elm or oak
Already both outside and in,
And cannot, therefore, counsel folk
Who have their unity to win.

Turn all tree-signals into speech,
And what comes out is a command:
'Keep running if you want to reach
The point of knowing where you stand.'

A truth at which one should arrive,
Forbids immediate utterance,
And tongues to speak it must contrive
To tell two different lies at once.

My chance of growing would be slim,
Were I with wooden honesty
To show my hand or heart to Him
Who will, if I should lose, be Me.

Our race would not have gotten far,
Had we not learned to bluff it out
And look more certain than we are
Of what our motion is about;

Nor need one be a cop to find
Undressing before others rude:
The most ascetic of our kind
Look naked in the buff, not nude.

                                                        1957

Hands

We don't need a face in the picture to know
That palms downward, thumbs a little out,
        Have a paternal status,
        With blessing to bestow
On some filial or penitent head,
        Their signal is obvious—

Nor a tradesman's calendar to recognize
A gift season when palms look skyward
    And ten serried fingers curl,
    Eager to grasp the size,
Texture and weight of a lollipop,
    Tobacco-pouch or pearl;

And abroad where nothing is called by its right name,
Thanks to a flexible wrist and digits,
    We command a rhetoric
    Which makes us glad we came:
Hands will reckon, beckon, demonstrate
    Why we are angry or where sick.

Without them, what should we talk of anyway?
They built the gear and worldly fabric
    Which to us mean Home, will repair
    A torn jacket or play
A difficult sonata right through
    While the mind is elsewhere.

Strange, then, that these busybodies should have no
Feel for the quality of an absence,
    Should never twitch in regret
    For dear dead So-and-So
Or the Fall of the Roman Empire,
    Never itch to play Hamlet.

For peace, pardon, true love and finer weather
Trinitarian, Arian, Gnostic lips
    Pray to a *Deus Absconditus*,
    But, folded together,
All hands do homage to the god of hands,
    Tangible *Terminus*.

Lines on a face betoken a mounting care
For the ifs and buts of Time, a growing grief
    At lost opportunity,
    But lines on a hand declare,
Day after wasted day: 'I am just what I am,
    There is no one else like Me.'

No wonder poor hunted fugitives are afeard
Of every footfall and shadow:
    What help are ten aliases,
    Forged papers, a fake beard,
If hands are too good or bad to cheat
    Even their enemies?

Eyes can often be taken in, hands never:
At once, whether gripped in a greeting
    Or lightly pressed in a waltz,
    One hand knows another
And, spite of vows or rage or heartbreak,
    Blurts out: 'This hand is false!'

We may find a verse, a letter, as we sort,
We refuse to believe ('No!' heart swears,
    'I never wrote such rubbish!'),
    Would deny the words in court,
Were handwriting, like a memory,
    A fact we could unwish.

1959

The Sabbath

Waking on the Seventh Day of Creation,
    They cautiously sniffed the air:
The most fastidious nostril among them admitted
    That fellow was no longer there.

Herbivore, parasite, predator scouted,
    Migrants flew fast and far—
Not a trace of his presence: holes in the earth,
    Beaches covered with tar,

Ruins and metallic rubbish in plenty
    Were all that was left of him
Whose birth on the Sixth had made of that day
    An unnecessary interim.

Well, that fellow had never really smelled
    Like a creature who would survive:
No grace, address of faculty like those
    Born on the First Five.

Back, then, at last on a natural economy,
    Now His Impudence was gone,
Looking exactly like what it was,
    The Seventh Day went on,

Beautiful, happy, perfectly pointless. . . .
    A rifle's ringing crack
Split their Arcadia wide open, cut
    Their Sabbath nonsense short.

For whom did they think they had been created?
    That fellow was back,
More bloody-minded than they remembered,
    More godlike than they thought.

? July 1959

Walks

I choose the road from here to there
When I've a scandalous tale to bear,
Tools to return or books to lend
To someone at the other end.

Returning afterwards, although
I meet my footsteps toe to toe,
The road looks altogether new
Now that is done I meant to do.

But I avoid it when I take
A walker's walk for walking sake:
The repetition it involves
Raises a doubt it never solves.

What good or evil angel bid
Me stop exactly when I did?
What would have happened had I gone
A kilometer further on?

No, when a fidget in the soul
Or cumulus clouds invite a stroll,
The route I pick goes roundabout
To finish where it started out.

It gets me home, this curving track,
Without my having to turn back,
Nor does it leave it up to me
To say how long my walk shall be,

Yet satisfies a moral need
By turning behavior into deed,
For I have boxed the compass when
I enter my front door again.

The heart, afraid to leave her shell,
Demands a hundred yards as well
Between my personal abode
And either sort of public road,

Making, when it is added too,
The straight a T, the round a Q,
Allowing me in rain or shine
To call both walks entirely mine,

A lane no traveler would use,
Where prints that do not fit my shoes
Have looked for me and, like enough,
Were made by someone whom I love.

? 1958

Friday's Child

(In memory of Dietrich Bonhoeffer,
martyred at Flossenburg, April 9th, 1945)

He told us we were free to choose
But, children as we were, we thought—
'Paternal Love will only use
   Force in the last resort

On those too bumptious to repent'—
Accustomed to religious dread,
It never crossed our minds He meant
   Exactly what He said.

Perhaps He frowns, perhaps He grieves,
But it seems idle to discuss
If anger or compassion leaves
   The bigger bangs to us.

What reverence is rightly paid
To a Divinity so odd
He lets the Adam whom He made
   Perform the Acts of God?

It might be jolly if we felt
Awe at this Universal Man
(When kings were local, people knelt);
   Some try to, but who can?

The self-observed observing Mind
We meet when we observe at all
Is not alarming or unkind
   But utterly banal.

Though instruments at Its command
Make wish and counterwish come true,
It clearly cannot understand
   What It can clearly do

Since the analogies are rot
Our senses based belief upon,
We have no means of learning what
   Is really going on,

And must put up with having learned
All proofs or disproofs that we tender
Of His existence are returned
   Unopened to the sender.

Now, did He really break the seal
And rise again? We dare not say;
But conscious unbelievers feel
   Quite sure of Judgment Day.

Meanwhile, a silence on the cross,
As dead as we shall ever be,
Speaks of some total gain or loss,
    And you and I are free

To guess from the insulted face
Just what Appearances He saves
By suffering in a public place
    A death reserved for slaves.

? 1958

Academic Graffiti
(*In Memoriam Ogden Nash*)

My First Name, Wystan,
Rhymes with Tristan,
*But—O dear!—I do hope
I'm not quite such a dope.*

*　　*　　*

Henry Adams
Was mortally afraid of Madams:
In a disorderly house
He sat quiet as a mouse.

*　　*　　*

St. Thomas Aquinas
Always regarded wine as
A medicinal juice
That helped him to deduce.

*　　*　　*

Johann Sebastian Bach
Was a master of his *Fach:*
Nothing could be more *kluge*
Than his *Kunst der Fuge.*

*　　*　　*

Thomas Lovell Beddoes
Could never walk through meadows
Without getting the glooms
And thinking of tombs.

*　　*　　*

Ludwig van Beethoven
Believed it proven
That, for mortal dust,
What must be, must.

*　　*　　*

Good Queen Bess
Couldn't have liked it less,
When Burghley and Cecil
Drank out of the same vessel.

      *   *   *

William Blake
Found Newton hard to take,
And was not enormously taken
With Francis Bacon.

      *   *   *

Said Robert Bridges,
When badly bitten by midges:
'They're only doing their duty
As a testament to my beauty.'

      *   *   *

Robert Browning
Immediately stopped frowning
And started to blush,
When fawned on by Flush.

      *   *   *

Martin Buber
Never said 'Thou' to a tuber:
Despite his creed,
He did not fool the need.

      *   *   *

Lord Byron
Once succumbed to a Siren:
His flesh was weak,
Hers Greek.

      *   *   *

Among the prosodists, Bysshe
Was the syllable-counting old sissy,
Guest
The accentual pest.

      *   *   *

When Arthur Hugh Clough
Was jilted by a piece of fluff,
He sighed 'Quel dommage!',
And wrote *Amours de Voyage*.

Dante
Was utterly *enchanté*
When Beatrice cried in tones that were peachy:
Noi siamo amici.

*   *   *

Hugo De Vries
During a visit to Greece
Composed a pastoral poem,
Xylem and Phloem.

*   *   *

Charles Dickens
Could find nothing to say to chickens,
But gossipping with rabbits
Became one of his habits.

*   *   *

Desiderius Erasmus
Always avoided chiasmus,
But grew addicted as time wore on
To oxymoron.

*   *   *

Fulke Greville
Wrote beautifully at sea level:
With each rising contour his verse
Got progressively worse.

*   *   *

The *Geheimrat* in Goethe
Made him all the curter
With *Leute* who were leery
Of his Color Theory.

*   *   *

Sir Rider Haggard,
Was completely staggered
When his bride-to-be
Announced 'I AM SHE!'

*   *   *

Georg Friedrich Händel
Was highly respected in Kendal:
It was George Frederick Handel
Who caused all the scandal.

Thomas Hardy
Was never tardy
When summoned to fulfill
The Immanent Will.

* * *

Joseph Haydn
Never read Dryden
Nor did John Dryden
Ever hear Haydn.

* * *

No one could ever inveigle
Georg Wilhelm Friedrich Hegel
Into offering the slightest apology
For his *Phenomenology*.

* * *

George Herbert
Once tried ordering sherbet
On Salisbury plain:
He ordered in vain.

* * *

Robert Herrick
Certainly did not write *Eric*:
So far
As we know, It was Dean Farrar.

* * *

Henry James
Abhorred the word *Dames*,
And always wrote *'Mommas'*
With inverted commas.

* * *

When the young Kant
Was told to kiss his aunt,
He obeyed the Categorical Must,
But only just.

* * *

Søren Kierkegaard
Tried awfully hard
To take The Leap
But fell in a heap.

Karl Kraus
Always had some grouse
Among his bêtes noires
Were Viennese choirs.

*   *   *

Archbishop Laud
Was High, not Broad:
He could never descend
To celebrating the North End.

*   *   *

Edward Lear
Was haunted by a fear
While travelling in Albania
Of contracting kleptomania.

*   *   *

Joseph Lister,
According to his sister,
Was not an alcoholic:
His vice was carbolic.

*   *   *

Mr. Robert Liston
Used the saw like a piston:
He was *that* elated
When he amputated.

*   *   *

Luther & Zwingli
Should be treated singly:
L hated the Peasants,
Z the Real Presence.

*   *   *

Mallarmé
Had too much to say:
He could never quite
Leave the paper white.

*   *   *

Mary, Queen of Scots,
Could tie the most complicated knots,
But she couldn't bake
The simplest cake.

Queen Mary (The Bloody)
Had an understudy
Who was a Prot:
She was not.

* * *

When Karl Marx
Found the phrase 'financial sharks,'
He sang a Te Deum
In the British Museum.

* * *

John Milton
Never stayed in a Hilton
Hotel,
Which was just as well.

* * *

William Henry Monk
Lived in a perpetual blue funk
Of being taken on hikes
By John Bacchus Dykes.

* * *

Thomas More
Caused a furore
Every time he bellowed his
Irish Melodies.

* * *

Cardinal Newman
Was being only human
When he dreamed of panning
The latest contract by Cardinal Manning.

* * *

Nietzsche
Had the habit as a teacher
Of cracking his joints
To emphasize his points.

* * *

Oxbridge philosophers, to be cursory,
Are products of a middle-class nursery:
Their arguments are anent
What Nanny really meant.

Louis Pasteur,
So his colleagues aver,
Lived on excellent terms
With most of his germs.

*　　*　　*

Alexander Pope
Never gave up hope
Of finding a motto
To affix to his Grotto.

*　　*　　*

Christina Rossetti
Thought it rather petty,
When her brother, D.G.,
Put laudanum in her tea.

*　　*　　*

When Sir Walter Scott
Made a blot,
He stamped with rage
And started a new page.

*　　*　　*

'*Ma foi!*', exclaimed Stendhal,
'*Ce Scarpia n'est pas si mal*,
But he's no Count Mosca,
Unluckily for Tosca.'

*　　*　　*

Adalbert Stifter
Was no weight-lifter:
He would hire old lags
To carry his bags.

*　　*　　*

William Makepeace Thackeray
Wept into his daiquiri,
When he heard St. John's Wood
Thought he was no good.

*　　*　　*

Thomas the Rhymer
Was probably a social climber:
He should have known Fairy Queens
Were beyond his means.

Thomas Traherne
Could always discern
The Angel in boys,
Even when they made a noise.

    *   *   *

Paul Valéry
Earned a meager salary,
Walking through the *Bois*,
Observing his *Moi*.

    *   *   *

Good Queen Victoria
In a fit of euphoria
Commanded Disraeli
To blow up the Old Bailey.

    *   *   *

James Watt
Was the hard-boiled kind of Scot:
He thought any dream
Sheer waste of steam.

    *   *   *

Oscar Wilde
Was greatly beguiled,
When into the Café Royal walked Bosie
Wearing a tea-cosy.

    *   *   *

Sir Thomas Wyatt
Never went on a diet,
Unlike the Earl of Surrey,
Who ate nothing but curry.

    *   *   *

Whenever Xantippe
Wasn't feeling too chippy,
She would bawl at Socrates:
'Why aren't you Hippocrates?'

    *   *   *

T. S. Eliot is quite at a loss
When clubwomen bustle across
   At literary teas,
    Crying: 'What, if you please,
Did you mean by *The Mill on the Floss*?'

To get the Last Poems of Yeats,
You need not mug up on dates;
    All a reader requires
    Is some knowledge of gyres
And the sort of people he hates.

1952, 1970

Thanksgiving for a Habitat

Funes ceciderunt mihi in praeclaris:
etenim hereditas mea praeclara est mihi.

PSALM XVI, 6

I. PROLOGUE: THE BIRTH OF ARCHITECTURE
(for John Bayley)

From gallery-grave and the hunt of a wren-king
    to Low Mass and trailer camp
is hardly a tick by the carbon clock, but I
    don't count that way nor do you:
already it is millions of heartbeats ago
    back to the Bicycle Age,
before which is no *After* for me to measure,
    just a still prehistoric *Once*
where anything could happen. To you, to me,
    Stonehenge and Chartres Cathedral,
the Acropolis, Blenheim, the Albert Memorial
    are works by the same Old Man
under different names: we know what He did,
    what, even, He thought He thought,
but we don't see why. (To get that, one would have
    to be selfish in His way,
without concrete or grapefruit.) It's our turn now
    to puzzle the unborn. No world
wears as well as it should but, mortal or not,
    a world has still to be built
because of what we can see from our windows,
    that Immortal Commonwealth
which is there regardless: It's in perfect taste
    and it's never boring but
it won't quite do. Among its populations
    are masons and carpenters
who build the most exquisite shelters and safes,
    but no architects, any more
than there are heretics or bounders: to take
    umbrage at death, to construct
a second nature of tomb and temple, lives
    must know the meaning of *If*.

? 1962

Some thirty inches from my nose
The frontier of my Person goes,
And all the untilled air between
Is private *pagus* or demesne.
Stranger, unless with bedroom eyes
I beckon you to fraternize,
Beware of rudely crossing it:
I have no gun, but I can spit.

II. THANKSGIVING FOR A HABITAT
(for Geoffrey Gorer)

Nobody I know would like to be buried
   with a silver cocktail shaker,
a transistor radio and a strangled
   daily help, or keep his word because

of a great-great-grandmother who got laid
   by a sacred beast. Only a press lord
could have built San Simeon: no unearned income
   can buy us back the gait and gestures

to manage a baroque staircase, or the art
   of believing footmen don't hear
human speech. (In adulterine castles
   our half-strong might hang their jackets

while mending their lethal bicycle chains.
   luckily, there are not enough
crags to go round.) Still, Hetty Pegler's Tump
   is worth a visit, so is Schönbrunn,

to look at someone's idea of the body
   that should have been his, as the flesh
Mum formulated shouldn't: that whatever
   he does or feels in the mood for,

stocktaking, horseplay, worship, making love,
   he stays the same shape, disgraces
a Royal I. To be overadmired is not
   good enough: although a fine figure

is rare in either sex, others like it
   have existed before. One may
be a Proustian snob or a sound Jacksonian
   democrat, but which of us wants

to be touched inadvertently, even
   by his beloved? We know all about graphs
and Darwin, enormous rooms no longer
   superhumanize, but earnest

519

city planners are mistaken: a pen
   for a rational animal
is no fitting habitat for Adam's
   sovereign clone. I, a transplant

from overseas, at last am dominant
   over three acres and a blooming
conurbation of country lives, few of whom
   I shall ever meet, and with fewer

converse. Linnaeus recoiled from the Amphibia
   as a naked gruesome rabble,
Arachnids give me the shudders, but fools
   who deface their emblem of guilt

are germane to Hitler: the race of spiders
   shall be allowed their webs. I should like
to be to my water-brethren as a spell
   of fine weather: Many are stupid,

and some, maybe, are heartless, but who is not
   vulnerable, easy to scare,
and jealous of his privacy? (I am glad
   the blackbird, for instance, cannot

tell if I'm talking English, German or
   just typewriting: that what he utters
I may enjoy as an alien rigmarole.) I ought
   to outlast the limber dragonflies

as the muscle-bound firs are certainly
   going to outlast me: I shall not end
down any esophagus, though I may succumb
   to a filter-passing predator,

shall, anyhow, stop eating, surrender my smidge
   of nitrogen to the World Fund
with a drawn-out *Oh* (unless at the nod
   of some jittery commander

I be translated in a nano-second
   to a c.c. of poisonous nothing
in a giga-death). Should conventional
   blunderbuss war and its routiers

invest my bailiwick, I shall of course
   assume the submissive posture:
but men are not wolves and it probably
   won't help. Territory, status,

and love, sing all the birds, are what matter:
   what I dared not hope or fight for
is, in my fifties, mine, a toft-and-croft
   where I needn't, ever, be at home *to*

those I am not at home *with*, not a cradle,
   a magic Eden without clocks,
and not a windowless grave, but a place
   I may go both in and out of.

August 1962

III. THE CAVE OF MAKING
(*In Memoriam Louis MacNeice*)

For this and for all enclosures like it the archetype
   is Weland's Stithy, an antre
more private than a bedroom even, for neither lovers nor
   maids are welcome, but without a
bedroom's secrets: from the Olivetti portable,
   the dictionaries (the very
best money can buy), the heaps of paper, it is evident
   what must go on. Devoid of
flowers and family photographs, all is subordinate
   here to a function, designed to
discourage daydreams—hence windows averted from plausible
   videnda but admitting a light one
could mend a watch by—and to sharpen hearing: reached by an
   outside staircase, domestic
noises and odors, the vast background of natural
   life are shut off. Here silence
is turned into objects.
                    I wish, Louis, I could have shown it you
   while you were still in public,
and the house and garden: lover of women and Donegal,
   from your perspective you'd notice
sights I overlook, and in turn take a scholar's interest
   in facts I could tell you (for instance,
four miles to our east, at a wood palisade, Carolingian
   Bavaria stopped, beyond it
unknowable nomads). Friends we became by personal
   choice, but fate had already
made us neighbors. For Grammar we both inherited
   good mongrel barbarian English
which never completely succumbed to the Roman rhetoric
   or the Roman gravity, that nonsense
which stood none. Though neither of our dads, like Horace's,
   wiped his nose on his forearm,
neither was porphyry-born, and our ancestors probably
   were among those plentiful subjects
it cost less money to murder. Born so, both of us
   became self-conscious at a moment
when locomotives were named after knights in Malory,
   Science to schoolboys was known as
Stinks, and the Manor still was politically numinous:
   both watched with mixed feelings
the sack of Silence, the churches empty, the cavalry
   go, the Cosmic Model
become German, and any faith, if we had it, in immanent
   virtue died. More than ever

life-out-there is goodly, miraculous, lovable,
    but we shan't, not since Stalin and Hitler,
trust ourselves ever again: we know that, subjectively,
    all is possible.
                            To you, though,
ever since, last Fall, you quietly slipped out of Granusion,
    our moist garden, into
the Country of Unconcern, no possibility
    matters. I wish you hadn't
caught that cold, but the dead we miss are easier
    to talk to: with those no longer
tensed by problems one cannot feel shy and, anyway,
    when playing cards or drinking
or pulling faces are out of the question, what else is there
    to do but talk to the voices
of conscience they have become? From now on, as a visitor
    who needn't be met at the station,
your influence is welcome at any hour in my ubity,
    especially here, where titles
from *Poems* to *The Burning Perch* offer proof positive
    of the maker you were, with whom I
once collaborated, once at a weird Symposium
    exchanged winks as a juggins
went on about Alienation.
                            Who would, for preference,
    be a bard in an oral culture,
obliged at drunken feasts to improvise a eulogy
    of some beefy illiterate burner,
giver of rings, or depend for bread on the moods of a
    Baroque Prince, expected,
like his dwarf, to amuse? After all, it's rather a privilege
    amid the affluent traffic
to serve this unpopular art which cannot be turned into
    background noise for study
or hung as a status trophy by rising executives,
    cannot be 'done' like Venice
or abridged like Tolstoy, but stubbornly still insists upon
    being read or ignored: our handful
of clients at least can rune. (It's heartless to forget about
    the underdeveloped countries,
but a starving ear is as deaf as a suburban optimist's:
    to stomachs only the Hindu
integers truthfully speak.) Our forerunners might envy us
    our remnant still able to listen:
as Nietzsche said they would, the *plebs* have got steadily
    denser, the *optimates*
quicker still on the uptake. (Today, even Talleyrand
    might seem a naïf: he had so
little to cope with.) I should like to become, if possible,
    a minor atlantic Goethe,
with his passion for weather and stones but without his silliness
    re the Cross: at times a bore, but,
while knowing Speech can at best, a shadow echoing
    the silent light, bear witness

to the Truth it is not, he wished it were, as the Francophile
   gaggle of pure songsters
are too vain to. We're not musicians: to stink of Poetry
   is unbecoming, and never
to be dull shows a lack of taste. Even a limerick
   ought to be something a man of
honor, awaiting death from cancer or a firing squad,
   could read without contempt: (at
that frontier I wouldn't dare speak to anyone
   in either a prophet's bellow
or a diplomat's whisper).
               Seeing you know our mystery
   from the inside and therefore
how much, in our lonely dens, we need the companionship
   of our good dead, to give us
comfort on dowly days when the self is a nonentity
   dumped on a mound of nothing,
to break the spell of our self-enchantment when lip-smacking
   imps of mawk and hooey
write with us what they will, you won't think me imposing if
   I ask you to stay at my elbow
until cocktail time: dear Shade, for your elegy
   I should have been able to manage
something more like you than this egocentric monologue,
   but accept it for friendship's sake.

                                  July 1964

POSTSCRIPT

Timeless fictional worlds
Of self-evident meaning
Would not delight,

Were not our own
A temporal one where nothing
Is what it seems.

      *   *   *

A poem—a tall story:
But any good one
Makes us want to know.

      *   *   *

Only tuneless birds,
Inarticulate warriors,
Need bright plumage.

      *   *   *

In a brothel, both
The ladies and gentlemen
Have nicknames only.

      *   *   *

Speechless Evil
Borrowed the language of Good
And reduced it to noise.

*   *   *

A dry sad day.
What pirate falsehood
Has beheaded your stream of Truth?

*   *   *

At lucky moments we seem on the brink
Of really saying what we think we think:
But, even then, an honest eye should wink.

*   *   *

Nature, consistent and august,
Can't teach us what to write or do:
With Her the real is always true,
And what is true is also just.

*   *   *

Time has taught you
                how much inspiration
your vices brought you,
                   what imagination
can owe temptation
              yielded to,
that many a fine
              expressive line
would not have existed,
                had you resisted:
as a poet, you
           know this is true,
and though in Kirk
              you sometimes pray
to feel contrite,
          it doesn't work.
Felix Culpa, you say:
              perhaps you're right.

You hope, yes,
           your books will excuse you,
save you from hell:
              nevertheless,
without looking sad,
              without in any way
seeming to blame
            (He doesn't need to,
knowing well
           what a lover of art

like yourself pays heed to),
God may reduce you
on Judgment Day
to tears of shame,
reciting by heart
the poems you would
have written, had
your life been good.

IV. DOWN THERE
(for Irving Weiss)

A cellar underneath the house, though not lived in,
Reminds our warm and windowed quarters upstairs that
Caves water-scooped from limestone were our first dwellings,
A providential shelter when the Great Cold came,
Which woke our feel for somewhere fixed to come back to,
A hole by occupation made to smell human.

Self-walled, we sleep aloft, but still, at safe anchor,
Ride there on caves; lamplit we dine at street level:
But, deep in Mother Earth, beneath her key-cold cloak,
Where light and heat can never spoil what sun ripened,
In barrels, bottles, jars, we mew her kind commons,
Wine, beer, conserves and pickles, good at all seasons.

Encrust with years of clammy grime, the lair, maybe,
Of creepy-crawlies or a ghost, its flagstoned vault
Is not for girls: sometimes, to test their male courage,
A father sends the younger boys to fetch something
For Mother from down there; ashamed to whimper, hearts pounding,
They dare the dank steps, re-emerge with proud faces.

The rooms we talk and work in always look injured
When trunks are being packed, and when, without warning,
We drive up in the dark, unlock and switch lights on.
They seem put out: a cellar never takes umbrage;
It takes us as we are, explorers, homebodies,
Who seldom visit others when we don't need them.

July 1963

V. UP THERE
(for Anne Weiss)

Men would never have come to need an attic.
Keen collectors of glass or Roman coins build
Special cabinets for them, dote on, index
Each new specimen: only women cling to
Items out of their past they have no use for,
Can't name now what they couldn't bear to part with.

525

Up there, under the eaves, in bulging boxes,
Hats, veils, ribbons, galoshes, programs, letters
Wait unworshipped (a starving spider spins for
The occasional fly): no clock recalls it
Once an hour to the household it's part of,
No Saint's Day is devoted to its function.

All it knows of a changing world it has to
Guess from children, who conjure in its plenum,
Now an eyrie for two excited sisters,
Where, when Mother is bad, her rage can't reach them,
Now a schooner on which a lonely only
Boy sails north or approaches coral islands.

July 1963

VI. THE GEOGRAPHY OF THE HOUSE
(*for Christopher Isherwood*)

Seated after breakfast
In this white-tiled cabin
Arabs call *the House where
Everybody goes,*
Even melancholics
Raise a cheer to Mrs.
Nature for the primal
Pleasures She bestows.

Sex is but a dream to
Seventy-and-over,
But a joy proposed un-
-til we start to shave:
Mouth-delight depends on
Virtue in the cook, but
This She guarantees from
Cradle unto grave.

Lifted off the potty,
Infants from their mothers
Hear their first impartial
Words of worldly praise:
Hence, to start the morning
With a satisfactory
Dump is a good omen
All our adult days.

Revelation came to
Luther in a privy
(Crosswords have been solved there)
Rodin was no fool
When he cast his Thinker,
Cogitating deeply,
Crouched in the position
Of a man at stool.

526

All the Arts derive from
This ur-act of making,
Private to the artist:
Makers' lives are spent
Striving in their chosen
Medium to produce a
De-narcissus-ized en-
-during excrement.

Freud did not invent the
Constipated miser:
Banks have letter boxes
Built in their façade
Marked *For Night Deposits*,
Stocks are firm or liquid,
Currencies of nations
Either soft or hard.

Global Mother, keep our
Bowels of compassion
Open through our lifetime,
Purge our minds as well:
Grant us a kind ending,
Not a second childhood,
Petulant, weak-sphinctered,
In a cheap hotel.

Keep us in our station:
When we get pound-noteish,
When we seem about to
Take up Higher Thought,
Send us some deflating
Image like the pained ex-
-pression on a Major
Prophet taken short.

(Orthodoxy ought to
Bless our modern plumbing:
Swift and St. Augustine
Lived in centuries
When a stench of sewage
Ever in the nostrils
Made a strong debating
Point for Manichees.)

Mind and Body run on
Different timetables:
Not until our morning
Visit here can we
Leave the dead concerns of
Yesterday behind us,
Face with all our courage
What is now to be.

? September 1963

VII. ENCOMIUM BALNEI
(for Neil Little)

it is odd that the English
           a rather dirty people
   should have invented the slogan
Cleanliness is next to Godliness
              meaning by that
   a gentleman smells faintly of tar
persuaded themselves that constant cold hydropathy
   would make the sons of gentlemen
pure in heart
         (not that papa or his chilblained offspring can
   hope to be gentry)
             still John Bull's
hip-bath it was
         that made one carnal pleasure lawful
   for the first time since we quarreled
over Faith and Works
         (Shakespeare probably stank
                  Le Grand
   Monarque certainly did)
            thanks to him
shrines where a subarctic fire-cult could meet and marry
   a river-cult from torrid Greece
rose again
        resweetened the hirsute West
               a Roman though
   bath addict
        amphitheater fan
would be puzzled
        seeing the caracallan acreage
   compressed into such a few square feet
mistake them for hideouts
           warrens of some outlawed sect
   who mortify their flesh with strange
implements
        he is not that wrong
             if the tepidarium's
   barrel vaulting has migrated
to churches and railroad stations
            if we no longer
   go there to wrestle or gossip
or make love
        (you cannot purchase a conjugal tub)
   St. Anthony and his wild brethren
(for them ablutions were tabu
           a habit of that doomed
   behavioral sink this world)
         have been
just as he thought
      at work
        we are no more chaste
           obedient

nor
if we can possibly help it
poor than he was but
enthusiasts who were have taught us
(besides showing lovers of nature
how to carry binoculars instead of a gun)
the unclassical wonder of being
all by oneself
though our dwellings may still have a master
who owns the front-door key
a bathroom
has only an inside lock
belongs today to whoever
is taking a bath
among us
to withdraw from the tribe at will
be neither Parent
Spouse nor Guest
is a sacrosanct
political right
where else shall the Average Ego
find its peace
not in sleep surely
the several worlds we invent are quite as pugnacious
as the one into which we are born
and even more public
on Oxford Street or Broadway
I may escape notice
but never
on roads I dream of
what Eden is there for the lapsed
but hot water
snug in its caul
widows
orphans
exiles may feel as self-important
as an only child
and a sage
be silly without shame
present a Lieder Abend
to a captive audience of his toes
retreat from rhyme and reason into some mallarmesque
syllabic fog
for half an hour
it is wise to forget the time
our daily peril
and each other
good for the soul
once in the twenty-four hour cycle of her body
whether according to our schedule
as we sit down to breakfast
or stand up to welcome
folk for dinner
to feel as if

the Pilgrim's Way
>or as some choose to call it
>>the War Path
>were now a square in the Holy City
that what was wrong has been put right
>>as if Von Hügel's
>hoggers and lumpers were extinct
thinking the same as thanking
>>all military hardware
>already slighted and submerged

>>>*April 1962*

VIII. GRUB FIRST, THEN ETHICS (Brecht)
(*for Margaret Gardiner*)

Should the shade of Plato
visit us, anxious to know
how *anthropos* is, we could say to him: 'Well,
>we can read to ourselves, our use
of holy numbers would shock you, and a poet
>may lament—where is Telford
whose bridged canals are still a Shropshire glory,
>where Muir who on a Douglas spruce
rode out a storm and called an earthquake noble,
>where Mr. Vynyian Board,
thanks to whose lifelong fuss the hunted whale now suffers
>a quicker death?—without being
called an idiot, though none of them bore arms or
>made a public splash,' then 'Look!'
we would point, for a dig at Athens, 'Here
>is the place where we cook.'

Though built in Lower Austria,
>do-it-yourself America
prophetically blueprinted this
>palace kitchen for kingdoms
where royalty would be incognito, for an age when
>Courtesy might think: 'From your voice
and the back of your neck I know we shall get on
>but cannot tell from your thumbs
who is to give the orders.' The right note is harder
>to hear than in the Age of Poise
when She talked shamelessly to her maid and sang
>noble lies with Him, but struck
it can be still in New Cnossos where if I am
>banned by a shrug it is my fault,
not Father's, as it is my taste whom
>I put below the salt.

The prehistoric hearthstone,
>round as a birthday-button
and sacred to Granny, is as old
>stuff as the bowel-loosening

530

nasal war cry, but this all-electric room
    where ghosts would feel uneasy,
a witch at a loss, is numinous and again
    the center of a dwelling
not, as lately it was, an abhorrent dungeon
    where the warm unlaundered meiny
belched their comic prose and from a dream of which
    chaste Milady awoke blushing.
House-proud, deploring labor, extolling work,
    these engines politely insist
  that banausics can be liberals,
    a cook a pure artist

    who moves everyman
    at a deeper level than
  Mozart, for the subject of the verb
    to-hunger is never a name:
dear Adam and Eve had different bottoms,
    but the neotene who marches
upright and can subtract reveals a belly
    like the serpent's with the same
vulnerable look. Jew, Gentile or pigmy,
    he must get his calories
before he can consider her profile or
    his own, attack you or play chess,
and take what there is however hard to get down:
    then surely those in whose creed
  God is edible may call a fine
    omelette a Christian deed.

    The sin of Gluttony
    is ranked among the Deadly
  Seven, but in murder mysteries
    one can be sure the gourmet
didn't do it: children, brave warriors out of a job,
    can weigh pounds more than they should
and one can dislike having to kiss them yet,
    compared with the thin-lipped, they
are seldom detestable. Some waiter grieves
    for the worst dead bore to be a good
trencherman, and no wonder chefs mature into
    choleric types, doomed to observe
Beauty peck at a master-dish, their one reward
    to behold the mutually hostile
  mouth and eyes of a sinner married
    at the first bite by a smile.

    The houses of our City
    are real enough but they lie
  haphazardly scattered over the earth,
    and her vagabond forum
is any space where two of us happen to meet
    who can spot a citizen
without papers. So, too, can her foes. Where the

power lies remains to be seen,
the force, though, is clearly with them: perhaps only
       by falling can She become
Her own vision, but we have sworn under four eyes
       to keep Her up—all we ask for,
should the night come when comets blaze and meres break,
       is a good dinner, that we
    may march in high fettle, left foot first,
       to hold her Thermopylae.

1958

IX. FOR FRIENDS ONLY
(for John and Teckla Clark)

Ours yet not ours, being set apart
As a shrine to friendship,
Empty and silent most of the year,
This room awaits from you
What you alone, as visitor, can bring,
A weekend of personal life.

In a house backed by orderly woods,
Facing a tractored sugar-beet country,
Your working hosts engaged to their stint,
You are unlike to encounter
Dragons or romance: were drama a craving,
You would not have come.

Books we do have for almost any
Literate mood, and notepaper, envelopes,
For a writing one (to 'borrow' stamps
Is a mark of ill-breeding):
Between lunch and tea, perhaps a drive;
After dinner, music or gossip.

Should you have troubles (pets will die,
Lovers are always behaving badly)
And confession helps, we will hear it,
Examine and give our counsel:
If to mention them hurts too much,
We shall not be nosey.

Easy at first, the language of friendship
Is, as we soon discover,
Very difficult to speak well, a tongue
With no cognates, no resemblance
To the galimatias of nursery and bedroom,
Court rhyme or shepherd's prose,

And, unless often spoken, soon goes rusty.
Distance and duties divide us,
But absence will not seem an evil
If it make our re-meeting
A real occasion. Come when you can:
Your room will be ready.

In Tum-Tum's reign a tin of biscuits
On the bedside table provided
For nocturnal munching. Now weapons have changed,
And the fashion in appetites:
There, for sunbathers who count their calories,
A bottle of mineral water.

Felicissima notte! May you fall at once
Into a cordial dream, assured
That whoever slept in this bed before
Was also someone we like,
That within the circle of our affection
Also you have no double.

June 1964

X. TONIGHT AT SEVEN-THIRTY
(*for M. F. K. Fisher*)

The life of plants
is one continuous solitary meal,
and ruminants
hardly interrupt theirs to sleep or to mate, but most
predators feel
ravenous most of the time and competitive
always, bolting such morsels as they can contrive
to snatch from the more terrified: pack-hunters do
dine *en famille*, it is true,
with protocol and placement, but none of them play host
to a stranger whom they help first. Only man,
supererogatory beast,
Dame Kind's thoroughbred lunatic, can
do the honors of a feast,

and was doing so
before the last Glaciation when he offered
mammoth-marrow
and, perhaps, Long Pig, will continue till Doomsday
when at God's board
the saints chew pickled Leviathan. In this age farms
are no longer crenellated, only cops port arms,
but the Law of the Hearth is unchanged: a brawler may not
be put to death on the spot,
but he is asked to quit the sacral dining area
instanter, and a foul-mouth gets the cold
shoulder. The right of a guest
to standing and foster is as old
as the ban on incest.

For authentic
comity the gathering should be small
and unpublic:
at mass banquets where flosculent speeches are made
in some hired hall
we think of ourselves or nothing. Christ's cenacle

seated a baker's dozen, King Arthur's rundle
the same, but today, when one's host may well be his own
    chef, servitor and scullion,
when the cost of space can double in a decade,
   even that holy Zodiac number is
    too large a frequency for us:
  in fact, six lenient semble sieges,
     none of them perilous,

     is now a Perfect
Social Number. But a dinner party,
    however select,
is a worldly rite that nicknames or endearments
    or family
diminutives would profane: two doters who wish
to tiddle and curmurr between the soup and fish
belong in restaurants, all children should be fed
    earlier and be safely in bed.
Well-liking, though, is a must: married maltalents
   engaged in some covert contrast can spoil
    an evening like the glance
  of a single failure in the toil
    of his bosom grievance.

    Not that a god,
  immune to grief, would be an ideal guest:
    he would be too odd
to talk to and, despite his imposing presence, a bore,
    for the funniest
mortals and the kindest are those who are most aware
of the baffle of being, don't kid themselves our care
is consolable, but believe a laugh is less
    heartless than tears, that a hostess
prefers it. Brains evolved after bowels, therefore,
   great assets as fine raiment and good looks
    can be on festive occasions,
  they are not essential like artful cooks
    and stalwart digestions.

    I see a table
at which the youngest and oldest present
    keep the eye grateful
for what Nature's bounty and grace of Spirit can create:
    for the ear's content
one raconteur, one gnostic with amazing shop,
both in a talkative mood but knowing when to stop,
and one wide-traveled worldling to interject now and then
    a sardonic comment, men
and women who enjoy the cloop of corks, appreciate
   dapatical fare, yet can see in swallowing
    a sign act of reverence,
  in speech a work of re-presenting
    the true olamic silence.

? 1963

XI. THE CAVE OF NAKEDNESS
(for Louis and Emmie Kronenberger)

Don Juan needs no bed, being far too impatient to undress,
nor do Tristan and Isolda, much too in love to care
    for so mundane a matter, but unmythical
mortals require one, and prefer to take their clothes off,
    if only to sleep. That is why bedroom farces
must be incredible to be funny, why Peeping Toms
    are never praised, like novelists or bird watchers,
for their keenness of observation: where there's a bed,
    be it a nun's restricted cot or an Emperor's
baldachined and nightly-redamselled couch, there are no
    effable data. (Dreams may be repeatable,
but our deeds of errantry in the wilderness of wish
    so often turn out, when told, to be less romantic
than our day's routine: besides, we cannot describe them
    without faking.) Lovers don't see their embraces
as a viable theme for debate, nor a monk his prayers
    (do they, in fact, remember them?): O's of passion,
interior acts of attention, not being a story
    in which the names don't matter but the way of telling,
with a lawyer's wit or a nobleman's assurance,
    does, need a drawing room of their own. Bed-sitting-rooms
soon drive us crazy, a dormitory even sooner
    turns us to brutes: bona fide architects know
that doors are not emphatic enough, and interpose,
    as a march between two realms, so alien, so disjunct,
the no-man's-land of a stair. The switch from personage,
    with a state number, a first and family name,
to the naked Adam or Eve, and vice versa,
    should not be off-hand or abrupt: a stair retards it
to a solemn procession.
                    Since my infantile entrance
    at my mother's bidding into Edwardian England,
I have suffered the transit over forty thousand times,
    usually, to my chagrin, by myself: about
blended flesh, those midnight colloquia of Derbies and Joans,
    I know nothing therefore, about certain occult
antipathies perhaps too much. Some perks belong, though
    to all unwilling celibates: our rooms are seldom
battlefields, we enjoy the pleasure of reading in bed
    (as we grow older, it's true, we may find it prudent
to get nodding drunk first), we retain the right to choose
    our sacred image. (That I often start with sundry
splendors at sundry times greened after, but always end
    aware of one, the same one, may be of no importance,
but I hope it is.) Ordinary human unhappiness
    is life in its natural color, to cavil
putting on airs: at day-wester to think of nothing
    benign to memorize is as rare as feeling
no personal blemish, and Age, despite its damage,
    is well-off. When they look in their bedroom mirrors,
Fifty-plus may be bored, but Seventeen is faced by

a frowning failure, with no money, no mistress,
no manner of his own, who never got to Italy
    nor met a great one: to say a few words at banquets,
to attend a cocktail party in honor of N or M,
    can be severe, but Junior has daily to cope
with ghastly family meals, with dear Papa and Mama
    being odd in the wrong way. (It annoys him to speak,
and it hurts him not to.)
                        When I disband from the world,
    and entrust my future to the Gospel Makers,
I need not fear (not in neutral Austria) being called for
    in the waist of the night by deaf agents, never
to be heard of on earth again: the assaults I would be spared
    are none of them princely—fire, nightmare, insomnia's
Vision of Hell, when Nature's wholesome genial fabric
    lies utterly discussed and from a sullen vague
wafts a contagious stench, her adamant minerals
    all corrupt, each life a worthless iteration
of the general loathing (to know that, probably,
    its cause is chemical can degrade the panic,
not stint it). As a rule, with pills to help them, the Holy Four
    exempt my nights from nuisance, and even wake me
when I would be woken, when, audible here and there
    in the half-dark, members of an avian orchestra
are already softly noodling, limbering up for
    an overture at sunrise, their effort to express
in the old convention they inherit that joy in beginning
    for which our species was created, and declare it
good.
        We may not be obliged—though it is mannerly—to bless
    the Trinity that we are corporal contraptions,
but only a villain will omit to thank Our Lady or
    her henwife, Dame Kind, as he, she, or both ensemble,
emerge from a private cavity to be reborn,
    reneighbored in the Country of Consideration.

                                                June 1963

Only look in the glass to detect a removable blemish:
As for the permanent ones, already you know quite enough.

                    *   *   *

        Our bodies cannot love:
        But, without one,
        What works of Love could we do?

                    *   *   *

        Money cannot buy
        The fuel of Love:
        But is excellent kindling.

                    *   *   *

Nightmare of the base,
Silence to lovers
Is the welcome third party.

* * *

No winter in Dreamland:
Thermometers there
Stand always at blood-heat.

* * *

Since he weighs nothing,
Even the stoutest dreamer
Can fly without wings.

* * *

To dreamers who never
Travel by rail, I must be
An old fogey.

XII. THE COMMON LIFE
(for Chester Kallman)

A living room, the catholic area you
    (Thou, rather) and I may enter
without knocking, leave without a bow, confronts
    each visitor with a style,

a secular faith: he compares its dogmas
    with his, and decides whether
he would like to see more of us. (Spotless rooms
    where nothing's left lying about

chill me, so do cups used for ashtrays or smeared
    with lipstick: the homes I warm to,
though seldom wealthy, always convey a feeling
    of bills being promptly settled

with checks that don't bounce.) There's no *We* at an instant,
    only *Thou* and *I*, two regions
of protestant being which nowhere overlap:
    a room is too small, therefore,

if its occupants cannot forget at will
    that they are not alone, too big
if it gives them any excuse in a quarrel
    for raising their voices. What,

quizzing ours, would Sherlock Holmes infer? Plainly,
    ours is a sitting culture
in a generation which prefers comfort
    (or is forced to prefer it)

537

to command, would rather incline its buttocks
    on a well-upholstered chair
than the burly back of a slave: a quick glance
    at book titles would tell him

that we belong to the clerisy and spend much
    on our food. But could he read
what our prayers and jokes are about, what creatures
    frighten us most, or what names

head our roll call of persons we would least like
    to go to bed with? What draws
singular lives together in the first place,
    loneliness, lust, ambition,

or mere convenience, is obvious, why they drop
    or murder one another
clear enough: how they create, though, a common world
    between them, like Bombelli's

impossible yet useful numbers, no one
    has yet explained. Still, they do
manage to forgive impossible behavior,
    to endure by some miracle

conversational tics and larval habits
    without wincing (were you to die,
I should miss yours). It's a wonder that neither
    has been butchered by accident,

or, as lots have, silently vanished into
    History's criminal noise
unmourned for, but that, after twenty-four years,
    we should sit here in Austria

as cater-cousins, under the glassy look
    of a Naples Bambino,
the portrayed regards of Strauss and Stravinsky,
    doing British crossword puzzles,

is very odd indeed. I'm glad the builder gave
    our common-room small windows
through which no observed outsider can observe us:
    every home should be a fortress,

equipped with all the very latest engines
    for keeping Nature at bay,
versed in all ancient magic, the arts of quelling
    the Dark Lord and his hungry

animivorous chimeras. (Any brute
    can buy a machine in a shop,
but the sacred spells are secret to the kind,
    and if power is what we wish

they won't work.) *The ogre will come in any case:*
    so Joyce has warned us. Howbeit,
fasting or feasting, we both know this: without
    the Spirit we die, but life

without the Letter is in the worst of taste,
    and always, though truth and love
can never really differ, when they seem to,
    the subaltern should be truth.

? July 1963

Shorts I

Between those happenings that prefigure it
And those that happen in its anamnesis
Occurs the Event, but that no human wit
Can recognize until all happening ceases.

? 1959

*   *   *

PARABLE

The watch upon my wrist
Would soon forget that I exist,
If it were not reminded
By days when I forget to wind it.

*   *   *

We've covered ground since that awkward day
When, thoughtlessly, a human mind
Decided to leave the apes behind,
Come pretty far, but who dare say
If far be forward or astray,
Or what we still might do in the way
Of patient building, impatient crime,
Given the sunlight, salt and time.

? 1964

*   *   *

ECONOMICS

In the Hungry Thirties
boys used to sell their bodies
for a square meal.

In the Affluent Sixties
they still did:
to meet Hire-Purchase Payments.

February 1965

*   *   *

At Twenty we find our friends for ourselves, but it takes Heaven
To find us one when we are Fifty-Seven.

*   *   *

Each year brings new problems of Form and Content,
new foes to tug with: at Twenty I tried to
vex my elders, past Sixty it's the young whom
   I hope to bother.

May 1969

*   *   *

LOST

Lost on a fogbound spit of sand
In shoes that pinched me, close at hand
I heard the plash of Charon's oar,
Who ferries no one to a happy shore.

? 1963

*   *   *

TO GOETHE: A COMPLAINT

How wonderfully your songs begin
With praise of Nature and her beauty,
But then, as if it were a duty,
You drag some god-damned sweetheart in.
Did you imagine she'd be flattered?
They never sound as if they mattered.

May 1969

*   *   *

CONTRA BLAKE

The Road of Excess
leads, more often than not, to
The Slough of Despond.

*   *   *

METAPHOR

Nose, I am free
To turn up or thumb
At my neighbor, stick into
His business, it's You
Also, through Whom
For my liberties he
With like insolence may
Make me pay.

*   *   *

540

A moon profaned by
Sectarian din, death by
Fervent implosion:—
Possibles. But here and now
Our oath to the living word.

1964

Two *Don Quixote* Lyrics

I. THE GOLDEN AGE

The poets tell us of an age of unalloyed felicity,
The Age of Gold, an age of love, of plenty and simplicity,
When summer lasted all the year and a perpetual greenery
Of lawns and woods and orchards made an eye-delighting scenery.

There was no pain or sickness then, no famine or calamity,
And men and beasts were not afraid but lived in perfect amity,
And every evening when the rooks were cawing from their rookery,
From every chimney rose the smell of some delicious cookery.

Then flowers bloomed and fruits grew ripe with effortless fertility,
And nymphs and shepherds danced all day in circles with agility;
Then every shepherd to his dear was ever true and amorous,
And nymphs of seventy and more were lovely still and glamorous.

O but alas!
Then it came to pass
The Enchanters came
Cold and old,
Making day gray
And the age of gold
Passed away,
For men fell
Under their spell,
Were doomed to gloom.
Joy fled,
There came instead
Grief, unbelief,
Lies, sighs,
Lust, mistrust,
Guile, bile,
Hearts grew unkind,
Minds blind,
Glum and numb,
Without hope or scope.
There was hate between states,
A life of strife,
Gaols and wails,
Donts, wonts,
Cants, shants,
No face with grace,
None glad, all sad.

541

It shall not be! Enchanters, flee! I challenge you to battle me!
Your powers I with scorn defy, your spells shall never rattle me.
Don Quixote de la Mancha is coming to attend to you,
To smash you into smithereens and put a final end to you.

II. RECITATIVE BY DEATH

Ladies and gentlemen, you have made most remarkable
   Progress, and progress, I agree, is a boon;
You have built more automobiles than are parkable,
   Crashed the sound-barrier, and may very soon
   Be setting up juke-boxes on the Moon:
But I beg to remind you that, despite all that,
I, Death, still am and will always be Cosmocrat.

Still I sport with the young and daring; at my whim,
   The climber steps upon the rotten boulder,
The undertow catches boys as they swim,
   The speeder steers onto the slippery shoulder:
   With others I wait until they are older
Before assigning, according to my humor,
To one a coronary, to one a tumor.

Liberal my views upon religion and race;
   Tax-posture, credit-rating, social ambition
Cut no ice with me. We shall meet face to face,
   Despite the drugs and lies of your physician,
   The costly euphemisms of the mortician:
Westchester matron and Bowery bum,
Both shall dance with me when I rattle my drum.

? 1964

A Change of Air

Corns, heartburn, sinus headaches, such minor ailments
Tell of estrangement between your name and you,
Advise a change of air: heed them, but let
The modesty of their discomfort warn you
Against the flashy errands of your dreams.

To grow a sailor's beard, don monkish garb,
Or trade in an agglutinative tongue
With a stone-age culture, would be mollycoddling:
To go Elsewhere is to withdraw from movement,
A side step, a short one, will convey you thither.

Although its chaffinches, maybe, have learned
The dialect of another river basin,
A fault transformed the local building stone,
It has a priest, a postmistress, an usher,
Its children know they are not to beg from strangers.

542

Within its average elsewhereishness
Your name is as a mirror answers, yourself
How you behave in shops, the tips you give:
It sides with neither, being outside both,
But welcomes both with healing disregard.

Nor, when you both return here (for you will)
Where luck and instinct originally brought you,
Will it salute your reconciliation
With farewell rites, or populate your absence
With reverent and irreverent anecdote.

No study of your public reappearance
Will show, as judgment on a cure demands,
A sudden change in love, ideas, or diet:
Your sojourn Elsewhere will remain a wordless
Hiatus in your voluble biography.

Fanatic scholarship at most may prove
That you resigned from some Committee, unearth
A letter from the Grand Duke to his cousin,
Remarking, among more important gossip,
That you seem less amusing than you were.

September 1961

You

Really, must you,
Over-familiar
Dense companion,
Be there always?
The bond between us
Is chimerical surely:
Yet I cannot break it.

Must I, born for
Sacred play,
Turn base mechanic
So you may worship
Your secular bread,
With no thought
Of the value of time?

Thus far I have known your
Character only
From its pleasanter side,
But you know I know
A day will come
When you grow savage
And hurt me badly.

543

Totally stupid?
Would that you were:
But, no, you plague me
With tastes I was fool enough
Once to believe in.
Bah!, blockhead:
I know where you learned them.

Can I trust you even
On creaturely fact?
I suspect strongly
You hold some dogma
Of positive truth,
And feed me fictions:
I shall never prove it.

Oh, I know how you came by
A sinner's cranium,
How between two glaciers
The master-chronometer
Of an innocent primate
Altered its tempi:
That explains nothing.

Who tinkered and why?
Why am I certain,
Whatever your faults are,
The fault is mine,
Why is loneliness not
A chemical discomfort,
Nor Being a smell?

September 1960

Et in Arcadia Ego

Who, now, seeing Her so
Happily married,
Housewife, helpmate to Man,

Can imagine the screeching
Virago, the Amazon,
Earth Mother was?

Her jungle growths
Are abated, Her exorbitant
Monsters abashed,

Her soil mumbled,
Where crops, aligned precisely,
Will soon be orient:

Levant or couchant,
Well-daunted thoroughbreds
Graze on mead and pasture,

A church clock subdivides the day,
Up the lane at sundown
Geese podge home.

As for Him:
What has happened to the Brute
Epics and nightmares tell of?

No bishops pursue
Their archdeacons with axes,
In the crumbling lair

Of a robber baron
Sightseers picnic
Who carry no daggers.

I well might think myself
A humanist,
Could I manage not to see

How the autobahn
Thwarts the landscape
In godless Roman arrogance,

The farmer's children
Tiptoe past the shed
Where the gelding knife is kept.

? 1964

Hammerfest

For over forty years I'd paid it atlas homage,
  The northernmost township on earth, producing
The best deep-frozen fish sticks you can buy: for three days,
  I pottered round, a monolingual pilgrim,
And drank the beer of the world's most northern brewery.
  Though miles beyond the Moral Circle, I saw
No orgies, no great worms, nor dreamed of any during
  Three sunny nights: louts, though—German this time—
Had left their usual mark. How much reverence could I,
  Can anyone past fifty, afford to lose?

Was it as worldly as it looked? I might have thought so
  But for my ears: something odd was happening
Soundwise. A word, a laugh, a footstep, a truck's outcry,
  Each utterance rang singular, staccato,

N.B. *The Moral Circle:* a jocular term, used by southern Norwegians, for the Arctic
Circle. *German this time:* in 1945 the retreating *Wehrmacht* burnt down every single
house.

545

To be cut off before it could be contradicted
   Or confused by others: a listening terrain
Seized on them all and never gave one back in echo,
   As if to land as desolate, as far up,
Whatever noise our species cared to make still mattered.
   Here was a place we had yet to disappoint.

The only communities it had to judge us by
   Were cenobite, mosses and lichen, sworn to
Station and reticence: its rocks knew almost nothing,
   Nothing about the glum Reptilian Empire
Or the epic journey of the Horse, had heard no tales
   Of that preglacial Actium when the huge
Archaic shrubs went down before the scented flowers,
   And earth was won for color. For all it knew,
Religion had begun with the Salvation Army,
   Warfare with motorized resentful conscripts.

Ground so bare might take a century to realize
   How we behave to regions or to beings
Who have anything we're after: to have disgusted
   Millions of acres of good-natured topsoil
Is an achievement of a sort, to fail to notice
   How garden plants and farmyard beasts look at us,
Or refuse to look, to picture all of them as dear
   Faithful old retainers, another, but why
Bring that up now? My intrusion had not profaned it:
   If innocence is holy, it was holy.

May 1961

Iceland Revisited
(for Basil and Susan Boothby)

Unwashed, unshat,
He was whisked from the plane
To a lunch in his honor.

*   *   *

He hears a loudspeaker
Call him well-known:
But knows himself no better.

*   *   *

Twenty-eight years ago
Three slept well here.
Now one is married, one dead,

Where the harmonium stood
A radio:—
Have the Fittest survived?

*   *   *

Unable to speak Icelandic,
He helped instead
To do the dishes.

*   *   *

The bondi's sheep dog
And the visitor from New York
Conversed freely.

*   *   *

Snow had camouflaged
The pool of liquid manure:
The town mouse fell in.

*   *   *

The desolate fjord
Denied the possibility
Of many gods.

*   *   *

A blizzard. A bare room.
Thoughts of the past.
He forgot to wind his watch.

*   *   *

The gale howled over lava. Suddenly
In the storm's eye
A dark speck,

Perseus in an air-taxi,
Come to snatch
Shivering Andromeda

Out of the wilderness
And bring her back
To hot baths, cocktails, habits.

*   *   *

Once more
A child's dream verified
The magical light beyond Hekla.

*   *   *

Fortunate island,
Where all men are equal
But not vulgar—not yet.

April 1964

On the Circuit

Among pelagian travelers,
Lost on their lewd conceited way
To Massachusetts, Michigan,
Miami or L.A.,

An airborne instrument I sit,
Predestined nightly to fulfill
Columbia-Giesen-Management's
Unfathomable will,

By whose election justified,
I bring my gospel of the Muse
To fundamentalists, to nuns,
To Gentiles and to Jews,

And daily, seven days a week,
Before a local sense has jelled,
From talking-site to talking-site
Am jet-or-prop-propelled.

Though warm my welcome everywhere,
I shift so frequently, so fast,
I cannot now say where I was
The evening before last,

Unless some singular event
Should intervene to save the place,
A truly asinine remark,
A soul-bewitching face,

Or blessed encounter, full of joy,
Unscheduled on the Giesen Plan,
With, here, an addict of Tolkien,
There, a Charles Williams fan.

Since Merit but a dunghill is,
I mount the rostrum unafraid:
Indeed, 'twere damnable to ask
If I am overpaid.

Spirit is willing to repeat
Without a qualm the same old talk,
But Flesh is homesick for our snug
Apartment in New York.

A sulky fifty-six, he finds
A change of mealtime utter hell,
Grown far too crotchety to like
A luxury hotel.

The Bible is a goodly book
I always can peruse with zest,
But really cannot say the same
For Hilton's *Be My Guest*,

Nor bear with equanimity
The radio in students' cars,
Muzak at breakfast, or—dear God!—
Girl-organists in bars.

Then, worst of all, the anxious thought,
Each time my plane begins to sink
And the No Smoking sign comes on:
What will there be to drink?

Is this a milieu where I must
How grahamgreeneish! How infra dig!
Snatch from the bottle in my bag
An analeptic swig?

Another morning comes: I see,
Dwindling below me on the plane,
The roofs of one more audience
I shall not see again.

God bless the lot of them, although
I don't remember which was which:
God bless the U.S.A., so large,
So friendly, and so rich.

? June 1963

Symmetries & Asymmetries

Deep in earth's opaque mirror,
The old oak's roots
Reflected its branches:

Astrologers in reverse,
Keen-eyed miners
Conned their scintillant gems.

* * *

The underground roads
Are, as the dead prefer them,
Always tortuous.

* * *

When he looked the cave in the eye,
Hercules
Had a moment of doubt.

* * *

549

Fords may have demons,
But no spring is watched by
A malevolent nymph.

*   *   *

The brook's impromptu babble
Suggested to Orpheus
A cunning song.

*   *   *

The water of the sleeping lake
Dreamed kindly
Of earth and fire and air.

*   *   *

The flowers danced for the wind
Gladly, knowing
That was all he needed.

*   *   *

Metal, extorted from stone
In a paroxysm of fire,
Was beaten,

Then ducked in water:
Outrage sealed into the sword
Fury for battle.

*   *   *

Old Brandy in the heated spoon
Looked dignified at first, but soon
Went off his head and, lost to shame,
Lay wallowing in a fit of flame.

*   *   *

After Krakatoa exploded, the first living thing to return
Was the ant, Tridomyrex, seeking in vain its symbiot fern.

*   *   *

To grow:—like the vine
That instinctively rations
Its water intake.

*   *   *

Leaning out over
The dreadful precipice,
One contemptuous tree.

*   *   *

Shod and saddled,
The horses of the Tartars
Could out-gallop the drought.

*   *   *

Like spoiled rich women,
The swallows follow
Their congenial isotherm.

*   *   *

When we fondle one,
Our other cats are jealous:
But they don't envy

Nor admire either,
Ignorant of why
Another can be more loved.

*   *   *

Could any tiger
Drink martinis, smoke cigars,
And last as we do?

*   *   *

Chirm and skimmer of insects
In the coy noon heat:
He smiled at himself.

*   *   *

Self and Shadow:
By day a comic pair,
At moonprime one and somber.

*   *   *

Flattered by Pleasure, accused by Pain,
Which of the two
Should he believe?

*   *   *

To himself the Brute Fact:
To others (sometimes)
A useful metaphor.

* * *

Because the level table
Made him think of steppes,
He knew it was there.

* * *

Like the redstart,
He recalls but a formless fragment
Of his real tune.

* * *

A signpost points him out his road:
But names no place,
Numbers no distance.

* * *

Not daring to saunter,
He made forced marches,
Uphill, against the wind.

* * *

Hunting for some lost object
He was meant to forget,
He lost himself.

* * *

Making it easy to boil,
The tinker's art
Ruined the tribe's cuisine.

* * *

The yoke permitted
Gentle dray horses to build
Coercive castles.

* * *

At chess, before gunpowder,
The Queen took only
Diagonal steps.

* * *

From the Eastern Campaign
They returned with forks
And a more flamboyant rite.

*   *   *

The iconoclast's home
Was hung with many
Pornographic pictures.

*   *   *

Mental parasites,
They took up
A universal vague religion.

*   *   *

How image today
The Knight's lonely Quest? On all roads
Laute Leute.

*   *   *

Honest democrats,
They would die rather
Than touch their caps to a lord:

But they know better
Than to get fresh
With Customs & Immigration.

*   *   *

Their lives were boring and undignified:
They worked a little, they consumed, they died.

*   *   *

Life wrong already:
Each life an amateur sleuth,
Asking *Who did it?*

*   *   *

Behind the perversions
Not lust for pleasure,
But a cry for justice.

*   *   *

Finding Echo repellent,
Narcissus ate his snot,
Pee'd in his bath.

*   *   *

Their daydreams were the same:
A blood brother, a comrade-in-arms,
Plus sex.

So were their natures:
Both wish to play *Officer*,
Neither *Other Ranks*.

*   *   *

Loneliness waited
For Reality
To come through the glory hole.

*   *   *

Cigars. Scotch.
They recalled (inexactly)
How many, how big, how much.

*   *   *

Pride has always despised Pleasure,
Left gluttony, lust,
To underdogs:

Sought Joy and found it,
Taking life, destroying things,
Moving at high speed.

*   *   *

The God of Love
Will never withdraw our right
To grief and infamy.   *? 1963–1964*

The Maker

Unmarried, nearsighted, rather deaf,
This anonymous dwarf,
Legendary ancestor
Of Gunsmiths to His Majesty
And other bespoke houses:—
Every museum visitor knows him.

554

Excluded by his cave
From weather and events, he measures
Days by the job done, and at night
Dreams of the Perfect Object, war to him
A scarcity of bronze, the fall of princes
A change of customer.

Not a musician: songs
Encourage laboring demes, amuse the idle,
But would distract a self-appointed worker
From listening to his hammer's dactyl.
And not an orator: sophists
Don't do metallurgy.

His prices are high and, if he doesn't like you,
He won't oblige: once more the Quality
Are made to learn that charm is useless,
A threat fatal. He will deliver
In his good time, not yours: he has no rival,
And he knows you know it.

His love, embodied in each useful wonder,
Can't save them in our world from insult,
But may avenge it: beware, then, maladroit,
Thumb-sucking children of all ages,
Lest on your mangled bodies the court verdict
Be Death by Misadventure.

? 1961

At the Party

Unrhymed, unrhythmical, the chatter goes:
Yet no one hears his own remarks as prose.

Beneath each topic tunelessly discussed
The ground-bass is reciprocal mistrust.

The names in fashion shuttling to and fro
Yield, when deciphered, messages of woe.

You cannot read me like an open book.

I'm more myself than you will ever look.

Will no one listen to my little song?

Perhaps I shan't be with you very long.

A howl for recognition, shrill with fear,
Shakes the jam-packed apartment, but each ear
Is listening to its hearing, so none hear.

? 1962

Bestiaries Are Out

A sweet tooth taught us to admire
The bees before we'd made a fire:
Nemorivagrant tribes at least
Could serve wild honey at a feast.

Accustomed in hard times to clem,
We started soon to envy them
An industry that stocks their shelves
With more food than they need themselves.

By Estimation, too, inclined
Towards a social stead of kind,
We sought from study of their hives
To draw some moral for our lives,

And when conspiracy, revolt,
Gave Princes of this world a jolt,
Philosopher and Christian Preacher
Upheld the Bee as Civics Teacher.

Now bestiaries are out, for now
Research has demonstrated how
They actually behave, they strike us
As being horridly unlike us:

Though some believe (some even plan
To do it) that from Urban Man,
By Advertising plus the aid
Of drugs, an insect might be made.

No. Who can learn to love his neighbor
From neuters whose one love is labor,
To rid his Government of knaves
From commonwealths controlled by slaves?

How, for us children of the word,
Anthropomorphic and absurd
To ask what code they satisfy
When they swoop out to sting and die,

Or what catharsis undergo
When they put on their biggest show,
A duel to the death between
A tooting and a quacking Queen.

? July 1964

After Reading a Child's Guide to Modern Physics

If all a top physicist knows
About the Truth be true,
Then, for all the so-and-so's,
Futility and grime,
Our common world contains,
We have a better time
Than the Greater Nebulae do,
Or the atoms in our brains.

Marriage is rarely bliss
But, surely it would be worse
As particles to pelt
At thousands of miles per sec
About a universe
In which a lover's kiss
Would either not be felt
Or break the loved one's neck.

Though the face at which I stare
While shaving it be cruel
For, year after year, it repels
An ageing suitor, it has,
Thank God, sufficient mass
To be altogether there,
Not an indeterminate gruel
Which is partly somewhere else.

Our eyes prefer to suppose
That a habitable place
Has a geocentric view,
That architects enclose
A quiet Euclidean space:
Exploded myths—but who
Would feel at home astraddle
An ever expanding saddle?

This passion of our kind
For the process of finding out
Is a fact one can hardly doubt,
But I would rejoice in it more
If I knew more clearly what
We wanted the knowledge for,
Felt certain still that the mind
Is free to know or not.

It has chosen once, it seems,
And whether our concern
For magnitude's extremes
Really become a creature
Who comes in a median size,
Or politicizing Nature
Be altogether wise,
Is something we shall learn.

1961

Ascension Day, 1964

From leaf to leaf in silence
The year's new green
Is passed along northward:

A bit, though, behind schedule,
For the chestnut chandeliers
Are still dim.

But today's atmosphere
Is encouraging,
And the orchard peoples,

Naïve in white
Or truculent in pink,
Aspect an indulgent blue.

Pleased with his one good remark,
A cuckoo repeats it,
Well-satisfied,

Some occasional heavy feeder
Obliges
With a florid song.

Lives content
With their ecological niche
And relevant objects,

Unable to tell
A hush before storms
From one after massacres,

As warriors, as lovers,
Without mixed feelings:
What is our feast to them?

This Thursday when we must
Go through the ritual
Formulae of farewell,

The words, the looks,
The embraces, knowing
That this time they are final.

Will as we may to believe
That parting should be
And that a promise

Of future joy can be kept,
Absence remains
The factual loss it is:

Here on out as permanent,
Obvious to all,
As the presence in each

Of a glum Kundry,
Impelled to giggle
At any crucifixion.

May 1964

Whitsunday in Kirchstetten
(for H. A. Reinhold)

Grace dances. I would pipe. Dance ye all.
ACTS OF JOHN

Komm Schöpfer Geist I bellow as Herr Beer
picks up our slim offerings and Pfarrer Lustkandl
    quietly gets on with the Sacrifice
as Rome does it: outside car-worshippers enact
    the ritual exodus from Vienna
their successful cult demands (though reckoning time
    by the Jewish week and the Christian year
like their pedestrian fathers). When Mass is over,
    although obedient to Canterbury,
I shall be well gruss-gotted, asked to contribute
    to *Caritas*, though a metic come home
to lunch on my own land: no doubt, if the Allies had not
    conquered the Ost-Mark, if the dollar fell,
the *Gemütlichkeit* would be less, but when was peace
    or its concomitant smile the worse
for being undeserved?
                        In the onion-tower overhead
    bells clash at the Elevation, calling
on Austria to change: whether the world has improved
    is doubtful, but we believe it could
and the divine Tiberius didn't. Rejoice, the bells
    cry to me. Blake's Old Nobodaddy
in his astronomic telescopic heaven,
    the Big White Christian upstairs, is dead,
and won't come hazing us no more, nor bless our bombs:
    no more need sons of the menalty,
divining their future from plum stones, count aloud

559

Army, Navy, Law, Church, nor a Prince
say who is *papabile.* (The Ape of the Living God
   knows how to stage a funeral, though,
as penitents like it: Babel, like Sodom, still
   has plenty to offer, though of course it draws
a better sort of crowd.) Rejoice: we who were born
   congenitally deaf are able
to listen now to rank outsiders. The Holy Ghost
   does not abhor a golfer's jargon,
a Lower-Austrian accent, the cadences even
   of my own little Anglo-American
musico-literary set (though difficult,
   saints at least may think in algebra
without sin): but no sacred nonsense can stand Him.
   Our magic syllables melt away,
our tribal formulae are laid bare: since this morning,
   it is with a vocabulary
made wholesomely profane, open in lexicons
   to our foes to translate, that we endeavor
each in his idiom to express the true *magnalia*
   which need no hallowing from us, loaning terms,
exchanging graves and legends. (Maybe, when just now
   Kirchstetten prayed for the dead, only I
remembered Franz Joseph the Unfortunate, who danced
   once in eighty-six years and never
used the telephone.)
                 An altar bell makes a noise
   as the Body of the Second Adam
is shown to some of his torturers, forcing them
   to visualize absent enemies
with the same right to grow hybrid corn and be wicked
   as an Abendlander. As crows fly,
ninety kilometers from here our habits end,
   where minefield and watchtower say NO EXIT
from peace-loving Crimtartary, except for crows
   and agents of peace: from Loipersbach
to the Bering Sea not a living stockbroker,
   and church attendance is frowned upon
like visiting brothels (but the chess and physics
   are still the same). We shall bury you
and dance at the wake, say her chiefs: that, says Reason
   is unlikely. But to most people
I'm the wrong color: it could be the looter's turn
   for latrine duty and the flogging block,
my kin who trousered Africa, carried our smell
   to germless poles.
                 Down a Gothic nave
comes our Pfarrer now, blessing the West with water:
   we may go. There is no Queen's English
in any context for *Geist* or *Esprit:* about
   catastrophe or how to behave in one
what do I know, except what everyone knows—
   if there when Grace dances, I should dance.

                                   July 1962

Three Posthumous Poems

I. GLAD

Hugerl, for a decade now
My bed-visitor,
An unexpected blessing
In a lucky life,
For how much and how often
You have made me glad.

Glad that I know we enjoy
Mutual pleasure:
Women may cog their lovers
With a feigned passion,
But males are so constructed
We cannot deceive.

Glad our worlds of enchantment
Are so several
Neither is tempted to broach:
I cannot tell a
Jaguar from a Bentley,
And you never read.

Glad for that while when you stole
(You burgled me too),
And were caught and put inside:
Both learned a lesson,
But for which we well might still
Be *Strich* and *Freier*.

Glad, though, we began that way,
That our life-paths crossed,
Like characters in Hardy,
At a moment when
You were in need of money
And I wanted sex.

How is it now between us?
Love? Love is far too
Tattered a word. A romance
In full fig it ain't,
Nor a naked letch either:
Let me say we fadge,

And how much I like Christa
Who loves you but knows,
Good girl, when not to be there.
I can't imagine
A kinder set-up: if mims
Mump, *es ist mir Wurscht*.

March 1965

II. AUBADE

At break of dawn
he takes a street-car, happy
after a night of love.

Happy,
but sleepily wondering
how many away is the night

when an ecto-endomorph
cock-sucker must put on
The Widow's Cap.

July 1964

III. MINNELIED

When one is lonely (and You,
My Dearest, know why,
as I know why it must be),
steps can be taken, even
a call-boy can help.

To-night, for instance, now that
Bert has been here, I
listen to the piercing screams
of palliardising cats
without self-pity.

? 1967

City Without Walls

...'Those fantastic forms, fang-sharp,
bone-bare, that in Byzantine painting
were a shorthand for the Unbounded
beyond the Pale, unpolicied spaces
where dragons dwelt and demons roamed,

'colonized only by ex-worldlings,
penitent sophists and sodomites,
are visual facts in the foreground now,
real structures of steel and glass:
hermits, perforce, are all to-day,

'with numbered caves in enormous jails,
hotels designed to deteriorate
their glum already-corrupted guests,
factories in which the functional
Hobbesian Man is mass-produced.

562

'A key to the street each convict has,
but the Asphalt Lands are lawless marches
where gangs clash and cops turn
robber-barons: reckless he
who walks after dark in that wilderness.

'But electric lamps allow nightly
cell-meetings where sub-cultures
may hold palaver, like-minded,
their tongues tattooed by the tribal jargon
of the vice or business that brothers them;

'and mean cafés to remain open,
where in bad air belly-talkers,
weedy-looking, work-shy,
may spout unreason, some ruthless creed
to a dozen dupes till dawn break.

'Every work-day Eve fares
forth to the stores her foods to pluck,
while Adam hunts an easy dollar:
unperspiring at eventide
both eat their bread in boredom of spirit.

'The week-end comes that once was holy,
free still, but a feast no longer,
just time out, idiorhythmic,
when no one cares what his neighbor does:
now newsprint and network are needed most.

'What they view may be vulgar rubbish,
what they listen to witless noise,
but it gives shelter, shields them from
Sunday's Bane, the basilisking
glare of Nothing, our pernicious foe.

'For what to Nothing shall nobodies answer?
Still super-physiques are socially there,
frequently photographed, feel at home,
but ordinary flesh is unwanted:
engines do better what biceps did.

'Quite soon computers may expel from the world
all but the top intelligent few,
the egos they leisure be left to dig
value and virtue from an invisible realm
of hobbies, sex, consumption, vague

'tussles with ghosts. Against Whom
shall the Sons band to rebel there,
where Troll-Father, Tusked-Mother,
are dream-monsters like dinosaurs
with a built-in obsolescence?

'A Gadgeted Age, but as unworldly
as when the faint light filtered down
on the first men in Mirkwood,
waiting their turn at the water-hole
with the magic beasts who made the paths.

'Small marvel, then, if many adopt
cancer as the only offered career
worth while, if wards are full of
gents who believe they are Jesus Christ
or guilty of the Unforgiveable Sin:

'if arcadian lawns where classic shoulders,
baroque bottoms, make *beaux gestes*,
is too tame a dream for the dislocated,
if their lewd fancies are of flesh debased
by damage, indignities, dirty words:

'if few now applaud a play that ends
with warmth and pardon the word to all,
as, blessed, unbamboozled, the bridal pairs,
rustic and oppidan, in a ring-dance,
image the stars at their stately bransles:

'if all has gone phut in the future we paint,
where, vast and vacant, venomous areas
surround the small sporadic patches
of fen or forest that give food and shelter,
such home as they have, to a human remnant,

'stunted in stature, strangely deformed,
numbering by fives, with no zero,
worshipping a ju-ju *General Mo*,
in groups ruled by grandmothers,
hirsute witches who on winter nights

'fable them stories of fair-haired Elves
whose magic made the mountain dam,
of Dwarves, cunning in craft, who smithied
the treasure-hoards of tin-cans
they flatten out for their hut roofs,

'nor choice they have nor change know,
their fate ordained by fore-elders,
the Oldest Ones, the wise spirits
who through the mouths of masked wizards
blessing give or blood demand.

'Still monied, immune, stands Megalopolis:
happy he who hopes for better,
what awaits Her may well be worse. . . .'

Thus I was thinking at three A.M.
in Mid-Manhattan till interrupted,
cut short by a sharp voice.

'What fun and games you find it to play
Jeremiah-cum-Juvenal:
Shame on you for your *Schadenfreude*.'

'My!', I blustered, 'How moral we're getting.
A pococurante? Suppose I were,
so what, if my words are true.'

Thereupon, bored, a third voice:
'Go to sleep now for God's sake!
You both will feel better by breakfast-time.'

1967

Eleven Occasional Poems

I. A TOAST
(Christ Church Gaudy, 1960)

What on earth does one say at a Gaudy,
   On such an occasion as this,
O what, since I may not be bawdy,
   Can I do except reminisce?
Middle-age with its glasses and dentures
   (There's an opera about it by Strauss)
Puts an end to romantic adventures,
   But not to my love of *The House*.

Ah! those Twenties before I was twenty,
   When the news never gave one the glooms,
When the chef had minions in plenty,
   And we could have lunch in our rooms.
In *Peck* there were marvelous parties
   With bubbly and brandy and grouse,
And the aesthetes fought with the hearties:
   It was fun, then, to be at *The House*.

National Service had not been suggested,
   O-Level and A were called Certs,
Our waistcoats were cut double-breasted,
   Our flannel trousers like skirts.
One could meet any day in Society
   Harold Acton, Tom Driberg or *Rowse*:
May there always, to lend their variety,
   Be some rather odd fish at *The House*.

The *Clarendon*'s gone—I regret her—
   The *George* is closed and forgot;
Some changes are all for the better,
   But *Woolworth*'s is probably not.
May the *Meadows* be only frequented
   By scholars and couples and cows:
God save us from all these demented
   Plans for a road through *The House*.

All those who wish well to our College
Will wish her *Treasurer* well;
May Mammon give him foreknowledge
Of just what to buy and to sell,
That all his investments on which her
Income depends may be wows:
May She ever grow richer and richer,
And the gravy abound at *The House.*

God bless and keep out of quarrels
The *Dean*, the *Chapter* and *D*,
The *Censors* who shepherd our morals,
Roy, Hooky, Little and me.
May those who come up next October
Be *anständig*, have *esprit* and *nous*:
And now, though not overly sober,
I give you a toast— TO THE HOUSE!

II. A SHORT ODE TO A PHILOLOGIST
(1962)

Die Sprache ist die Mutter, nicht die Magd, des Gedankens.
K. KRAUS

Necessity knows no Speech. Not even
Shakespeare can say
What must be said so well as Frisch's bees convey
Vital instructions by ballet,
Nor do Jack and Jill, like thrushes,
Grow outspoken under May's compulsion:
A scream can be uncontrollable, and yawning a rudeness
One has to be excused, but free
Speech is a tautology.

Who means *Good Morning* reveals he is not
Napoleon or
Napoleon's cook, but quite as born, a new author,
Ready in turn to answer for
A story he cannot invent
But must leave to others to tell with what
Prejudice they prefer. Social climbers daren't invite comment,
And a chatterbox doesn't: in
Speech, if true, true deeds begin.

If not, there's International Babel,
In which murders
Are sanitary measures and stockbrokers
Integrity-ridden, for sirs
Who think big, where noises abound
For throats to hire whose doom is to compel
Attention: Its Void costs money, being flood-lit, wired for sound,
With banner headlines guaranteed,
And applause prerecorded.

But Dame Philology is our Queen still,
Quick to comfort
Truth-loving hearts in their mother tongue (to report
On the miracles She has wrought
In the U.K., the O.E.D.
Takes fourteen tomes): She suffers no evil,
And a statesman still, so her grace prevent, may keep a treaty,
A poor commoner arrive at
The Proper Name for his cat.

No hero is immortal till he dies:
Nor is a tongue.
But a lay of Beowulf's language too can be sung,
Ignoble, maybe, to the young,
Having no monsters and no gore
To speak of, yet not without its beauties
For those who have learned to hope: a lot of us are grateful for
What J. R. R. Tolkien has done
As bard to Anglo-Saxon.

III. ELEGY FOR J.F.K.
(November 22nd, 1963)

Why *then*, why *there*,
Why *thus*, we cry, did he die?
The heavens are silent.

What he was, he was:
What he is fated to become
Depends on us.

Remembering his death,
How we choose to live
Will decide its meaning.

When a just man dies,
Lamentation and praise,
Sorrow and joy, are one.

February 1964

IV. LINES FOR ELIZABETH MAYER
on the occasion of her eightieth birthday, April 6th, 1964

Withdrawn from the Object-World
A Grand Duke's glass coach,
His Chaplain's *Sand-Uhr*,

And extinct
The governesses who played
Chopin, Opus 31:

(Two of the Six
Noble Gases have, I hear,
Already been seduced.)

While for those who still remember them,
The minutes are long,
The day short.

Here, now, as bodies,
We have no option:
Dates, locations divide us.

As You, as I, though, each
Is born with the right
Of liberal passage

To Dame Philology's Realm
Where, in singular,
Name may call to Name,

And Name to Name respond,
Untaunted by
Numerical haphazard.

So, today, I think that sound
To which you have answered
For eighty years

With this intent:
That you shall think it happily,
As *Elizabeth*

Through twenty-five has been
For a happiness of mine
Its Proper Name.

V. JOSEF WEINHEBER
     (1892–1945)

Reaching my gate, a narrow
lane from the village
passes on into a wood:
when I walk that way
it seems befitting to stop
and look through the fence
of your garden where (under
the circs they had to)
they buried you like a loved
old family dog.

Categorised enemies
twenty years ago,
now next-door neighbors, we might
have become good friends,
sharing a common ambit
and love of the Word,
over a golden *Kremser*

568

had many a long
language on syntax, commas,
versification.

Yes, yes, it has to be said:
men of great damage
and malengine took you up.
Did they for long, though,
take you in, who to Goebbels'
offer of culture
countered—*in Ruah lossen*?
But Rag, Tag, Bobtail
prefer a stink, and the young
condemn you unread.

What, had you ever heard of
Franz Jägerstätter,
the St. Radegund peasant,
who said his lonely
Nein to the Aryan State
and was beheaded,
would your heart, as Austrian,
poet, have told you?
Good care, of course, was taken
you should hear nothing,

be unprepared for a day
that was bound to come,
a season of dread and tears
and dishevolment
when, transfixed by a nightmare,
you destroyed yourself.
Retribution was ever
a bungler at it:
*dies alles ist furchtbar, hier
nur Schweigen gemäss.*

Unmarked by me, unmourned for,
the hour of your death,
unhailed by you the moment
when, providence-led,
I first beheld Kirchstetten
on a pouring wet
October day in a year
that changed our cosmos,
the *annus mirabilis*
when Parity fell.

Already the realms that lost
were properly warm
and over-eating, their crimes
the pedestrian
private sort, those nuisances,
corpses and rubble,
long carted away: for their raped
the shock was fading,
their kidnapped physicists felt
no longer homesick.

To-day we smile at weddings
where bride and bridegroom
were both born since the Shadow
lifted, or rather
moved elsewhere: never as yet
has Earth been without
her bad patch, some unplace with
jobs for torturers
(In what bars are they welcome?
What girls marry them?),

or her nutritive surface
at peace all over.
No one, so far as we know,
has ever felt safe:
and so, in secret regions,
good family men
keep eye, devoted as monks,
on apparatus
inside which harmless matter
turns homicidal.

Here, though, I feel as at home
as you did: the same
short-lived creatures re-utter
the same care-free songs,
orchards cling to the regime
they know, from April's
rapid augment of color
till boisterous Fall,
when at each stammering gust
apples thump the ground.

Looking across our valley
where, hidden from view,
Sichelbach tottles westward
to join the Perchling,
humanely modest in scale
and mild in contour,
conscious of grander neighbors
to bow to, mountains
soaring behind me, ahead
a noble river,

I would respect you also,
Neighbor and Colleague,
for even my English ear
gets in your German
the workmanship and the note
of one who was graced
to hear the viols playing
on the impaled green,
committed thereafter *den
Abgrund zu nennen*.

February 1965

VI. EPITHALAMIUM
(for Peter Mudford and Rita Auden, May 15, 1965)

All folk-tales mean by ending
with a State Marriage,
feast and fireworks, we wish you,
Peter and Rita,
two idiosyncrasies
who opt in this hawthorn month
to common your lives.

A diffy undertaking,
for to us, whose dreams
are odorless, what is real
seems a bit smelly:
strong nerves are an advantage,
an accurate wrist-watch too
can be a great help.

May Venus, to whose caprice
all blood must buxom,
take such a shine to you both
that, by her gifting,
your palpable substances
may re-ify those delights
they are purveyed for:

cool Hymen from Jealousy's
teratoid phantasms,
sulks, competitive headaches,
and Pride's monologue
that won't listen but demands
tautological echoes,
ever refrain you.

As genders, married or not,
who share with all flesh
a left-handed twist, your choice
reminds us to thank
Mrs. Nature for doing
(our ugly looks are our own)
the handsome by us.

571

For we're better built to last
than tigers, our skins
don't leak like the ciliates',
our ears can detect
quarter-tones, even our most
myopic have good enough
vision for courtship:

and how uncanny it is
we're here to say so,
that life should have got to us
up through the City's
destruction layers after
surviving the inhuman
Permian purges.

Wherefore, as Mudfords, Audens,
Seth-Smiths, Bonnergees,
with civic spear and distaff
we hail a gangrel
Paleocene pseudo-rat,
the Ur-Papa of princes
and crossing-sweepers:

as Adams, Eves, commanded
to nonesuch being,
answer the One for Whom all
enantiomorphs
are super-posable, yet
Who numbers each particle
by its Proper Name.

April 1965

VII. EULOGY
(for Professor Nevill Coghill on the occasion of his retirement in 1966)

In our beginning
was a snuffling life without
sky or horizon,
full of objects and not-theres,
too close, over-big,
and not all of them friendly,
lit up at moments
from an invisible source
by shafts of sunlight
or a split-second levin:
childhood remembered
as a row of cloudless days
is a revision

we make later on,
after we've learned from noting
the habits of stars
to annal births, bereavements,

572

manage dimensions
with standard weights and measures,
derive our rages
into useful leats, and know,
without knowing when,
we've made our bed. Whoever
is waiting for us
at ford or cross-roads cannot
be avoided now:

and we must pray for
a good death, whatever
world we are destined
to look on last. It could be
a field of battle,
or a vista of terse lawns
and tantalised yews,
or a forgotten province
of sagging fences,
weeds and pecker-wood saw-mills,
where an ill-nourished
sullen people vegetate
in some gloomy schism.

But Then was also
an Age of Care: what Nature
was doing to us
had to be coped with, the frown
of crag or cupboard
no more to be laughed away
than a Cruel Fair,
wife-trouble, debts, or public
crises when the State
trots out its Higher Clergy.
Between, though, with luck,
for a columbine season
we are free to play,

swains of a pasture
where neither love nor money
nor clocks are cogent,
a time to wear odd clothing,
behave with panache
and talk nonsense as I did,
ambling in Oxford's
potamic meadows with friends:
one austere dogma
capped another, abstract noun
echoed abstract noun,
to voice our irreverent
amoebaean song.

Blessed be Christ Church
for having been so snooty
forty years ago
about E. Lit. (What reason
had I to suppose
Exeter worth a visit?):
now of the body
I brashly came to my first
tutorial in
not a molecule remains,
but to its mind's eye
optically definite
is our meeting still.

This Nevill, I knew,
was not a *Heldentenor*
of the lecture-hall,
not a disciple-hunting
Socratic bully,
not a celibate glutton
averse to pupils
as to mal-edited texts,
yet a don distinct
as these from the common plump,
and as a Privy
Councillor more deserving
of our vail and verge.

Endowed with the charm
of your Irish provenance
but no proper-false,
you countenanced all species,
the alphas, the bone-
-idle, the obstreperous
and the really rum,
never looked cross or sleepy
when our essays were
more about us than Chaucer,
and no unfinished
shy production felt afraid
to knock on your door.

Among the ageing
too large a group disappoint
by looking a mess,
and even Aphrodite's
ex-darlings who once
swanned through crowds, the stare of all,
turn lipless vipers
or red-nosed stertorous bores,
but you have induced
your structure of carbon-rings
and brine to assume
a face that features a self
serene yet haggard,

574

a life lived droitly,
with a license from now on
for any conduct
in mild Gloucestershire, whither
our love shall follow:
may sunbeams, falling across
your breakfast-table,
forecast new agreeable hours
to paint in, re-thumb
a pet author, night by night
through your dreams the sound
of lapsing brooks assure you
that you pass muster.

July 1965

VIII. ELEGY
(*In Memoriam Emma Eiermann, ob. November 4, 1967*)

Liebe Frau Emma,
na, was hast Du denn gemacht?
You who always made
such conscience of our comfort,
oh, how could you go and die,

as if you didn't know
that in a permissive age
so rife with envy,
a housekeeper is harder
to replace than a lover,

and die, too, when we
were thousands of miles away,
leaving no one there
to prune and transplant before
the winter cold should set in.

Good witch that you were,
Surely you should have foreseen
the doom that your death
would spell for your cats and ours:
all had to be put away.

You came with the house,
you and your brother Josef,
Sudetendeutsche
made homeless paupers when Czechs
got their turn to be brutal:

but catastrophe
had failed to modernize you,
Child of the Old World,
in which to serve a master
was never thought ignoble.

Children of the New,
we had to learn how to live
in the older way,
well tendered and observed by
loyal but critical eyes.

From the first, I think,
you liked us, but to the last
assumed most callers
knocked with some evil intent
(now and again you were right).

When guests were coming,
there was always the worry:—
would you disallow?
Greeks, in your censure, were rogues,
all teen-agers delinquent.

Nor were you ever
one to behave your temper:
let Youth pick a fruit
or flower, out you would storm,
arms whirling, screaming abuse

in peasant German
at startled Americans
who had meant no harm,
and, after they'd gone, for days
you would treat us to the sulks.

But when in good form,
how enchanting your shy grin,
your soft cat-language:
no, no, Frau E, dear oddling,
we shall always be grateful.

After Josef died
(siblings can live in a bond
as close as wedlock),
you were all amort, your one
wish to rejoin him quickly.

You have, and we're left
with ten years to consider,
astonished at how
vivid they are to recall:
Du gute, schlaf in Ruhe.

                                    June 1968

IX. A MOSAIC FOR MARIANNE MOORE
(on the occasion of her eightieth birthday, November 15, 1967)

The concluded gardens of personal liking
are enchanted habitats
where real toads may catch imaginary flies
and the climate will accommodate the tiger
and the polar-bear.

So in the middle of yours (where it is human
to sit) we see you sitting
in a wide-brimmed hat beneath a monkey-puzzle,
at your feet the beasts you animated for us
by thinking of them.

Your lion with ferocious chrysanthemum head,
your jerboa, erect on
his Chippendale claw, your pelican behaving
like charred paper, your musk-ox who smells of water,
your fond nautilus,

cope with what surprises them and greet the stranger
in a mid-western accent,
even that bum, the unelephantine creature
who is certainly here to worship and often
selected to mourn.

Egocentric, eccentric, he will name a cat
Peter, a new car *Edsel*,
emphasize his own birthday and a few others
ho thinks deserve it, as to-day we stress your name,
Miss Marianne Moore

who, fastidious but fair, are unaffronted
by those whose disposition
it is to affront, who beg the cobra's pardon,
are always on time and never would yourself write
error with four *r*'s.

For poems, dolphin-graceful as carts from Sweden,
our thank-you should be a right
good salvo of barks: it's much too muffled to say
'how well and with what unfreckled integrity
it has all been done.'

August 1967

X. LINES TO DR. WALTER BIRK ON HIS RETIRING FROM GENERAL PRACTICE

When you first arrived in Kirchstetten, trains had
long been taken for granted, but electric
light was still a surprise and as yet no one
      had seen a tractor.

To-day, after forty-five years, as you leave us,
autobahns are a must, mid-wives are banished,
and village doctors become museum pieces
        like the horse-and-buggy.

I regret. The specialist has his function,
but, to him, we are merely banal examples of
what he knows all about. The healer I faith is
        someone I've gossipped

and drunk with before I call him to touch me,
someone who admits how easy it is to misconster
what our bodies are trying to say, for each one
        talks in a local

dialect of its own that can alter during
its lifetime. So children run high fevers on
slight provocation, while the organs of old men
        suffer in silence.

When summer plumps again, our usual sparrows
will phip in the eaves of the patulous chestnuts
near your old home, but none will ask: 'Is Doctor
        Birk around to hear me?'

For nothing can happen to birds that has not
happened before: we though are beasts with a sense of
real occasion, of beginnings and endings,
        which is the reason

we like to keep our clocks punctual as Nature's
never is. Seasons She has but no Calendar:
thus every year the strawberries ripen
        and the autumn crocus

flares into blossom on unpredictable
dates. Such a *Schlamperei* cannot be allowed an
historian: with us it's a point of honor
        to keep our birth-days

and wedding-days, to rejoice or to mourn, on
the right one. Henceforth, the First of October
shall be special for you and us, as the Once when
        you quit the Public

Realm to private your ways and snudge in a quiet
you so deserve. Farewell, and do not wince at
our sick world: it is genuine in age to be
        happily selfish.

September 1970

XI. A TOAST

(to Professor William Empson on the occasion of his retirement in 1971)

As *quid pro quo* for your enchanting verses,
when approached by Sheffield, at first I wondered
    if I could manage *Just a Smack at Empson*,
        but nothing occurred.

All I could fault was your conceit that Milton's
God, obtrusive prolix baroque Olympian,
    is our Christian one. Who, though, but you has pondered
        so deeply on *Alice*?

Good voices are rare, still rarer singers with
perfect pitch: if Graves was right, if at Cambridge
    the tuning's a wee bit sharp, then at Oxford
        it well may be flat.

Our verbal games are separate, thank heaven,
but Time twins us: both learned to person Life in
    an open-hearthed, nannied, un-T-V'd world, where
        cars looked peculiar.

To wish you long years would be heartless (may you
leave when you want to, no earlier): but I gladly,
    dear Bill, dear fellow mandarin, smile to your
        future holidays.

The Horatians

Into what fictive realms can imagination
translate you, Flaccus, and your kin? Not the courts of
    Grand Opera, that *galère*
    of lunatics, power-famished

or love-ravenous, belting out their arias,
nor the wards of *Buffa*, either, where abnormal
    growths of self-love are excised
    by the crude surgery of a

practical joke. Perhaps the only invented
story in which your appearance seems credible
    is the Whodunit: I can
    believe in one of you solving

a murder which has the professionals baffled,
thanks to your knowledge of local topography.
    In our world all of you share
    a love for some particular

place and stretch of country, a farm near Tivoli
or a Radnorshire village: what the Capital
    holds out as a lure, a chance
    to get into Society,

does not tempt you, who wry from crowds, traffic-noises,
blue-stockings and millionaires. Your tastes run to
    small dinner-parties, small rooms,
    and the tone of voice that suits them,

neither truckle nor thrasonical but softly
certain (a sound wood-winds imitate better
    than strings), your most worldly wish
    a genteel sufficiency of

land or lolly. Among those I really know, the
British branch of the family, how many have
    found in the Anglican Church
    your Maecenas who enabled

a life without cumber, as pastors adjective
to rustic flocks, as organists in trollopish
    cathedral towns. Then, in all
    labyrinthine economies

there are obscure nooks into which Authority
never pokes a suspicious nose, *embusqué* havens
    for natural bachelors
    and political idiots,

Zoological and Botanical Gardens,
museum-basements displaying feudal armor
    or old coins: there, too, we find
    you among the custodians.

Some of you have written poems, usually
short ones, and some kept diaries, seldom published
    till after your deaths, but most
    make no memorable impact

except on your friends and dogs. Enthusiastic
Youth writes you off as cold, who cannot be found on
    barricades, and never shoot
    either yourselves or your lovers.

You thought well of your Odes, Flaccus, and believed they
would live, but knew, and have taught your descendants to
    say with you: 'As makers go,
    compared with Pindar or any

of the great foudroyant masters who don't ever
amend, we are, for all our polish, of little
    stature, and, as human lives,
    compared with authentic martyrs

like Regulus, of no account. We can only
do what it seems to us we were made for, look at
   this world with a happy eye
   but from a sober perspective.'

April 1968

Profile

He thanks God daily
that he was born and bred
a British Pharisee.

*   *   *

A childhood full of love
and good things to eat:
why should he not hate change?

*   *   *

Gluttony and Sloth
have often protected him
from Lust and Anger.

*   *   *

In his cups neither savage nor maudlin,
but all too prone
to hold forth.

*   *   *

Too timid to cruise,
in his feudal day-dream no
courage is needed.
The Cardinal halts his coach:
'Dear Child, you please me. Hop in!'

*   *   *

The way he dresses
reveals an angry baby,
howling to be dressed.

*   *   *

He has often stamped his feet,
wept on occasion,
but never been bored.

*   *   *

Vain? Not very, except
about his knowledge of metre,
and his friends.

*   *   *

Praise? Unimportant,
but jolly to remember
while falling asleep.

*   *   *

He likes giving presents,
but finds it hard to forget
what each one cost.

*   *   *

He envies those who have learned,
when reading newspapers,
how to fold them.

*   *   *

He wishes he were
Konrad Lorenz and had written
Firbank's novels.

*   *   *

Reaching a cross-roads,
he expects the traffic-lights
to turn green for him.

*   *   *

So obsessive a ritualist
a pleasant surprise
makes him cross.

*   *   *

Without a watch
he would never know when
to feel hungry or horny.

*   *   *

His guardian-angel
has always told him
What and Whom to read next.

*   *   *

Conscious of his good-luck,
he wonders why so few
people kill themselves.

    *   *   *

Scanning his fellow
Subway passengers, he asks:
'Can I really be
the only one in this car
who is glad to be alive?'

    *   *   *

On waking, he thinks:
'Precious, Precious Me!
A fig for your detractors!'

On going to bed:
'What *am* I to do?
Again You have let Us down.'

? 1965–1966

ADDENDA

In anxiety dreams,
at the moment he gives up hope,
he ejaculates.

    *   *   *

By nature monandrous,
he finds it hard to desert
a piece of trade.

    *   *   *

In a coughing-fit
he felt he was throwing up
hard Capital *F*'s.

    *   *   *

Why, when passively borne
by train or car, does he feel
less urge to smoke?

    *   *   *

He has never seen God,
but, once or twice, he believes
he has heard Him.

1973

Since

On a mid-December day,
frying sausages
for myself, I abruptly
felt under fingers
thirty years younger the rim
of a steering-wheel,
on my cheek the parching wind
of an August noon,
as passenger beside me
You as then you were.

Slap across a veg-growing
alluvial plain
we raced in clouds of white dust,
and geese fled screaming
as we missed them by inches,
making a bee-line
for mountains gradually
enlarging eastward,
joyfully certain nightfall
would occasion joy.

It did. In a flagged kitchen
we were served broiled trout
and a rank cheese: for a while
we talked by the fire,
then, carrying candles, climbed
steep stairs. Love was made
then and there: so halcyoned,
soon we fell asleep
to the sound of a river
swabbling through a gorge.

Since then, other enchantments
have blazed and faded,
enemies changed their address,
and War made ugly
an uncountable number
of unknown neighbors,
precious as us to themselves:
but round your image
there is no fog, and the Earth
can still astonish.

Of what, then, should I complain,
pottering about
a neat suburban kitchen?
Solitude? Rubbish!
It's social enough with real

faces and landscapes
for whose friendly countenance
I at least can learn
to live with obesity
and a little fame.

January 1965

Amor Loci

I could draw its map by heart,
showing its contours,
strata and vegetation,
name every height,
small burn and lonely sheiling,
but nameless to me,
faceless as heather or grouse,
are those who live there,

its dead too vague for judgement,
tangible only
what they wrought, their giant works
of delve and drainage
in days preterite: long since
their hammering stopped
as the lodes all petered out
in the Jew Limestone.

Here and there a tough chimney
still towers over
dejected masonry, moss,
decomposed machines,
with no one about, no chance
of buttering bread,
a land postured in my time
for marginal farms.

Any musical future
is most unlikely.
Industry wants Cheap Power,
romantic muscle
a perilous wilderness,
Mr. Pleasure pays
for surf-riding, claret, sex:
it offers them none.

To me, though, much: a vision,
not (as perhaps at
twelve I thought it) of Eden,
still less of a New
Jerusalem but, for one,
convinced he will die,
more comely, more credible
than either day-dream.

How, but with some real focus
of desolation
could I, by analogy,
imagine a love
that, however often smeared,
shrugged at, abandoned
by a frivolous worldling,
does not abandon?

July 1965

Bird-Language

Trying to understand the words
   Uttered on all sides by birds,
I recognize in what I hear
   Noises that betoken fear.

Though some of them, I'm certain, must
   Stand for rage, bravado, lust,
All other notes that birds employ
   Sound like synonyms for joy.

May 1967

Two Songs

I. SONG OF THE OGRES

Little fellow, you're amusing,
Stop before you end by losing
   Your shirt:
Run along to Mother, Gus,
Those who interfere with us
   Get hurt.

Honest Virtue, old wives prattle,
Always wins the final battle.
   Dear, Dear!
Life's exactly what it looks,
Love may triumph in the books,
   Not here.

We're not joking, we assure you:
Those who rode this way before you
   Died hard.
What? Still spoiling for a fight?
Well, you've asked for it alright:
   On guard!

Always hopeful, aren't you? Don't be.
Night is falling and it won't be
    Long now:
You will never see the dawn,
You will wish you'd not been born.
    And how!

II. SONG OF THE DEVIL

Ever since observation taught me temptation
Is a matter of timing, I've tried
To clothe my fiction in up-to-date diction,
The contemporary jargon of Pride.
    I can recall when, to win the more
      Obstinate round,
    The best bet was to say to them: 'Sin the more
      That Grace may abound.'

Since Social Psychology replaced Theology
The process goes twice as quick,
If a conscience is tender and loth to surrender
I have only to whisper: 'You're sick!
    Puritanical morality
      Is madly Non-U:
    Enhance your personality
      With a Romance, with two.

'If you pass up a dame, you've yourself to blame,
For shame is neurotic, so snatch!
All rules are too formal, in fact they're abnormal,
For any desire is natch.
    So take your proper share, man, of
      Dope and drink.
    Aren't you the Chairman of
      Ego, Inc.?

'Free Will is a mystical myth as statistical
Methods have objectively shown,
A fad of the Churches: since the latest researches
Into Motivation it's known
    That Honor is hypocrisy,
      Honesty a joke.
    You live in a Democracy:
      Lie like other folk.

'Since men are like goods, what are shouldn'ts or shoulds
When you are the Leading Brand?
Let them all drop dead, you're way ahead,
Beat them up if they dare to demand
    What may your intention be,
      Or what might ensue:
    There's a difference of dimension be-
      -tween the rest and you.

'If in the scrimmage of business your image
Should ever tarnish or stale,
Public Relations can take it and make it
Shine like a Knight of the Grail.
    You can mark up the price that you sell at, if
        Your package has glamour and show:
    Values are relative.
    Dough is dough.

'So let each while you may think you're more O.K.,
More yourself than anyone else,
Till you find that you're hooked, your goose is cooked,
And you're only a cipher of Hell's.
    Believe while you can that I'm proud of you,
        Enjoy your dream:
    I'm so bored with the whole fucking crowd of you
        I could *scream!*'

? 1967

Forty Years On

Except where blast-furnaces and generating-stations
        have inserted their sharp profiles,
or a Thru-Way slashes harshly across them, Bohemia's contours
        look just as amiable now
as when I saw them first (indeed, her coast is gentler,
        for tame hotels have ousted
the havocking bears), nor have her dishes lost their flavor
        since Florizel was thwacked into exile
and we and Sicily discorded, fused into rival amalgams,
        in creed and policy oppugnant.
Only to the ear is it patent something drastic has happened,
        that orators no more speak
of primogeniture, prerogatives of age and sceptre:
        (for our health we have had to learn
the fraternal shop of our new Bonzen, but that was easy).
        For a useful technician I lacked
the schooling, for a bureaucrat the *Sitzfleisch*: all I had
        was the courtier's agility to adapt
my rogueries to the times. It sufficed. I survived and prosper
        better than I ever did under
the old lackadaisical economy: it is many years now
        since I picked a pocket (how deft
my hand was then!), or sang for pennies, or traveled on foot.
        (The singing I miss, but to-day's
audience would boo my ballads: it calls for Songs of Protest
        and wants its bawdry straight
not surreptitious.) A pedlar still, for obvious reasons
        I no longer cry my wares,
but in ill-lit alleys coaxingly whisper to likely clients:
        Anything you cannot buy
        In the stores I will supply,
        English foot-wear, nylon hose,

Or transistor radios;
Come to me for the Swiss Francs
Unobtainable in banks;
For a price I can invent
Any official document,
Work-Permits, Driving-Licenses,
Any Certificate you please:
Believe me, I know all the tricks,
There is nothing I can't fix.
Why, then, should I badger?
No rheum has altered my gait, as ever my cardiac muscles
    are undismayed, my cells
perfectly competent, and by now I am far too rich
    for the thought of the hangman's noose
to make me oggle. But how glib all the faces I see about me
    seem suddenly to have become,
and how seldom I feel like a hay-tumble. For three nights running
    now I have had the same dream
of a suave afternoon in Fall. I am standing on high ground,
    looking out westward over
a plain run smoothly by Jaguar farmers. In the eloignment,
    a-glitter in the whelking sun,
a sheer bare cliff concludes the vista. At its base I see,
    black, shaped like a bell-tent,
the mouth of a cave by which (I know in my dream) I am to
    make my final exit,
its roof so low it will need an awkward duck to make it.
    'Well, will that be so shaming?'
I ask when awake. Why should it be? When has Autolycus
ever solemnod himself?

                           1968

Marginalia

I
Fate succumbs
many a species: one alone
jeopardises itself.

    *   *   *

The gregarious
and mild-tempered never know
each other by name:
creatures who make friends are shy
and liable to anger.

    *   *   *

Unable to see
a neighbor to frown at,
Eutroplus beat his wife.
                (*after* KONRAD LORENZ)
    *   *   *

Afraid or ashamed to say
I don't like you,
he yawned and scratched himself.

* * *

The palm extended in welcome:
Look! for you
I have unclenched my fist.

* * *

Afraid after long
separation of meeting
a hostile stranger,
the two old friends re-affirmed
their pact with peals of laughter.

* * *

Brashly triumphant,
over-dogmatic, a sneeze
asserts without proof
some ritual connection
between breathing and loving.

* * *

Born with high voices
and first responding to one,
even as basses
we feel an operatic
hero must be a tenor.

* * *

Few can remember
clearly when innocence came
to a sudden end,
the moment at which we ask
for the first time: *Am I loved?*

* * *

Fear and Vanity
incline us to imagine
we have caused a face
to turn away which merely
happened to look somewhere else.
(*after* ERIK ERIKSON)

* * *

590

Everyone thinks:
'I am the most important
Person at present.'
The sane remember to add:
'Important, I mean, to me.'

*   *   *

Wooziness that knows it is woozy
may tell truths
Logic is deaf to.

*   *   *

True Love enjoys
twenty-twenty vision,
but talks like a myopic.

*   *   *

Justice: permission to peck
a wee bit harder
than we have been pecked.

*   *   *

The introvert is deaf
to his neighbor's cry
at the extrovert's pinch.

*   *   *

Needing above all
silence and warmth, we produce
brutal cold and noise.

*   *   *

Wicked deeds have their glamour,
but those who commit them
are always bores.

*   *   *

When we do evil,
we and our victims
are equally bewildered.

*   *   *

The decent, probably,
outnumber the swine,
but few can inherit

the genes, or procure
both the money and time,
to join the civilised.

                    II
A dead man
who never caused others to die
seldom rates a statue.

            *   *   *

The last king
of a fallen dynasty
is seldom well spoken of.

            *   *   *

Few even wish they could read
the lost annals
of a cudgeled people.

            *   *   *

The tyrant's device:
*Whatever Is Possible
Is Necessary*.

            *   *   *

Small tyrants, threatened by big,
sincerely believe
they love Liberty.

            *   *   *

No tyrant ever fears
his geologists or his engineers.

            *   *   *

Tyrants may get slain,
but their hangmen usually
die in their beds.

            *   *   *

Patriots? Little boys,
obsessed by Bigness,
Big Pricks, Big Money, Big Bangs.

            *   *   *

In States unable
to alleviate Distress,
Discontent is hanged.

*   *   *

In semi-literate countries
demagogues pay
court to teen-agers.

*   *   *

When Chiefs of State
prefer to work at night,
let the citizens beware.

III
Ancestorless,
the upstart warrior proclaimed
the Sun his Father.

*   *   *

Their gods:—like themselves
greedy skirt-chasing blackguards
without compunction,
but (as, thank God, they were not)
forever young and intact.

*   *   *

On their stage swords, horses
were sacred persons, the poor
farting bumpkins.

*   *   *

Wars, revolts, plagues, inflation:
no wonder they dreamed of God
as a Logical
One, for Whom to be solid
or moved was vulgar.

*   *   *

He praised his God
for the expertise
of his torturer and his chef.

*   *   *

Voracious eater,
shrewd diplomat though he was,
when playing checkers
he forgot about meal-times,
kept ambassadors waiting.

*   *   *

While the Empire went to pot,
he amused himself
extemporizing moral,
highly moral, iambics,
deficient in rhythm.

*   *   *

A neglected wife,
she refused to mope, but filled
her lonely bedroom
with costly apparatus
for distilling new perfumes:

had made to order
a metal icon of Christ
which answered questions
and foretold future events
by a change in its colors.

(*after* PSELLUS)

*   *   *

With silver mines,
recruiting grounds,
a general of real genius,

he thought himself invulnerable:
in one battle
he lost all three.

*   *   *

After the massacre
they pacified their conscience
by telling jokes.

*   *   *

Reluctant at first
to break his sworn promise
of Safe Conduct, after

consulting his confessor,
in good spirits
he signed a death-warrant.

*   *   *

Be godly, he told his flock,
bloody and extreme
like the Holy Ghost.

　　　　*　　*　　*

When their Infidel
Paymaster fell in arrears,
the mercenaries
recalled their unstained childhoods
in devout Christian homes.

　　　　*　　*　　*

After the Just War,
the Holy War that had saved
Christendom, there were
more palaces and clergy,
fewer scholars and houses.
　　　　　　　　　(*after* ILSA BAREA)

　　　　*　　*　　*

The Huguenot church-bells
were flogged, then baptized
as Roman Catholics.
　　　　　　　　　(*after* FRIEDRICH HEER)

　　　　*　　*　　*

The Queen fled, leaving
books behind her
that shocked the pious usurper.

　　　　*　　*　　*

Intelligent, rich,
humane, the young man dreamed of
posthumous glory
as connoisseur and patron
of Scholarship and the Arts.

An age bent on war,
the ambitions of his king,
decreed otherwise:
he was to be remembered
as a destroyer of towns.

　　　　*　　*　　*

Born to flirt and write light verses,
he died bravely
by the headsman's axe.

　　　　*　　*　　*

Into the prosperous quiet
between two wars
came *Anopheles*.

* * *

Under a Sovereign
who despised culture
Arts and Letters improved.

* * *

War-time. English schoolboys
killing the white butterflies
they called Frenchmen.

* * *

Rumors ran through the city
that the Tsar's bodyguard
was not house-trained.

* * *

Assembling
with ceremonial pomp,
the Imperial Diet

gravely debated
legislation
it had no power to reject.

* * *

He hid when he saw
a Minister approaching
with a worried look.

* * *

In the intervals between
bathing and tennis
he sought new allies.

* * *

Ready any day
to pistol each other
on a point of honor,

night after night
they staked their fortunes, knowing
there were money-lenders

they could always cheat
by absconding to Dieppe
or shooting themselves.

              *   *   *

The tobacco farmers
were Baptists who considered
smoking a sin.

              *   *   *

Abandoning his wives,
he fled with their jewels
and two hundred dogs.

              *   *   *

To maintain a stud
of polo-ponies he now
was too stout to ride,
he slapped taxes on windows,
hearth-stones and door-steps and wives.

              *   *   *

He walked like someone
who'd never had to
open a door for himself.

              *   *   *

Victorious over
the foreign tyrant,
the patriots retained

his emergency
police regulations,
devised to suppress them.

              *   *   *

Providentially
right for once in his life-time
(his reasons were wrong),
the old sod was permitted
to save civilisation.

              IV
Animal femurs
ascribed to saints who never
existed, are still

more holy than portraits
of conquerors who,
unfortunately, did.

*   *   *

Like any Zola
they poked their noses into
prisons and brothels,
not, though, in search of copy
but to comfort their equals.

*   *   *

To shock pagan purists
he never avoided
a metacismus.

*   *   *

With equal affection
he bathed the sick
and studied Greek papyri.

*   *   *

The young scamp turned into
a hermit, renowned for
his way with vipers.

*   *   *

A choleric type,
he was always butting in
to defend the Jews
against the mob, or the poor
against the King's warreners.

*   *   *

Knowing that God knew
that what she really liked best
was not the stable
but the crowded inn, she built
a fine hospice for pilgrims.

*   *   *

Getting up to pray
in the middle of the night,
she told her husband
(a heathen and a bad hat):
I must go to the bathroom.

*   *   *

On his return from foreign parts
where he had suffered
and learned mercy,

he abrogated at once
the Penal Code
his knavish gamekeeper,

his ignorant housemaids,
had enacted against
innocent barn-owls.
                    (*after* CHARLES WATERTON)

               *   *   *

Who died in Nineteen-Sixty-Five
more worthy of honors
than *Lark*, a cow

who gave to mankind
one-hundred-and-fifteen-thousand
litres of milk?

                    V
Once having shat
in his new apartment,
he began to feel at home.

               *   *   *

Another entire day wasted.
What is called for?
The Whip? Pills? Patience?

               *   *   *

His thoughts pottered
from verses to sex to God
without punctuation.

               *   *   *

Mulberries dropping,
twinges of lumbago,
as he read *Clarendon*.

               *   *   *

Round the ritual bonfire
on Midsummer Eve
another generation,
who never walk, drink no wine,
carry transistors.

* * *

A September night:
just the two of them, eating
corn from their garden,
plucked thirty minutes ago.
Outside: thunder, siling rain.

* * *

On the bushes
St. Martin's gossamer,
in the bathroom a stray toad.

* * *

Leaf-fall. A lane. A rogue,
driving to visit
someone who still trusts him.

* * *

Imaged in the bar-mirror
during their lunch-hour,
a row of city faces,
middle-aged, mute, expecting
no death of their own.

* * *

How cheerful they looked,
the unoccupied bar-stools
in mid-afternoon,
freed for some hours from the weight
of drab defeated bottoms.

* * *

How could he help him?
Miserable youth! in flight
from a non-father,
an incoherent mother,
in pursuit of—what?

* * *

The Marquis de Sade and Genet
Are highly thought of to-day,
　　But torture and treachery
　　Are not his kinds of lechery,
So he's given his copies away.

　　　　*　　*　　*

Americans—like omelettes:
there is no such thing
as a pretty good one.

　　　　*　　*　　*

Even Hate should be precise:
very few White Folks
have fucked their mothers.

　　　　*　　*　　*

As a Wasp, riding
the Subway, he wonders why
it is that nearly
all the aristocratic
faces he sees are Negro.

　　　　*　　*　　*

Passing Beauty
still delights him, but he no longer
has to turn round.

　　　　*　　*　　*

Post coitum homo tristis.
What nonsense! If he could,
he would sing.

　　　　*　　*　　*

Listening to the *Études*
of Chopin, entranced
by such a love-match of Craft
and Utterance, he forgot
his Love was not there.

　　　　*　　*　　*

Lonely he may be
but, each time he bolts his door
the last thing at night,
his heart rejoices: 'No one
can interfere with me now.'
　　　　*　　*　　*

He woke in the small hours,
dismayed by a wilderness
of hostile thoughts.

*   *   *

The shame in ageing
is not that Desire should fail
(Who mourns for something
he no longer needs?): it is
that someone else must be told.

*   *   *

Thoughts of his own death,
like the distant roll
of thunder at a picnic.

*   *   *

Pulling on his socks,
he recalls that his grand-pa
went pop in the act.

*   *   *

How odd it now seems
that, when he was born, there seemed
nothing odd about writing:
I traveled alone
to Bonn with a boring maid.

*   *   *

Years before doctors
had invented the jargon,
he knew from watching
his maiden-aunts that illness
could be psychosomatic.

*   *   *

Father at the wars,
Mother, tongue-tied with shyness,
struggling to tell him
the Facts of Life he dared not
tell her he knew already.

*   *   *

The class whose vices
he pilloried was his own,
now extinct, except
for lone survivors like him
who remember its virtues.

1965–1968

In Due Season

Spring-time, Summer and Fall: days to behold a world
Antecedent to our knowing, where flowers think
Theirs concretely in scent-colors and beasts, the same
Age all over, pursue dumb horizontal lives
On one level of conduct and so cannot be
Secretary to man's plot to become divine.

Lodged in all is a set metronome: thus, in May
Bird-babes still in the egg click to each other *Hatch!*;
June-struck cuckoos go off-pitch; when obese July
Turns earth's heating up, unknotting their poisoned ropes,
Vipers move into play; warned by October's nip,
Younger leaves to the old give the releasing draught.

Winter, though, has the right tense for a look indoors
At ourselves, and with First Names to sit face-to-face,
Time for reading of thoughts, time for the trying-out
Of new metres and new recipes, proper time
To reflect on events noted in warmer months
Till, transmuted, they take part in a human tale.

There, responding to our cry for intelligence,
Nature's mask is relaxed into a mobile grin,
Stones, old shoes, come alive, born sacramental signs,
Nod to us in the First Person of mysteries
They know nothing about, bearing a message from
The invisible sole Source of specific things.

September 1968

Rois Fainéants

On High Feast-Days they were given a public airing:
Their shoulder-length blond hair combed and braided,
In carts drawn by white oxen they were paraded
Before the eyes of the people, children bearing
The names of fabulous ancestors, Chlotar, Chilperic,
Clovis, Théodoric, Dagobert, Childeric,
In whose veins ran the royal blood, declared descended
In unbroken line (the facts were sometimes amended)
From sea-gods or sea-monsters of old, on which succession
The luck of the Franks, though now Catholic, still depended.
Everyone knew, of course, it was a staged play,
Everyone knew where the real power lay,
That it was the Mayor of the Palace who had the say,
But Mayors were only bishops. (Grimoald had tried
To rule without them: he soon and violently died.)
So from dawn till dusk they made their triumphal progression,
While war-horns dindled the heavens, silken banners
Flapped in the wind, and the rapt tribes shouted away.

But when darkness fell and their special outing was ended,
Off they were packed again to their secluded manors,
Closely watched day and night to prevent the danger
Of their escaping or talking too much to a stranger,
With nothing to do but affix their seals to charters
They had never been taught to read, and supplied with plenty
Of beef and beer and girls from which, as was intended,
They died young, most before they were twenty.

May we not justly call them political martyrs?

1968

Partition

Unbiassed at least he was when he arrived on his mission,
Having never set eyes on this land he was called to partition
Between two peoples fanatically at odds,
With their different diets and incompatible gods.
'Time,' they had briefed him in London, 'is short. It's too late
For mutual reconciliation or rational debate:
The only solution now lies in separation.
The Viceroy thinks, as you will see from his letter,
That the less you are seen in his company the better,
So we've arranged to provide you with other accommodation.
We can give you four judges, two Moslem and two Hindu,
To consult with, but the final decision must rest with you.'

Shut up in a lonely mansion, with police night and day
Patrolling the gardens to keep assassins away,
He got down to work, to the task of settling the fate
Of millions. The maps at his disposal were out of date
And the Census Returns almost certainly incorrect,
But there was no time to check them, no time to inspect
Contested areas. The weather was frightfully hot,
And a bout of dysentery kept him constantly on the trot,
But in seven weeks it was done, the frontiers decided,
A continent for better or worse divided.

The next day he sailed for England, where he quickly forgot
The case, as a good lawyer must. Return he would not,
Afraid, as he told his Club, that he might get shot.

May 1966

August 1968

The Ogre does what ogres can,
Deeds quite impossible for Man,
But one prize is beyond his reach,
The Ogre cannot master Speech.
About a subjugated plain,
Among its desperate and slain,
The Ogre stalks with hands on hips,
While drivel gushes from his lips.

September 1968

Fairground

Thumping old tunes give a voice to its whereabouts
long before one can see the dazzling archway
of colored lights, beyond which household proverbs
cease to be valid,

a ground sacred to the god of vertigo
and his cult of disarray: here jeopardy,
panic, shock, are dispensed in measured doses
by fool-proof engines

As passive objects, packed tightly together
on Roller-Coaster or Ferris-Wheel, mortals
taste in their solid flesh the volitional
joys of a seraph.

Soon the Roundabout ends the clumsy conflict
of Right and Left: the riding mob melts into
one spinning sphere, the perfect shape performing
the perfect motion.

Mopped and mowed at, as their train worms through a tunnel,
by ancestral spooks, caressed by clammy cobwebs,
grinning initiates emerge into daylight
as tribal heroes.

Fun for Youth who knows his libertine spirit
is not a copy of Father's, but has yet to
learn that the tissues which lend it stamina,
like Mum's, are bourgeois.

Those with their wander-years behind them, who are rather
relieved that all routes of escape are spied on,
all hours of amusement counted, requiring
caution, agenda,

keep away:—to be found in coigns where, sitting
in silent synods, they play chess or cribbage,
games that call for patience, foresight, manoeuvre,
like war, like marriage.

June 1966

River Profile

Our body is a moulded river
NOVALIS

Out of a bellicose fore-time, thundering
head-on collisions of cloud and rock in an
up-thrust, crevasse-and-avalanche, troll country,
deadly to breathers,

it whelms into our picture below the melt-line,
where tarns lie frore under frowning cirques, goat-bell,
wind-breaker, fishing-rod, miner's-lamp country,
already at ease with

the mien and gestures that become its kindness,
in streams, still anonymous, still jumpable,
flows as it should through any declining country
in probing spirals.

Soon of a size to be named and the cause of
dirty in-fighting among rival agencies,
down a steep stair, penstock-and-turbine country,
it plunges ram-stam,

to foam through a wriggling gorge incised in softer
strata, hemmed between crags that nauntle heaven,
robber-baron, tow-rope, portage-way country,
nightmare of merchants.

Disemboguing from foothills, now in hushed meanders,
now in riffling braids, it vaunts across a senile
plain, well-entered, chateau-and-cider-press country,
its regal progress

gallanted for a while by quibbling poplars,
then by chimneys: led off to cool and launder
retort, steam-hammer, gasometer country,
it changes color.

Polluted, bridged by girders, banked by concrete,
now it bisects a polyglot metropolis,
ticker-tape, taxi, brothel, foot-lights country,
à-la-mode always.

Broadening or burrowing to the moon's phases,
turbid with pulverized wastemantle, on through
flatter, duller, hotter, cotton-gin country
it scours, approaching

the tidal mark where it puts off majesty,
disintegrates, and through swamps of a delta,
punting-pole, fowling-piece, oyster-tongs country,
wearies to its final

acts of surrender, effacement, atonement
in a huge amorphous aggregate no cuddled
attractive child ever dreams of, non-country,
image of death as

a spherical dew-drop of life. Unlovely
monsters, our tales believe, can be translated
too, even as water, the selfless mother
of all especials.

July 1966

Insignificant Elephants

Although He was the greatest, Our Lord Jesus Christ
was made the Most Insignificant of all the Elephants.

THE BESTIARY

Talented creatures, on the defensive because
Glory, Real Estate, Girls, are not in Virtue's gift,
translate into verse or prose,

do equally well in tragic and comic parts,
give story-tellers the nudge to invent that cooks
get from slightly-tainted meat.

But a *Hugh of Lincoln* or a *Peter Claver*
are only game for reporters, news, like *Auschwitz*,
Dickens could not have made up

nor *Halley* have predicted: genetic typos
bring forth infant prodigies, imbeciles, midgets,
but no Prime Numbers, no Saints.

Nor would a snapshot reveal a halo: they hide
their incandescence like tasty moths who mimic
unpalatable cousins.

Wild converts, at sea on a collapsing culture,
concocted one or two viable folk-tales—*George*
cuts a dash with his Dragon—

but a deal of bosh, semi-gnostic compost-heaps
where spurious cults could mushroom: there never was
a *Catherine* with a Wheel,

nor a *Barbara* to bless the Artillery,
nor an *Uncumber* for English wives to invoke
against lickerous husbands.

Some anecdotes, even from those dark years, have reached us
that are odd enough to be true:—*Perpetua*,
with a beastly end to face,

trying to convince, *Papa, if that is a jug,*
I am a Christian, and dreaming of a shepherd
who consoled her with cream cheese.

With all our flair for research we are still nonplussed:
what shifted members of our species to become
insignificant elephants?

A hard life, often a hard death, and side-effects
that a humanist finds hard to stomach, are signs
which divulge nothing. A trait

which might cannot be checked on: all who met them speak
of joy which made their own conveniences
mournfulness and a bad smell.

If their hunch was not mistaken, it would explain
why there is something fishy about a High Style
and the characters it suits,

why we add the embarrassing prefix *super*-
to a natural life which nothing prevents us
living except our natures.

May 1966

Ode to Terminus

The High Priests of telescopes and cyclotrons
keep making pronouncements about happenings
    on scales too gigantic or dwarfish
    to be noticed by our native senses,

discoveries which, couched in the elegant
euphemisms of algebra, look innocent,
    harmless enough but, when translated
    into the vulgar anthropomorphic

tongue, will give no cause for hilarity
to gardeners or house-wives: if galaxies
    bolt like panicking mobs, if mesons
    riot like fish in a feeding-frenzy,

it sounds too like Political History
to boost civil morale, too symbolic of
    the crimes and strikes and demonstrations
    we are supposed to gloat on at breakfast.

How trite, though, our fears beside the miracle
that we're here to shiver, that a Thingummy
    so addicted to lethal violence
    should have somehow secreted a placid

tump with exactly the right ingredients
to start and to cocker Life, that heavenly
    freak for whose manage we shall have to
    give account at the Judgement, our Middle-

-Earth, where Sun-Father to all appearances
moves by day from orient to occident,
    and his light is felt as a friendly
    presence not a photonic bombardment,

where all visibles do have a definite
outline they stick to, and are undoubtedly
    at rest or in motion, where lovers
    recognize each other by their surface,

608

where to all species except the talkative
have been allotted the niche and diet that
   become them. This, whatever micro-
   -biology may think, is the world we

really live in and that saves our sanity,
who know all too well how the most erudite
   mind behaves in the dark without a
   surround it is called on to interpret,

how, discarding rhythm, punctuation, metaphor,
it sinks into a drivelling monologue,
   too literal to see a joke or
   distinguish a penis from a pencil.

Venus and Mars are powers too natural
to temper our outlandish extravagance:
   You alone, Terminus the Mentor,
   can teach us how to alter our gestures.

God of walls, doors and reticence, nemesis
overtakes the sacrilegious technocrat,
   but blessed is the City that thanks you
   for giving us games and grammar and metres.

By whose grace, also, every gathering
of two or three in confident amity
   repeats the pentecostal marvel,
   as each in each finds his right translator.

In this world our colossal immodesty
has plundered and poisoned, it is possible
   You still might save us, who by now have
   learned this: that scientists, to be truthful,

must remind us to take all they say as a
tall story, that abhorred in the Heav'ns are all
   self-proclaimed poets who, to wow an
   audience, utter some resonant lie.

May 1968

Six Commissioned Texts

I. RUNNER
(Commentary for a film, directed by Donald Owen
and produced by The National Film Board of Canada)

FIRST VOICE   Excellence is a gift: among mankind
                To one is assigned a ready wit,
                To another swiftness of eye or foot.

Art which raises Nature to perfection
Itself demands the passion of the elect
Who expect to win.

As Pindar long ago in Greece was proud to hail
Thessalian Hippokleas, even so
It is meet we praise in our days fleet-footed
Bruce Kidd from Toronto.

ANNOUNCER   The Place of Training: The East York Track Club.
               The Trainer: Fred Foote.
               The Training Schedule: two hours a day, six days a
                   week.
               Average distance run per week: one hundred miles.

SECOND VOICE   All visible visibly
               Moving things
               Spin or swing,
               One of the two,
               Move, as the limbs
               Of a runner do,
               To and fro,
               Forward and back,
               Or, as they swiftly
               Carry him,
               In orbit go
               Round an endless track:
               So, everywhere, every
               Creature disporting
               Itself according
               To the law of its making,
               In the rivals' dance
               Of a balanced pair,
               Or the ring-dance
               Round a common centre,
               Delights the eye
               By its symmetry
               As it changes place,
               Blessing the unchangeable
               Absolute rest
               Of the space all share.

FIRST VOICE   Speed is inborn in sprinter's muscle,
               But long learning alone can build
               Stamina and strength.
SECOND VOICE   By instruction only
               Can limbs learn to live their movements
               Without thinking.
FIRST VOICE   All important
               Is leg-action: arms are for balance.
SECOND VOICE   Of more moment is mileage run
               Than time taken.

ANNOUNCER   Now for the main event of this Dominion Day
             Celebration in East York:
             The Two-mile Invitation Race.

             We have three international track stars here this
             afternoon:
             Lt. Max Truex of the United States Navy in the dark
             trunks,
             Laszlo Tabori, late of Hungary, in the light trunks,
             And, of course,
             Toronto's own Bruce Kidd.

             The runners are lining up for the start mark:
             The officials are ready.
             They're off!

             They're jockeying for position round the first bend.
             Tabori's taking a strong lead.
             Kidd's right after him.
             Now Truex is moving out in front.
             Tabori's coming up strong behind him.
             Coming down the straightway now, it's
             Tabori
             Truex
             Kidd.

FIRST VOICE   Rivals should ride to the race together,
                 Be firm friends.
SECOND VOICE   Foolish is he
                 Who, greedy for victory, grits his teeth,
                 Frowns fiercely before contests,
                 And no neighbor.
FIRST VOICE   It is nice to win,
                 But sport shall be loved by losers also:
                 Foul is envy.
SECOND VOICE   False are those
                 With warm words for the winner after
                 A poor race.
FIRST VOICE   Pleasing to the ear
                 Are clapping crowds, but the cold stop-watch
                 Tells the truth.
SECOND VOICE   There is time and place
                 For a fine performance: Fate forbids
                 Mortals to be at their best always.
                 God-given is the great day.

ANNOUNCER   Truex is spurting ahead,
             But Tabori and Kidd are hot on his heels.
             One mile to go.
             The runners are maintaining a grueling pace.

             Now we have the official standing in the two-mile event.
             KIDD first
             TABORI second
             TRUEX third.

611

The camera's eye
Does not lie,
But it cannot show
The life within,
The life of a runner,
Or yours or mine,
That race which is neither
Fast nor slow,
For nothing can ever
Happen twice,
That story which moves
Like music when
Begotten notes
New notes beget,
Making the flowing
Of Time a growing,
Till what it could be
At last it is,
Where Fate is Freedom,
Grace and Surprise.

May 1962

II. THE TWELVE

Anthem for the Feast of any Apostle. Music by Sir William Walton
(for Cuthbert Simpson)

1

RECITATIVE   Without arms or charm of culture,
Unimportant persons
From an unimportant Province,
They did as the Spirit bid,
Went forth into a joyless world
Of swords and rhetoric
To bring it joy.

CHORUS   When they heard the Word, some demurred, some were
shocked, some mocked. But many were stirred, and the
Word spread. Dead souls were quickened to life; the sick
were healed by the Truth revealed; released into peace
from the gin of old sin, men forgot themselves in the glory
of the story told by the Twelve.

Then the Dark Lord, adored by this world, perceived the
threat of the light to his might. From his throne he spoke
to his own. The loud crowd, the sedate engines of State,
were moved by his will to kill. It was done. One by one they
were caught, tortured and slain.

2

SOLO   O Lord, my God,
Though I forsake Thee,
Forsake me not,
But guide me as I walk
Through the Valley of Mistrust,

And let the cry of my disbelieving absence
Come unto Thee,
Thou who declared unto Moses
I SHALL BE THERE.

3

CHORUS   Children play about the ancestral graves: the dead no
longer walk.
Excellent still in their splendor are the antique statues:
but can do neither good nor evil.
Beautiful still are the starry heavens: but our Fate is not
written there.
Holy still is Speech, but there is no sacred tongue: the
Truth may be told in all.

Twelve as the winds and months are those who taught us
these things:
Envisaging each in an oval glory, let us praise them all
with a merry noise.

January 1965

III. MORALITIES
(Text after Aesop. Music by Hans Werner Henze)

1

SPEAKER   In the First Age the frogs dwelt
At peace in their pond: they paddled about,
Flies they caught and fat grew.

Courts they knew not, nor kings nor servants,
No laws they had, nor police nor jails:
All were equal, happy together.

The days went by in unbroken calm:
Bored they grew, ungrateful for
Their good luck, began to murmur.

CHORUS   Higgledy-Piggledy,
What our Society
Needs is more Discipline,
Form and Degree.
Nobody wants to live
Anachronistically:
Lions have a Hierarchy,
Why shouldn't we?

SPEAKER   To mighty Jove on his jeweled throne
Went the Frog-Folk, the foolish people:
Thus they cried in chorus together.

CHORUS   Hickory-Dockery,
Greatest Olympian,
Graciously grant the pe-
-tition we bring.

613

                    Life as we know it is
                    Unsatisfactory,
                    We want a Monarchy,
                    Give us a King!

BASS SOLO   Foolish children, your choice is unwise.
               But so be it: go back and wait.

SPEAKER   Into their pond from the heavens above,
               With a splendid splash that sprayed them all,
               Something fell, then floated around.

               From the edge of their pond in awe they gazed,
               The Frog-Folk, the foolish people:
               Words they waited, but no words came.

CHORUS   He has no legs. He has no head.
               Is he dumb? Is he deaf? Is he blind? Is he dead?
               It's not a man. It's not a frog.
               Why, it's nothing but a rotten old log!
               Silly stump, watch me jump!
               Tee-hee-hee, you can't catch me!
               Boo to you! Boo! Boo! Boo!

SPEAKER   Back to Jove on his jeweled throne
               Went the Frog-Folk, the foolish people:
               Thus they cried in chorus together.

CHORUS   Jiggery-Pokery,
                           Jove, you've insulted the
                           Feelings of every
                           Sensitive frog:
                           What we demand is a
                           Plenipotentiary
                           Sovereign, not an in-
                           -animate log.

BASS SOLO   By the hard way must the unwise learn.
               So be it: go back and wait.

SPEAKER   Onto their pond from the heavens above,
               Cruel-beaked, a crane alighted.
               Fierce, ravenous, a frog-eater.

               Doom was upon them, Dread seized
               The Frog-Folk, the foolish people:
               They tried to escape. It was too late.

CHORUS   No! No! Woe! Woe! O! O! O . . .

SPEAKER   If people are too dumb to know when all is well with them,
               The gods shrug their shoulders and say:—To Hell with
                    them.

2

SPEAKER   When first had no second, before Time was,
           Mistress Kind, the Mother of all things,
           Summoned the crows: they crowded before Her.

ALTO SOLO Dun must you be, not dainty to behold,
           For your gain, though, I grace you with the gift of song:
           Well shall you warble, as welcome to the ear
           As the lively lark or loud nightingale.
           Go in peace.

SPEAKER   Gaily they went,
           And daily at dawn with dulcet voices
           Tooted in the tree-tops a tuneful madrigal.

CHORUS   Now, glorious in the East, the day is breaking:
           Creatures of field and forest, from your sleep awaking,
           Consort your voices, fearless of exposure,
           And of yourselves now make a free disclosure,
           Your pitch of presence to the world proclaiming,
           Expressing, affirming, uttering and naming,
           And each in each full recognition finding,
           No scornful echo but a warm responding,
           Your several notes not harsh nor interfering,
           But all in joy and concord co-inhering.

SPEAKER   So they chanted till by chance one day
           Came within earshot where the crows were nesting
           A stand of horses, stallions and mares,
           Whinnying and neighing as their wont in Spring is.

CHORUS   How strange! How astonishing! What astonishing sounds!
           Never have we heard such noises as these.
           It's so . . . so . . . so . . . so . . . so IT!
           How new, How new! We must be too. What a break-through!
           Away with dominant and tonic!
           Let's be chic and electronic.
           Down with the Establishment!
           Up with non-music, the Sound-Event!
           Arias are out and neighing is in:
           Hurrah for horses! Let us begin.

SPEAKER   But crows are no more horses than chutney is tabasco:
           Their efforts at *aggiornamento* ended in fiasco.

CHORUS   CAW! CAW! CAW! CAW! CAW!

3

SPEAKER   A ship put to sea, sailed out of harbor
           On a peaceful morning with passengers aboard.
           The sun was shining, but the ship's Captain,
           Weather-wise, watching the sky,
           Warned his crew.

BASS SOLO	Wild will be to-night With a gurling gale and great waves. To your storm stations! Stand by!
CHORUS	O Captain, Captain, tell us the truth! Are we doomed to drown in the deep sea?
BASS SOLO	While my body breathes I will battle for our lives, But our fate lies now in Neptune's hands.
CHORUS	Ah! What shall we do? The ship is about to founder, Overwhelmed by the waves that so wildly surround her. Neptune at our sins is righteously offended: Over the deck his dreadful trident is extended. Neptune, Neptune, forgive us! We confess it sadly, We have neglected Thy worship and acted very badly. Forgive us! Have mercy, have mercy, and be our Saviour, And for ever after we will alter our behavior. Neptune, thou Strong One, stop this outrageous welter, Restrain the wind and waft us safely into shelter: Bulls we will bring to Thine altar and incense offer, With treasures of great pride fill up Thy temple coffer.
BASS SOLO	The wind is falling, the waves are less, The clouds scatter, the sky lightens: By the kindness of Neptune we have come through.
CHORUS	We knew He was joking, not serious: Who would harm nice people like us?

          In this merry month of May,
             Dew on leaves a-sparkle,
          Of youth and love and laughter sing,
             Dancing in a circle.

          Over hill, over dale,
             Over the wide water,
          Jack McGrew is come to woo
             Jill, the oil-king's daughter.

          Come from afar in his motorcar,
             Eager to show devotion,
          Looking so cute in his Sunday Suit,
             And smelling of shaving-lotion.

          Here comes the Bride at her Father's side,
             Fresh as thyme or parsley:
          Blushing now, to the Bridegroom's bow
             She answers with a curtsey.

BOYS' SEMI-CHORUS   Kiss her once, kiss her twice,
            Bring her orchids on a salver,
        Spit in her eye if she starts to cry,
            And send her to Charlie Colver.

GIRLS' SEMI-CHORUS   Feed the brute eggs and fruit,
            Keep him clean and tidy,
        Give him what-for if he starts to snore,
            And scold him every Friday.

CHORUS   We wish you health, we wish you wealth,
            And seven smiling children,
        Silver-bright be every night,
            And every day be golden.

        Captain, why do you sit apart,
        Frowning over your nautical chart?
        Blue is the sky and bright is the sun:
        Leave your bridge and join the fun.

BASS SOLO   The sky is blue, the sun is bright,
        But who laughs in the morning may weep before night.

CHORUS   Your gloom does not enlighten us:
        We will not let you frighten us.

        An acid-drop for the Corner Cop,
            A crab-apple for Teacher,
        Some mouldy fudge for His Honor the Judge,
            And a Bronx Cheer for the Preacher.

SPEAKER   When afraid, men pray to the gods in all sincerity,
        But worship only themselves in their days of prosperity.

1967

IV. A REMINDER
(*Prologue for Christ Church* Son et Lumière, *Summer 1968*)

Mr. Dean, Canons and Students of Christ Church, Ladies and Gentlemen, in lieu of prologue a reminder.

Truth is a single realm, but its governance is a Dual Monarchy.

Tonight we are to take our pleasure in that moiety which lies under the especial care of DAME PHILOLOGY, where persons with Proper Names choose to say and do certain things when, had they so wished, they could have said and done others, where to hear is to translate and to know is to be known.

But, before settling down to enjoy Her lively company, it is meet that we remember to give homage and fair attribution to one who cannot be with us on this occasion, Her co-parcener in wisdom and in this University co-regent, Her younger but no less august and humane sister, DAME ALGEBRA.

Praise Her because, mute but full of sentence, Her written structures exemplify the patterns it is their purpose to convey, and so are read the same by all minds.

Praise Her because She can so elegantly summarize the average effect of anonymous and seemingly disorderly occurrences.

Hers the pure joy of knowing what at all times and in all places is the case: Hers the music, silent and uncarnal, of immortal necessity.

Woe to us if we speak slightingly of Her. Except Her grace prevent, we are doomed to idolatry, to worship imaginary gods of our own childish making, creatures of whim both cruel and absurd.

For She it is, and She alone who, without ambiguity or palter, can teach us to rejoice in the holy Providence of our Creator and our Judge.

Honor to Her, then, and delight to those who serve Her faithfully.

But to Her Sister's revels now. Let music strike!

1968

V. THE BALLAD OF BARNABY
(for Chuck Turner)

(to Guitar accompaniment)

Listen, good people, and you shall hear
A story of old that will gladden your ear,
The Tale of Barnaby, who was, they say,
The finest tumbler of his day.

In every town great crowds he drew,
And all men marvelled to see him do
The French Vault, the Vault of Champagne,
The Vault of Metz, and the Vault of Lorraine.

His eyes were blue, his figure was trim,
He liked the girls and the girls liked him;
For years he lived a life of vice,
Drinking in taverns and throwing the dice.

It happened one day he was riding along
Between two cities, whistling a song,
When he saw what then was quite common to see,
Two ravens perched on a gallows-tree.

'Barnaby,' the first raven began,
'Will one day be as this hanging man':
'Yes,' said the other, 'and we know well
That when that day comes he will go to Hell.'

Then Barnaby's conscience smote him sore;
He repented of all he had done heretofore:
'Woe is me! I will forsake
This wicked world and penance make.'

The evening air was grave and still
When he came to a monastery built on a hill:
As its bells the Angelus did begin,
He knocked at the door and they let him in.

(*Choral music*)

The monks in that place were men of parts,
Learned in the sciences and the arts:
The Abbot could logically define
The place of all creatures in the Scheme Divine.

Brother Maurice then wrote down all that he said
In a flowing script that it might be read,
And Brother Alexander adorned the book
With pictures that gave it a beautiful look.

There were brothers there who could compose
Latin Sequences in verse and prose,
And a brother from Picardy, too, who sung
The praise of Our Lady in the vulgar tongue.

(*Choral music*)

Now Barnaby had never learned to read,
Nor *Paternoster* knew nor *Creed*;
Watching them all at work and prayer,
Barnaby's heart began to despair.

Down to the crypt at massing-time
He crept like a man intent on crime:
In a niche there above the altar stood
A statue of Our Lady carved in wood.

'Blessed Virgin,' he cried, 'enthroned on high,
Ignorant as a beast am I:
Tumbling is all I have learnt to do;
Mother-of-God, let me tumble for You.'

Straightway he stripped off his jerkin,
And his tumbling acts he did begin:
So eager was he to do Her honor
That he vaulted higher than ever before.

(*Ballet music*)

The French Vault, the Vault of Champagne,
The Vault of Metz and the Vault of Lorraine,
He did them all till he sank to the ground,
His body asweat and his head in a swound.

Unmarked by him, Our Lady now
Steps down from her niche and wipes his brow.
'Thank you, Barnaby,' She said and smiled;
'Well have you tumbled for me, my child.'

From then on at the Office-Hours
Barnaby went to pay Her his devoirs.
One brother thought to himself: 'Now where
Does Barnaby go at our times of prayer?'

And so next day when Barnaby slipped
Away he followed him down to the crypt.
When he saw how he honored the Mother-of-God,
This brother thought: 'This is very odd.

It may be well: I believe it is,
But the Abbot, surely, should know of this.'
To the Abbot he went with reverent mien
And told him exactly what he had seen.

The Abbot said to him: 'Say no word
To the others of what you have seen and heard.
I will come to-morrow and watch with you
Before I decide what I ought to do.'

Next day behind a pillar they hid,
And the Abbot marked all that Barnaby did.
Watching him leap and vault and tumble,
He thought, 'This man is holy and humble.'

            (*Ballet music*)

'Lady,' cried Barnaby, 'I beg of Thee
To intercede with Thy Son for me!',
Gave one more leap, then down he dropped,
And lay dead still, for his heart had stopped.

Then grinning demons, black as coal,
Swarmed out of Hell to seize his soul:
'In vain shall be his pious fuss,
For every tumbler belongs to us.'

            (*Ballet music*)

But Our Lady and Her angels held them at bay,
With shining swords they drove them away,
And Barnaby's soul they bore aloft,
Singing with voices sweet and soft.

CHORUS: *Gloria in excelsis Deo.*

                                                    1969

VI. UNITED NATIONS HYMN
(*Music by Pablo Casals*)

Eagerly, Musician,
Strike your string,
So we may sing,
Elated, optative,
Our several voices
Interblending,
Playfully contending,
Not interfering
But co-inhering,
For all within
The cincture of the sound
Is holy ground,
Where all are Brothers,
None faceless Others.

Let mortals beware
Of words, for
With words we lie,
Can say peace
When we mean war,
Foul thought speak fair
And promise falsely.
But song is true:
Let music for peace
Be the paradigm,
For peace means to change
At the right time,
As the World-Clock
Goes tick and tock.

So may the story
Of our human city
Presently move
Like music, when
Begotten notes
New notes beget,
Making the flowing
Of time a growing,
Till what it could be
At last it is,
Where even sadness
Is a form of gladness,
Where Fate is Freedom,
Grace and Surprise.

March 1971

N.B.: Some of the lines in the last stanza I wrote for a Canadian Film Board documentary, *Runner*. I found I needed them again.

Prologue at Sixty
(for Friedrich Heer)

Dark-green upon distant heights
the stationary flocks foresters tend,
blond and fertile the fields below them:
browing a hog-back, an oak stands
post-alone, light-demanding.

Easier to hear, harder to see,
limbed lives, locomotive,
automatic and irritable,
social or solitary, seek their foods,
mates and territories while their time lasts.

Radial republics, rooted to spots,
bilateral monarchies, moving frankly,
stoic by sort and self-policing,
enjoy their rites, their realms of data,
live well by the Law of their Flesh.

All but the youngest of the yawning mammals,
Name-Giver, Ghost-Fearer,
maker of wars and wise-cracks,
a rum creature, in a crisis always,
the anxious species to which I belong,

whom chance and my own choice have arrived
to bide here yearly from bud-haze
to leaf-blush, dislodged from elsewhere,
by blood barbarian, in bias of view
a Son of the North, outside the *limes*.

Rapacious pirates my people were,
crude and cruel, but not calculating,
never marched in step nor made straight roads,
nor sank like senators to a slave's taste
for grandiose buildings and gladiators.

But the Gospel reached the unroman lands.
I can translate what onion-towers
of five parish churches preach in Baroque:
to make One, there must be Two,
Love is substantial, all Luck is good,

Flesh must fall through fated time
from birth to death, both unwilled,
but Spirit may climb counterwise
from a death, in faith freely chosen,
to resurrection, a re-beginning.

And the Greek Code got to us also:
a Mind of Honor must acknowledge
the happy eachness of all things,
distinguish even from odd numbers,
and bear witness to what-is-the-case.

East, West, on the Autobahn
motorists whoosh, on the Main Line
a far-sighted express will snake by,
through a gap granted by grace of nature:
still today, as in the Stone Age,

our sandy vale is a valued passage.
Alluvial flats, flooded often,
lands of outwash, lie to the North,
to the South litters of limestone alps
embarrass the progress of path-seekers.

Their thoughts upon ski-slope or theatre-opening,
few who pass us pay attention
to our squandered hamlets where at harvest time
chugging tractors, child-driven,
shamble away down sheltered lanes.

Quiet now but acquainted too
with unwelcome visitors, violation,
scare and scream, the scathe of battle:
Turks have been here, Boney's legions,
Germans, Russians, and no joy they brought.

Though the absence of hedge-rows is odd to me
(no Whig landlord, the landscape vaunts,
ever empired on Austrian ground),
this unenglish tract after ten years
into my love has looked itself,

added its names to my numinous map
of the *Solihull* gas-works, gazed at in awe
by a bronchial boy, the *Blue John Mine*,
the *Festiniog* railway, the *Rhayader* dams,
Cross Fell, Keld and *Cauldron Snout*,

of sites made sacred by something read there,
a lunch, a good lay, or sheer lightness of heart,
the *Fürbringer* and the *Friedrich Strasse*,
Isafjördur, Epomeo,
Poprad, Basel, Bar-le-Duc,

of more modern holies, *Middagh Street,*
Carnegie Hall and the *Con-Ed* stacks
on *First Avenue*. Who am I now?
An American? No, a New Yorker,
who opens his *Times* at the obit page,

whose dream images date him already,
awake among lasers, electric brains,
do-it-yourself sex manuals,
bugged phones, sophisticated
weapon-systems and sick jokes.

Already a helpless orbited dog
has blinked at our sorry conceited O,
where many are famished, few look good,
and my day turned out torturers
who read *Rilke* in their rest periods.

Now the Cosmocrats are crashed through time-zones
in jumbo jets to a Joint Conference:
nor sleep nor shit have our shepherds had,
and treaties are signed (with secret clauses)
by Heads who are not all there.

Can Sixty make sense to Sixteen-Plus?
What has my camp in common with theirs,
with buttons and beards and Be-Ins?
Much, I hope. In *Acts* it is written
Taste was no problem at Pentecost.

To speak is human because human to listen,
beyond hope, for an Eighth Day,
when the creatured Image shall become the Likeness:
Giver-of-Life, translate for me
till I accomplish my corpse at last.

April 1967

Epistle to a Godson
(for Philip Spender)

DEAR PHILIP: 'Thank God for boozy godfathers'
you wrote in our guest-book, which was flattering:
    though I've reached the years when discretion
    calls for a yearly medical check-up,

who am I to avouch for any Christian
baby, far less offer ghostly platitudes
    to a young man? In yester times it
    was different: the old could still be helpful

when they could nicely envisage the future
as a named and settled landscape their children
    would make the same sense of as they did,
    laughing and weeping at the same stories.

Then sheep and goats were easy to recognize,
local fauna: good meant Giles the shoemaker
    taking care of the village ninny,
    evil Count ffoulkes who in his tall donjon

indulged in sinister eccentricities.
But *I speak from experience*, how could I
    say that to you, who can't remember
    when everyone travelled by railway,

and the poor were what they were used to being,
the creators of wealth not, as now they are,
    an expensive nuisance? (Nobody
    has dared suggest gassing them, but someone

surely will.) You don't need me to tell you what's
going on: the ochlocratic media,
    joint with under-the-dryer gossip,
    process and vent without intermission

all to-day's ugly secrets. Imageable
no longer, a featureless anonymous
    threat from behind, to-morrow has us
    gallowed shitless: if what is to happen

occurs according to what Thucydides
defined as 'human', we've had it, are in for
    a disaster that no four-letter
    words will tardy. I've beheld in nightmares

(who hasn't?) likely abominations: seething
behavioral sinks, the Muses scuttering,
    smelly, from eutrophied Helicon,
    the Witches' Sabbath on Garbage Mountain,

Herod's genetic engineers commanded
to modify the Innocents. By then, with
    any luck, the tangible Me should
    be mineral, too set in my habits

to distinguish light from darkness, and valued
in current prices at three-dollars-fifty:
    but you might well be there, if what is
    ripely is not promptly done. Yet who can

issue proper instructions? Not, certainly,
our global Archons, whose top-lofty slogans
    are as off the beam as their syntax
    is vague: (they would be figures of fun, if

very clever little boys had not found it
amusing to build devices for them, more
    apt at disassembly than any
    old fire-spewing theogonic monster.)

To be responsible for the happiness
of the Universe is not a sinecure:
    in elite lands your generation
    may be called to opt for a discipline

that out-peers the monks, a Way of obedience,
poverty and—good grief!—perhaps chastity,
    yet in this world's ill-weathered open,
    a stern venture pre-figured in folk-tales

as the Quest Perilous. For such wayfarers,
what should we write to give them the nourishment,
    warmth and shelter they'll be in need of?
    Nothing obscene or unpleasant: only

the unscarred overfed enjoy Calvary
as a verbal event. Nor satiric: no
    scorn will ashame the Adversary.
    Nor shoddily made: to give a stunning

display of concinnity and elegance
is the least we can do, and its dominant
    mood should be that of a Carnival.
    Let us hymn the small but journal wonders

of Nature and of households, and then finish
on a serio-comic note with legends
    of ultimate eucatastrophe,
    regeneration beyond the waters.

But perhaps you think poems are as foolish
as most poets, and would rather spend your spare
    moments romping around in Cantor's
    logical paradise, or beseeching

such knotty points as *Can we hang a robber*
who is not there? or *What is the color of*
    the number Three? Why not? All pleasures
    come from God. Since I *am* your godfather,

I'll close this letter with some worldly maxims:
Be glad your being is unnecessary,
    then turn your toes out as you walk, dear,
    and remember who you are, a Spender.

                                            April 1969

The Art of Healing
(*In Memoriam David Protetch, M.D.*)

        Most patients believe
    dying is something they do,
        not their physician,
        that white-coated sage,
    never to be imagined
        naked or married.

Begotten by one,
I should know better. 'Healing,'
    Papa would tell me,
    'is not a science,
but the intuitive art
    of wooing Nature.

    Plants, beasts, may react
according to the common
    whim of their species,
    but all humans have
prejudices of their own
    which can't be foreseen.

    To some, ill-health is
a way to be important,
    others are stoics,
    a few fanatics,
who won't feel happy until
    they are cut open.'

    Warned by him to shun
the sadist, the nod-crafty,
    and the fee-conscious,
    I knew when we met,
I had found a consultant
    who thought as he did,

    yourself a victim
of medical engineers
    and their arrogance,
    when they atom-bombed
your sick pituitary
    and over-killed it.

    'Every sickness
is a musical problem,'
    so said Novalis,
    'and every cure
a musical solution':
    You knew that also.

    Not that in my case
you heard any shattering
    discords to resolve:
    to date my organs
still seem pretty sure of their
    self-identity.

    For my small ailments
you, who were mortally sick,
    prescribed with success:
    my major vices,
my mad addictions, you left
    to my own conscience.

Was it your very
predicament that made me
sure I could trust you,
if I were dying,
to say so, not insult me
with soothing fictions?

Must diabetics
all content with a nisus
to self-destruction?
One day you told me:
'It is only bad temper
that keeps me going.'

But neither anger
nor lust are omnipotent,
nor should we even
want our friends to be
superhuman. Dear David,
dead one, rest in peace,

having been what all
doctors should be, but few are,
and, even when most
difficult, condign
of our biassed affection
and objective praise.

May 1969

A New Year Greeting

After an article by Mary J. Marples in Scientific American, *January, 1969*
(for Vassily Yanowsky)

On this day tradition allots
to taking stock of our lives,
my greetings to all of you, Yeasts,
Bacteria, Viruses,
Aerobics and Anaerobics:
A Very Happy New Year
to all for whom my ectoderm
is as Middle-Earth to me.

For creatures your size I offer
a free choice of habitat,
so settle yourselves in the zone
that suits you best, in the pools
of my pores or the tropical
forests of arm-pit and crotch,
in the deserts of my fore-arms,
or the cool woods of my scalp.

Build colonies: I will supply
    adequate warmth and moisture,
the sebum and lipids you need,
    on condition you never
do me annoy with your presence,
    but behave as good guests should,
not rioting into acne
    or athlete's-foot or a boil.

Does my inner weather affect
    the surfaces where you live?
Do unpredictable changes
    record my rocketing plunge
from fairs when the mind is in tift
    and relevant thoughts occur
to fouls when nothing will happen
    and no one calls and it rains.

I should like to think that I make
    a not impossible world,
but an Eden it cannot be:
    my games, my purposive acts,
may turn to catastrophes there.
    If you were religious folk,
how would your dramas justify
    unmerited suffering?

By what myths would your priests account
    for the hurricanes that come
twice every twenty-four hours,
    each time I dress or undress,
when, clinging to keratin rafts,
    whole cities are swept away
to perish in space, or the Flood
    that scalds to death when I bathe?

Then, sooner or later, will dawn
    A Day of Apocalypse,
when my mantle suddenly turns
    too cold, too rancid, for you,
appetising to predators
    of a fiercer sort, and I
am stripped of excuse and nimbus,
    a Past, subject to Judgement.

May 1969

Smelt and Tasted

The nose and palate never doubt
Their verdicts on the world without,
But instantaneously condemn
Or praise each fact that reaches them:

Our tastes may change in time, it's true,
But for the fairer if they do.

Compared with almost any brute,
Our savouring is less acute,
But, subtly as they judge, no beast
Can solve the mystery of a feast,
Where love is strengthened, hope restored,
In hearts by chemical accord.

May 1969

Heard and Seen

Events reported by the ear
Are soft or loud, not far or near,
In what is heard we only sense
Transition and impermanence:
A bark, a laugh, a rifle-shot,
These may concern us or may not.

What-has-been and what-is-to-be
To vision form a unity:
The seen hill stays the way it is,
But forecasts greater distances,
And we acknowledge with delight
A so-on after every sight.

May 1969

I Am Not a Camera

Photographable life is always either trivial or already sterilised.
EUGEN ROSENSTOCK-HUESSY

To call our sight Vision
implies that, to us,
all objects are subjects.

*   *   *

What we have not named
or beheld as a symbol
escapes our notice.

*   *   *

We never look at two people
or one person twice
in the same way.

*   *   *

It is very rude to take close-ups and, except
when enraged, we don't:
lovers, approaching to kiss,
instinctively shut their eyes before their faces
can be reduced to
anatomical data.

*   *   *

Instructive it may be to peer through lenses:
each time we do, though, we should apologise
to the remote or the small for intruding
upon their quiddities.

*   *   *

The camera records
visual facts: i.e.,
all may be fictions.

*   *   *

Flash-backs falsify the Past:
they forget
the remembering Present.

*   *   *

On the screen we can only
witness human behavior:
Choice is for camera-crews.

*   *   *

The camera may
do justice to laughter, but must
degrade sorrow.

A Bad Night
(A LEXICAL EXERCISE)

In his dream zealous
To attain his home,
But ensorcelling powers
Have contorted space,
Odded the way:
Instead of a facile
Five-minute trot,
Far he must hirple,
Clumsied by cold,
Buffeted often
By blouts of hail

Or pirries of rain,
On stolchy paths
Over glunch clouds,
Where infrequent shepherds,
Sloomy of face,
Snudge of spirit,
Snoachy of speech,
With scaddle dogs
Tend a few scrawny
Cag-mag sheep.

Fetched into conscience
By a hoasting fit,
He lies darkling,
Senex morosus,
Too ebb of verve
Even to monster
Social trifles,
Or violent over
The world's wrongs,
While time drumbles,
A maunder of moments,
Wan, haphazard,
And unaccented:
To re-faith himself,
He rummages lines,
Plangent or pungent,
By bards of sentence,
But all to his sample
Ring fribble or fop,
Not one of them worth
A hangman's wages.

June 1969

Moon Landing

It's natural the Boys should whoop it up for
so huge a phallic triumph, an adventure
    it would not have occurred to women
    to think worth while, made possible only

because we like huddling in gangs and knowing
the exact time: yes, our sex may in fairness
    hurrah the deed, although the motives
    that primed it were somewhat less than *menschlich*.

A grand gesture. But what does it period?
What does it osse? We were always adroiter
    with objects than lives, and more facile
    at courage than kindness: from the moment

the first flint was flaked this landing was merely
a matter of time. But our selves, like Adam's,
    still don't fit us exactly, modern
    only in this—our lack of decorum.

Homer's heroes were certainly no braver
than our Trio, but more fortunate: Hector
    was excused the insult of having
    his valor covered by television.

Worth *going* to see? I can well believe it.
Worth *seeing*? Mneh! I once rode through a desert
    and was not charmed: give me a watered
    lively garden, remote from blatherers

about the New, the von Brauns and their ilk, where
on August mornings I can count the morning
    glories, where to die has a meaning,
    and no engine can shift my perspective.

Unsmudged, thank God, my Moon still queens the Heavens
as She ebbs and fulls, a Presence to glop at,
    Her Old Man, made of grit not protein,
    still visits my Austrian several

with His old detachment, and the old warnings
still have power to scare me: Hybris comes to
    an ugly finish, Irreverence
    is a greater oaf than Superstition.

Our apparatniks will continue making
the usual squalid mess called History:
    all we can pray for is that artists,
    chefs and saints may still appear to blithe it.

August 1969

The Garrison

Martini-time: time to draw the curtains and
choose a composer we should like to hear from,
before coming to table for one of your
    savoury messes.

Time crumbs all ramparts, brachypod Nemesis
catches up sooner or later with hare-swift
Achilles, but personal song and language
    somehow mizzle them.

Thanks to which it's possible for the breathing
still to break bread with the dead, whose brotherhood
gives us confidence to wend the trivial
    thrust of the Present,

so self-righteous in its assumptions and so
certain that none dare out-face it. We, Chester,
and the choir we sort with have been assigned to
    garrison stations.

Whoever rules, our duty to the City
is loyal opposition, never greening
for the big money, never neighing after
    a public image.

Let us leave rebellions to the choleric
who enjoy them: to serve as a paradigm
now of what a plausible Future might be
    is what we're here for.

May 1969

Pseudo-Questions

Who could possibly approve of Metternich
and his Thought Police? Yet in a liberal
milieu would Adalbert Stifter have written
    his noble idylls?

Vice-versa, what God-fearing Magistrate
would dream of shaking hands with a financial
crook and Anti-Semite? Yet Richard Wagner
    wrought masterpieces.

Wild horses could not drag me to debates on
Art and Society: critics with credos,
Christian or Marxist, should keep their trap shut,
    lest they spout nonsense.

June 1969

Stark bewölkt
(for Stella Musulin)

I'm no photophil who burns
his body brown on beaches:
foolish I find this fashion
of modern surf-riding man.
Let plants by all means sun-bathe,
it helps them to make their meals:
exposure, though, to ultra-
-violet vapids the brain,
bids us be stodge and stupid.
Still, safe in some sheltered shade,
or watching through a window,
an ageing male, I demand
to see a smiling summer,
a sky bright and wholly blue,
save for a drifting cloudlet

634

like a dollop of whipped cream.
This year all is unthuswise:
O why so glum, weather-god?

Day after day we waken
to be scolded by a scowl,
venomous and vindictive,
a flat frowning Friday face,
horrid as a hang-over,
and mean as well: if you must
so disarray the heavens,
at least you might let them rain.
(Water is always welcome,
for trees to take neat and men
to make brandy or beer with.)
But, no, we don't get a drop,
dry you remain and doleful
in a perpetual pique.

Fowls mope, flowers are wretched,
the raspberry-canes are forced
into phyllomania.
To ignore you, not be cross,
one would have to be either
drunk, lit on amphetamines,
or a feverish lover:
being dead sober all day,
I find your bearing boorish,
by four in the afternoon
frequently close the curtains
to shut your shabbiness out.

Who or what are you mad at?
What has poor Austria done
to draw such disapproval?
The *Beamterei*, it's true,
is as awful as ever,
the drivers are dangerous,
standards at the *Staatsoper*
steadily decline each year,
and *Wien*'s become provincial
compared to the pride She was.
Still, it's a cosy country,
unracked by riots or strikes
and backward at drug-taking:
I've heard of a dozen lands
where life sounds far more ugsome,
fitter goals for your disgust.
(I needn't name them, for you, whose
glance circumspects the whole globe,
ken at first-hand what's cooking.)

Have done! What good does it do,
dumb god, just to deject us?
Foul our function may be, but
foul weather won't reform it.
If you merely wish our world
to mend its ways, remember:
when happy, men on the whole
behave a wee bit better,
when unhappy, always worse.

? 1971

Natural Linguistics
(for Peter Salus)

Every created thing has ways of pronouncing its ownhood:
    basic and used by all, even the mineral tribes,
is the hieroglyphical *koine* of visual appearance
    which, though it lacks the verb, is, when compared with our own
heaviest lexicons, so much richer and subtler in shape-nouns,
    color-adjectives and apt prepositions of place.
Verbs first appear with the flowers who utter imperative odors
    which, with their taste for sweets, insects are bound to obey:
motive, too, in the eyes of beasts is the language of gesture
    (urban life has, alas, sadly impoverished ours),
signals of interrogation, friendship, threat and appeasement,
    instantly taken in, seldom, if ever, misread.
All who have managed to break through the primal barrier of Silence
    into an audible world find an indicative AM:
though some carnivores, leaving messages written in urine,
    use a preterite WAS, none can conceive of a WILL,
nor have they ever made subjunctive or negative statements,
    even cryptics whose lives hang upon telling a fib.
Rage and grief they can sing, not self-reproach or repentance,
    nor have they legends to tell, though their respect for a rite
is more pious than ours, for a complex code of releasers
    trains them to walk in the ways which their ur-ancestors trod.
(Some of these codes remain mysteries to us: for instance,
    fish who travel in huge loveless anonymous turbs,
what is it keeps them in line? Our single certainty is that
    minnows deprived of their fore-brains go it gladly alone.)
Since in their circles it's not good form to say anything novel,
    none ever stutter on *er*, guddling in vain for a word,
none are at loss for an answer: none, it seems, are bilingual,
    but, if they cannot translate, that is the ransom they pay
for just doing their thing, not greedily trying to publish
    all the world as we do into our picture at once.
If they have never laughed, at least they have never talked drivel,
    never tortured their own kind for a point of belief,
never, marching to war, inflamed by fortissimo music,
    hundreds of miles from home died for a verbal whereas.

'Dumb' we may call them but, surely, our poets are right in assuming
    all would prefer that they were rhetorized *at* than *about*.

June 1969

The Aliens
(for William Gray)

Wide though the interrupt be that divides us, runers and counters,
from the Old World of the Plants, all lapped in a tolerant silence,
where, by the grace of chlorophyll, few of them ever have taken
life and not one put a sceptical question, we nod them as neighbours
who, to conclude from their friendly response to a gardener's handling,
like to be given the chance to get more than a self-education.
As for the hot-blooded Beasts, we didn't need Darwin to tell us
horses and rabbits and mice are our cognates, the double-voiced song-
   birds
cousins, however removed: unique as we seem, we, too, are
shovelled out into the cold, poodle-naked, as male or as female,
grab at and gobble up proteins, drop dung, perform the ungainly
brute-with-two-backs until, dared and doddered by age, we surrender,
lapse into stagnant stuff, while they by retaining a constant
visible shape through a lifetime, accord with our human idea of
having a Self. They also, we cannot but fancy, are peering
at a horizon as we do, aware of, however obscurely,
more than they must be concerned with, and vaguely elated at being
someone who's up and about: yes, even their humblest have, surely,
nosed a few steps on the hazardous foreright to courage,
utterance, joy and collateral love. That is why, in our folk-tales,
toads and squirrels can talk, in our epics the great be compared to
lions or foxes or eagles.
                         But between us and the Insects,
namely nine-tenths of the living, there grins a prohibitive fracture
empathy cannot transgress: (What Saint made a friend of a roach or
preached to an ant-hill?) Unrosed by a shame, unendorsed by a sorrow,
blank to a fear of failure, they daunt alike the believer's
faith in a fatherly providence and the atheist's dogma of purely
random events. To begin as a crawling insatiable eater,
then to be buried and mortify, then to emerge from the cere-cloth
winged and mateable, brilliantly coloured, a sipper of juices,
yet a compulsive hunter and hoarder, must do havoc to any
unitive sense. To insert them, excuse those unamiable towns where
sex is reserved for the Few and the many animate tool-kits
perish from overwear, one is tempted to cook up a Gnostic
myth of an earlier Fall, preceding by aeons the Reptiles:
Adam, a crab-like creature who'd just wriggled out of a steamy
ocean where he had failed at making a living and now lay
moribund, choked, on a shore without song. Unto whom the Seducer,
not our romantic Satan but a clever cartesian Archon,
coaxingly thus: *Not doing very well, are you, poor deathling,*
no, and unlikely to do any better, thanks to the schemes of
We-Know-Whom. (He's a Precious but logic was never his forte.)
Freedom may manage in Heaven with Incorporeals, but for
ghosted extended matter the consequence is to be doomed to
err where an error is mortal. But trust me and live, for I do know
clearly what needs to be done. If I programme your ganglia for you,
you shall inherit the earth.

Such a myth, we all know, is no answer.
What they mean to themselves or to God is a meaningless question:
they to us are quite simply what we must never become.

May 1970

Doggerel by a Senior Citizen
(for Robert Lederer)

Our earth in 1969
Is not the planet I call mine,
The world, I mean, that gives me strength
To hold off chaos at arm's length.

My Eden landscapes and their climes
Are constructs from Edwardian times,
When bath-rooms took up lots of space,
And, before eating, one said Grace.

The automobile, the aeroplane,
Are useful gadgets, but profane:
The enginry of which I dream
Is moved by water or by steam.

Reason requires that I approve
The light-bulb which I cannot love:
To me more reverence-commanding
A fish-tail burner on the landing.

My family ghosts I fought and routed,
Their values, though, I never doubted:
I thought their Protestant Work-Ethic
Both practical and sympathetic.

When couples played or sang duets,
It was immoral to have debts:
I shall continue till I die
To pay in cash for what I buy.

The Book of Common Prayer we knew
Was that of 1662:
Though with-it sermons may be well,
Liturgical reforms are hell.

Sex was, of course—it always is—
The most enticing of mysteries,
But news-stands did not yet supply
Manichaean pornography.

Then Speech was mannerly, an Art,
Like learning not to belch or fart:
I cannot settle which is worse,
The Anti-Novel or Free Verse.

Nor are those Ph.D's my kith,
Who dig the symbol and the myth:
I count myself a man of letters
Who writes, or hopes to, for his betters.

Dare any call Permissiveness
An educational success?
Saner those class-rooms which I sat in,
Compelled to study Greek and Latin.

Though I suspect the term is crap,
If there *is* a Generation Gap,
Who is to blame? Those, old or young,
Who will not learn their Mother-Tongue.

But Love, at least, is not a state
Either *en vogue* or out-of-date,
And I've true friends, I will allow,
To talk and eat with here and now.

Me alienated? Bosh! It's just
As a sworn citizen who must
Skirmish with it that I feel
Most at home with what is Real.

May 1969

Shorts II

A poet's hope: to be,
like some valley cheese,
local, but prized elsewhere.

* * *

A disappointed
politician, he became
obsessed in age with
the social virtues of rooks,
and adopted two leeches.

* * *

Who can picture
Calvin, Pascal or Nietzsche,
as a pink chubby boy?

* * *

Deprived of a mother to love him,
Descartes divorced
Mind from Matter.

* * *

When engineers drink together,
what professional
jokes can they tell?

* * *

The glass-lens
desanctified Sight: men believed
they had seen through Nature.

* * *

Space was holy to
pilgrims of old, till the plane
stopped all that nonsense.

* * *

When gales assault them,
trees are always astonished,
but never ask why.

* * *

The fire mumbles on
to itself, but allows us
to overhear it.

* * *

Rivers, sooner or later,
all reach some ocean,
and in due season all men
arrive at a death-bed, but
neither on purpose.

* * *

Youth, like the Press, is excited when Nature
throws one of her tantrums, but Age approves Her
when She's courteous: earthquakes, floods, eruptions,
    seem a bit vulgar.

* * *

Our tables and chairs and sofas
know things about us
our lovers can't.

* * *

What we touch is always
an Other: I may fondle
my leg, not Me.

* * *

In moments of joy
all of us wished we possessed
a tail we could wag.

* * *

Why must Growth rob us
of the infant's heavenly
power to bellow?

* * *

When I was little . . .
Why should this unfinished phrase
so pester me now?

* * *

Who, upon hearing
a tape of his speaking voice,
is not revolted?

* * *

Their senses cannot
teach the tired: they can only
feel in general.

* * *

Oncers do no damage;
only those who could love
can really corrupt.

* * *

Only bad rhetoric
can improve this world:
to true Speech it is deaf.

* * *

The words of liars
blush, but a statistician's
figures are shameless.

* * *

Virtue is always
more expensive than Vice, but
cheaper than Madness.

*   *   *

Cosmic trivia
we all are, but none of us
are unessential.

*   *   *

What is Death? A Life
disintegrating into
smaller simpler ones.

*   *   *

It is the unimportant
who make all the din:
both God and the Accuser
speak very softly.

*   *   *

God never makes knots,
but is expert, if asked to,
at untying them.

*   *   *

Does God ever judge
us by appearances? I
suspect that He does.

*   *   *

How many ravishing things whose innocent beauty astounds us
   owe their existence to Greed, Fear or Vainglory or Guilt.

*   *   *

Lucky the poets of old; for half their work was done for them:
   all would applaud when they named places or heroes or gods.
Proper Names are *an-sich* poetic, but now there is hardly
   one that a poet will dare pen without adding a gloss.

*   *   *

Blessed be all metrical rules that forbid automatic responses,
   force us to have second thoughts, free from the fetters of Self.

*   *   *

No, Surrealists, no! No, even the wildest of poems
    must, like prose, have a firm basis in staid common-sense.

           *   *   *

I suspect that without some undertone of the comic
    genuine serious verse cannot be written to-day.

           *   *   *

What should I write at Sixty-Four? is a question, a folly
    What should I write in Nineteen-Hundred-and-Seventy-One?

           *   *   *

To-day two poems begged to be written: I had to refuse them.
    Sorry, no longer, my dear! Sorry, my precious, not yet!

           *   *   *

Like it is among all wild men and repetitive creatures,
    eyed from a singular stand-point, is the Why of the Arts.
Poet, employ your vocative talent to utter exactly
    what you were graced to behold: leave us to judge for ourselves.

           *   *   *

Psychological critics, do be more precise in your language:
    symbols must not be confused with allegorical signs.

           *   *   *

Shameless envious Age!, when the Public will shell out more cash for
    note-books and sketches that were never intended for them
than for perfected works. Observing erasures and blunders,
    every amateur thinks: *I could have done it as well.*

           *   *   *

Gossip-Columnists I can forgive for they make no pretences,
    not Biographers who claim it's for Scholarship's sake.

           *   *   *

Autobiographer, please don't tell me the tale of your love-life:
    much as it mattered to you, nothing could marvel me less.

           *   *   *

Why is pornography boring? Because it can never surprise us.
    All of us know the few things Man as a mammal can do.

           *   *   *

Knowing artists, you think that you know all about Prima Donnas:
   boy!, just wait till you hear scientists get up and sing.

*   *   *

Why should the cleverest minds so often hold the religion
   Sacred is any Machine, all that's alive is profane?

*   *   *

Those who run to the apes to explain our behaviour are chuckle-
   -heads too dumb to know their arse from a hole-in-the-ground.

*   *   *

If all our acts are conditioned behaviour, then so are our theories:
   yet your behaviourist claims his is objectively true.

*   *   *

Horse-Flies, why didn't Nature bring you up to respect us?
   Bite us you can, but it is usually fatal for you.

*   *   *

What we mean when we say that So-and-So's *a good person,*
   no psychologist can tell, for we certainly don't
mean that He has no problems: all that is clear is that, when we
   say this, nobody says, shaking his head—*He is bad!*

*   *   *

Talent calls for display, some public space to perform in:
   Virtue hills itself, even from virtuous men.

*   *   *

When two persons discover that they have a passion in common,
   Sex, Donizetti or Chows, Class is no barrier at all:
secret to every class, though, its code of polite conversation,
   how one should carry on when talking to strangers and bores.

*   *   *

Violence is never just, though Justice may sometimes require it:
   tyrants are persons to whom requisite evil is fun.

*   *   *

Alienation from the Collective is always a duty:
   every State is the Beast who is Estrangement itself.

*   *   *

Is it Progress when T.V.'s children know all the names
Of politicians, but no longer play children's games?

*   *   *

Yes, a Society so obsessed with rabid consumption
    stinks, I entirely agree: but, student radicals, why,
why protest in its own dehumanised language of Ad-Mass?
    If you would civil our land, first you should civil your speech.

*   *   *

Why strip naked and bellow words of four letters in public?
    Poor young things, can it be none of you have any friends?

*   *   *

Somebody shouted, I read: *We are ALL of us marvelously gifted!*
    Sorry, my love, but I am: You, though, have proved that You ain't.

*   *   *

In adolescence, of course, at times I was cross or unhappy,
    but I cannot recall once having ever been bored.

*   *   *

I'm for Freedom because I mistrust the Censor in office:
    but, if I held the job, my!, how severe I should be.

1069 1971

Old People's Home

All are limitory, but each has her own
nuance of damage. The elite can dress and decent themselves,
    are ambulant with a single stick, adroit
to read a book all through, or play the slow movements of
    easy sonatas. (Yet, perhaps their very
carnal freedom is their spirit's bane: intelligent
    of what has happened and why, they are obnoxious
to a glum beyond tears.) Then come those on wheels, the average
    majority, who endure T.V. and, led by
lenient therapists, do community-singing, then
    the loners, muttering in Limbo, and last
the terminally incompetent, as improvident,
    unspeakable, impeccable as the plants
they parody. (Plants may sweat profusely but never
    sully themselves.) One tie, though, unites them: all
appeared when the world, though much was awry there, was more
    spacious, more comely to look at, its Old Ones
with an audience and secular station. Then a child,
    in dismay with Mamma, could refuge with Gran
to be revalued and told a story. As of now,

645

we all know what to expect, but their generation
is the first to fade like this, not at home but assigned
    to a numbered frequent ward, stowed out of conscience
as unpopular luggage.
                        As I ride the subway
    to spend half-an-hour with one, I revisage
who she was in the pomp and sumpture of her hey-day,
    when week-end visits were a presumptive joy,
not a good work. Am I cold to wish for a speedy
    painless dormition, pray, as I know she prays,
that God or Nature will abrupt her earthly function?

April 1970

Circe

Her Telepathic-Station transmits thought-waves
the second-rate, the bored, the disappointed,
and any of us when tired or uneasy,
        are tuned to receive.

So, though unlisted in atlas or phone-book,
Her Garden is easy to find. In no time
one reaches the gate over which is written
        large: MAKE LOVE NOT WAR.

Inside it is warm and still like a drowsy
September day, though the leaves show no sign of
turning. All around one notes the usual
        pinks and blues and reds,

a shade over-emphasised. The rose-bushes
have no thorns. An invisible orchestra
plays the Great Masters: the technique is flawless,
        the rendering schmaltz.

Of Herself no sign. But, just as the pilgrim
is starting to wonder 'Have I been hoaxed by
a myth?', he feels Her hand in his and hears Her
        murmuring: *At last!*

With me, mistaught one, you shall learn the answers.
What is Conscience but a nattering fish-wife,
the Tree of Knowledge but the splintered main-mast
        of the Ship of Fools?

Consent, you poor alien, to my arms where
sequence is conquered, division abolished:
soon, soon, in the perfect orgasm, you shall, pet,
        be one with the All.

She does not brutalise Her victims (beasts could
bite or bolt), She simplifies them to flowers,
sessile fatalists who don't mind and only
        can talk to themselves.

All but a privileged Few, the elite She
guides to Her secret citadel, the Tower
where a laugh is forbidden and DO HARM AS
    THOU WILT is the Law.

Dear little not-so-innocents, beware of
Old Grandmother Spider: rump Her endearments.
She's not quite as nice as She looks, nor you quite
    as tough as you think.

                                        May 1969

Short Ode to the Cuckoo

No one now imagines you answer idle questions
—How long shall I live? How long remain single?
*Will butter be cheaper?—*nor does your shout make
    husbands uneasy.

Compared with arias by the great performers
such as the merle, your two-note act is kid-stuff:
our most hardened crooks are sincerely shocked by
    your nesting habits.

Science, Aesthetics, Ethics, may huff and puff but they
cannot extinguish your magic: you marvel
the commuter as you wondered the savage.
    Hence, in my diary,

where I normally enter nothing but social
engagements and, lately, the death of friends, I
scribble year after year when I first hear you,
    of a holy moment.

                                        June 1971

Ode to the Medieval Poets

Chaucer, Langland, Douglas, Dunbar, with all your
brother Anons, how on earth did you ever manage,
    without anaesthetics or plumbing,
    in daily peril from witches, warlocks,

lepers, The Holy Office, foreign mercenaries
burning as they came, to write so cheerfully,
    with no grimaces of self-pathos?
    Long-winded you could be but not vulgar,

bawdy but not grubby, your raucous flytings
sheer high-spirited fun, whereas our makers,
    beset by every creature comfort,
    immune, they believe, to all superstitions,

647

even at their best are so often morose or
kinky, petrified by their gorgon egos.
    We all ask, but I doubt if anyone
    can really say why all age-groups should find our

Age quite so repulsive. Without its heartless
engines, though, you could not tenant my book-shelves,
    on hand to delect my ear and chuckle
    my sad flesh: I would gladly just now be

turning out verses to applaud a thundery
jovial June when the judas-tree is in blossom,
    but am forbidden by the knowledge
    that you would have wrought them so much better.

June 1971

An Encounter

The Year: 452. The Place: the southern
bank of the River Po. The Forelook: curtains
on further hopes of a Western and Christian
    civilisation.

For Attila and his Hun Horde, slant-eyed, sallow,
the creatures of an animist horse-culture,
dieted on raw-meat and goat-cheese, nocent to
    cities land letters,

were tented there, having routed the imperial
armies and preyed the luscious North, which now lay
frauded of mobile goods, old sedentary
    structures distorted.

Rome was ghastly. What earthly reason was there
why She should now not be theirs for the taking?
The Pope alone kept his cool, to the enemy
    now came in person,

sequenced by psalm-singing brethren: astonished,
Attila stared at a manner of men so
unlike his. 'Your name?', he snapped at their leader.
    'Leo,' he answered, raising

his right hand, the forefinger pointed upwards,
the little finger pressed to the thumb, in the
Roman salute: 'I ask the King to receive me
    in private audience.'

Their parley was held out of earshot: we only
know it was brief, that suddenly Attila
wheeled his horse and galloped back to the encampment,
    yelling out orders.

Next morning the site was vacant: they had vanished,
never to vex us again. What can Leo have
actually said? He never told, and the poets
    can only imagine

speeches for those who share a common cosmos:
all we can say is that he rose to the occasion,
that for once, and by His own standards, the Prince of
    this world showed weakness.

July 1970

A Shock

Housman was perfectly right.
Our world rapidly worsens:
nothing now is so horrid
or silly it can't occur.
Still, I'm stumped by what happened
to upper-middle-class me,
born in '07 when Strauss
was starting on *Elektra*,
gun-shy myopic grandchild
of Anglican clergymen,
suspicious of all passion,
including passionate love,
day-dreaming of leafy dells
that shelter carefree shepherds,
averse to violent weather,
pained by the predator beasts,
shocked by boxing and blood-sports,
when I, I, I, if you please,
at Schwechat Flughafen was
frisked by a cop for weapons.

September 1971

Loneliness

Gate-crashing ghost, aggressive
invisible visitor,
tactless gooseberry, spoiling
my *tête-à-tête* with myself,
blackmailing brute, behaving
as if the house were your own,
so viciously pursuing
your victim from room to room,
monotonously nagging,
ungenerous jabberer,
dirty devil, befouling
fair fancies, making the mind
a quagmire of disquiet,
weakening my will to work,
shadow without shape or sex,

649

excluding consolation,
blotting out Nature's beauties,
grey mist between me and God,
pestilent problem that won't
be put on the back-burner,
hard it is to endure you.

Routine is the one technique
I know of that enables
your host to ignore you now:
while typing business letters,
laying the table for one,
gobbling a thoughtless luncheon,
I briefly forget you're there,
but am safe from your haunting
only when soundly asleep.

History counsels patience:
tyrants come, like plagues, but none
can rule the roost for ever.
Indeed, your totter is near,
your days numbered: to-morrow
Chester, my chum, will return.
Then you'll be through: in no time
he'll throw you out neck-and-crop.
We'll merry-make your cadence
with music, feasting and fun.

August 1971

Talking to Dogs
(In memoriam Rolfi Strobl, run over, June 9th, 1970)

From us, of course, you want gristly bones
and to be led through exciting odorscapes
    —their colors don't matter—with the chance
of a rabbit to chase or of meeting
    a fellow arse-hole to snuzzle at,
but your deepest fury is to be accepted
    as junior members of a Salon
suaver in taste and manners than a pack,
    to be scratched on the belly and talked to.
Probably, you only hear vowels and then only if
    uttered with lyrical emphasis,
so we cannot tell you a story, even
    when it is true, nor drily dissect
in the third person neighbors who are not there
    or things which can't blush. And what do we,
those of us who are householders, not shepherds
    or killers or polar explorers,
ask from you? The admiration of creatures
    to whom mirrors mean nothing, who never
false your expression and so remind us
    that we as well are still social retards,

650

who have never learned to command our feelings
and don't want to, really. Some great men,
Goethe and Lear, for instance, have disliked you,
which seems eccentric, but good people,
if they keep one, have good dogs. (The reverse
is not so, for some very bad hats
handle you very well.) It's those who crave
a querulous permanent baby,
or a little detachable penis,
who can, and often do, debase you.
Humor and joy to your thinking are one,
so that you laugh with your whole body,
and nothing dismays you more than the noise
of our local superior titters.
(But then our young males are dismayed by yours
to whom, except when a bitch is air-borne,
chastity seems to present no problem.)
Being quicker to sense unhappiness
without having to be told the dreary
details or who is to blame, in dark hours
your silence may be of more help than many
two-legged comforters. In citizens
obedience is not always a virtue,
but yours need not make us uneasy
because, though child-like, you are complete, no New
Generation whom it's our duty
to disappoint since, until they notice
our failings, they will never bother
to make their own mistakes. Let difference
remain our bond, yes, and the one trait
both have in common, a sense of theatre.

July 1970

Talking to Mice

Plural the verdicts we cast on the creatures we have to shake hands
    with:
Creepy! Get HER! Good Lord, what an oddity! One to steer clear of!
Fun! Impossible! Nice, but a bore! An adorable monster!
But those animates which we call in our arrogance *dumb* are
judged as a species and classed by the melodramatic division,
either *Goodies* or *Baddies*. So spiders and roaches and flies we
excommunicate as—ugh!—all irredeemably evil,
Dreck to be stamped on or swatted, abolished without any hover.
Mice, *per contra*, except to a few hysterical women,
rank among the most comely of all the miniature mammals
who impinge on our lives, for our smell doesn't seem to alarm them,
visitors whom we can jump with, co-agents it doesn't seem phoney
we should endow with a *You*, as from now on I shall in these verses,
though my grammatical shift will be out of your ken for, alas, you
never have managed, as all successful parasites must, to
crack the code of your host, wise up on what habits can travel.

651

Ah!, if only you had, with what patience we would have trained you
how to obtemper your greeds, recalling the way that our Nannies
moulded our nursery *moeurs*, bechiding whenever we turned our
noses up at a dish—*Now remember the starving Armenians!*—
and when we gobbled—*Enough! Leave something for nice Mr. Manners!*—
cited you suitable maxims. *Good Little Mice never gnaw through*
wood-work or nibble at packages. Good Little Mice never scatter
droppings that have to be swept up. Good Little Mice get a tid-bit,
Bad Little Mice die young. Then, adapting an adage of lovers,
Two Little Mice are a company, Three Little Mice are a rabble.

All through the Spring and the Summer, while you were still only a
    couple,
fit-sides we dwelt in a peace as idyllic as only a Beatrix
Potter could paint. In September, though, this was abrupted: you must
    have
littered for, lo! quite suddenly, there were a swarm of you, messing
everything up until no cache was aloof to your insults.
What occurred now confirmed that ancient political axiom:
When Words fail to persuade, then Physical Force gives the orders.
Knowing you trusted in us, and would never believe an unusual
object pertaining to men could be there for a sinister purpose,
traps were baited and one by one you were fatally humbugged.
All fourteen of you perished. To move from where we'd been sipping
cocktails and giving ear, translated out of ourselves, to
Biedermeier Duets or Strauss in *Metamorphosen*,
mourning the end of his world, and enter the kitchen to find there
one more broken cadaver, its black eyes beadily staring,
obumbated a week. We had felt no talent to murder,
it was against our pluck. Why, why then? For *raisons d'État*. As
householders we had behaved exactly as every State does,
when there is something It wants, and a minor one gets in the way.

May 1971

Talking to Myself
(*for Oliver Sacks*)

Spring this year in Austria started off benign,
the heavens lucid, the air stable, the about
sane to all feeders, vegetate or bestial:
the deathless minerals looked pleased with their regime,
where what is not forbidden is compulsory.

Shadows of course there are, Porn-Ads, with-it clergy,
and hubby next door has taken to the bottle,
but You have preserved Your poise, strange rustic object,
whom I, made in God's Image but already warped,
a malapert will-worship, must bow to as Me.

My mortal manor, the carnal territory
allotted to my manage, my fosterling too,
I must earn cash to support, my tutor also,
but for whose neural instructions I could never
acknowledge what is or imagine what is not.

652

Instinctively passive, I guess, having neither
fangs nor talons nor hooves nor venom, and therefore
too prone to let the sun go down upon Your funk,
a poor smeller, or rather a censor of smells,
with an omnivore palate that can take hot food.

Unpredictably, decades ago, You arrived
among that unending cascade of creatures spewed
from Nature's maw. A random event, says Science.
Random my bottom! A true miracle, say I,
for who is not certain that he was meant to be?

As You augmented and developed a profile,
I looked at Your looks askance. *His architecture*
should have been much more imposing: I've been let down!
By now, though, I've gotten used to Your proportions
and, all things considered, I might have fared far worse.

Seldom have You been a bother. For many years
You were, I admit, a martyr to horn-colic
(it did no good to tell You—*But I'm not in love!*):
how stoutly, though, You've repelled all germ invasions,
but never chastised my tantrums with a megrim.

You are the Injured Party for, if short-sighted,
I am the book-worm who tired You, if short-winded
as cigarette addicts are, I was the pusher
who got You hooked. (Had we been both a bit younger,
I might well have mischiefed You worse with a needle.)

I'm always amazed at how little I know You.
Your coasts and outgates I know, for I govern there,
but what goes on inland, the rites, the social codes,
Your torrents, salt and sunless, remain enigmas:
what I believe is on doctors' hearsay only.

Our marriage is a drama, but no stage-play where
what is not spoken is not thought: in our theatre
all that I cannot syllable You will pronounce
in acts whose *raison-d'être* escapes me. Why secrete
fluid when I dole, or stretch Your lips when I joy?

Demands to close or open, include or eject,
must come from Your corner, are no province of mine
(all I have done is to provide the time-table
of hours when You may put them): but what is Your work
when I librate between a glum and a frolic?

For dreams I, quite irrationally, reproach You.
All I know is that I don't choose them: if I could,
they would conform to some prosodic discipline,
mean just what they say. Whatever point nocturnal
manias make, as a poet I disapprove.

Thanks to Your otherness, Your jocular concords,
so unlike my realm of dissonance and anger,
You can serve me as my emblem for the Cosmos:
for human congregations, though, as Hobbes perceived,
the apposite sign is some ungainly monster.

Whoever coined the phrase *The Body Politic*?
All States we've lived in, or historians tell of,
have had shocking health, psychosomatic cases,
physicked by sadists or glozing expensive quacks:
when I read the papers, You seem an Adonis.

Time, we both know, will decay You, and already
I'm scared of our divorce: I've seen some horrid ones.
Remember: when *Le Bon Dieu* says to You *Leave him!*,
please, please, for His sake and mine, pay no attention
to my piteous *Dont*'s, but bugger off quickly.

April 1971

Part XIII

1972–1973

Thank You, Fog

Grown used to New York weather,
all too familiar with Smog,
You, Her unsullied Sister,
I'd quite forgotten and what
You bring to British winters:
now native knowledge returns.

Sworn foe to festination,
daunter of drivers and planes,
volants, of course, will curse You,
but how delighted I am
that You've been lured to visit
Wiltshire's witching countryside
for a whole week at Christmas,
that no one can scurry where
my cosmos is contracted
to an ancient manor-house
and four Selves, joined in friendship,
Jimmy, Tania, Sonia, Me.

Outdoors a shapeless silence,
for even those birds whose blood
is brisk enough to bid them
abide here all the year round,
like the merle and the mavis,
at Your cajoling refrain
their jocund interjections,
no cock considers a scream,
vaguely visible, tree-tops
rustle not but stay there, so
efficiently condensing
Your damp to definite drops.

Indoors specific spaces,
cosy, accommodate to
reminiscence and reading,
crosswords, affinities, fun:
refected by a sapid
supper and regaled by wine,
we sit in a glad circle,
each unaware of our own
nose but alert to the others,
making the most of it, for
how soon we must re-enter,
when lenient days are done,
the world of work and money
and minding our p's and q's.

No summer sun will ever
dismantle the global gloom
cast by the Daily Papers,
vomiting in slip-shod prose
the facts of filth and violence
that we're too dumb to prevent:
our earth's a sorry spot, but
for this special interim,
so restful yet so festive,
Thank You, Thank You, Thank You, Fog.

May 1973

Aubade
(In Memoriam Eugen Rosenstock-Huessy)

Beckoned anew to a World
where wishes alter nothing,
expelled from the padded cell
of Sleep and re-admitted
to involved Humanity,
again, as wrote Augustine,
I know that I am and will,
I am willing and knowing,
I will to be and to know,
facing in four directions,
outwards and inwards in Space,
observing and reflecting,
backwards and forwards through Time,
recalling and forecasting.

Out there, to the Heart, there are
no dehumanised Objects,
each one has its Proper Name,
there is no Neuter Gender:
Flowers fame their splendid shades,
Trees are proud of their posture,
Stones are delighted to lie
just where they are. Few bodies
comprehend, though, an order,
few can obey or rebel,
so, when they must be managed,
Love is no help: We must opt
to eye them as mere Others,
must count, weigh, measure, compel.

Within a Place, not of Names
but of Personal Pronouns,
where I hold council with Me
and recognise as present
Thou and Thou comprising We,
unmindful of the meinie,
all those We think of as They.
No voice is raised in quarrel,

but quietly We converse,
by turns relate tall stories,
at times just sit in silence,
and on fit occasion I
sing verses *sotto-voce*,
made on behalf of Us all.

But Time, the domain of Deeds,
calls for a complex Grammar
with many Moods and Tenses,
and prime the Imperative.
We are free to choose our paths
but choose We must, no matter
where they lead, and the tales We
tell of the Past must be true.
Human Time is a City
where each inhabitant has
a political duty
nobody else can perform,
made cogent by Her Motto:
Listen, Mortals, Lest Ye Die.

August 1972

Unpredictable But Providential
(*for Loren Eiseley*)

Spring with its thrusting leaves and jargling birds is here again
to remind me again of the first real Event, the first
genuine Accident, of that Once when, once a tiny
corner of the cosmos had turned indulgent enough
to give it a sporting chance, some Original Substance,
immortal and self sufficient, knowing only the blind
collision experience, had the sheer audacity
to become irritable, a Self requiring a World,
a Not-Self outside Itself from which to renew Itself,
with a new freedom, to grow, a new necessity, death.
Henceforth, for the animate, to last was to mean to change,
existing both for one's own sake and that of all others,
forever in jeopardy.   The ponderous ice-dragons
performed their slow-motion ballet: continents cracked in half
and wobbled drunkenly over the waters: Gondwana
smashed head on into the under-belly of Asia.
But catastrophes only encouraged experiment.
As a rule, it was the fittest who perished, the mis-fits,
forced by failure to emigrate to unsettled niches, who
altered their structure and prospered. (Our own shrew-ancestor
was a Nobody, but still could take himself for granted,
with a poise our grandees will never acquire.)
                                        Genetics
may explain shape, size and posture, but not why one physique
should be gifted to cogitate about cogitation,
divorcing Form from Matter, and fated to co-habit

659

on uneasy terms with its Image, dreading a double death,
a wisher, a maker of asymmetrical objects,
a linguist who is never at home in Nature's grammar.

Science, like Art, is fun, a playing with truths, and no game
should ever pretend to slay the heavy-lidded riddle,
What is the Good Life?
                    Common Sense warns me of course to buy
neither but, when I compare their rival Myths of Being,
bewigged Descartes looks more *outré* than the painted wizard.

June 1972

Address to the Beasts

For us who, from the moment
we first are worlded,
lapse into disarray,

who seldom know exactly
what we are up to,
and, as a rule, don't want to,

what a joy to know,
even when we can't see or hear you,
that you are around,

though very few of you
find us worth looking at,
unless we come too close.

To you all scents are sacred
except our smell and those
we manufacture.

How promptly and ably
you execute Nature's policies,
and are never

lured into misconduct
except by some unlucky
chance imprinting.

Endowed from birth with good manners,
you wag no snobbish elbows,
don't leer,

don't look down your nostrils,
nor poke them into another
creature's business.

Your own habitations
are cosy and private, not
pretentious temples.

660

Of course, you have to take lives
to keep your own, but never
kill for applause.

Compared with even your greediest,
how Non-U
our hunting gentry seem.

Exempt from taxation,
you have never felt the need
to become literate,

but your oral cultures
have inspired our poets to pen
dulcet verses,

and, though unconscious of God,
your Sung Eucharists are
more hallowed than ours.

Instinct is commonly said
to rule you: I would call it
Common Sense.

If you cannot engender
a genius like Mozart,
neither can you

plague the earth
with brilliant sillies like Hegel
or clever nasties like Hobbes.

Shall we ever become adulted,
as you all soon do?
It seems unlikely.

Indeed, one balmy day,
we might well become,
not fossils, but vapour.

Distinct now,
in the end we shall join you
(how soon all corpses look alike),

but you exhibit no signs
of knowing that you are sentenced.
Now, could that be why

we upstarts are often
jealous of your innocence,
but never envious?

June 1973

Archaeology

The archaeologist's spade
delves into dwellings
vacancied long ago,

unearthing evidence
of life-ways no one
would dream of leading now,

concerning which he has not much
to say that he can prove:
the lucky man!

Knowledge may have its purposes,
but guessing is always
more fun than knowing.

We do know that Man,
from fear or affection,
has always graved His dead.

What disastered a city,
volcanic effusion,
fluvial outrage,

or a human horde,
agog for slaves and glory,
is visually patent,

and we're pretty sure that,
as soon as palaces were built,
their rulers,

though gluttoned on sex
and blanded by flattery,
must often have yawned.

But do grain-pits signify
a year of famine?
Where a coin-series

peters out, should we infer
some major catastrophe?
Maybe. Maybe.

From murals and statues
we get a glimpse of what
the Old Ones bowed down to,

but cannot conceit
in what situations they blushed
or shrugged their shoulders.

Poets have learned us their myths,
but just how did They take them?
That's a stumper.

When Norsemen heard thunder,
did they seriously believe
Thor was hammering?

No, I'd say: I'd swear
that men have always lounged in myths
as Tall Stories,

that their real earnest
has been to grant excuses
for ritual actions.

Only in rites
can we renounce our oddities
and be truly entired.

Not that all rites
should be equally fonded:
some are abominable.

There's nothing the Crucified
would like less
than butchery to appease Him.

CODA

From Archaeology
one moral, at least, may be drawn,
to wit, that all

our school text-books lie.
What they call History
is nothing to vaunt of,

being made, as it is,
by the criminal in us:
goodness is timeless.

August 1973

Progress?

Sessile, unseeing,
the Plant is wholly content
with the Adjacent.

Mobilised, sighted,
the Beast can tell Here from There
and Now from Not-Yet.

Talkative, anxious,
Man can picture the Absent
and Non-Existent.

A Curse

Dark was that day when Diesel
conceived his grim engine that
begot you, vile invention,
more vicious, more criminal
than the camera even,
metallic monstrosity,
bale and bane of our Culture,
chief woe of our Commonweal.

How dare the Law prohibit
hashish and heroin yet
licence your use, who inflate
all weak inferior egos?
Their addicts only do harm
to their own lives: you poison
the lungs of the innocent,
your din dithers the peaceful,
and on choked roads hundreds must
daily die by chance-medley.

Nimble technicians, surely
you should hang your heads in shame.
Your wit works mighty wonders,
has landed men on the Moon,
replaced brains by computers,
and can smithy a 'smart' bomb.
It is a crying scandal
that you cannot take the time
or be bothered to build us,
what sanity knows we need,
an odorless and noiseless
staid little electric brougham.

July 1972

Ode to the Diencephalon
(*after A. T. W. Simeons*)

How *can* you be quite so uncouth? After sharing
the same skull for all these millennia, surely
you should have discovered the cortical *I* is
    a compulsive liar.

He has never learned you, it seems, about fig-leaves
or fire or ploughshares or vines or policemen,
that bolting or cringing can seldom earth a
    citizen's problems.

We are dared every day by guilty phobias,
nightmares of missing the bus or being laughed at,
but goose-flesh, the palpitations, the squitters
  won't flabbergast them.

When you could really help us, you don't. If only,
whenever the trumpet cries men to battle,
you would flash to their muscles the urgent order
  ACUTE LUMBAGO!

June 1972

Shorts

None of us are as young
as we were. So what?
Friendship never ages.

*   *   *

Pascal should have been soothed, not scared by his infinite spaces:
  God made the All so immense, stellar collisions are rare.

*   *   *

Earth's mishaps are not fatal,
Fire is not quenched by the dark,
no one can bottle a *Breeze*,
no friction wear out *Water*.

*   *   *

The conversations of birds
say very little,
but mean a great deal.

*   *   *

Butterflies, alas,
ignore us, but midges don't,
unfortunately.

*   *   *

When did the bed-bug
first discover
that we were tastier than bats?

*   *   *

Some beasts are dumb,
some voluble, but only
one species can stammer.

*   *   *

Among the mammals
only Man has ears
that can display no emotion.

*   *   *

Many creatures make nice noises,
but none, it seems,
are moved by music.

*   *   *

Beasts, Birds, Fish, Flowers do what
the Season insists They must,
but Man schedules the Days on
which He may do what He should.

*   *   *

Bound to ourselves for life,
we must learn how to
put up with each other.

*   *   *

Consciousness should be a parlour
where words are well-groomed
and reticent.

*   *   *

Man must either fall in love
with Someone or Something,
or else fall ill.

*   *   *

Nothing can be loved too much,
but all things can be loved
in the wrong way.

*   *   *

When truly brothers,
men don't sing in unison
but in harmony.

*   *   *

Whatever their personal faith,
all poets, as such,
are polytheists.

*   *   *

Envy we must those bards who compose in Italian or German:
  apposite Feminine Rhymes give them no bother at all.
We, though, thanks to a Tongue deprived of so many inflexions,
  can very easily turn Nouns, if we wish, into Verbs.

* * *

Met individually, most men appear friendly and gentle,
  but collectively, Man commonly acts like a cad.

* * *

Policy ought to conform to Liberty, Law and Compassion,
  but, as a rule, It obeys Selfishness, Vanity, Funk.

* * *

Where are brigands
most commonly to be found?
Where boundaries converge.

* * *

Wherever there is gross
inequality, the Poor
corrupt the Rich.

1972–1973

Posthumous Letter to Gilbert White

It's rather sad we can only meet people
whose dates overlap with ours, a real shame that
you and Thoreau (we know that he read you)
never shook hands. He was, we hear, a rabid

Anti-Clerical and quick-tempered, you the
quietest of curates, yet I think he might well have
found in you the Ideal Friend he wrote of
with such gusto, but never ran into.

Stationaries, both of you, but keen walkers,
chaste by nature and, it would seem, immune to
the beck of worldly power, kin spirits,
who found all creatures amusive, even

the tortoise in spite of its joyless stupors,
aspected the vagrant moods of the Weather,
from the modest conduct of fogs to
the coarse belch of thunder or the rainbow's

federal arch, what fun you'd have had surveying
two rival landscapes and their migrants, noting
the pitches owls hoot on, comparing
the echo-response of dactyls and spondees.

Selfishly, I, too, would have plumbed to know you:
I could have learned so much. I'm apt to fancy
myself as a lover of Nature,
but have no right to, really. How many

birds and plants can I spot? At most two dozen.
You might, though, have found such an ignoramus
a pesky bore. Time spared you that: I
have, though, thank God, the right to re-read you.

August 1973

A Contrast

How broad-minded were Nature and My Parents
in appointing to My Personal City
exactly the sort of *Censor* I would have
   Myself elected,

Who bans from recall any painful image:
foul behaviour, whether by Myself or Others,
days of dejection, breakages, poor cooking,
   are suppressed promptly.

I do wish, though, They had assigned Me a less hostile
Public Prosecutor, Who in the early morning
cross-questions Me with unrelenting venom
   about My Future—

'How will You ever pay Your taxes?' 'Where will You
find a cab?' 'Won't Your Speech be a flop?'—and greets My
answers with sarcastic silence. Well, well, I
   must grin and bear it.

July 1973

The Question

All of us believe
we were born of a virgin
(for who can imagine

his parents copulating?),
and cases are known
of pregnant Virgins.

But the Question remains:
from where did Christ get
that extra chromosome?

668

No, Plato, No

I can't imagine anything
    that I would less like to be
than a disincarnate Spirit,
    unable to chew or sip
or make contact with surfaces
    or breathe the scents of summer
or comprehend speech and music
    or gaze at what lies beyond.
No, God has placed me exactly
    where I'd have chosen to be:
the sub-lunar world is such fun,
    where Man is male or female
and gives Proper Names to all things.

    I can, however, conceive
that the organs Nature gave Me,
    my ductless glands, for instance,
slaving twenty-four hours a day
    with no show of resentment
to gratify Me, their Master,
    and keep Me in decent shape,
(not that I give them their orders,
    I wouldn't know what to yell),
dream of another existence
    than that they have known so far:
yes, it well could be that my Flesh
    is praying for 'Him' to die,
so setting Her free to become
    irresponsible Matter.

                              May 1973

Nocturne
(for E. R. Dodds)

Do squamous and squiggling fish,
down in their fireless houses,
notice nightfall? Perhaps not.
But any grounded goer,
and all to whom feathers grant
the sky's unbounded freedom,
alter their doings at dusk,
each obsequious to its
curiosity of kind.
The commons mild their movements
and mew all their senses, but
there are odd balls: for instance,
the owl and the pussy-cat,
as soon as day has thestered,
increase their thinking and jaunt
to kill or to engender.

669

No couple of our kindred
obey the same body-clock:
for most the law is to shut
their minds up before midnight,
but someone in the small hours,
for the money or love, is
always awake and at work.
Here young radicals plotting
to blow up a building, there
a frowning poet rifling
his memory's printer's-pie
to form some placent sentence,
and overhead wanderers
whirling hither and thither
in bellies of overbig
mosquitoes made of metal.

Over oceans, land-masses
and tree-tops the Moon now takes
her dander through the darkness,
to lenses a ruined world
lying in its own rubbish,
but still to the naked eye
the Icon of all mothers,
for never shall second thoughts
succumb our first-hand feelings,
our only redeeming charm,
our childish drive to wonder:
spaced about the firmament,
planets and constellations
still officiously declare
the glory of God, though known
to be uninfluential.

Out there still the Innocence
that we somehow freaked out of
where *can* and *ought* are the same:
so comely to our conscience,
where nothing may happen twice,
its timely repetitions,
so variant from our ways,
immodest scandal-mongers,
the way its fauna respect
the privacy of others.
How else shall mannerless minds
in ignorance imagine
the Mansion of Gentle Joy
it is our lot to look for,
where else weak wills find comfort
to dare the Dangerous Quest?

? 1972

A Thanksgiving

When pre-pubescent I felt
that moorlands and woodlands were sacred:
  people seemed rather profane.

Thus, when I started to verse,
I presently sat at the feet of
  Hardy and *Thomas* and *Frost*.

Falling in love altered that,
now Someone, at least, was important:
  Yeats was a help, so was *Graves*.

Then, without warning, the whole
Economy suddenly crumbled:
  there, to instruct me, was *Brecht*.

Finally, hair-raising things
that Hitler and Stalin were doing
  forced me to think about God.

Why was I sure they were wrong?
Wild *Kierkegaard*, *Williams* and *Lewis*
  guided me back to belief.

Now, as I mellow in years
and home in a bountiful landscape,
  Nature allures me again.

Who are the tutors I need?
Well, *Horace*, adroitest of makers,
  booking in Tivoli, and

Goethe, devoted to stones,
who guessed that—he never could prove it—
  Newton led Science astray.

Fondly I ponder You all:
without You I couldn't have managed
  even my weakest of lines.

                                        ? May 1973

A Lullaby

The din of work is subdued,
another day has westered
and mantling darkness arrived.
Peace! Peace! Devoid your portrait
of its vexations and rest.
Your daily round is done with,
you've gotten the garbage out,
answered some tiresome letters
and paid a bill by return,
all *frettolosamente*.
Now you have licence to lie,
naked, curled like a shrimplet,
jacent in bed, and enjoy
its cosy micro-climate:
Sing, Big Baby, sing lullay.

The old Greeks got it all wrong:
Narcissus is an oldie,
tamed by time, released at last
from lust for other bodies,
rational and reconciled.
For many years you envied
the hirsute, the he-man type.
No longer: now you fondle
your almost feminine flesh
with mettled satisfaction,
imagining that you are
sinless and all-sufficient,
snug in the den of yourself,
Madonna and *Bambino*:
Sing, Big Baby, sing lullay.

Let your last thinks all be thanks:
praise your parents who gave you
a Super-Ego of strength
that saves you so much bother,
digit friends and dear them all,
then pay fair attribution
to your age, to having been
born when you were. In boyhood
you were permitted to meet
beautiful old contraptions,
soon to be banished from earth,
saddle-tank loks, beam-engines
and over-shot waterwheels.
Yes, love, you have been lucky:
Sing, Big Baby, sing lullay.

Now for oblivion: let
the belly-mind take over
down below the diaphragm,
the domain of the Mothers,
They who guard the Sacred Gates,
without whose wordless warnings
soon the verbalising I
becomes a vicious despot,
lewd, incapable of love,
disdainful, status-hungry.
Should dreams haunt you, heed them not,
for all, both sweet and horrid,
are jokes in dubious taste,
too jejune to have truck with.
Sleep, Big Baby, sleep your fill.

April 1972

Appendices
and
Indices

Appendix I

Titles of Poems Excluded from this Edition

This appendix lists pieces excluded by Auden from his *Collected Shorter Poems 1927–1957* (other than the four restored poems noted in the editor's preface), although published in his earlier volumes. Not listed are poems published only in periodicals, or in privately printed pamphlets such as the 1928 *Poems* printed by Stephen Spender; nor are those poems listed that were printed only as parts of longer works such as *The Orators* or the notes to 'New Year Letter' in *The Double Man*. Full information may be found in *W. H. Auden: A Bibliography*, second edition, by B. C. Bloomfield and Edward Mendelson (University Press of Virginia, 1972).

Poems are listed under the volumes in which they first appeared. If Auden also published a poem in one of his later collections, the date of the later volume is noted together with any new or altered titles. Poems that first appeared untitled are listed by first lines. The parenthetical dates in this appendix refer to reprintings in the following volumes:

- 1933 *Poems*, second edition (Faber, reprinted in the 1934 Random House *Poems*)
- 1945 *The Collected Poetry of W. H. Auden* (Random House)
- 1950 *Collected Shorter Poems 1930–1944* (Faber)
- 1958 *W. H. Auden: A Selection by the Author* (Penguin; reprinted by the Modern Library as *Selected Poetry of W. H. Auden*)

1945 and *1950* are similar collections; poems appearing in both, with the same title, are noted *1945/50*.

Most of the poems in this list will be included in a forthcoming selection of Auden's early work, printed according to the original texts.

POEMS (*1930*)

Which of you waking early and watching daybreak . . .
To have found a place for nowhere . . .
The crowing of the cock . . .
Bones wrenched, weak whimper, lids wrinkled . . .
Sentries against inner and outer . . . (*1933, 1945/50* Shut Your Eyes and Open Your Mouth)
Get there if you can and see the land . . . (*1933*)
Nor was that final, for about that time . . .
Suppose they met, the inevitable procedure . . .
No trenchant parting this . . .
Under boughs between our tentative endearments . . . (*1933, 1945/50* When the Devil Drives)
Sir, no man's enemy . . . (*1933, 1945/50* Petition)

POEMS (*1933*)

It's no use raising a shout . . .

677

ON THIS ISLAND (*1936*)[1]

Since the external disorder . . .
Prologue (*1945/50* Perhaps)
Brothers, who when the sirens roar . . .
The chimneys are smoking . . . (*1950* Two Worlds)
Here on the cropped grass . . . (*1950* The Malverns)
The sun shines down . . .
To lie flat on the back . . . (*1945/50* What's the Matter?)
Night covers up the rigid land . . .
To settle in this village of the heart . . . (*1945/50* It's So Dull Here)
August for the people and their favourite islands . . . (*1950* Birthday Poem)
Epilogue (*1945* As We Like It, *1950* Our City)

LETTERS FROM ICELAND (*1937*)
(*with Louis MacNeice*)

Letter to R. H. S. Crossman, Esq.
Letter to William Coldstream, Esq.
Auden and MacNeice: Their Last Will and Testament

JOURNEY TO A WAR (*1939*)
(*with Christopher Isherwood*)

The Traveller (*1945/50*)
In Time of War: A Sonnet Sequence with a Verse Commentary
(*1945/50; Collected Shorter Poems 1927–1957*, and the present edition, omit
sonnets IX, X, XIV, XV, XX, XXVI, and the verse Commentary, and
severely revise the remainder as 'Sonnets from China')

ANOTHER TIME (*1940*)

Every eye must weep alone ⊙ . .
The Creatures (*1945/50*)
Pascal (*1945/50*)
Matthew Arnold (*1945/50*)
Spain 1937 (*1945/50*)
September 1, 1939 (*1945/50*)
Epithalamion (*1945/50*)

---

[1] The title of the British edition, *Look, Stranger!*, was chosen by the publishers while
Auden was in Iceland, and was used over his strong objections.

THE DOUBLE MAN (*1941*)[2]

Prologue (*1945* Spring 1940)

THE COLLECTED POETRY OF W. H. AUDEN
(Random House, *1945*)

In War Time (*1950*)
The Cultural Presupposition[3] (*1950* Culture)
Christmas 1940 (*1950*)
January 1, 1931[4] (*1950*)
Letter to a Wound[4]
Gold in the North . . . (*1950*)
Not, Father, further do prolong . . .[4] (*1950*)
Now through night's caressing grip . . .[3] (*1950*)
Depravity: A Sermon[3]

COLLECTED SHORTER POEMS 1930–1944 (Faber, *1950*)

Prothalamion[3]

THE SHIELD OF ACHILLES (*1955*)

Barcarolle (from *The Rake's Progress*)

NOTE: The present collection also excludes the translations printed in two of Auden's later volumes— the 'Four Transliterations' of Polish and Russian poems in *About the House*, and the 'Eight Songs from *Mother Courage*' in *City Without Walls*. An antimasque written in collaboration with Chester Kallman, 'The Entertainment of the Senses', appeared in *Thank You, Fog*; this will be reprinted in a forthcoming collection of Auden's dramatic writings.

---

[2] The title of the British edition, *New Year Letter*, was chosen by the publishers.
[3] Reprinted from the play *The Dog Beneath the Skin* (with Christopher Isherwood, 1935).
[4] Reprinted from *The Orators* (1932).

Appendix II

Variant Titles

The method of this appendix should for the most part be self-explanatory. If Auden previously used a title when publishing a poem, but collected it for this edition without a title, its first line is given in the right-hand column. Volumes in which the earlier title appeared are indicated by dates of publication:

1936 *Look, Stranger!* (American edition, *On this Island*)
1939 *Journey to a War*
1940 *Another Time*
1941 *The Double Man* (British edition, *New Year Letter*)[1]
1945 *The Collected Poetry of W. H. Auden* (Random House)
1950 *Collected Shorter Poems 1930–1944* (Faber)
1951 *Nones*
1955 *The Shield of Achilles*
1958 *W. H. Auden: A Selection by the Author* (Penguin; published by the Modern Library as *Selected Poetry of W. H. Auden*)
1966 *Collected Shorter Poems 1927–1957*

1945 and *1950* are similar collections; titles appearing in both are indicated *1945/50*.

Alternative Title	Title in This Edition
Able At Times to Cry (*1958*)	As He Is
Adventure (*1941, 1945*)	The Quest XVII
The Adventurers (*1941, 1945*)	The Quest XVIII
Aera sub Lege (*1945*)	The Hidden Law
Air Port (*1951*)	In Transit
All Over Again (*1945*)	*From* Paid on Both Sides
Alonso to Ferdinand (*1958*)	*From* The Sea and the Mirror
Always in Trouble (*1945*)	*From* Paid on Both Sides
Are You There? (*1945*)	Alone
As Well as can be Expected (*1945*)	Taller To-day
Autumn 1940 (*1945*)	The Dark Years
The Average (*1941, 1945*)	The Quest XI
Barbed Wire (*1958*)	*From* Memorial to the City
The Bard (*1958*)	Sonnets from China VII
Better Not (*1945/50*)	No Change of Place
But I Can't (*1945*)	If I Could Tell You
Caliban to the Audience (*1958*)	*From* The Sea and the Mirror
Chorus (*1958*)	The Wanderer
The City (*1941, 1945*)	The Quest V
The Climbers (*1945/50*)	Two Climbs
Crisis (*1940*)	They
The Crossroads (*1941, 1945*)	The Quest III
The Dead Echo (*1958*)	Death's Echo
Do Be Careful (*1945*)	Between Adventure
Doomsday Song (*1958*)	Domesday Song

[1] In the sonnet sequence 'The Quest', separate titles for each of the sonnets appear only in the American edition (see editor's preface).

The Door (*1941, 1945*) — The Quest I

A Dream (*1958*) — 'Dear, though the night is gone . . .'

Embassy (*1958*) — Sonnets from China XV

Epilogue (*1941*) — The Dark Years

The First Temptation (*1941, 1945*) — The Quest VI

Footnotes to Dr. Sheldon 1 (*1951*) — 'Behold the manly mesomorph...'

Footnotes to Dr. Sheldon 2 (*1951*) — 'Give me a doctor...'

For the Last Time (*1945*) — The Council

Funeral Blues (*1940*) — 'Stop all the clocks . . .'

Ganymede (*1958*) — Sonnets from China IX

The Garden (*1941, 1945*) — The Quest XX

The Hard Question (*1950*) — The Question (*in Part II*)

The Hero (*1941, 1945*) — The Quest XVI

I Shall Be Enchanted (*1945*) — Legend

In Father's Footsteps (*1945*) — Our Hunting Fathers

In Legend (*1958*) — Legend

In Time of War (*1939, 1945/50*)[2] — Sonnets from China

Invocation to Ariel (*1958*) — *From* The Sea and the Mirror

It's Too Much (*1945*) — *From* Paid on Both Sides

Johnny (*1940*) — 'O the valley in the summer...'

The Journey (*1958*) — *From* Paid on Both Sides

The Labyrinth (*1945*) — The Maze

Like a Dream (*1950*) — This Lunar Beauty

Like Us (*1945/50*) — 'These had stopped seeking...'

The Love Letter (*1945/50*) — The Letter

The Lucky (*1941, 1945*) — The Quest XV

Madrigal (*1940, 1958*) — 'O lurcher-loving collier . . .'

Make Up Your Mind (*1945*) — Easy Knowledge

Miranda's Song (*1958*) — *From* The Sea and the Mirror

Music Ho (*1951*) — 'The Emperor's favorite concubine...'

A New Age (*1958*) — Sonnets from China X

Nobody Understands Me (*1945/50*) — A Misunderstanding

Nocturne II (*1955*) — 'Make this night loveable . . .'

Not All the Candidates Pass (*1945/50*) — The Watchers

O Tell Me the Truth about Love (*1940*) — 'Some say that love's a little boy...'

'O who can ever praise enough . . .' (*1945/50*) — The Price

One Evening (*1958*) — As I Walked Out One Evening

The Pilgrim (*1945*) — The Quest IV

Please Make Yourself at Home (*1945*) — Like a Vocation

The Preparations (*1941, 1945*) — The Quest II

The Presumptuous (*1941, 1945*) — The Quest X

The Proof (*1955*) — 'When rites and melodies begin . . .'

Pur (*1945*) — This Lunar Beauty

The Quarry (*1958*) — O What is That Sound

Refugee Blues (*1940*) — 'Say this city . . .'

Remember (*1945*) — *From* Paid on Both Sides

A Sanguine Thought (*1955*) — 'O where would those choleric boys...'

Seascape (*1958*) — On This Island

[2] In Time of War XXV *becomes in the present edition* A Major Port.

The Second Temptation (*1941, 1945*)	The Quest VII
Serenade (*1951*)	'On and on and on ...'
Something is Bound to Happen (*1945*)	The Wanderer
Song for St. Cecilia's Day (*1945/50*)	Anthem for St. Cecilia's Day
Song of the Master and Boatswain (*1958*)	*From* The Sea and the Mirror
Song of the Old Soldier (*1958*)	*From* For the Time Being
Stephano's Song (*1958*)	*From* The Sea and the Mirror
Such Nice People (*1945/50*)	On Sunday Walks
'The summer quickens all...' (*1945*)	*From* Paid on Both Sides
Surgical Ward (*1958*)	Sonnets from China XIV
The Third Temptation (*1945*)	The Quest VIII
This One (*1945/50, 1958*)	This Loved One
The Three Companions (*1958*)	'O where are you going...'
Three Dreams (*1958, 1966*)	*From* The Age of Anxiety
To E. M. Forster (*1939, 1950*)	Sonnets from China XXI
To You Simply (*1945/50*)	'For what as easy ...'
The Tower (*1941, 1945*)	The Quest IX
The Traveler (*1941*)	The Quest IV
Trinculo's Song (*1958*)	*From* The Sea and the Mirror
True Enough (*1945*)	'His ageing nature is the same...'
Two's Company (*1945*)	Never Stronger
The Useful (*1941, 1945*)	The Quest XIII
Vocation (*1941, 1945*)	The Quest XII
The Voyage (*1939, 1945/50*)	Whither?
The Walking Tour (*1945*)	*From* Paid on Both Sides
The Waters (*1941, 1945*)	The Quest XIX
The Way (*1941, 1945*)	The Quest XIV
We All Make Mistakes (*1945*)	A Free One
We're Late (*1945*)	No Time
What Do *You* Think? (*1945*)	The Question
'When the Sex War ended...' (*1966*)	*From* For the Time Being
Which Side am I Supposed to be On? (*1945/50*)	Ode
The Willow-Wren and the Stare (*1955*)	'A starling and a willow-wren...'
Year after Year (*1945*)	*From* Paid on Both Sides

NOTE: In the American edition of *The Double Man* and in *1945*, the sonnets in 'The Quest' have the following titles (see editor's preface):

I	The Door
II	The Preparations
III	The Crossroads
IV	The Pilgrim (*1941* The Traveler)
V	The City
VI	The First Temptation
VII	The Second Temptation
VIII	The Third Temptation
IX	The Tower
X	The Presumptuous
XI	The Average
XII	Vocation

XIII	The Useful
XIV	The Way
XV	The Lucky
XVI	The Hero
XVII	Adventure
XVIII	The Adventurers
XIX	The Waters
XX	The Garden

Index of Titles

A. E. Housman, 148
Academic Graffiti, 510
Address to the Beasts, 660
Adolescence, 64
After Reading a Child's Guide to
    Modern Physics, 557
The Age of Anxiety, 343
The Aliens, 637
Alone, 243
Amor Loci, 585
Another Time, 218
Anthem, 257
Anthem for St. Cecilia's Day, 220
Archaeology, 662
The Art of Healing, 626
As He Is, 142
As I Walked Out One Evening, 114
Ascension Day, 1964, 558
At the Grave of Henry James, 242
At the Party, 555
Atlantis, 245
Aubade (1964), 562
Aubade (1972), 658
August 1968, 604
Autumn Song, 118

A Bad Night, 631
The Ballad of Barnaby, 618
Bathtub Thoughts, 461
Bestiaries Are Out, 556
Between Adventure, 46
Bird-Language, 586
Blessed Event, 238
The Bonfires, 53
A Bride in the 30's, 111
Brussels in Winter, 146
Bucolics, 126

Calypso, 211
Canzone, 256
The Capital, 145
Casino, 123
Cattivo Tempo, 419
The Cave of Making, 521
The Cave of Nakedness, 535
A Change of Air, 542
The Chimeras, 466
Circe, 646
City Without Walls, 562
The Common Life, 537
Compline, 484

The Composer, 148
Consider, 61
Contra Blake, 540
A Contrast, 668
The Council, 236
A Curse, 664

Dame Kind, 503
Danse Macabre, 130
The Dark Years, 222
Death's Echo, 128
The Decoys, 66
Detective Story, 127
Diaspora, 234
Dichtung und Wahrheit, 489
Doggerel by a Senior Citizen, 638
Domesday Song, 213
Dover, 124
Down There, 525
The Duet, 264

Easy Knowledge, 44
Economics, 539
Edward Lear, 149
Elegy, 575
Elegy for J. F. K., 567
Encomium Balnei, 528
An Encounter, 648
The Epigoni, 460
Epistle to a Godson, 624
Epitaph for the Unknown Soldier,
    435
Epitaph on a Tyrant, 149
Epithalamium, 571
Et in Arcadia Ego, 544
Eulogy, 572
The Exiles, 61

Fairground, 605
The Fall of Rome, 257
Family Ghosts, 47
Few and Simple, 253
First Things First, 444
Fleet Visit, 420
For Friends Only, 532
For the Time Being, 269
Forty Years On, 588
A Free One, 46
Friday's Child, 509

Gare du Midi, 147

The Garrison, 633
The Geography of the House, 526
Glad, 561
The Golden Age, 541
Good-Bye to the Mezzogiorno, 486
Grub First, Then Ethics, 530

Half Way, 67
Hammerfest, 545
Hands, 505
Happy Ending, 57
Have a Good Time, 66
A Healthy Spot, 254
Heard and Seen, 630
Heavy Date, 205
Hell, 219
Herman Melville, 200
The Hidden Law, 209
His Excellency, 122
The History of Science, 462
The History of Truth, 463
Homage to Clio, 463
Hong Kong, 144
Horae Canonicae, 475
The Horatians, 579
A Household, 469
Hunting Season, 420

I Am Not a Camera, 630
Iceland Revisited, 546
If I Could Tell You, 244
In Due Season, 603
In Memoriam L. K.-A. 1950–1952, 435
In Memory of Ernst Toller, 198
In Memory of Sigmund Freud, 215
In Memory of W. B. Yeats, 197
In Praise of Limestone, 414
In Schrafft's, 259
In Sickness and in Health, 247
In Transit, 413
Insignificant Elephants, 607
Ischia, 416
An Island Cemetery, 421
Islands, 431

James Honeyman, 134
Josef Weinheber, 568
Journey to Iceland, 126

Kairos and Logos, 238

Lady Weeping at the Crossroads, 219

Lakes, 430
Lauds, 485
Law Like Love, 208
Leap Before You Look, 244
Legend, 70
The Lesson, 253
Let History Be My Judge, 42
The Letter, 39
Letter to Lord Byron, 75
Like a Vocation, 203
Limbo Culture, 468
Lines Addressed to Dr. Claude Jenkins, 443
Lines for Elizabeth Mayer, 567
Lines to Dr. Walter Birk, 577
Loneliness, 649
Lost, 540
The Love Feast, 466
Lullaby, 131
A Lullaby, 672
Luther, 235

Macao, 145
A Major Port, 145
The Maker, 554
Makers of History, 456
The Managers, 459
Many Happy Returns, 249
Marginalia, 589
May, 110
The Maze, 236
Meiosis, 108
Memorial for the City, 450
Merax & Mullin, 467
Metalogue to The Magic Flute, 441
Metaphor, 540
Minnelied, 562
Miss Gee, 132
Missing, 40
A Misunderstanding, 109
The Model, 255
Montaigne, 235
Moon Landing, 632
Moralities, 613
The More Loving One, 445
A Mosaic for Marianne Moore, 577
Mountains, 428
Mundus et Infans, 252
Musée des Beaux Arts, 146
Music is International, 263

Natural Linguistics, 636
Never Stronger, 43
A New Year Greeting, 628

New Year Letter, 159
Night Mail, 113
1929, 50
No Change of Place, 42
No, Plato, No, 669
No Time, 234
Nocturne (1951), 446
Nocturne (1972), 669
Nones, 480
Not in Baedeker, 422
The Novelist, 147
Numbers and Faces, 473
Nursery Rhyme, 258

O What is That Sound, 105
Objects, 473
Ode, 68
Ode to Gaea, 423
Ode to Terminus, 608
Ode to the Diencephalon, 664
Ode to the Medieval Poets, 647
The Old Man's Road, 461
Old People's Home, 645
On Sunday Walks, 54
On the Circuit, 548
On This Island, 112
One Circumlocution, 474
Orpheus, 132
Our Bias, 218
Our Hunting Fathers, 106
Oxford, 124

Paid on Both Sides, 19
Parable, 539
Partition, 604
Paysage Moralisé, 104
A Permanent Way, 445
Plains, 432
Pleasure Island, 265
Posthumous Letter to Gilbert
   White, 667
Precious Five, 447
The Price, 129
Prime, 475
Profile, 581
Progress, 663
Prologue at Sixty, 622
Prologue: The Birth of
   Architecture, 518
The Prophets, 203
Pseudo-Questions, 634

The Quest, 224
The Question (1930), 58

The Question, 668
The Questioner Who Sits So Sly, 47

Recitative By Death, 542
Reflections in a Forest, 504
A Reminder, 617
The Riddle, 204
Rimbaud, 148
River Profile, 605
Rois Fainéants, 603
Roman Wall Blues, 121
Runner, 609

The Sabbath, 507
Schoolchildren, 109
The Sea and the Mirror, 309
Secondary Epic, 455
The Secret Agent, 41
Secrets, 472
Sext, 477
The Shield of Achilles, 454
The Ship, 143
A Shock, 649
A Short Ode to a Philologist, 566
Short Ode to the Cuckoo, 647
Shorts (1927–1932), 55
Shorts (1939–1947), 231
Shorts (1948–1957), 435
Shorts I (1958–1971), 539
Shorts II (1958–1971), 639
Shorts (1972–1973), 665
Since, 584
Smelt and Tasted, 029
The Song, 474
Song of the Beggars, 116
Song of the Devil, 587
Song of the Ogres, 586
Sonnets from China, 149
The Sphinx, 144
Stark bewölkt, 634
Streams, 433
A Summer Night, 103
Symmetries & Asymmetries, 549

T the Great, 457
Talking to Dogs, 650
Talking to Mice, 651
Talking to Myself, 652
Taller To-day, 39
Terce, 476
Thank You, Fog, 657
A Thanksgiving, 671
Thanksgiving for a Habitat, 518
Their Lonely Betters, 444

There Will Be No Peace, 468
They, 201
This Loved One, 44
This Lunar Beauty, 57
Through the Looking-Glass, 107
To Goethe: A Complaint, 540
To T. S. Eliot on his Sixtieth
  Birthday, 440
A Toast (1960), 565
A Toast (1971), 579
Tonight at Seven-Thirty, 533
Too Dear, Too Vague, 45
'The Truest Poetry is the Most
  Feigning', 470
The Twelve, 612
Two Climbs, 108

Uncle Henry, 60
Under Sirius, 417
Under Which Lyre, 259
United Nations Hymn, 621
The Unknown Citizen, 201
Unpredictable But Providential,
  659

Up There, 525

Venus Will Now Say a Few Words, 49
Vespers, 482
Victor, 138
Voltaire at Ferney, 199
A Voyage, 143

A Walk After Dark, 267
Walks, 507
The Wanderer, 62
The Watchers, 63
The Watershed, 41
We Too Had Known Golden Hours,
  471
Whither?, 143
Whitsunday in Kirchstetten, 559
Who's Who, 109
Winds, 426
The Witnesses, 71
Woods, 427
Words, 473

You, 543

Index of First Lines

Among the various 'Shorts,' 'Symmetries & Asymmetries,' and 'Marginalia,' only poems of more than ten lines, or that have titles of their own, are indexed here.

A cellar underneath the house, though not lived in, 525
A cloudless night like this, 267
A lake allows an average father, walking slowly, 430
A living room, the catholic area you, 537
A nondescript express in from the South, 147
A sentence uttered makes a world appear, 473
A shilling life will give you all the facts, 109
A shot: from crag to crag, 420
A starling and a willow-wren, 438
A sweet tooth taught us to admire, 556
A weed from Catholic Europe, it took root, 145
About suffering they were never wrong, 146
Absence of heart—as in public buildings, 466
Across the Great Schism, through our whole landscape, 461
After shaking paws with his dog, 476
Again in conversations, 43
All are limitory, but each has her own, 645
All fables of adventure stress, 462
All folk tales mean by ending, 571
All had been ordered weeks before the start, 224
All of us believe, 668
All streets are brightly lit; our city is kept clean, 143
All that which lies outside our sort of why, 473
All the others translate: the painter sketches, 148
All winter long the huge sad lady, 264
Almost happy now, he looked at his estate, 199
Among pelagian travelers, 548
Among the leaves the small birds sing, 485
Anthropos apteros for days, 236
Appearing unannounced, the moon, 446
Ares at last has quit the field, 259
Around them boomed the rhetoric of time, 238
As evening fell the day's oppression lifted, 155
As I listened from a beach-chair in the shade, 444
As I walked out one evening, 114
As it is, plenty, 122
As *quid pro quo* for your enchanting verses, 579
Ashamed to be the darling of his grief, 225
At break of dawn, 562
At last the secret is out, as it always must, 119
At peace under this mandarin, sleep, Lucina, 435

Babies in their mothers' arms, 231
Be patient, solemn nose, 447
Beckoned anew to a World, 658
Before this loved one, 44
Begot like other children, he, 457
Behold the manly mesomorph, 436

Being set on the idea, 245
Between attention and attention, 44
By all means sing of love but, if you do, 470
By landscape reminded once of his mother's figure, 64

Carry her over the water, 212
Castle and crown are faded clean away, 241
Certainly praise: let song mount again and again, 153
Chaucer, Langland, Douglas, Dunbar, with all your, 647
Chilled by the Present, its gloom and its noise, 156
Clocks cannot tell our time of day, 234
Consider this and in our time, 61
Control of the passes was, he saw, the key, 41
Corns, heartburn, sinus headaches, such minor ailments, 542

Dark was that day when Diesel, 664
Dark-green upon distant heights, 622
Dear, all benevolence of fingering lips, 247
DEAR PHILIP: 'Thank God for boozy godfathers', 624
Dear, though the night is gone, 117
Deep, deep below our violences, 426
Deep water, clear water, playful in all your streams, 433
Deftly, admiral, cast your fly, 437
Did it once issue from the carver's hand, 144
Do squamous and squiggling fish, 669
Don Juan needs no bed, being far too impatient, 535
Doom is dark and deeper than any sea-dingle, 62
Driver drive faster and make a good run, 211

Each lover has a theory of his own, 243
Each traveller prays *Let me be far from any*, 126
Eagerly, Musician, 621
Earth has turned over; our side feels the cold, 107
Easily you move, easily your head, 111
Encased in talent like a uniform, 147
Enter with him, 70
Events reported by the ear, 630
Ever since observation taught me temptation, 587
Every created thing has ways of pronouncing its ownhood, 636
Excellence is a gift: among mankind, 609
Except where blast-furnaces and generating-stations, 588
Excuse, my lord, the liberty I take, 77
Eyes look down into the well, 212

Far from a cultural centre he was used, 154
Fish in the unruffled lakes, 118
Fleeing from short-haired mad executives, 108
For over forty years I'd paid it atlas homage, 545
For this and for all enclosures like it the archetype, 521
For us like any other fugitive, 218
For us who, from the moment, 660
For what as easy, 59
Fresh addenda are published every day, 228
From gallery-grave and the hunt of a wren-king, 518

From leaf to leaf in silence, 558
From scars where kestrels hover, 40
From the very first coming down, 39
From this new culture of the air we finally see, 423
From us, of course, you want grisly bones, 650

Gate-crashing ghost, aggressive, 649
Generally, reading palms or handwriting or faces, 255
Grown used to New York weather, 657

Hail, future, friend, whose present I, 461
Having abdicated with comparative ease, 67
Having finished the Blue-plate Special, 359
He disappeared in the dead of winter, 197
He looked in all His wisdom from His throne, 152
He parried every question that they hurled, 229
He stayed, and was imprisoned in possession, 150
He thanks God daily, 581
He told us we were free to choose, 509
He turned his field into a meeting-place, 152
He was found by the Bureau of Statistics to be, 201
He was their servant (some say he was blind), 152
He watched the stars and noted birds in flight, 151
He watched with all his organs of concern, 226
Hearing of harvests rotting in the valleys, 104
Hell is neither here nor there, 219
Her Telepathic-Station transmits thought-waves, 646
Here are all the captivities, the cells are as real, 109
Here war is harmless like a monument, 153
His care-free swagger was a fine invention, 151
His library annoyed him with its look, 226
His peasant parents killed themselves with toil, 227
Housman was perfectly right, 649
How broad-minded were Nature and My Parents, 668
How *can* you be quite so uncouth? After sharing, 664
How he had survived them they could never understand, 234
How wonderfully your songs begin, 540
Hugerl, for a decade now, 561

I can imagine quite easily ending up, 432
I can't imagine anything, 669
I choose the road from here to there, 507
I could draw its map by heart, 585
I know a retired dentist who only paints mountains, 428
If all a top physicist knows, 557
If it form the one landscape that we, the inconstant ones, 414
If one could name the father of these things, 240
If the hill overlooking our city has always been known as, 482
I'm no photophil who burns, 634
In a garden shady this holy lady, 220
In an upper room at midnight, 466
In gorgeous robes befitting the occasion, 236
In his dream zealous, 631
In our beginning, 572

691

In that ago when being was believing, 463
In the bad old days it was not so bad, 459
In the First Age the frogs dwelt, 613
In the Hungry Thirties, 539
In villages from which their childhoods came, 225
Incredulous, he stared at the amused, 228
Into what fictive realms can imagination, 579
it is odd that the English, 528
It was Easter as I walked in the public gardens, 50
It's farewell to the drawing-room's mannerly cry, 130
Its leading characters are wise and witty, 144
It's natural the Boys should whoop it up for, 632
It's rather sad we can only meet people, 667

James Honeyman was a silent child, 134
Johnny, since to-day is, 249
Jumbled in one common box, 213
Just as his dream foretold, he met them all, 109

Kicking his mother until she let go of his soul, 252
Komm Schöpfer Geist I bellow as Herr Beer, 559

Ladies and gentlemen, you have made most remarkable, 542
Lady, weeping at the crossroads, 219
Law, say the gardeners, is the sun, 208
Lay your sleeping head, my love, 131
Left by his friend to breakfast alone on the white, 149
Let a florid music praise, 117
Let both our Common Rooms combine to cheer, 443
Let me tell you a little story, 132
Let out where two fears intersect, a point selected, 413
Let us praise our Maker, with true passion extol Him, 257
Liebe Frau Emma, 575
Listen, good people, and you shall hear, 618
Little fellow, you're amusing, 586
Look, stranger, on this island now, 112
Look there! The sunk road winding, 53
Looking up at the stars, I know quite well, 445
Lost on a fogbound spit of sand, 540
Love by ambition, 45
Love had him fast but though he fought for breath, 108

Make this night loveable, 440
Martini-time: time to draw the curtains and, 633
May with its light behaving, 110
Men would never have come to need an attic, 525
Most patients believe, 626
My First Name, Wystan, 510
My second thoughts condemn, 214

Nature invades: old rooks in each college garden, 124
Necessity knows no Speech. Not even, 566
No guidance can be found in ancient lore, 145
No one, not even Cambridge, was to blame, 148

No one now imagines you answer idle questions, 647
No use invoking Apollo in a case like theirs, 460
No, Virgil, no, 455
No window in his suburb lights that bedroom where, 225
Nobody I know would like to be buried, 519
Nose, I am free, 540
Not as that dream Napoleon, rumour's dread and centre, 203
Now, as desire and the things desired, 484
Now from my window-sill I watch the night, 63
Now the leaves are falling fast, 118

'O for doors to be open and an invite with gilded edges', 116
O lurcher-loving collier, black as night, 116
O the valley in the summer where I and my John, 120
O what is that sound which so thrills the ear, 105
'O where are you going?' said reader to rider, 60
'O who can ever gaze his fill', 128
Old saints on millstones float with cats, 431
On a mid-December day, 584
On and on and on, 215
On High Feast-Days they were given a public airing, 603
On Sunday walks, 54
On this day tradition allots, 628
Only a smell had feelings to make known, 150
Only their hands are living, to the wheel attracted, 123
Orchestras have so long been speaking, 263
Others had found it prudent to withdraw, 229
Our earth in 1969, 638
Our global story is not yet completed, 155
Our hill made its submission and the green, 463
Our hunting fathers told the story, 106
Ours yet not ours, being set apart, 532
Out of a bellicose fore-time, thundering, 605
Out of a gothic North, the pallid children, 486
Out of it steps our future, through this door, 224
Out on the lawn I lie in bed, 103
Outside his library window he could see, 235
Over the heather the wet wind blows, 121

Perfection, of a kind, was what he was after, 149
Perhaps I always knew what they were saying, 203
Plural the verdicts we cast on the creatures, 651
Poet, oracle, and wit, 230

Quarter of pleasures where the rich are always waiting, 145
Quite suddenly her dream became a word, 239

Reaching my gate, a narrow, 568
Really, must you, 543
Relax, Maestro, put your baton down, 441
Returning each morning from a timeless world, 222
Round the three actors in any blessed event, 238

Say this city has ten million souls, 210

Seated after breakfast, 526
Seen when nights are silent, 60
Self-drivers may curse their luck, 445
Serious historians care for coins and weapons, 456
Sessile, unseeing, 663
Sharp and silent in the, 205
She looked over his shoulder, 454
Should the shade of Plato, 530
Simple like all dream-wishes, they employ, 155
Simultaneously, as soundlessly, 475
Since you are going to begin to-day, 49
Sirocco brings the minor devils, 419
So an age ended, and its last deliverer died, 153
So from the years their gifts were showered: each, 149
So large a morning so itself to lean, 474
Some say that love's a little boy, 121
Sometimes we see astonishingly clearly, 474
Spinning upon their central thirst like tops, 230
Spring this year in Austria started off benign, 652
Spring with its thrusting leaves and jargling birds, 659
Spring-time, Summer and Fall: days to behold a world, 603
Steatopygous, sow-dugged, 503
Steep roads, a tunnel through chalk downs, 124
Stop all the clocks, cut off the telephone, 120
Suppose he'd listened to the erudite committee, 229
Sylvan meant savage in those primal woods, 427

Talented creatures, on the defensive because, 607
Taller to-day, we remember similar evenings, 39
That night when joy began, 59
That we are always glad, 472
The archaeologist's spade, 662
The concluded gardens of personal liking, 577
The din of work is subdued, 672
The Emperor's favorite concubine, 438
The eyes of the crow and the eye of the camera open, 450
The first time that I dreamed, we were in flight, 253
The Hidden Law does not deny, 209
The High Priests of telescopes and cyclotrons, 608
The hour-glass whispers to the lion's roar, 218
The Kingdom of Number is all boundaries, 473
The life of plants, 533
The nights, the railway-arches, the bad sky, 148
The nose and palate never doubt, 629
The ogre does what ogres can, 604
The over-logical fell for the witch, 228
The piers are pummelled by the waves, 257
The poets tell us of an age of unalloyed felicity, 541
The Road of Excess, 540
The sailors come ashore, 420
The sense of danger must not disappear, 244
The shining neutral summer has no voice, 198
The silly fool, the silly fool, 57
The single creature leads a partial life, 212
694

The snow, less intransigeant than their marble, 242
The strings' excitement, the applauding drum, 47
The tribes of Limbo, travellers report, 468
The watch upon my wrist, 539
The Year: 452. The Place: the southern, 648
Their learned kings bent down to chat with frogs, 258
There are some birds in these valleys, 66
There is a time to admit how much the sword decides, 416
There is one devil in the lexicon, 467
There were lead-mines here before the Romans, 422
These had stopped seeking, 56
They are and suffer; that is all they do, 154
They noticed that virginity was needed, 227
They wondered why the fruit had been forbidden, 150
They're nice—one would never dream of going over, 254
This graveyard with its umbrella pines, 421
This is an architecture for the odd, 227
This is the Night Mail crossing the Border, 113
This lunar beauty, 57
Those fantastic forms, fang-sharp, 562
Though aware of our rank and alert to obey orders, 68
Though determined Nature can, 213
Though Italy and King's are far away, 157
Though mild clear weather, 468
Thumping old tunes give a voice to its whereabouts, 605
Time will say nothing but I told you so, 244
To ask the hard question is simple, 58
To call our sight vision, 630
To save your world, you asked this man to die, 435
Towards the end he sailed into an extraordinary mildness, 200
Trying to understand the words, 586
Two friends who met here and embraced are gone, 224

Unbiassed at least he was when he arrived on his mission, 604
Under the familiar weight, 161
Underneath an abject willow, 119
Underneath the leaves of life, 204
Unmarried, nearsighted, rather deaf, 554
Unrhymed, unrhythmical, the chatter goes, 555
Unwashed, unshat, 546
Upon this line between adventure, 46

Victor was a little baby, 138

Waking on the Seventh Day of Creation, 507
Wandering through cold streets tangled like old string, 146
Warm are the still and lucky miles, 211
Watch any day his nonchalant pauses, see, 46
We don't need a face in the picture to know, 505
'We have brought you,' they said, 'a map of the country', 66
We made all possible preparations, 42
We, too, had known golden hours, 471
What does the song hope for? And his moved hands, 132
What on earth does one say at a Gaudy, 565

What siren zooming is sounding our coming, 64
What there is as a surround to our figures, 265
What we know to be not possible, 480
What's in your mind, my dove, my coney, 59
When all our apparatus of report, 156
When one is lonely (and You, 562
When pre-pubescent I felt, 671
'When rites and melodies begin', 439
When shall we learn, what should be clear as day, 256
When the Flyin Scot, 60
When there are so many we shall have to mourn, 215
When things began to happen to our favourite spot, 440
When, to disarm suspicious minds at lunch, 469
When you first arrived in Kirchstetten, trains had, 577
Whenever you are thought, the mind, 253
Where do they come from? Those whom we so much dread, 201
Where does this journey look which the watcher upon the quay, 143
Who can ever pause enough, 129
Who could possibly approve of Metternich, 634
Who is ever quite without his landscape, 127
Who needs their names? Another genus built, 156
Who, now, seeing Her so, 544
Who stands, the crux left of the watershed, 41
Who will endure, 42
Why *then*, why *there*, 567
Wide though the interrupt be that divides us, 637
Will you turn a deaf ear, 47
With conscience cocked to listen for the thunder, 235
Withdrawn from the Object-World, 567
Within a shadowland of trees, 504
Within these gates all opening begins, 230
Without arms or charm of culture, 612
Woken, I lay in the arms of my own warmth, 444
Wrapped in a yielding air, beside, 142

Yes, these are the dog-days, Fortunatus, 417
You need not see what someone is doing, 477
Young men late in the night, 71